PHYSIOLOGY OF TREES

McGRAW-HILL PUBLICATIONS IN
THE BOTANICAL SCIENCES

Edmund W. Sinnott, *Consulting Editor*

There are also the related series of McGraw-Hill Publications in the Zoological Sciences, of which E. J. Boell is Consulting Editor, and in the Agricultural Sciences, of which R. A. Brink is Consulting Editor.

PHYSIOLOGY OF TREES

Paul J. Kramer
JAMES B. DUKE PROFESSOR OF BOTANY
DUKE UNIVERSITY

Theodore T. Kozlowski
PROFESSOR OF FORESTRY
UNIVERSITY OF WISCONSIN

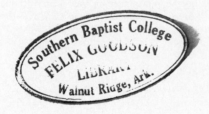
McGRAW-HILL BOOK COMPANY, INC.

New York   Toronto   London   1960

PHYSIOLOGY OF TREES

III

35351

TO
EDITH
AND
MAUDE

Preface

This book was written to be used either as a textbook or as a reference by all who want a better understanding of how trees grow. They include practicing foresters, arborists, horticulturists, botanists, and agronomists, as well as teachers, students, and investigators. It is difficult to write for such a varied audience because of the wide differences in their training, knowledge, and interests, but the importance to everyone who works with trees of a better understanding of the role of physiological processes in tree growth seems to justify the effort. We assume that the reader has at least some knowledge of elementary botany and plant physiology. Some readers with a limited background in these fields may find parts of the book rather technical. Others with more extensive training in plant physiology may find certain sections rather elementary. The latter group should remember that this book was not written primarily for specialists in plant physiology, but rather to show how physiological processes are involved in the growth of trees.

For several years the authors have realized the need for a book on the physiology of trees, partly to summarize what is known and partly to stimulate further research on the numerous problems about which we know little or nothing. We postponed the writing from year to year because it seemed that too little information was available, but it finally appeared that the usefulness of a summary of what we now know would more than compensate for the lack of information in certain fields. Of course, many serious deficiencies in information exist, but perhaps pointing out their existence will encourage investigations to supply the needed information.

The viewpoint of this book is rather different from that of conventional textbooks of plant physiology which deal primarily with mechanisms of physiological processes. Our approach has been influenced somewhat by Bailey and Spoehr who suggested that tree physiology should deal with both individual trees and stands of trees, as well as with their processes.

vii

This is desirable because in nature the behavior of a tree is greatly influenced by the neighboring trees with which it competes. The most useful approach seems to be an ecological one in which emphasis is placed on the effects of evironmental conditions on physiological processes of the organism as a whole, rather than a wholly biochemical one in which emphasis is placed on the details of the processes themselves.

We have emphasized the close interrelationships between structure and function because it is quite impossible to understand the processes of a tree without first understanding its structure. Furthermore the structure of a tree comes into existence as the result of a complex series of physiological processes which too often are hidden behind the term "growth." We have therefore given considerable attention to the structure of a tree and the manner in which growth occurs, as a desirable preliminary to discussing its physiological processes. Vegetative and sexual reproduction and seed germination also are discussed in detail because these processes consist of interesting and important groups of physiological processes.

We have attempted to evaluate the sometimes divergent views held in the literature and have presented what seem to us the most probable conclusions, based on our present state of knowledge. We realize, however, that as more information is acquired some of these conclusions will require revision. We therefore urge our readers to be critical, but open-minded and ready to change their views when new information makes changes necessary.

The entire manuscript was read by Dr. R. M. Barnes, Dr. W. H. D. McGregor, and Dr. T. Satoo and most of it was read by Dr. R. M. Allen and Dr. R. Zahner. Considerable portions were reviewed by Dr. P. Bourdeau, Dr. H. B. Tukey, and Dr. H. Wilcox. Individual chapters were read by Dr. A. C. Gentile, Dr. E. S. Harrar, Dr. L. Leyton, Dr. R. B. Livingston, Dr. H. J. Oosting, Dr. K. F. Wenger, and Dr. J. P. Decker. Their help is deeply appreciated. We also express our gratitude to Miss Gladys Miner who assisted with the bibliography, Mrs. Patricia James who assisted with the typing, and Mr. H. M. Tschinkel who assisted in preparing the illustrations. We alone, however, are responsible for any errors which may appear in the text.

A short list of collateral readings has been added to the end of each chapter. Papers cited in the text and those from which data have been used are listed in the bibliography. We have attempted to represent the significant worldwide literature but admit that we have omitted many important papers for lack of space and probably have overlooked others. In general, research papers cited in well-known journals have been given priority over those which are less readily accessible, but some obscure papers are cited because of their importance.

In the text common names generally are used for well-known species and Latin names for less common ones. Both common and Latin names of species mentioned in the text are listed in the Appendix. Names of North American forest trees are based on E. L. Little, *Check List of Native and Naturalized Trees of the United States,* Agriculture Handbook No. 41, U.S. Forest Service, Washington, D.C., 1953. Names of other species are from various sources.

Paul J. Kramer
Theodore T. Kozlowski

Contents

xi

Contents

CHAPTER 1

Introduction

A tree means different things to different people. For our ancestors it was the chief source of fuel and shelter and occasionally an object of worship. To the average man on the street it may be a source of pleasant shade in the summer but a nuisance which sheds leaves on his lawn in the autumn. To an arborist it is an ornamental object in the landscape, and to a forester a source of timber and pulpwood. To a physiologist, however, a tree is a complex biochemical factory which starts from a seed and literally builds itself, and physiologists are therefore interested in the manner in which the complex of processes that we call "growth" is carried on.

An acre of forest produces several thousand pounds of new dry matter each year from the simple raw materials water, carbon dioxide, and a few pounds of nitrogen and mineral salts. The success of trees depends primarily on their efficiency in manufacturing carbohydrates by photosynthesis and their ability to convert these simple carbohydrates into new tissues. This involves translocation of the products of photosynthesis to various parts of the plant, their conversion into other substances such as proteins and fats, and their use in assimilation and respiration.

The Role of Physiology

The general objective of plant physiology is to explain how plants grow in terms of the internal processes and conditions which control growth. Study of these processes is carried on for two principal reasons. One reason is to satisfy the scientific curiosity of physiologists who simply wish to understand various aspects of growth. They are challenged by the existence of an unsolved problem, just as a mountain climber is challenged by an unclimbed mountain, without much regard for the practical applications of their findings. Such so-called basic research often proves to be very valuable in the long run because the more basic

1

the research the broader its possible practical applications. The second reason for research on the physiology of plants is to provide a basis for developing better methods of growing them.

Plant physiologists are interested primarily in learning how trees grow, while foresters and horticulturists are interested primarily in how to grow trees more efficiently. These two approaches are more closely related than many people suppose. There really is no conflict between long-term research on basic processes and principles and short-term research on applied problems. Each type actually contributes to the other, and the greatest over-all progress will occur when physiologists learn more about the growing of trees, foresters and horticulturists learn more about the physiology of trees, and the two work together to solve the many problems which exist.

Physiological Processes and Growth

Measurements of physiological processes such as photosynthesis, respiration, and transpiration may seem far removed from the practice of forestry cr horticulture, but in order to grow trees efficiently it is necessary to understand how trees grow and why they react as they do to the various environmental factors and cultural treatments to which they are subjected. Growth is the end result of the interaction of numerous physiological processes, and in order to understand why trees grow differently under various environmental conditions and cultural treatments, it is necessary to understand how the basic processes which control growth are affected by the environment.

Nearly everyone knows that the growth of trees, like that of all other organisms, is controlled by their inherited genetic potentialities and their environment, but too little consideration is given to the means by which this control is exerted. To say that shade or drought reduces growth, or that a new combination of genes is responsible for rapid growth of a hybrid, does not really explain how the observed effects are brought about. We need a better understanding of how various causes produce their respective effects. The following diagram shows how heredity and environment interact through the internal physiological processes and conditions of trees to control the quantity and quality of growth. It also shows the relationships of several fields of science which are involved in the study of these phenomena.

Klebs' Concept. This scheme sometimes is called Klebs' concept because the German plant physiologist Klebs (1913–1918) was one of the first to point out that environmental factors can affect plant processes only by changing internal processes and conditions. Lundegardh (1931) also made important contributions to this viewpoint. This concept was introduced to the United States by the mycologist Kauffman (1926), and it was further developed by H. C. Sampson of The Ohio State University, who first brought it to the attention of the senior author.

Klebs' concept emphasizes the basic biological principle that the only way in which heredity or environment can affect the growth of an organism is by affecting its internal processes and conditions. The physiological processes of a tree constitute the machinery through which heredity and environment operate to control growth. Therefore, in order to understand why trees are affected by any particular factor or treatment, we must learn how this factor or treatment affects their physiological processes.

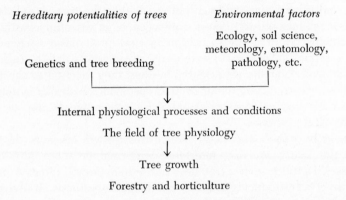

Hereditary potentialities of trees   *Environmental factors*

Ecology, soil science,
meteorology, entomology,
Genetics and tree breeding   pathology, etc.

Internal physiological processes and conditions

The field of tree physiology

Tree growth

Forestry and horticulture

Application of Klebs' Concept. The application of this concept can be illustrated by some specific examples. For instance, if a hybrid grows faster than its parents in the same environment, it is because a new combination of genes has produced a more efficient balance of physiological processes, resulting in more food being converted into plant tissue. This may result from increased efficiency either of structures or of processes, or both. The rate of photosynthesis per unit of leaf area might be increased by increased chlorophyll content, or by structural changes which increase the intake of carbon dioxide or the exposure of leaves to light. A more extensive root system or a thicker layer of cutin might result in maintenance of a higher level of turgidity in the tree, which in turn would be favorable for photosynthesis and also for cell enlargement.

If a certain slash pine produces more gum than its neighbors in the same environment, it probably is because a different genetic constitution results in higher rates of those processes which cause food to be converted into gum. Another possibility is that structural differences increase the rate of gum flow. If one species exhibits greater cold or drought resistance or greater shade tolerance than another, it is because its genetic constitution produces differences in structures or processes which result in more resistance to unfavorable environmental conditions.

Even though a change in rate of growth can be attributed to some structural modification, basically it is dependent on a change in processes. Structures are the products of biochemical processes included in the physiological processes involved in growth, and changes in structure result from changes in processes. Thus processes control structure even though they also are modified by changes in structure.

Unfavorable environmental conditions reduce tree growth because they interfere with various essential physiological processes. For example, water deficits reduce growth because they cause closure of stomates, reduction in photosynthesis, loss of turgidity, cessation of cell enlargement, and other unfavorable conditions within the tree. A deficiency of nitrogen reduces growth because nitrogen is an essential constituent of the proteins required for formation of new protoplasm, enzymes, and other essential substances. Phosphorus, potassium, calcium, sulfur, and other mineral elements are essential because they function as constituents of various essential compounds such as coenzymes, in buffer systems, and in other biochemical systems essential for proper functioning of various physiological processes.

Attacks by insects and fungi reduce tree growth or cause death only when the injury severely interferes with one or more physiological processes. Defoliation of a tree does not reduce growth directly, but does so indirectly by reducing the amount of photosynthesis. If the phloem is attacked, injury to the tree results from decreased translocation of food to the roots, and damage to the root system is harmful to the tree because it reduces the absorption of water and nutrients from the soil. Forest pathologists and entomologists probably have been too much concerned with the description and classification of the causal organisms and often have tended to overlook the fact that they were really dealing with physiological problems. Resistance to attacks of insects and fungi is largely biochemical in nature, and injury is the result of disturbance of biochemical and physiological processes. Just as the control of human diseases has progressed enormously through the use of biochemical and physiological approaches, so the control of tree diseases will become more successful when entomologists and pathologists become more aware of the physiological aspects of their problems instead of merely describing organisms and applying sprays.

We repeat, for the sake of emphasis, that the only way in which genetic differences, environmental factors, cultural practices, and diseases and insects can affect tree growth is by affecting their internal physiological processes and conditions. The operations of arborists, foresters, and horticulturists should be aimed at producing the most favorable genotypes and environments possible for the operation of the physiological machinery which really controls growth. To do this effectively and efficiently they must understand the nature of the principal physiological processes, their roles in growth, and their reactions to various environmental factors.

Special Characteristics of Trees

As Huber (1937) stated, trees have always been regarded by non-botanists as representing the apex of development in the plant kingdom. Because of their size and beauty they have often been credited with a special personality and have even been worshiped. The peculiar characteristics of trees are a matter of degree rather than of kind, however. They go through the same stages of growth and carry on the same processes as other plants, but their larger size, slower maturity, and longer life accentuate certain problems as compared with smaller plants with a shorter life span. The most obvious difference between trees and herbaceous plants is the great distance over which water, minerals, and food must be translocated in the former. Also, because of their longer life span, they usually are exposed to greater variations and extremes of temperature and other climatic and soil conditions than annuals or biennials. Thus, just as trees are notable for their large size, they are also notable for their special physiological development.

Some Important Physiological Processes and Conditions

The successful growth of trees depends on the interaction of a large number of processes and conditions. Some of the more important physiological processes are listed:

Photosynthesis. The synthesis of carbohydrates from carbon dioxide and water in the chlorophyllous tissue of trees provides the basic food materials for all other processes.

Nitrogen metabolism. The incorporation of inorganic nitrogen into organic compounds makes possible the synthesis of proteins and protoplasm itself.

Fat metabolism. Synthesis of fats and related compounds.

Respiration. The oxidation of food in living cells releases the energy used in assimilation, mineral absorption, and other energy-using processes.

Assimilation. The conversion of food into new protoplasm, cell walls, and other substances. A basic process in growth.

Accumulation of food. The storage of food in seeds and in the woody structure of trees.

Accumulation of salt. Concentration of salt in cells and tissues by an active transport mechanism dependent on expenditure of metabolic energy.

Digestion. Conversion by enzyme action of complex or insoluble forms of food such as starch into simpler, soluble forms which can be translocated and used in respiration and other processes.

Absorption. The intake of water and minerals from the soil and oxygen and carbon dioxide from the air.

Translocation. The movement of water, minerals, foods, and hormones from place to place in trees.

Transpiration. The loss of water from trees in the form of vapor.

Growth. Permanent increase in size, which results from the interaction of the various processes just listed.

Reproduction. Production of cones or flowers and finally of seeds. This also results from the interaction of a number of physiological processes. Vegetative reproduction plays an important role in some species.

Some of the important physiological conditions are as follows:

Amount and efficiency of chlorophyll.

Kinds and amounts of carbohydrates present and their interconversion, for example, change of starch to sugar and the reverse.

Kinds and amounts of nitrogen compounds and the ratio of carbohydrates to nitrogen.

Kinds and amounts of other constituents, such as fats.

Protoplasmic characteristics. Cold and drought resistance probably are at least partly dependent on special characteristics of protoplasm.

Permeability of cell membranes. Related to uptake of minerals, translocation, and cold resistance.

Osmotic pressure of cell sap. Increased osmotic pressure often associated with exposure to drought and cold.

Turgidity of cells. Loss of turgidity causes cessation of growth and affects rates of various physiological processes.

To physiologists belongs the task of measuring these conditions and processes, studying their mechanisms, observing their reaction to various environmental conditions, and identifying their role in tree growth. The more physiologists can learn about the mechanisms of the principal physiological processes, the better they can assist foresters and horticulturists in solving their practical problems. If we knew enough about the physiological requirements of trees, we could predict how a particular species will behave in a particular soil or climatic condition, or how it would react to a particular treatment.

Complexity of Physiological Processes

A physiological process such as photosynthesis, respiration, or transpiration actually is an aggregation of chemical and physical processes. In order to understand the mechanism of a physiological process it is necessary to resolve it into its physical and chemical components, and plant physiology depends more and more on the methods of biochemistry in its efforts to accomplish this. The biochemical approach has been very fruitful, as shown by the progress made toward a better understanding of such complicated processes as photosynthesis and respiration.

As the primary objective of this book is to increase the reader's understanding of how trees grow, we shall emphasize the physiology of the entire tree rather than detailed descriptions of the chemistry and physics of physiological processes. Our approach might be termed ecological rather than biochemical because we have given more attention to the manner in which processes are modified by environmental factors and in turn modify growth than to the mechanism of the processes themselves. Nevertheless, some knowledge of the mechanisms of processes is essential for a clear understanding of how they react to various environmental factors and how they affect growth; hence brief descriptions of many processes are included. For more detailed descriptions readers should turn to textbooks of plant physiology and monographs such as Bonner and Galston (1952), Meyer and Anderson (1952), Thomas et al. (1956), and Bonner (1950), as well as the several volumes of the Encyclopedia of Plant Physiology.

Processes Controlling Various Stages of Growth

It has been recognized ever since the time of Sachs that different physiological processes are most important at various stages of growth. For example, conditions often are so favorable for seed germination under pine stands that numerous pine seedlings appear, but conditions are unfavorable for seedling establishment and they die within a year or two. Climatic and soil conditions in a region might be favorable for vegetative growth but so unfavorable for reproduction that although trees of a certain species thrive when planted, they are unable to reproduce themselves. In Table 1.1 are indicated the principal processes which seem to dominate each stage of growth and the environmental factors which are most important. We lack a full understanding of these processes, and it is probable that our ideas about the role of some of them will be revised after further study.

Different Objectives of Foresters, Horticulturists, and Arborists

Trees are grown for quite different reasons by foresters, horticulturists, and arborists, and the types of physiological problems which are of greatest importance to each of them vary accordingly.

Foresters are concerned chiefly with trees in stands; hence they are most interested in problems of competition between individuals which affect the stand as a whole. Their problems may also differ somewhat, depending on whether their chief objective is production of pulpwood, saw timber, or seed. The trend toward more intensive forestry is rapidly

Table 1.1. Important processes and environmental factors at various stages of growth.

Stage	Processes and conditions	Most important environmental factors
Seed germination	Absorption of water Digestion Respiration Assimilation	Temperature Water Oxygen
Seedling establishment	Photosynthesis Assimilation Internal water balance	Light Water Temperature Nutrients
Vegetative growth	Photosynthesis Respiration Assimilation Translocation Internal water balance	Light Water Nutrients Temperature
Reproduction	Photosynthesis C/N balance Readiness to flower Initiation of flower primordia Accumulation of food	Light Nutrients Temperature
Senescence	Unknown (possibly water and hormonal relations, transloca-tion, and balance between photosynthesis and respiration)	Water Nutrients Insects and diseases

increasing the number of problems which require a knowledge of tree physiology for their solution.

Among these problems are methods of producing seedlings with the highest possible likelihood of survival when outplanted and some understanding of the processes which control differences in growth rate, quality of wood, drought and cold resistance, tolerance of root systems to poor aeration, shade tolerance, and length of growing season. Recent interest in tree improvement programs raises problems concerning induction of early and abundant seed production in trees. The success of various practical operations such as debarking of trees, fertilizing, girdling, and pruning and cutting in the season when sprouting is least likely to occur depends on performing them at a time when trees are in a particular physiological condition. For example, easy mechanical removal of bark occurs only when the cambium is physiologically active. It is probable that all silvicultural problems have a physiological basis and can be solved effectively only after foresters obtain a good understanding of the physiological processes of the trees with which they are working.

Horticulturists are interested primarily in the production of fruits; hence they are interested in getting trees into flowering at as early an age as possible and keeping them bearing fruit as steadily as possible. Like the arborists, they often must deal with soil problems, and because of the high value of orchard trees they, like the arborists, can afford to deal with problems of individual trees. Horticulturists have made more progress in the study of tree physiology, especially mineral nutrition, than any other group, but they have many more problems to solve.

Arborists are concerned principally in growing individual trees of good form and appearance to fit into ornamental plantings, regardless of the suitability of the soil and other environmental conditions. They often are faced with problems resulting from poor drainage, inadequate aeration, excessive root pruning or filling during construction, gas leaks, toxic fumes in the air, and other specialized conditions.

Among the general physiological processes of particular interest to arborists and horticulturists is aging. The short life span of many fruit and ornamental trees comprises an important practical problem which deserves serious study, but unfortunately practically nothing is known about the physiology and biochemistry of aging.

Historical Background

Although modern plant physiology usually is assumed to have begun about the middle of the nineteenth century with Sachs, its beginnings actually go back much further. One of the first books dealing with trees was John Evelyn's *Sylva,* published in 1670, in an attempt to interest English landowners in planting more trees. Although it contained little on the physiology of trees, mention is made of sap flow of birch and requirements for the growth of various tree species are discussed. Several papers were published in the *Proceedings of the Royal Society of London* between 1668 and 1671 by Beale, Lister, Ray, Tonge, and Willoughby on the ascent of sap in trees, but no satisfactory conclusions were reached. Nehemiah Grew, who published important works on anatomy in 1671 and 1682, described the anatomy of tree trunks in some detail and discussed the probable function of various structures. Another early anatomist, Malpighi (*Anatomes plantarum,* 1675), distinguished between heartwood and sapwood and observed the formation of annual rings, but apparently did not understand the function of cambium.

The first important physiological work on trees was done by Stephen Hales (1727), who also made the first measurements of blood pressure in animals. He measured transpiration and root and stem pressures, decided that water moves upward in the wood rather than the bark, and demonstrated that there is no circulation of sap in trees comparable with that of blood in animals. Hales' work is important because he emphasized the experimental approach and attempted to explain plant processes in terms of physical laws.

Forest botany sometimes is said to have begun with the publication of *La physique des arbres* by Duhamel du Monceau in 1758, but his work contains no important original contributions on the physiology of trees. Few new contributions to tree physiology were made until more than a century after Hales, when Theodor Hartig began work in Germany. Hartig studied phloem and named the sieve tubes. He also studied food storage and translocation, phloem exudation, and water content of wood and mineral nutrition and published numerous papers. His best-known book, *Anatomie und Physiologie der Holzpflanzen,* appeared in 1878. Theodor Hartig was the first of a distinguished group of German forest botanists who have added much to our understanding of the physiology of trees. Among these were Theodor Hartig's son Robert, a distinguished forest pathologist; Büsgen, who wrote the notable volume entitled *Bau und Leben unserer Waldbäume,* which first appeared in 1897; Münch, who revised it in 1926; and Huber, who for over thirty years has contributed to our understanding of how trees live and grow.

One little-known American, W. S. Clark, should be mentioned because he was not only one of the first men to carry on physiological research in this country but was also the first to study sap flow of trees exhaustively. His studies were published in the *Annual Reports* of the Massachusetts State Board of Agriculture in 1874 and 1875 and still constitute very interesting reading. G. W. Scarth of McGill University should also be mentioned both because of his own work and because several of his students continued to work in the field of tree physiology. The more important contributors of the present century will be cited in the text; hence we need not mention them here. It should be acknowledged that we owe more to the early workers than most of us realize. Because we fail to give sufficient attention to the earlier work, we sometimes laboriously rediscover facts which we learn later were known many years ago.

In the following chapters we shall discuss the important processes of trees and other woody plants, such as growth, synthesis, translocation and uses of foods, mineral nutrition and metabolism, and water relations. We shall also discuss the ways in which various internal and external factors affect internal processes and conditions and thereby affect growth. Unfortunately, we know much less than we ought to know concerning many of these processes. This will be disappointing to many readers, but it also should challenge them to assist in filling in the deficiencies in our knowledge of how trees grow.

GENERAL REFERENCES

Bailey, I. W., and H. A. Spoehr, 1929, The role of research in the development of forestry in North America, The Macmillan Company, New York.

Barrett, L. I., 1946, The status of silvical research, Jour. Forestry, 44:972–977.

Bonner, J., 1950, Plant biochemistry, Academic Press, Inc., New York.

—— and A. W. Galston, 1952, Principles of plant physiology, W. H. Freeman, San Francisco.

Büsgen, M., and E. Münch, 1931, The structure and life of forest trees, transl. by T. Thomson, John Wiley & Sons, Inc., New York.

Kaufert, F. H., and W. H. Cummings, 1955, Forestry and related research in North America, Society of American Foresters, Washington.

Kramer, P. J., 1956, The role of physiology in forestry, Forestry Chronicle, 32:297–308.

Mason, H. L., and P. R. Stout, 1954, The role of plant physiology in plant geography, Ann. Rev. Plant Physiology, 5:249–270.

Meyer, B. S., and D. B. Anderson, 1952, Plant physiology, 2d ed., D. Van Nostrand Company, Inc., Princeton, N.J.

Ruhland, W. (ed.), 1955, Encyclopedia of plant physiology, 18 vols., Springer-Verlag, Berlin.

Thimann, K. V. (ed.), 1958, The physiology of forest trees, The Ronald Press Company, New York.

Thomas, M., S. L. Ranson, and J. A. Richardson, 1956, Plant physiology, 4th ed., J. and A. Churchill, London.

Toumey, J. W., and C. F. Korstian, 1937, Foundations of silviculture upon an ecological basis, 2d ed., John Wiley & Sons, Inc., New York.

CHAPTER 2 *Growth and Structure*

Knowledge of tree structure is as essential to the understanding of physiological processes as is knowledge of chemistry. For example, it is necessary to know something about leaf structure in order to understand how photosynthesis and transpiration are affected by various environmental factors. A knowledge of root structure is important for an appreciation of the mechanism of water and salt absorption, and information on stem structure is basic to an understanding of the ascent of sap and translocation of food. Because every physiological process is more or less affected by the structure of the tissues and organs in which it occurs, a knowledge of structure is essential to an understanding of the process of growth in trees.

A tree may be regarded as consisting of six organs. Three of these—roots, stems, and leaves—are vegetative structures, while the other three—flowers, fruits, and seeds—are reproductive structures. Each of these organs is composed of a number of tissues. Xylem and phloem are particularly important because they form continuous conducting systems for water, salts, and food between the tips of the deepest roots and the uppermost leaves in the top of the crown. This chapter deals principally with the growth and structure of roots and stems. Reproductive structures will be discussed in Chapter 13, and leaf anatomy will be considered in relation to photosynthesis (Chapter 3) and transpiration (Chapter 10).

GROWTH AND STRUCTURE OF STEMS

As may be seen in Figure 2.1, a mature tree stem consists of a tapering column of wood composed of a series of layers or annual increments, added one above another, like a series of overlapping cones, and enclosed in a covering of bark. At the apex of the stem and of each of its branches is a terminal growing point where increase in length occurs. Between the bark and the wood is the cambium, a meristematic tissue which each year gives rise to additional wood and bark cells and causes increase in diameter of the stem. The orientation of the different parts of a tree stem is shown in Figure 2.2. The bark consists of a dead outer layer (*A*) and an inner living layer (*B*). The wood consists of an outer layer of sapwood containing some living cells (*C*) and the inner heartwood (*D*) in which no cells are living. The pith or central core (*E*) is a parenchymatous tissue arising from the apical meristem.

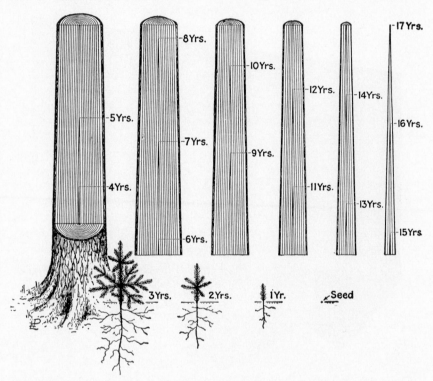

Figure 2.1 Diagram of a 17-year-old coniferous tree showing increase in diameter of the trunk by addition of annual increments or rings. (*From Brown, Panshin, and Forsaith, 1949.*)

Gross Structure of Wood

When wood cells are first formed by division of the cambium their walls are flexible and expand readily as the cells enlarge. During enlargement and differentiation of cells their walls become thickened and lignified, causing them to become rigid, inelastic, and incapable of further enlargement. After their maturation the majority of the parenchyma cells in the wood die, but about 10 per cent (from 5 to 40 per cent in different species) remain alive in the sapwood for several years. Many of the living cells occur in the wood rays, which are bands of parenchyma cells oriented horizontally and radiating outward from the first annual ring like spokes in a wheel. The wood rays are connected through the cambium with the phloem rays and form important avenues for the translocation and storage of food. Wood rays are said to comprise an average of about 17 per cent of the volume of hardwoods and 7.8 per cent of the volume of conifers (Myer, 1922). The vessels and tracheids are oriented longitudinally, and although dead, they are important physiologically

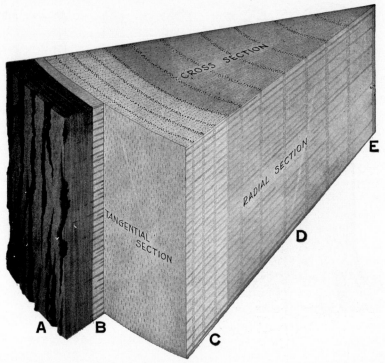

Figure 2.2 A wedge-shaped block cut from the trunk of a young hardwood tree. A. Outer dead bark. B. Inner living bark. C. Sapwood, composed in this example of four growth increments or annual rings. D. Heartwood, composed in this example of seven growth increments or annual rings. (*From Brown, Panshin, and Forsaith, 1949.*)

because they constitute the pathway for water movement from the roots to the leaves. Fibers and longitudinal parenchyma cells also are longitudinal elements. Thus a tree stem consists largely of dead cells interspersed with living cells in the outer part of the wood and the inner part of the bark, all enclosed in a layer of dead outer bark.

Growth Increments

Growth in diameter is most rapid early in the season, and as the growing season advances, growth slows down considerably. The part of the annual increment which is produced later in the growing season, called latewood or summerwood, usually is darker in color and frequently is composed of more cells per unit of area. The terms "earlywood" and "latewood" are now used in preference to the old terms springwood and summerwood by many writers. Young (1952) found that the percentage of latewood in the annual increments of loblolly pine decreased from the ground level upward. Latewood began to be formed at the ground level in June and gradually appeared up the bole until it occurred near the tip in September. At any given place on the bole, latewood as a percentage of the annual ring width increased from the pith toward the cambium. For such reasons Young suggested that the terms springwood and summerwood are really misnomers and should be abandoned, as was suggested by Chalk (1937) some years ago.

In cross sections of stems, growth increments take the form of annual rings. They are prominent as rings because of the differences in density of early growth of one year compared with the adjoining late growth of the previous year. The amount of woody tissue produced varies in width and density in different trees and at different heights in the same tree.

False Rings. Normally one ring is produced in each year by a tree, but occasionally more than one ring is formed in a year (Weakley, 1943). Tingley (1936) found two rings formed in Red Astrachan apple trees in years when a heavy fruit crop was produced, apparently because of heavy utilization of carbohydrates by maturing fruits. One ring was formed in off years. When multiple or false rings are formed earlywood appears to grade into latewood and then back to earlywood. However, in a normal ring earlywood grades into latewood, which ends abruptly where it abuts on the earlywood of the following year. False rings, which occur within the boundaries of the total annual increment, can sometimes be recognized by their poorly defined outer borders (Glock, 1955). Because of the occurrence of multiple, missing, or discontinuous rings, counts of rings obviously do not always indicate accurately the age of a tree. In longleaf pine ring counts are especially inadequate because this species does not form annual rings in its youth. Height growth of longleaf pine seedlings often does not begin until seedlings are 4 to 15 years or more of age, and during this period no distinct annual rings are evident in roots or stems. Only after height growth begins do the young trees form annual rings. Thus ring counts merely show the years that have elapsed since the stem began to grow in height but do not account for the years the seedlings remained in the grass stage (Pessin, 1934).

Severe freezes after mild winters often produce "frost" rings, which differ histologically from normal rings (Figure 16.8). Among the changes that occur in frost rings are distorted xylem elements, formation of parenchymatous tissue, gummosis, formation of traumatic parenchym-

atous tissue, and widening of xylem rays (Harris, 1934). Frost rings are
most often found near the center of a tree because young shoots are more
susceptible to frost injury than are old stems (Stone, 1940).

Annual rings usually form a complete circle. Occasionally, however,
the cambium remains dormant on one side of a tree, so no wood cells
are cut off on the dormant side. The resulting discontinuous ring does not
encircle the stem but runs into an older ring. One-sided cambial dormancy often occurs in trees with one-sided crowns (Fritz and Averell,
1924). Sometimes cambial activity is discontinuous vertically, resulting
in "islands" of ring discontinuities (Larson, 1956). These discontinuities
might be caused by local deficiencies of auxin or food or both.

Sapwood and Heartwood

As a tree stem ages, all the living cells of the central core die. Oils,
gums, resins, tannins, and other substances often accumulate in the
heartwood, causing it to become darker than the sapwood. Some of these
materials are distributed in cell cavities, while others impregnate the cell
walls. Some heartwood deposits are toxic or at least repellent to fungi and
insects. Examples of trees possessing unusually durable heartwood are
black locust, cypress, redwood, red mulberry, catalpa, osage-orange, and
cedars. The amount of heartwood which forms varies with species and
site. Spruces and firs do not form a visibly differentiated heartwood, while
wood of locust (*Robinia*) is mostly heartwood. Maples and ashes form
relatively little heartwood. Once heartwood starts to form, it increases in
diameter throughout the life of the tree. Heartwood provides mechanical
support but does not participate in physiological processes. Sapwood is
much more important from a physiological standpoint because its cells
store food and transport water and minerals. The living cells of the sapwood also carry on metabolic processes such as respiration and digestion.

Growing Regions

There are three growing regions in trees: apical meristems in stem and
root tips, primary cambiums, and secondary or cork cambiums. Growth
consists of three phases: cell division, cell enlargement, and then differentiation and maturation into final form. Growth occurring at apical
meristems usually is classified as "primary growth," and the resulting
tissues are called primary tissues. Growth from lateral meristems results
in increase in diameter. It is called "secondary growth," and the new
xylem and phloem formed are called secondary xylem and phloem.
Growth in height at apical meristems and growth in diameter at lateral
meristems will be discussed separately.

Apical Meristems. A bud is an embryonic axis with its appendages.
Height growth results from the activity of apical meristems or growing

points. These are enclosed in bud scales during the dormant season, but are exposed while growth is occurring. Such a growing point at the stem tip contains groups of meristematic cells called "initials." These divide rapidly and produce cells whose elongation accounts for growth in length. Division occurs in several planes simultaneously so that the stem retains its essentially cylindrical form as it elongates. Apical growth may be considered to consist of three phases: cell division, elongation, and differentiation and maturation, which may be seen in order progressively back from the tip. Whereas cell division occurs only at the tip, elongation may

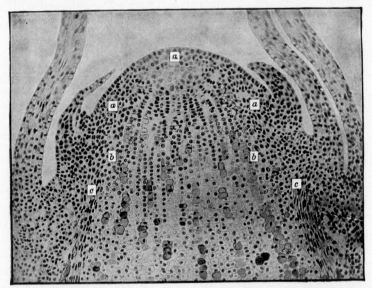

Figure 2.3 Photomicrograph of a longitudinal section through the dormant growing region at the tip of a white pine stem. Promeristem, *a-a-a;* pith, *b-b;* procambium, *c-c.* (*Photograph by W. M. Harlow,* 50×. *From Brown, Panshin, and Forsaith,* 1949.)

extend over several internodes. Elongation slows down, however, with increasing distance from the tip. The initials of the apical meristem build up an undifferentiated primary tissue which differentiates as it ages by changes in size, shape, and wall thickness of its cells.

The tissues produced by the apical initials give rise to tissues which differentiate into epidermis, pith, pericycle, cortex, primary xylem, and primary phloem. Since they owe their origin to an apical meristem they are classed as primary tissues.

An embryo contains two such meristems, one of which initiates stem growth and the other produces root tissues. Some idea of the cellular organization of a multicellular growing point of a white pine stem tip may be gained from Figure 2.3. The first-formed meristem, a region of

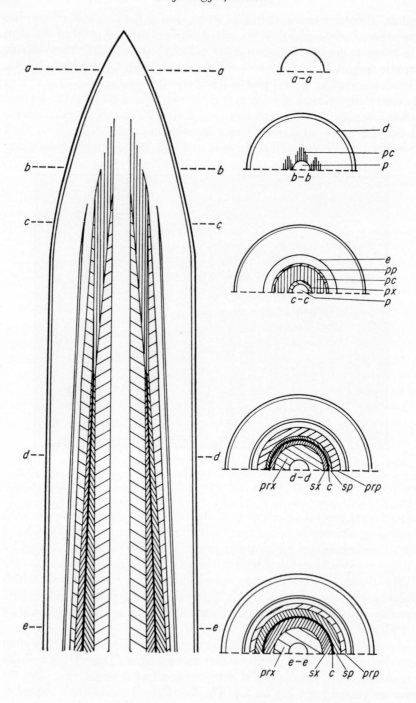

initiating cells, is located in the area bounded by the letters *a-a-a*. The tissue between the letters *b-b* is the pith, and farther back in the growing point, at *c-c*, is the procambium layer, which elongates vertically to form a primary tissue which encloses the pith. Patterns of cell zonation in apical meristems may vary considerably in different species and even within a species.

The early development of primary tissues at the apex and the addition of secondary or cambium-produced tissues farther back from the tip in a young stem or twig are shown in Figure 2.4. The tip contains only primary tissues which result from apical cell divisions, but at *e-e*, part of the procambium has become cambium, which starts to thicken the stem by producing secondary xylem and secondary phloem through tangential division. The zonal relation of primary tissues to the youngest tissues produced by the cambium may be seen in greater detail in cross sections of a white pine twig about an inch back from the tip (Figure 2.5). Before secondary thickening begins, primary xylem and primary phloem, which were originally transformed from part of the procambium, are quite prominent. Before the end of the first year, however, secondary thickening has begun through divisions of the cambium and most of the first annual ring already consists of secondary xylem or wood. The primary xylem tissue remains unaltered and continues to surround the pith. Production of secondary phloem by cambial division pushes the primary phloem outward so that it becomes crushed and eventually is sloughed off from the tree. In each succeeding year secondary xylem and secondary phloem cells continue to be built up by divisions of the cambium. The sequence of events in the development of the axis of a young tree from the embryo is essentially similar for conifers and broadleaf trees.

Lateral Meristems. The lateral meristems include the vascular cambium and secondary or cork cambium. These will be discussed separately.

Primary Cambium. Growth in thickness of trees is traceable to the primary cambium, a lateral meristem located between the bark and wood, which each year gives rise to xylem cells to the inside and phloem cells

---

Figure 2.4 Diagrams showing development of a young tree stem or twig. The apex *a-a* is the promeristem shown in Figure 2.3. At the level of section *b-b* the dermatogen (*d*), procambium (*pc*), and pith (*p*) are beginning to differentiate. At *c-c* the procambium has formed a complete cylinder and the outer part has become protophloem (*pp*) and the inner part protoxylem (*px*). The endodermis (*e*) sometimes becomes differentiated at this stage. The amount of procambium decreases as it is converted into primary phloem (*prp*) and primary xylem (*prx*). Between *c-c* and *d-d* the remaining layer of procambium becomes cambium and begins to produce secondary phloem (*sp*) and secondary xylem (*sx*) as shown at *d-d*. At level *e-e* the secondary xylem and phloem has increased in amount and the primary phloem has begun to be crushed by the increase in secondary tissues. Eventually, all of the tissues outside of the secondary phloem are split off, as shown in Figure 2.7. (*Redrawn from Eames and MacDaniels, 1947.*)

to the outside. The term "cambium" is used by some writers to designate the unicellular layer of cambial initials, while others use it to identify the entire meristematic or cambial zone which produces xylem and phloem. However, the broader usage of cambium to include the self-perpetuating layer as well as xylem and phloem mother cells is more generally accepted. The self-perpetuating, unicellular layer of cambial cells is composed of

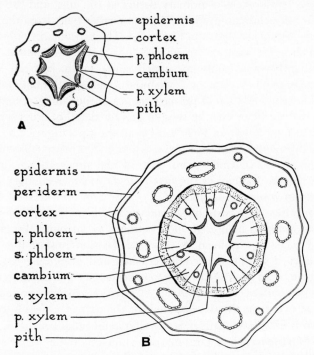

Figure 2.5 Diagrammatic drawings of cross sections through young white pine twigs showing arrangement of tissues before (*A*) and after (*B*) secondary thickening occurs. *A.* About 1 inch from the apex the primary tissues are complete, but secondary thickening has not begun. *B.* At the end of the growing season considerable secondary thickening has occurred. (*From Brown, Panshin, and Forsaith, 1949.*)

two types of cells, fusiform initials and ray initials. The predominating fusiform initials are elongated, spindle-shaped cells which give rise through tangential divisions to longitudinally arranged elements such as fibers, vessel elements, sieve tubes, and longitudinal parenchyma of the wood and inner bark. The short, cubical ray initials give rise by tangential divisions to xylem ray cells inwardly and phloem ray cells outwardly, which form the transverse elements of the tree. Cambial cells often are highly vacuolated and exhibit protoplasmic streaming.

Fusiform initials vary greatly in shape and size, those in gymnosperms being much larger than those in broadleaf trees. In conifers and less specialized broadleaf trees there is marked increase in length of cambial cells for a number of years, after which no further significant increase occurs. In contrast, cambial elements of some broadleaf trees show virtually no increase in length with increasing age of the tree (Bailey, 1954). As fusiform initials change in size with age of the tree, the xylem and phloem elements which are cut off from them are similarly altered in length. These elements also undergo changes in size during differentiation.

As a tree increases in diameter, the circumference of the cambium must also increase. This is accomplished by increase in number and size of cambial cells by divisions in a manner that varies with the kind of tree. In a few genera of angiosperms, division is radiolongitudinal (anticlinal) and produces initials which lie side by side. In all other angiosperms and in gymnosperms division appears to be pseudotransverse. In pseudotransverse division an oblique wall is formed across the center of the initial and cuts off two daughter cells. The daughter initials then grow at the tips until they are about as large as the cambial initial which produced them (Figure 2.6).

Pseudotransverse division in conifers produces many more initials than are necessary for increase in cambial circumference.

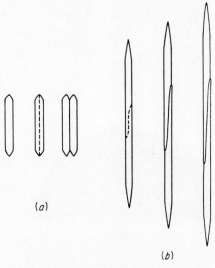

(a)

(b)

Figure 2.6 Cambial initials in tangential section showing stages of division. *a.* Radiolongitudinal division which occurs in some angiosperms. *b.* Pseudotransverse division which occurs in most angiosperms and in conifers.

Usually the largest cells, which have the most ray contacts, survive and the shortest ones fail to grow and finally die. This suggests the existence of internal competition for carbohydrates and water during the growing season (Bannan, 1956).

Initials which divide pseudotransversely often undergo elongation. Several ideas have existed concerning how this takes place. One view visualized walls of adjoining cells sliding by one another in "sliding growth." Priestley (1930) believed that such slipping of adjoining cells by one another was unlikely to occur and that cells expanded in unison, a pattern termed "symplastic growth." One present view is that fusiform initials elongate at the tips only and intrude or force their way between cells above and below (Bannan, 1956). This type of growth has been called "intrusive growth" by Sinnott and Bloch (1939a) and "interposition growth" by Schoch-Bodmer (1945). The greatest elongation of cambial cells often occurs after diameter growth slows down (Bannan, 1956). The rate and amount of elongation vary greatly among neighboring initials, and growth may proceed steadily or in spurts (Bannan, 1951).

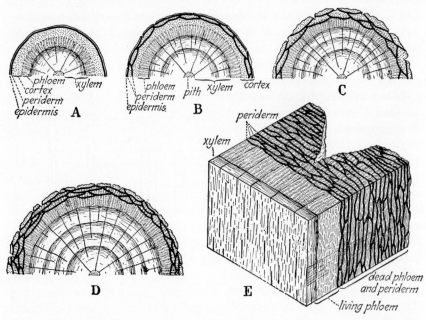

Figure 2.7 Diagrams showing formation of successive periderm layers in bark of a typical woody stem. *A* is a 1-year-old twig in which the first periderm forms a complete cylinder inside of the epidermis. *B* is a 2-year-old twig in which the epidermis and first periderm have been ruptured and new arc-shaped layers have formed deeper in the cortex. In *C*, a 3-year-old stem, the outer tissues have weathered away and periderm has begun to develop in the secondary phloem. This process continues in *D*, a 4-year-old stem. *E* is the outer part of a mature tree trunk, showing a narrow band of living phloem and the deeply fissured outer bark made up of dead phloem and periderm layers. Considerable tissue has weathered away from the outside of the bark. (*From Eames and MacDaniels, 1947.*)

Elongation of cambial cells usually is greatest at their morphologically lower ends (Bannan, 1956).

Cork Cambium. The cork cambium or phellogen is a secondary meristem one cell in thickness which forms in subepidermal or other mature parenchyma tissues of stems, roots, and even in fruits (Figure 2.7). It gives rise by tangential divisions to cork cells or phellem to the outside and phelloderm cells to the inside. Collectively the three layers (phellogen, phellem, and phelloderm) are called a "periderm." The phelloderm is a layer of loosely arranged living cells which sometimes carry on photosynthesis and store starch. More cork than phelloderm cells usually are formed, but the amount of cork formed varies greatly with species. Some species lose external cork by cracking and peeling, so the cork layer on a tree remains of about the same thickness. Other species such as cork oak build up thick cork layers but form very few phelloderm cells.

Cork cells are dead. They have highly suberized cellulose walls and are closely packed with no intercellular spaces. Because of its cell structure cork has many valuable properties such as resistance to liquid penetration, resilience, compressibility, buoyancy, low thermal conductivity, and chemical inertness (Panshin et al., 1950). Two distinct types of cork cells occur, a thin-walled type and a thick-walled type. An individual tree may have either type, or it may have both types distributed in adjacent bands. Splitting of birch bark into thin sheets is caused by easy separation of layers of thin-walled cells lying between layers of thick-walled cells (Eames and MacDaniels, 1947). Cork also forms readily in the vicinity of wounds. Apparently cutin and suberin seal off the exposed surface of a wound and create conditions which are conducive to cork formation. Physiological aspects of cork formation in relation to wounding are discussed by Bloch (1941, 1952).

Development of Bark Characteristics. A periderm develops in most trees during the first growing season, usually in the cortex just inside the epidermis, but sometimes from the epidermis (*Acer pensylvanicum*) or the pericycle (*Thuja*). Shortly thereafter the epidermis breaks and disintegrates (Eames and MacDaniels, 1947). With added diameter growth the first periderm and other outer tissues split and new periderm layers form deeper in the cortex and finally in the secondary phloem. Tissues outside of the periderms soon die because they are cut off from food and water by the impermeable layers of cork. The first periderm is a complete cylinder, but subsequent periderms are small arcs or lunes with overlapping edges so that they cut off scales of bark tissue (Figure 2.7). In many species the outer overlapping periderms weather and slough off, while in other species such as redwood they are persistent and build up a very thick bark.

The smoothness and degree of exfoliation of bark are related to the persistence of the first periderm. In smooth-barked trees such as beech and birch the first periderm may persist for a long time, or even for the life of the tree. In such species the periderm increases in circumference by radial division and by increase in size of cork cambium cells. Stems of beech trees are covered with a very thin periderm except near lenticels. In rough-barked species the first periderm ruptures as the stem grows, a new cork cambium develops deeper in the cortex, and deep cork formation begins. Tissues of the older periderms die and make up the rough outer bark of such species as oaks and hackberries. Various characteristic patterns of exfoliation may develop later. For example, small isolated periderm layers may cut off scales of tissue in a "scale-bark" pattern as in red maple or there may be a vertical splitting of periderm as in hickory because of many fibers in the phloem. Some species shed bark in sheets as the periderms form abscission layers.

Some normally smooth-barked species form rough bark in response to abnormal conditions due to fungi, lichens, or mechanical injury. Kaufert (1937) found very little difference between the periderm structure of a 20-year-old aspen with smooth bark and that of a 1-year-old twig. A constant thickness of periderm with age was maintained since sloughing off of surface cells kept pace with production of new cells. Fungus invasion caused rough bark in this species. Bark beneath lichens was also invariably rougher than bark on the exposed side of the tree. He also observed that the thin periderm could be broken by continued whipping of brush, resulting in rough bark near the base of mature trees. Formation of rough bark was attributed also to hail and sleet injury.

Hardness of bark reflects the degree of sclerification which occurs. In oaks, hickories, and maples parenchyma cells of the bark become sclereids or stone cells, thus giving these species a hard bark. The soft bark of trees such as American elm is associated with the presence of soft corky layers and limited sclerification.

Growth Periodicity

Tree growth involves many complex biochemical processes which occur simultaneously. The rates of these individual processes vary with time, and as a result of these variations and of variations in the environment, trees manifest diurnal, seasonal, and lifetime growth periodicities. Growth of stems is most rapid in the early part of the frost-free season and by midsummer either stops or slows up considerably. Trees grow rapidly in their youth, but more slowly with increasing age. Height and diameter growth of a tree begin and end at different times. Diameter growth usually continues later in the summer than height growth. Roots have an even longer growing season, and in southern states often grow all winter (Reed, 1939; Huberman, 1940). Seasonal growth periodicity of various parts of a white pine tree in New England is shown in Figure 2.8. While seasonal periodicity in height growth is controlled mostly by internal genetic factors, growth in diameter is more sensitive to environmental fluctuations. The important features of height growth and diameter growth will be discussed separately.

Knowledge of the seasonal periodicity in growth has both physiological and practical importance. The need to relate irrigation and fertilization to growth seems obvious. The relation of cambial activity and cell maturation to bark peeling has been studied extensively (Huber, 1948; Wilcox et al., 1954). It generally is necessary to know the growth status of trees in order to understand the effects of cultural treatments and weather, because they often react quite differently when dormant and when growing.

Diurnal Periodicity in Height Growth. In general, more shoot elongation occurs at night than during the day. During unusually cold nights, however, growth at night may be less than during the day. Growth of red pine shoots in New Hampshire averaged 5.93 millimeters per night and

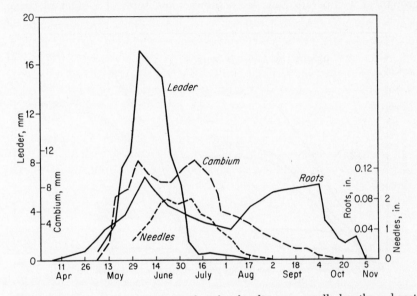

Figure 2.8 Seasonal course of growth in height, diameter, needle length, and root length of 10-year-old white pine in southern New Hampshire. (*After Kienholz, 1934.*)

4.77 millimeters per day, a ratio of 4:3, over the growing season (Kienholz, 1934). Illick (1919) noted a similar pattern for several species in Pennsylvania. For example, white pine shoots averaged 30 per cent more growth at night than during the day. In North Carolina Reed (1939) measured height growth of loblolly and shortleaf pines at 6:30 A.M. and 6:30 P.M. from June 12 to July 2. The average total daytime and nighttime growth per tree for this period follow.

	Average day growth, inches	Average night growth, inches
Loblolly pine	1.64	3.21
Shortleaf pine	1.27	2.13

According to Kienholz (1934), there is a high degree of correlation between night growth and minimum temperature. On cold nights when the temperature dropped to 42°F or lower, growth of shoots was negligible. Thus there is relatively less night growth at the beginning of the growing season when nights are unusually cold. Tolsky (1914) found this was true in southern Russia.

Seasonal Periodicity in Height Growth. Height-growth data usually are plotted either as cumulative growth over time or as actual growth at a particular time during the growing season. When plotted cumulatively, growth of Temperate Zone trees shows some form of a sigmoid curve.

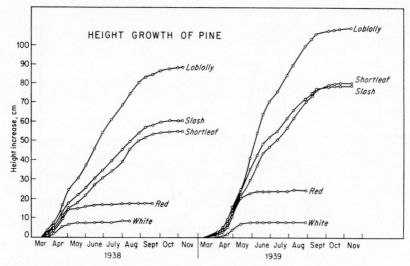

Figure 2.9 Height growth of pines in North Carolina during two growing seasons. (*From Kramer,* 1943.)

Growth starts slowly, then accelerates rapidly, and finally levels off sometime during the summer (Figure 2.9). Curves showing actual growth at different times of the season generally show a grand period pattern. A slow increase in the spring is followed quickly by acceleration at an increasing rate to a maximum, and then a rapid decline, with growth tapering off before it stops completely. As may be seen in Figure 2.10, growth curves rarely are symmetrical. They may be modified so one side is drawn out longer than the other, or double peaks may occur. Curves of some species show sharp peaks in midsummer, while others show a flat plateau. Some Temperate Zone species tend to put on a final burst of growth in late summer just before dormancy. Such late growth often occurs from bursting of current-year buds. The shoots thus formed are called "lammas shoots" after the English festival of Lammas on August 1.

In Germany these shoots are called *Johannistriebe* because the midsummer festival is named in honor of St. John. Lammas shoots are formed commonly by oaks, hickories, alders, elders, and elms as a result of an abundance of available water. Lammas shoot growth, which often exceeds early spring growth, may render a tree susceptible to frost injury since new shoots do not always have time to harden off before frosts occur. It may also produce poorly formed trees.

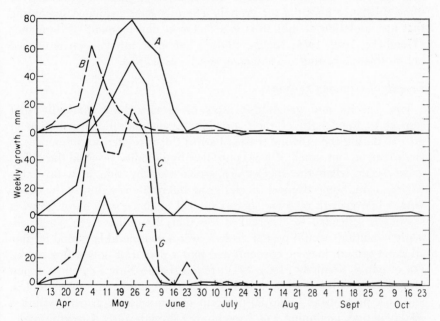

Figure 2.10 Types of growth curves found in pines growing in Indiana, based on measurements of red, white, jack, and Scotch pine 3 to 8 years old. Type *C* was most common, and type *G* with two equal peaks was rare. (*From Friesner,* 1942a.)

Recurrent Flushes of Growth. Even in the most favorable environment trees rarely if ever grow continuously during the entire year. In an air-conditioned greenhouse with adequate water and minerals loblolly pine seedlings do not grow continuously (Kramer, 1957b), as shown in Figure 15.10. Shoots elongate for a few weeks, cease growth for a time, then resume elongation, and this may occur three, four, or even more times during the season. Recurrent flushes of shoot growth have been reported for lemons (Reed, 1928), oranges (Reed and MacDougal, 1937), cacao (Humphries, 1947), tea (Bond, 1942), and other tropical or subtropical plants, but it also is common in the Temperate Zone. Lammas shoots are really an example of this type of growth. The common occurrence of this type of growth often is overlooked because most growth curves are averages of a number of trees and some of them are growing even when others have temporarily ceased.

The causes of intermittent growth are not yet understood. Klebs (1915) observed it in both tropical and Temperate Zone plants and attributed it to a temporary deficiency of mineral nutrients. This is not the cause, however, because it occurs in tree seedlings receiving an adequate supply of mineral nutrients. The general behavior of trees suggests that they may either accumulate an inhibitor or suffer a deficiency of some substance essential for growth. There is some evidence suggesting that accumulation of inhibitors is a factor in development of dormancy (Hemberg, 1949, 1958; Nitsch, 1957a), but more information is needed before this interesting phenomenon can be explained.

Length of Growing Season

Tree species and geographic races of species differ markedly with respect to the length of their growing season and the distribution of growth during the growing season. Part of this is related to differences in environment, but much of it is controlled by heredity because the differences occur when the species are grown side by side in a favorable environment. Some tropical species grow intermittently during the entire year, while growth of some species in cool climates with short growing seasons is restricted to a period of less than 2 months. Even where climatic conditions would permit growth over a considerable period of time all shoot growth may be concentrated into a period of only a few weeks. For example, Kienholz (1934, 1941) found that in New England a group of species, including white ash, beech, red oak, and red, white, Scotch, and jack pine, make up to 90 per cent of the season's growth within a 30-day period, beginning 1 or 2 weeks after growth starts. Growth usually ceases in this group of trees in late June. Another group, including aspen, gray and white birch, and yellow-poplar, start growth more slowly and make 90 per cent of the season's growth in a period of 60 days, beginning 3 or 4 weeks after growth starts in the spring. Growth ceases in these species by mid-August. Johnston (1941) reported that black, white, and post oak had a growing season of only 19 days in the Missouri Ozarks and made 90 per cent of their growth in only 11 days in late April and early May.

Even when moved from upper New York to the longer growing season of North Carolina, red and white pine and balsam fir made most of their growth in April and almost ceased growth by the end of May. In contrast, the southern species—loblolly, slash, and shortleaf pine—made 10 to 20 per cent of the season's growth in each of 5 months and had a total growing period of 200 days. Yellow-poplar and white ash both had a somewhat longer growing season in North Carolina than farther north, but preserved their individual differences, white ash making half of its total growth in April, while yellow-poplar made 20 per cent or more of its total growth in each of four months and had a growing season of 160 days (Kramer, 1943).

These individual differences occur even under the most favorable environmental conditions, as for example in a nursery where the trees are grown with uniform spacing in fertile soil. Under these very favorable conditions Kozlowski and Ward (1957b) found that some species grew for 10 weeks and others for twice as long (Table 2.1). Likewise, in an air-conditioned greenhouse with adequate water and nutrients the growing season for red oak was only a few weeks while that for loblolly pine was over 30 weeks (Kramer, 1958b).

Table 2.1. Variations in length of growing season for deciduous species in Westfield, Massachusetts, during 1954. (*After Kozlowski and Ward, 1957b.*)

Species	Date height growth began	Date height growth stopped	Weeks of height growth	No. of days for middle 90% of growth
Acer saccharum	May 1	Aug. 28	17	75
Acer saccharinum	Apr. 24	Sept. 11	20	80
Gymnocladus dioicus	Apr. 19	June 26	10	36
Pyrus americana	Apr. 19	Aug. 7	16	39
Betula papyrifera	Apr. 19	Sept. 11	21	98
Cornus florida	Apr. 24	Sept. 4	19	95

In general, most species in a given locality begin growth within a short time span in the spring but they cease growth over a wide range of time (Figure 2.9). It seems likely that growth usually starts as soon as temperatures are high enough; hence there is a wide range in dates from south to north. In the southern part of the United States growth of many species starts in March, but in the north it may not start until June. As mentioned previously, the time of cessation of growth is highly variable among species and usually occurs long before temperatures are low enough to hinder growth.

Height-growth patterns of various species are remarkably similar from year to year in spite of minor variations in weather (Hiley and Cunliffe, 1922). Tryon and Finn (1937) and Kienholz (1934) found that the peak of growth of several coniferous and broadleaf species occurred at nearly the same time for several successive years. Species with long growing seasons showed more variability in this respect than those with short growing seasons. Kramer (1943) found essentially the same pattern of growth in two successive seasons in several species of conifers and hardwoods growing out of doors. Numerous studies of height growth have been made for different species and in different parts of the country. Among them are those of Baldwin (1931), Cook (1941a and b), Kienholz (1934, 1941), Fowells (1941), Johnston (1941), Friesner (1942a, 1943a), Kramer (1943), Bonck and Penfound (1944), Farnsworth (1955), and Kozlowski and Ward (1957a and b).

Most of these studies have been made on seedlings or young trees because of the obvious difficulties of measuring large trees, and it may be questioned whether seedlings and mature trees behave in the same manner. Wareing (1956) found that seedlings of black locust grew well into the autumn although mature trees ceased growth by the end of July. Young and Kramer (1952) found that 13-year-old loblolly pine trees about 35 feet tall ceased growth a few weeks earlier than the younger trees measured by Reed (1939) or the seedlings measured by Kramer (1943). Büsgen and Münch (1931, pp. 67–68) state that the date of resumption of shoot growth is retarded with increasing age up to 16 to 25 years, at which time it may be a month later than in seedlings.

It is well known that water deficits and other unfavorable environmental conditions cause premature cessation of growth. It has been demonstrated also that improving the environment by irrigation, fertilization, or removal of competing vegetation increases the length of the growing season and the amount of shoot growth (Harris and Boynton, 1952; Meginnis, 1934; Merrill and Kilby, 1952; Schreiner, 1940).

Rate of Height Growth

Rates of shoot growth vary with species, age of the tree, and location of the shoot. Growth over the life span of a tree shows a sigmoid pattern with a short period of acceleration by the seedling, very fast growth of the young tree, and a rather long period of negligible height growth of the old tree (Baker, 1950).

In North Carolina yellow-poplar and white ash seedlings grew faster than red and white oak and black walnut seedlings. Loblolly pine grew more than slash and shortleaf pine, while red and white pines grew much less. Eight years after planting, the average heights of trees in adjacent plantations in Durham, North Carolina, were loblolly pine, 18.1; slash pine, 12.6; red pine, 2.3; and white pine, 3.8 feet (Kramer, 1943). Growth rates also vary in different parts of the stem. According to Friesner (1943b), a primary axis in white pine and red pine starts to grow sooner, grows later in the season, and elongates more than a secondary axis. He noted that branches near the top of a tree began to grow earlier and elongated more than those lower on the tree. Stump sprouts often grow

much faster and have a longer growing season than seedling shoots. For
example, Kienholz (1941) noted that red maple sprouts had a growing
season that was nearly twice as long as that of trees.

Conifers of the Pacific Northwest attain the greatest ultimate heights
and continue to grow to much greater ages than conifers in other regions

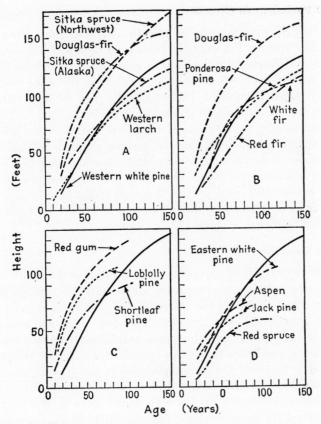

Figure 2.11 Patterns of height growth typical of various species native to different
regions of the United States. *A*. Pacific Northwest. *B*. California and West. *C*. The
South. *D*. Lake states and Northeast. The solid line on each graph is the growth
curve for western white pine. (*From Baker, 1950.*)

(Figure 2.11). An occasional redwood, Douglas-fir, or Sitka spruce may
exceed 300 feet in height (Baker, 1950). Trees with a short life span often
grow faster than those with a long life span. Young gray birch trees grow
much faster than Douglas-firs of the same age, but the short-lived birch
rarely exceeds 50 feet in height (Toumey and Korstian, 1947).

Many examples of very rapid growth rates are reported, chiefly from
tropical and subtropical areas. Bamboo is one of the most rapid growers,

Phyllostachys edulis being reported to grow 15 to 20 meters in 4 or 5 weeks in southern China. Bradley (1922) reported that *Albizia moluccana* in the Andaman Islands grew from seed to a height of 86 feet and a diameter of 9.8 inches in only 7 years. *Albizia* is also a very rapid grower in the Temperate Zone.

Ecotypic Variations in Growth

Races which vary greatly in growth characteristics often develop within a tree species. For example, trees from high and low elevations or from widely different latitudes vary in amounts of growth and length of growing season, even when brought together in the same site (Pauley and Perry, 1954; Critchfield, 1957). According to Billings (1957), ecotypic variation in response to a number of environmental factors can be shown, but usually the response is related to the photoperiodic or temperature regime to which the race has become adapted. Billings attributes such ecotypic variation to environmental selection operating on mixed genotypes in local populations. This obviously has great practical importance in considering seed sources from altitudes or latitudes that are different from those in which the trees are to be grown. Ecotypic variation is discussed further in Chapter 15.

Diameter Growth

Diameter growth is of particular interest because the width of annual rings and the relative proportions of early- and latewood in each ring have important effects on the quantity and quality of wood produced. Diameter growth, like shoot growth, shows both daily and seasonal periodicity, but diameter growth seems considerably more sensitive to environmental conditions than shoot growth. For example, Mikola (1950) stated that in northern Europe temperature of the growing season markedly affects diameter growth but there is no strong correlation of short-term variations in climatic factors with height growth. This situation has been observed by many workers. The sensitivity of diameter growth to soil moisture forms the basis for the science of dendrochronology.

Diurnal Periodicity in Diameter Growth. Numerous studies of diameter growth have indicated that diurnal variations in diameter of tree trunks occur regularly (Figure 15.2). Part of this variation is caused by changes in volume resulting from changes in water content. Heavy midday transpiration removes water faster than it is absorbed, causing shrinkage, while uptake of water at night causes rehydration and swelling. This has been observed by many workers and is discussed in detail by MacDougal (1921, 1938). The extent of shrinkage and swelling seems to depend on the type of wood, as it is reported to be greater in a softwood such as white pine than in conifers with harder woods (Daubenmire and Deters, 1947). Seasonal shrinkage and swelling also occur (Haasis, 1933; Fielding and Millett, 1941; Byram and Doolittle, 1950) because the water content of tree trunks usually decreases during the summer and increases during the winter (Gibbs, 1939; Clark and Gibbs, 1957). Changes in diameter caused by changes in water content are discussed further in Chapter 12.

The diurnal variations in diameter caused by variations in water content tend to obscure the diurnal variations in rate of growth, which doubtless occur. It is probable that when water deficits become large enough to reduce the tree diameter they also reduce diameter growth, but it is quite possible that even when the tree trunk as a whole is shrinking the growth continues in the cambial region because growing regions often are able to obtain water at the expense of nongrowing regions.

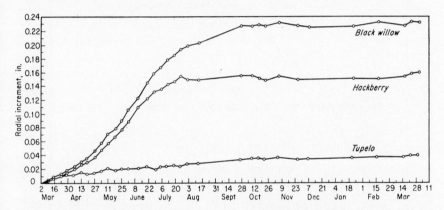

Figure 2.12 Differences in radial growth and length of growing season of three species of hardwood in southern Louisiana. (*From Eggler*, 1955.)

Seasonal Periodicity in Diameter Growth. Diameter growth during a given season follows a modified sigmoid curve (Figure 2.12). The length of the season during which diameter growth occurs varies with species and with latitude, but in general it occurs over a longer period than shoot growth. According to Jackson (1952), grand periods of radial growth for trees of the Georgia Piedmont varied from 70 to 209 days. In Indiana, Friesner (1942b) noted that beech increased in diameter for only 5 weeks while other broadleaf species grew for varying periods up to 15 weeks. Fritts (1958) observed diameter growth in beech in Ohio for over 3 months. Reimer (1949) found growth of several species of Indiana hardwoods to vary from 8 to 19 weeks. Many southern species have very long growing seasons. A black willow in Louisiana grew for 8 months (Eggler, 1955), and slash pine in Florida has an equally long growing period (Schopmeyer, 1955). In southern Canada diameter growth of four hardwood and two conifer species was completed in less than 4 months (Belyea et al., 1951). Byram and Doolittle (1950) followed the course of diameter growth of a 65-foot-high shortleaf pine tree in North Carolina. As may be seen in Figure 2.13, diameter growth followed a modified sigmoid curve, with greatest diameter increase occurring in the spring. Daily stem shrinkage occurred on sunny days because of excess transpiration, but this was more than made up at night. During June, soil moisture apparently became limiting and growth slowed down, until by July 9 drought caused a shrinkage in diameter of about 0.06 millimeter per day. Growth probably was taking place during this time, but it was obscured by shrinkage caused by decreased moisture content in the stem. When

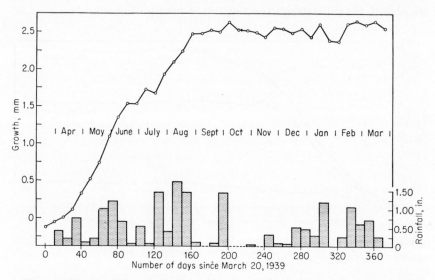

Figure 2.13 Rainfall and diameter growth of shortleaf pine in western North Carolina. (*From Byram and Doolittle, 1950.*)

soil moisture was replenished by rain the tree continued to show radial increase until the curve finally leveled off after about 200 days of diameter growth.

Environment in Relation to Diameter Growth. Diameter growth apparently proceeds largely at the expense of current photosynthate and is sensitive to environmental conditions, especially water supply. Decreases in diameter caused by dehydration often are superimposed on a seasonal-growth curve and may mask small amounts of diameter growth during periods of drought. Friesner and Walden (1946) reported such diameter decrease for white pine. Stems of black locust were reported by Daubenmire and Deters (1947) to shrink as much as 30 per cent of total annual increment in diameter, and Jackson (1952) observed such shrinkage in 13 of 21 species studied. Fritts (1958) also found shrinkage in beech.

MacDougal (1938) emphasized the close relationship between available moisture and diameter increase. When he irrigated an evergreen oak which had not shown any growth for 3 weeks, an increase in diameter was observed within 2 hours after irrigation, but this may have been merely the result of rehydration of the tissues rather than real growth. Because of the marked response of diameter growth to climatic factors, there is less similarity in diameter-growth curves during successive years than there is in height-growth curves of the same tree. In Indiana, beech trees increased in diameter for 9 weeks one year but for only 5 weeks the next year (Friesner, 1942b). Conifers apparently respond similarly, because a white pine tree increased in diameter for 20 weeks one year and for 28 weeks another year (Friesner and Walden, 1946).

There is a wide range in dates both of initiation and of cessation of diameter growth of different species. There appears to be less spread in the North than in the South with respect to the time at which growth of individual trees of a species resumes (Belyea et al., 1951; Jackson, 1952). Eggler (1955) reported that in southern Louisiana there was a spread of 3 months between the times when the first and last tupelo-gum began diameter growth and a similar spread between cessations of growth of the first and last tree. In contrast, diameter growth of eight coniferous and eight broadleaf species in Idaho began at about the same time (Daubenmire and Deters, 1947). However, even in the North several weeks may elapse before all trees on a particular site begin growing. In Indiana five species of broadleaf trees started to grow within a month (Reimer, 1949).

Rate of Diameter Growth. The rate of diameter growth varies greatly with species, age, and site. In southern Louisiana cottonwood grew 0.63 inch in diameter in one growing season while trident red maple grew only 0.05 inch. Other species were intermediate (Eggler, 1955). An example of phenomenally rapid growth was cited by Parham (1941), who noted that the average diameter at breast height of 3-year-old *Albizia falcata* trees was 7 inches, and Bradley (1922) reported that a tree of *A. moluccana* grew from seed to a diameter of 9.8 inches in 7 years. There seems to be no consistent relationship between the starting date and rate of growth. Species that have a long life span usually grow less in a given period than do species with a short life span. The short-lived aspens and willows grow faster than oaks, which are longer-lived and larger at maturity. Tolerant species apparently grow slower than intolerant ones (Toumey and Korstian, 1947). The marked variation in diameter growth caused by site factors is discussed in Chapter 16.

Although lifetime growth curves are basically sigmoid, they are much flatter than seasonal curves (Baker, 1950). Wide variation in diameter increase during the life span of several conifers is shown in Figure 2.14.

Forms of Tree Stems. Tree trunks tend to grow like cylinders below the crown and like a cone within the crown (Young and Kramer, 1952). However, entire tree trunks may vary from paraboloids to neiloids because of differences in diameter growth at different stem heights. In exposed trees annual rings increase in thickness from the base of the crown downward, but in suppressed trees annual rings narrow from the base of the crown downward and then increase again near the base of the trunk (Baker, 1950; Satoo et al., 1955). Young and Kramer (1952), however, found growth in trunk diameter of loblolly pine to decrease from the base of the crown downward regardless of the total amount of crown. The zone of increased diameter growth below the crown moves upward as trees increase in height, tending to maintain trunks with a cylindrical rather than a conical form (Baker, 1950). The actual bending of trees under wind stress apparently also influences the height at which most wood is laid down, and trees guyed to prevent swaying are said to make less growth than those allowed to sway (Jacobs, 1954).

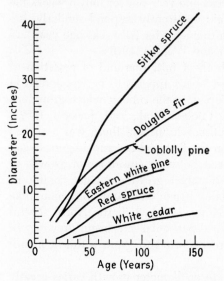

Figure 2.14 Rate of diameter growth of various species at various ages. (*From Baker*, 1950.)

According to Labyak and Schumacher (1954), the contribution of individual branches to growth of the main stem varies greatly with the height of the branches on the stem. In loblolly pine, branches located at a distance below the top equal to 15 per cent of the total height contributed most to volume growth of the main stem. The lowermost branches contributed nothing to growth of the stem except when they had a large number of branchlets. Many lower branches with small leaf areas and poor lighting require all the carbohydrates they synthesize for their own growth and in addition constitute a drain on food elaborated by other branches.

Methods of Measuring Diameter Growth

Large increases in diameter may be measured by calipers, tapes, or increment borers. Direct histological examinations have been made to ascertain when cambial cell division begins (Priestley et al., 1933; Ladefoged, 1952). For measuring small amounts of growth over short time intervals dendrographs and dendrometers are used. Whereas dendrographs give a continuous and permanent record of tree growth on a chart driven by a clock mechanism, dendrometers provide growth data only at the time they are read by an observer.

Early dendrographs are discussed by MacDougal (1921). Many improvements have been made over the years. A dendrograph which meas-

Figure 2.15 A dendrograph for recording radial growth of tree trunks. (*Fritts and Fritts, 1955. Photograph courtesy of H. C. Fritts.*)

ures and records changes in radius of a tree trunk as small as 0.0001 inch has been described by Fritts and Fritts (1955) and is shown in Figure 2.15. Measurements of radial growth were greatly simplified when Reineke (1932) introduced a dial-gauge dendrometer which made it possible to take observations on a large number of trees. Daubenmire (1945) also used a dial-gauge dendrometer with improved fittings that enabled inexperienced operators to make accurate measurements. A useful and inexpensive modification of the dendrometer, described by Byram and Doolittle (1950), involves a simple metal mounting on a tree trunk and use of micrometer calipers for determining radial increase by measuring the distance between two pieces of metal which are part of the mounting (Figure 2.16). Young (1952) observed that radial increase varied on different sides of a tree and occasionally might even be positive on one side and negative on another. He therefore suggested that when dendrometers are used several radii should be selected at the same height above the ground so that average diameter growth and an estimate of its error can be calculated.

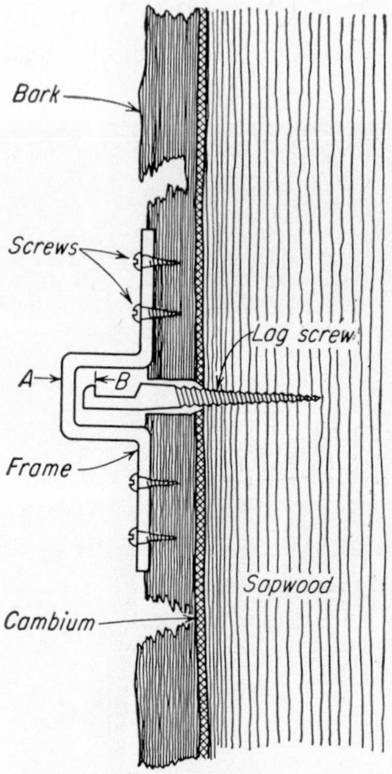

A useful type of dendrometer is the tree-ring band described by Hall (1944) and modified by Liming (1957). It consists of an aluminum band which encircles a tree and is held firmly in place by a coil spring. The band is graduated by inches and tenths of inches and is fitted with a vernier which permits readings of changes in circumference to 0.01 inch, as shown in Figure 2.17.

Such bands have been used successfully in following diameter growth throughout a whole season (Schopmeyer, 1955; Young and Kramer, 1952).

Relation between Height Growth and Diameter Growth

Trees usually grow in diameter for a longer period of time than they grow in height. In most species diameter growth of the lower trunk starts later and continues longer than does height growth. In some species, however, diameter growth of the lower trunk starts at about the same time as height growth, or only shortly thereafter. In still other species

Figure 2.16 Device for measuring radial growth of tree trunks. Measurements of the distance *A-B* are made periodically with micrometer calipers. (*From Byram and Doolittle, 1950.*)

diameter growth near the base of the tree does not even begin until the peak of height growth is over (Table 2.2). Büsgen and Münch (1931, pp. 98–105) gave a good review of the older literature on this subject.

In both hardwoods and conifers the cambium apparently is stimulated to meristematic activity by naturally occurring growth hormones. As early as 1891 Jost demonstrated dependence of cambial activation on a substance, presumably hormonal in nature, which was translocated downward from a growing tip. Snow (1935) activated a cambium with pure synthetic hormones and concluded that cambial growth was normally activated by the same growth hormone which is formed by the young leaves and promotes extension of cells in stems. Söding (1936) showed that introduction of a crystal of indoleacetic acid into the cambium of trees led to rapid cambial growth below the point of insertion of the crystal. Zimmerman (1936) demonstrated that opening buds were rich

Figure 2.17 Tree ring band for measuring changes in circumference of tree trunks. (*Liming,* 1957. *U.S. Forest Service photograph.*)

reservoirs of auxin which moved downward from the tips. Brown and Cormack (1937) were able to bring the dormant cambium of balsam poplar into activity by applications of heteroauxin. Bannan (1955) cites several investigators who concluded that the cambium itself may produce growth hormones after receiving an initial supply from the expanding buds. Messeri (1948) felt that hormones were stored in the cambium from the preceding summer.

In many species debudding or defoliation prevents cambial activity in the treated shoots. Furthermore, the removal of a ring of bark inhibits cambial activity below the ring. If a branch is pruned above a node, cambial activity occurs below the node, beginning in the nodal bud and moving downward. The cambium is not active in the stub above the node. Such observations emphasize a close relationship between presence of hormonal substances and diameter growth in trees. These relationships will be discussed separately for angiosperms and gymnosperms.

Angiosperms. In hardwoods two distinct patterns of cambial growth have been demonstrated. In diffuse-porous species a cambial growth wave progresses downward rather slowly from the expanding buds. Thus diameter growth in the lower trunk usually is observed much later than is the beginning of height growth (Priestley and Scott, 1936). In ring-porous species, however, there is much more rapid initiation of cambial activity throughout the trunk. The ring-porous group apparently depends less on terminal buds as a hormone source. Although in many trees the start of cambial activity in the spring is related to bud activity, apparently cell division continues throughout the summer and is not controlled by terminal growth (Priestley, 1930).

Avery et al. (1937) observed that in *Aesculus* and *Malus* the terminal buds and new shoots developing from them were centers of hormone production. A movement of hormone occurred from the tips basipetally into older portions of the stem. Cambial activity began at the level of the terminal buds and progressed to older portions of the stem, thus following the translocation of the hormone into these regions. Reimer (1949) found that each of five diffuse-porous species began diameter growth at breast height several weeks after height growth began. Diameter growth also lasted much longer than did height growth (Table 2.2). In *Acer pseudoplatanus* 9 to 10 weeks may elapse between the beginning of xylem differentiation in the twigs and that in the roots (Cockerham, 1930). Friesner (1942b) reported differences in time of cambial growth of ring-porous and diffuse-porous species. Cambial growth in *Fagus* and *Acer* was not observed until leaves were expanded, while in *Ulmus* and *Quercus* growth began near the time of bud growth.

In debudded, ring-porous species formation of wide vessels has been shown by Wareing (1951b) to proceed actively throughout all parts of the trunk and the upper parts of the root. In contrast, Wareing observed that cambial activity of debudded diffuse-porous species was restricted to formation of a few isolated vessels, which extended only for a short distance. In both ring- and diffuse-porous species formation of new vessels apparently originated from the stimulus of adventitious buds which were caused to start growth by the debudding. Wareing concluded that ring-porous species have a high amount of auxin in terminal buds

Table 2.2. Correlation between height growth and diameter growth in diffuse-porous species. (*After Reimer, 1949.*)

Species	Height growth			Diameter growth		
	Period	*Weeks*	*Average amount, mm*	*Period*	*Weeks*	*Average amount, mm*
Prunus	Apr. 14–June 4	8	92.0	May 26–Sept. 30	19	2.30
Acer platanoides	Apr. 7–May 26	8	39.7	June 17–Aug. 4	8	1.42
Acer saccharum	Apr. 14–May 26	7	42.3	June 10–Aug. 25	12	1.46
Tilia	Apr. 21–June 17	9	48.8	June 17–Sept. 22	15	1.58
Fagus	Apr. 7–May 26	8	87.2	May 19–Aug. 25	15	1.79

because the first-formed vessels are the widest. He also suggested that whereas diffuse-porous species depend on translocation downward of auxin from terminal buds, ring-porous species have a reserve of auxin precursor in the cambium which makes possible the rapid spread of wide vessel formation throughout the tree, at an early stage of bud development. Ladefoged (1952) studied periodicity of wood formation of conifers and hardwoods in Denmark by histological techniques. He concluded that in ring-porous hardwoods cell division in the lower trunk was detectable some days before, or at the latest simultaneously with the bursting of the buds. In diffuse-porous species cell division in the lower stem did not start until the leaves were partially or completely expanded. At the base of the bud, however, cell division in both ring-porous and diffuse-porous species was often detectable before buds burst.

Gymnosperms. Diameter growth in conifers has been reported to occur both before and after shoot growth starts. Brown (1912, 1915) and Knudson (1913) concluded that cambial activity was initiated some distance below the apex and then moved both upward and downward. Korstian (1921) reported the beginning of diameter growth in conifers to be practically simultaneous with bursting of buds. Priestley (1930) disagreed with Brown and Knudson and reemphasized the hormonal relation of cambial growth to shoot growth. Fraser (1952) also questioned the work of Brown and Knudson and especially the possibility of an upward progression of cambial growth. He found cambial activity to progress only from the top downward or from the tips of branches inward in several conifers, including white pine, the same species Brown had reported on earlier. Young and Kramer (1952) found that height growth of loblolly pine started only a few days before measurable diameter growth occurred, and there was little difference in the time of initiation of cambial growth at four different heights of the stem. Ladefoged (1952) found considerable similarity in diameter growth of conifers and ring-porous hardwoods. Cambial cell division at the base of the bud began several days before buds burst and before cambium cells began to divide in the lower trunk. Cell division in the lower trunk began before or at about the same time as the breaking of the buds. In conifers it appears that hormones accumulate at the apex very early and are translocated downward quite rapidly, often before the buds burst. The possibility also exists that diameter growth of conifers, like that of ring-porous hardwoods, is not exclusively dependent on hormones translocated from terminal buds. This intriguing problem deserves further study.

Anatomy of Woody Stems

A knowledge of their structure is essential to an understanding of the processes which occur in stems.

Wood Structure of Gymnosperms. As may be seen in Figure 2.18, the wood structure of gymnosperms is quite simple and differs from that of angiosperms chiefly in the absence of vessels and the smaller proportion of longitudinally oriented parenchyma. The predominant elements in conifer wood are the tracheids, which may occupy up to 90 per cent of the volume. Tracheids are vertically oriented, thick-walled dead cells

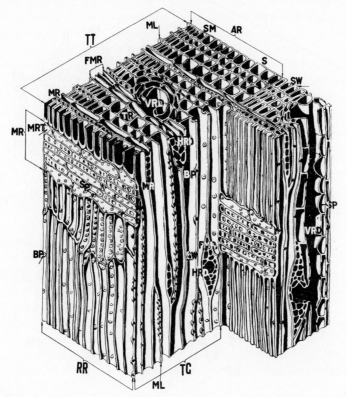

Figure 2.18 Structure of wood of a gymnosperm. *TT*, cross section; *RR*, radial section; *TG*, tangential section; *TR*, tracheids: *ML*, middle lamella; *S*, earlywood or "springwood"; *SM*, latewood or "summerwood"; *AR*, annual ring; *MR*, wood ray; *FMR*, fusiform wood ray; *HRD*, simple pit; *BP*, bordered pit. (*Courtesy of U.S. Forest Service, Forest Products Laboratory photograph.*)

varying in length from 0.5 to 15 millimeters. The tracheids of the early-wood have thinner walls and larger cavities than those formed later, which tend to be thicker-walled and compressed radially. In some species the tracheids show a gradual transition from early- to latewood, but in others, such as the hard pines, the transition is abrupt. Walls of adjoining tracheids contain numerous pit pairs which facilitate movement of water and solutes between tracheids (Bailey, 1954).

The chief transversely oriented elements in coniferous woods are the wood rays. In nonresinous species the rays are typically one cell wide (uniseriate), although in some species they tend to become two cells in width (biseriate). Rays become several cells wide when transverse resin canals occur in them, and then are called fusiform rays. In some conifer-

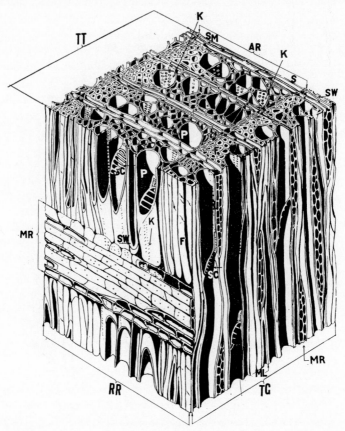

Figure 2.19 Wood structure of an angiosperm. *TT*, cross section; *RR*, radial section; *TG*, tangential section; *P*, vessel; *SC*, perforation plate at vessel end; *F*, wood fibers; *K*, pit; *MR*, wood ray; *AR*, annual ring; *S*, earlywood or "springwood"; *SM*, latewood or "summerwood"; *ML*, middle lamella. (*Courtesy of U.S. Forest Service, Forest Products Laboratory photograph.*)

ous species limited amounts of vertically oriented parenchyma occur in long strands. These occur commonly in redwood and baldcypress, occasionally in some other species, but never in pines.

Wood Structure of Angiosperms. The wood of angiosperms or so-called hardwoods contains vessels, tracheids, various types of fibers, longitudinally oriented wood parenchyma cells, and xylem rays (Figure 2.19). A few genera, mostly tropical, also have gum canals. The most prominent feature of the wood of angiosperms is the vessel, although a few genera such as *Drimys* and *Trochodendron* lack vessels. The wood of angiosperms also contains more parenchymatous tissue than the wood of gymnosperms.

Each vessel consists of a vertical series of vessel members from which the end walls have disappeared, forming tubular structures ranging from 20 to 400 microns or more in diameter and varying in length from a few centimeters to many meters. In some species, such as the oaks, elms, ashes, and chestnuts, the vessels of the spring- or earlywood are much larger than those formed later in the season. Such woods are described as ring-porous in contrast to the diffuse-porous woods such as the maples and willows, where the vessels are of fairly uniform diameter throughout each annual ring. The physiological significance of ring- and diffuse-porous structure is discussed in Chapter 11 in connection with the ascent of sap.

The chief function of xylem vessels is water conduction, but older vessels often are blocked by tyloses. Tyloses are formed when the pressure developed in a parenchyma cell causes the protoplast to balloon out through a pit pair into the cavity of an adjacent vessel. Tyloses are much more abundant in some species such as black locust and white oak than in others such as red oak. The presence of numerous tyloses in white oak wood makes it less permeable to liquids than red oak; hence the former is used in whisky barrels but not the latter. In certain species vessels sometimes are blocked by gum and amorphous deposits of inorganic matter (maple, mahogany, and other tropical species).

Tracheids are smaller than vessels and are individual cells. Because of their smaller size and numerous cross walls they offer more resistance to water movement than vessels and usually are less important as a pathway for conduction. The greater part of the woody xylem tissue often consists of wood fibers which somewhat resemble tracheids but have thicker walls, fewer pits, and smaller cavities. They are of negligible importance in conduction but contribute mechanical strength.

Vessels, tracheids, and fibers lose their protoplasts as soon as they mature, but parenchyma cells often remain alive and physiologically active for a number of years. Strands of longitudinal wood parenchyma are interspersed through the wood in amounts varying from up to 18 per cent of the volume in woods of the Temperate Zone to 50 per cent in the tropical woods (Brown and Panshin, 1940). The radiating, ribbon-shaped wood rays form a characteristic part of the grain of many woods. Rays may be one to several cells in thickness and vary in height from 1 cell to 200 or more cells in certain oaks where rays 20 to 30 cells wide are common. The volume of ray tissue is of some physiological impor-

tance because rays function in food storage and transverse translocation.

Gum canals develop in certain tropical hardwoods, and they develop
as a result of injury in sweetgum and a few other species of the Temperate
Zone. These canals are lined by specialized parenchymatous elements
called "epithelial cells," which produce the gum found in them.

Structure of Phloem

Bark is located outside of the cambium and consists of outer dead
tissue and an inner living layer of phloem. The living phloem is important as the tissue through which upward and downward translocation of
carbohydrates takes place. However, the dead outer bark which sloughs
off with time does not have a physiological role in translocation. Whereas
wood cells are lignified and retain their shape, the sieve tubes and companion cells of the phloem are never woody. In most species the sieve
tubes remain alive and functional for only one season and then collapse,
but in a few species such as basswood, yellow-poplar, and grape they are
functional for 2 or more years. Sieve tubes of inactive phloem may
resemble active phloem tissue as in basswood (*Tilia*), or they may be
completely disorganized as in locust (*Robinia*). Collapse of sieve tubes
in conifers is striking. The amount of inactive phloem that accumulates is related to the depth and functioning of the cork cambium.
If the cork cambium is close to the surface, a large amount of inactive
phloem may accumulate. Normally the bark of a mature tree is not very
thick because more xylem than phloem cells are cut off each year by the
cambium, the phloem elements collapse, and eventually old phloem
tissues of the dead, outer bark are shed.

Phloem of Gymnosperms. Phloem of conifers, which is of relatively
simple structure, contains sieve cells, parenchyma cells, and often fibers
for vertical elements, but no companion cells. Each long, narrow sieve
cell is connected with transversely oriented, uniseriate rays. Longitudinal
parenchyma cells commonly occur. They may contain resins, crystals,
and tannins, and during certain seasons they store starch (Esau, 1953).
Conifer phloem may also contain resin canals and cysts. The phloem cells
of some conifers remain active for 2 years (Huber, 1939).

Phloem of Angiosperms. Phloem of hardwoods differs from conifer
phloem in having a more variable cell arrangement involving more types
of elements. In addition to sieve tubes, it contains companion cells, and
it may contain fibers as in yellow-poplar; or they may be absent as in
sycamore. Longitudinal parenchyma cells and transversely oriented
parenchyma rays also occur. The structure of sieve tubes, the chief path
for movement of foods, is considered in greater detail in Chapter 8.

STRUCTURE AND GROWTH OF ROOTS

The characteristics of a root system depend partly on its heredity and partly on the environment in which it develops. Growing roots usually are considered to possess four distinct regions: the root cap, the meristematic region, the region of cell elongation, and the region of differentiation and maturation; but in at least some roots these regions are by no means so clearly defined as is often supposed. While the root cap usually is well defined, it is absent from some roots such as the short roots of pine. The meristematic region typically consists of numerous small, compactly arranged, thin-walled cells, almost completely filled with cytoplasm. It is difficult to delimit a definite zone of differentiation because different types of cells are differentiated at different distances behind the root apex. Phloem often becomes differentiated before the xylem as in Valencia oranges (Hayward and Long, 1942) and in pear roots (Esau, 1943). The rate of elongation has some bearing on the location of the zones, because in slowly growing roots differentiation of tissues extends closer to the root tips than it does in rapidly growing roots; and when growth is checked or ceases, differentiation extends almost to the apex, only a small meristematic region being left (Wilcox, 1954).

Supported by the older, more rigid tissue and on the sides by soil particles, the root tip is pushed forward through the soil by the elongating cells. Usually its course is somewhat tortuous, as it follows the path of least resistance between soil particles and around pebbles and other obstacles. Although cells of the root cap are torn off by contact with soil particles, they are replaced with new ones formed at the apex of the meristematic zone. Very considerable pressures are developed by enlarging roots, as is evidenced by the lifting of sidewalks and cracking of masonry walls.

As the newly formed, thin-walled cells at the base of the zone of cell enlargement lose their ability to elongate, they become differentiated into the epidermis, cortex, and stele, which constitute the primary structure of a root.

Epidermis and Root Hairs

The epidermis is composed of thin-walled elongated cells which are often slightly smaller than the cortical parenchyma cells. Sometimes a second layer of cells, the hypodermis, lies within the epidermis. The walls of young epidermal cells consist of an inner layer of cellulose and an outer layer of pectic material, probably pectic acid (Cormack, 1935, 1944). Ordinarily as the epidermis matures the cell walls become suberized, and consequently less permeable to water. The most distinctive characteristic of the root epidermis is the production of root hairs, which usually arise as protrusions from the external, lateral cell walls, although in a few species, including roots of citrus and pine, they sometimes arise from cortical cells one or two layers beneath the epidermis. In some species any or all of the epidermal cells can produce root hairs, but in other species the rudimentary epidermal cells divide, giving rise to long epidermal cells and to short ones known as trichoblasts, which usually produce the root hairs (Sinnott, 1939; Sinnott and Bloch, 1939b).

According to Miller (1938), root hairs vary in length from a mere protuberance to about 10 millimeters and have an average diameter of about 10 microns. They are absent on certain conifers (Büsgen and Münch, 1931) and on pecan (Woodroof and Woodroof, 1934). Their absence on many forest trees probably is the result of extensive development of mycorrhizae. Roots of 7-week-old black locust seedlings, grown in fertile soil in the greenhouse, had 520 root hairs per square centimeter of root surface, while loblolly pine roots of the same age and grown under the same conditions bore only 217 root hairs per square centimeter (Kozlowski and Scholtes, 1948). Richardson (1953) showed that roots of sycamore maple developed more root hairs than did roots of northern red oak. Nutman (1934) reported that root hairs of coffee trees increased the absorbing surfaces on which they are produced by about 8.5 times. There undoubtedly are hereditary differences between species with respect to numbers of root hairs per unit of root surface, as well as differences caused by environmental factors.

Root hairs usually are assumed to be short-lived, being destroyed in a few days or weeks by the changes associated with secondary thickening, such as suberization or lignification of epidermis or hypodermis. On some species, however, root hairs may become suberized or lignified and persist for months or even for years. Persistent root hairs have been observed in Valencia orange seedlings (Hayward and Long, 1942), *Cercis, Gleditsia,* and *Gymnocladus* (McDougall, 1921). It is questionable if such root hairs are of importance in the absorption of water and solutes, although Muller (1946) reported that old root hairs of guayule, empty of cytoplasm, absorbed water when brought into contact with it.

Origin of Lateral Roots

Lateral roots arise in the pericycle, a parenchymatous outer layer of the stele. In forming lateral roots pericycle cells become meristematic. As may be seen in Figure 2.20, a definite growing point forms with initials and a root cap and begins to force its way through the endodermis, cortex, and epidermis. This involves partial digestion of the surrounding tissue, but mechanical pressure is largely responsible for the outgrowth

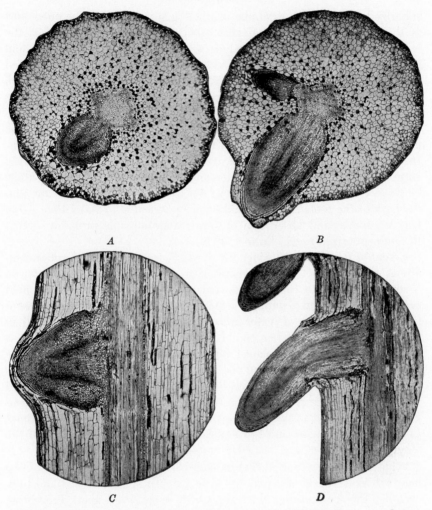

Figure 2.20 Stages in development of branch roots in black willow. *A* and *B* are cross sections, *C* and *D* longitudinal sections. In *A* the tip of a young branch root is passing through the cortex; in *B* it has broken out through the cortex and epidermis. In *C* the branch root is just breaking out, and in *D* it has broken out, although its attachment to the central cylinder is obvious. (*From Eames and MacDaniels,* 1947.)

of the new lateral from the deep-seated meristem (Eames and Mac-Daniels, 1947).

Secondary Growth of Roots

Increase in diameter caused by cambial activity generally destroys the epidermis and the root hairs. Sometimes the hypodermal cells become suberized and the cork cambium or phellogen develops in the outer part of the cortex. In roots of Valencia orange and some other species, the hypodermal cells sometimes produce secondary root hairs, lenticels, and absorbing areas consisting of groups of thin-walled radially elongated cells (Hayward and Long, 1942). Water presumably is absorbed through all these structures. Usually as cambial activity increases the diameter of the stele, the cortex and epidermis are split off and disappear. Frequently a cork cambium arises from the pericycle and the roots become covered with a thin layer of corky tissue containing numerous lenticels. In woody roots, successive cork cambiums usually develop until the cortex has disappeared; the arrangement of tissues in large, woody roots becomes essentially similar to that in woody stems. Apparently, however, the bark of the roots is considerably more permeable to water than is the bark of stems, and absorption of water and minerals probably occurs through suberized roots (Kramer, 1949).

Extent of Root Systems. Since the most efficient zone of absorption usually is near the root tip, the number of tips is an important factor in absorption. Because capillary movement of water in soils below field capacity is very slow, continual extension of roots through soil is essential to the absorption of water and minerals from soils much drier than field capacity. The water in the areas of soil not penetrated by roots is relatively unavailable to plants; hence those plants which develop the most extensively branched and the most deeply penetrating root systems are able to utilize most effectively soil water and minerals. Büsgen and Münch (1931) cite Nobbe as stating that the ability of pine to succeed where silver fir and spruce failed is the result of the pines having 24 times as many root branches and tips and 8 times the absorbing surface of the other species.

Wiggans (1936) reported that roots of 18-year-old apple trees in a deep loess soil in Nebraska had penetrated to a depth of over 30 feet and fully occupied the area between the rows, which were 33 feet apart. Proebsting (1943) studied root distribution of apricot, almond, cherry, peach, pear, and prune on a deep sandy loam soil at Davis, California. Very few roots occurred in the surface foot of soil, probably because of cultivation, and the chief concentration of roots was from 2 to 5 feet, but many roots probably penetrate 15 feet or more. It should be remembered that such deep penetration by roots occurs only in relatively coarse textured, well drained, well aerated soils, but never in heavy clay or where a heavy subsoil, a hardpan layer, or shallow water table exists. In contrast to the deep rooting of apples in Nebraska and of other fruits in California, pears growing on a heavy adobe soil in Oregon developed, out of all the roots occurring in the upper 4 feet of soil, 35 per cent in the surface foot, 68 per cent in the upper 2 feet, and 89 per cent in the upper 3 feet, with only

11 per cent in the 3- to 4-foot horizon. Absorption of water at various depths by these trees was proportional to the concentration of roots.

The extent of the branching and rebranching of root systems is truly remarkable. Kozlowski and Scholtes (1948) found over 2,600 roots on a 6-month-old greenhouse-grown dogwood seedling (Table 2.3). Kalela

Table 2.3. Orders, numbers, and lengths of roots of one 6-month-old dogwood and one loblolly pine seedling grown in the greenhouse in absence of competition. (*After Kozlowski and Scholtes,* 1948.)

Order	Dogwood		Loblolly pine	
	No. of roots	Length, cm	No. of roots	Length, cm
First	1	44.1	1	32.2
Second	93	859.7	71	187.5
Third	1,035	2,714.4	496	146.1
Fourth	1,336	1,357.0	199	21.2
Fifth	191	168.1	0	0.0
Sixth	1	0.6	0	0.0
Total	2,657	5,143.9	767	387.0
Length, ft		168.76		12.70

(1954) reported that the total length of a root system of a 100-year-old pine tree was 50,000 meters. This tree had 5 million root tips. Many of the small absorbing roots of forest trees are located close to the soil surface. Their location and number are important because they constitute the water- and salt-absorbing surface of trees (Scholtes, 1953). Coile (1937b) found that there were as many as 250 roots less than 0.1 inch in diameter per square foot of trench face in the top 5 inches of soil in an oak forest in North Carolina. This was more than 90 per cent of all roots of that size class which occurred to a depth of 36 inches. In a 35-year-old loblolly pine stand, there were about 160 small roots per square foot of trench face in the top 5 inches, again more than 90 per cent of the small roots of this size. Scully (1942) noted that the 0- to 8-inch level of soil contained 80 per cent or more of the total root volume in a maple-oak forest in Wisconsin. Lateral roots of red pine were observed by Day (1941) to occur within 1 foot of the surface, and only the sucker roots and taproots extended below this depth. Nutman (1934) studied the root system of 3-year-old coffee trees growing in the open. He found that 80 per cent of the roots were in a cylinder of soil 5 feet deep, with a radius of 3.5 feet from the tree trunk, and that this cylinder of soil contained an average of 22,675 meters of roots, equivalent to about 118 meters per cubic foot of soil. In contrast, Roberts (1948) found only slightly over 21 meters of roots per cubic foot of soil in the *A* horizon under a 20-year-

old loblolly pine stand. It is common for roots of trees to extend out two
or three times the radius of the branches, although the region of maximum
concentration of absorbing roots is, as a rule, probably under the periphery
of the crown.

   Rate and Periodicity of Root Growth. Because of the difficulties involved in studying roots, much less is known about their growth behavior
than has been learned about shoot growth. Data on diameter growth are
especially meager. Reed (1939) observed that the roots of young loblolly
and shortleaf pine trees growing under field conditions in North Carolina
elongated at a rate of nearly 25 millimeters per day during the period of
maximum growth. Roots of loblolly pine made considerably more growth
in the season than did those of shortleaf pine. In New York State growth
in length of sugar maple roots averaged 0.6 to 1 millimeter per day from
the middle of March to the end of June (Morrow, 1950). Rogers (1939)
noted that apple roots often grew 3 millimeters per day during active
growth periods. Barney (1951) measured root elongation of loblolly pine
seedlings under controlled conditions in the greenhouse and observed
that the maximum rate of growth was 3.4 to 5.2 millimeters per day at the
optimum temperature of 20 to 25°C. In the Cloquet Forest of Minnesota
25- to 28-year-old jack pine roots averaged 9 to 12 inches of elongation
in a season, but individual roots grew as much as 26 inches (Kaufman,
1945). In New York State yearly growth in length of roots of 35- and
50-year-old sugar maple trees was from 3 to 4 inches (Morrow, 1950).
Holch (1931) reported that bur oak roots penetrated to a depth of
60 inches in heavy soil during the first growing season but that red oak
roots penetrated only 28 inches under the same conditions, illustrating
differences in rates of growth for different species.

   There has been considerable discussion as to the length of the growing
season of tree roots. Diameter growth of roots begins later than diameter
growth in the lower stem and continues later in the season. Some evidence
of periodicity of growth in length has been found, and several investigators
have reported two principal periods of growth, one in the spring and the
other in the autumn. Woodroof and Woodroof (1934) reported as many
as four to eight cycles in pecan roots in Georgia. According to Reed and
MacDougal (1937), roots of citrus trees in California had two periods of
growth, one from late March to late June, another in July and August.
While rising temperature was doubtless responsible for the resumption
of growth in March, these investigators did not believe that the cessation
and resumption of growth during the summer could be attributed to environmental factors. Reed (1939) found that roots of loblolly pine and of
shortleaf pine elongated during every month of the year in North Carolina but that they made the best growth in April and May and the least
during January and February. The periods of slowest root growth during

the winter coincided with the periods of lowest soil temperature, while the periods of slowest root growth in the summer coincided with the periods of lowest soil moisture. Huberman (1940) found root growth of southern pines to continue through the winter in Louisiana. Turner (1936) observed that root growth of loblolly and shortleaf pine in Arkansas occurred during every 8-day period for 2 years. The least elongation occurred in the winter, the most in the spring and again in early autumn or mid-autumn, with less growth during dry periods in the summer.

Morrow (1950) found 80 per cent of growth of sugar maple roots to take place from the middle of March to the end of June in New York State. The roots grew throughout a mild winter. Harris (1926) reported that in Oregon and British Columbia apple and filbert roots grow throughout the year if they are not subjected to freezing, drought, or submersion in water. These studies were made in a mild climate where the soil seldom freezes below the surface.

The number of growing root tips varies markedly with season. In New England Stevens (1931) found all the root tips of white pine to be growing in May while by midsummer only a few tips were growing. No growth of white pine roots occurred from November 15 to April 1, but roots of trees kept in the greenhouse grew as rapidly in the winter as in summer. When dormant potted tree seedlings are brought into the greenhouse in the winter, root elongation often begins within a few days. Apparently roots, unlike the stems of many plants, have no inherent dormant period. It seems doubtful whether there is any inherent periodicity in root elongation. It is more likely that the periodicity observed is the result of variations in soil temperature, soil moisture, oxygen supply, or supply of food, though this view has been questioned by Reed and MacDougal (1937) and by others. The effects of various factors on root growth were discussed by Kramer (1949, chap. 6).

Longevity of Roots

It is generally assumed that tree roots are perennial. This undoubtedly is true of the larger roots. The primary root, for example, often develops into a taproot and attains great size and age. Even casual examination by means of trenching shows, however, that many of the smaller roots die each year and, according to Hatch, short roots of pine normally live but 1 year. Probably most of this loss occurs during periods when the soil is too wet for good aeration, and unless these roots are rapidly replaced, tree growth may be seriously handicapped by lack of sufficient absorbing roots. It is well known that many of the fine absorbing roots of fruit trees die during the winter or after the soil has become saturated by irrigation or by heavy rains. This probably is also true of forest trees. Childers and White (1942) found the average life of small branches on apple roots to be only a week, even though environmental conditions seemed favorable to growth. Kinman (1932) reported the presence on fruit trees of numerous fine lateral roots that died in a few days when the roots from which they were growing began to become suberized.

Heredity and Initial Root Habit

The type of growth of the root systems of seedlings of many trees is firmly fixed by their heredity. This has an important bearing on their ability to absorb water and hence to survive droughts. Toumey (1929) concluded from extensive studies that most tree seedlings can be classified in one of two general groups, those with taproots which grow rapidly downward and penetrate deeply and those with slowly growing, shallow primary roots and extensive, rapidly growing lateral roots. Baldcypress and yellow birch can become established only in wet areas, because their shallow seedling root systems do not enable them to survive where the soil dries out during the first year or two after germination. Upland hickories, redcedar, longleaf pine, and many other upland species produce rapidly growing, deeply penetrating taproots, which enable them to obtain water even after the surface soil has dried out during summer droughts. Red maple has a root system which is readily modified by the environment. It develops numerous shallow laterals in swamps and a deep taproot system in dry upland soils; hence it is able to thrive on both dry and wet sites. When grown under unfavorable conditions, as in the shade, root systems tend to be miniature replicas of those produced under favorable conditions.

Holch (1931) also found each of the several species of tree seedlings which he studied to have its characteristic root system. The roots of bur oak, which occurs normally on dry ridges, reached a depth of 5.7 feet the first season, while those of linden, which usually grows on moist sites, penetrated only 1.2 feet but spread out laterally. Because of the shallow root system, the majority of the seedlings of linden died during the first summer in the comparatively dry soil of the open prairie. Albertson and Weaver (1945) studied the survival of trees in the prairie region after the great droughts of the 1930s. They concluded that root habit is one of the most important factors determining the drought resistance of trees, deep-rooted species surviving much better than shallow-rooted species. Coile (1940) concluded that the deep taproots of oak and hickory seedlings, which extend below the horizon of most intense root competition, enable them to survive droughts much better than do the more shallow-rooted pine seedlings. The relatively lower shoot/root ratios of hardwoods also enable them to survive droughts better than do pines (Kozlowski, 1949). It has been found also that shallow-rooted seedlings, such as western hemlock and western cedar, suffer much greater mortality during droughts than do seedlings of such deep-rooted species as western white pine, western larch, Douglas-fir, and lowland fir (Haig, 1936). Eastern hemlock and redcedar both germinate freely in open sites in southern New England during moist springs, but hemlock seedlings have shallow roots and die from desiccation as the surface soil dries, while the deep-rooted seedlings of redcedar survive and become permanently established (Toumey, 1929).

As seedlings grow older the form of the root system often tends to be increasingly modified by environmental factors. A few species, however, possess root systems whose forms are so firmly fixed by heredity that they are maintained regardless of the environment. Lodgepole pine typically develops a much more shallow root system than does western yellow pine; hence it is restricted to moister sites than are required by the latter (Gail and Long, 1935).

Mycorrhizae

The root systems of most forest trees and many other woody plants often are modified by the development of mycorrhizae, formed as a result of the invasion of young roots by hyphae of a fungus. Two principal types occur, endotrophic mycorrhizae, in which the mycelium penetrates into the epidermal and cortical parenchyma but affects the external appearance of the roots very little, and ectotrophic mycorrhizae, in which the mycelium penetrates between the cortical cells and produces marked hypertrophy and extensive branching of the roots. A feltlike covering of fungal hyphae (the so-called "sheath") usually is produced over the root surface, and hyphae extend from this out into the soil. Combinations of the two types of mycorrhizae also occur. Hacskaylo (1957) has a good discussion of the two types of mycorrhizal roots. Mycorrhizal roots of pine are shown in Figure 2.21.

According to Hatch (1937), the type of root system as well as the fungus determines the type of mycorrhizae. Trees such as sweetgum, yellow-poplar, maple, and members of the Ericaceae which have roots that can be differentiated only as coarse and fine roots have endotrophic mycorrhizae. Trees of the Abietineae, Salicaceae, Betulaceae, Fagaceae, and a few other groups have roots of two types, long roots and short roots. Long roots elongate fairly rapidly, produce root hairs usually from sub-epidermal layers, branch racemosely, exhibit secondary growth, are long-lived, and seldom are converted into mycorrhizae. Their branches form short roots which grow very slowly, produce few root hairs, are short-lived, often become mycorrhizal, and then branch dichotomously. The mycorrhizal rootlets are blunt, thickened, and much branched, sometimes even forming coralloid clusters, as shown in Figure 2.21. This branching probably is caused by auxin produced by the fungus (Slankis, 1958).

Development of mycorrhizal roots considerably increases their surface, and the fungal hyphae extending out from them increase contact with the soil. Thus the absorbing surface for minerals is materially increased, and this is believed to be of considerable importance for the growth of trees in soil low in nutrients, especially phosphorus. The function of mycorrhizal roots in mineral absorption is discussed further in Chapter 9.

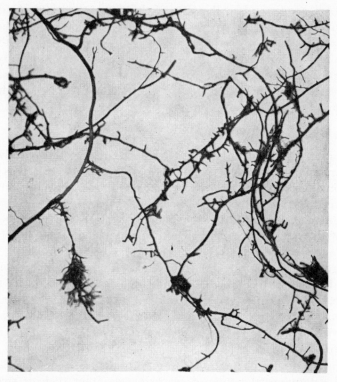

Figure 2.21 Mycorrhizal roots on loblolly pine. Note coralloid cluster at lower left and dichotomous branching of short roots. (*Photograph by H. Tschinkel.*)

GENERAL REFERENCES

Bailey, I. W., 1954, Contributions to plant anatomy, Chronica Botanica Co., Waltham, Mass.

Brown, H. P., and A. J. Panshin, 1940, Commercial timbers of the United States, McGraw-Hill Book Company, Inc., New York.

Desch, H. E., 1953, Timber, its structure and properties, 3d ed., St. Martin's Press, Inc., New York.

Eames, A. J., and L. H. MacDaniels, 1947, An introduction to plant anatomy, 2d ed., McGraw-Hill Book Company, Inc., New York.

Esau, K., 1953, Plant anatomy, John Wiley & Sons, Inc., New York.

Glock, W. S., 1955, Tree growth. II. Growth rings and climate, Bot. Rev., 21:73–188.
MacDougal, D. T., 1938, Tree growth, Chronica Botanica Co., Waltham, Mass.
Record, S. J., 1934, Identification of the timbers of temperate North America, John
    Wiley & Sons, Inc., New York.
Studhalter, R. A., 1955, Tree growth. I. Some historical chapters, Bot. Rev., 21:1–72.

CHAPTER 3 *Photosynthesis*

Photosynthesis is the process by which carbohydrates are manufactured from carbon dioxide and water in the chlorophyll-containing tissues of plants exposed to light. It undoubtedly is the most important physiological process occurring in trees because their growth is dependent on the carbohydrates produced by photosynthesis. Photosynthesis is an energy-storing process in which light energy is converted into chemical energy, which is stored in the carbohydrates. It occurs only in the green tissues because chlorophyll plays an essential role in the absorption of light energy and its conversion into chemical energy. In Europe photosynthesis often is called "assimilation" or "carbon assimilation," but most American plant physiologists prefer to apply the term assimilation to the production of new protoplasm and cell walls from food (Chapter 7).

The amount of food produced by photosynthesis seldom is fully appreciated, even by botanists and foresters. Polster (1950) estimated that forest stands in central Europe synthesize the equivalent of 75 to 300 kilograms of glucose per day per hectare (30 to 120 kilograms per acre) in excess of that used in respiration. The net photosynthesis for a season is estimated by Polster to be 21.8 to 77 metric tons per hectare (8 to 31 metric tons per acre). Schroeder (1919) estimated that land plants produce 16.6×10^9 metric tons of organic carbon per year, and two-thirds of this is produced by trees. The total energy converted and stored by plants in photosynthesis is about 100 times greater than that in all the coal mined in the entire world during a year. Polster (1950) estimated that 25 to 45 per cent of the total product of photosynthesis is converted into usable wood. Until coal came into general use most of the heat energy used by man came from the combustion of wood. Today we are concerned more with the use of wood as a building material than with its use as fuel. Regardless of its use, we must remember that the energy required for wood production is light energy which has been transformed into chemical energy in the process of photosynthesis.

58

The Chloroplast Pigments

The pigments found in trees deserve our attention both because of the essential role of the chlorophylls in photosynthesis and also because of their importance in giving color to the earth's surface. The predominantly green aspect of the earth during the growing season results from the fact that chlorophyll is the most conspicuous pigment in nearly all plants. Occasionally the yellow carotenoid pigments are conspicuous, as in certain ornamental strains of trees and shrubs, and if conditions become unfavorable for growth, leaves usually turn yellow because the yellow pigments are more resistant than chlorophyll to unfavorable conditions. Leaves of a few varieties of trees such as copper beech and Japanese maple are red or purple because of the presence of anthocyanin in the cell sap of their leaves. Many other trees develop anthocyanin in the autumn, but the development of autumn coloration will be discussed in Chapter 4.

The chlorophyll and carotenoid pigments are concentrated in chloroplasts which apparently originate by division of preexisting chloroplasts. These typically are ovoid, disc-, or saucer-shaped bodies about 5 microns in diameter and 2 or 3 microns in thickness. They consist of a colorless framework or stroma of protein in which are embedded 50 or more cylindrical bodies called "grana." Each plastid is an organelle surrounded by a differentially permeable membrane. The pigments occur in the grana, which are cylinders composed of 15 or more thin discs of protein and lipid material, on the surfaces of which the chlorophyll molecules are densely packed, probably in a monomolecular layer. Starch granules often develop in the plastids during periods of rapid photosynthesis. This complex organization is not necessarily maintained permanently, and it is reported that in at least some evergreens the chloroplasts lose their organization during the winter. This may be a factor in the low capacity for photosynthesis found in some species in the winter and is discussed later in this chapter. More details and numerous references on chloroplast structure can be found in papers by Granick (1955), Rabinowitch (1956), and Weier and Stocking (1952).

Chlorophyll does not develop in all plastids. For instance, none is found in the plastids of epidermal cells, except for the guard cells. Chlorophyll commonly occurs in the cortical parenchyma of young twigs and in the phelloderm of older stems of some species. It occasionally develops in roots exposed to light and is common in flower parts, young fruits, and even sometimes in the embryos of seeds. Chloroplasts tend to become somewhat oriented in the mesophyll cells of leaves of some plants so that at low intensities their broad surfaces face the light but at high intensities their edges face the light.

Chlorophylls. Although several kinds of chlorophyll occur in the plant kingdom, chlorophylls *a* and *b* are of most importance in trees. Chlorophyll *a* has the formula $C_{55}H_{72}O_5N_4Mg$; the formula of chlorophyll *b* is $C_{55}H_{70}O_6N_4Mg$. The structural formula of chlorophyll *a* is shown in Figure 3.1. It has a ring structure consisting of four pyrrole rings with side chains, with magnesium in the center. Chlorophyll is fluorescent, absorbing certain wavelengths of visible light and reradiating red light of longer wavelengths.

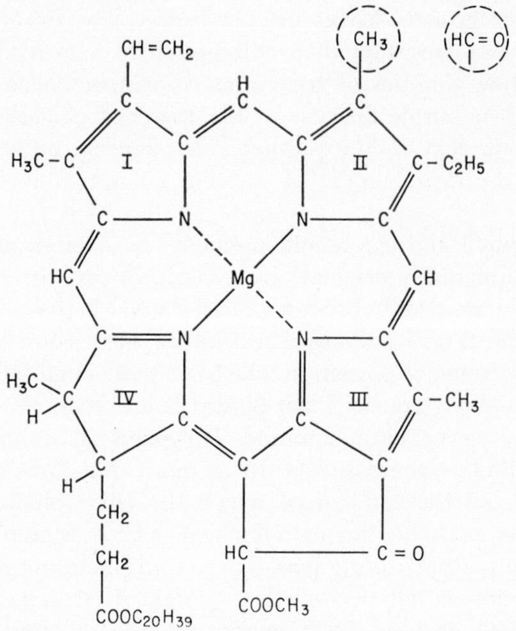

Figure 3.1 Structural formula for chlorophyll *a*. The formula for chlorophyll *b* is the same except that an HC—O group occurs in place of the CH_3 group enclosed in a dashed circle on pyrrole ring II. Another arrangement of double bonds is possible, and an alternative linkage of magnesium is indicated by the dashed lines.

Carotenoids. The yellow color sometimes observed in variegated leaves or those kept in darkness is caused by carotene and xanthophyll, two groups of fat-soluble pigments which also occur in chloroplasts. More than 60 different carotenoids occur in plants. Carotene is a hydrocarbon with the empirical formula $C_{40}H_{56}$, composed of eight isoprene units (Chapter 6). There are several isomers, of which beta carotene, the precursor of vitamin A, is most abundant. The red pigment, lycopene, found in ripe tomatoes, rose fruits, and other plant parts, is an isomer of carotene.

Most xanthophylls have the formula $C_{40}H_{56}O_2$. They are yellowish to brownish in color. Xanthophylls can be separated from carotenes because they are more soluble in alcohol and much less soluble in petroleum ether than the carotenes.

The carotenoids, unlike chlorophyll, are formed in darkness; hence seedlings grown in darkness usually are yellow in color. As they are also more resistant to destruction under unfavorable conditions, leaves kept in darkness for several days usually become yellow because destruction of the chlorophyll exposes the yellow carotenoid pigments. The same process brings about the yellow color in the leaves of some species in the autumn.

Relative Amounts of Various Leaf Pigments. The total chlorophyll content of healthy green leaves approximates nearly 1 per cent of the dry

Table 3.1. Concentration of plastid pigments in leaves of trees. (*Adapted from Willstätter and Stoll, 1913.*)

Chlorophyll Content, Per Cent of Dry Weight

Species	Chlorophylls			
	$a + b$	a	b	Ratio a/b
Pinus spp.	0.26	0.19	0.07	2.7
Platanus acerifolia:				
Sun leaves	0.68	0.53	0.15	3.5
Shade leaves	1.12	0.85	0.27	3.2
Sambucus nigra:				
Sun leaves	0.80	0.58	0.22	2.6
Shade leaves	1.18	0.79	0.39	2.0

Carotenoid Content, Per Cent of Dry Weight

Species	Carotene + xanthophyll	Carotene	Xanthophyll	Ratio of xanthophyll to carotene
Platanus acerifolia:				
Sun leaves	0.135	0.043	0.092	2.1
Shade leaves	0.176	0.051	0.125	2.5
Aesculus hippocastanum:				
Sun leaves	0.207	0.082	0.125	1.5
Shade leaves	0.148	0.037	0.111	3.0

weight (Willstätter and Stoll, 1913). The amounts and proportions of pigments vary with species, environment, and age of leaves. Some of the absolute and relative amounts of the chlorophylls and carotenoids in trees are given in Table 3.1. Generally there is about three times as much of the chlorophylls as of the carotenoids. Chlorophyll *a* usually is two to three times as abundant as chlorophyll *b*, and xanthophyll exceeds carotene by a similar amount.

The chloroplast pigments can be extracted fairly easily by the use of solvents such as acetone, and the various pigments can then be separated by differential solubility (Schertz, 1928; Zscheile, 1941) or by chromatographic methods. In fact, one of the first applications of chromatography to biological studies was the separation of leaf pigments by Tswett (1906). The concentrations of the various pigments can be determined spectrophotometrically after extraction.

Factors Affecting Chlorophyll Formation

Failure to develop chlorophyll results in such obvious yellowing or chlorosis that it has been studied extensively and found to depend on a number of internal and environmental factors.

Internal Factors. The most important factor is the genetic potentiality of the tree, because occasionally mutations result in complete loss of the ability to form chlorophyll and short-lived albino seedlings result. More often the process is only partly disturbed, resulting in lack of chlorophyll in certain areas of leaves (variegated leaves) or a uniformly low chlorophyll content which causes leaves to assume the yellowish hue of the aurea varieties often used for ornamental trees and shrubs. Occasionally mutations result in albino or variegated branches on otherwise normal trees and shrubs. Cytoplasmic inheritance of abnormalities in chlorophyll formation also is common. Apparently changes in the plastids themselves occur which may be regarded as a kind of mutation (Granick, 1955).

Even though a plant possesses the hereditary capacity to produce chlorophyll, this is not expressed in all its tissues. Chloroplasts are abundant in the mesophyll tissue of leaves, for example, but the plastids in the epidermal cells remain small and colorless, except for the guard cells. The plastids in the root cells of many species do not develop chlorophyll even when exposed to light, although the roots of some species become pale green when illuminated.

Viruses often interfere with chlorophyll formation, resulting in chlorotic areas and variegated leaves. For example, yellow mottling of camellia leaves often is caused by a virus (Milbraith and McWhorter, 1946), and Plakidas (1948) suggests that virus infection also causes variegation in camellia flowers, as it is known to do in Rembrandt tulips.

An adequate supply of carbohydrates seems essential for chlorophyll formation, and leaves containing little soluble carbohydrate may fail to become green even if all other conditions are favorable. If such leaves are allowed to absorb sugar, they often begin to form chlorophyll.

Enviromental Factors. The chief environmental factors affecting chlorophyll formation are light, temperature, minerals, and water, but chlorophyll formation is very sensitive to almost any factor which disturbs metabolic processes. For this reason chlorosis is associated with many disturbances of normal metabolism.

Light. In general, light is essential for the formation of chlorophyll, although some conifer seedlings and a few other plant structures develop chlorophyll in darkness. Bright light causes the decomposition of chlorophyll, and Shirley (1929a) found that above a rather low intensity the concentration of chlorophyll decreased with increasing light intensity. Apparently chlorophyll simultaneously is being synthesized and destroyed, and in bright light equilibrium is established at a lower concentration than in light of low intensity. Shade leaves usually have a higher concentration of chlorophyll than sun leaves.

Temperature. Synthesis of chlorophyll apparently occurs over a wide range of temperatures. Evergreens of the Temperate Zone must synthesize chlorophyll from temperatures near freezing up to the highest temperatures of midsummer. Many conifers become somewhat chlorotic during the winter, presumably because destruction exceeds synthesis of chlorophyll at very low temperatures. According to Pack (1921), maximum formation of chlorophyll in seedlings of eastern redcedar occurred at 15°C and no visible chlorophyll formation occurred at 1 or 30°C.

Minerals. One of the most common causes of chlorosis in trees is deficiency of one of the essential elements. Nitrogen deficiency is a common cause of chlorosis in trees, especially in the older leaves. Iron deficiency is another common cause of chlorosis, especially in the younger leaves. Apparently an adequate supply of iron is essential for chlorophyll synthesis even though it is not a chlorophyll constituent. Magnesium is a constituent of chlorophyll; hence a deficiency of it naturally causes chlorosis. In fact, a deficiency of most of the major elements and several of the minor ones results in chlorosis. This suggests that almost any disturbance of normal metabolism is likely to interfere with the synthesis of chlorophyll. Chlorosis caused by mineral deficiency is discussed in more detail in Chapter 9.

Water. Severe dehydration of plant tissues not only interferes with chlorophyll formation but also causes destruction of that already present. As a result leaves suffering from drought tend to turn yellow. Unfortunately, leaves on trees and shrubs also turn yellow when the soil around their roots is saturated with water. The effects of both drought and poor aeration probably are indirect, chlorophyll formation being hindered by the general disturbance of metabolism.

Oxygen. Seedlings will not develop chlorophyll in the absence of oxygen, but it is not clear whether this is an indirect effect or if chlorophyll synthesis itself is hindered.

The Mechanism of Photosynthesis

Like many other physiological processes, photosynthesis really consists of a number of steps, some of which are not yet well understood. Because of their rather complex nature a thorough discussion of these processes lies outside the scope of this book, and the reader is referred to works such as those of Rabinowitch (1945, 1951, 1956) and Hill and Whittingham (1955) for more details. In spite of its complexity, the great importance of photosynthesis requires that the mechanism of the process be discussed. Some knowledge of the nature of the process is necessary in order to understand how it is affected by various environmental factors.

In simple terms photosynthesis consists of the oxidation of water and the reduction of carbon dioxide. For many years it was thought that the oxygen released in photosynthesis came from the carbon dioxide. More recent experiments with water containing the heavy isotope of oxygen, O^{18}, indicate that the oxygen released probably comes from the water rather than from the carbon dioxide. This means that at least 12 molecules of water are used per molecule of hexose sugar formed, and the summary equation should be written as follows:

$$6CO_2 + 12H_2O \xrightarrow[\text{chlorophyll}]{\text{673 kg-cal light energy}} C_6H_{12}O_6 + 6H_2O + 6O_2$$

This equation is based on the assumption that the end product is a hexose sugar. For some purposes the process may be shown by the following equation:

$$CO_2 + 2H_2O \rightarrow CH_2O + H_2O + O_2$$

This is a generalized equation which omits a number of intermediate steps and merely indicates the type of carbohydrate unit from which more complex compounds can be formed. Although the carbon from carbon dioxide goes through a number of intermediates, of which phosphoglyceric acid probably is a key substance, for our purposes it is satisfactory to regard the final product as glucose, because it occurs almost universally in plants and can be converted easily into other substances.

Neither water nor carbon dioxide absorbs energy in the wavelengths effective in photosynthesis, but chloroplasts absorb visible light and use some of the energy to split water molecules and transfer hydrogen to the carbon dioxide. The energy necessary to cause hydrogen to combine with the carbon dioxide probably comes from ATP (adenosine triphosphate) produced by energy transfer in the illuminated chloroplasts.

These two processes can be indicated as follows:

$$2H_2O + 2A \xrightarrow[\text{chlorophyll}]{\text{light}} 2AH_2 + O_2$$

In this scheme A represents a hydrogen acceptor to which hydrogen is transferred from water by light energy absorbed by the chloroplasts. This is known as the "Hill reaction" because Hill (1937) first demonstrated that illumination of suspensions of chloroplasts in the presence of a suitable hydrogen acceptor resulted in the release of oxygen. The second stage of the process, the reduction of carbon, can be shown as follows:

$$CO_2 + 2AH_2 \rightarrow CH_2O + 2A + H_2O$$

Photosynthesis therefore includes a photochemical stage requiring light and a stage involving chemical reactions which use no light. Experiments with intermittent illumination at various temperatures indicate that the photochemical stage occurs very rapidly (in 0.00001 second) and is independent of temperature but is affected by the concentration of carbon dioxide. The dark stage occurs more slowly, requiring about 0.04 second at 25°C, and is slowed down by lower temperatures but is independent of carbon dioxide concentration.

Obviously, the rate of photosynthesis will be limited by the stage which is occurring most slowly. In bright light the chemical or dark stage is likely to be the limiting one and the process is sensitive to temperature, but at low light intensities the photochemical stage is more likely to be limiting and carbon dioxide concentration is more often a limiting factor than temperature.

The successful occurrence of photosynthesis depends on other processes in addition to those usually considered under the mechanism of the process. Foremost among these is intake of sufficient carbon dioxide. This depends largely on the behavior of stomates and on the permeability of the cuticle and epidermal layers to carbon dioxide. The role of leaf structure will be discussed later. An important factor in the availability of carbon dioxide is the large amount accumulated in the cells. The amount present in cells is much greater than would be expected if it were merely dissolved in the cell sap, and it occurs in nongreen tissue and in darkness, as well as in photosynthetic tissue. Apparently it reacts with phosphates and carbonates in addition to dissolving in the cell sap.

Measurement of Photosynthesis

Unfortunately, measurements of photosynthesis are complicated by the fact that respiration occurs simultaneously with photosynthesis and produces carbon dioxide and uses carbohydrate. Furthermore, some of the carbohydrate produced by photosynthesis is translocated out of the leaves, reducing their dry weight. Thus measurements of photosynthesis give only the apparent or net photosynthesis, which is total or gross photosynthesis minus the amount of carbon dioxide produced or food used in respiration or translocated to other organs. Attempts to calculate gross total photosynthesis by adding a correction for respiration are complicated by uncertainty as to whether respiration occurs at the same rate in light and darkness. Decker (1957), for example, claims that respiration probably is much more rapid in light than in darkness, but this is difficult to determine because respiration of green tissue can be measured only in darkness.

There are three general methods available for measuring photosynthesis: measurement of carbon dioxide uptake, measurement of oxygen production, and measurement of increase in dry weight. Measurement of oxygen production is useful only for aquatic plants, but the other two methods can be used on woody plants. Some of the older methods of measuring photosynthesis are described by Spoehr (1926) and Miller (1938). The two methods most commonly used on trees will be described, and their advantages and disadvantages discussed.

Measurement of Dry-weight Increase. According to Pickett (1937), Sachs (1884) was the earliest investigator to use the dry-weight-increase method. This involves cutting out a number of discs from leaves and determining their dry weight. A second sample of leaf discs is cut out at the end of a predetermined time period, and the dry weight of this sample also is obtained. Any gain in dry weight of the second sample over the first represents carbohydrate accumulation in the leaves during the interval between sampling. Sachs recognized that the method was inaccurate because of loss by respiration and by translocation of photosynthetic products from the leaves. Brown and Escombe (1905) measured photosynthesis of catalpa by measuring carbon dioxide uptake and also by dry-weight increase. Their values for dry-weight increase were two to three times greater than those obtained by carbon dioxide absorption. They believed that the dry-weight-increase method gave misleading values. However, Ganong (1905) believed the method could be very useful if standardized as much as possible, and he designed a leaf punch which removed circular leaf discs with an area of 1 square centimeter. He concluded that injury due to removal of test discs from leaves was not serious. The Ganong leaf punch is now standard laboratory equipment for leaf sampling to determine rates of photosynthesis by dry-weight increase. The dry-weight-increase method offers the simplest means of measuring photosynthesis and, with proper sampling technique and a sufficient number of discs, can be very useful in certain kinds of studies. Pickett (1937) used it with apple leaves because he considered it to be the method best suited to orchard conditions. A useful variation of this method is the twin-leaf method of Denny (1930), in which members of pairs of opposite leaves or leaflets are used as paired samples.

Measurement of Carbon Dioxide Uptake. Most measurements of photosynthesis of trees are made by determining the amount of carbon dioxide absorbed. Early use of this method is attributed to Kreusler (1885), but it has undergone numerous modifications. The plant or plant part to be measured is enclosed, an air stream of known volume is passed over it, and the difference in carbon dioxide concentration of the air before and after passing over the plant is determined. The rate of photosynthesis can be calculated from the volume of air and the change in carbon dioxide concentration. This method was used on parts of leaves (Freeland, 1948), whole leaves (Heinicke and Hoffman, 1933; Schneider and Childers, 1941; Wilson, 1948a; Decker and Tio, 1958), pine needles (Kramer and Clark, 1947; Bormann, 1956), entire tree seedlings (Kramer and Decker, 1944; Kozlowski, 1949, 1957; Bormann, 1953; Negisi and Satoo, 1954; Bourdeau, 1954; Tranquillini, 1957), and even trees of considerable size (Heinicke and Childers, 1937). According to Clark (1954), photosynthesis can be measured reliably on detached Norway spruce branches for short periods of time.

An open system in which a continuous stream of air is drawn over the plant or plant part requires the use of gas meters or flow meters to measure the rate of air flow. Accurate measurement of air flow often is difficult, and the rate of flow may affect the rate of photosynthesis (Decker, 1947). The procedure can be simplified by use of a closed system in which the plant or plant part is enclosed in a chamber in which the carbon dioxide concentration is measured from time to time. This system was used by Burns (1923) to determine the compensation point for seedlings of several species. Decker (1954) and Bourdeau (1954) used closed systems in which the air was circulated through an infrared gas analyzer. Small closed chambers are particularly useful for measurements on small amounts of photosynthetic tissue, such as seedlings.

Huber (1952) measured daily and seasonal changes in carbon dioxide concentration of the air at various distances above the soil surface and calculated the amount removed by photosynthesis and released by respiration of the vegetation. Koch (1957) measured gradients in carbon dioxide and water vapor above vegetation and calculated both photosynthesis and transpiration.

A wide variety of methods has been used to measure changes in the carbon dioxide concentration of the air. Some of the earliest studies, such as those of de Saussure and Boussingault in the nineteenth century and those of Burns (1923), were made by analyzing the air in a closed container with a volumetric type of gas analysis apparatus. Another and more commonly used method, said to have been introduced by Kreusler (1885), is to pass an air stream through an absorption tower containing dilute alkali. For many years the change in concentration of the alkali caused by reaction with carbon dioxide was determined by titration. This method was used by Stålfelt, Müller, Kostychev, and others in their pioneer work. More recently change in concentration of alkali has been determined by measuring the change in electrical conductivity (Thomas, 1933; Waugh, 1939; Leach et al., 1944; Kramer and Decker, 1944; Kozlowski, 1949, 1957). Holdheide et al. (1936) described a portable conductivity apparatus which gave a great impetus to field measurements of photosynthesis. Interferometry, spectrophotometry, and thermal conductivity also have been used. Infrared gas analyzers are now coming into increasing use because of their high sensitivity and the rapidity with which measurements can be made (Huber, 1950, 1958b; Parker, 1953b; Bourdeau and Laverick, 1958).

Although simple in principle, measurement of photosynthesis by measuring the absorption of carbon dioxide involves troublesome problems of controlling air flow, temperature, light, and carbon dioxide concentration. As stated previously, carbon dioxide uptake measures only net or apparent photosynthesis, and a somewhat uncertain correction for respiration must be made in order to estimate total photosynthesis. Nevertheless, it is the best method available for most studies of photosynthesis of trees.

Methods of Expressing Rates of Photosynthesis

The choice of a satisfactory basis for expressing photosynthesis of different species is difficult. Most data are expressed as carbon dioxide uptake per unit of leaf surface or leaf dry weight, but Polster (1950) expressed it in terms of leaf fresh weight. Pickett (1937) found photosynthesis to be closely correlated to the area of internal exposed surface. However, since it is difficult to measure the internal mesophyll surface, this method is not extensively used.

Photosynthesis often is expressed per unit of stomated surface. However, Freeland (1948) found nonstomated surfaces of some species to be very much involved in photosynthesis. Therefore the assumption that nonstomated surfaces may be disregarded probably is not valid for species with thin cuticles. When photosynthesis is expressed per unit of leaf tissue the assumption usually is made that a unit of tissue of one species is physiologically similar to a unit of tissue of another species. This is not always true, especially when comparing morphologically dissimilar trees. Sometimes the rate is calculated per unit of chlorophyll or per unit of nitrogen because these are the tissue fractions most directly involved (McGregor, 1958). Photosynthesis of oaks was found to be higher than that of loblolly pine on both a leaf area and leaf dry-weight basis, but the magnitude of the difference varied with the choice of the physiological unit used (Kozlowski, 1949). When studying effects of environmental stress on photosynthesis, much difficulty can be eliminated by subjecting the same plant or plants to varying environmental factors and expressing all observations as percentages of the observed maximum. Decker (1955a) has called attention to some of the logical difficulties that arise in interpreting the ecological significance of photosynthetic data expressed on a leaf area or weight basis.

Determination of leaf areas often is difficult, especially for conifers. Leaf areas of broadleaf species can be determined by drawing or blueprinting the outline of each leaf and measuring the area with a planimeter, or cutting out the leaf tracing and weighing the paper. Several investigators have described photoelectric devices to measure areas of leaves more rapidly than is possible by older methods (Frear, 1935; Withrow, 1935; Mitchell, 1936; Kramer, 1937b; Miller et al., 1956). Another rapid method was described by Negisi et al. (1957). Kozlowski and Schumacher (1943) described a method of measuring surface areas of pine needles. It should be remembered that measurable photosynthesis often occurs in twigs (Pearson and Lawrence, 1958).

Variations in Rates of Photosynthesis

Wide variations in rates of photosynthesis occur between individuals of the same species and between species, even when growing under similar conditions. The rate varies with position in the crown, and seasonal variations in rate also occur.

Species Variations. A few examples of the differences in rates among species will be given. Kramer and Decker (1944) observed photosynthesis of seedlings of two species of oak to be about twice that of dogwood on a leaf area basis over a wide range of light intensities. They also found the rate of photosynthesis of oak seedlings to be much higher per unit of area than that of loblolly pine at all light intensities up to and including full sun. Kozlowski (1949) found photosynthesis to be more rapid in oak than in pine seedlings. Some idea of the wide range in rates of photosynthesis occurring among various species of trees may be obtained from the data of Polster (1950), summarized in Table 3.2. It will be seen from this table that plants with high rates of photosynthesis also have relatively high rates of respiration. It should be remembered that trees of different species vary considerably in leaf area and a large leaf area compensates for a low rate per unit of area in some species (Table 10.2).

Investigations in Germany show marked differences in photosynthesis of different clones of poplar species and hybrids. Daily photosynthesis varied from 2.29 grams of carbon dioxide per plant for *Populus nigra* to

23.26 grams of carbon dioxide for a Wettstein hybrid. These differences were correlated with amounts of wood produced (Huber and Polster, 1955).

Table 3.2. Daily rates of respiration and photosynthesis of trees of several species, in milligrams of CO_2 per gram fresh weight. (*After Polster, 1950.*)

Species	Respiration	Apparent photosynthesis
Betula verrucosa	22.9	66.9
Quercus robur	17.5	43.2
Fagus sylvatica	11.1	52.9
Pinus sylvestris	7.9	17.1
Pseudotsuga taxifolia	7.5	18.8
Picea abies	5.5	14.2

Diurnal Variations. In the early morning of a bright, clear, warm day photosynthesis is low because of low light intensity and low temperature, despite a high leaf moisture content and high carbon dioxide concentration in intercellular spaces of leaves. As light intensity increases and the air warms up, photosynthesis begins to increase rapidly and may reach a daily maximum sometime before noon. The maximum often is followed by a midday decrease which may be slight or severe. This midday slump often is followed by an increase in photosynthesis in the late afternoon, and then a final subsidence, which generally follows the late-afternoon and early-evening decrease in light intensity and temperature (Figure 3.2).

The actual course of photosynthesis varies somewhat from the idealized diurnal pattern described here. Some species, especially conifers, may show only a morning maximum and may not show the afternoon rise at all (Uhl, 1937; Polster, 1950). The pattern for a single leaf may be different from that of a whole seedling or tree. Heinicke and Hoffman (1933) found the rate of photosynthesis of an apple leaf to differ at different times of the day and to vary widely on different days. Furthermore, they found that two leaves of about equal size and appearance in the same section of a shoot had different rates of photosynthesis when tested at the same time. Waugh (1939) reported that photosynthesis in apple leaves fluctuated by as much as 100 per cent under apparently uniform environmental conditions. He also found several maxima of photosynthesis on some days and concluded that internal factors were very important in controlling photosynthesis. Except for the midday dip, most diurnal changes in photosynthesis appear to be fairly well correlated with light intensity (Heinicke and Childers, 1937; Parker, 1953b).

Midday Decrease in Photosynthesis. Photosynthesis often slows down in varying amount during the middle of the day. McLean (1920) observed such a severe midday decrease in photosynthesis of coconut trees that carbon dioxide was actually released by the leaves. Such midday slowing down of photosynthesis often is attributed to stomatal closure caused by high transpiration (Maskell, 1928; Stålfelt, 1935, 1956a). Nutman (1937) attributed the midday decrease in coffee trees to closure of stomates caused by bright light. Another internal factor which may cause midday inhibition of photosynthesis is carbohydrate accumulation. Definite correlations between accumulation of starch and sugar and diurnal

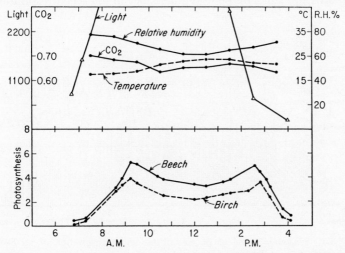

Figure 3.2 Midday reduction in photosynthesis of beech and birch on a clear September day in Germany. Early in the morning and late in the afternoon the rate of photosynthesis was related to light intensity, but it was depressed by the high midday light intensity. Also notice midday reduction in both photosynthesis and transpiration shown in Figure 10.3. (*Redrawn from Polster, 1950.*)

fluctuation in photosynthesis have been shown (Kursanov, 1933; von Guttenberg and Buhr, 1935; Mönch, 1937). Von Guttenberg and Buhr (1935) and Polster (1950) have emphasized the difficulty of attributing all midday slumps in photosynthesis to a single cause. In young leaves in spring, midday depression can often be best ascribed to carbohydrate accumulation. In the hot days of midsummer much midday inhibition of synthesis is the result of excessive transpiration, causing loss of turgor and stomatal closure. Böhning (1949) found that decreased carbon dioxide concentration of the atmosphere may sometimes also be important in depressing photosynthesis during the middle of the day.

Seasonal Variations. The seasonal course of photosynthesis in trees was studied by Heinicke and Childers (1937). They determined the rate of apparent photosynthesis of an 8-year-old McIntosh apple tree in central New York State. The tree had over ten thousand leaves, and the determinations were carried out continuously for 188 days. Leaf development was rapid from May 20 to June 10, after which leaves were added slowly. Leaves began to fall in mid-October, and 90 per cent had fallen by November 17 when photosynthesis was still measured. The seasonal course of apparent photosynthesis for this tree is given in Figure 3.3.

When the experiment started in mid-May, respiration exceeded photosynthesis. Respiration was high because of rapid metabolism associated with production of new shoots, expanding foliage, and maturing of flower parts. Shortly after bloom, photosynthesis began to exceed respiration and

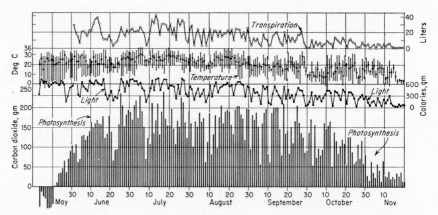

Figure 3.3 Seasonal course of photosynthesis and transpiration of an 8-year-old McIntosh apple tree at Ithaca, New York. Variations in photosynthesis were correlated with variations in light intensity during most of the season. During the early part of May the tree was starting growth and released more carbon dioxide in respiration than it used in photosynthesis. (*From Heinicke and Childers, 1937.*)

became detectable. Apparent photosynthesis then increased rapidly from mid-May through June.

By June 25 the highest rates were recorded even though the tree had not yet produced its maximum leaf area. During the remainder of the summer there was much fluctuation in photosynthesis, which appeared to be correlated with variations in light intensity. Although the highest rate occurred in late June, more total photosynthesis occurred during the months of July, August, or September than in June because of the smaller leaf surface in June. A gradual decline in photosynthesis began in mid-September and continued during October. By early November photosynthesis had dropped to a very low ebb. The few leaves left on the tree in November were surprisingly efficient during the short periods of high light intensity.

Figure 3.3 shows a strong correlation between photosynthesis and light, high photosynthesis occurring on the brightest days. The general slow decline at the end of the season reflects the decrease in light intensity, the decreasing photoperiod, and the decreasing temperature and leaf area.

Evergreen species would be expected to carry on photosynthesis throughout the year when light and temperature permit, but it has been reported that there is a loss of photosynthetic capacity during very cold weather (Ivanov and Kossovitsch, 1929; Zeller, 1951; Tranquillini, 1957). Experiments by McGregor (1958) indicate that this occurs even in mild climates. He found that loblolly and white pine seedlings kept outdoors but brought in at intervals during the year for measurement of photo-

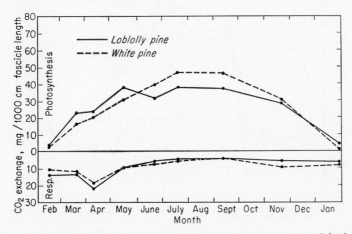

Figure 3.4 Seasonal changes in photosynthetic capacity per unit of leaf surface of loblolly and white pine seedlings. The seedlings were kept out of doors, but photosynthesis was measured indoors at 25°C and a light intensity of 4,000 foot-candles. (*From McGregor, 1958.*)

synthesis under standard conditions showed a distinct decrease in photosynthetic capacity during the autumn and winter. Some of his results are presented in Figure 3.4.

Saeki and Nomoto (1958) measured the seasonal course of photosynthesis in a deciduous species (*Zelkowa serrata*) and three broadleaf evergreens (*Cinnamomum camphora, Shiia sieboldii,* and *Pittosporum tobira*). Some of their data are shown in Figure 3.5. During the late spring and summer all the species carried on photosynthesis at about the same rate per unit of leaf surface. In the autumn the rates declined slowly until leaf fall brought an end to photosynthesis in *Zelkowa*. The evergreens carried on photosynthesis slowly all winter. The old leaves of *Pittosporum* regained their photosynthetic activity for a time in the spring before they were shed and new leaves took over. The authors concluded that the winter photosynthesis of the evergreens gave them a considerable advantage in competition with deciduous species, especially in regions with warm winters.

Factors Affecting Photosynthesis

Large variations in rate of photosynthesis are to be expected because it is influenced by a complex of environmental and tree factors, which often are interacting. During a typical day first one and later another

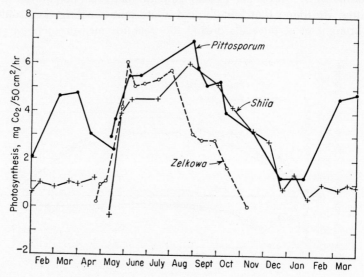

Figure 3.5 Seasonal course of photosynthetic capacity in leaves of deciduous (*Zelkowa serrata*) and evergreen trees (*Shiia sieboldii, Pittosporum tobira*). Rates were measured on detached leaves at 25°C in the summer and 20° in the winter. Old leaves of *Pittosporum* recovered their photosynthetic capacity in early spring before abscission, but leaves of *Shiia* did not. Rates of very young leaves were below the compensation point. (*From Saeki and Nomoto, 1958.*)

factor may be limiting. For example, photosynthesis in the morning often is correlated with light intensity, but later in the day it is controlled by leaf water content as it affects stomatal aperture and entrance of carbon dioxide. Similarly, during the growing season there may be a shift from one controlling factor to another (Kozlowski, 1949, 1955). Sometimes several environmental factors are near limiting values, and changes in these together with internal changes cause abrupt changes in photosynthesis which do not correlate well with any environmental factor (Shirley, 1935). The principal environmental factors that influence photosynthesis of trees are light, temperature, carbon dioxide concentration of the air, soil moisture, soil fertility, fungicides and insecticides, and disease

(Kramer, 1958a). The important internal factors include age of leaves, structure and arrangement of leaves, stomatal distribution and behavior, chlorophyll content, and carbohydrate accumulation. These factors will be discussed separately.

Light. Effects of light on photosynthesis are exerted through light intensity, quality, and duration of exposure or photoperiod. However, the light intensity to which trees normally are exposed controls photosynthesis to a much greater extent than either light quality or photoperiod.

Light Intensity. In the dark there is no photosynthesis; therefore carbon dioxide produced in respiration is released from leaves. With added light increments a compensation point is reached at which photosynthesis and

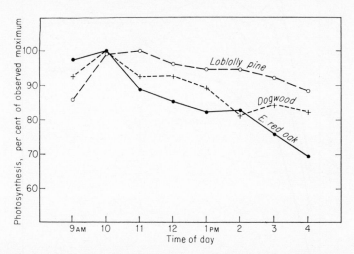

Figure 3.6 Effect of prolonged exposure to light of high intensity on rate of photosynthesis. Measurements were made at 25°C and 10,000 foot-candles. Graphs are averages of eight seedlings of each species. (*From Kozlowski, 1957.*)

respiration are equal and there is no net gas exchange. Light intensity at the compensation point varies among species, for sun and shade leaves of the same species, and with the temperature. With additional light above the compensation point, photosynthesis is proportional to light intensity until light saturation occurs, and the ascending part of a photosynthesis curve then becomes horizontal. In some species very high light intensities may even cause a decline in photosynthesis. For example, when Kozlowski (1957) exposed tree seedlings to a light intensity of 10,000 foot-candles throughout the day, photosynthesis was high for an hour or two, then decreased during the rest of the day (Figure 3.6).

Some trees show increase in photosynthesis with each addition of light up to full light intensity. Others apparently reach maximum photosynthesis at relatively low light intensity. Heinicke and Childers (1937) found

that during a whole growing season light was the factor that most frequently limited photosynthesis of apple trees in New York State. They
found that in general the greater the amount of sunlight during a short
or long interval, the more the amount of photosynthate produced. On
sunny days photosynthesis was high; on cloudy days it was low. Kramer
and Decker (1944) compared photosynthesis of eastern red oak, white
oak, flowering dogwood, and loblolly pine at light intensities varying

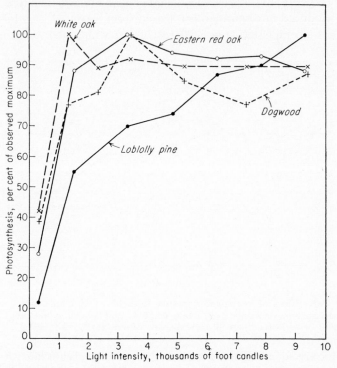

Figure 3.7 Effects of light intensity on photosynthesis of pine and hardwood
seedlings. Data are averages of at least seven seedlings of each species. Measurements were made at 30°C. (*From Kramer and Decker,* 1944.)

from 300 to 10,000 foot-candles. All four species showed rapid increase in
photosynthesis with increase in light intensity at the lower intensities.
Photosynthesis of loblolly pine increased with increased light intensity
up to full light. The hardwoods, however, achieved maximum photosynthesis at one-third or less of full light, and any further increase in light
intensity produced no further increase in photosynthesis (Figure 3.7).
Other hardwoods reach maximum rates of photosynthesis at relatively
low light intensities (Kozlowski, 1949; Bourdeau, 1954). Decker (1954)

found that variation in light intensity affected photosynthesis of Scotch pine and loblolly pine similarly.

The response of photosynthesis of some trees to light intensity varies with the age of the leaves. Loblolly pine seedlings with foliage composed of juvenile needles, alone or mixed with developing secondary needles, reached maximum photosynthesis at relatively low light intensity. As may be seen in Figure 3.8, this response was different from that of older seedlings, which reached maximum photosynthesis at light intensities corresponding to full light only (Bormann, 1956, 1958). Apparently the

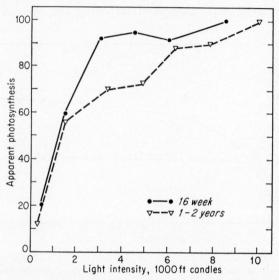

Figure 3.8 Effects of light intensity on apparent photosynthesis of 16-week-old loblolly pine seedlings with juvenile needles and 2-year-old seedlings with mature secondary needles. Juvenile needles are more efficient at intermediate light intensities, probably because of less self-shading. (*From Bormann, 1956.*)

radial arrangement of juvenile needles gives much better exposure and less self-shading than the clusters of needles found on older seedlings.

Effect of Mutual Shading of Leaves. The relative efficiency of photosynthesis of some trees at low light intensities is related to mutual shading of their leaves. Heinicke and Childers (1937) found that the maximum rate of photosynthesis of individual, fully exposed apple leaves was attained at only one-fourth to one-third of full sun, but photosynthesis of entire trees continued to increase with increased light up to full sun. They concluded that much of the leaf area of the tree was too heavily shaded to carry on maximum photosynthesis except during the middle of very bright days. Such mutual shading apparently also limits photosynthesis in conifers. The rate of photosynthesis of two-, three-, and five-needled pines per unit of leaf tissue decreased as the number of needles per fascicle increased because the more needles there are in a fascicle the more they shade each other (Uhl, 1937). Kramer and Clark (1947) also found that mutual shading of loblolly pine needles was an important factor in inhibiting photosynthesis of pine at low light intensities. Relatively low rates of photosynthesis of entire pine seedlings in the shade seemed to result principally from mutual shading of the needles.

Adaptation to Light Intensity. Light saturation intensity also may vary between species and between trees of the same species because of differences in optical density of the leaves. The light intensity at which the most deeply embedded chlorophyll molecules are affected depends on

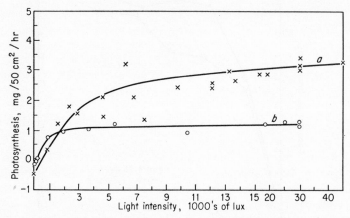

Figure 3.9 Rates of photosynthesis of sun leaves (*a*) and shade leaves (*b*) of European beech at various light intensities. The latter are saturated at a much lower light intensity than the former. (*From Boysen-Jensen, 1932.*)

leaf thickness. Adaptation of leaves to sun and shade affects photosynthesis over a range of light intensity. Shade-adapted leaves are darker green than light-adapted ones, and they absorb light more efficiently. As may be seen in Figure 3.9, shade leaves show a lower maximum rate and earlier leveling off of photosynthesis or light saturation with increasing light. Sun leaves of apple trees showed no decline of photosynthesis for 18 days when continuously illuminated at 3,800 foot-candles, while photosynthesis of shade leaves declined rapidly under the same conditions (Böhning, 1949).

Tranquillini (1954) found that at low light intensities shade leaves of beech produced four to five times as much carbohydrate as sun leaves. In another study (1955) he reported that the light intensity which was necessary for *Pinus cembra* seedlings to reach the compensation point depended on temperature and adaptation to light. Photosynthesis of shade-tolerant trees was always regulated by light intensity, while photosynthesis of sun trees was affected by light only on overcast days. The shade trees, however, made better use of light of low intensity than did the sun trees. Seedlings of sycamore maple grown in high light intensity have a higher saturation light intensity and higher maximum rate of photosynthesis than seedlings grown with low light intensity (Wassink et al., 1956). Bourdeau and Laverick (1958) found that shade leaves of white and red pine had higher rates of photosynthesis per unit of leaf weight than sun leaves at low light intensities but there was no significant difference between sun and shade leaves of hemlock. Takahara (1954) reported that shade leaves of *Cryptomeria japonica* and *Chamaecyparis obtusa* carry on photosynthesis more efficiently than sun leaves at low light intensities, presumably because of their higher chlorophyll concentration.

Photosynthesis and Tolerance. For convenience many foresters formerly defined "tolerance" as the ability of a species to survive under shade. Currently this term is used more often to express the ability of a tree to endure the whole complex of environmental factors which affect its growth and ultimate survival. Relative photosynthetic capacities of trees are involved in each of these definitions. Failure of a species to survive usually is the result of inability to carry on photosynthesis under environmental stress, whether caused by shade alone or by all the factors of the environmental complex. In one accepted usage, that which defines tolerance as capacity to endure shade, a tree which reaches maximum photosynthesis at relatively low light intensity is tolerant while one whose rate of photosynthesis continues to increase with each added increment of light up to full sun is considered intolerant. Thus tolerance ratings may be assigned to species. It is not the intent of the authors to defend a chosen definition of tolerance but merely to indicate that reactions of photosynthetic mechanisms of different species to environment are implicit in the term, however it is used. Kusumoto (1957a) studied photosynthesis of sun and shade leaves of broadleaf evergreens from various plant associations and concluded that there was a relationship between efficiency of photosynthesis and success in sun or shade. Monsi and Saeki (1953) suggest that the composition of plant communities depends on the relative photosynthetic efficiencies of the various competing species. For consideration of the basis for varying viewpoints regarding tolerance, the reader is referred to Toumey and Korstian (1947), Shirley (1943), Baker (1950), and Decker (1952). The broader aspects of tolerance are discussed in Chapter 16.

Light Quality. The light quality which reaches an understory tree in the forest is different from that which strikes a tree in the open. In hardwood forests the light which reaches the understory is low in blue, high in yellow and green, similar to sunlight in the orange red, and exceptionally rich in the far red. Under coniferous trees, however, no great changes occur in light quality (Toumey and Korstian, 1947). Burns (1934) showed that conifers are able to use all the visible spectrum except part of the blue and all the violet. The entire visible spectrum appears to be better for growth than any part of it. Photosynthesis is not seriously affected by the slight increase in green light under hardwood canopies as long as light intensity is not decreased too much.

Photoperiod. Growth of trees often is influenced by the number of hours of exposure to light. Trees will accumulate more total photosynthate if exposed to a long day than if exposed to a short one (Wareing, 1956). Böhning (1949) exposed young apple trees to continuous illumination at a light intensity of 3,200 foot-candles and found the rate of apparent photosynthesis to be fairly uniform for 18 days. Müller (1928) has reported that arctic plants carry on photosynthesis throughout a 24-hour day during the summer. It is surprising that accumulation of carbohydrates does not reduce carbon dioxide uptake during such long periods of illumination.

Temperature. Since only apparent photosynthesis can be measured and since temperature affects actual photosynthesis and respiration differently, the precise influence of temperature on photosynthesis is difficult to characterize. The role of the temperature factor usually is modified by existing light intensity, carbon dioxide availability, water supply, and a "time" factor.

Under field conditions photosynthesis would often be greater at the existing temperature if some other factor or combination of factors were not limiting. Thus photosynthesis of intolerant understory trees is little affected by fluctuations in air temperature because light is limiting. Trees also often fail to carry on maximum possible photosynthesis on a warm day even though they are in bright light and have adequate soil moisture, because the concentration of carbon dioxide may be limiting.

Effects of Low Temperature. Photosynthesis occurs in trees over wide temperature ranges. In the colder parts of the Temperate Zone conifers apparently carry on some photosynthesis into midwinter. Ehlers (1915) found that starch accumulated in conifers in winter while starch of evergreen broadleaf plants was depleted during the same time. This suggested the occurrence of winter photosynthesis in the conifers. Norway spruce trees showed high photosynthetic activity on warm, clear days in November and December, when leaves of neighboring deciduous trees had already fallen (Parker, 1953b). Some apparent photosynthesis occurred even on days when the temperature was several degrees below freezing. Freeland (1944) found some apparent photosynthesis in Scotch pine, black spruce, and black pine (*Pinus nigra* var. *austriaca*) at temperatures down to −6°C. Actual photosynthesis undoubtedly occurred at considerably lower temperatures, but below −6°C respiration exceeded photosynthesis, so apparent photosynthesis was negative. Ivanov and Orlova (1931) found photosynthesis occurring in pine trees down to −7°C, and Printz (1933) down to −2 or −3°C. Matthaei (1902, 1905) observed photosynthesis in detached cherry laurel leaves at −6°C and stated that respiration occurred at lower temperatures than apparent photosynthesis. Pisek and Tranquillini (1954) and Tranquillini (1957) also found that with the onset of winter and temperatures below freezing, photosynthesis ceased before respiration. Respiration also increased more rapidly than photosynthesis during the first warm days of spring.

Photosynthesis of conifers has been reported to take place at −30°C (Jumelle, 1892), but more recent research with improved instrumentation does not substantiate this earlier report. Reports of occurrence of photosynthesis in trees when air temperatures are below freezing are not surprising because leaves of trees in winter may be warmer than the surrounding air. Ehlers (1915) found that conifer leaves maintained winter temperatures of from 2 to 10°C higher than the surrounding air because of absorption of radiant energy. These temperatures were determined for the leaf as a whole and were not necessarily those of the chloroplasts, which absorb most of the radiant energy. The differences between chloroplast temperature and air temperature may often be even greater than suggested by Ehlers.

Indirect evidence indicates that in warm parts of the Temperate Zone conifers probably can synthesize some carbohydrates throughout the year. Shortleaf pine in the southeastern United States accumulated maximum amounts of carbohydrates in the roots during the winter months (Hepting, 1945). This suggests that photosynthesis is occurring in excess of use of carbohydrates in respiration and assimilation. On the other hand, the data presented in Figures 3.4 and 3.5 indicate a considerable reduction in photosynthetic capacity of evergreen trees during the winter.

Effects of High Temperature. With adequate carbon dioxide and high light intensities, apparent or net photosynthesis usually increases with increasing temperature up to some critical temperature, at which it begins to decline rapidly (Figures 3.10 and 8.10). Above the critical high temperature, respiration continues to increase while actual photosynthesis probably levels off or decreases. Therefore apparent photosynthesis decreases above this temperature.

Matthaei (1905) found that photosynthesis of both woody and herbaceous plants increased regularly from −6 to approximately 25°C, but only if neither carbon dioxide nor light intensity were limiting. Over this range photosynthesis of cherry laurel was slightly more than doubled for a 10°C rise in temperature. At low light intensities temperature did not influence uptake of carbon dioxide.

Nightingale (1935) found that peach and apple trees accumulated more carbohydrates at moderate temperatures than at higher temperatures. Decker (1944) found that apparent photosynthesis of red and loblolly pine seedlings was about the same at 20 and 30°C but decreased about 45 per cent when the temperatures were raised from 30 to 40°C.

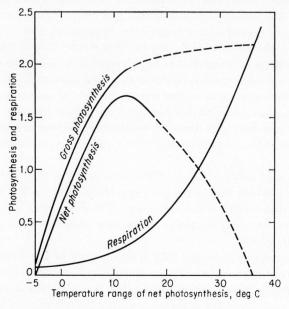

Figure 3.10 Effects of temperature on photosynthesis, respiration, and net or apparent photosynthesis of *Pinus cembra* seedlings. Solid parts of lines are from actual measurements; broken parts are estimated. (*After Tranquillini, 1955.*)

Tranquillini (1955) noted that apparent photosynthesis of *Pinus cembra* seedlings increased steadily to a maximum at 10 to 15°C and fell thereafter with rising temperatures. At approximately 35°C carbon dioxide was given off by the leaves, indicating that respiration was exceeding photosynthesis at that temperature. Poor development of tree seedlings in nurseries also has been noted under conditions of unusually high temperatures. Such depressed growth probably results largely because respiration increases faster than photosynthesis with increasing temperatures above a certain critical value (Figure 3.10).

At unusually high temperatures a "time" factor sets in and photosynthesis decreases with time (Matthaei, 1905). The higher the temperature, the more rapid the drop in photosynthesis. Such a time factor reflects internal conditions which may involve enzyme inactivation, accumulation of photosynthetic end products, or an inadequate rate of diffusion inward of carbon dioxide (Meyer and Anderson, 1952). This probably is more serious in detached leaves or twigs than in intact plants.

In the field some trees often respond less to wide temperature fluctuation than to some other environmental factors such as light intensity. In an environment of high light intensity, high soil fertility, and abundant soil moisture, photosynthesis of apple trees was not affected greatly by

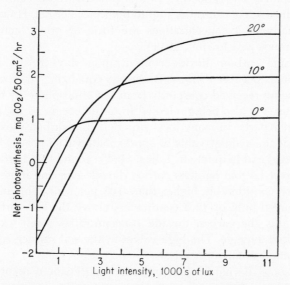

Figure 3.11 Effect of light intensity on net photosynthesis of the arctic willow *Salix glauca*, at various temperatures. Maximum photosynthesis occurs at low temperature in weak light, at a much higher temperature in brighter light. (*After Müller, 1928.*)

wide variation in temperature. Carbon dioxide uptake occurred during the hottest days as well as at temperatures near freezing, even though the leaves had been previously frozen (Heinicke and Childers, 1937).

Thermal Adaptations. Lower, optimal, and upper limits of photosynthesis are dissimilar in trees from different climatic areas. Cold-adapted trees often show maximum photosynthesis at low temperatures. For instance, Müller (1928) showed that photosynthesis of *Salix glauca* in Greenland was greatest at 0°C in weak light. At somewhat higher light intensities the optimum temperature was 10°C, and at the highest intensities tested it was 20°C or higher (Figure 3.11). Studies by Kusumoto (1957b) indicate that the optimum temperature for photosynthesis of evergreen trees may be lower in the winter than in the summer.

Carbon Dioxide. Photosynthesis of Temperate Zone trees that are well exposed to light probably is inhibited most frequently by the low carbon dioxide concentration of the air, which averages about 3 parts in 10,000, or about 0.03 per cent by volume. During much of the time photosynthesis varies directly with carbon dioxide concentration at levels present in the field (Thomas and Hill, 1949). Decker (1947) found a linear relationship between photosynthesis and carbon dioxide concentration in the range of 0.52 to 0.45 milligram per liter for both hardwoods and conifers in the laboratory. The short-time rate of photosynthesis can be increased by carbon dioxide concentrations up to ten times normal. However, either such unusually high concentrations are toxic or other factors become limiting (Franck and Loomis, 1949).

The average carbon dioxide concentration stays relatively constant over large areas because the oceans serve as equalizing reservoirs. Carbon dioxide is being received constantly from the atmosphere by colder parts of oceans, but it is also being released from the oceans to the atmosphere in the warmer parts. In many local situations the carbon dioxide content often exceeds the average value of approximately 0.03 per cent, especially at ground level and in quiet air. Fuller (1948) found that in forests, grassland, and river-bottom habitats carbon dioxide concentrations at the soil surface were considerably higher than 0.03 per cent. This high concentration occurred only up to 8 centimeters above the soil surface, and at greater heights the carbon dioxide concentrations rarely exceeded the generally cited average. The high values at the soil surface result largely from respiration of microorganisms.

There is some diurnal fluctuation in carbon dioxide content of air, and this affects photosynthesis adversely because carbon dioxide content usually reaches a daily minimum early in the afternoon (Huber, 1952; Chapman et al., 1954). This afternoon reduction presumably is caused by removal of carbon dioxide by photosynthesis. Böhning (1949) found decrease in photosynthesis to be caused by low carbon dioxide content in the air during the middle of the day. When he substituted tanks of compressed air in which carbon dioxide concentration was nearly constant, instead of subjecting apple leaves to the usual fluctuations in atmospheric carbon dioxide, no cyclic variation in photosynthesis occurred. Increased photosynthesis may occur on foggy days if light is not limiting because the carbon dioxide content of air is higher on such days than on clear days (Wilson, 1948a). Fog often is considered to favor plant growth through its effect on moisture content, but the high carbon dioxide concentration associated with fog may also be quite favorable for photosynthesis.

It often has been supposed that because volume percentage concentration of carbon dioxide in air is essentially similar at different altitudes, carbon dioxide has no influence in determining altitudinal species distribution. However, as Decker (1947) has pointed out, diffusion of carbon dioxide into a leaf is a function of carbon dioxide pressure rather than concentration, and the pressure of carbon dioxide in air varies directly as does total atmospheric pressure. Normal pressure of atmospheric carbon dioxide is approximately 0.228 millimeter of mercury at sea level and only 0.130 millimeter of mercury at an altitude of 15,000 feet. This altitudinal gradient in carbon dioxide pressure may well be one of the complex of factors which govern altitudinal zonation of species.

Soil Moisture. Soil moisture can become an important factor in photosynthesis because the rate is reduced by a water deficit in leaves. Either an excess or a deficiency of soil moisture can produce a water deficit. Since only a very small amount of the water absorbed by trees is used directly in photosynthesis, moisture supply affects photosynthesis indirectly by influencing stomatal closure, impeding uptake of carbon dioxide, and reducing the hydration of protoplasm. The reduction in photosynthesis varies with the severity and duration of the unfavorable soil moisture supply as well as with the dryness of the air.

Reduction of photosynthesis in drying soil has been observed in orchard trees (Schneider and Childers, 1941; Loustalot, 1945; Allmendinger et al., 1943) and in forest trees (Kozlowski, 1949; Bormann, 1953; Bourdeau, 1954; Negisi and Satoo, 1954).

Photosynthesis is depressed in many plants before the onset of wilting. Stålfelt (1921) found that when a rain during the night was followed by a clear day, maximum photosynthesis of Scotch pine and Norway spruce was attained at 10 or 11 A.M. and this high rate continued for several hours. When no further rain fell on the next day, the high rate did not continue as long as it had just after the rain. Continued drought for several days reduced the maximum rate as well as the length of time that the maximum was maintained during the day.

Uptake of carbon dioxide by apple trees in a drying soil declined as much as a week before actual wilting of leaves occurred (Allmendinger et al., 1943). Similarly, in both light and heavy soils photosynthesis of pecan trees was reduced as the soil dried and the reduction was apparent before wilting percentage was reached (Loustalot, 1945). The amount of reduction in photosynthesis depended on soil moisture content and atmospheric conditions. Photosynthesis was reduced more in the afternoon than in the morning because the leaves were drier in the afternoon when transpiration was highest. After the plants were subjected to severe drought, rewatering the soil to field capacity caused a rapid increase in photosynthesis but normal rates were not attained immediately. Ten days after rewatering, photosynthesis had recovered to only about two-thirds of the normal rate (Figure 3.12). Trees subjected to severe drought

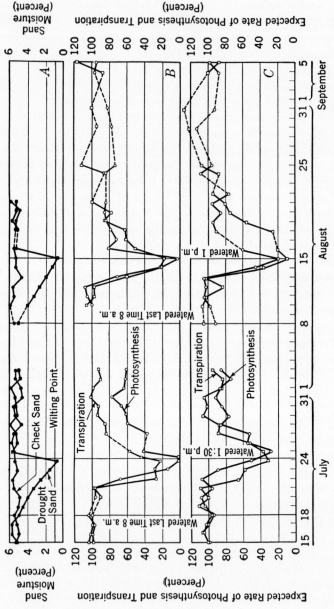

Figure 3.12 Effect of decreasing soil moisture on photosynthesis and transpiration of pecan seedlings growing in sand. A. Moisture content of sand. B. Rates of photosynthesis and transpiration during the afternoon, expressed as percentages of the rate expected with well-watered plants. C. Similar rates during the forenoon. Effects of dry soil were greater in the afternoon because more rapid transpiration produced a larger water deficit in leaves in the afternoon. (*From Kramer, 1949; after Loustalot, 1945.*)

apparently suffer physiological damage from which they do not recover readily.

Kozlowski (1949) studied response of potted loblolly pine seedlings in soil allowed to dry down almost to the wilting percentage. He found that photosynthesis was depressed before the wilting percentage was reached and almost stopped near the wilting percentage. Photosynthesis of oak also was depressed in drying soil, but less rapidly than that of pine. Bormann (1953) found that sweetgum behaved in the same manner in drying soils as the loblolly pine studied by Kozlowski (Figure 3.13). Photosynthesis of northern red oak and blackjack oak seedlings also began

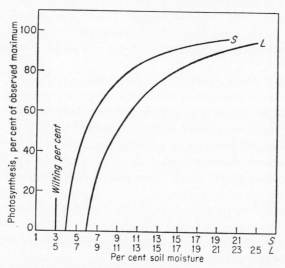

Figure 3.13 Apparent photosynthesis of sweetgum (S) and loblolly pine (L) with high light intensity and decreasing soil moisture content. (*Sweetgum data from Bormann, 1953; loblolly pine data from Kozlowski, 1949.*)

to fall off as soil dried down from field capacity (Bourdeau, 1954). In Japan, Negisi and Satoo (1954) noted a slight increase in photosynthesis of *Pinus densiflora* seedlings from considerably above to just below field capacity. Photosynthesis was seriously reduced, however, when the soil continued to dry. The depressing effect was evident long before the wilting percentage was approached. Recovery was rapid and was evident 1 day after watering. Schneider and Childers (1941) observed a small increase in photosynthesis of apple leaves with slight moisture decrease below field capacity in a fairly heavy soil. Experiments with herbaceous plants also show that more carbohydrate reserves build up when soil moisture contents are maintained near the field capacity than when their moisture contents are allowed to decrease almost to the wilting percentage before they are reirrigated (Woodhams and Kozlowski, 1954).

Excess Soil Moisture. In flooded soils the excess gravitational water displaces air from the pore space and the resulting poor aeration impedes water uptake by roots, causing leaves to dry out (Chapter 11). Leaf desiccation associated with flooding acts to reduce photosynthesis. Loustalot (1945) found that a few days of root submersion caused substantial reduction in photosynthesis of pecan leaves. The amount of reduction was greater in the afternoon than in the morning, suggesting that the reduction was caused by water deficit. Photosynthesis of flooded trees in sand was reduced to a low of 11 per cent of normal, while in leaves of trees in a heavier soil it was reduced to a value so low that it could not be measured. This differential response suggests that oxygen supply to roots was reduced less in the sand than in the heavier soil. When excess water was removed, photosynthesis increased but did not return to normal for several days.

Childers and White (1942) found that flooding reduced photosynthesis of apple leaves, usually within 2 to 7 days after the roots were submerged. Furthermore, the leaves from submerged trees contained less water than those from control trees which were in unflooded soil.

Soil Fertility. Deficiencies of essential nutrients have both direct and indirect effects on photosynthesis. It is reduced directly by the decreased synthesis of chlorophyll which often accompanies mineral deficiencies, but it also is reduced by decreased leaf area, possibly by changes in leaf structure, and even by decreased stomatal activity. Effects on enzymes and other internal processes also doubtless occur, as indicated by the fact that photosynthesis sometimes is reduced by mineral deficiencies although no visible symptoms occur.

The depressing effects of mineral deficiencies on photosynthesis, and consequently on growth, often are more serious in the management of forests than of orchards. Deficiencies in orchards are corrected by fertilization, but applications of fertilizers to large forest areas have not been regarded as economically feasible, at least until very recently (Chapter 9). Application of fertilizer, especially nitrogen, to apple and tung trees has been shown to increase photosynthesis materially (Heinicke, 1934; Loustalot et al., 1950; Tompkins, 1934). This resulted both from increase in leaf area and from increase in photosynthesis per unit of leaf area.

Nitrogen and magnesium are components of the chlorophyll molecule, and a deficiency of either inhibits photosynthesis. Iron deficiency also reduces photosynthesis since iron is necessary for chlorophyll formation. Insufficient amounts of other elements decrease photosynthesis, but deficiencies of some elements do not seem to affect photosynthesis appreciably. In one study deficiencies of copper and zinc caused low rates of photosynthesis in tung leaves, but manganese deficiency had somewhat different effects. Manganese deficiency caused a disease known as "frenching," and when photosynthesis of frenched leaves of tung was compared with photosynthesis of leaves treated with manganese sulfate, no great differences were apparent per unit of surface. However, the manganese-deficient trees had smaller leaves and less total leaf surface, so the total amount of photosynthate produced by them was less than that of normal trees (Reuther and Burrows, 1942). Decrease in photosynthesis of mineral-deficient trees is not confined to leaves showing necrosis or chlorosis. Copper- and zinc-deficient tung seedlings had lower photosynthetic rates per unit of leaf area than normal seedlings. The rate of photosynthesis in copper-deficient plants was often less than half the normal rate. Reduction was greatest for leaves showing definite deficiency symptoms, but photosynthesis also was reduced in leaves that showed no visible evidence of deficiency (Loustalot et al., 1945).

Nitrogen deficiency appears to have a greater inhibitory effect on photosynthesis than does the deficiency of any other element. For example, nitrogen deficiency decreased photosynthesis of young McIntosh apple leaves by over 60 per cent, while phosphorus and potassium deficiencies either alone or combined decreased the rate much less (Childers and Cowart, 1935). Similar effects were noted in tung seedlings. Whenever the nitrogen content of leaves dropped to 2 per cent, there was a change in the color of foliage, decreased photosynthesis, and decreased growth. In leaves with nitrogen content of 1.60 to 1.40 per cent, photosynthesis was at a low ebb, growth was stopped, leaves began to abscise, and dry-weight increment was negligible. Reduction of potassium in leaves to 0.55 per cent did not affect leaf color but reduced apparent photosynthesis somewhat, although to a much lesser extent than did nitrogen deficiency (Loustalot et al., 1950).

Spray Materials. Many fungicidal and insecticidal sprays reduce photosynthetic efficiency. The reduction usually is greater when only the lower leaf surface is sprayed than when only the upper surface is sprayed. The amount of reduction varies with species and increases with increasing temperature. Photosynthesis is reduced primarily because of clogging of stomates and interference with inward diffusion of carbon dioxide. Some of the effect probably is due to decreasing light intensity, and some to direct chemical effects (Southwick and Childers, 1941).

Oils. Saturated-petroleum-oil insecticides are not toxic in the usual sense but often cause metabolic disturbances because of entrance of oil into plant tissue. Knight et al. (1929) found that oils applied to surfaces of citrus leaves were absorbed through both stomated and nonstomated leaf surfaces. During rapid oil penetration photosynthesis was severely reduced and some of the chlorophyll was dissolved in the oil. Recovery was most rapid when light oils were used, and it was characterized by build-up of abnormally high amounts of carbohydrates in leaves, possibly because the phloem was still blocked with oil and could not translocate recently elaborated carbohydrates. Photosynthesis of leaf discs of citrus trees was depressed rapidly by petroleum-oil sprays in amounts commonly used as insecticides (Wedding et al., 1952). Some inhibition of photosynthesis persisted for the entire length of the determination—59 days (Figure 3.14). Young (1934) found that photosynthesis of Jonathan apple leaves returned to normal after one spray application of fish oil. When more than one application was made, there was a definite decrease in carbon dioxide intake following each spray (Schroeder, 1936).

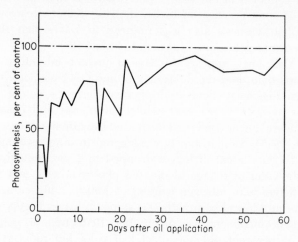

Figure 3.14 Influence of an oil spray on photosynthesis of Eureka lemon leaves. (*From Wedding et al., 1952.*)

Sulfur and Copper Fungicides. Sulfur fungicides reduce photosynthesis in varying amounts. Bordeaux mixture has been shown to have almost no effect on photosynthesis (Clore, 1935) or to reduce it only slightly (Hyre, 1939). Some sprays reduce photosynthesis mechanically by cutting off light or by plugging stomates. The influence of bordeaux mixture, however, has been reported to be primarily physiological rather than mechanical. The soluble-copper fraction seems to be directly responsible for the reduction in photosynthesis (Southwick and Childers, 1941).

Lime sulfur reduces photosynthesis considerably. When Baldwin apple trees were sprayed with lime sulfur, photosynthesis was reduced by about half during the first 5 days after the spray. This represented reduced production of dry matter equivalent to that found in $\frac{1}{2}$ bushel of apples (Heinicke, 1937a).

Hyre (1939) made a comprehensive study of the effects of 22 different sulfur fungicides on photosynthesis of McIntosh and Baldwin apple trees in an environment controlled with respect to temperature, light, and humidity. Reduction of apparent photosynthesis was greater at 100°F than at lower temperatures. All spray materials decreased apparent photosynthesis. As may be seen in Figure 3.15, bordeaux mixture caused only

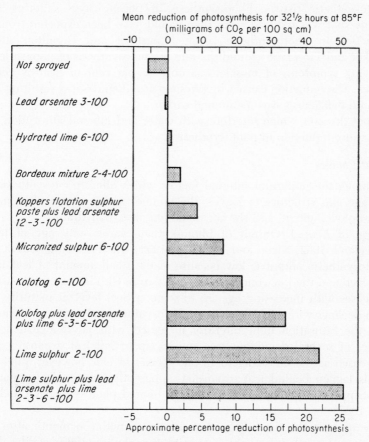

Figure 3.15 Effect of various spray materials on apparent photosynthesis of Baldwin and McIntosh apple leaves. Negative values indicate increased photosynthesis. (*From Hyre, 1939.*)

slight reduction, wettable sulfurs were next in order, and lime-sulfur solution reduced photosynthesis more than did the wettable sulfurs. Mixtures of sulfur fungicides had the most depressing effects. Apparently the use of milder sprays which cause less reduction in photosynthesis will bring benefits in terms of increased yields, provided that control of disease can be achieved with such sprays.

Inhibition of photosynthesis by 2,4-dichlorophenoxyacetic acid has been observed in citrus leaves. This appears to be related to the concentration of undissociated 2,4-D acid molecules in the spray solution (Wedding et al., 1954).

Disease. Leaf diseases often reduce photosynthesis by reducing the photosynthetic area and by reducing the efficiency of the remaining photosynthetic tissues. Photosynthesis of pecan leaves suffering from downy spot was reduced more than would have been expected from the reduction in photosynthetic tissue (Loustalot and Hamilton, 1941). Decker and Tio (1958) found the rate of photosynthesis of papaya leaves showing symptoms of mosaic was only 36 per cent of healthy control leaves. The reduction caused by physiological disturbances resulting from mineral deficiences was mentioned earlier.

Root diseases which interfere with water and mineral absorption may also cause reduction in photosynthesis.

Plant Factors

Among the important internal factors which affect photosynthesis are the age and structure of leaves, the number and response of stomates, chlorophyll content, and the accumulation of carbohydrates.

Age of Leaves. Output of photosynthate varies with age of leaves (Freeland, 1952; Nixon and Wedding, 1956). In very young leaves total photosynthetic output is low because of the small amount of leaf tissue involved and the low concentration of chlorophyll. Photosynthesis usually increases with increasing age up to some critical level of maturity, and then declines with age. The rate of photosynthesis per unit of leaf surface and the saturation light intensity increased with physiological age of leaves of several deciduous tree species up to full leaf expansion, then decreased as the leaves aged. In one species of oak, however, photosynthesis lagged behind leaf expansion, apparently because leaf expansion outstripped some internal factor which limited photosynthesis (Richardson, 1957).

In apple leaves the foliage that developed within a month after bud opening showed remarkable capacity for photosynthesis. Older basal leaves were soon forced to compete with younger terminal leaves for light, water, and nutrients, resulting in decrease of their photosynthetic capacity. The younger leaves produced most of the total photosynthate during the season (Heinicke and Childers, 1937). Leaves of conifers apparently respond in the same manner as deciduous leaves during their first year, for McGregor (1958) found that the photosynthetic efficiency of white and loblolly pine needles began to decrease soon after they attained full size.

Nixon and Wedding (1956) observed that photosynthetic efficiency of date palm leaves appeared to increase during the first year until maturity, then declined progressively during the next 3 years. Similar changes have been observed in photosynthesis of citrus leaves (Rhoads and Wedding, 1953). Freeland (1952) measured the rates of photosynthesis of 1-, 2-, and 3-year-old needles of several species of conifers and found that the rate decreased with increasing age (Figure 3.16).

Structure and Arrangement of Leaves. Photosynthesis is correlated with the differences in leaf structure that occur between species, between environmental adaptations of the same species, and even between leaves in different parts of the same branch. Photosynthesis of sun-grown leaves often is higher in bright light than that of shade-grown

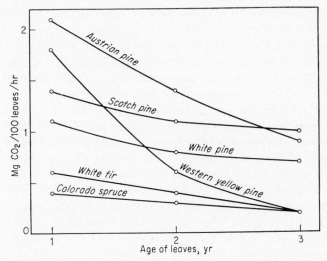

Figure 3.16 Effect of age of needles on apparent or net photosynthesis. (*From Freeland, 1952.*)

leaves of the same species, probably because sun-grown leaves have more exposed internal leaf surface (Turrell, 1936, 1944). Sun-grown leaves may also have more water-conducting tissue and smaller but more numerous stomates.

Pickett (1933) found large variations in amounts of exposed mesophyll in several varieties of apple leaves. The variety Delicious had only 58 per cent as much internal surface as the variety Liveland. In a later study Pickett (1937) found that leaves with extensive intercellular space made the greatest dry-weight increases. The amount of internally exposed surface of apple leaves has been reported to be much more important in influencing photosynthesis than normal variations in chlorophyll content (Pickett and Kenworthy, 1939).

The high rates of photosynthesis of apple leaves located near a shoot apex could be partially accounted for by their structure (Cowart, 1935). Leaf thickness decreased from the base toward the median portion of the shoot, and then increased from that point to the shoot tip. Palisade layers of leaves near the tip of the shoot were more compact and occupied more of the mesophyll tissue. Furthermore, stomatal frequency increased progressively from leaf to leaf from the base of the shoot toward the tip. Leaves near the apex had more internal cell surface and more chlorophyll per unit area of leaf surface than did basal leaves. These anatomical differences conditioned photosynthesis only partially because differences in water supply and light intensity were also involved.

It was mentioned earlier that the highest rates of photosynthesis of individual exposed leaves of some trees are reached at a low light intensity, but photosynthesis of entire trees increases with increased light (Heinicke and Childers, 1937; Kramer and Clark, 1947). In these species the leaves apparently are so arranged that their mutual shading is an important factor in controlling photosynthesis. Leaf arrangement also is discussed in the section on mutual shading in this chapter.

Stomatal Distribution and Behavior. It often has been claimed that entrance of carbon dioxide into leaves occurs mainly through stomates. Much support for this long-held view came from the work of Blackman (1895), who claimed that normally the amount of gas which entered through a nonstomated epidermis was negligible and could be disregarded in photosynthesis. Maskell (1928) and Nutman (1937) supported this view by reporting that photosynthesis in trees was correlated with stomatal movement. The problem was reinvestigated by Freeland (1948) with several woody and herbaceous plants that were selected for wide variation in stomatal frequency and distribution as well as thickness of cuticle. He found considerable variation in carbon dioxide uptake through epidermal cells during photosynthesis. In plants with stomates on the lower surface only, apparent photosynthesis through the stomated surface always exceeded photosynthesis through the nonstomated side. However, carbon dioxide absorption did occur through the nonstomated side in varying amounts. In one species carbon dioxide uptake through a nonstomated epidermis was as much as 70 per cent of that through the stomated layer. Plants with heavily cutinized leaves showed negligible carbon dioxide uptake through nonstomated epidermal surfaces. Dugger (1952) found further that a nonstomated, cutinized epidermis was permeable to gaseous carbon dioxide and that its degree of permeability was proportional to the partial pressure of the gas above the epidermis. In some instances the amount of gas which penetrated the nonstomated epidermis was about equal to the amount entering the stomated lower surface. Dugger used rather high concentrations of carbon dioxide in his experiments; nevertheless it seems likely that in at least some species both leaf surfaces, including those without stomates, are involved in varying degrees in photosynthesis. In general, it seems probable that entrance of carbon dioxide into heavily cutinized leaves occurs principally through the stomates. In such leaves stomatal opening is more important in controlling photosynthesis than in leaves with thin cuticles.

Satoo (1955a) found that stomatal aperture and photosynthesis of *Quercus acutissima* were decreased by exposure to artificial wind. When soil moisture was low, the effect of wind was more intense. Apparently drying of the leaves caused stomatal closure and decreased available carbon dioxide to the chloroplasts, thus reducing photosynthesis. Stomatal behavior is discussed further in Chapter 10.

Chlorophyll Content. Photosynthesis in leaves with an abnormally light green color usually is less than that in leaves with a healthy, dark green color. The amount of reduction may not vary much over a considerable range of color, and it appears that chlorophyll content is often less important in limiting photosynthesis than are other factors. For instance, Pickett and Kenworthy (1939) concluded that leaf structure was more important in controlling photosynthesis than was chlorophyll content. Nevertheless, leaves with pronounced chlorosis from severe mineral deficiency will show greatly reduced photosynthesis. Slight yellowing resulting from poor soil aeration, accumulation of photosynthetic products, root/shoot imbalance, or other causes may not reduce photosynthesis much. Willstätter and Stoll (1918) found that photosynthesis was slightly higher in green varieties of elm and alder than in yellow ones, but they also found that the yellow-leaved varieties were more efficient per unit of chlorophyll. However, when Heinicke and Hoffman (1933) compared photosynthesis of similarly located leaves selected from trees with light green and dark green foliage, they found the dark green ones to have about three times the rate of photosynthesis of the light green ones. The selected yellow leaves probably were markedly nitrogen-deficient.

Carbohydrate Accumulation. Carbohydrates produced in photosynthesis may accumulate much faster than they can be assimilated, used up in respiration, or translocated out of leaves. Under some circumstances such accumulations of carbohydrates in leaves reduce photosynthesis. A high sugar content in apple leaves reduced photosynthesis significantly whether sugar content of leaves was increased artificially through cut stems or whether translocation of sugars from leaves was prevented by girdling the stem (Kursanov, 1933). Substantial reduction of apparent photosynthesis was also found in pecan leaflets on ringed branches within 1 to 2 days after girdling (Loustalot, 1943). Apparent photosynthesis was reduced up to 100 per cent by the second afternoon following girdling, and reduced photosynthesis was still evident 50 days after ringing. The reduction was less in the morning than in the afternoon, suggesting that leaf water deficits were involved. Respiration of leaves was also increased by ringing of branches, so that the observed reductions in apparent photosynthesis probably reflected not only inhibition of true photosynthesis but also increased respiration.

Tranquillini (1957) reported that chlorophyll content of pine seedlings in an alpine habitat decreased during the winter and that in the spring photosynthetic capacity was related to chlorophyll content. Seasonal changes in photosynthesis of a deciduous species, *Zelkowa serrata,* also show some relation to changes in chlorophyll content (Saeki and Nomoto, 1958).

In some instances where accumulation of carbohydrates might be expected to reduce photosynthesis, little or no reduction is observed. For example, Böhning (1949) found apple trees to maintain about the same rate of photosynthesis during a period of 18 days of continuous illumination at 3,200 foot-candles. McGregor (1958) observed a constant rate of photosynthesis for up to 16 hours at 30°C and 4,000 foot-candles of light. Respiration also was constant in darkness for 16 hours at 23°C.

GENERAL REFERENCES

Baker, F. S., 1950, Principles of silviculture, McGraw-Hill Book Company, Inc., New York.
Bassham, J. A., and M. Calvin, 1957, The path of carbon in photosynthesis, Prentice-Hall, Inc., Englewood Cliffs, N.J.
Franck, J., and W. E. Loomis (eds.), 1949, Photosynthesis in plants, Iowa State College Press, Ames, Iowa.
Hill, R., and C. P. Whittingham, 1955, Photosynthesis, Methuen & Co., Ltd., London.
Kramer, P. J., 1958, Photosynthesis of trees as affected by their environment, chap. 8 in K. V. Thimann (ed.), The physiology of forest trees, The Ronald Press Company, New York.
Polster, H., 1950, Die physiologischen Grundlagen der Stofferzeugung im Walde, Bayerischen Landwirtschaftsverlag Gmbh., Munich.
Rabinowitch, E. I., 1945, Photosynthesis and related processes, vol. 1, and vol. 2, parts 1 and 2, 1951, Interscience Publishers, Inc., New York.

CHAPTER 4 *Carbohydrate Metabolism*

This chapter deals with the kinds of carbohydrates found in trees, the uses made of them, and the accumulation of surplus. Carbohydrates are of special importance because they are direct products of photosynthesis and are therefore the basic organic substances from which all other organic compounds found in plants are synthesized. They are the chief constituents of cell walls; they form the starting point for the synthesis of fats and proteins; large amounts are oxidized in respiration; and whatever is left accumulates as reserve food. Soluble carbohydrates increase the osmotic pressure of the cell sap, and such carbohydrates as the pentosans, pectic compounds, gums, and mucilages increase the water-holding capacity. Quantitatively they are the most important constituents of trees, comprising about 75 per cent of the dry weight.

Kinds of Carbohydrates

The carbohydrates include sugars, polysaccharides, and compound carbohydrates.

Although a wide variety of carbohydrates occur in trees, only a few occur in sufficient quantity to deserve special mention. Figure 4.1 shows the classification of the more important carbohydrates. In monosaccharides the hydrogen and oxygen occur in the same proportions as in water, although this is not true of all carbohydrates. Sugars containing 2, 3, 4, 5, 6, and 7 carbon atoms are known, but only those containing 5 (pentoses) or 6 (hexoses) carbon atoms occur in appreciable quantities. Often 2, 3, 4, or many sugar molecules are linked together to form di-, tri-, tetra-, or polysaccharides. Of these only the disaccharides and polysaccharides are of much importance in trees, although tri- and tetrasaccharides occur in the phloem exudate of some trees (Chapter 8).

Monosaccharides. The monosaccharides are the basic carbohydrate units from which other more complex compounds are formed. Although only traces of pentose sugars are found free in plants, their condensation

97

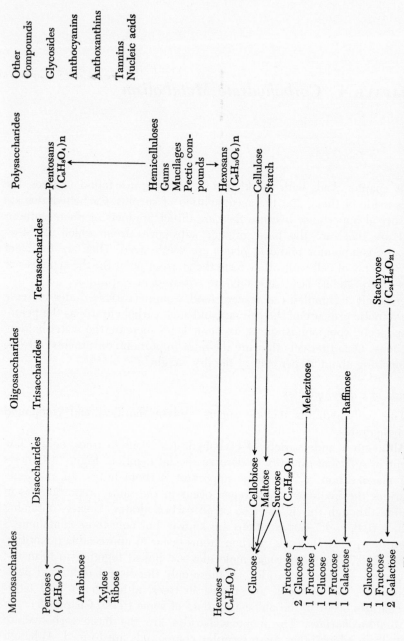

Figure 4.1 Relationships among some important carbohydrates and products of their hydrolysis.

products, the pentosans, are important constituents of cell walls. The pentose sugar ribose occurs not only in plants but in all living cells, as a constituent of certain respiratory coenzymes and nucleic acids. Some of the hexose sugars occur chiefly in their condensed forms, galactose and mannose for example, as galactans and mannans. Glucose, in contrast, probably occurs in every living cell and is found in plant tissues in large quantities. It occurs in condensed form in cellulose and starch. Fructose also is common, although it usually occurs in lower concentrations than glucose. Glucose and fructose occur not only in living cells but also in the xylem sap of certain trees such as maple and birch. Derivatives of glucose and fructose which have been phosphorylated, i.e., have had phosphate groups attached to them, form the starting point for many metabolic transformations of carbohydrates.

Disaccharides. The disaccharide sucrose is a very abundant sugar in trees. It is the chief solute in the xylem sap of maple and some other species in the winter and early spring and probably occurs in the vacuolar sap of all plants. Sucrose yields glucose and fructose when hydrolyzed. Maltose also is common, but it usually occurs in lower concentrations than sucrose. It is an important intermediate substance in the digestion of starch by amylase and therefore occurs wherever starch is being hydrolyzed. Maltose yields 2 molecules of glucose when hydrolyzed to monosaccharide units.

Tri- and Tetrasaccharides. Zimmerman (1957a) found considerable amounts of the trisaccharide raffinose in the phloem exudate of white ash and American elm and smaller amounts or traces in exudate from trees of several other species. Melezitose is another trisaccharide found in exudates of certain trees. Considerable amounts of the tetrasaccharide stachyose also occur in the phloem exudate of elm and white ash, and traces of it are found in a few other species.

Polysaccharides. The most important polysaccharides in trees are cellulose and starch. Cellulose is the chief constituent of the cell walls which form the framework of a tree. Each cellulose molecule consists of 1,000 or more glucose residues linked together by oxygen bridges between the 1 and 4 carbon atoms of adjacent molecules to form long, straight, unbranched chains. The chains are packed together into micelles, which in turn are organized into microfibrils. Considerable spaces occur between the micelles and microfibrils. These spaces are occupied by water in pure cellulose walls such as cotton fibers, but become partly filled with lignin in woody tissue and with pectic compounds, cutin, or suberin if these substances are present. Among the notable characteristics of cellulose are its high degree of resistance to dilute acids and its insolubility in water and organic solvents.

Starch is the most abundant reserve carbohydrate in trees. Starch grains cannot pass from cell to cell; hence starch must have been synthe-sized in those tissues where it is found. It is formed by the condensation of hundreds of glucose molecules into long spiral chains. As in cellulose, the glucose residues are linked together by oxygen bridges between the 1 and 4 carbon atoms, but starch has an alpha linkage while cellulose has a beta linkage. Starch consists of two components which differ in some physical properties. The most abundant component of most starch is amylopectin, which consists of very long molecules with numerous branched side chains. The other component is amylose, which consists of unbranched chains containing 300 to 1,000 residues. Amylose gives a deeper blue color with iodine and is more water-soluble and more vis-cous than amylopectin. Starch accumulates in definite grains formed of many layers, which give them a laminated appearance. Starch grains often occur in the sapwood but not in the heartwood of trees. They also occur in the living phloem cells of the inner bark. The amount of starch in the woody structure of trees varies seasonally, as will become apparent later. Starch grains also occur in large numbers in almost all leaves.

The hemicelluloses are a somewhat poorly defined group of polysac-charides which occur in all woody tissues. They include arabans, xylans, galactans, and mannans. Unlike cellulose, hemicelluloses are soluble in dilute acids and alkalies and they are sometimes digested and used as reserve foods by plants. Hemicelluloses occur in some seeds, persimmon and certain palms for example, and these are digested and used during germination. There is some debate concerning the extent to which hemi-celluloses found in cell walls of the woody structure are used as reserve food, and this will be discussed in a later section.

Pectic compounds are hydrophilic substances which occur in the middle lamella and in the primary walls of cells but are not present in woody tissues in large amounts. Gums and mucilages are compound carbo-hydrates which somewhat resemble pectic compounds. Spruce gum is a well-known example. Examples of mucilages are the slimy substance from the inner bark of slippery elm and the sticky substances found in the seed pods of the carob (*Ceratonia siliqua*) and honey locust. The well-known gum arabic, also known as gum acacia, comes from an African acacia, and most readers are familiar with the gum which exudes from the stems of cherry, peach, and plum trees.

In prunes, peaches, citrus, and some other trees, excessive gum forma-tion as a result of wounding is called gummosis. It is caused by hydroly-sis of cell wall constituents.

Enzymes

Before discussing carbohydrate transformations it is desirable to con-sider briefly the general nature of the enzymes which are involved in these reactions. The numerous chemical reactions which occur in living cells are controlled by enzymes, hundreds of which probably are contained in each cell. Enzymes usually are defined as organic catalysts produced by living cells. They are highly specific, each enzyme being effective in only one or a few related reactions. They resemble inorganic catalysts in being effective at very low concentrations, but they differ in being inactivated at moderately high temperatures.

All enzymes thus far isolated basically are proteins, but there are two general types. Some enzymes, including many involved in hydrolytic processes, are simply protein molecules. Other enzymes consist of a protein molecule plus an associated nonprotein called a "prosthetic group" or "coenzyme." The prosthetic group can be a metal ion such as copper with ascorbic acid oxidase or iron with cytochrome oxidase. Sometimes the prosthetic group or coenzyme is a complex organic molecule such as one of the B vitamins, or the phosphopyridine nucleotides associated with dehydrogenases.

Enzymes can be classified in several ways, but it will suffice here to group them as hydrolytic or desmolyzing enzymes. Hydrolyzing enzymes cause substrate molecules to split with the addition of water, as when starch is digested to sugar, or sucrose to glucose and fructose. Desmolyzing enzymes are involved in a variety of reactions such as the splitting of linkages between carbon atoms (carboxylases), splitting off of hydrogen atoms (dehydrogenases), and transfer of atoms or groups from one part of a molecule or one molecule to another (transaminase). Many of these reactions are reversible. The types of compounds formed in plants (e.g., sucrose, starch, inulin) depend on the kinds of enzymes present, and the kinds of enzymes formed are controlled basically by heredity although their formation sometimes is affected by environmental factors ("adaptive" enzymes).

Enzyme activity is affected by various factors, of which temperature, pH, hydration of tissue, and concentration are most important. Increasing temperature tends to increase the rate of most chemical reactions, but high temperatures tend to inactivate enzymes. At high temperatures the rates of enzyme-catalyzed processes often decrease rapidly because of enzyme inactivation. Examples of the effect of various factors on enzyme action will be mentioned later in this book in connection with various processes.

Carbohydrate Transformation

Many of the carbohydrates found in plants are less stable than once supposed and actually are continually undergoing conversion from one form to another or being transformed into compounds used in respiration or the synthesis of fats, proteins, and other noncarbohydrates. This is

shown by the fact that if plants are supplied with carbon dioxide containing radioactive C^{14}, the radioactive carbon is quickly incorporated into a
wide variety of carbohydrates, organic acids, and other compounds. Some
carbon fixation occurs even in darkness.

Phosphorylation. The first step in many of the carbohydrate transformations is phosphorylation, a process in which glucose or fructose molecules
react with adenosine triphosphate (ATP) to form the phosphate esters,
glucose-6-phosphate and fructose-6-phosphate, while ATP is converted to
ADP (adenosine diphosphate). From glucose-6-phosphate, by transfer of
the phosphate group from carbon atom 6 to carbon atom 1, is formed
glucose-1-phosphate, which is the starting point for synthesis of both

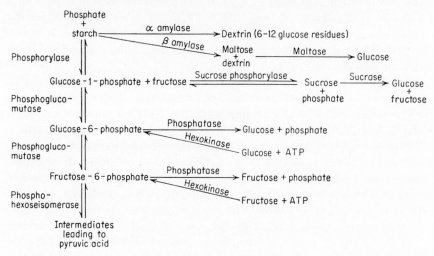

Figure 4.2 Some transformation of carbohydrates which occur in plants. The
transformations leading to pyruvic acid and the Krebs cycle are shown in Figure 7.1.

starch and sucrose. Some of the important transformations of carbohydrates and the enzymes involved are shown diagrammatically in Figure 4.2. Only the synthesis and breakdown of starch and sucrose will be
discussed in detail.

Starch—Sugar. The most important transformation involving reserve
carbohydrates is that between starch and sugar. In most woody plants of
the Temperate Zone starch accumulates in late summer and early
autumn; then after the beginning of cold weather it tends to disappear
and sugar, usually sucrose, increases. It generally is supposed that starch
is synthesized as follows:

$$\text{Glucose-1-phosphate} \underset{\text{phosphorolysis}}{\overset{\text{starch synthesis}}{\rightleftarrows}} \text{starch} + H_3PO_4$$

This usually is regarded as a reversible process, the breakdown of starch in this scheme being termed phosphorolysis. The enzyme involved is starch phosphorylase, which is found in a variety of plant tissues. The direction in which this reaction goes probably is determined by the supply of glucose-1-phosphate, starch synthesis being favored by a high concentration and starch degradation by a low concentration. Ewart et al. (1954) isolated glucose-1-phosphate from the inner bark of black locust and were able to demonstrate starch synthesis in sections of bark by adding glucose-1-phosphate. They doubt, however, that phosphorylase is involved in normal starch synthesis in living bark because the ratios of inorganic phosphate and glucose-1-phosphate were unfavorable to synthesis even in tissues where starch was actually accumulating. Conditions were favorable for its participation in starch degradation, however.

The more familiar hydrolysis of starch to dextrins and maltose is brought about by quite different enzymes and in a different manner, water entering into the reaction.

$$
\begin{array}{c}
\overbrace{\text{Diastase}} \\
\overbrace{\text{Amylase}}\ \ \overbrace{\text{Maltase}} \\
\text{Starch} \rightarrow \text{dextrins} \rightarrow \text{maltose} \rightarrow \text{glucose}
\end{array}
$$

The diastase often used in laboratories is a mixture of enzymes.

Sucrose. The exact mechanism of sucrose synthesis in trees is unknown, but it occurs in a series of steps involving phosphorylation of glucose and the formation of complex intermediates, followed by combination with fructose. The hydrolysis of sucrose into glucose and fructose by sucrase is better known, but it is not reversible.

$$
\begin{array}{c}
\text{Sucrase} \\
\text{Sucrose} \rightarrow \text{glucose} + \text{fructose}
\end{array}
$$

Most of these reactions are combined in Figure 4.2.

Factors Affecting Carbohydrate Transformations. Considerable attention has given to the factors which affect the carbohydrate transformations occurring in trees and other woody plants. Both internal factors such as pH, concentration of sugar, and hydration of cells and environmental factors such as temperature are known to affect the process.

All enzymes are sensitive to the pH of the medium; hence enzymatic processes are usually affected by variations in pH. A well-known example of this occurs in the guard cells of stomates, where decrease in pH is accompanied by conversion of sugar to starch and increase in pH causes the reverse.

Presumably, the concentration of sugar ought to affect the direction in which these reactions proceed. For instance, when sugar concentration is kept high by photosynthesis, starch formation ought to be favored, but when photosynthesis stops and the sugar concentration drops, the conversion of starch to sugar might be expected. Etiolated, detached leaves often can be caused to accumulate starch by floating them on sucrose solution in darkness.

It has been reported by several investigators that in some plants reduction in water content causes conversion of starch to sugar, resulting in rapid disappearance of starch from wilting leaves (Ahrns, 1924; Spoehr and Milner, 1939).

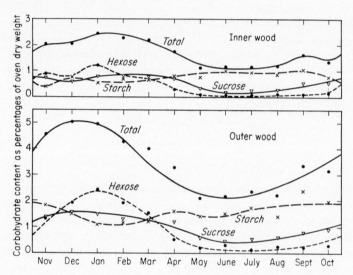

Figure 4.3 Seasonal changes in hexose sugars, sucrose, starch, and total carbohydrates of inner and outer wood of sugar maple in northern Vermont. What is termed outer wood in this study corresponds approximately to the outer part of the sapwood. (*After Jones and Bradlee,* 1933.)

The relations between temperature and starch content have been observed many times. It appears that starch accumulates in late summer and autumn in most woody species of the Temperate Zone but that when the temperature falls the starch content drops and the sugar content goes up (Figure 4.3). This change definitely is related to temperature, because when woody plants are kept in a warm greenhouse the starch often remains unchanged instead of being converted into sugar (Coville, 1920). Ewart et al. (1954) reported that if locust logs containing starch are stored at 3°C, the starch disappears and an equivalent amount of sugar appears.

It is very puzzling to find starch digestion speeded up at low temperatures because one would expect chemical reactions to be slowed down by temperatures near freezing. Perhaps some inhibitor of enzyme action is present at high temperatures which disappears during a period of low temperature. This situation deserves further study.

Uses of Carbohydrates by Trees

The carbohydrates formed by photosynthesis in the leaves have several possible fates. The largest fraction is used in growth, being translocated to the cambium of the roots and stems and to the root and stem tips, where it is converted into new protoplasm, cell walls, and other products of protoplasm. Another large fraction is oxidized in respiration, releasing the energy needed in the synthetic processes associated with growth (Chapter 7). The remainder is accumulated and eventually used in growth and respiration during periods when little or no photosynthesis is occurring.

Few data are available on the actual amounts of food used in these various ways, and the proportions must differ considerably in different trees and under various conditions. Heinicke and Childers (1937) measured the carbon dioxide uptake and estimated the increase in dry weight and the respiration of an 8-year-old McIntosh apple tree slightly over 10 feet tall, with a spread of over 6 feet. This tree produced about 19 kilograms of sugar during the growing season of 188 days. It was estimated that 10.9 kilograms (57 per cent) was used in growth and fruiting, 3 kilograms was used in root respiration, 4.4 kilograms was used in shoot respiration (a total of 38 per cent in respiration), and the remaining 0.7 kilogram (5 per cent) was accumulated.

Table 4.1 shows the amount of food used in various processes by a bearing apple tree (Heinicke, 1937b). About 35 per cent of the total

Table 4.1. Estimated carbohydrate requirements of an apple tree. (*After Heinicke*, 1937b.)

Use	Pounds carbohydrates used	Per cent of total
Fruit crop	192.40	35.47
Leaf production	62.50	11.52
Formation of structural tissues	187.50	34.57
Loss in respiration	100.00	18.44
Total	542.40	100.00

carbohydrate went into the fruit, 45 per cent into growth, and 18 per cent into respiration. Baker (1950) estimated that only 1 per cent of the food goes into fruit and seed in forest trees, 10 per cent into respiration,

Physiology of Trees

and the remainder into vegetative growth (Figure 4.4). This allocation seems to neglect accumulation as a separate process, and it probably assigns too little food to respiration (Figure 7.2).

Reproduction. The production of a heavy crop of fruit or seed certainly uses a large amount of carbohydrate. The proportion required for fruit production doubtless is ordinarily much higher in fruit trees where large fruits high in carbohydrates are formed than in forest trees which usually produce much smaller fruits. Nevertheless, production of a heavy crop of seed does deplete the carbohydrate reserve of trees, and many foresters believe that this depletion is responsible for the failure of forest trees to produce heavy seed crops each year. Gäumann (1935) found

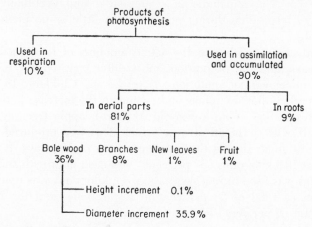

Figure 4.4 The uses of carbohydrates in various parts of a tree, according to Baker (1950). According to data presented in Table 4.1 and Figures 7.2 and 7.3, considerably more than 10 per cent of the food is used in respiration.

that during a year of flowering and fruiting in beech there was an unusually large drain on reserve carbohydrates. He estimated that during a seed year the reproductive parts of beech required 40 to 50 times as much food reserve as did the leafy branches. Murneek (1939) reported that starch and nitrogen were completely removed from the 20 outer annual rings of mature beech and oak trees in years of heavy seed production but only from a few outer rings in years when no seed was produced. Apparently both reserves and products of current photosynthesis are used in a fruit crop, as shown by the relation of fruit size to leaf area (Widdowson, 1932; Murneek, 1932). This will be discussed later.

Vegetative Growth. Vegetative growth also depends on both reserve and currently produced carbohydrates. Height growth starts before any photosynthetic apparatus is available in deciduous trees; hence it must depend on stored reserve food, at least early in the season. Burger (1926) reported that shoot growth of trees depends so much on food synthesized the preceding year that growth is more closely related to the weather of the preceding summer than to the weather of the current summer. Secondary or diameter growth, in contrast, is largely dependent on current photosynthesis for its supply of carbohydrate. Loomis (1935) found that cambial activity of several species did not begin until the leaves were one-third open, and he concluded that diameter growth depends principally on the photosynthetically active leaf area connected through uninterrupted phloem to the growing region. Cambial activity also may be influenced by hormones produced in the leaves. Although some reserve carbohydrates stored in the xylem parenchyma are used in diameter growth early in the season, most of the diameter growth of trunks and roots depends on carbohydrates produced currently by photosynthesis and moved down from the crown.

Accumulation of Carbohydrates

Many studies have been made of the accumulation of starch and sugars in various tissues and organs and at various times of year. As might be expected, there are marked variations in the amount of carbohydrate present in the various parts of a tree and there also are large seasonal variations in both amounts and kinds of carbohydrates present. Furthermore, there are differences between deciduous and evergreen species with respect to the seasonal trends in carbohydrate accumulation.

Carbohydrate Content of Stems, Leaves, and Roots. The leaves of trees usually contain a fairly high concentration of carbohydrate. In young apple trees in October the carbohydrate concentration of the leaves was as high as that of the young wood, as shown in Table 4.2. Shortleaf pine needles in April contained about 16.6 per cent of carbohydrates, the stem bark 12.4 per cent, and the stemwood 2.4 per cent on a dry-weight basis (Hepting, 1945). Nevertheless, the leaves usually contain a very small proportion of the total reserve carbohydrate in the tree. Murneek (1942) found only 3.09 pounds of starch and sugar in the leaves compared with 51 pounds in the remainder of an 18-year-old Grimes Golden apple tree in October. There is a high concentration of hemicelluloses in trees, but it is doubtful that they serve as reserve foods.

In dealing with food reserves in tree trunks it is desirable to distinguish between sapwood and heartwood because the latter contains no living cells and ordinarily accumulates no food. It also is necessary to distinguish between wood and bark. A good summary of the distribution of carbohydrates in the various parts of an 18-year-old Grimes apple tree in October is given in Table 4.2. Expressed as percentages of dry weight, there was about three times as high a concentration of starch and twice the concentration of sugar in roots as in shoots. The total amount of carbohydrates in the shoots was greater than that in the roots, however, because the shoots weighed nearly three times as much as the roots. Jones and Bradlee (1933) found about twice as high a concentration of carbohydrate in the roots as in the shoots of sugar maple, and Hepting (1945) found a mueh higher concentration of carbohydrate in the roots than in the shoots of shortleaf pine. Wenger (1953a) also found a higher concentration in the roots than in the shoots of sweetgum.

Table 4.2. Distribution of starch and sugars in Grimes apple trees in mid-October. (*Adapted from Murneek,* 1942.)

	Dry weight, lb	Starch and sugar	Per cent of oven-dry weight	Starch, lb	Per cent of oven-dry weight	Sugar, lb	Per cent of oven-dry weight
Leaves	32.82	3.09	9.41	0.92	2.80	2.17	6.61
Spurs	6.33	0.69	10.90	0.37	5.85	0.32	5.05
Wood aged:							
1 year	5.94	0.65	10.94	0.35	5.89	0.30	5.05
2 years	7.12	0.73	10.25	0.45	6.32	0.28	3.93
3 years	8.74	0.85	9.73	0.51	5.84	0.34	3.89
4–6 years	46.27	2.48	5.36	1.32	2.85	1.16	2.51
7–10 years	124.00	7.20	5.81	4.46	3.60	2.74	2.21
11–18 years	101.20	5.95	5.88	4.01	3.96	1.94	1.92
Main stem	68.19	7.57	11.10	6.14	9.00	1.43	2.10
Total above-ground	400.61	29.21	7.29 *	18.53	4.63 *	10.68	2.67 *
Root stump	62.80	9.94	15.83	6.91	11.00	3.03	4.83
Roots aged:							
18–14 years	46.90	8.22	17.53	6.34	13.52	1.88	4.01
13–7 years	22.52	5.52	24.51	3.97	17.63	1.55	6.88
6–1 year	5.40	1.10	20.37	0.86	15.93	0.24	4.44
Total in soil	137.62	24.78	18.01 *	18.08	13.14 *	6.70	4.87 *
Total for tree	538.23	53.99	10.03 *	36.61	6.75 *	17.38	3.23 *

* Mean.

The relation of age of wood to carbohydrate concentration was investigated by Murneek (1942). The concentration of starch and sugar was higher in wood 1 to 3 years old than in wood 4 to 18 years old, but the total amount present was much greater in the older wood because it forms a much larger percentage of the total volume of the tree. Jones and Bradlee (1933) found the concentration of carbohydrates to be about twice as high in the outer as in the inner wood of sugar maple. According to Wenger (1953a), there was no difference in carbohydrate concentration between the outer and inner wood of sweetgum saplings up to 3 inches in diameter, but trees of this size have not yet developed any heartwood.

The carbohydrate concentration in the bark and wood of the upper part of the stem of sugar maple was higher than in the bark and wood of the lower part of the stem, and the concentration in the bark was higher than in the wood at the same level. In cacao trees, the concentration of starch is higher in the bark than in the wood, both near the ground and at a height of 12 feet (Humphries, 1947). In shortleaf pine Hepting (1945) found a much higher concentration of carbohydrate in the root bark than in the stem bark, and the concentration was higher in the bark than in the wood of both roots and stems. In pine roots 1 inch in diameter, 68 per cent of the total carbohydrate occurred in the bark. According to Gäumann (1935), the concentration of carbohydrates in beech during the winter is much higher in the rootwood than in the stemwood, but the total amount present in the stem is much greater than that in the roots. Wenger (1953a) also found a higher concentration in the bark than in the wood of sweetgum.

Although the concentration of carbohydrate is typically higher in the roots, it seems probable that in most forest trees the tops contain more total reserves than the roots because the tops are larger than the roots. Even in the apple trees studied by Murneek, the total amount of carbohydrate in the tops exceeded that in the roots because the tops were about three times as heavy as the roots. According to Baker (1950), the ratio of tops to roots may be as large as 16:1 in mature forest trees; hence the roots do not constitute a sufficiently large fraction of the tree to store the major part of the carbohydrate reserves.

Seasonal Cycles in Carbohydrate Content. Seasonal cycles in carbohydrate content are particularly well defined in deciduous trees of the Temperate Zone. The seasonal cycle for sugar maple is shown in Figure 4.3, and these trends probably are typical of those for many deciduous species. Total carbohydrate content reaches a maximum in the autumn about the time of leaf fall, begins to decrease in late winter, and decreases rapidly in early spring when food is being used for growth of new twigs and leaves. Rising temperatures at this season probably also greatly increase the use of food in respiration. Gibbs (1940) found a rather similar cycle in sucrose and total sugar content of gray birch. Gäumann's data for beech also indicate a higher carbohydrate content of roots, stems, and twigs early in the winter than at other seasons of the year. Wenger (1953a) measured the total carbohydrate concentration of the wood of roots and stems of sweetgum growing in South Carolina at monthly intervals from early March to early October. There was a marked decrease in concentration in the roots during March, followed by an upward trend during the summer and early autumn, but there was no significant change in concentration in the stems.

Hepting (1945) studied the seasonal changes in carbohydrate concentration of shortleaf pine trees and found the seasonal trend to be quite different from that in deciduous species. The carbohydrate reserve of the roots was at a minimum in the autumn and increased during the winter to a concentration in the early spring about three times that present in the autumn. There was much less seasonal variation in the stems, and they reached their highest concentration from March to June and were at a more or less constant low level from July to March. The seasonal

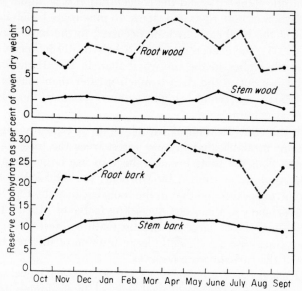

Figure 4.5 Seasonal variations in total reserve carbohydrate content of wood and bark of roots and stems of healthy shortleaf pine trees growing in North Carolina. (*After Hepting, 1945.*)

trends are shown in Figure 4.5. They resemble the seasonal trends reported for a European pine by Sablon (1904).

Satoo and Takegosi (1952) compared the starch content of various parts of *Quercus acutissima*, a deciduous species of oak, and *Q. myrsinae-folia*, an evergreen species, at 2-week intervals for a year. There was little change in the amount of starch in the trunk of the deciduous species, but there was a marked decrease in starch content in the trunk of the evergreen species from July until October. The starch content of the roots, branches, and twigs of the deciduous species reached a maximum in the spring and was relatively low the remainder of the year, but the starch content of these parts of the evergreen species was lower in the winter and spring and rose in the late summer and autumn. Unfortunately, no data on total carbohydrates were obtained in this study; hence it is impossible to follow changes in total amount of carbohydrate, and the results cannot be compared with those mentioned previously.

In general, it seems that the carbohydrate content shows much greater fluctuations in concentration in deciduous species than in evergreen species. The latter seem to be more dependent on current photosynthesis for shoot growth in the spring than on stored food. Deciduous species accumulate carbohydrates during the summer, but evergreen species accumulate them during the winter, presumably because of reduced respiration and cessation of growth at that season.

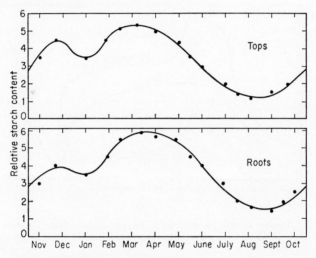

Figure 4.6 Seasonal changes in starch content of tops and roots of avocado trees growing in California. Relative amounts of starch were estimated by staining sections with I₂KI. (*From Cameron and Borst, 1938.*)

Even tropical and subtropical species show yearly cycles in carbohydrates although they are likely to be much more limited in range than the cycles occurring in trees of cooler climates. Figure 4.6 shows the variations in starch concentration in roots and tops of avocado trees, studied by Cameron and Borst (1938). These trees made three flushes of growth which had little effect on the starch content of the larger branches, trunk, and roots. According to Humphries, cacao trees in Trinidad show decreases in carbohydrate content each time a flush of growth occurs but the decreases are relatively smaller than the spring decrease in deciduous trees of the Temperate Zone.

Changes in Proportions of Various Carbohydrates. Studies of changes in one kind of carbohydrate give a very incomplete picture of trends with respect to total carbohydrates, because sugars may be converted into starch or starch into sugar and the proportions of hexose and sucrose may vary from time to time. The study of sugar maple made by Jones and Bradlee (1933) is particularly useful because they followed sucrose, hexose, and starch simultaneously. The starch content of the wood varied relatively less than the total sugar content, and the hexose content varied more than the sucrose content. Hexoses reached a peak in midwinter, fell rapidly in the spring, and remained low all summer. Sucrose showed similar but smaller fluctuations. Sucrose was the principal carbohydrate in the bark of maple, but there was a noticeable peak of hexose concentration in late winter and of starch in early autumn. Sucrose also is the domi-

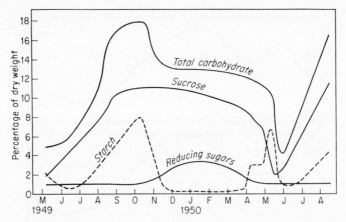

Figure 4.7 Average seasonal variations in various carbohydrate constituents of the living inner bark of black locust trees growing near Ottawa, Canada. (*From Siminovitch et al.*, 1953.)

nant carbohydrate in the bark of black locust. In black locust there was a sharp decrease in the total carbohydrate content in June and a peak in starch in October, a decrease during the winter, and another increase in May (Ewart et al., 1954). Winkler and Williams (1945) found starch to be very low in the wood of grape in spring and early summer, but it rose rapidly from August to November. Reducing sugar was high in April, fell rapidly in May, and remained low during the remainder of the season.

It has been suggested that height growth and phloem activity are causally related to fluctuations in starch reserves. As may be seen in Figure 4.7, two seasonal maxima of starch occur in many species, one in late summer or early autumn and the other in spring just before the beginning of shoot growth (Cockerham, 1930; Siminovitch et al., 1953). Bimodal seasonal curves for phloem activity also occur. Some of the phloem cells cut off during one season mature before the onset of dormancy, while the remainder mature the following spring. The autumn maximum in starch content occurs at the time phloem begins to differentiate, and when starch content falls to a minimum in late autumn phloem differentiation ceases. According to Gibbs (1940), the winter increase in sucrose does not account for all the missing starch and it has been suggested by Wilcox (1958) that this fraction is used in phloem differentiation. With initiation of apical growth in the spring the starch content drops rapidly.

The possibility of transformation of hemicellulose into soluble sugars

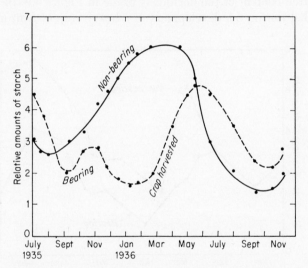

Figure 4.8 Effect of bearing fruit on starch content of evergreen avocado trees. Relative amounts of starch were estimated by staining sections of twigs with I_2KI. (*From Cameron and Borst, 1938.*)

usable in metabolic processes has been widely debated. Sablon (1904) reported that an incrustation of what was presumed to be cellulose on the cell walls of willow twigs disappeared in the spring. Murneek (1929) reported that in apple, hemicellulose decreased and sugar increased at flowering, and he thought that the hemicellulose had been converted to sugar. Bennett (1924) and others reported seasonal changes in hemicellulose content. Winkler and Williams (1938), after reexamining the literature and studying carbohydrate changes in grape, decided there was no definite evidence that hemicelluloses function as reserve foods. Gooding (1947) studied the cells of five woody species and found no evidence of seasonal changes in thickness of cell walls. It seems unlikely that the hemicelluloses found in the vegetative structure of trees are important reserve foods, and possibly they never function in this way. The hemicelluloses of seeds of some species (date, vegetable ivory palm), however, do seem to be an important source of food for the seedling plant.

Fruiting and Carbohydrate Accumulation. Horticulturists and foresters have long known that production of a heavy crop of fruit or seeds tends to deplete carbohydrate reserves. As shown in Table 4.1, Heinicke (1937b) estimated that 35 per cent of the carbohydrate used by a bearing apple tree went into fruit production. This was equal to the amount which went into the production of new wood. The effects of fruiting on the starch content of the evergreen avocado tree are shown in Figure 4.8 and on the starch content of the deciduous prune in Figure 4.9. In general, it appears that during the development of a heavy crop of fruit most of the

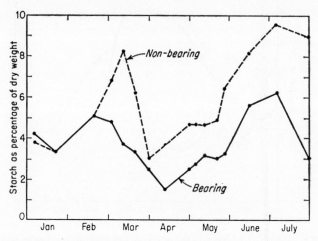

Figure 4.9 Effect of bearing fruit on starch content of spurs of sugar prune, a deciduous tree, growing in California. (*From Davis,* 1931.)

current photosynthate plus some reserve carbohydrate is used in fruit growth.

The total amount of carbohydrate used in seed production by forest trees may not be so large as in fruit trees, but the effects on accumulation probably are just as serious. It generally is believed that several years often are required to replace the carbohydrate reserves removed by a heavy seed crop and that this is an important factor in the irregular seed production of forest trees. This subject will be discussed later in relation to reproduction.

There is competition among the various organs and processes for the carbohydrate produced by photosynthesis. Apparently fruits and seeds have precedence over vegetative regions such as stem tips and cambium, and accumulation in the vegetative structure of the tree occurs only after other demands are satisfied. The factors governing the distribution of food among various organs and processes are complex, but apparently involve hormones as well as relative rates of metabolic activity.

Autumn Coloration

Autumn coloration will be discussed at this time because the anthocyanins which are responsible for the pink, red, and purple colors are related to the carbohydrates, and carbohydrate accumulation favors their formation. Anthocyanin pigments are responsible for the red or purplish colors of leaves of copper beech, the Crimson King variety of Norway maple, and other trees with red foliage. In many trees anthocyanins form only in the autumn when cool weather prevails and trees have accumulated an excess of soluble sugars. Anthocyanins are glycosides, formed by reactions between various sugars and cyclic compounds called anthocyanidins. They are water-soluble and usually occur in the cell sap. Anthocyanins usually are red in acid solution and may become purplish to blue as the pH is increased. Production of anthocyanin depends first of all on the possession of certain hereditary potentialities, but the amount produced is affected by environmental factors.

With declining autumn temperatures the leaves of trees cease producing chlorophyll, and at the same time some species which have large amounts of carbohydrates and the genetic potentiality begin to form anthocyanins in their leaves. As anthocyanins form and chlorophyll synthesis stops, the chlorophyll already present begins to disintegrate and the anthocyanins are unmasked. In those trees which do not form anthocyanins the autumn breakdown of chlorophyll unmasks the stable yellow to orange carotene and xanthophyll pigments, resulting in clear-yellow-colored leaves, as in yellow-poplar or hickory, or there may be an admixture of red anthocyanin with yellow carotene to give a bright orange color as in some maples. Thus by disintegration of green pigment and unmasking of yellow, the formation of red, or both, the leaves may assume various shades of yellow, orange, crimson, purple, or red.

Such species as alders and locusts show little change. Others, such as poplars, tulip tree, ginkgo, honey locust, beech, and birches, show various degrees of yellow. But by far the most dazzling displays are seen in the reds of maples, sassafras, tupelo, staghorn sumac, white oak, shadbush, and others which form large amounts of anthocyanin. The maples show much gradation from yellow to deep red.

Trees of the same species growing together often show much difference in color because of individual variation in amounts of soluble carbohydrates. Some reach their peak of color later than others. Oaks color late in the fall, usually after the best maple color has gone by. The yellow-brown colors of beeches and some oaks have been linked to the presence of tannins in leaves in addition to yellow carotenoids.

The brightest colors occur under conditions of clear, dry, and cool but not freezing weather. Severe early frosts actually make autumn color less brilliant. Any factor which influences either the synthesis of carbohydrate or conversion of insoluble to soluble carbohyrate will influence autumn color. Most important of these factors are light, temperature, water supply, and hydrogen-ion concentration.

GENERAL REFERENCES

Blank, F., 1947, The anthocyanin pigments of plants, Bot. Rev., 13:241–317.

Bonner, J., 1950, Plant biochemistry, Academic Press, Inc., New York.

Fruton, J. S., and S. Simmonds, 1953, General biochemistry, John Wiley & Sons, Inc., New York.

Pigman, W., 1957, The carbohydrates: chemistry, biochemistry, physiology, Academic Press, Inc., New York.

Ruhland, W. (ed.), 1958, Encyclopedia of plant physiology, vol. 6, Formation, storage, mobilization, and transformation of carbohydrates, A. Arnold (subed.), Springer-Verlag, Berlin.

CHAPTER 5   *Nitrogen Relations of Trees*

Although compounds containing nitrogen constitute only a small proportion of the total dry weight of trees, they are exceedingly important constituents physiologically. Cellulose forms more than half of the dry weight of a tree, but it occurs in the cell walls, which are relatively inactive in physiological processes. Nitrogen compounds, in contrast, are concentrated chiefly in the leaves, meristematic regions, and other areas of living cells which carry on the complex processes associated with growth. First in importance among nitrogen-containing compounds are the proteins which form the structure of protoplasm and the enzymes which catalyze metabolic processes. Nitrogen also occurs in various products of protoplasm such as amino acids, amides, alkaloids, hormones, and other substances which are essential in growth, are of economic importance, or sometimes are merely by-products of metabolism.

From the seedling stage to mature trees, nitrogen is required for growth and a deficiency seriously limits it. The largest amount is required for the production of protein used in formation of protoplasm for new cells. Another important use is in the formation of chlorophyll. One of the most common symptoms of nitrogen deficiency is the pale green color of leaves resulting from inadequate synthesis of chlorophyll. Lack of chlorophyll reduces photosynthesis and thus indirectly reduces growth.

The demand for nitrogen is closely related to the amount of growth. Trees which make a large part of their annual growth early in the season require large amounts of nitrogen at that time. Although few data are available, much of this must come from the reserves in the tree because the average forest soil is rather low in available nitrogen and absorption must be slow. Orchardists commonly supply nitrogen to fruit trees to ensure an adequate supply during this critical period of growth. Foresters cannot afford to do so; hence growth of forest trees commonly is limited by the supply of nitrogen. This is less serious where the growing season is long and absorption occurs over a considerable period of

117

time than it would be for annual crop plants which require most of their nitrogen within a few weeks.

Distribution and Seasonal Fluctuations

Because of its physiological importance numerous studies have been made of the relative amounts of seasonal fluctuations in nitrogen content of various parts of trees. The amount of nitrogen present varies with the tissue, the age or stage of development, and the season. Much of the nitrogen occurs in the protoplasm and associated compounds such as enzymes, vitamins, nucleic acids, and other physiologically active substances. Thus the highest concentrations of nitrogen are found in those tissues which are composed chiefly of physiologically active cells, including leaves and meristematic tissues such as cambiums and root and stem tips. Seeds also are often high in nitrogen, but this occurs chiefly as reserve food and is relatively inactive physiologically.

Concentration in Various Tissues. Table 5.1 shows the distribution of nitrogen in various parts of an 18-year-old apple tree sampled in mid-

Table 5.1. Distribution of nitrogen in apple trees in mid-October. (*After Murneek*, 1942.)

Average of 3 Varieties—Grimes, Jonathan, and Delicious

	Oven-dry weight, lb	N, lb	N as per cent of dry weight
Leaves	29.60	0.365	1.23
Spurs	5.66	0.059	1.04
Wood aged:			
1 year	10.06	0.094	0.93
2 years	12.23	0.082	0.67
3 years	11.85	0.064	0.54
4–6 years	43.82	0.154	0.35
7–10 years	144.36	0.390	0.27
11–18 years	138.73	0.225	0.16
Main stem	67.80	0.098	0.14
Total above ground	464.11	1.531	0.33
Root stump	50.15	0.130	0.26
Roots aged:			
18–14 years	46.20	0.147	0.32
13–7 years	29.33	0.176	0.60
6–1 year	5.39	0.067	1.24
Total in roots below ground	131.07	0.520	0.40
Total for tree	595.18	2.051	0.34

October. The concentration in the leaves was higher than in any other part of the tree, except possibly the younger roots, and it decreased from the youngest to the oldest wood. Of the total nitrogen in the tree, 75 per cent was in the shoots and nearly 20 per cent was in the leaves. Earlier

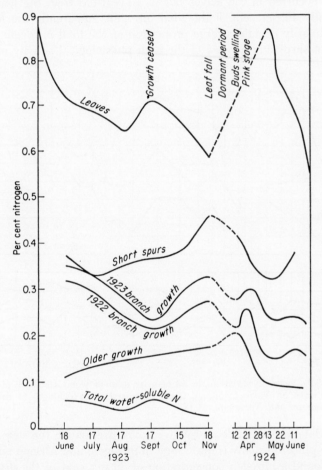

Figure 5.1 Seasonal variations in total nitrogen content of leaves, short spurs, 1-year, 2-year, and older branches of apple as percentages of fresh weight. (*From Thomas*, 1927.)

in the season even more of the total nitrogen content probably would have been in the leaves, because the outward movement which occurs before leaf fall probably would have already started in mid-October. The concentration in the fruit spurs also was relatively high. Essentially the same situation apparently exists in evergreen trees, because Cameron and Compton (1945) found that nearly 50 per cent of the total nitrogen present in bearing orange trees was in the leaves, about 10 per cent in twigs, and 25 per cent in the branches and trunk. Less than 20 per cent of the total was in the roots. In another study Cameron and Appleman (1933) found that in 3.5-year-old orange trees 60 per cent of the total nitrogen occurred in the leaves but in 10-year-old trees the leaves contained only 40 per cent of the total nitrogen. Apparently the leaves of trees ordinarily contain a large proportion of the total nitrogen. Perhaps this is not surprising in view of the high physiological activity of leaves.

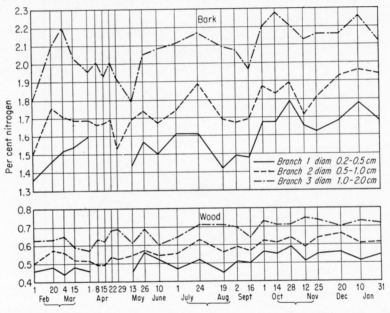

Figure 5.2 Seasonal variations in nitrogen content of wood and bark of branches of various sizes on Valencia orange trees, expressed as percentages of dry weight. (*From Cameron and Appleman, 1933.*)

Some data are available on relative concentrations in the stem. Apparently the phloem usually is quite high in nitrogen, and Allsopp and Misra (1940) found a nitrogen concentration of 30 per cent of the dry weight in the cambium of ash and elm but only 20 per cent in Scotch pine. The newly formed xylem of ash and elm contained about 5 per cent nitrogen, the older sapwood 1.3 and 1.7 per cent, respectively, while the sapwood of Scotch pine contained only 0.8 per cent.

Seeds often contain considerable nitrogen because in some species the principal reserve food is protein. Several species of acorns averaged about 1.1 per cent, pinyon pine 2 per cent, digger pine 5 per cent, and longleaf pine 6 per cent. Data on the chemical composition of a number of tree seeds are presented in Table 14.1.

Seasonal Changes. Seasonal fluctuations in nitrogen content of leaves, twigs, bark, and wood have been observed in many trees and probably are of universal occurrence. The migration of nitrogen out of leaves in the autumn will be discussed later. Figure 5.1 shows seasonal fluctuations in nitrogen content of various parts of 15-year-old Stayman Winesap apple trees over an entire year (Thomas, 1927). The amount of total nitrogen and of various fractions in the wood decreased when growth was rapid and increased when growth ceased. Apparently much of the nitrogen in the leaves was translocated to the spurs during the autumn before

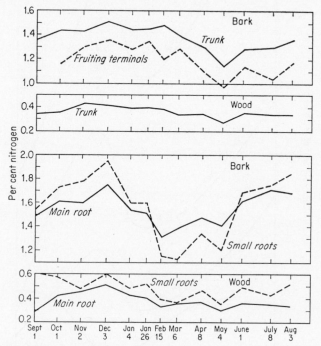

Figure 5.3 Seasonal variations in nitrogen content of root- and stemwood and bark of young Valencia orange trees. (*From Cameron and Appleman,* 1933.)

leaf fall occurred. Mulay (1931) observed that in Bartlett pear the nitrogen content of the bark was greatly decreased when growth began but built up again after growth slowed down and reached its maximum in the winter. Each flush of growth in orange trees also produces a decrease in the nitrogen content of the adjacent tissues, as shown in Figure 5.2 from Cameron and Appleman (1933). Apparently the branch bark (actually the phloem) is the principal source of nitrogen for growth because the wood shows much smaller fluctuations in nitrogen content than the bark. Figure 5.3 shows the seasonal fluctuations in nitrogen content of root and stemwood and bark of young Valencia orange trees.

Some seasonal variations have been observed in the kinds of nitrogen compounds present in trees. In Figure 5.4 are shown the seasonal variations in several forms of nitrogen in apple leaves. Mulay (1931) reported that the seasonal changes in nitrogen content of the bark of pear mainly involved the insoluble nitrogen, but in the wood the soluble fraction

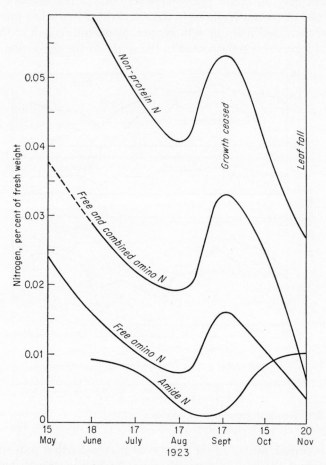

Figure 5.4 Seasonal variations in various forms of nitrogen in apple leaves, expressed as percentage of fresh weight. (*From Thomas, 1927.*)

showed most of the variation. Siminovitch and Briggs (1949) studied changes in nitrogen fractions in stems of trees in relation to cold hardiness and found that exposure to cold was associated with a marked increase in water-soluble proteins.

Parker (1958a) reported that total protein nitrogen in the inner bark of several tree species increased from August to December. The concentration of a number of free amino acids decreased over this period, but the concentration of proline increased.

Aging of Tissues. Changes associated with aging are somewhat confounded with the effects of season. For example, as leaves grow older the proportion of cell wall material increases and this tends to modify the apparent nitrogen content. Sampson and Samisch (1935) found that most of the nitrogen absorption by leaves of *Quercus gambelii* and *Q. kelloggii* in California occurred very early in their development. Leaf expansion continued, resulting in gradual decrease in protein content per unit of leaf area during the summer, followed by a rapid decrease in the autumn, which was attributed to translocation of nitrogenous compounds out of the leaves. Chapman (1935) found progressive decrease in the concentration of total nitrogen per unit of dry weight in elm leaves from June 23 to November 10. The increase in the nonnitrogenous constituents and accompanying decrease in concentration of nitrogenous compounds are especially noticeable in the woody part of trees. This is shown in Table 5.2, based on work of Gardner et al. (1952). There is little difference in the nitrogen concentration of the new growth and of fruits of young and old apple trees, but the concentration in the trunk and branches and in the roots is considerably lower in the older trees.

Autumn Movement from Leaves

In the autumn a considerable part of the nitrogen and minerals in the leaves is translocated into the twigs before abscission occurs. Apparently, as the leaves become senescent they are no longer able to retain the substances against the competition of regions which are more active physiologically, and the normal summer translocation stream therefore is reversed. This movement back into twigs and branches is quite important to trees because otherwise a large fraction of the nitrogen in the plant would be lost temporarily by leaf fall. In forest trees this might be disastrous, and in orchards it certainly would require even larger applications of nitrogen fertilizers than are now necessary.

Among the earlier investigators who observed loss of nitrogen compounds from aging forest tree leaves were Rissmüller (1874), Ramann (1912), and Molliard (1913). The latter reported that chestnut leaves contained the following percentages of nitrogen: September 13, 2.26 per cent; October 10, 2.22 per cent; November 1, 1.21 per cent; November 2, 0.94 per cent. Some of the early studies are suspect because it was not shown that the nitrogen moved back into the woody part of the trees and it was possible that some of the loss might be caused by leaching by rain. Combes (1927a and b) therefore determined the nitrogen content of leaves, stems, and roots of young forest trees while the leaves were yellowing. He found that the transfer of nitrogen out of the leaves occurred

Table 5.2. Effect of age on nitrogen content of leaves, new growth, trunks and branches, roots, and fruit of apple trees. (After Gardner, Bradford, and Hooker, 1952.)

Age, years	Leaves		New growth		Trunks and branches		Roots		Fruit	
	% oven-dry weight	N, g	% oven-dry weight	N, g	% oven-dry weight	N, g	% oven-dry weight	N, g	% oven-dry weight	N, g
1	1.71	0.44			0.30	0.29	0.39	0.20		
2	2.09	1.51			0.57	1.36	0.88	1.14		
5	1.76	7.84	0.89	1.93	0.48	17.20	0.64	9.85		
9	1.70	61.50	0.82	9.08	0.35	85.50	0.58	81.00	0.31	10.55
30	2.09	394.00	0.95	13.60					0.31	258.00
100	1.04	435.00	1.04	390.00	0.27	2,863.00	0.22	417.00		

124

over a period of about 8 weeks and leaves of beech lost 40 per cent, chestnut 50 per cent, and horsechestnut 65 per cent of their nitrogen to the stems. Tamm (1951) reported that the nitrogen content of birch leaves was fairly constant from July to the end of September, but when they began to turn yellow they lost one-third to one-half of their nitrogen in slightly over 2 weeks.

The autumn movement of nitrogen out of leaves has been observed in many fruit trees, including apple, cherry, pear, and plum. Thomas (1927) reported that in apple most of the nitrogen which moved out of the leaves was stored in the spurs and youngest wood (Figure 5.1). Murneek and Logan (1932) made a careful study of this process in 17-year-old Grimes, Delicious, and Stayman apple trees. They showed the nitrogen concen-

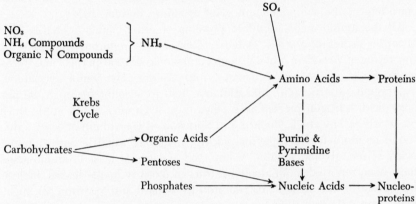

Figure 5.5 Relationships among important nitrogen-containing compounds. (*Modified from Meyer and Anderson, 1952.*)

tration of leaves to decrease from the time active growth ceased until time of complete defoliation. Nitrogen removal was greater from yellowed leaves than from green ones collected at the same time. Nitrogen in non-bearing spurs and twigs increased uniformly during the abscission period. Much of the absorbed nitrogen was later translocated to older wood tissues and probably to the roots. Leaves that had dropped early in October contained 1.29 per cent nitrogen, while leaves of the mid-November collection contained only 0.96 per cent nitrogen. Murneek and Logan concluded that although considerable nitrogen of apple leaves moves back into the tree prior to abscission, about one-half to three-fourths of it is lost, at least temporarily, in the dropped leaves.

Important Nitrogen Compounds

Having discussed the general distribution of nitrogen in trees, we shall now turn to a consideration of the principal compounds in which nitrogen occurs and their synthesis. The most important of these compounds are amino acids, proteins, nucleoproteins, amides, and alkaloids. The inter-relationships among some of the compounds are shown in Figure 5.5, modified from Meyer and Anderson (1952).

Amino Acids

The amino acids are the basic building blocks of protoplasmic proteins. Most amino acids have the basic formula $R \cdot CHNH_2 \cdot COOH$ and have properties of both amines and acids because each amino acid has an amino group (NH_2) and a carboxyl group ($COOH$). In the simplest amino acid, glycine, R is represented by a hydrogen atom (CH_2NH_2COOH). In others R may be very complex and may contain additional amino or carboxyl groups. Some 22 amino acids are commonly considered to be components of plant proteins (Bonner, 1950).

All the amino acids found in proteins of other plants probably also occur in proteins of trees. Bollard (1956, 1958) reported that most of the nitrogen in xylem sap of monocotyledons, gymnosperms, and ferns occurred as amino acids, ureides, and amides. He found glutamine, asparagine, aspartic acid, and glutamic acid to account for up to 90 per cent of all nitrogen present in tracheal sap of Granny Smith apple trees on Northern Spy stock. Pollard and Sproston (1954) found at least 7 different amino acids in sugar maple sap, including aspartic and glutamic acids, serine, glycine, alanine, valine, and leucine. At least 14 amino acids have been reported in an alcohol extract of Norway maple leaves, including several of the same acids reported by Pollard and Sproston for sugar maple sap (Plaisted, 1956).

Amino Acid Synthesis. Most of the biochemical information about amino acid synthesis comes from work with animal tissues. Very little basic work has been done with woody plants, but it is generally considered that in trees the mode of origin is similar to that in other higher plants.

Amino acids can be produced in several ways, including reductive amination, transamination, chemical transformation of acid amides or other nitrogen compounds, and hydrolysis of proteins by enzymes. The first two methods probably are most important.

Nitrate Reduction. Nitrate is the most common source of nitrogen for plants, and reduction of nitrate to ammonia is an important step in nitrogen metabolism. Nitrate is absorbed readily by trees and usually is quickly reduced, although it may accumulate if the carbohydrate supply and level of metabolic activity are low. The steps in nitrate reduction have been studied extensively in microorganisms, and presumably the process follows a similar path in woody plants. One possible pathway follows:

$$NO_3^- \rightarrow NO_2^- \rightarrow N_2O_2^= \rightarrow NH_2OH \rightarrow NH_3$$

Nitrate   Nitrite   Hyponitrite   Hydroxylamine   Ammonia

The energy for nitrate reduction is supplied by oxidation of carbohydrates, and the ammonia produced is finally combined with organic acids to form amino acids, as shown later. The intermediates are toxic in moderate concentrations, but they ordinarily do not accumulate in sufficient quantities to cause injury.

It has been shown that in several tree species nitrate reduction occurs in the roots and the organic nitrogen is translocated to the shoots in the xylem as amides, amino acids, and ureides (Bollard, 1957b, 1958; Thomas, 1927). It is doubtful if nitrates and nitrites are found in the tops of trees under normal conditions.

Reductive Amination. The ammonia resulting from nitrate reduction can react with an organic acid to produce an amino acid.

$$
\begin{array}{ccc}
\text{COOH} & & \text{COOH} \\
| & & | \\
\text{C=O} & & \text{CHNH}_2 \\
| & \xrightarrow[\text{dehydrogenase}]{\text{glutamic}} & | \\
\text{CH}_2 + \text{NH}_3 + \text{DPN·H}_2 & & \text{CH}_2 + \text{H}_2\text{O} + \text{DPN} \\
| & & | \\
\text{CH}_2 & & \text{CH}_2 \\
| & & | \\
\text{COOH} & & \text{COOH} \\
\alpha\text{-Ketoglutaric acid} & & \text{Glutamic acid}
\end{array}
$$

This process is catalyzed by glutamic dehydrogenase, and diphosphopyridine nucleotide (DPN) acts as a coenzyme.

Transamination. Transamination involves the transfer of an amino group from one molecule to another. This is exemplified by the reaction between glutamic acid and oxalacetic acid to produce alpha ketoglutaric acid and aspartic acid. A transaminase enzyme is involved:

$$
\begin{array}{cccc}
\text{COOH} & \text{COOH} & \text{COOH} & \text{COOH} \\
| & | & | & | \\
\text{CHNH}_2 & \text{C=O} & \text{C=O} & \text{CHNH}_2 \\
| & | \quad \xrightarrow{\text{transaminase}} \quad & | & | \\
\text{CH}_2 + \text{CH}_2 & \rightleftharpoons & \text{CH}_2 + \text{CH}_2 \\
| & | & | & | \\
\text{CH}_2 & \text{COOH} & \text{CH}_2 & \text{COOH} \\
| & & | & \\
\text{COOH} & & \text{COOH} & \\
\text{Glutamic} \quad \text{Oxalacetic} & & \alpha\text{-Ketoglutaric} \quad \text{Aspartic} \\
\text{acid} \qquad \text{acid} & & \text{acid} \qquad\quad \text{acid}
\end{array}
$$

Proteins

Proteins are the principal organic constituents of protoplasm. They are exceedingly complex nitrogenous substances of high molecular weight which differ from one another in shape, size, surface properties, and even in function. They all, however, have in common the fact that they are built up from amino acids, are amphoteric, and have colloidal properties. An amphoteric compound acts as an acid or a base. Proteins possess basic NH_2 and acidic $COOH$ groups. They are positively charged at pH values below the critical "neutral" value known as the isoelectric point and negatively charged at pH values above the isoelectric point. In addition to forming the structural framework of protoplasm, proteins also occur as enzymes and reserve foods, especially in seeds.

Although molecular weights of proteins are always high, there is considerable variation in weights of the various types. Some of the seed proteins have molecular weights of 200,000 to 400,000 (Bonner, 1950). Amandin, a protein of almond, has a molecular weight of 329,000, and hippocastanum, a protein found in horsechestnut seed, has a molecular weight of 430,000.

On a dry-weight basis proteins usually contain 50 to 55 per cent carbon, 6 to 7 per cent hydrogen, 20 to 23 per cent oxygen, and 12 to 19 per cent nitrogen. All plant proteins contain small amounts of sulfur, and certain plant proteins also contain phosphorus.

Proteins have been classified in a number of ways. The classical schemes (Gortner, 1938) are based on differences in solubility in various reagents, but Bonner (1950) emphasized the convenience of dealing with plant proteins on a more functional basis. For example, they might be divided into structural or protoplasmic proteins and reserve proteins. The former include enzymes and the proteins which form the structure of protoplasm; the latter are mostly foods, such as those in seeds. The latter usually are more easily hydrolyzed than protoplasmic proteins.

When decomposed by acids, alkalies, or enzymes, proteins produce a mixture of amino acids, but during the course of hydrolysis several products of intermediate complexity are formed as follows:

Proteins → proteoses → peptones → polypeptides → dipeptides → amino acids

Enzymatic degradation is more specific, the enzymes usually attacking certain specific chemical bonds and splitting off specific amino acids or groups of amino acids, rather than the large poorly defined groups or compounds split off by acid or alkali hydrolysis.

Protein Synthesis. A protein molecule consists of a long chain of amino acids brought together by peptide linkages or bonds in which the carboxyl group of an amino acid unites with the amino group of another amino acid and water is split off in the reaction. An example of a peptide linkage is the union of 2 molecules of glycine (CH_2NH_2COOH).

$$
\begin{array}{cccc}
 & & \overset{\displaystyle CH_2COOH}{\underset{}{|}} & \\
 & \overset{\displaystyle CH_2COOH}{\underset{}{|}} & CH_2CONH & \\
CH_2COOH + H\!-\!\overset{}{\underset{|}{N}} & & | & +\ HOH \\
\underset{}{\overset{|}{NH_2}} \quad \overset{|}{H} & & \underset{}{\overset{|}{NH_2}} & \\
\text{Glycine} \quad\quad \text{Glycine} & & \text{Dipeptide} & \text{Water}
\end{array}
$$

Inspection of the dipeptide formed in this reaction shows a free carboxyl and a free amino group for possible linkage to other amino acids. No matter how many additional amino acids are linked to such a dipeptide, there are always free amino and carboxyl groups in the resulting complex molecule. Thus, with the union of several hundred amino acids in peptide linkages, a protein is formed. The skeleton of a protein molecule might be pictured as follows (Bonner, 1950):

$$\begin{array}{cccccc} R_1 & O & & R_3 & O & \\ | & \| & H & | & \| & H \\ CH & C & N & CH & C & N \\ \diagdown\diagup & \diagdown\diagup & \diagdown\diagup & \diagdown\diagup & \diagdown\diagup & \diagdown \\ C & N & CH & C & N & CH \\ \| & H & | & \| & H & | \\ O & & R_2 & O & & R_4 \end{array}$$

In this chain R_1, R_2, and R_3 represent residues of different amino acids. In the case of glycine (CH_2NH_2COOH) $R = H$; in alanine (CH_3CH-NH_2COOH), $R = CH_3$.

In a living plant proteins are in a dynamic state and are constantly being broken down and reformed. The total amount of protein may remain constant over considerable periods of time, but new proteins are being formed and degradation is being balanced by synthesis.

Nucleoproteins

In recent years a group of proteins of exceedingly high molecular weights have received particular attention because of their relationship with genes which control cell metabolism and the transmission of hereditary characteristics. These are the nucleoproteins which are found in every living cell and involve a linkage of a protein to a nucleic acid. Their molecular weights may run into the millions. When hydrolyzed they produce phosphoric acid, a pentose sugar, and cyclical nitrogen compounds in the forms of purine and pyrimidine bases. Two types of nucleoprotein are commonly found: (1) deoxyribonucleoprotein, found primarily in cell nuclei, and (2) ribonucleoprotein, found primarily in cytoplasm. In the nuclei the sugar radical of nucleoproteins is deoxyribose, a pentose, while in the cytoplasm the nucleoprotein sugar radical is another pentose, D-ribose. Workers in this field commonly refer to the nucleic acids rather than to the nucleoproteins of which they are components; hence we find numerous references in the literature to deoxyribonucleic acid (DNA) and ribonucleic acid (RNA).

Amides

Two of the most important nitrogen compounds in plants are the amides asparagine and glutamine. They are formed from the corresponding acids by substitution of an amino group for the hydroxyl group of the carboxyl radical of the acid. Although the exact mechanism of this conversion is unknown, it occurs in a wide variety of plants. The formulas for the two principal amides and the corresponding amino acids follow:

$$
\begin{array}{cc}
\text{COOH} & \text{COOH} \\
| & | \\
\text{CHNH}_2 & \text{CHNH}_2 \\
| & | \\
\text{CH}_2 & \text{CH}_2 \\
| & | \\
\text{COOH} & \text{CONH}_2 \\
\text{Aspartic acid} & \text{Asparagine}
\end{array}
$$

$$
\begin{array}{cc}
\text{COOH} & \text{COOH} \\
| & | \\
\text{CHNH}_2 & \text{CHNH}_2 \\
| & | \\
\text{CH}_2 & \text{CH}_2 \\
| & | \\
\text{CH}_2 & \text{CH}_2 \\
| & | \\
\text{COOH} & \text{CONH}_2 \\
\text{Glutamic acid} & \text{Glutamine}
\end{array}
$$

Baldwin (1938) reported that when reserve proteins of tree seeds are hydrolyzed during germination, large amounts of asparagine are formed. Asparagine and glutamine have been considered important in plant metabolism because their synthesis prevents accumulation of free ammonia. Under conditions of low carbohydrate level, amino acids may be oxidized in respiration. This releases ammonia, which in turn is rapidly utilized in amide synthesis, thereby preventing the toxic effects of free ammonia in living cells. Amides are easily translocated, and most of the nitrogen translocation in plants probably occurs in this form.

Alkaloids

The alkaloids are complex bases which contain nitrogen and, in addition, carbon, hydrogen, and usually oxygen. They are widely distributed in herbaceous plants but are also common in many woody species, especially certain tropical groups. Alkaloids are commonly concentrated in leaves, bark, and roots but may also be found in wood and thus account for toxicity of various tropical woods. Some woods of the families Anacardiaceae, Apocynaceae, Euphorbiaceae, Leguminosae, Rutaceae, and Rubiaceae contain so much alkaloid that they are toxic and cause dermatitis. McNair (1935) found that 57 of the 295 families of angiosperms and gymnosperms which he studied contained alkaloids. Their physiological function in trees is not known, and many physiologists believe they are merely by-products of metabolism which in themselves are of no importance in vital processes.

Because of their widespread use in medicine, the cinchona alkaloids are probably the best-known group. They occur in the Andean genera

Cinchona and *Remijia* of the family Rubiaceae. Cinchona alkaloids obtained from bark are an extreme example of the fact that often the same tree will produce several closely related alkaloids. Quinine, quinidine, cinchonine, and cinchonidine are of greatest importance in this group, but more than 20 other alkaloids have been extracted from species of *Cinchona*.

For further discussion of alkaloids and toxicity of tropical woods the reader is referred to a paper by Garratt (1922) and for data on chemistry, distribution, synthesis, and pertinent literature to the excellent treatment by Henry (1949).

Nitrogen Requirements

It is of interest to consider how much nitrogen must be absorbed by trees to enable them to manufacture their nitrogen-containing compounds. Baker (1950) estimated that forest trees generally take up 38 to 45 pounds of nitrogen per acre per year and return all but 8 pounds of this nitrogen in leaf fall. The actual annual drain on forests in the United States appears to be of the order of 5 pounds per acre each year. In Europe Rebel (1920) reported that forest stands annually take up 30 to 55 pounds of nitrogen per acre and that 80 per cent of this amount is returned to the soil each year in litter. His values support Ramann's (1890) earlier data. Combes's data, cited earlier in this chapter, suggest that considerably less nitrogen is returned to the soil by leaf fall because about half is translocated out of the leaves before abscission occurs.

These data show the relatively low amounts of nitrogen that are required for forest trees and provide a sharp contrast with the amounts taken up by agricultural crops. Alfalfa in some areas may take up almost 200 pounds of nitrogen from each acre of land.

Nitrogen requirements are much higher for orchard trees than for forest trees. Whereas forest trees acquire most of their nitrogen from fixation of atmospheric nitrogen and that returned by way of leaf litter, orchard trees receive large amounts from added fertilizer. According to Murneek, apple trees 20 to 25 years old take up 1.31 to 1.51 pounds of nitrogen per tree each year. The amounts annually taken up per acre by the trees alone in apple orchards will generally vary between 50 and 150 pounds, depending on the number of trees.

A comparison of the data in Table 5.3 for nitrogen requirements of 20- and 25-year-old apple trees indicates that almost a third of the nitrogen which is necessary for the development of such trees, exclusive of leaf development in spring, is used for the fruit crop and a similar or slightly lesser amount for vegetative enlargement of the top and roots. As the tree gets older, proportionally less nitrogen is used for development of fruit and a higher proportion for stem and root tissues. Temporary loss

Table 5.3. Estimated annual nitrogen requirements of apple trees. (*After Murneek, 1942, and Magness and Regeimbal, 1938.*)

	Murneek 20-yr-old trees		Magness and Regeimbal 25-yr-old trees	
	Pounds	Per cent of total	Pounds	Per cent of total
For fruit crop	0.40	30.53	0.33	21.57
Loss (temporary) from abscised blossoms and fruit	0.06	4.59	0.09	5.88
Loss (temporary) from abscised leaves	0.40	30.53	0.60	39.22
For top and root growth (maintenance)	0.35	26.72	0.51	33.33
Removed by pruning	0.10	7.63		
Total	1.31	100.00	1.53	100.00

from fallen leaves is very high, and about 30 to 40 per cent of the 1.3 to 1.5 pounds of nitrogen required is returned to the soil with shedding of flowers and young fruits in the spring and the abscission of leaves in the autumn. The amount of nitrogen returned to the soil in the autumn by way of the leaves is at least six times as great as that returned by shedding of flowers and young fruit in the spring.

Murneek (1930) has shown that in years of heavy bearing very little nitrogen is stored in trees and reserves stored in the prior year or years may become seriously or completely depleted. This results in decreased vegetative growth and inhibited flower bud formation during the current year as well as lessened growth and fruit setting the following year. Often more than one year is required for complete recovery. These effects are analogous to effects of fruiting on carbohydrate reserves discussed in Chapter 4.

Sources of Nitrogen for Trees

Trees are able to use nitrogen in the form of nitrates, nitrites, ammonium salts, and organic nitrogen compounds, but most nitrogen probably is absorbed in the form of nitrates. Addoms (1937) found that loblolly pine was able to utilize nitrogen in the form of either nitrate or ammonium. Nitrate was used more successfully at low pHs, but at more nearly neutral reactions ammonium nitrogen was better. Cranberry plants also did well with ammonium nitrogen (Addoms, 1931). According to Nemec and Kvapil (1927), European conifers absorb most of their nitrogen as ammonia while hardwoods, especially beech, oak, and ash, obtain nitrogen chiefly as nitrates.

Primary nitrogen sources for trees are atmospheric nitrogen which has been "fixed" by microorganisms in soil, leaf and twig litter, nitrogen fertilizers, and nitrogen fixed in the atmosphere by electrical storms and carried down in rain and snow. Commercial nitrogen fertilizers are the most important source for orchard trees but are not used extensively as a source of nitrogen for forest trees. Nitrogen may be lost from soil by harvesting plants and by fire, leaching, and denitrification. Some ammonia escapes into the atmosphere and is returned to the soil by precipitation.

Nitrogen Fixation. Although the atmosphere consists of about 80 per cent nitrogen, atmospheric nitrogen is very inert and this potential source can be used by trees only after it is "fixed" or combined with other elements. Nitrogen fixation by microorganisms replaces that lost from the soil by leaching, fire, and absorption by plants and prevents its ultimate exhaustion.

Fixation by Bacteria. Nitrogen fixation in soils occurs largely as the result of the activities of saprophytic bacteria of the genera *Azotobacter* and *Clostridium* and symbiotic nitrogen-fixing bacteria of the genus *Rhizobium,* which are associated with root nodules of various plants, chiefly legumes. The nodule bacteria are far less important than the saprophytic genera for making nitrogen available to forest trees.

The saprophytic bacteria fix nitrogen by combining carbohydrates with gaseous nitrogen of the air. The *Clostridium* bacteria are rod-shaped anaerobes, while those of the *Azotobacter* group are aerobic cocci. Waksman (1932) reported that forest soils may have from 100 to 10,000 anaerobic nitrogen-fixing bacteria per gram of soil. The anaerobic forms are more common in forest soils than are the aerobic organisms. Apparently high acidity is largely responsible for the fact that aerobic nitrogen-fixing bacteria are scarce in forest soils. The occurrence and activity of *Azotobacter* may also be influenced by mineral supply and availability of carbon compounds as a source of energy (Waksman and Starkey, 1931).

Fixation by Legumes. Many species of the family Leguminosae, including herbaceous and woody types, produce root nodules which are involved in symbiotic nitrogen fixation. Rod-shaped bacteria of the genus *Rhizobium* penetrate roots of leguminous plants through root hairs and cause tubercles or nodules to form on the roots. Less commonly the bacteria enter roots through broken epidermal and cortical cells or ruptured tissue in areas where rootlets emerge (Allen and Allen, 1958). Two distinct types of nodules may form. The more common exogenous type develops from infection of cortical parenchyma cells, while an endogenous type occasionally forms by proliferation of the pericycle (Allen and

Allen, 1958). The bacteria reside in large numbers inside the nodules and there synthesize organic nitrogen compounds from carbohydrates of the invaded plant and gaseous nitrogen from the air. The reader is referred to Wilson (1940) and to Allen and Allen (1958) for detailed descriptions of infective stages leading to nodule formation and of nodule structure.

Root nodule fixation is probably most important to trees in the southeastern United States, where forest trees normally are associated with wild herbaceous legumes.

Chapman (1935) found increased height and diameter growth of several species of hardwoods planted beside black locust trees. He also found that total nitrogen in the soil was greatest near the black locust trees and concluded that the improved growth was the result of nitrogen fixation by the locust.

Fixation in Nodulated Nonlegumes. Nitrogen-fixing root nodules have been classically identified with the family Leguminosae. However, root nodules occur on a number of nonleguminous dicotyledons and have been reported on 65 species of trees and shrubs in 8 families including Betulaceae, Eleagnaceae, Myricaceae, Rhamnaceae, Casuarinaceae, Coriariaceae, Zygophyllaceae, and Rubiaceae (Allen and Allen, 1958). All the plants in these families are adapted to growth on poor sites. Bond and his coworkers have demonstrated appreciable nitrogen fixation by several nodulated nonleguminous woody plants, including *Alnus, Myrica, Hippophaë, Shepherdia,* and *Casuarina* (Figure 5.6) (Bond, 1955–1957; Ferguson and Bond, 1953; Gardner and Bond, 1957). Alder plants, grown from seed in the greenhouse and caused to develop nodules by inoculation with a suspension of crushed nodules from field seedlings, made excellent growth in a rooting medium free of combined nitrogen, indicating that fixation of elemental nitrogen is associated with the nodulated plant. In another experiment Bond (1956) showed that field nodules of alder, like those of greenhouse-grown plants, regularly fix nitrogen and concluded that the amount of nitrogen fixed is substantial. Bond and Gardner (1957) reported that under experimental conditions fixation of European alder and *Myrica gale* during the first year of growth exceeded that of annual legumes and of black locust.

Nitrogen fixation by nodulated nonlegumes appears to be of considerable ecological significance in certain areas. For example, Crocker and Major (1955) noted that at Glacier Bay, Alaska, an average of 55 pounds of nitrogen accumulated per acre under alder thickets. This undoubtedly created a favorable site for Sitka spruce, which succeeded alder. The practice of interplanting alder in conifer plantations to improve growth of the conifers has long been recognized by Europeans and is also practiced extensively in Japan. The beneficial effects are undoubtedly due to greater nitrogen availability. Virtanen (1957) demonstrated that when spruce was planted beside alder, it obtained nitrogen fixed in the root nodules of the alder. He calculated that in a grove of alders about 2.5 meters high and with 10,000 trees per hectare, the leaf fall and roots remaining in the soil would add about 200 kilograms of nitrogen per

Figure 5.6 Effect of nitrogen-fixing bacteria on growth of *Casuarina equisetifolia.* Both sets of plants were grown for 6 months in a solution free of combined nitrogen. Plants on the left had bacterial nodules on their roots. Those on the right were free of nodules. (*From Bond, 1957.*)

hectare. Nitrogen losses were not taken into account in his calculations.

It should not be assumed that all nodulated nonlegumes are nitrogen fixers. The possibility exists that tubercles of some plants may be merely pathological growths and that more work needs to be done with such species to ascertain whether or not they are really involved in nitrogen fixation.

Atmospheric Nitrogen Fixation. Some inorganic nitrogen is added to the soil by rain and snow. It is reported that in England 4.4 pounds per acre of nitrogen is returned annually in rain, enough to balance the loss by leaching. Baker (1950) estimated that 5 pounds of nitrogen per acre per year is returned to the soil in the United States, all of it readily available.

Release from Litter. Some of the nitrogen absorbed by trees is returned to the soil in fallen litter. Maintenance of forest soil fertility is partly dependent on return of nitrogen and mineral nutrients by decay of litter. Leaves and twigs which are annually added to the forest floor may add up to several thousand pounds of organic material containing approximately 1 per cent of nitrogen-containing compounds. Baker (1950) gives 3,000 pounds per acre for fully stocked forests on good sites in the United States as a reasonable average annual amount of leaf and twig deposit. Wide variations occur, however, and values as low as 500 pounds have been measured on poor beech sites while the best European beech stands return as much as 6,000 pounds of leaf and twig debris to each acre of soil.

The amount of nitrogen in litter varies greatly with species. Chandler (1941) found the nitrogen content of leaf litter of hardwoods in central New York State to vary from 0.43 to 1.04 per cent with an average of 0.65 per cent, while Coile (1937a), working with conifers and hardwoods in the Piedmont of North Carolina, found values ranging from 0.50 per cent to 1.25 per cent. Hardwood leaves in litter generally have higher average nitrogen contents than do coniferous leaves. Conifer leaves which have been shed have about 0.6 to 1.0 per cent nitrogen, while fallen hardwood leaves generally range from 0.8 to 2.0 per cent nitrogen (Baker, 1950). However, values considerably lower than 0.8 per cent have been reported for several hardwoods (Coile, 1937a; Chandler, 1941; Alway et al., 1933).

With an average addition of 3,000 pounds of litter by forest trees and an average nitrogen content of 0.6 to 2.0 per cent, the return of nitrogen is actually 18 to 60 pounds per acre. Foresters often use 30 pounds per acre as an average figure and in general think of hardwoods as returning 5 pounds of nitrogen more per acre than do conifers.

The rate of decomposition of litter varies with species, nutrient conditions of the soil, aeration, moisture conditions, and temperature. In general, hardwood leaves decompose more rapidly than do coniferous leaves. Decomposition is slow in northern latitudes and most rapid in tropical areas (Lutz and Chandler, 1946). In northern forests up to 50 years may be required to release all the nitrogen from a year's twig and leaf litter, while in tropical forests fallen leaves and twigs decay within a few weeks.

Only a small part of the nitrogen which is returned to the soil in leaf litter becomes immediately reavailable. Therefore unless more nitrogen is continually added to the soil, by soil and atmospheric fixation, a serious deficit will soon develop.

Nitrogen Fertilizers. It is common orchard practice to apply nitrogen fertilizer in order to increase yield of fruit trees. The increased yield may result from more vegetative growth, more fruit buds, better fruit setting, larger fruit, or from some combination of these. For an excellent discussion of the application of nitrogen-carrying fertilizers the reader is referred to the book by Gardner et al. (1952).

High-nitrogen fertilizers such as 10-8-6 or 10-6-4 are routinely used by arborists for shade-tree maintenance. Recommendations vary, but 2 to 4 pounds of fertilizer for each inch of trunk diameter at breast height has been recommended as a safe dosage. For a discussion of fertilizer materials and formulas used in shade-tree maintenance, readers are referred to the book by Pirone (1941).

The use of fertilizers in forestry has been restricted thus far to nurseries, but fertilization of plantations may become practical. This subject is discussed in Chapter 9.

The Nitrogen Cycle

It has already been mentioned that specific microorganisms are involved in converting atmospheric nitrogen to available forms. Other specific organisms effect the decomposition of organic material, including plant litter and some animal material, into usable forms through ammonification and nitrification.

In the process of ammonification, nitrogen compounds of plants and animals are broken down and nitrogen is released as ammonia. This is a rather generalized process inasmuch as several species of bacteria and fungi may be involved. Much of the ammonia which is thus released is acted on by specific genera of nitrifying bacteria and converted in two stages to nitrates, a process known as nitrification. The first stage of nitrification involves a conversion of ammonia to nitrites through the activity of bacteria of the genera *Nitrosomonas* and *Nitrosococcus*. These bacteria cannot convert ammonia beyond the nitrite stage, and the conversion of nitrite to nitrate is accomplished by bacteria of the genus *Nitrobacter*. It is emphasized that these are specific reactions which are carried out in stages and the bacteria involved have specific roles which they cannot exceed.

The oxidations which are carried on in these two stages by the chemosynthetic bacteria both produce energy, as indicated in the following type reactions (Bonner, 1950):

(1) Production of nitrite:

$$NH_4^+ + 1.5\,O_2 \rightarrow NO_2^- + H_2O + 2H^+$$
Nitrosomonas

(2) Production of nitrate:

$$NO_2^- + 0.5\,O_2 \rightarrow NO_3$$
Nitrobacter

The organisms involved grow and synthesize organic matter for their own cell substance from carbon dioxide, using energy from the oxidation of ammonia or nitrite.

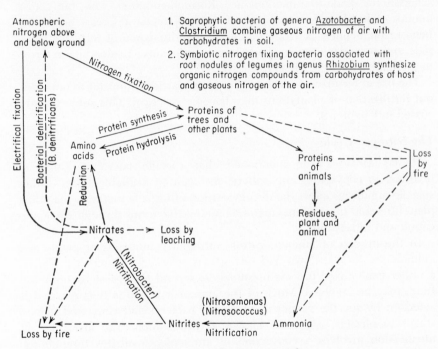

1. Saprophytic bacteria of genera <u>Azotobacter</u> and <u>Clostridium</u> combine gaseous nitrogen of air with carbohydrates in soil.

2. Symbiotic nitrogen fixing bacteria associated with root nodules of legumes in genus <u>Rhizobium</u> synthesize organic nitrogen compounds from carbohydrates of host and gaseous nitrogen of the air.

Figure 5.7 The nitrogen cycle.

Another group of anaerobic bacteria, the denitrifying bacteria, are able to reduce nitrates to molecular nitrogen in still another type of reaction. Several species are involved, but the most commonly known one is *Bacterium denitrificans*. Denitrification is accomplished best under conditions of large carbohydrate supplies. It results in a net loss of available nitrogen.

Various aspects of the nitrogen cycle with some of the organisms involved are summarized in Figure 5.7.

GENERAL REFERENCES

Bonner, J., 1950, Plant biochemistry, Academic Press, Inc., New York.

Chibnall, A. C., 1939, Protein metabolism in the plant, Yale University Press, New Haven, Conn.

Henry, T. A., 1949, The plant alkaloids, McGraw-Hill Book Company, Inc., Blakiston Division, New York.

McElroy, W. D., and H. B. Glass, 1955, A symposium on amino acid metabolism, Johns Hopkins Press, Baltimore.

———— and H. B. Glass, 1956, Inorganic nitrogen metabolism, Johns Hopkins Press, Baltimore.

Ruhland, W. (ed.), 1958, Encyclopedia of plant physiology, vol. 8, Nitrogen, K. Mothes (subed.), Springer-Verlag, Berlin.

Steward, F. C., and J. K. Pollard, 1957, Nitrogen metabolism in plants: ten years in retrospect, Ann. Rev. Plant Physiology, 8:65–114.

Wilson, P. W., and R. H. Burris, 1953, Biological nitrogen fixation: a reappraisal, Ann. Rev. Microbiology, 7:415–432.

CHAPTER 6 *Fats, Oils, Terpenes, and Related Substances*

The fats and other lipids which occur in trees are of both physiological and economic importance. They are physiologically important because fats and phospholipids are essential constituents of protoplasm and occur at least in small quantities in all living cells. Fats also are important storage forms of food in seeds and occur in varying quantities in the vegetative organs of most trees. Fats and oils differ principally in that the former are solids and the latter are liquids at ordinary temperatures, and the terms will be used synonymously in this discussion. The seeds of some trees such as palm and tung yield oils of great economic importance. The terpenes obtained from certain pines are important as the source of turpentine. Essential oils, extracted from the wood and leaves of various trees and shrubs such as camphor, cedar, eucalyptus, sassafras, sweetgum, and witch-hazel, usually are included although they are not closely related to true fats and oils. The latex from which rubber is made is often also included in this group of compounds.

Most of the substances treated in this chapter actually have little in common except that they are insoluble in water and soluble in so-called fat solvents such as benzene, chloroform, and ether. The general relationships of this group of ether-extractable substances are shown in Figure 6.1.

Importance of Fats

Fats are esters of fatty acids and glycerol, a trihydric alcohol. They are one group of a larger class of organic compounds called lipids, which can be defined as esters of fatty acids and alcohols or products of the hydrolysis of such esters. Lipids include many substances which are insoluble in water but soluble in ether, chloroform, hot alcohol, benzene, carbon tetrachloride, and acetone. In addition to true fats, the lipids

140

Crude Lipids
or
Ether Extract
All substances
extracted by
benzene,
chloroform,
ether, etc.

True Lipids
Esters of fatty acids
and alcohols and products
of their hydrolysis

Simple Lipids
- True fats–Esters of fatty acids and oils and glycerol
- Waxes–Esters of fatty acids and alcohols other than glycerol

Compound Lipids
- Esters of fatty acids containing groups in addition to alcohols and fatty acids
- Phospholipids

Derived Lipids
- Fatty acids
  - Saturated
    - Lauric
    - Palmitic
    - Stearic
  - Unsaturated
    - Oleic
    - Linolenic
- Sterols

Substances not esters of fatty acids

Terpenes
- Essential Oils
- Resins
- Latex
- Carotenes
- Rubber
- Gutta Percha

Figure 6.1 Classification of the substances found in ether extracts from plants.

include such compounds as waxes, sterols, and phospholipids. Ether extracts often include essential oils, resins, and other substances not classified as true lipids.

Fats, like carbohydrates and proteins, serve as an important form of storage food for trees. Their high concentration in many tree seeds makes them an important respiratory substrate during germination (Chapter 14). Fats also serve as a respiratory substrate in buds, twigs, and bark. Disappearance of fats from the apical meristem downward into the twigs has been noted during growth periods. According to Kostychev (1926), Ivanov found that fats were metabolically consumed from the

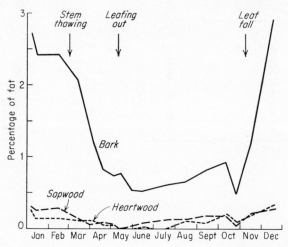

Figure 6.2 Seasonal variations in fat content of bark, sapwood, and heartwood of beech in Switzerland. Notice the decrease during the period when growth was being resumed and the increase in the autumn. (*From Gäumann, 1935.*)

bark of trees during spring growth flushes and that this process was analogous to utilization of fats in germinating seeds.

Gäumann (1935) has shown that when beech trees begin to grow, oil reserves in the bark and buds are rapidly depleted (Figure 6.2). Kostychev (1926) believed that reserve fats in twigs were converted to soluble substances in the spring and utilized in growth. Ishibe (1935) also demonstrated disappearance of fats from twigs in the spring (Figure 6.3).

Fats are especially important as reserve foods because they contain more energy per unit of weight than do carbohydrates or proteins. The heat of combustion of 1 gram dry weight of fat is 9.3 kilogram-calories, of proteins 5.7 kilogram-calories, and of carbohydrates 5.1 kilogram-calories.

Distribution and Seasonal Fluctuation

Fats are widely distributed throughout trees and may be found in varying quantity in leaves, stems, roots, fruits, flowers, and seeds. By far the greatest concentrations are found in reproductive structures, including seeds and mature fruits. Some seeds contain well over 70 per cent oil on a dry-weight basis, but vegetative parts rarely contain over 5 per cent and often have much less than this.

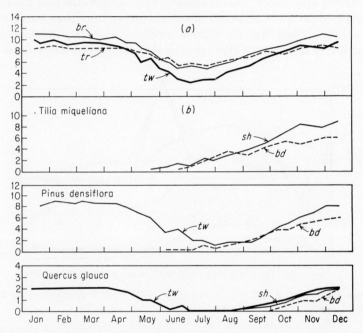

Figure 6.3 Seasonal variations in fat content of various parts of the tops of trees of three Japanese tree species. The ordinates indicate relative rather than absolute amounts. *a. br*, 5-year-old branch; *tw*, 1-year-old twig; *tr*, trunk. *b. bd*, bud; *sh*, current year's shoot. (*From Ishibe, 1935.*)

Fats are dispersed as small droplets in the cytoplasm and occur as liquids at ordinary temperatures, so they might more properly be called oils although the terms "fats" and "oils" in common usage are interchangeable. In seeds and fruits the fats are present in much larger globules than they are in vegetative tissues of low fat content.

Very little reliable quantitative research has been done on fats in tree foliage, but that which has been done indicates that the concentrations are very low. In leaves total lipids, as determined by ether extraction, very seldom exceed 4 to 5 per cent of the dry weight. Included in such an extract are waxes, sterols, phospholipids, and other substances in addition to fats, so the content of true fat is quite low. Several investigators have reported that in winter fats accumulate in leaves at the expense of carbohydrates (Tuttle, 1919, 1921; Lewis and Tuttle, 1920, 1923). The substance reported as fat was demonstrated microchemically with neutral red and osmic acid. Further observations have shown that the substances earlier reported as fats did not react with Sudan III in a specific fat test or give other normal fat reactions; hence doubt has been expressed concerning the conversion of carbohydrates to fats (Meyer, 1918; Doyle and Clinch, 1927). Doyle (1938) concluded that the earlier tests showed presence of resiniferous substances rather than true fats. He reported that there was no reliable evidence that fat accumulated in conifer leaves in winter or that fat at any season played a significant part

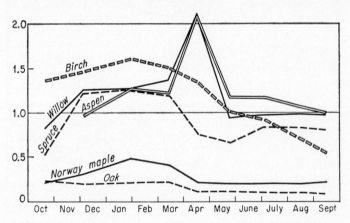

Figure 6.4 Seasonal and species variations in fat content of wood of six species of trees in Sweden. (*From Arrhenius*, 1942.)

in their metabolism. It has been demonstrated, however, that ether-soluble substances increase with age of pine and fir needles (Clements, 1938).

Fat contents may vary from less than 1 per cent to 8 per cent in the wood of different trees, but the concentration rarely exceeds 2 or 3 per cent and often is much less than this. Sapwood generally contains less fat than heartwood, while the bark contains more than either sapwood or heartwood. Fat content of wood usually is highest in the winter and lowest in midsummer, but the wood of some species which are low in fats shows almost no seasonal fluctuation. Some trees, such as pines, birches, and lindens, have conspicuously high fat contents during the winter (Figure 6.5).

Fischer (1891) attempted to classify trees as "starch trees" and "fat trees" on the basis of the predominant reserves in their wood during winter. In his "fat trees" starch disappeared and fats constituted the only visible winter food reserve of woody tissues. Preston and Phillips (1911) substantiated these findings. They also found fat content to be lowest at the time of unfolding of buds and to increase slowly through the summer to a maximum in late autumn or early winter and to decline again to the spring minimum. Among the trees which contained considerable fat were eastern cottonwood, black walnut, American basswood, and American elm. Those showing little fat were white willow and pignut hickory. Largest amounts of fats were found in the phloem and rays of twigs. Roots of all trees examined had no more than traces of fat in any of the tissues.

Sinnott (1918) found that "starch trees" usually have heavy woods of high density while "fat trees" have woods of lower density, although there are a number of exceptions to this rule. He stated that diffuse-porous species either are usually "fat trees" or have an abundance of fat in winter while ring-porous species are almost always "starch trees." Trees with narrow rays may be in either group, but those with compound rays are usually "starch trees." Thus he identified oaks, ashes, and hickories as "starch trees" and pines and lindens as "fat trees." He also found several genera which are intermediate and store both starch and fat in the wood during the winter season (Table 6.1).

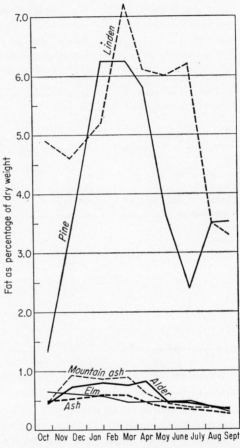

Figure 6.5 Seasonal and species variations in fat content of wood of pine and various deciduous species in Sweden. (*From Arrhenius,* 1942.)

Whereas carbohydrate depletion of twigs is very closely coordinated with the growth cycle, the relation of fat depletion in twigs to growth is somewhat less well correlated since minimum fat content is often attained in young branches in early or midsummer when most of the growth is over. Furthermore, fat is never completely depleted even from young twigs in which the decrease is most pronounced.

Table 6.1. Classification of tree genera based on types of food reserves in pith and wood of young twigs and branches during midwinter. (*Modified from Sinnott, 1918.*)

Predominantly fat	Both starch and fat	Predominantly starch
Hardwoods	Hardwoods	Hardwoods
Aesculus	Betula (some species)	Acer
Betula (some species)	Juglans (some species)	Carpinus
Catalpa	Populus (some species)	Carya
Cornus (some species)	Prunus	Castanea
Juglans (some species)	Rhus (most species)	Celtis
Populus (most species)	Robinia	Cladrastis
Tilia	Salix	Cornus (some species)
Rhus (some species)	Sambucus	Crataegus
Viburnum (some species)	Viburnum (some species)	Diospyros
		Fagus
Softwoods	Softwoods	Fraxinus
Pinus	Abies	Gleditsia
Picea	Ginkgo	Hamamelis
Pseudotsuga		Ilex
Tsuga		Liquidambar
Taxus		Liriodendron
		Magnolia
		Nyssa
		Platanus
		Quercus
		Syringa
		Ulmus
		Zanthoxylum

Gäumann (1935) found a slight seasonal fluctuation of fat content in wood of beech. His study showed the common pattern of winter maximum and summer minimum and further showed that fat content was exceedingly low and was always less than 0.5 per cent in the wood but was much higher in the bark (Figure 6.2).

Ishibe (1935) studied seasonal changes in fat and carbohydrate reserves of several deciduous tree species and one conifer, *Pinus densiflora*, in Japan. The sample trees varied in age from 4 to 14 years, but most of them were at least 10 years old. Fresh tissue sections were treated with Sudan III to bring out fat reserves, and the relative amounts were plotted as ordinate values. These values have no significant quantitative meaning but are useful to indicate relative differences between species as well as seasonal fluctuations. Most of his classification agrees with that of Sinnott. Representative data are given in Figure 6.3.

Ishibe divides trees into three distinct groups, using fat storage at midwinter as a criterion:

1. Fat trees: species showing much fat throughout stem tissue: *Tilia, Populus,* and *Pinus*

2. Starch trees: species showing fat confined to bark: *Castanea, Robinia,* and *Quercus*

3. Intermediate trees: species showing both fat and starch in wood: *Alnus*

In *Tilia miqueliana,* fat was found in considerable quantity all through the stem tissues, especially in the inner bark and young wood. Vegetative buds showed a very high fat content at dormancy, but this rapidly disappeared with growth inception and was completely gone when buds were opened. Disappearance of fat from buds was followed by disappearance from young twigs. Such exhaustion of fat apparently progressed basipetally down the branches to tissues of the main stem. It was not until the beginning of May that fat disappeared from the trunk in appreciable quantities.

In the trunk the cambial zone was depleted first, and this was followed by loss of fat from the phloem adjoining the cambium. In the remaining tissues of the trunk decrease in fat took place at a much reduced rate. This was especially true in the inner wood and pith. The amount of fat in the pith was very small, and there was little seasonal fluctuation in this tissue.

By the middle of August the young parts showed a slight increase in fat content. In new shoots and buds fat appeared in late May and June. A steady rise was then evident until the winter maximum. In new shoots fats began to accumulate first in the ray cells of the wood.

Castanea pubinervis, a "starch tree," manifested considerable fat in the bark of branches and the stem and negligible amounts in the wood and pith. Buds were rich in fat but quite free of starch. The seasonal fluctuation of fat was very similar to that of *Tilia* even though the amounts involved were different.

Seasonal fat content of *Pinus densiflora* is of particular interest. During the dormant period the branches and the trunk had a high fat content. Unlike other "fat trees," there was a relatively large seasonal decrease, and by the August minimum none of the tissues contained more than very small amounts. Ishibe regarded the parallelism of starch disappearance and fat appearance in this species as a mere coincidence.

There is a striking difference between stems and roots in their ability to produce fats. Ishibe showed that tree roots contain only negligible amounts of fats and often the seasonal fluctuation is so slight that roots can be disregarded as fat-storage organs. Most of the fat present in roots usually occurs in the thickened basal parts, and the fat content diminishes toward the tips. Several investigators have emphasized that roots contain little or no fat, but none have explained why stems are much more efficient than roots in their ability to produce and accumulate fats (Weber, 1909; Sinnott, 1918; Ishibe, 1935).

Arrhenius (1942) analyzed the wood of 12 species of 20-year-old forest trees near Stockholm, Sweden, for fat content at various seasons of the year. There was considerable variation between species as well as considerable seasonal variation, but the maximum fat content usually occurred in winter and the minimum in summer. Arrhenius classified the trees he studied into four classes:

1. Oak and maple, with very low fat content in winter as well as in summer.

2. Alder, elm, ash, and mountain-ash, with about 0.5 per cent fat content in the summer and 1 per cent in the winter.

3. Aspen, birch, spruce, and willow, with about 0.75 to 2.00 per cent fat content. Aspen and willow deviate from the general pattern and show an especially marked maximum in April.

4. Linden and pine, with winter values around 6 to 7 per cent.

The seasonal distribution of fat in the trees studied by Arrhenius is shown in Figures 6.4 and 6.5. Unquestionably the values are too high, at least in some species, since he was dealing with total ether extractables rather than fats or oils alone. Nevertheless, this study reinforces the work of Fischer, who considered oak and maple as typical "starch trees" and linden and pine as typical "fat trees."

Fat content of tree bark is usually higher than that of either the sapwood or heartwood of the same species. Thus Gäumann (1935) found that fats and fatty acids were consistently several times higher in the bark than the wood of twigs, stem, and roots of 33-year-old beech trees (Table 6.2). He further found that although fat content of the bark decreased markedly during the spring, it never decreased to as low a value as the fat content of wood (Figure 6.2).

Greatest capacity for storage of fats and oils in trees is localized in reproductive structures, including both fruits and seeds. In some trees like avocado and olive, fats accumulate in the parenchymatous cells of the fruit pericarp. Fleshy coats of many tree fruits are high in oil content and are important sources for commercial extraction of oil. In trees of the *Rosaceae*, fats accumulate in the tissues of the receptacle. Seeds may store fat either in embryo tissues as in red oak acorns or chiefly in the endosperm as in coconut. The reproductive structures of some trees have unusually high oil contents. Brazil nuts, coconuts, and pecans contain 60 to 75 per cent of oil, pinyon pine seed 64 per cent, and olive fruits 25 to 28 per cent.

Synthesis of fats and oils takes place very rapidly during a short time

Table 6.2. Distribution of carbohydrates, fats, and proteins in beech during the winter. (*After Gäumann*, 1935.)

Material	Dry weight, kg	Total, %	Carbo-hydrates, kg	Fats and fatty acids %	Fats and fatty acids kg	Raw protein %	Raw protein kg
Twigs	10	8.2	0.8	1.5	0.2	5.8	0.6
Branches:							
Bark	10	8.4	0.8	1.5	0.2	5.9	0.6
Wood	130	3.6	4.7	0.1	0.1	1.5	2.0
Stem:							
Bark	75	9.7	7.3	2.5	1.9	5.4	4.1
Sapwood	300	2.5	7.5	0.3	0.9	1.1	3.3
Heartwood	1,100	2.0	22.0	0.2	2.2	0.9	9.9
Stump and roots:							
Bark	20	9.7	1.9	0.8	0.2	5.1	1.0
Wood	130	5.2	6.8	0.3	0.4	1.3	1.7
Total	1,775		51.8		6.1		23.2

Table 6.3. Development of fats in tree fruits and seeds.

Walnut seed * Date	Walnut seed * Oil, %	Almond seed * Date	Almond seed * Oil, %
July 6	3	June 9	2
Aug. 1	16	July 4	10
Aug. 15	42	Aug. 1	37
Oct. 4	62	Oct. 4	46

Black walnut kernels † Date	Black walnut kernels † Oil, %	Tung fruit ‡ Date	Tung fruit ‡ Oil, %
June 15	3.54	July 15	3.88
July 15	13.44	Aug. 15	58.29
July 29	39.26	Sept. 15	64.18
Aug. 12	51.12	Oct. 15	63.83
Aug. 26	61.92	Nov. 15	63.19

* After Sablon (1896).
† After M'Clenahan (1909).
‡ After Sell et al. (1948).

period in the development of fruits and seeds. Thor and Smith (1935) found that as late as September 1 oil formation had hardly begun in pecan but during the next 30 days 75 to 80 per cent of the eventual oil content was laid down in the kernel. By September 19 oil content of the kernel was already 70 per cent on a dry-weight basis. After this there was a gradual increase until harvest, when the Burkett variety of pecan contained 74 per cent and the Stuart variety 76 per cent oil on a dry-weight basis. Similarly, Sell et al. (1948) found the oil content of tung kernels to increase from 3.88 to 58.29 per cent over a 4-week period from mid-July to mid-August. For 12 weeks thereafter there was only an insignificant change in oil content over the mid-August content. The same pattern of rapid fat formation was shown to occur in almond and walnut by Sablon (Table 6.3).

Fat is formed in seeds and fruits and is not translocated to reproductive organs from the leaves or stem. This view is reinforced by the varying compositions of leaf and fruit fats and, perhaps more importantly, by the fact that in some species fats are synthesized in fruits even after they have been removed from the tree.

Chemistry of Fat Formation

Fats are esters of fatty acids with glycerol, a trihydric alcohol with the molecular formula $C_3H_5(OH)_3$. Fat molecules are made up of approximately 10 per cent glycerol and 90 per cent fatty acids.

Fatty acids may be divided into saturated and unsaturated acids on the basis of presence or absence of double bonds. If double bonds are present, the acids are unsaturated. The empirical formula of a saturated fatty acid is $C_nH_{2n+1}COOH$. Fatty acids of tree fats are straight-chain compounds with even numbers of carbon atoms. Palmitic acid is the most

Table 6.4. Some fatty acids found in plant fats.

Saturated Acids

Caproic	$C_6H_{12}O_2$	$CH_3(CH_2)_4COOH$
Caprylic	$C_8H_{16}O_2$	$CH_3(CH_2)_6COOH$
Capric	$C_{10}H_{20}O_2$	$CH_3(CH_2)_8COOH$
Lauric	$C_{12}H_{24}O_2$	$CH_3(CH_2)_{10}COOH$
Myristic	$C_{14}H_{28}O_2$	$CH_3(CH_2)_{12}COOH$
Palmitic	$C_{16}H_{32}O_2$	$CH_3(CH_2)_{14}COOH$
Stearic	$C_{18}H_{36}O_2$	$CH_3(CH_2)_{16}COOH$
Arachidic	$C_{20}H_{40}O_2$	$CH_3(CH_2)_{18}COOH$

Unsaturated Acids

Oleic	$C_{18}H_{34}O_2$	$CH_3(CH_2)_7CH:CH(CH_2)_7COOH$
Linoleic	$C_{18}H_{32}O_2$	$CH_3(CH_2)_4CH:CHCH_2CH:CH(CH_2)_7COOH$
Linolenic	$C_{18}H_{30}O_2$	$CH_3CH_2CH:CHCH_2CH:CHCH_2CH:CH(CH_2)_7COOH$

widely distributed saturated fatty acid in tree fats. Lauric, stearic, myristic, and arachidic acids are other members of the saturated series which occur in tree fats. The formulas of some important fatty acids are shown in Table 6.4.

Most of the fatty acids in tree fats are unsaturated. Two such acids, oleic and linoleic, are the most important and most abundant. Unsaturated acids have the capacity of combining with oxygen of the air, and this property is responsible for drying characteristics of many oils, such as that obtained from the seed of the tung tree.

Fats have the following skeleton formula:

$$R—COO—CH_2$$
$$R^1—COO—CH$$
$$R^2—COO—CH_2$$

in which R, R^1, and R^2 represent carbon chains of the same or of three different fatty acids. Glycerol is a trihydric alcohol, and each molecule can unite with three fatty acid molecules to form triglycerides. Most fats are triglycerides, although mono- and diglycerides exist, compounds in which only one or two fatty acids unite with a molecule of glycerol. Typical esterification may be illustrated in the reaction between glycerol and palmitic acid to produce the glyceride tripalmitin, a typical fat. The enzyme lipase serves as the catalyst.

$$3C_{15}H_{31}COOH + \begin{array}{c} CH_2OH \\ | \\ CHOH \\ | \\ CH_2OH \end{array} \xrightleftharpoons{\text{lipase}} \begin{array}{c} C_{15}H_{31}COOCH_2 \\ | \\ C_{15}H_{31}COOCH \\ | \\ C_{15}H_{31}COOCH_2 \end{array} + 3H_2O$$

Palmitic acid   Glycerol   Tripalmitin   Water

Fats can be hydrolyzed, producing 3 molecules of fatty acids plus 1 molecule of glycerol according to the type reaction:

$$\begin{array}{c} R—COO—CH_2 \\ | \\ R^1—COO—CH \\ | \\ R^2—COO—CH_2 \end{array} + 3H_2O \xrightleftharpoons{\text{lipase}} \begin{array}{c} R—COOH \\ R^1—COOH \\ R^2—COOH \end{array} \begin{array}{c} HOCH_2 \\ | \\ HOCH \\ | \\ HOCH_2 \end{array}$$

Fat   Water   Fatty acids   Glycerol

This reaction can be carried out in the laboratory in boiling water or with mineral acids. In living plant tissues the reaction is catalyzed by lipase, the same enzyme system involved in fat synthesis.

Fats also are decomposed by alkalies in a process called "saponification." End products of saponification are soaps and glycerol. Saponification normally occurs in plant tissues where soaps serve as emulsifiers. The following is a typical saponification reaction:

$$
\begin{array}{lll}
\text{RCOOCH}_2 & R\text{—COONa} & \text{HOCH}_2 \\
\mid & & \mid \\
R^1\text{COOCH} + 3\text{NaOH} \rightarrow & R^1\text{—COONa} + & \text{HOCH} \\
\mid & & \mid \\
R^2\text{COOCH}_2 & R^2\text{—COONa} & \text{HOCH}_2 \\
\text{Fat} \quad \text{Sodium} & \text{Soap} & \text{Glycerol} \\
\quad\quad \text{hydroxide}
\end{array}
$$

Fats apparently are synthesized in seeds and fruits from a precursor which is relatively rich in oxygen, presumably a carbohydrate (Bonner, 1950), but the ratio of carbon to oxygen is much higher in a fat than in a carbohydrate. A probable pathway for fat synthesis is shown in Figure 7.1. When a substrate low in oxygen is oxidized in respiration, the respiratory quotient (also called respiratory ratio), or ratio of carbon dioxide evolved to oxygen absorbed, is less than when a substrate high in oxygen is oxidized. The respiratory quotient for oxidation of a hexose sugar is normally 1, and for oxidation of fatty substances, considerably less than 1.

Sablon (1896) long ago showed that sugars disappeared from tree seeds while oils increased and interpreted this to mean that they were converted into oil. Thor and Smith (1935) showed that in pecan, sugar decreases while fat accumulates in the seed, but the amount of sugar which disappears cannot account for more than 5 per cent of the fat which appears in the same period of time. Thus it seems that the substrate from which the fats are formed is translocated into the seed during fat formation. During germination of the seed the process is reversed and fats are converted to sugars which are translocated to growing tissues of the young seedling.

Several early investigators concluded that during the normal seasonal cycle starch is converted directly to fat, or fat directly to starch, and that such conversions are promoted by temperature changes (Fischer, 1891; Tuttle, 1919, 1921). There is considerable evidence, however, which indicates that seasonal fat cycles are internally controlled metabolic phenomena and are not influenced directly by temperature. Arrhenius (1942) found that fat breakdown in the wood did not begin in all species at the same time of year and questioned the importance of temperature alone. Gäumann (1935) found that in beech the use of fat as a respiratory substrate was high shortly after the stem thawed but the conversion of oils to carbohydrates during this season was too small to measure. Ishibe (1935) summarized considerable evidence indicating that annual changes in starch and fat reserves of deciduous trees represent two distinct cycles. Other investigators have questioned the existence of a close relationship between temperature and changes in fat content (Weber, 1909; Niklewski, 1906; Gardner, 1929a; Sinnott, 1918).

Composition of Tree Fats

Oleic acid seems to be the most widely distributed and most abundant fatty acid in tree fats. Oleic, palmitic, linoleic, and occasionally linolenic acids occur in the fats of both seeds and vegetative structures. Oleic acid is reported to be the chief constituent of bark fats in several species (Hilditch, 1949; Eckey, 1954), but Kurth and Hubbard (1951) found chiefly saturated fatty acids in the fat from bark of ponderosa pine. The fatty acids most commonly found in tree fats are shown in Table 6.4.

In addition to the fatty acids almost universally present, fats of some trees contain a fatty acid characteristic of the botanical family to which they belong. According to Hilditch (1949), the fatty acid components of seed fats might be used as a basis for a system of classification. The American elm is an interesting exception to the general rule that related species produce similar fats, because its seed fat contains about 50 per cent of capric acid (Hilditch, 1949), a fatty acid not found in seeds of other species of elm.

Trees of cool climates tend to produce more unsaturated fatty acids than trees of warm climates. Furthermore, a species with a wide climatic range usually produces more unsaturated fatty acids, such as linoleic and linolenic acid, in the cooler part of its range than in the warmer part.

Waxes

Waxes may occur as leaf cuticles, fruit cuticles, and seed coat covers. Like fats they may also be dispersed in cells. Since waxes are resistant to decomposition and are insoluble in water they make an excellent protective covering and reduce water loss from plant tissues. For the most part they are found outside of cells. The "bloom" of fruits, such as plums, consists of wax deposits.

Waxes are esters in which simple fatty acids are combined with monohydric alcohols of high molecular weight. These alcohols generally contain from 24 to 36 carbon atoms. The term "wax" is often extended to include other chemical compounds that have physical properties similar to the waxes as here defined. Some waxes are fatty acid esters of sterols.

The same fatty acids which frequently occur in fats are often found in waxes. Thus acids such as lauric, myristic, palmitic, and stearic occur frequently. All these are relatively short chain acids, while the bulk of the acids in wax esters have longer chains than C_{18}. Unsaturated acids are relatively unimportant in waxes.

Among the best-known commercial waxes obtained from trees is carnauba wax obtained from the leaves of the palm *Copernicia cerifera* of Brazil. Carnauba wax contains about 80 per cent alkyl esters of wax acids and 10 per cent free monohydric alcohols, with small amounts of other materials.

Palm wax obtained from the wax palm (*Ceroxylon andicola*) occurs on the tree trunk in layers up to an inch in thickness. As much as 25 pounds can be obtained from a single tree. Palm wax consists of about one-third true wax, while the remainder is resin. Other commercial palm waxes are ouricuri wax, obtained from the undersurface of the leaves of the Attalea palm (*Attalea excelsa*) and raffia wax, obtained from the dried leaves of the Madagascar raffia palm, *Raphia pedunculata* (Deuel, 1951).

Among the broadleaf trees which yield wax are species of *Eucalyptus,* notably *Eucalyptus gunni* var. *acervula* of Tasmania. Another wax is obtained from the leaves of white sandalwood (*Santalum album*).

Much knowledge about the structure of waxes comes from work on the wax of the apple cuticle. Sando (1923) showed that the amount of wax varied with the species of apple. Markley and coworkers (1932) showed that the principal hydrocarbon present in apple cuticle wax was *n*-nona-cosane, $CH_3(CH_2)_{27}CH_3$. In addition to hydrocarbons several alcohols were found, the most important of which was a secondary alcohol, 10-nonacosanol. The wax of the pear skin was studied by Markley et al. (1935), who reported on its chemical composition and found it similar in some respects to the wax of the apple cuticle.

Citrus waxes are found in the pulp and peel of the fruit. The composition of the wax of Florida grapefruit was reported by Markley et al. (1937).

Terpenes

The terpenes are plant products which may be regarded as being built up of multiples of isoprene units, C_5H_8. Among the important terpenes are essential oils, resins, carotene, latex, gutta-percha, and rubber. These compounds are not considered to be important food reserves in plants. In fact, most of them appear to have no essential functions, but they include some commercially important substances. The relationship of various terpene classes to isoprene, as summarized by Bonner (1950), is given in Figure 6.6.

Essential Oils. The substances that give aromatic odors to leaves and twigs of many trees, especially conifers, are chemically classed as essential oils, also sometimes termed volatile oils or ethereal oils. Essential oils are highly variable and complex in composition, as indicated by the fact that over 500 specific compounds have been isolated from them. Most essential oils, however, are considered to be primarily lower members of the terpenes. They are straight-chain or cyclic compounds and may be monoterpenes ($C_{10}H_{16}$), sesquiterpenes ($C_{15}H_{24}$), or diterpenes

($C_{20}H_{32}$). The characteristics of various essential oils are determined by the chemical groups associated with them.

Essential oils are not restricted to conifers, but also are commonly found in broadleaf trees such as *Citrus* and *Eucalyptus*, and in fact they occur in about 0.5 per cent of all higher plants. The families Pinaceae, Umbelliferae, Myrtaceae, Lauraceae, Rutaceae, Labiatae, and Compositae often produce essential oils. Although most commonly found in bark, wood, and leaf tissue of trees, these compounds may also be found in fruits and flowers. They are formed in specialized ducts, glands, glandular hairs, or other specialized cells. Many essential oils are steam-volatile, although some, such as citrus oils, are expressible. In contrast to the fats,

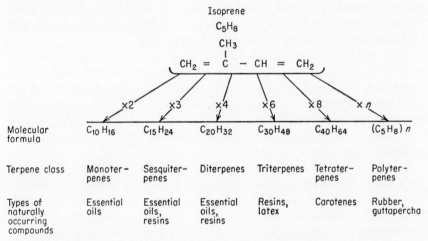

Figure 6.6 Diagram showing relationships of essential oils, resins, carotene, and rubber. (*Adapted from Bonner, 1950.*)

they do not serve as reserve foods in plants but are considered to be by-products of metabolism with no established metabolic role. Since many are volatile, they are continuously lost from trees by evaporation, especially during the day (Bonner, 1950). Examples are the odors associated with many conifers and fragrant flowers.

Essential oils are commercially extracted from conifer leaves for use as scenting agents. The attractive odors are due mainly to the presence of borneol and bornyl esters. Conifer leaf oils are found in longitudinal ducts. They are typically steam-distilled, and oil yields of conifers generally range from 0.4 to 0.6 per cent but yields exceeding 1 per cent have been commonly recorded (Bailey, 1948). Oils are extracted on a commercial scale from leaves of eastern arborvitae, black spruce, balsam fir, and eastern hemlock; and from cedar wood, sweet birch bark, and sassafras roots and buds by steam distillation. Tall oil and turpentine are also obtained in this manner.

Resins. Resins are a heterogeneous mixture of resin acids ($C_{20}H_{30}O_2$), fatty acids, esters of these acids, sterols, alcohols, waxes, and resenes (Wise and Jahn, 1952).

Conifers and hardwoods both synthesize resins, but conifers usually produce much larger amounts. Resin yields of 0.8 to 25 per cent have been reported for coniferous woods as against only 0.7 to 3 per cent for hardwoods (Wise and Jahn, 1952). Most resin used commercially comes from the families Pinaceae, Leguminosae, and Dipterocarpaceae. Copals are a group of resins extracted from forest trees of the Leguminosae and are known for their hardness and high melting point. Trees of the Dipterocarpaceae produce a resin called "dammar" in commerce. Another commercially important resin is "Kauri gum," obtained from the Kauri tree (*Agathis australis*) of New Zealand (Howes, 1949).

Most resins are secreted in special ducts or canals. Such ducts are lined with specialized cells which secrete resin into them through a thin membrane. The canals often are much branched, so that when one of the branches is tapped or wounded, resins will flow toward the cut area from considerable distances. Resins may also be found occasionally in cell interiors and in cell walls. They are not used as reserve foods, and their metabolic role in trees is obscure.

Haaglund (1951) distinguishes between physiological and pathological resin, the former occurring normally inside the woody tissue while formation of the latter is a result of bark or wood injury. Büsgen and Münch (1931) have emphasized the protective nature of resins. They point out that sapwood of resinous pine does not decay readily while spruce wood, which is low in resin, is more easily infected with decay fungi.

An abnormal flow of resin, called "resinosis," may be stimulated by wounds or presence of fungus disease. Resinosis is a characteristic of stem parts of conifers that are affected with white pine blister rust, larch canker, and red ring rot of spruce. Root collars of pines may show pronounced resinosis when shoestring rot caused by *Armillaria mellea* is present. A fungus disease of planted white and red pines known as "resinosis disease" is characterized by copious resin flow from the butts of trees (Boyce, 1948).

Oleoresins. The most important resins commercially are the oleoresins obtained from pines. Oleoresin is a term applied to the viscous liquid secreted by cells bordering the resin ducts of conifers. Its composition is approximately 66 per cent resin acids, 7 per cent nonvolatile neutral material, 25 per cent turpentine, an essential oil, and 2 per cent water (Wise and Jahn, 1952).

Oleoresin-yielding tissues are parenchymatous and occur in roots, leaves, stemwood, and inner bark. Oleoresin is produced by living cells, so-called epithelial cells, which separate to form resin canals or ducts which are especially active in the outer sapwood. Longitudinal and transverse resin canals are a normal feature of pines, spruces, larches, and Douglas-fir, while traumatic or wound canals may occur in hemlock, true firs, and redwood. Streaking, boring, or scarifying the tree exposes the resin canals, and oleoresin oozes out. Oleoresin yield varies not only between species but also between different trees of the same species. Bourdeau and Schopmeyer (1958) found the amount of flow in slash pine to be controlled by the number and size of resin ducts, resin pressures, and viscosity of the exudate. Resin pressures vary diurnally in the same tree and appear to be related to changes in stem hydration. Bourdeau and Schopmeyer (1958) found that the highest resin pressures occurred about dawn and the lowest pressures in the afternoon when moisture stresses are likely to develop in rapidly transpiring trees. The ability of individual trees to produce large quantities of oleoresin appears to be an inherited characteristic (Mergen et al., 1955).

Composition of turpentine of southeastern and western pines of the United States varies considerably. Turpentine of southeastern pines is of relatively simple composition and consists essentially of two monoterpenes, alpha and beta pinenes. Turpentines of western pines are complex and contain, in addition to the pinenes, some aliphatic hydrocarbons, aliphatic aldehydes, Δ-3-carene, and sesquiterpenes. Turpentine of southeastern pines resembles that of European species, while that of western areas resembles turpentine from pines of southeast Asia (Mirov, 1954).

After the volatile turpentine has been removed from the oleoresin by distillation, the remaining substance, a hard resin, varying in color from amber to almost black, is called rosin. Its chief constituent is abietic acid.

Other commercially important oleoresins are "Canada balsam" and "Oregon balsam." The former, obtained from balsam fir, is secreted in resin canals formed by separation of cells in the bark and found in small blisters under the bark. Oregon balsam, obtained from Douglas-fir, is found in cavities of the tree which were produced by wind shake.

Rubber

Rubber is formed by about 2,000 species of plants, including herbs, shrubs, trees, and vines. According to Bonner and Galston (1947), rubber is formed only in dicotyledonous angiosperms and is not synthesized by monocotyledons, gymnosperms, or lower plants. Especially well represented with rubber-producing species are the families Euphorbiaceae, Moraceae, Apocynaceae, Asclepiadaceae, and Compositae. Most rubber-producing woody plants are tropical, and guayule is said to be the only Temperate Zone woody plant that produces enough rubber for commercial extraction. The chief source of natural rubber is the tropical tree *Hevea brasiliensis*.

Rubber may be characterized as a polyterpene composed of 500 to 5,000 isoprene units joined linearly in the following pattern:

$$\underset{\text{Isoprene}}{-CH_2-\underset{\underset{CH_3}{|}}{C}=CH-CH_2-}\ \underset{\text{Isoprene}}{-CH_2-\underset{\underset{CH_3}{|}}{C}=CH-CH_2-}$$

Rubber occurs in plants as suspended particles in latex, a liquid produced in specialized cells or ducts. Latex is a complex system containing a variety of substances in solution or suspension. Among these are terpene derivatives, sugars, starch grains, organic acids, sterols, and enzymes. The exact composition varies widely among species and even among individual plants of the same species. Starch grains occur in latex of *Euphorbia*, but not in *Hevea* latex. *Ficus* latex is high in protein, the latex of *Papaver somniferum* is high in the alkaloids of opium, and the latex of *Carica papaya* is the commercial source of the enzyme papain. The chicle used in chewing gum is obtained from latex of a tropical tree, *Achras zapota*.

Rubber does not occur in the latex of all plants and when present usually is found in very low concentrations. It occurs in commercially useful quantities in only a few species, notably in *Hevea brasiliensis*, where it comprises 20 to 60 per cent of the latex on a dry-weight basis, and in guayule, where it sometimes amounts to over 20 per cent of the dry weight of the plant. Neither latex nor rubber is used as reserve food by plants.

Latex occasionally is formed in parenchyma cells, as in guayule, but usually is formed in latex vessels. These are ducts produced by the elongation of single cells or the union of many specialized cells to form complex systems (Esau, 1953). In woody plants such as *H. brasiliensis* the latex ducts occur chiefly in the bark as vertically oriented tubes up to several meters in length.

When the vessels are opened, as by tapping a rubber tree, the latex flows out because of the turgor pressure which was imposed on it. According to Frey-Wyssling (1952), latex flow obeys Poiseuille's law for flow of liquids through capillaries, the elasticity of the walls of the vessels producing the pressure gradient. When first tapped latex of high viscosity flows slowly, but decreased turgor results in increased intake of water, diluting the latex and increasing the rate of flow (Spencer, 1939b). If the latex coagulates at the point of tapping, turgor pressure in the tubes increases, the diffusion pressure deficit decreases, and water moves out of the vessels. When flow stops, latex tends to regain its original concentration (Moyer, 1937).

The pressure and rate of flow seem to depend at least in part on the internal water balance of the tree and therefore vary with season, site conditions, and time of day, as well as with the tree. Curtis and Blondeau (1946) found maximum yields of latex and rubber in the morning and low yields in the afternoon. Bangham (1934) observed that latex actually spurted out to a distance of several feet from trees tapped early in the morning. No latex vessels occur in guayule, and it cannot be tapped; hence rubber is obtained by mechanical extraction of the entire plant.

GENERAL REFERENCES

Bonner, J., 1950, Plant biochemistry, Academic Press, Inc., New York.
—— and A. W. Galston, 1947, The physiology and biochemistry of rubber formation in plants, Bot. Rev., 13:543–596.
Eckey, E., 1954, Vegetable fats and oils, Reinhold Publishing Corporation, New York.
Esau, K., 1953, Plant anatomy, chap. 13, Laticifers, John Wiley & Sons, Inc., New York.
Frey-Wyssling, A. (ed.), 1952, Deformation and flow in biological systems, chap. 5, Latex flow, North-Holland Publishing Co., Amsterdam.
Guenther, E., et al., 1948–1952, The essential oils, vols. 1 to 6, D Van Nostrand Company, Inc., Princeton, N.J.
Hilditch, T. P., 1949, Chemical constitution of natural fats, John Wiley & Sons, Inc., New York.
Howes, F. N., 1949, Vegetable gums and resins, Chronica Botanica Co., Waltham, Mass.
Ruhland, W. (ed.), 1957, Encyclopedia of plant physiology, vol. 7, The metabolism of fats and related compounds, M. Steiner (subed.), Springer-Verlag, Berlin.
Wise, L. E., and E. C. Jahn, 1952, Wood chemistry, Reinhold Publishing Corporation, New York.

CHAPTER 7 *Assimilation and Respiration*

The food manufactured by plants is used in assimilation and respiration. In fact, foods often are defined as substances which can be used as a substrate in respiration or as building materials in assimilation. The surplus not used in these two processes is accumulated in fruits, seeds, and the vegetative structures.

ASSIMILATION

The conversion of food into new protoplasm and cell walls by the existing protoplasm is called "assimilation." It is an integral part of growth and therefore is concentrated in the meristematic regions such as the cambiums and root and stem tips. The simple carbohydrates translocated to these regions are converted into cellulose, pectic compounds, and lignin in new cell walls, and the amino acids and amides into the protein framework of new protoplasm. Small amounts of fats, mineral nutrients, and growth-promoting substances also are used. A variety of enzymes is involved in these complex transformations, which also require large amounts of chemical energy.

Assimilation might be termed the "crossroads" of plant metabolism because of the extensive interconversion of compounds that occurs during the complex biochemical syntheses which characterize the process. The existing protoplasm not only produces new protoplasm and new cell walls, but it also produces a wide variety of other substances. Among these are the alkaloids, the anthocyanins, carotenes, chlorophylls and other pigments, isoprene derivatives such as essential oils, oleoresins, and rubber, the sterols, the tannins, and many other substances. Some of these play important roles in plant metabolism, but others such as the alkaloids and rubber seem to have no useful role.

The formation of lignin is a good example of assimilation. It is of special interest to physiologists and foresters because of its importance as a

160

constituent of cell walls in woody plants. In spite of many decades of research and many hundreds of publications on lignin, neither its composition nor its synthesis has been completely worked out. Many of the problems of lignin formation are discussed in the series of papers presented at the Third Lignin Round Table, published in Volume 40 of *Tappi* (1957). Apparently lignin consists of phenyl propane units linked with carbohydrates. Coniferyl and sinapyl alcohols generally are regarded as important precursors; but Kremers (1957) claims that the glucosides of these alcohols occur much less extensively than does lignin; hence other precursors must be involved.

Kremers (1957) pointed out that lignification requires large amounts of energy because the heat of combustion of lignin is 6.3 calories per gram, compared with 3.7 calories per gram for glucose. Large amounts of food are used in cell wall formation. Kremers estimated that for each gram of cell wall material present in the primary stage, 20 grams is added by maturity. Of this about 11 grams is added as cellulose and 5 grams as lignin. Stewart (1957) summarized the available information on the chemical processes occurring in active cambium.

It seems that more work is desirable on the relation between environmental factors and the structure and composition of cell walls. It might prove possible to modify the course of assimilation and thereby change both the quantity and the quality of wood produced.

Basically, the course of assimilation and the substances produced by plants are controlled by their heredity. Heredity probably operates by controlling the kinds of enzymes produced. Each species of pine produces its own specific kind of oleoresin, and geographic races may even show characteristic differences in their resins (Mirov, 1954, 1958). Zobel (1951) found differences in oleoresins useful in identifying hybrid pines, and Gibbs (1945, 1958) and Towers and Gibbs (1953) attempted to correlate chemical characteristics with the taxonomic position of various tree species. McNair (1945) has done considerable work on the relation between environment, taxonomic classification, and the kinds of fats produced by various plants.

Various aspects of assimilation are discussed in other chapters, although they are not always so designated. Almost every discussion of metabolism deals with processes which may be termed assimilation because they contribute to the formation of the plant structure and its products.

RESPIRATION

Respiration is essential because it supplies the energy required for assimilation and other energy-using processes such as fat and protein synthesis, mineral absorption, and maintenance of protoplasmic structure. An understanding of the process of respiration is necessary for a good understanding of various phases of plant behavior. Root growth and seed germination often are hindered by soil conditions which limit respiration. Successful storage of many kinds of fruits and seeds depends at least partly on maintenance of an environment which controls respiration at a suitable rate. Furthermore, respiration sometimes becomes a competitor of assimilation and accumulation for food, resulting in reduced growth and inadequate accumulation of reserves.

Some Characteristics of Respiration

Respiration is difficult to define precisely, but it can be described as the oxidation of food in living cells, accompanied by the release of energy. The energy released was stored as chemical energy in the bonds between atoms and groups of the substrate molecules. Part of the energy is stored as chemical energy of high-energy phosphate bonds which can be used to drive energy-requiring reactions. Some is released as mechanical energy, such as that exhibited in protoplasmic streaming, some in the form of electrical energy, and some as heat, and some is used to maintain the structure of protoplasm. Respiration usually is accompanied by the uptake of oxygen, release of carbon dioxide, and decrease in dry weight.

Respiration occurs continuously in all living cells of plants, but the rate is extremely low in some structures such as dormant seeds. It is most rapid in meristematic regions such as cambiums and root and stem tips and in young leaves. It sometimes is very rapid in maturing fruits. In growing tissues some of the energy released is used in synthetic processes, but much or even most escapes as heat. In mature tissues such as ripe fruits practically all the energy is released as heat which serves no useful function in plants (James, 1953). Much of the energy released in anaerobic respiration also is unavailable for plant processes. Furthermore, anaerobic respiration releases only a small fraction of the energy released by aerobic respiration. Fermentation of glucose to alcohol, for example, releases slightly over 3 per cent of the energy released by its complete oxidation to carbon dioxide and water, while aerobic respiration releases about 65 per cent in a usable form.

Although some minimal level of respiration is essential for cell survival and a somewhat higher rate is needed for growth, the rate of respiration often rises far above the essential level. This results in useless consumption of food which might have been used in assimilation to produce new tissue or accumulated in storage organs. As respiration occurs in all living tissues all the time and photosynthesis occurs only in the light and chiefly in the leaves, the rate of photosynthesis must be several times as rapid as the rate of respiration per unit of tissue, if any net increase in dry weight is to occur. As shown in Figures 7.2 and 7.3, a large fraction of the food produced by trees is used in respiration. Polster (1950) suggested that the productivity of a forest might be increased more by treatments which reduce respiration than by treatments to increase photosynthesis.

If atmospheric oxygen is absent, anaerobic respiration or fermentation occurs, no atmospheric oxygen being used. At low oxygen concentrations both aerobic and anaerobic respiration often occur. Anaerobic respiration occurs in roots and rhizomes in poorly aerated soils and in tissues where entrance of oxygen is restricted by impermeable structures such as fruit and seed coats and by bud scales. Anaerobic respiration generally is undesirable because most of the energy released is not available for growth (James, 1953) and because its products often are toxic to the tissues in which they are formed.

The first stages of aerobic and anaerobic respiration of carbohydrates are the same, and the relationship can be shown as follows:

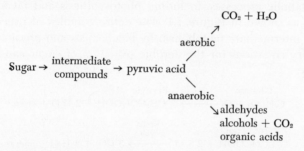

Biological Oxidations. Respiration is an oxidation process, and oxidations basically involve the removal of electrons from the substance being oxidized. They usually are transferred to some acceptor, which thereby is reduced. Occasionally oxygen is actually added to the system, as when carbon monoxide is oxidized to carbon dioxide and the electrons are moved from the carbon atom to the carbon-oxygen bond. More often hydrogen atoms (electrons plus protons) are split off from the substrate, as shown in the Krebs cycle, and transferred to a hydrogen acceptor. In the oxidation of food the hydrogen atoms usually are split off in pairs by enzymes known as dehydrogenases and are transferred through a series of acceptors, finally combining with oxygen to form water. Much of the energy released is used to form high-energy phosphate bonds which are coupled to adenosinediphosphate (ADP) to form adenosinetriphosphate (ATP).

According to current views, 38 high-energy phosphate bonds are formed in the aerobic oxidation of a molecule of glucose. A total of 10 are formed during glycolysis, but 2 are used, making a net gain of 8. An average of 3 high-energy phosphate bonds are formed for each of the

5 pairs of hydrogen atoms oxidized to water in the Krebs cycle, or a total of 30 for 2 molecules of pyruvic acid which result from a molecule of glucose. If the energy of such a bond is 12,000 calories, about 456,000 calories, or about 65 per cent of the total energy in the glucose, is transferred to these high-energy phosphate bonds, where they are available as an energy source for other chemical reactions. The remainder of the energy is dissipated as heat.

Readers who are interested in the biochemistry of respiration should turn to more advanced texts for detailed descriptions of these processes.

Mechanism of Respiration

Respiration is not a single independent process, but consists of a series of steps. These steps fall into two groups, a preliminary group known as glycolysis which terminates in pyruvic acid and a second group concerned with the oxidation of pyruvic acid. Some of the steps are linked to other metabolic processes, including photosynthesis and fat and protein synthesis, as shown in Figure 7.1. The entire complex of processes often is termed intermediary metabolism by biochemists and physiologists.

Summary equations for the aerobic oxidation of sugar can be written as follows:

$$\text{Glucose} \quad \xrightarrow{\text{glycolysis}} \quad \text{Pyruvic acid}$$
$$C_6H_{12}O_6 + O_2 \longrightarrow 2\ CH_3COCOOH + 2\ H_2O + \text{energy}$$

$$\text{Pyruvic acid} \quad \xrightarrow{\substack{\text{Krebs} \\ \text{cycle}}}$$
$$CH_3COCOOH + 2.5\ O_2 \longrightarrow 3\ CO_2 + 2\ H_2O + \text{energy}$$

Thus a molecule of glucose yields 2 molecules of pyruvic acid and 2 molecules of water and each molecule of pyruvic acid when completely oxidized yields 3 molecules of carbon dioxide and 2 molecules of water, or a total 6 molecules of carbon dioxide and 6 molecules of water per molecule of glucose.

As indicated in Figure 7.1, in the early stages of carbohydrate respiration, or glycolysis, hexose sugars undergo phosphorylation. Phosphate esters are formed by transfer of phosphate ion from ATP to sugar, producing glucose phosphate and fructose phosphate and ADP. Later in this series of processes phosphate groups are transferred from the sugars to form ATP. The energy stored in the high-energy phosphate bonds of ATP is available for driving various energy-using reactions in physiological processes. A relatively small fraction of the total energy is released during glycolysis.

Pyruvic acid, the end product of glycolysis, is a key compound in this series of reactions. Under aerobic conditions a molecule of carbon dioxide and 2 hydrogen atoms are split off and a derivative of pyruvic acid called acetyl coenzyme A is produced. Acetyl coenzyme A combines with oxaloacetic acid to form a 6-carbon atom acid, probably citric acid. Citric acid is successively converted to 5- and 4-carbon atom acids as carbon dioxide molecules and hydrogen atoms are split off, and the cycle finally returns to oxaloacetic acid, as shown in Figure 7.1. This is known as the Krebs or tricarboxylic acid cycle.

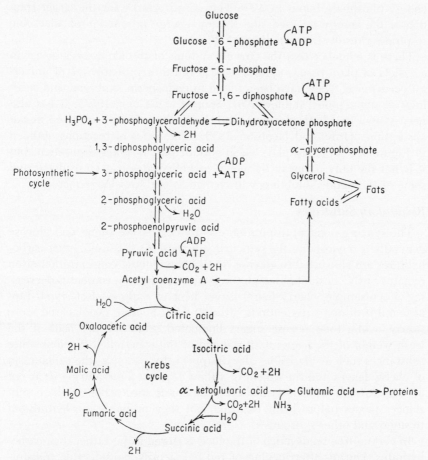

Figure 7.1 An abbreviated outline of the principal steps in glycolysis and the Krebs cycle.

According to this scheme carbon atoms are split off by decarboxylase enzymes in the formation of acetyl coenzyme A, α-ketoglutaric acid, and succinic acid, producing 3 molecules of carbon dioxide per molecule of pyruvic acid oxidized. Pairs of hydrogen atoms are split off in the formation of acetyl coenzyme A, α-ketoglutaric acid, succinic, fumaric, and oxaloacetic acids by dehydrogenase enzymes. These hydrogen ions are passed through a series of acceptors and finally are combined with oxygen to form water by the action of enzyme systems known as "oxidases." A total of five pairs of hydrogen ions are split off in this series of reactions, but 3 molecules of water are used in the cycle, resulting in a net release of 2 molecules of water per molecule of pyruvic acid.

The energy released during the formation of water is stored as high-energy phosphate bonds in ATP. This constitutes by far the larger fraction of the energy released, and the low-energy production of anaerobic respiration results from omission of this stage.

There is evidence that the enzyme systems of the Krebs cycle occur in a variety of plant tissues (James, 1953), and they probably are of universal occurrence. They have been found in endosperm, embryos, and seedlings of sugar pine (Stanley, 1957; Stanley and Conn, 1957). It has also been shown that both glycolysis and the Krebs cycle are involved in salt absorption (Ordin and Jacobson, 1955). The series of reactions outlined in Figure 7.1 probably plays an important part in plant respiration, but it is not the only pathway by which carbohydrates can be oxidized and some of the details doubtless will change as our knowledge increases.

Respiratory Substrates

The starting point in respiration usually is a hexose sugar, and glucose generally is regarded as the principal substrate. As it is used, other carbohydrates are converted to glucose, so that the glucose concentration often remains fairly constant although the total carbohydrate content is decreasing. For example, cherry laurel leaves kept in darkness lost starch rapidly and it disappeared entirely after 10 days. Sucrose disappeared more slowly, while total hexose sugars fluctuated around 1 per cent of the fresh weight of the leaves until the end of the experiment. Various other substances such as glycosides also disappear, for example, the prulaurasin of cherry leaves and the salicin of willow leaves (James, 1953). It is not certain through what intermediate compounds the carbon in these substances passes before being oxidized, but they probably are hydrolyzed to sugar and other substances.

In certain tree seeds much of the food is stored as fat rather than carbohydrates. During afterripening of red oak acorns, considerable transformation of fats to carbohydrates occurs (Korstian, 1927; Miller, 1938; Brown, 1939). It generally is stated that fats are transformed to carbohydrates before being used as a respiratory substrate (Murlin, 1933), but fatty acids might enter the Krebs cycle by way of acetyl coenzyme A, as indicated in Figure 7.1.

Respiratory Quotient

The respiratory quotient is the ratio of carbon dioxide produced to oxygen consumed, and it is a useful indicator of the type of substrate being used in respiration. The respiratory quotient is approximately 1 for complete oxidation of carbohydrates, about 0.7 for proteins, and as low as 0.6 for fats because of their low initial oxygen content. On the other hand, if certain organic acids are being oxidized, the respiratory quotient will be greater than 1. Thus measurement of the respiratory quotient aids in determining what kind of material constitutes the principal substrate.

Brown (1939) found the ratio of carbon dioxide produced to oxygen used in acorns to be about 0.5 when they matured, but it decreased gradually during the afterripening period and reached 0.1 to 0.2 by the time the acorns were ready to germinate. These low ratios were believed to be caused by heavy consumption of oxygen, resulting from conversion of fats to carbohydrates during afterripening.

Measurement of Respiration

Because of its importance as an indicator of metabolic activity and of the reaction of trees and seeds to their environment, it often is desirable to measure respiration. This is done most frequently by measuring the uptake of oxygen or the production of carbon dioxide. It can also be done by measuring the change in dry weight of successive samples or even by estimating the change in organic matter in comparable samples by means of a bomb calorimeter.

Carbon dioxide production can be measured by essentially the same methods used in measuring photosynthesis, i.e., by measuring the change in carbon dioxide concentration in a stream of air passed over the respiring material. The carbon dioxide concentration of the air stream can be measured either by absorption in alkali and titration of the alkali (Heinicke and Childers, 1937), by change in conductivity of a dilute alkali solution (Decker, 1944), or by passage through an infrared gas analyzer (Huber, 1950; Parker, 1953b). Carbon dioxide production by small samples of seeds or other tissue can be measured in Warburg respirometers and their various modifications (Umbreit et al., 1957) or in microrespirometers such as those described by Scholander (1947) and by Pollock and Steward (1949).

Oxygen consumption of small samples can also be measured in Warburg and other small respirometers of the type just mentioned for measurement of carbon dioxide. Changes in oxygen concentration in closed systems also can be measured rapidly and conveniently by various models of Beckman oxygen analyzers. The classical method of measuring carbon dioxide and oxygen concentrations in closed systems by means of an Orsat-type gas analyzer is so tedious that it has been supplanted by more rapid methods.

Although it is comparatively easy to measure gas exchange, it sometimes is difficult to interpret the results. For example, afterripened red oak acorns show much greater oxygen consumption in proportion to carbon dioxide production than recently collected acorns (Figure 14.8), and it may be questioned whether oxygen uptake or carbon dioxide production is the better indicator of respiration. In this instance carbon dioxide production may be the better basis because much of the oxygen absorbed appears to have been used in the conversion of fats to carbohydrates. Of course, in a certain sense conversion of fats to carbohydrates is a form of respiration, because it involves oxidation of food in living cells. Questions may also arise as to whether respiration should be expressed in terms of fresh weight, dry weight, per unit of nitrogen, or some other basis. This usually must be decided in terms of the objectives of the experiments.

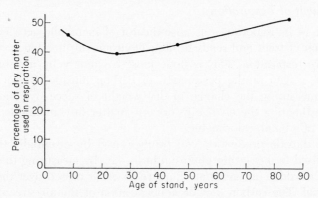

Figure 7.2   The percentage of food produced which is used in respiration by stands of beech trees of various ages. (*From Möller et al., 1954.*)

Amount of Food Used in Respiration

The total amount of food used in respiration by a tree is of interest because it affects the amount available for assimilation and accumulation. Practically all the food is manufactured in the leaves, but it is used in respiration by every living tissue in the plant. The total used in respiration by leaves, twigs, and the living tissues of trunks and roots amounts to a considerable fraction of the total food produced.

The Tree as a Whole. It was estimated that about one-third of the food produced by photosynthesis was used in respiration by the 8-year-old apple tree studied by Heinicke and Childers (1937). According to Möller et al. (1954), the proportion of food used in respiration by trees increases with age. As shown in Figure 7.2, about 40 per cent of the product of photosynthesis is used in respiration by 25-year-old trees but about 50 per cent is used in 85-year-old trees. This occurs because the ratio of respiring tissue to photosynthetic tissue increases with age, while the efficiency per unit of leaf area decreases somewhat. The leaf area remains fairly constant; the volume of living tissue increases. Perhaps one reason young trees grow more rapidly than older ones is that they have a higher ratio of photosynthetic surface to respiring tissue than older trees, providing more food for growth. According to Möller et al. (1954), decrease in net dry-matter production of older stands is caused partly by decreased photosynthesis and partly by a small increase in loss of dry matter by respiration and loss of roots, branches, and twigs. Figure 7.3

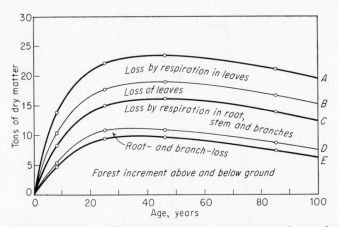

Figure 7.3 The amounts of dry matter used in various processes by stands of European beech of various ages growing on good sites in Denmark. The ordinate represents metric tons of dry matter per hectare per year. The upper heavy curve (A) indicates total or gross production by photosynthesis. The middle heavy curve (C) indicates net photosynthesis, and the lower heavy curve (E) indicates the amount of dry matter added in growth each year. The area between curves A and B represents loss of dry matter by leaf respiration, that between B and C loss by leaf fall. The area between curves C and D represents loss of dry matter by respiration in roots, stems, and branches, and the area between D and E represents dry matter lost by death of roots and branches. (*From Möller et al., 1954.*)

shows Möller's estimates of total apparent photosynthesis, losses by respiration, and net increase in dry weight in stands of beech trees of various ages in Denmark. Möller (1946) also calculated the annual loss by respiration for stands of different species and concluded that a larger percentage of the food manufactured is used in respiration by hardwoods than by spruce.

It seems probable that in healthy, vigorously growing trees both photosynthesis and respiration are more rapid than in less vigorous trees of the same age; hence it is likely that the percentage of carbohydrate used by respiration is relatively constant for trees of the same age, within a species (Baker, 1950).

It might be expected that a tree growing in the open with a large crown would have a higher ratio of photosynthesis to respiration and hence would grow more rapidly than a tree growing in a closed stand and having a small crown. This is generally true, but it has been found that in some species the larger, lower branches apparently contribute little to trunk growth. For example, it appears that the branches can be pruned from the lower two-thirds of the trunks of loblolly pine without causing any serious reduction in diameter growth. Apparently most of the food manufactured by the leaves on the lower branches of loblolly pine is used

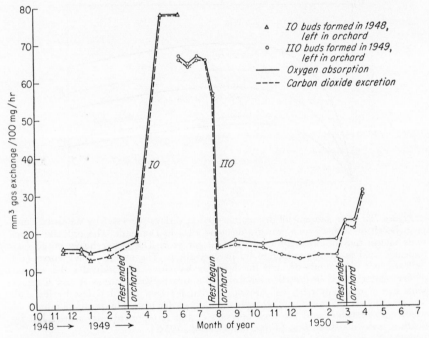

Figure 7.4 Seasonal cycle in respiration of pear buds. (*From Thom*, 1951.)

locally in growth and respiration and does not reach the main stem (Labyak and Schumacher, 1954; Young and Kramer, 1952; Takahara, 1954).

Respiration of Various Parts. The rates of respiration of various parts of a tree vary widely, and this will be discussed separately for the different structures.

Leaves. In general, young leaves have high rates of respiration, but as they mature the amount of nonliving cell wall material increases in relation to the amount of protoplasm and the rate of respiration per unit of dry weight decreases. According to Wedding et al. (1952), the respiration rate of navel orange leaves was 19 per cent and that of Eureka lemon was 15.5 per cent of the rate of photosynthesis. These rates of respiration, if maintained during the entire 24 hours, would result in the leaves using 30 to 40 per cent of all the food which they had manufactured. This seems quite unlikely. Actually, the lower night temperatures would reduce the rate of respiration at night. It is estimated that the leaves of the apple tree studied by Heinicke and Childers (1937) used considerably less than 10 per cent of the total photosynthate in respiration.

Buds. Although buds constitute a very small part of the volume of a tree, they are regions of relatively high physiological activity during the growing season. There is, of course, a well-defined seasonal cycle in the respiration of buds. This is shown in Figure 7.4 from Thom (1951), where it can be seen that the respiration rate of growing pear buds is more than five times that of dormant buds. Kozlowski and Gentile (1958) reported that the rate of respiration of white pine buds increased rapidly at the time of bud break in the spring.

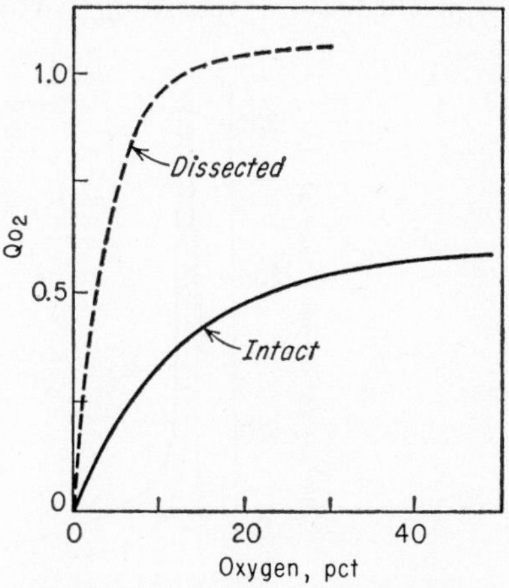

Figure 7.5 Effect of removal of bud scales on respiration of Norway maple buds. The curve for dissected buds was calculated from the respiration of its separate components for comparison with intact buds. (*From Pollock, 1953.*)

Although respiration of dormant buds is low, Gäumann (1935) found that buds of European beech lost about 6 per cent of their total dry weight and 16 per cent of their carbohydrate from mid-October to mid-December. Later much of the fat stored in them also disappeared, but after January the dry weight increased until April, when increased respiration caused a 25 per cent decrease.

According to Thom (1951), terminal buds of pear showed a more rapid increase in respiration and a higher rate than lateral buds. The behavior of the buds seemed to be independent of that of the twigs on which they were located, because twig respiration of pear remained high all summer, then decreased slowly until January, while bud respiration decreased abruptly in August when the buds became dormant, as shown in Figure 7.4.

Bud scales hinder the entrance of oxygen in Norway maple buds (Pollock, 1953) and white pine buds (Kozlowski and Gentile, 1958). Respiration of an intact maple bud is only about half as great as that of a bud from which the scales have been removed (Figure 7.5). Respiration of growing buds appears to be limited by oxygen supply because the rate increased with increasing oxygen concentration up to 100 per cent. Respiration of dormant buds was not increased by oxygen concentrations above 20 per cent. During much of the growing season the respiratory quotient of maple buds was higher than 1 and apparently anaerobic respiration occurred. Pollock thought that inhibitors were formed as a result of this anaerobic respiration, causing cessation of growth.

Stems. Respiration in tree stems is confined largely to the cambium and adjacent tissues. According to Goodwin and Goddard (1940), respiration

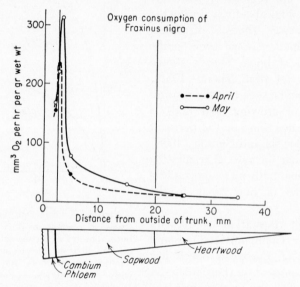

Figure 7.6 Rates of respiration (oxygen consumption) of various parts of a trunk of black ash before and after buds opened. (*From Goodwin and Goddard, 1940.*)

was highest in the cambium of red maple but in black ash it was even higher in the differentiating xylem adjacent to the cambium (Figure 7.6). Respiration was higher in the phloem than in all but the newest sapwood. In the inner sapwood the living ray and longitudinal parenchyma cells have high rates of respiration, but the number is so small that total respiration is very low.

Even the heartwood absorbed small amounts of oxygen, but this probably resulted from oxidation of organic compounds in dead cells rather than from respiration, because boiled pieces of heartwood absorbed nearly as much oxygen as unboiled wood (Table 7.1).

Möller (1946) also found the least respiration in the oldest part of the

Table 7.1. The effect of killing by boiling on oxygen consumption in various tissues of black ash. (*Goodwin and Goddard,* 1940.)

Tissue	Mm³ O₂ per hr per g wet weight		Percentage residual O₂ consumption after boiling
	Unboiled	Boiled 10 min	
Phloem	89.0	1.4	1.6
Cambium	181.0	0.0	0.0
Sapwood	18.7	2.1	11.2
Heartwood	2.3	2.0	87.0

tree trunk, and he reported that respiration was concentrated near the cambium to a greater extent in oak than in beech. In beech there was a very gradual decrease in respiration from the cambium inward and apparently some living cells existed even in the center of old trees. This might be expected in diffuse-porous species such as beech where heartwood seldom is formed.

Seasonal Variations. Marked seasonal variations in respiration occur, accompanying seasonal differences in growth, food supply, and temperature. Johansson (1933) measured respiration of stems and branches of intact trees throughout the growing season. In Figure 7.7 are shown curves for a hardwood and a conifer. As the carbon dioxide production of the surface was measured, the values probably represent largely the respiration of the inner bark and recently formed wood. Maximum respiration occurred at the same time that maximum diameter growth occurred. In some species diameter growth occurred in cycles and respiration followed the same pattern. Respiration of English oak and European beech declined rapidly during August, and by September it was only about 5 per cent of the July peak. Goodwin and Goddard (1940) reported that opening of buds was not accompanied by changes in respiration of the phloem, cambium, or older sapwood but there was a strong increase in the differentiating xylem. Probably this was the chief source of carbon dioxide in the study by Johansson (1933). Respiration of tree stems also varies diurnally, and it varies with exposure and stem height. Geurten (1950) found respiration of *Betula verrucosa* stems in Germany to be considerably higher on the south side than on other sides.

Gases in Tree Trunks

Considerable carbon dioxide is produced by the living cells in the cambium and wood, and this accumulates in vessels and tracheids, so that an appreciable fraction of the xylem may become filled with gas.

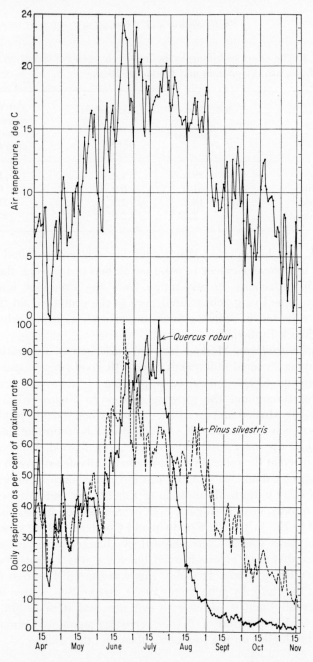

Figure 7.7 Seasonal variations in respiration of stems of *Quercus robur* and Scotch pine. A value of 100 on the ordinate is equivalent to 2.04 milligrams carbon dioxide per hour. Stems and portions of stems were enclosed in containers, and the carbon dioxide production of the enclosed area was measured. The behavior of Scotch pine is typical of most species studied in showing a good correlation with temperature. Oak is somewhat atypical because respiration decreases abruptly in late summer. (*From Johansson*, 1933.)

There is more gas in hardwoods than in conifers because the larger pores in the xylem elements of hardwoods result in more of them losing their water under tension. In general, the larger vessels tend to become filled with gas first, so there often are alternating water- and gas-filled regions in adjacent parts of an annual ring. MacDougal and Working (1933) claimed that in willow water occupied the summerwood and gas the

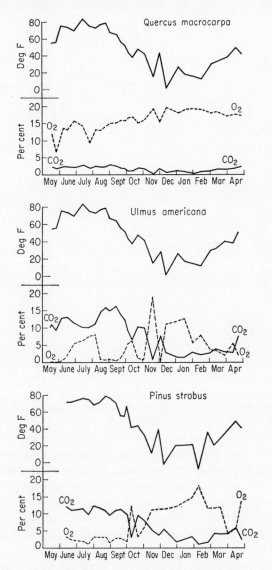

Figure 7.8 Seasonal variations in composition of gases in tree stems. (*From Chase,* 1934.)

springwood of several annual rings, resulting in concentric cylinders of water-filled tissue separated by cylinders of gas-filled tissue. In walnut, gas occupied chiefly the wood formed in midseason, but in pine and red-wood most of the cylinder within the outer three or four annual rings was occupied by gas.

The cylinder of cambium which encloses the wood offers such a barrier to the diffusion of gas that the concentration of oxygen generally is con-

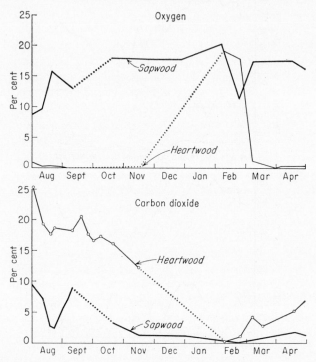

Figure 7.9 Seasonal variations in carbon dioxide and oxygen content of gas in sapwood and heartwood of poplar. Dotted lines indicate periods when samples were too small for analysis. (*From Chase*, 1934.)

siderably lower and the concentration of carbon dioxide generally is considerably higher inside the cambium than in the outside air. Chase (1934) studied seasonal fluctuations of gases in ring-porous, diffuse-porous, and nonporous tree stems. A definite relationship was found between metabolism and internal gas content, carbon dioxide content being higher in all species during the growing season and lowest during the winter. The carbon dioxide concentration was lower in oak stems than in white pine, poplar, or elm. Oxygen content varied inversely with carbon dioxide content during the year (Figure 7.8). There was more oxygen and less carbon dioxide in the sapwood than in the heartwood, as shown in Figure 7.9. Although respiration is most rapid in or near the cambium, the outer sapwood is filled with water and therefore accumulates little gas while the heartwood serves as a sort of gas-storage reservoir.

Chase found that rapidly growing trees such as cottonwood contained more carbon dioxide in their stem gas than more slowly growing species such as bur and red oak. There appeared to be no correlation between height and gas content.

The situation in the bark is quite different from that in the wood because the intercellular spaces of the cortex and phloem usually are connected with the outside air through lenticels. The gas pressure and composition in the bark therefore usually is similar to that of the outside air.

Abnormally high gas pressures are reported occasionally in tree stems. Abell and Hursh (1931) found in making increment borings in scarlet oak that gas escaped with a hissing sound, and even blew out the core. Similar positive pressures have been reported for blackgum, northern red oak, chestnut, pignut hickory, and two species of poplar (Gates, 1931; Haasis, 1931). In some instances the gas was inflammable. High gas pressures also have been found in elm trees suffering from the disease known as wet wood. Such gas pressures seem to result from the activities of organisms which are decaying the wood and have nothing to do with normal respiration. That they occur is evidence, however, that the outer wood is relatively impermeable to gases, even under pressure.

Roots and Pneumatophores

The respiration rate of roots and other underground structures is of particular interest because they often are exposed to low concentrations of oxygen (Chapter 16).

Roots. Meristematic regions of elongating root tips probably have among the highest respiration rates occurring in trees. Since root tips continue to grow much later in the season than do stem tips or the cambium of stems, a high respiratory activity is maintained by root tips for most of the frost-free season. In roots cambial cells and parenchyma cells also have high respiration rates. Respiration rates of root tips seem to vary among species (Voigt, 1953), probably because of differences in amounts of meristematic tissue present.

Some comparisons have been made of the respiration rates of mycorrhizal and nonmycorrhizal roots. Routien and Dawson (1943) reported that oxygen uptake and carbon dioxide production of 1-inch segments of mycorrhizal roots of shortleaf pine were two to four times greater than those of nonmycorrhizal roots. Mycorrhizal roots also respired more rapidly under anaerobic conditions. Kramer and Hodgson (1954) found that although mycorrhizal roots of loblolly pine absorb considerably more oxygen per unit of fresh weight, they absorb only half as much per unit of dry weight as nonmycorrhizal roots. This occurs because mycorrhizal roots contain about twice as much dry matter per unit of fresh weight as nonmycorrhizal roots. Azide (0.001 M) reduced respiration of both types of roots about 50 per cent.

Harley and his colleagues have worked on respiration and salt absorption of beech roots. Both the mycorrhizal sheaths and the root cores stored in water for a few days showed increases in respiration after being supplied with salt or sugar, as do various other types of tissue (Harley et al., 1954). Harley and McCready (1953) found that azide stimulates respiration of aerated mycorrhizal roots of beech while reducing uptake of phosphorus. This led to the suggestion that perhaps cytochrome oxidase is not involved in respiration, but Rees (1958) found evidence that cytochrome oxidase plays a part in respiration of nonmycorrhizal as well as mycorrhizal beech roots.

Pneumatophores. Trees of swampy habitats or those subject to tidal flooding and drying, such as mangroves, often have specialized root systems called "pneumatophores" which are involved in gas exchange.

Mangroves of a type represented by *Avicennia nitida* may produce several thousand air roots or pneumatophores which protrude from the mud around the base of the tree. These air roots, which average about a centimeter thick, are covered with small lenticels. They arise from submerged, porous, main roots that contain large amounts of air (Figure 7.10). Scholander et al. (1955) reported that air is sucked in through lenticels of vertical pneumatophores in *Avicennia* when the tide falls and is forced out when the tide rises. Another mangrove, *Rhizophora mangle*, has arching stilt roots which end in many long, spongy, air-filled roots (Figure 7.10). The stilt roots have lenticels on the surface which are connected to mud roots. Plugging the lenticels with grease caused oxygen content of mud roots to decrease, indicating that the stilt roots serve as aerating mechanisms for the submerged roots (Scholander et al., 1955).

Roots of cypress trees growing in frequently flooded soil develop conical, vertical growths or "knees" because of active, localized cambial activity which adds thick layers of wood on upper surfaces of roots. Although many claims have been made that cypress knees, like other pneumatophores, serve as aerating organs which supply oxygen to submerged roots, the evidence that they play such a role is not convincing. If oxygen transfer commonly occurs through the knees to the root system, then when knees are detached the amount of oxygen they absorb should be immediately reduced. Kramer et al. (1952) found, however, that respiration of detached knees was higher than in attached knees for 2 days but decreased with time. Because of the large amount of active cambial tissue in knees, it appears that most of the oxygen is utilized locally and that cypress knees do not serve as aerating organs.

Cypress knees do not develop in deep water or when the period of flooding is very short (Kurz and Demaree, 1934; Penfound, 1934). Under conditions of periodic flooding they grow to a height approximating high water level. Apparently cypress knees develop as a result of localized cambial activity in regions which are better aerated than the remainder of the root (Whitford, 1956).

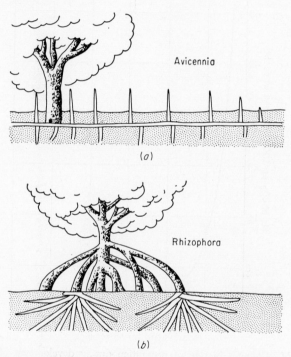

Avicennia

(a)

Rhizophora

(b)

Figure 7.10 Pneumatophores of mangroves. *a.* Vertical branches of roots extending into the air found in *Avicennia*. *b.* Stilt or prop roots of *Rhizophora*. (*From Scholander et al.,* 1955.)

Respiration of Fruits

Respiration of fruits is of both theoretical and practical importance. Much has been learned about respiration from studies of fruits, and their life in storage depends largely on control of respiration.

Respiration of Attached Fruits. Respiration of fruits varies during their development and is correlated with ontogenetic stages of cell division, enlargement, maturation, senescence, and death. Highest respiration occurs immediately after fruits are set and then decreases rapidly during the early summer. Respiration of developing apples in mid-June was about 10 times that at the beginning of September. Rapid decline in respiration occurred in June during rapid cell multiplication (Krotkov, 1941). Later in the autumn the rate of decline was much more gradual and was followed by an abrupt increase called the "climacteric." This

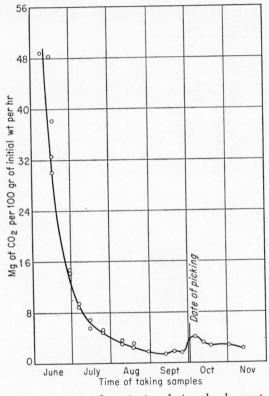

Figure 7.11 Changes in rate of respiration during development of apple fruits. (*From Krotkov, 1941.*)

rise often occurs shortly after picking and is followed by a decline until death occurs (Figure 7.11).

Many fruits are capable of respiring anaerobically. Carbon dioxide production by apples occurs in the absence of oxygen (Blackman and Parija, 1928). Apple peels are covered with a thick cuticle which is quite impervious to gases. Although pierced by many lenticels, the peel allows less gaseous exchange than would take place without it. Apples with skins removed produce more carbon dioxide than those with intact skins (Kidd, 1935).

Respiration of Harvested Fruits. Prior to senescence many harvested fruits undergo a climacteric or burst of carbon dioxide evolution, which represents a crucial metabolic change separating stages of maturation and development from senescence, disorganization, and breakdown. Susceptibility to fungi and disease is increased after the climacteric. Climacteric rise occurs in many immature and mature fruits of the Tropical and

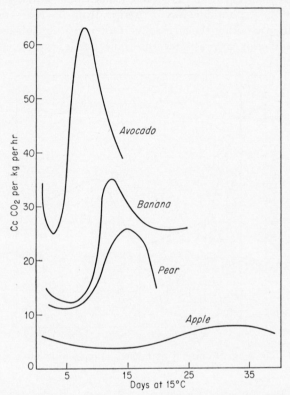

Figure 7.12 The climacteric rise in respiration of various kinds of fruit. (*From Biale*, 1950.)

Temperate Zones which are normally ripened after being harvested in a horticulturally mature condition. Citrus fruits, which do not ripen after picking, do not normally show a postharvest carbon dioxide burst unless exposed to abnormally high oxygen atmospheres (Biale, 1950).

Climacteric rises occur in many fruits before they are harvested, but there is considerable variation in time of climacteric onset in unpicked fruits. Some fruits like avocado do not show a climacteric unless removed from the tree (Biale, 1950). The magnitude of the climacteric varies greatly. Apples and pears show less marked rises than bananas and avocados (Figure 7.12). Papaw fruits gave off 30 milligrams of carbon dioxide per kilogram per hour at the preclimacteric minimum and up to four times as much at the height of their climacteric (Wardlaw and Leonard, 1938).

Ripening in fruits is associated with a variety of changes in metabolism. Odors and flavors develop as well as changes in color and texture, which are identified with ripening. As stored fruits ripen, ethylene is evolved and may cause respiration rates of unripe fruits in the same room to increase, thus promoting their ripening. Other volatile substances which affect taste and odor, such as esters of formic, acetic, caproic, and caprylic

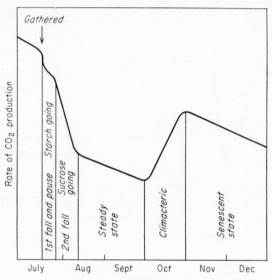

Figure 7.13 The normal course of respiration in apple fruits after harvest. (*From Kidd*, 1935.)

acid, are also produced. During senescence the mechanism controlling aerobic respiration becomes ineffective. With disorganization, anaerobic respiration becomes evident and produces ethyl alcohol and acetaldehyde, which affect fruit taste. Softening is associated with changes in pectic compounds. These sometimes are caused by ethylene emanations. Cells may separate as a result of conversion of insoluble to soluble pectins. Eventually cell walls may be digested and protoplasts disintegrated in the final stages of metabolic collapse. Senescence may be postponed by artificially delaying the climacteric (Biale, 1950). Final breakdown of fruits apparently does not result from any lack of food but rather from some metabolic disorganization (Biale, 1950). The course of normal respiratory activity of apple fruits after harvest is shown in Figure 7.13.

Successful storage of harvested fruits is related to control of the rate of respiration; hence much research has been done on methods of controlling the environment to reduce respiration and undesirable chemical changes and to prolong storage life and edibility of fruit. It has been found that the beneficial effects of low temperature often can be supplemented by use of an atmosphere low in oxygen and high in carbon dioxide. Sufficient ventilation to prevent accumulation of high concentrations of ethylene is desirable with some fruits. Smock and Neubert (1950) discuss in detail the various factors which affect the respiration of harvested apples, and Ulrich (1958) has recently reviewed the literature on the physiology of harvested fruits.

Respiration of Seeds

Tree seeds show wide variations in respiration during their ontogeny. Young, developing seeds have very high rates of respiration, but as the seeds mature the rate decreases to a minimum in fully mature seeds. Dry seeds in storage have very low rates of respiration, and it has been questioned if seeds which remain viable for 100 years or more (*Cassia*, for example) respire at all. It was stated earlier in this chapter that every living cell respires all the time, but the rate must be extremely low in very long lived seeds.

The low respiration rate of dormant seeds may result from various causes. Some seeds show a rapid increase in respiration and resumption of growth as soon as they are allowed to absorb water. In some instances the seed coats are impermeable to water or oxygen, but respiration increases and germination begins as soon as the seed coat is broken. In other instances the physiological condition of the embryo prevents germination. This is discussed in Chapter 14.

During germination, respiration invariably increases many times above the rate of dormant or nongerminating seeds. The use of food in respiration causes a considerable decrease in dry weight of germinating seeds despite the increase in volume and fresh weight which occurs. No increase in dry weight can occur until the leaves expand to the point where the weight of dry matter produced by photosynthesis exceeds that lost in respiration.

Respiration of tree seeds varies greatly among species. Sherman (1921) found that in rosaceous seeds of hawthorn, peach, apricot, cherry, and plum, respiration rates were quite variable for different species and for different groups of seeds of the same species under controlled conditions. Internal protoplasmic changes may alter respiratory capacity. Harrington (1923) found respiration of dormant apple seeds to be low and to increase greatly with afterripening. Apparently the seed coats also inhibited respiration. Their removal increased respiration and speeded up germination. Some data on seed respiration are given in Chapter 14.

Factors Affecting Respiration

Respiration of living trees may be influenced by several internal or tree factors and environmental factors which often are interacting. Among the most important internal factors are age and physiological condition of tissues, amount of oxidizable substrate, and hydration. The important environmental factors include soil and air temperature, light, gaseous composition of soil and air, soil moisture, injury and mechanical disturbances, and chemicals such as fungicides, insecticides, fertilizers, and enzyme inhibitors. These factors will be considered separately.

Age and Physiological Condition of Tissues. It is well known that young tissues which contain a relatively high proportion of protoplasm in relation to cell wall material have higher respiration rates than mature tissue which contains less physiologically active material. Thus, as pointed out in the previous section, all active meristems have high oxygen consumption compared with older tissues.

Respiration of root tips shows a definite longitudinal gradient with the highest rate near the apex and a gradual decrease toward the base, which is correlated with the decrease in protoplasm per unit of volume. According to Voigt (1953), the age of the seedling affects the rate of respiration of the root tips. He reported that 10-millimeter apical segments from roots of 10-day-old jack pine seedlings respired about 40 per cent faster than similar segments from roots of 40-day-old seedlings. The younger leaves on elongating apple shoots respire more rapidly per unit of surface than older leaves (Kelley, 1930), and this probably is generally true. Respiration of twigs also is higher per unit of dry weight than respiration of older woody stems (Möller, 1946). It already has been shown (Figure 7.4) that the respiration of buds decreases abruptly when they become dormant, and it is well known that respiration of seeds increases rapidly as they begin to germinate.

In general, respiration is a good index to physiological activity, and measurements of respiration often serve as indicators of the relative toxicity of various sprays, herbicides, and other chemicals to trees. This will be discussed in more detail in connection with the effects of various chemicals on respiration. The rate of respiration of twigs was found to serve as a good indicator of relative cold hardiness of different varieties, the most hardy variety having the lowest carbon dioxide production and the least hardy the highest, as shown in Figure 7.14 (De Long et al., 1930). In general, younger tissues serve as better physiological indicators than older tissues because they react more vigorously. For example, the respiration of younger apple leaves is affected more by oil sprays (Green,

1936), and biocides affect the respiration of younger roots more than older roots (Voigt, 1953).

Amount of Oxidizable Substrate. Respiration usually increases with increase in the amount of available substrate. In detached leaves of cherry laurel respiration was very high immediately after removal and remained

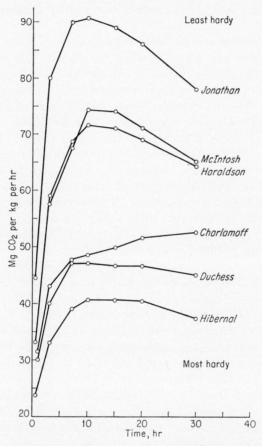

Figure 7.14 Respiration of apple twigs of varying degrees of winter hardiness. (*From De Long et al., 1930.*)

high for varying times up to 9 hours, after which it decreased rapidly over a 5-day period. The initial rapid drop represented a true starvation effect and reflected a utilization of relatively labile respiratory substrate. The second, slowly declining phase was linked to consumption of relatively nonlabile material (Audus, 1935).

Baker (1950) emphasized the correlation between rates of respiration and photosynthesis. Vigorous, healthy trees have higher respiration and photosynthetic rates than slow-growing or stunted trees, and the higher respiration rates possibly reflect the large amount of oxidizable substrates present in vigorous trees. Jones and Bradlee (1933) and Murneek (1942) showed that the outer sapwood of maple and apple trees had more carbohydrate than did the inner wood. This suggests that lower rates of respiration in the inner stem may be influenced not only by relatively fewer living cells and lower oxygen supply but also by a decreased amount of food.

Hydration. Within certain limits respiration increases with increased hydration of tissue and decreases when the tissue is dehydrated. This is particularly noticeable in dry seeds, which show an abrupt increase in respiration with a small increase in water content above a critical content. Faust (1936) observed that the respiration of seed of bigtooth aspen decreased rapidly when the water content was decreased.

Respiration of leaves is not usually affected as much as respiration of seeds by small variations in water content. If leaves and twigs are severely dehydrated, however, there often is temporary increase in respiration, probably because dehydration favors conversion of starch to sugar, resulting in a higher concentration of respiratory substrate (Parker, 1952). Kozlowski and Gentile (1958) found a good correlation between respiration and moisture content of white pine buds. Effects of hydration on respiration are discussed later in this chapter in connection with effects of soil moisture.

Soil and Air Temperatures. Measurable respiration of tree tissues occurs over a wide temperature range and even occurs at temperatures below freezing. With increase in temperature from -12 to $0°C$, respiration of pine needles increased some 25 times (Büsgen and Münch, 1931). Rapid increases in air temperatures that normally occur during the day probably account for many rapid increases in respiration rates. The respiratory acceleration with temperature is usually approximately exponential in the range from 0 to $30°C$ (James, 1953). Although temperature increase over a wide range causes increased respiration, the effects may be complicated by interactions with other factors such as amount of substrate, time, oxygen availability, prior treatment, etc.

Respiration apparently occurs at lower temperatures than does photosynthesis. Freeland (1944) found measurable rates of respiration in Scotch pine and black spruce at $-12°C$ but no net photosynthesis below $-6°C$. Tree growth may be seriously inhibited by excessive respiration at high temperatures because the most favorable temperature for photosynthesis usually is lower than that for respiration (Decker, 1944). Increasing temperature from 20 to $40°C$ caused a consistent increase in respiration of shoots of red and loblolly pine. Rates of apparent photosynthesis were similar at 20 to $30°C$, but decreased by almost 50 per cent when the temperature was increased from 30 to 40°C (Figure 8.10). The decreasing ratio of photosynthesis to respiration from 13 at 20°C to 3 at 40°C reduces the ability of these species to accumulate carbohydrates at the higher temperature.

Pollock (1953) found that respiration of intact maple buds increased with increased temperature. Temperature effects varied with available oxygen, and this suggested that low temperature may contract bud scales and decrease their permeability, thereby further limiting oxygen diffusion.

Northern red and white oak acorns show increase in CO_2 production and in respiratory quotient with increase in temperature from 5 to 30°C (Brown, 1939). The increasing respiratory quotients suggest the possibility that with rising temperature, conversion of fats to carbohydrates decreases while oxidation of carbohydrates increases. Similarly, Harrington (1923) found the respiratory quotient of apple seeds to increase with temperature. Temperature effects on respiration were also influenced by previous storage treatment of the seeds.

Respiration as measured at any temperature is conditioned by temperatures to which tissues were previously exposed. When the previous temperature was higher than the temperature at which respiration was measured, a constant level of CO_2 production was gradually attained by apple twigs, but if the previous temperature was lower, there was a peak of CO_2 production for several hours, and then a new level, higher than the original rate, was gradually reached (De Long et al., 1930).

Light. Effects of light on respiration usually are indirect because of the relation of light to temperature increase, influence on oxidizable substrates of photosynthesis, and influences on hydrolysis of reserve foods to immediate respiratory substrates. The effect of light on stomatal opening may have some effect on respiration.

Audus (1947) exposed cut shoots of cherry laurel to lights of varying intensity and duration and measured their subsequent respiration in the dark. Marked stimulation of respiration in the dark resulted from prior exposure to light, and the effect was greatest for the first 3 hours in the dark. After this the respiration curve fell away gradually. Audus postulated that light stimulated hydrolysis of reserves to an immediately oxidizable substrate, presumably hexose. Decker (1955b) also presented evidence that exposure to light stimulates respiration.

Composition of Atmosphere. Respiring plant tissues receive oxygen by diffusion. Diffusion of oxygen as a gas is slow, and it is even slower when the gas is dissolved in water. Cells in direct contact with air normally do not suffer from lack of oxygen, but the respiration of buds and internal tree tissues, such as living cells in the sapwood, often is limited by lack of oxygen. When insufficiently supplied with oxygen, such tissues often carry on anaerobic respiration, at least in part. Inner bark tissues probably suffer less from oxygen deficiency than do tissues inside the cambium because bark tissues are connected by lenticels to the outer atmosphere.

Effects of oxygen supply on buds vary with seasonal changes in their respiratory capacity (Figure 7.15). During warm weather respiration is high and is materially affected by increased oxygen content, but during the dormant season increase in the oxygen concentration above 20 per cent has little effect on respiration. The effect of bud scales on respiration was discussed earlier in this chapter and is shown in Figure 7.5.

It is well known that seed coats often interfere with oxygen uptake by embryos. In a recent study by Kozlowski and Gentile (1959), the coats

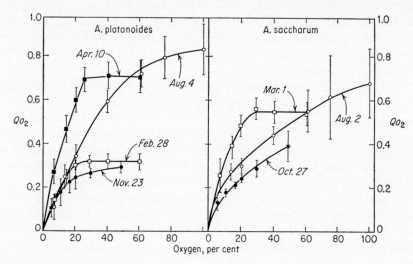

Figure 7.15 Effects of season and external oxygen concentration on oxygen uptake by maple buds at 25°C. Oxygen uptake (Q_{O_2}) is expressed in microliters of oxygen per milligram dry weight per hour. (*From Pollock,* 1953.)

of seeds of eastern white pine were found to inhibit oxygen uptake. This is discussed in more detail in Chapter 14.

Composition of the Soil Atmosphere. Respiration of roots and soil organisms tends to deplete the oxygen and increase the carbon dioxide concentration. The concentration of carbon dioxide in the soil normally tends to increase with depth, while oxygen concentration decreases. There also are marked seasonal variations, carbon dioxide concentration usually becoming much higher in the summer when roots and organisms are most active than in the winter. These relationships are shown in Figure 16.15.

An adequate supply of oxygen for respiration is essential to the survival and functioning of roots, and an excessively high concentration of carbon dioxide can also become injurious. In well-drained soils there usually is sufficient exchange of gases between the soil and the air by diffusion to prevent development of conditions seriously unfavorable to root respiration, but if the soil is flooded or the surface is compacted by trampling, gas exchange is greatly reduced. In fine-textured soils and in soils where hardpan layers occur, oxygen deficiency commonly exists.

In undisturbed forests soil aeration is seldom a serious problem because natural selection has eliminated those species not adapted to a particular site. Unfortunately, large-scale forestry operations often result in planting trees on areas to which they are poorly adapted. As a result there is an increasing incidence of "dieback" and poor growth in plantations in widely separated parts of the world, a considerable part of which probably can be attributed to soil conditions, especially aeration, unfavorable to the growth of a particular species. Arborists and landscape architects also often plant trees on particular sites, regardless of whether or not that species is adapted to the site. Such mistakes could be avoided if more were known about the aeration requirements of roots of different species and if aeration conditions were measured in the soil. Furthermore, poor management has resulted in deterioration of the soil in some areas, resulting in difficulties such as the little leaf disease of pines in the southeastern United States (Campbell and Copeland, 1954).

It is obvious that roots of different tree species vary widely in their oxygen requirements, because cypress and tupelo-gum thrive in swamps where the soil is flooded part or all of the year, but yellow-poplar, dogwood, peach, and cherry are easily injured by poor aeration. The reasons for the differences in tolerance of flooding are not fully understood, but work on herbaceous species suggests that two factors may be involved. In some instances oxygen may diffuse down to submerged roots through aerenchyma tissue, as in cattails, and the possible role of pneumatophores and cypress knees has already been mentioned. A second possibility is that roots which tolerate flooding have different physiological characteristics which enable them to survive periods of anaerobic respiration with less injury than intolerant root systems. This problem deserves further investigation.

Leyton and Rousseau (1958) found that respiration of excised root tips of several species of conifers was reduced in an atmosphere containing 5 per cent oxygen to about half of the rate in 20 per cent oxygen, but growth was reduced to about 20 per cent of the control rate. Conifer roots died in 2 days in an unaerated medium, but willow roots made about 50 per cent of normal growth in the absence of oxygen. Leyton and Rousseau suggest that willow roots obtain oxygen from the shoots. Harley et al. (1953) found that absorption of phosphorus by the root core was much less sensitive to low concentrations of oxygen than absorption by the fungal sheath of beech roots. This suggests that respiration of the root tissue might be less affected by lack of oxygen than respiration of the fungal sheath. According to Kramer and Hodgson (1954), mycorrhizal roots of pine have a higher rate of respiration per unit of fresh weight than nonmycorrhizal roots but they have a lower rate per unit of dry weight because the moisture content of mycorrhizal roots is much lower than that of nonmycorrhizal roots.

Filling in with soil over an established root system often injures or kills trees by cutting off the supply of oxygen to their roots. Arborists install wells, tile, and gravel fills to increase gas exchange and minimize injury. Use of a coarse-textured sandy soil in fills also will decrease injury. Some species are more tolerant of filling than others, presumably because their roots can better tolerate a reduced oxygen supply.

Inadequate aeration of tree roots sets in motion a series of metabolic disturbances. Decreased root respiration reduces root growth and mineral absorption and at least indirectly reduces water absorption. If the oxygen deficiency is very serious, anaerobic respiration occurs and some of its incompletely oxidized products are very toxic. Decreased nitrification results in less nitrogen being available for trees, also.

Actively growing trees are much more susceptible to injury from poor aeration of the root system than dormant ones. Flooding during the winter is therefore less injurious than flooding during the summer. The effects of inadequate aeration on roots are discussed further in Chapter 16.

Soil Moisture. Effects on Roots. As has already been pointed out, excess soil moisture influences respiration of roots largely by interfering with oxygen availability. Moisture content and air content of soils are inversely related, dry soils containing relatively larger amounts of air than wet soils, regardless of texture. As water contains only about 6 milliliters of oxygen per liter when saturated at temperatures which occur during the growing season, soil moisture in excess of field capacity depresses root respiration through oxygen deficiency. Thus respiration of roots in flooded soils may be largely anaerobic. Draining such soils to increase aeration should result in increased aerobic respiration of roots, improved root growth, and consequently better shoot growth.

It seems probable that fluctuations in soil moisture are more injurious than a high water content maintained continuously. Tree seedlings of most species can be grown in water culture with little or no supplemental aeration, indicating that water itself is not injurious. Unfortunately, many swampy areas are flooded during a part of the year but are dry during the remainder of the year. Trees growing in such areas have very shallow root systems; hence they suffer from drought injury when the soil dries out. If the water table could be maintained at a fairly high level, much better growth would occur than with a widely fluctuating water table which produces extreme variations in root environment.

Effects on Shoots. Soil moisture content affects respiration in tree tops by affecting their hydration. Leaf respiration apparently increases in soil that is drying down from field capacity toward wilting percentage. According to Schneider and Childers (1941), as moisture dropped below field capacity in a fairly heavy soil, respiration of leaves of apple trees increased greatly although photosynthesis and transpiration decreased. When the soil was rewatered to field capacity, respiration decreased again. The highest leaf respiration was recorded when transpiration and photosynthesis were lowest and the trees showed definite signs of wilting. Increased respiration of leaves with drying soil may have resulted from more available respiratory substrate because dehydration of the leaves favored conversion of starch to sugar.

Respiration of leaves also is increased by flooding of soil to a moisture content higher than field capacity, although photosynthesis and transpiration are decreased. Respiration of apple leaves was greatly increased within 2 days after submerging the roots, but when the soil was drained, respiration dropped to its normal level (Childers and White, 1942). Again these effects probably are linked to reduced leaf hydration because of decreased water uptake. Leaves from trees with flooded root systems contained less water than those from check trees.

Injuries and Mechanical Disturbances

Injury to respiring tissues usually causes increased respiration. This possibly reflects increased oxygen availability, although there is a possibility of the action of "wound" hormones. Möller (1946) stated that respiration of wood blocks cut out of forest trees was increased approximately 20 per cent by a traumatic stimulus. When tree stems are wounded, their respiration is apparently not as seriously affected as is that of other wounded tissues such as fruits. When sections of Jonathan apples were used for respiration determinations, the increased surface and wounding effects increased oxygen consumption 63 per cent over that of whole apples (Shaw, 1942).

Handling, bending, or rubbing of leaves also results in large increases in respiration (Audus, 1935; Godwin, 1935). Stimulation of cherry laurel leaves by rubbing increased respiration considerably, however, shortly thereafter there was a drop and respiration approached the previous rate (Figure 7.16). These observations suggest that care should be taken to avoid rough handling of plant material prior to measuring respiration or other physiological processes.

Chemicals

Respiration is affected by various chemicals, including insecticides, herbicides, fertilizers, fungicides, and inhibitors. The presence of volatile

Physiology of Trees

substances in the air, such as SO_2 and smog, also is of increasing importance. These effects are rather complex. Some chemicals stimulate respiration; others depress it. The effects of atmospheric pollution on physiological processes are discussed in Chapter 16.

Effects on Shoots. Hydrocarbon oils used as insecticides affect respiration of twigs and leaves in a complex manner, the effect often varying with age and dormancy of tissue and with the quality of oil used. Kelley (1930) found that effects of oil sprays on respiration of dormant twigs varied with the stage of dormancy. Before separation of bud scales all

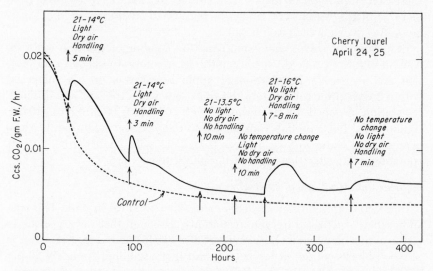

Figure 7.16 Effects of mechanical disturbance on respiration of cherry laurel leaves. The control set was subjected to minimum disturbance; the other group was subjected to some handling during measurements. (*From Audus, 1935.*)

the oils tested increased respiration. When applied at delayed dormancy (after scales separated but before the first of these unfolded) the oils retarded respiration.

Respiration of leaves was increased by hydrocarbon oils, young leaves being affected more than older leaves. Respiration was increased when oils were applied to either surface, but the effects were more marked when oils were applied to the underside and injury occurred only when oils were applied to the undersurface. Relative humidity and oil viscosity controlled the effect of the oil on respiration and influenced the amount of leaf injury. Wedding et al. (1952) found petroleum-oil spray to decrease respiration in discs of tissue taken from leaves of citrus trees. This effect probably was correlated with amounts of substrate since photosynthesis was also depressed.

Green (1936) found that apple twig respiration was influenced by degree of refinement of oils. When apple twigs were sprayed in the field with highly refined oils, respiration was retarded about 7.5 per cent, but when sprayed with poorly refined oils, respiration was increased by as much as 30 per cent. This effect extended over long periods. Apple leaves sprayed with lime sulfur showed slight or negligible increase in respiration (Hoffman, 1935).

Effects on Roots. Voigt (1953) found considerable variation in response of respiration of root tips of tree seedlings to several biocides and fertilizers (Table 7.2). Fertilizers, chlordane, and stoddard oil increased

Table 7.2. Oxygen uptake of excised root tips of tree seedlings in solutions or suspensions of various biocides and fertilizers. (*After Voigt,* 1953.)

Respiration as Per Cent of Control

Treatment	Jack pine	Red pine	White pine	Black locust
Calomel	60.0	82.4	102.1	113.4
Spergon	58.8	95.6	96.0	86.4
Thiosan	58.3	69.2	87.1	95.8
Stoddard oil	138.5	107.6	118.8	119.0
Chlordane	146.9	115.0	118.0	109.2
Fertilizer	116.8	115.2	102.2	93.5

respiration in all cases. Calomel, Spergon, and Thiosan had a depressing effect on root respiration in some species and an accelerating effect in others. Increased respiration caused by stoddard oil was probably the result of temporary injury. The seedlings responded to increased solution concentration of fertilizers by increased rates of respiration. The reaction of roots to biocides decreased with increasing age. Jack pine and red pine roots were more sensitive to presence of biocides than white pine and black locust roots.

Respiration Inhibitors

A number of enzyme inhibitors, including cyanide, azide, fluoride, malonate, iodoacetate, diethyldithiocarbamate, and carbon monoxide, reduce respiration. Differences in responses to different inhibitors often give useful clues to the enzyme systems and pathways involved in respiration. Kramer (1951a) found that phosphorus accumulation and presumably respiration were reduced more by azide and fluoride in mycorrhizal than in nonmycorrhizal roots of loblolly pine, but Kramer and Hodgson (1954) later found that respiration was reduced to about the same extent in both types of roots by azide and dinitrophenol. Harley and McCready (1953) reported that azide has three separate effects on mycorrhizal roots of beech. These are inhibition of phosphate accumulation, inhibition of carbon dioxide production in the absence of oxygen, and stimulation of carbon dioxide production in the presence of oxygen.

Barnes (1958) found that cyanide, iodoacetic acid, and fluoride all inhibited oxygen uptake of root callus cultures of sand pine. Growth of root cultures of pond pine was greatly reduced by these and other inhibitors. In general, it appears that tissues of trees are sensitive to the same substances which inhibit respiration in other plants and in animal tissues.

GENERAL REFERENCES

Anderson, L. (ed.). 1949, Respiratory enzymes, Burgess Publishing Co., Minneapolis.

Biale, J. B., 1950, Postharvest physiology and biochemistry of fruits, Ann. Rev. Plant Physiology, 1:183–206.

Dixon, M., 1951, Manometric methods as applied to the measurement of cell respiration and other processes, Cambridge University Press, New York.

James, W. O., 1953, Plant respiration, Oxford University Press, New York.

Möller, C. M., 1945, Untersuchungen über Laubmenge, Stoffverlust und Stoffproduktion der Waldes, Kandrup and Wunsch, Copenhagen.

Stiles, W., and W. Leach, 1952, Respiration in plants, 3d ed., John Wiley & Sons, Inc., New York.

Umbreit, W. W., R. H. Burris, and J. F. Stauffer, 1957, Manometric techniques, Burgess Publishing Co., Minneapolis.

CHAPTER 8 *Translocation and Food Accumulation*

TRANSLOCATION

Translocation refers to the movement of materials from cell to cell, tissue to tissue, and organ to organ within plants. Such movement may occur by mass flow in the xylem, by diffusion, or by active transport. The different kinds of processes involved in the movement of materials are discussed in more detail in Chapter 9, in connection with the absorption of minerals. Some translocation occurs within cells, and it has been suggested that under favorable conditions the rate of growth may be controlled by the rate of diffusion of materials within cells. There also is continual exchange of materials between individual cells and their environment, but in this chapter we are concerned chiefly with movement over longer distances, as between roots and shoots.

Importance

The translocation of water and minerals to the top and of organic compounds to the roots is just as essential for growth of a tree as its synthetic activities. The development of the xylem and phloem which function effectively in such translocation was as necessary to the evolution of trees and vines as was the development of a bony skeleton and circulatory system to the evolution of large animals.

In small, relatively undifferentiated organisms every cell can carry on all essential processes and no cell is far from the source of raw materials. In low-growing plants such as mosses and liverworts diffusion, perhaps aided by cytoplasmic streaming, suffices for such translocation as is necessary. In large land plants such as trees, rapid translocation is essential because there is much greater interdependence between roots and shoots and food and water must move over much greater distances. The top of a tree or large vine may be hundreds of feet from the roots which supply it with water and minerals, and many pounds of sugar must be translocated from leaves to roots if they are to grow and function properly.

195

Translocation begins in germinating seeds when minerals and organic compounds start moving from the storage tissue to the meristematic regions (Figure 8.1). Thus it begins at the cellular level, but as the plant grows it soon progresses to movement from organ to organ through the specialized translocation tissues of the xylem and phloem. Translocation occurs at all levels of organization, from cell to cell, from tissue to tissue, and from organ to organ. We shall concern ourselves chiefly with movement through xylem and phloem, but it also is necessary to discuss movement outside of the xylem and phloem.

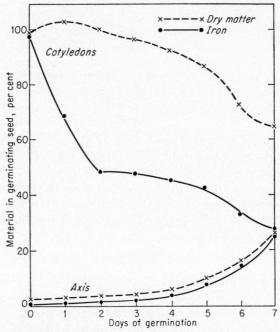

Figure 8.1 Translocation of iron and dry matter out of cotyledons into growing axis of germinating bean seeds. (*From Biddulph*, 1951.)

A wide variety of materials move in and out and from place to place in plants, including gases, water, minerals, soluble carbohydrates and nitrogen compounds, hormones, viruses, and even herbicides. The movement of water is discussed in Chapter 11. In this chapter attention is concentrated on translocation of minerals and organic compounds. The availability and convenience of using stable and radioactive isotopes has stimulated extensive research on translocation during the past few years. Nevertheless, many questions remain unanswered and much more research must be done before we shall be able to explain some aspects of translocation.

Pathways Used in Translocation

Xylem and phloem have been recognized as conducting tissues at least since the seventeenth century when Grew and Malpighi published their classical works in plant anatomy. Hales established the role of the xylem in water conduction early in the seventeenth century, but it was not until the nineteenth century that Theodor Hartig made a thorough study of phloem structure and the movement of materials through it.

The general arrangement of xylem and phloem was discussed in Chapter 2, and the structure of xylem is discussed in Chapter 11 in connection with the ascent of sap. Both phloem and xylem are continuous through plants from the tips of their roots to the tips of their stems and the smallest veins of their leaves. Translocation in phloem differs from translocation in xylem because in phloem it occurs through living sieve elements, whereas in xylem translocation occurs through dead elements.

Phloem consists of varying proportions of sieve elements, companion cells, parenchyma cells, and phloem fibers. The sieve elements which are the principal pathway for translocation are of two types, sieve tubes and sieve cells. In most angiosperms the sieve elements consist of thick-walled, elongated cells arranged end to end, forming sieve tubes. The end walls of the individual elements or cells are called sieve plates because they contain pores through which strands of cytoplasm extend from cell to cell. In gymnosperms the sieve cells are not regularly arranged end to end to form tubes and the sieve plates are not as well differentiated as in angiosperms. The protoplasts of mature sieve elements are unusual because they possess no nuclei and contain no starch grains but apparently are differentially permeable. The physiology of phloem has been reviewed recently by Esau et al. (1957).

It generally is assumed that upward movement of solutes occurs in the xylem and downward movement in the phloem, but some exceptions to this seem to occur. It was argued by some physiologists (Birch-Hirschfeld, 1920; Dixon, 1922) that downward as well as upward movement of solutes must occur in the xylem, because the phloem does not provide an adequate path for translocation. In contrast, Curtis claimed that both upward and downward movement of minerals and organic substances occurs principally in the phloem. Readers wishing more information on these controversial views are referred to the books by Curtis (1935) and Curtis and Clark (1950, chap. 27). Huber (1956, 1958b) has recently summarized a large amount of research on translocation.

It appears safe to state that upward movement of minerals and some organic compounds occurs chiefly in the xylem but some upward movement also occurs in the phloem. Downward movement of all kinds of solutes probably occurs almost exclusively in the phloem. In addition, considerable lateral movement of water and solutes occurs over short distances outside of the xylem and phloem. Various aspects of translocation will be discussed in more detail.

Movement of Minerals

Discussion of mineral translocation is complicated by the fact that certain elements, notably nitrogen, phosphorus, and sulfur, can move either as organic or inorganic compounds while others move only as inorganic ions. It has been suggested that organic compounds may move in the phloem while inorganic compounds move in the xylem. This now seems less likely because Bollard (1957a and b) and others find considerable amounts of amino acids and amides in the xylem sap of a variety of trees but nitrates are absent or present only in traces. Mothes and Engelbrecht (1952) reported that in maple nearly all nitrogen moves upward as allantoin or allantoic acid. Tolbert and Wiebe (1955) found an organic phosphorus compound in xylem sap which was identified by Maizel et al. (1956) as phosphoryl choline. These and other observations indicate that considerable translocation of minerals in the xylem probably occurs in the form of organic compounds.

Upward Movement. The magnitude of upward movement of minerals in trees is indicated in Table 8.1. Although it often is assumed that

Table 8.1. Weights in grams of various elements in old and new tissue of a 20-year-old apple tree and percentage of that used in new growth which comes from roots and soil. (*Burke and Morris,* 1933.)

	Dry wt.	N	P	K	Ca	Mg
Present in top of dormant tree, Apr. 9	33,908	116.25	25.67	60.96	267.91	21.89
Present in old growth, June 11	33,908	79.67	25.19	64.08	253.30	15.34
Present in new growth, June 11	6,147	110.65	22.87	113.10	87.16	16.84
Percentage obtained for new growth from roots and soil		67.0	98.0	100.0	83.2	61.1

upward movement of minerals occurs almost entirely in the xylem, this view was opposed by Curtis and there appear to be many instances of upward movement in the phloem (Curtis and Clark, 1950, chap. 27). In some experiments Curtis obtained evidence that less salt moved into shoots past girdles which cut the phloem than into shoots where the xylem was cut but the phloem was left intact and water for the shoot was provided by enclosing the cut portion in a tube filled with water. He concluded from these experiments that most upward movement of minerals occurs in the phloem.

Clements (1934) and Clements and Engard (1938) objected to the conclusions of Curtis because they found that girdling not only cuts the phloem but also hinders upward movement of water through the xylem of some species, which results in decreased salt movement. Chilling stem segments to reduce the activity of phloem cells also reduces water movement in the xylem. Clements and Engard (1938), Phillis and Mason (1940), and others have demonstrated that cutting the phloem does not hinder upward movement of minerals if the xylem is not partially blocked, but Mason and Phillis (1940) also showed that nitrogen compounds can move upward in the phloem, at least in some plants.

The availability of radioactive isotopes facilitated studies of mineral translocation, but only a few of the numerous experiments which have been published can be mentioned. Stout and Hoagland (1939) separated the bark from the xylem for a distance of several centimeters in stems of willow, cotton, and geranium and inserted strips of paraffined paper to prevent lateral movement of water or solutes. A radioactive tracer was then supplied to the roots, and after a few hours the wood and bark were cut into segments and their radioactivity measured. As shown in Figure 8.2, where xylem and phloem were in contact, the concentration of tracer in the bark was high, but where they were separated the concentration was very low in the bark. Experiments of this type do not exclude slow movement in the phloem, but they indicate that rapid upward movement occurs in the xylem. According to Biddulph et al. (1958), P^{32} applied to bean leaves moves out of them and up the stem in the phloem.

Fraser and Mawson (1953) observed that movement of radioactive rubidium and calcium in yellow birch and white pine occurred in rather narrow bands. In birch these usually spiraled upward as a result of spiral grain in the wood. Kuntz and Riker (1955) found that radioactive isotopes injected into trunks of oak trees moved not only upward but also downward into the roots and laterally through root grafts into adjacent trees. Although downward movement of injected substances often occurs in the xylem, it probably is uncommon in intact plants. Upward movement in northern pin oak was very diffuse, but in bur oak it occurred in narrow channels, as in the yellow birch and white pine studied by Fraser and Mawson. Movement in trees suffering from oak wilt was reduced because the xylem vessels were plugged with tyloses and gum.

Some measurements of the rate of upward movement of minerals in trees have been made. Moreland (1950) measured rates of translocation of radioactive phosphorus in loblolly pine of up to 1.4 meters per hour in roots and 1.2 meters in stems, and Fraser and Mawson (1953) found rates up to about 20 meters per hour in birch. According to Kuntz and Riker (1955), the rate in oak under conditions favorable for rapid transpiration was from 30 to 60 meters per hour. Minerals carried in the transpiration stream would be expected to move approximately as rapidly as the water, and these rates compare well with rates of ascent of sap measured by Huber and others, as reported in Chapter 11.

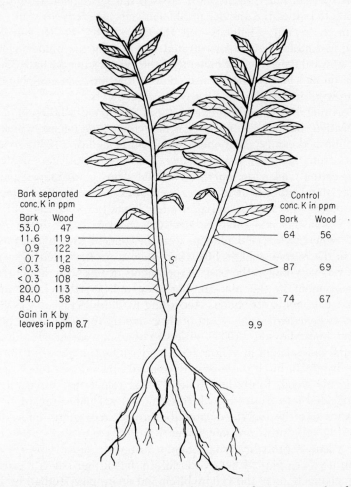

Bark separated
conc. K in ppm

Bark	Wood
53.0	47
11.6	119
0.9	122
0.7	11.2
< 0.3	98
< 0.3	108
20.0	113
84.0	58

Gain in K by
leaves in ppm 8.7

Control
conc. K in ppm

Bark	Wood
64	56
87	69
74	67

9.9

Figure 8.2 Experiment to determine path of upward movement of radioactive potassium in willow. The bark of the left-hand branch was separated from the wood by a layer of paraffined paper, while the right-hand branch was left intact. Very little potassium was found in the bark where it was separated from the wood, but large amounts where it was in normal contact. This experiment indicates that upward movement occurred chiefly in the xylem but that lateral movement from wood to bark also occurs. (*From Stout and Hoagland, 1939.*)

According to Biddulph (1951), the upward movement of minerals is controlled by the rate of transpiration and the rate at which they are used in metabolic processes. Those solutes which enter the xylem sap in the roots are carried upward at a rate controlled largely by the rate of transpiration, but considerable quantities diffuse out of the xylem along the way because a concentration gradient is produced by their use in growing regions along the way. The cells of growing leaves, stem tips, the cambial region, and other metabolically active regions all accumulate minerals and use them in metabolism, producing gradients which cause movement toward these regions. The importance of the transpiration stream is suggested by experiments in which radioactive phosphorus was injected into tree stems early in the spring. The phosphorus moved rapidly to the tips of the twigs of conifers, but very little movement occurred in the bare hardwood trees with low rates of transpiration (Graham, 1957).

Little interference with movement of minerals through the xylem would be expected, but Hewitt and Gardiner (1956) reported that considerable amounts of zinc are adsorbed on the walls of the xylem vessels in grapes. Iron also is precipitated in the xylem of leaf veins in the presence of phosphate and at a high pH (Biddulph, 1951).

Movement Out of Leaves. The continual movement of minerals carried into leaves by the transpiration stream is likely to supply more than can be accumulated or used in the leaf cells. The total salt content of leaves tends to increase during the growing season, as shown in Figure 9.6, and if the water supply contains a high concentration of salt, so much sometimes accumulates in the leaves that they are injured or killed. Under normal conditions excessive concentrations of salt seldom occur in leaves of growing plants because reexport to younger leaves and other growing regions keeps the concentration down to a safe level. Some salt also is removed by leaching in rain and dew (Chapter 9).

The amount of salt exported from leaves varies with their age and metabolic condition and the element involved. There is a tendency for some elements such as nitrogen, phosphorus, and potassium to move out of older leaves (Chapter 9, section on salt content of leaves). Relatively little retranslocation of calcium occurs, although Ferrell and Johnson (1956) found that radioactive calcium injected into white pine trees 1 year moved into new buds formed 1 or 2 years later. Rediske and Biddulph (1953) found very little retranslocation of iron out of leaves at high pH values and high concentrations of phosphorus, and according to Rediske and Selders (1953), little retranslocation of strontium occurs.

The translocation of minerals out of leaves and downward in stems occurs in the phloem and is blocked by girdling or killing the phloem. Downward movement could occur in the xylem if reversal of the normal upward movement of water occurred, but this rarely happens in intact plants. Outward movement of minerals from leaves seems to be related to outward movement of carbohydrates, more movement occurring during the day than at night (Biddulph, 1941). Helder and Bonga (1956) also concluded that movement of phosphorus out of leaves is coupled with the movement of carbohydrates. Biddulph and Markle (1944) observed that radioactive phosphorus supplied to leaves of cotton moved downward in the phloem at a rate in excess of 21 centimeters per hour. Upward movement of minerals also occurs in the phloem (Biddulph et al., 1958), but it is difficult to determine how much of the salt reaching new leaves comes directly from the roots and how much comes from the older leaves through the phloem or xylem.

The reexport of minerals from older regions of plants is particularly important where the supply is deficient because it ensures a continued supply of mobile elements such as phosphorus, potassium, and nitrogen to the growing regions. These regions often suffer from deficiencies of calcium, boron, and iron because these elements are less mobile. Biddulph (1951) suggests that symptoms of deficiencies occur as often because of failures in translocation as because of failures in initial absorption through the roots. New growth requires a large amount of minerals in a very limited period of time, as shown in Table 8.1, and this must remove large amounts of minerals from the older tissues. Outward translocation from leaves also is important in connection with the application of mineral nutrients in foliar sprays, and the movement of herbicides and other substances applied to leaves into the plant as a whole. It has been demonstrated that a wide variety of inorganic and organic substances applied to leaves will move throughout plants.

Lateral Movement. So much attention is given to movement of solutes through the xylem and phloem that the importance of translocation outside of the vascular system often is overlooked. The lateral movement of salts from the soil solution across the root tissues and into the root xylem is much more difficult to explain than upward movement in the xylem to the leaves. This problem is discussed in Chapter 9. Much lateral movement of salt out of the xylem into the cambium and young phloem must occur to supply these actively growing tissues. The extent of this movement is indicated by experiments such as those of Stout and Hoagland (1939) and by the amounts of calcium and other elements found in the bark. Movement from the phloem into the xylem also can occur under some conditions, as indicated in experiments of Biddulph and Markle (1944). Biddulph and Cory (1957) reported that 24 per cent of P^{32} and 31 per cent of tritiated water supplied to bean leaves and translocated downward in the phloem were lost to the xylem. Most of the cells of leaves lack direct contact with xylem and phloem, and solutes can reach them only by movement through intervening cells.

Little attention has been given to the pathway and mechanisms by which such movement occurs. Do substances move from protoplast to protoplast by active transport, or do they move passively by diffusion, or are they in some instances carried in the transpiration stream? It should be remembered that the water in the xylem and in the water-saturated cell walls forms a continuous system throughout the plant, which in effect is part of the apparent free space mentioned in Chapter 9 in connection with salt absorption by roots. Solutes can move freely in this system by diffusion or by mass flow in the transpiration stream, and if the cytoplasm is included in free space, movement can be speeded up by cytoplasmic streaming. Only the water in the vacuoles is unavailable for passive movement of solutes because it is enclosed within differentially permeable membranes. There is active accumulation of minerals in growing cells of root and stem tips and in the cambium, and this causes gradients along which minerals probably move by diffusion, perhaps aided by cytoplasmic streaming. Burstrom (1948a) found that enlarging buds of *Carpinus* accumulate potassium and phosphorus to an extent that requires movement from a distance of a meter or more.

When transpiration causes mass movement of water to the evaporating surfaces the water must carry salt with it to the extent that it does not pass through membranes impermeable to them. Strugger (1943) has been the principal supporter of the view that movement of water and salts occurs through cell walls, and there is little doubt that some movement of this type occurs. Thus it seems probable that salt movement outside of the vascular system can occur in three ways: (1) by active transport in the cytoplasm, (2) by diffusion, and (3) by mass movement in the transpiration stream.

As mentioned earlier, there usually is some interchange of materials between xylem and phloem, the direction of movement depending chiefly on relative concentrations in the two tissues. The occurrence of lateral translocation between xylem and phloem combined with upward movement of minerals in the xylem and downward movement in the phloem results in a sort of circulation. If a substance moving upward in the xylem is not used in the leaves, it may move down in the phloem, and if it is not used in the roots, it might move up again in the xylem, and so on indefinitely.

Movement of Organic Compounds

Serious study of the translocation of organic substances in plants began with the work of the forest botanist Theodor Hartig, who described sieve tubes in 1837. In 1859 he discovered that sap could be obtained by puncturing the sieve tubes, and this provided the methodology for many later studies of translocation. Some of Hartig's work was summarized recently by Zimmerman (1958). Work done during the present century has shown that in addition to carbohydrates a variety of organic substances move in plants, including nitrogenous compounds, vitamins, hormones, and such foreign substances as viruses and herbicides. The quantity of carbohydrates translocated from place to place in plants exceeds that of all other solutes combined. Most of this moves downward, but some upward movement also occurs.

Downward Movement. The downward movement of carbohydrates occurs in the phloem, as indicated by the fact that girdling trees by cutting through the phloem results in accumulation of carbohydrates above the girdle and decrease in them below the girdle. Baldwin (1934) obtained data on carbohydrate concentration above and below the girdle in a number of hardwoods and found consistent decreases below the girdles. Girdled trees die eventually, probably because starvation of the roots stops growth and reduces water absorption. Death probably actually occurs from dehydration rather than directly from starvation.

Occasionally puzzling situations occur where tops of trees remain alive for many years after the phloem has been effectively cut. In most of these instances the root system probably is kept alive by carbohydrates supplied through root grafts with adjacent trees, as suggested in the section on root grafts.

Upward Movement. Considerable upward movement of carbohydrates must occur under some conditions. Growth of the rapidly elongating twigs and new leaves of new growth is dependent on carbohydrates from the older parts of the branches. Later in the season when the new leaves begin to carry on photosynthesis, the direction of carbohydrate movement is reversed, but if additional new leaves are added during the summer, food must move up to them until they become independent.

Since the time of Hartig, it has been assumed by most botanists that the carbohydrate stored as starch in the roots and stems in late summer and early autumn is converted to sugar and moves upward to growing regions in the xylem. The concept of a rise of sap in the spring as the buds open has been almost universally accepted by botanists, and it has even inspired poets. Curtis (1935) questioned the amount of upward movement of carbohydrates in trees in the spring and concluded that what movement occurs must take place in the phloem rather than the xylem. This is based on the observation that girdling consistently prevented upward movement of carbohydrate from below the girdle in branches of trees, and if two girdles were made, the carbohydrate between them did not move out. Curtis claimed that disappearance of starch from below a girdle is not proof that it moved upward past the girdle in the xylem because it may be used where it occurs or it may be translocated downward. He concluded that the carbohydrate stored in stems either is used in the region where it occurs or moves into the phloem and is translocated through that tissue.

It seems reasonably certain that the products of current photosynthesis move upward through the phloem. Rabideau and Burr (1945) observed that both upward and downward movement of carbohydrate labeled with C^{13} was stopped by killing the phloem above or below the source, and Chen (1951) demonstrated upward movement in the phloem. Biddulph et al. (1958) found that C^{14}-labeled compounds moved out of leaves and were translocated both upward and downward in the phloem. Lateral movement from phloem to xylem also occurred. On the other hand, considerable amounts of sugar are found in xylem sap in the spring, and this almost certainly moves up in the transpiration stream. Even before the leaves open there is sufficient transpiration to cause upward movement of the xylem sap, which must carry with it whatever solutes it contains.

There are various other kinds of evidence that food can move either upward or downward. Winkler (1932) showed by defoliation experiments on grapes that organic substances moved readily in either direction from leaves to ripening fruits. Zimmerman and Connard (1934) grafted plants together by inarching and later cut the roots off of one and the top off of the other so water and solutes were forced to move in reverse of the usual direction through a segment of xylem and phloem (Figure 8.3). Somewhat similar experiments were performed by Hales and other early investigators.

There is some uncertainty concerning the distance over which carbohydrates are translocated upward in trees and other woody plants. Curtis (1935) found that girdles on the region of a stem 3 to 5 years old did not interfere with shoot growth of some plants. This led him to conclude that there usually was enough food stored in the growth of the last 2 to 4 years for bud development and that little upward translocation of food occurs in trees in the spring. On the other hand, Overholser and Claypool (1935) observed transport of food from one branch to another to cherry fruits, and Winkler (1932) caused movement back from a shoot into the spur and out another shoot over a distance of at least 3 feet to fruits on a defoliated grapevine. Miller (1938, pp. 892–894) has summarized considerable data which indicate that food is translocated fairly rapidly over distances of several feet, both upward and downward.

Composition of Xylem Sap. Numerous studies have been made of the composition of xylem sap, and these indicate that it contains a variety of organic and inorganic substances. Most of these studies were made on sap exuding from wounds of grape (Priestley and Wormall, 1925), birch (Ladefoged, 1948), and maple (Pollard and Sproston, 1954). These saps contain a variety of substances, including varying quantities of mineral salts, sugars (mono- and disaccharides), nitrogenous compounds, and enzymes. Some interesting studies have been made of seasonal changes in xylem sap composition by displacing it from cut stems by air pressure (Bollard, 1953). Anderssen (1929) found a high carbohydrate content in pear xylem sap in late winter and early spring which decreased rapidly to a low in late spring and early summer, then rose again in late summer, the rise continuing to the winter maximum. Bollard (1956, 1957a, 1958) found nitrate in the sap of only a few species of woody

Figure 8.3 An example of reversal in the usual direction of translocation produced by inarching one tomato plant to another, then cutting it free from its roots. The inked lines show the path followed by water and solutes. (*From Zimmerman and Connard, 1934.*)

plants, most of the nitrogen occurring as amides and amino acids. This extended and supported earlier work of Mothes and Engelbrecht (1952) and Reuter and Wolffgang (1954). Some data on seasonal variations in composition of xylem sap are shown in Figure 8.4.

It is obvious that solutes occurring in the xylem sap are translocated toward the leaves in the transpiration stream. This must be the principal path of upward movement of nitrogen in trees (Bollard, 1957b, 1958). Appreciable upward movement of carbohydrates must also occur, at least during the spring and late summer, when they occur in the xylem sap in measurable quantities. This probably represents a kind of recirculation, similar to that of minerals mentioned earlier, because the carbohydrates

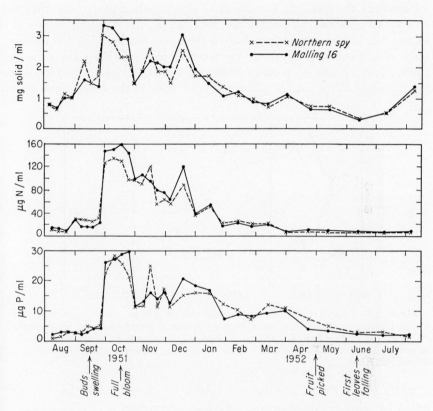

Figure 8.4 Seasonal changes in concentration of phosphorus, nitrogen, and total solids in xylem sap of two varieties of apple trees growing in New Zealand. (*From Bollard, 1953.*)

in the xylem presumably reached it by diffusion out of the phloem where the concentration is much higher.

Composition of Phloem Sap. Ever since Hartig (1861) discovered that sieve tube sap could be obtained by puncturing the phloem, there has been interest in its flow and composition. Only a few of the investigations can be mentioned here. Moose (1938), working at Ithaca, New York, found that flow of phloem exudate from the four species he studied started about June 15, increased until mid-July, and remained high until leaf fall, when it ceased. Best flow was observed in afternoons on sunny days. Zimmerman (1957b) found about the same situation in white ash at Petersham, Massachusetts.

Huber et al. (1937) measured diurnal changes in concentration of sieve tube sap at various heights in *Quercus rubra* by measuring the refractive index of the sap. The maximum concentration occurred at night, and the minimum in the morning, but the peak concentration moved downward at a speed of about 3.5 meters per hour during the night, as shown in Figure 8.5. This moving concentration peak was attributed to the downward movement each day of a new wave of photosynthate. Zimmerman (1958) found a sucrose peak in white ash which moved downward during the night at the rate of 1.25 meters per hour in the region from 9 to

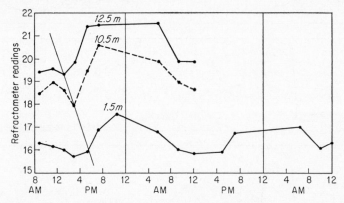

Figure 8.5 Diurnal variations in concentration of phloem sap of a northern red oak at various heights on the trunk, measured with a refractometer as percentages of sugar. The sloping line indicates the downward movement of the sap of minimum concentration at a rate of nearly 3 meters per hour. (*From Huber, Schmidt, and Jahnel, 1937.*)

1 meter aboveground, but he was unable to ascertain whether or not peaks for other sugars coincided with that for sucrose.

It has been reported that sucrose is the only sugar in phloem exudate, but other sugars sometimes are present, and in white ash stachyose is most abundant and the concentration of raffinose is equal to that of sucrose (Zimmerman, 1957a). The composition of phloem sap from trees of several species is shown in Table 8.2. No reducing sugars or sugar phosphates were found in phloem exudate of white ash, and only small quantities of amides and amino acids, but considerable mannitol sometimes was present (Zimmerman, 1957b). The amino acid content increased slightly late in the autumn, possibly because of withdrawal of nitrogen from the dying leaves.

Zimmerman (1957b, 1958) measured the concentration of the various sugars at different heights on the trunk and found that the concentration

Table 8.2. Sugars found in exudate from sieve tubes of trees, of various species. (*From Zimmerman,* 1957a.)

Family	Species	Sucrose	Raffinose	Stachyose	Verbascose
Salicaceae	*Populus tremuloides*	a	tr	tr	c
Fagaceae	*Fagus grandifolia*	a	tr	c	c
Fagaceae	*Quercus alba*	a	c	c	c
Fagaceae	*Quercus rubra*	a	c	c	c
Ulmaceae	*Ulmus americana*	b	b	b	c
Magnoliaceae	*Liriodendron tulipifera*	a	tr	tr	c
Leguminosae	*Robinia pseudoacacia*	a	c	c	c
Aceraceae	*Acer saccharum*	a	c	c	c
Oleaceae	*Fraxinus americana*	b	b	a	tr

Total sugar concentration of sieve tube sap varies from 20 to 25 per cent.

The sign [a] indicates over 10 per cent, [b] indicates 2 to 10 per cent, tr less than 0.5 per cent, and [c] less than 0.1 per cent.

generally decreased from above to below. The gradient was steeper in the evening than in the morning, and in the autumn it disappeared, the gradients for some of the constituents being reversed. The relative amounts of various constituents tend to change along the trunk, possibly because the complex sugars are being broken down and the galactose units removed (Zimmerman, 1958). Zimmerman suggests that an α-galactosidase occurs in the protoplasm of the sieve tubes which converts stachyose to raffinose, then converts raffinose to sucrose by splitting off galactose.

An interesting variation from the usual method of obtaining phloem sap involves the use of aphids. Certain aphids invariably insert their mouth parts into the sieve tubes to feed, and if the mouth parts are quickly cut off before they can be removed, phloem sap will flow out through them. Mittler (1958) found this a convenient method of obtaining samples of phloem sap for analysis at various stages of leaf development. He found that the number and kinds of amino acids were higher in young and senescent leaves than in leaves after growth ceased but before they became senescent.

Movement of Hormones and Vitamins. There seem to be two types of translocation of auxin in plants, the highly polarized downward movement from cell to cell, such as is found in oat coleoptiles and other undifferentiated tissue, and movement in xylem and phloem. If auxin is absorbed through the roots, it moves upward and throughout the plant in the transpiration stream, but if it is applied to the leaves, it moves downward in the phloem. Huber et al. (1937) found auxin in the phloem exudate of *Robinia, Fagus,* and *Aesculus* in July and August, but little or none was present in September. It was shown by Avery et al. (1937) that a wave of auxin moves downward in tree trunks from opening buds, apparently activating cambial activity. The path of movement was not studied, but one might expect it to move in the phloem. Gregory and Hancock (1955) estimated the rate of downward movement of auxin in short segments of apple twigs to be about 0.5 centimeter per hour, but the downward movement in intact tree stems probably is much more rapid. This is discussed in Chapter 2 in connection with the relation between shoot growth and cambial activity. The movement in apple stem segments was highly polar and was reduced by low temperature and low oxygen.

A number of studies of movement of flower-forming hormones in herbaceous species suggest that they also move in the phloem. Vitamins such as thiamin, riboflavin, pantothenic acid, and pyridoxine accumulate above girdles in tomato plants, along with sucrose and nitrogen compounds (Bonner, 1944), suggesting that these substances move downward in the phloem. They probably also move downward in the phloem of woody species, but apparently no studies of their translocation have been made on trees.

In recent years there has been active interest in the translocation of growth regulators because of their increased use as herbicides, and van Overbeek (1952) reviewed the literature in this field. Most of the work has been done on herbaceous plants, but some data are available from experiments on woody species. Crafts (1956) recently published on translocation of herbicides, and Leonard and Crafts (1956) dealt specifically with translocation of radioactive 2,4-D from leaves of woody species. They found large differences in uptake and translocation among plants of various species and also marked seasonal differences. Leaves of coyote bush (*Baccharis pilularis*) absorbed small amounts of radioactive 2,4-D in February and larger amounts in April, but absorption decreased in May and June and none occurred in July. In February and March movement was mostly downward from the treated leaves, but in April it was mostly upward. Little translocation occurred from arroyo willow (*Salix lasiolepis*) until April 15. After this date both upward and downward translocation occurred from treated leaves until September, but in October all movement was downward. Crafts (1956) states that 2,4-D migrates to the phloem and is transported in this tissue along with food. No 2,4-D was transported from young leaves which were still importing food from more mature parts of the plants.

Movement of Viruses. Many viruses move in the phloem. Some are limited to the phloem, and infection can be produced only by direct introduction into that tissue, usually by insect vectors. Other viruses can be introduced into parenchyma, where they spread very slowly until they reach the vascular bundles, and the rate of spread then becomes much more rapid. The curly top virus of beet has been observed to move 6 inches in 6 minutes, but rates of 0.5 to 7 inches per hour are more common (Bennett, 1956). Apparently movement of viruses out of leaves, like movement of minerals and growth regulators, is associated with the movement of food. Some viruses produce serious injury to the phloem, but others do not. Certain viruses move in the xylem, and those causing the phony disease of peach and Pierce's disease of grape apparently are restricted to the xylem.

Translocation around Wounds

In past years there was considerable interest in the amount of lateral translocation of water and solutes which occurs in plants. If water is supplied only to one side, there is some lateral transfer, as indicated by similar moisture contents of leaves on the watered and unwatered sides of the tree (Miller, 1938, p. 876). Auchter (1923) studied lateral movement of nitrates in several kinds of woody plants by supplying them to one side of the root system or by removing the roots on one side. In general, nitrates moved directly up to the branches above the roots to which they were supplied, and the nitrogen content of the foliage on that side was higher than on the other side. Carbohydrates also normally are translocated straight downward, and the annual rings often are wider under a large branch or on the sunny side of a tree than on the opposite side (Auchter, 1923).

It might be expected that serious injury to the phloem by fire or other causes would greatly interfere with translocation, but there is such a large safety factor in the capacity of conducting systems that most of it can be removed without causing serious interference with translocation. Furthermore, the interference is only temporary, because trees soon form new xylem and phloem around large wounds in which the elements are oriented so that they function effectively in both upward and downward translocation (MacDaniels and Curtis, 1930). Jemison (1944) found that severe injury from fire which killed both phloem and xylem on as much as 90 per cent of the circumference of trees caused little or no reduction in growth. It reduced neither the water, mineral, or nitrogen content of leaves on branches above the wound nor the carbohydrate content of roots below the wound. The temporary obstruction to translocation was quickly circumvented by new xylem and phloem laid down like a bridge around the wound, as shown in Figure 8.6.

Effects of Fungi and Insects on Translocation. Attacks of insects or fungi can girdle trees just as effectively as an axman. The American chestnut has been almost exterminated by the fungus which attacks the inner phloem and renders it useless in food conduction. White pine blister rust is another fungus which attacks the conducting system. Sometimes bark beetles destroy so much of the inner bark that they seriously hinder the translocation of food. Often insects and fungi act together. Pine bark beetles introduce a fungus into the sapwood which plugs up the xylem

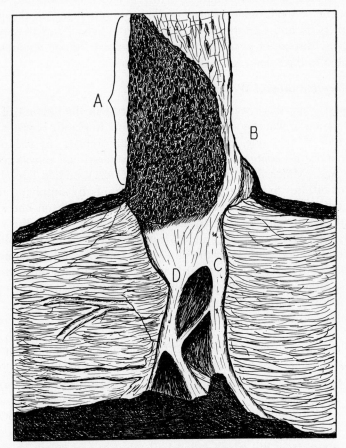

Figure 8.6 Translocation around a fire wound usually is maintained by formation of new xylem and phloem which rapidly form effective bypasses. A. Burned area. B. Living bark. C and D. Roots. (*From Jemison, 1944.*)

and causes dehydration in addition to injuring the phloem. The elm bark beetle was not a serious pest until the fungus causing Dutch elm disease was introduced to this country. It then became an active vector for the disease, and control of the disease is dependent on controlling the bark beetles. Dutch elm disease and oak wilt interfere with water conduction, while elm phloem necrosis interferes with food conduction.

Root Grafts

Connections between the root systems of adjacent trees by root grafts occur more frequently than is generally supposed. LaRue (1934, 1952) found root grafts common in many, but not all, species. Kuntz and Riker (1955) demonstrated that fungus spores, dyes, and radioactive materials are transferred from tree to tree through root grafts. They concluded that there are sufficient root grafts among oak trees to allow the rapid spread

Figure 8.7 Grafts between roots of two white pine trees. (*Photograph by F. S. Page, ret., Dartmouth College. Print courtesy of B. F. Graham, Jr.*)

of oak wilt from tree to tree in a stand. Grafts between the roots of two white pine trees are shown in Figure 8.7. A group of trees may be connected so effectively through root grafts that if all but one tree are cut, the root systems will survive on carbohydrates supplied by the remaining tree (Garner, 1958). Kuntz and Riker (1955) and Beskaravainyi (1958) also observed that if a tree is cut, neighboring trees often take over its root system through grafts. Bormann (1958) found so many root grafts in stands of white pine that he regards the entire stand as a physiological unit. Bormann (1957) also has demonstrated that transfer of water can occur between roots which are merely in close contact but not actually joined together. Figure 8.8 shows the occurrence of grafts in the root systems of a group of white pines.

Mechanisms of Translocation

One of the most puzzling problems in plant physiology is the mechanism by which translocation is brought about. It is particularly puzzling because of the large amounts of solutes which are moved through a conducting tissue of very small cross-section area in a short period of time. A good example is the development of the fruit of the sausage tree (*Kigelia africana*), studied by Clements (1940). A cluster of four fruits is developed at the end of a slender stem about a meter in length. The fruits under observation increased in dry weight over 1,450 grams in 72 days, or an average of over 20 grams per day, but we have no entirely

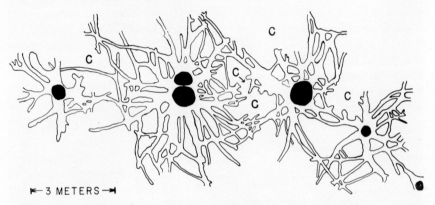

|←— 3 METERS —→|

Figure 8.8 Diagram showing occurrence of grafts among root systems of a group of six white pine trees. C. Grafts cut out. (*Courtesy of F. H. Bormann.*)

satisfactory explanation for the movement of over 20 grams of sugar per day through a long slender stem into the growing fruits.

The problem is further complicated by the fact that substances move either upward or downward through the phloem and the possibility that different substances may move in two directions simultaneously. There is, of course, the possibility that movement in opposite directions occurs in different sieve tubes.

The tendency toward polar translocation is another puzzling characteristic. For example, sugar moves into young growing leaves but out of older ones. It moves into developing fruits and seeds and into certain kinds of storage tissue against a concentration gradient. There seems to be competition among various tissues and organs for carbohydrates and an order of dominance, fruits having the advantage over apical buds, which have the advantage over lateral buds, while roots are lowest in competition for carbohydrates. The movement of natural auxin also is highly polar, always occurring in the downward direction.

Another puzzling feature is the apparently simultaneous and related movement of a variety of substances along with foods. The movement of minerals, dyes, growth regulators, vitamins, and viruses out of leaves seems to occur only under conditions where food is being translocated.

Several hypotheses have been proposed to explain the mechanism of translocation, but none of them is entirely satisfactory. The more important suggestions will be discussed separately.

Diffusion. Diffusion can explain movement of gases and even movement of solutes over distances of a few millimeters, but it is too slow to account for movement of foods and minerals over distances of many meters (Curtis and Clark, 1950, p. 453). Unfortunately, Sachs and Pfeffer both explained translocation as a diffusion process, and this delayed the advance of other possibilities for many years. Mason and Phillis (1936) found that sucrose moved along the phloem about 40,000 times as rapidly as it would move by diffusion. They proposed an "activated diffusion" by which the living protoplasm hastens diffusion in some manner, but no mechanism is known by which this could occur.

Movement along Interfaces. It is well known that substances can move very rapidly in thin films at interfaces, as oil spreads over water, and it has been suggested that substances may move through phloem in protoplasmic interfaces. Van Overbeek (1956) points out that spread along a solid interface is too slow, but that spread along liquid interfaces can be extremely rapid, and Esau et al. (1957) also mention this possibility. Crafts (1951) pointed out that spreading out translocation into thin films simply increases the difficulty of explaining how large masses of material are moved.

Protoplasmic Streaming. De Vries pointed out that diffusion is too slow to account for translocation, but suggested that it might be speeded up by protoplasmic streaming or cyclosis. Curtis (Curtis and Clark, 1950, pp. 458–463) supported this view because it allows for simultaneous movement in both directions and is consistent with the fact that translocation is correlated with metabolic activity. Some weaknesses are the low rate of streaming usually observed and the difficulty of reconciling it with the simultaneous movement of food, minerals, hormones, etc., out of leaves.

Mass Flow. The mass-flow hypothesis proposed by Münch (1930) and supported by Crafts (1938), Huber (1956, 1958b), and others seems to be increasingly popular. It assumes that sugar formed in photosynthesis usually maintains a high osmotic pressure in the leaf cells compared with the root cells where sugar is being used. Münch supposed that sugar is forced by turgor pressure into the sieve tubes along the plasmodesms, but it seems more probable that it is "secreted" into them by the surrounding cells or accumulated by them, because the concentration of sugar in the phloem sap sometimes is higher than in the leaf cells (Roeckl, 1949). If the concentration of solutes is kept at a higher level at one end of the system than the other, and if a supply of water is available, a turgor-pressure gradient will develop which tends to cause movement toward the region of lower concentration and lower turgor pressure. This is shown diagrammatically in Figure 8.9.

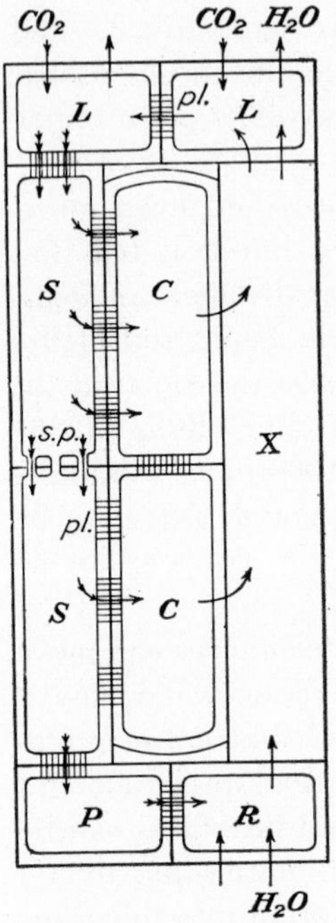

Huber et al. (1937) and Zimmerman (1957b, 1958) found that the concentration of sugar in the phloem decreases from top to bottom in trees, as is necessary if this mechanism is to work. Zimmerman also found that in white ash the cytoplasm lining the side walls of the sieve tubes is differentially permeable and the sieve plates are permeable to the solutes moving through the phloem. He therefore concluded that the downward movement of carbohydrates can be explained by the mass-flow hypothesis.

The mass-flow theory is consistent with the positive pressure which exists in the phloem of some plants and with the fact that movement of growth regulators, viruses, and other substances out of leaves is coupled with translocation of food. However, it is inconsistent with the fact that substances appear to move both upward and downward in the phloem, unless there is reversal of flow in at least a part of the phloem. The mechanical resistance to rapid mass flow through the phloem also would be very large, and there is some doubt if the rate attained would be sufficient to account for the amount of sugar known to be translocated.

Figure 8.9 Diagram showing operation of pressure flow mechanism of phloem translocation. *R*, root parenchyma; *X*, xylem; *L*, leaf parenchyma cells; *pl*, plasmodesms; *S*, sieve tubes; *C*, cambium cells; *P*, storage parenchyma. (*From Curtis and Clark*, 1950.)

Furthermore, positive pressures do not always exist in the phloem at times when translocation presumably is occurring.

All we are certain of is that translocation does occur through the phloem. Esau et al. (1957) and Zimmerman (1957b) suggest that perhaps more than one mechanism is involved. Certainly, much more research is necessary before we can fully explain this important process.

Factors Affecting Translocation

Some additional information concerning the rate, amount, and direction of translocation is summarized in this section. Unfortunately our knowledge of the process is so limited that it is impossible to present a very satisfactory picture of the situation. Most of the research has been done on herbaceous plants, but the general principles presumably apply equally well to woody plants.

Temperature. Increasing temperature would be expected to increase the rate of translocation, and experiments by Curtis and his colleagues (Curtis and Clark, 1950, p. 439) indicate that the rate increases with temperature from 4 to 20 or 30°C. At 40°C there is a sharp decrease, presumably because of high use of food in respiration. In contrast Went (1944) concluded that the rate of translocation increases with decreasing temperature, at least down to 8°C, but it seems possible that the apparent decrease in translocation at high temperatures results from the presence of less sugar because more is used in respiration. Several investigators have reported that reduced stem or petiole temperatures reduce the rate of translocation of both organic and inorganic substances.

Aeration. It has been demonstrated repeatedly that a supply of oxygen is necessary for translocation of food through stems of herbaceous plants (Curtis and Clark, 1950, p. 443). Presumably poor soil aeration hinders or prevents the movement of food in the roots of trees. It is probable that buttressed bases on tupelo and cypress growing in water are the result of physiological girdles caused by lack of oxygen. Inability of the phloem to function properly may cause food and auxin to accumulate at the water level and stimulate abnormal growth.

Internal Factors. Perhaps the most puzzling problem is polar transport. All the various growing regions of the plant, including root and stem tip, cambiums, and fruits and seeds compete for the products of photosynthesis. Their success in this competition seems to vary with age and stage of growth. Sideris and Krauss (1955) found that new shoots and fruits of pineapple were able to obtain water and food at the expense of the roots and leaves. The leader of a conifer seems to have an advantage over its side branches, young leaves get food and minerals from older leaves but lose some as they become senescent, while flowers, fruits, and seeds obtain food at the expense of roots and other vegetative structures. Perhaps the level of auxin production at least partly controls the direction of translocation because it affects metabolic activity, and food seems to move toward regions of high metabolic activity, but as yet this polarity is not fully explained.

ACCUMULATION OF FOODS

The topic of food accumulation rarely receives much space in textbooks of plant physiology. This is unfortunate because the accumulation of a reserve of food materials each growing season is as essential for growth and even for survival of trees as the use of food in metabolic processes. This is particularly true in deciduous trees where the maintenance of life during the winter and resumption of growth in the spring are entirely dependent on food accumulated during the previous growing season. The forms, places, and times of food accumulation will be discussed rather briefly because they were mentioned in the chapters on carbohydrates, fats, and proteins. Special attention will be given to factors affecting the amount of food accumulated since this depends on a complex interaction between environmental factors and physiological processes.

The food economy of a tree can be expressed as follows:

Income = food manufactured by photosynthesis
Expenditures = food used in assimilation and respiration
Balance = food accumulated

Uses of Reserve Foods

The most obvious use of reserve foods is in maintaining respiration and other processes at times when food is not supplied directly from photosynthesis. All metabolic activity at night is dependent on food accumulated during the day, and respiration and other processes are maintained in deciduous trees during the winter by the use of reserve foods. Considerable root growth occurs in the winter and early spring, and the production of new branches, flowers, and leaves in the spring is at the expense of food stored the previous summer.

Production of stump sprouts depends on the use of food stored in the roots and stumps, and the number and size of sprouts are believed to be related to the amount of stored food in many instances. Buell (1940), for example, found that dogwood trees cut in August when food reserves are low produced fewer and smaller stump sprouts than those cut in the winter when reserves presumably are higher. Sprouting of bushes after cutting also is often correlated with the amount of reserve food present in their roots and stumps (Aldous, 1929). Sprouting is not always related to food reserves, however, because Wenger (1953a) found no correlation between food reserves in the stumps and the number and size of sprouts produced by sweetgum. This might indicate that even the minimum amount of carbohydrates in the stumps of these trees was above the level which would be limiting to sprout growth.

Forms and Places in Which Food Accumulates

By far the largest part of the reserve food accumulated in trees is in the form of carbohydrates, chiefly starch. In many kinds of trees, as temperatures start to fall in late autumn and early winter, starch begins to be converted into sugar, and by spring large amounts of sugar, chiefly sucrose, are found in the xylem sap of birch, maple, and some other species. Some nitrogenous compounds and fats and oils also accumulate in the vegetative structures of trees, and in some species fats are an important storage form. According to Sinnott (1918), fats are most often the chief storage form in conifers and trees of a few genera of hardwoods, but carbohydrates are the chief storage form in hardwoods. More data on fat accumulation are given in Chapter 6.

Fats and proteins are relatively much more important reserve foods in seeds than in vegetative structures. Seeds of coconut palm, pecan, and Brazil nut often contain 65 to 75 per cent of fat on a dry-weight basis, and walnuts contain 50 to 65 per cent. Red oak acorns contain over 20 per cent of fat in the autumn, but the content decreases during the winter, apparently because it is gradually converted into carbohydrates. The fats and oils in seeds usually appear to be converted into carbohydrates during germination and then are used by the developing embryos. Proteins are an important storage form in many seeds. Korstian (1927) found 7 to 8 per cent of protein in acorns of several species of oaks.

In vegetative structures foods accumulate in the parenchyma cells, especially in those of the xylem and phloem and the rays. Accumulation in leaves usually is temporary, and much of the food in leaves moves out of them before they fall by natural abscission.

The form in which foods accumulate probably is determined chiefly by the enzyme systems in the storage organs. For example, grafting immature sour lemon fruits on sweet lemon trees, and vice versa, did not change materially the composition of the fruit (Erickson, 1957).

Time of Accumulation

Food obviously accumulates at that period in the seasonal cycle when the rate of manufacture by photosynthesis is highest relative to the rate of use in assimilation and respiration. This is likely to be late in the summer in deciduous species, after growth has slowed down but before the leaves become senescent. The cool nights of early autumn reduce respiration, further favoring food accumulation in the period just before leaf fall. Considerable data on seasonal changes in carbohydrate content are presented in Chapter 4. Gardner (1925) found that starch began to accumulate in the ends of pear twigs soon after growth in length ceased.

The situation in evergreen species is different from that in deciduous species. Considerable carbohydrate accumulation occurs during the winter in conifers, with the result that carbohydrate reserves usually reach a maximum in the autumn or early spring (Figures 4.5 and 4.8). Gäumann (1927) reported that the carbohydrate contents of the wood of *Abies pectinata* or *Picea excelsa* were at a maximum in October or November and again in April, while Hepting (1945) found the maximum carbohydrate content in the stems of shortleaf pine occurring from April to June, with a fairly uniform low level from July to March. Climatic conditions doubtless have some bearing on the time at which maximum reserve foods are found, and conditions are very different in Switzerland where Gäumann worked and in the Southeastern United States where Hepting's pine was growing.

Factors Affecting Food Accumulation

It was stated at the beginning of the section on food accumulation that the amount of food accumulated represents the difference between the amount manufactured by photosynthesis and the amount used in assimilation and respiration. This means that the amount of food accumulated is affected by all those factors which affect either photosynthesis or the use of food. A few of the more important relationships will be discussed.

Factors Affecting Photosynthesis. Many of the factors which affect the efficiency of photosynthesis or rate per unit of leaf area are discussed in Chapter 3. We shall consider some factors which affect the photosynthetic surface because this probably is most important in the production of dry matter. Watson (1956) states that leaf area is the principal factor controlling dry-matter production by crop plants, and Ovington (1956a) found that maximum production of dry matter by forest stands appeared to be at the pole stage when leaf area also is at its maximum for the stand. According to Watson (1956), yield of plants is increased by irrigation and fertilization more because these treatments increase the leaf area than because they increase the rate of photosynthesis per unit of leaf area. Maintenance of a large leaf area therefore is the most important requisite for providing the food necessary for good growth and fruit production (Heinicke, 1934).

Defoliation. Defoliation by insects, fungi, fires, and storms usually causes reduction in growth and even death of trees because it reduces the photosynthetic surface. The effects of defoliation vary widely with the species, the vigor of the individual trees, and the season at which it occurs. Defoliation by excessive pruning sometimes reduces both total growth and the root/shoot ratio. The effects of defoliation and shading on growth are discussed in more detail in Chapter 16.

Factors Affecting Use of Food. Food is used in respiration and in the production of new tissues by the group of processes which we term assimilation. If environmental or internal factors increase such use excessively, the trees may suffer from inadequate reserves and flowering, fruiting, and vegetative growth may be reduced.

Assimilation. It has been demonstrated repeatedly that excessive stimulation of vegetative growth in fruit trees uses so much carbohydrates that flower bud formation is reduced or prevented. Occasionally vigorously growing young nonbearing trees are girdled to keep more carbohydrates in the tops and stimulate flower bud formation (Kraybill, 1923). Since forest trees are seldom fertilized, excessive stimulation of growth has not been a problem, but it is likely to be if seed trees are overfertilized. Seedlings in nurseries probably suffer more often from deficiency than from excess of nitrogen, but an excess conceivably could produce seedlings with an undesirably low carbohydrate reserve and a low root/shoot ratio. More attention should be given to developing fertilizer regimes which will result in seedlings with characteristics which increase their chances of survival when outplanted.

Flowering and Fruiting. Production of flowers, fruits, and seeds uses large amounts of food. Heinicke (1934) stated that so much reserve food sometimes is used by a heavy crop of flowers that not enough is left to produce a large leaf surface early in the season. Fruit production therefore usually reduces vegetative growth, although perhaps not in proportion to the dry weight of fruit and seeds produced (Chandler, 1934). Morris (1951) found that production of seed practically always reduces the amount of shoot growth and foliage produced by balsam. Flowering also is accompanied by reduction in diameter growth of balsam fir (Mott et al., 1957).

It is well known that the individual fruits are smaller when a heavy crop is allowed to develop than when the leaf area per fruit is increased by removing part of the fruit. The relation between photosynthetic surface and fruit size is shown in Table 8.3, and the relationship between fruiting and carbohydrate accumulation is discussed further in the chapters on carbohydrate metabolism (Chapter 4) and reproduction (Chapter 13).

Respiration. Photosynthesis occurs only in the chlorophyll-containing tissue when exposed to light, but respiration occurs in every living cell all the time. Trees synthesize food only during daylight hours. In very cloudy weather, during droughts, or when temperatures are too low, they manufacture little or no food, but they use food every minute of their life. Anything which increases the rate of respiration above that necessary for growth represents a waste of food. In nature high temperature probably is the most common factor causing excessive respiration, because over a wide temperature range the rate tends to double with every increase of 10°C.

High night temperatures appear to be particularly unfavorable for growth of even southern tree species (Kramer, 1957b). Printz (1933) claims that in Europe the southward and eastward extension of Scotch pine is limited by high summer temperatures which reduce the amount of net photosynthesis. Heinicke (1939) presents some interesting data showing that net photosynthesis of apple trees is decreased about 20 per cent for a 10°C increase in temperature in the range from 20 to 35°C.

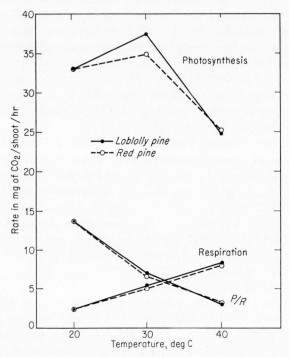

Figure 8.10 Effect of increasing temperature on ratio of photosynthesis to respiration in red and loblolly pine. (*From Decker, 1944.*)

Table 8.3. Relation between photosynthetic surface left above a girdle and the size of apples. (*From Magness, 1928.*)

No. of leaves per fruit	Weight of apple, g
10	93
20	134
30	170
50	201
75	211

Ratio of Photosynthesis to Respiration. The ratio of photosynthesis to respiration seems to be a very important factor in the success of trees and other plants, as suggested by Lundegardh (1931). Respiration continues to increase at high temperatures where photosynthesis begins to decrease, causing a very large decrease in food available for growth or accumulation. Some data on loblolly pine and red pine are shown in Figure 8.10 indicating how the ratio of photosynthesis to respiration decreases with increasing temperature. The similar behavior of *Pinus cembra* is shown in Figure 3.10. It seems possible that disturbance of the photosynthesis/respiration ratio may be an important factor in the reduced growth of trees grown with abnormally warm nights (Kramer, 1957b, 1958b). Heinicke and Childers (1936) estimated that the average night rate of respiration of an apple tree is less than 10 per cent of the average day rate of photosynthesis, but that because of higher day temperatures the day rate of respiration may be great enough to reduce net photosynthesis by 20 to 30 per cent on hot days. It is possible that some lower branches which are heavily shaded actually use more food than they manufacture. Polster (1950) suggested that there might be more opportunity to increase dry-matter production in a forest by reducing respiration than by increasing photosynthesis.

GENERAL REFERENCES

Crafts, A. S., 1951, Movement of assimilates, viruses, growth regulators, and chemical indicators in plants, Bot. Rev., 17:203–284.

Curtis, O. F., 1935, The translocation of solutes in plants, McGraw-Hill Book Company, Inc., New York.

—— and D. G. Clark, 1950, An introduction to plant physiology, McGraw-Hill Book Company, Inc., New York.

Esau, K., 1953, Plant anatomy, chap. 12, Phloem, John Wiley & Sons, Inc., New York.

——, H. B. Currier, and V. I. Cheadle, 1957, Physiology of phloem, Ann. Rev. Plant Physiology, 8:349–374.

Huber, B., 1956, Die Saftströme der Pflanzen, Springer-Verlag, Berlin.

——, 1958b, Anatomical and physiological investigations on food translocation in trees, chap. 17 in K. V. Thimann (ed.), The physiology of forest trees, The Ronald Press Company, New York.

Münch, E., 1930, Die Stoffbewegungen in der Pflanze, Gustav Fischer, Verlagsbuchhandlung, Jena, Germany.

Overbeek, J. van, 1956, Absorption and translocation of plant regulators, Ann. Rev. Plant Physiology, 7:355–372.

Zimmerman, M. H., 1958, Translocation of organic substances in the phloem of trees, chap. 18 in K. V. Thimann (ed.), The physiology of forest trees, The Ronald Press Company, New York.

CHAPTER 9 *Mineral Nutrition and*
Salt Absorption

MINERAL NUTRITION

Mineral nutrition is an important phase of tree physiology because an adequate supply of certain mineral elements is essential for successful growth. Plants require oxygen, water, carbon dioxide, nitrogen, and about a dozen mineral elements as reagents or raw materials in their various synthetic processes and for other purposes. Persons not trained in plant physiology often call mineral nutrients plant foods, and arborists speak of "feeding" trees when they apply fertilizers. Plant physiologists frown on such undiscriminating use of the term "food" because they usually restrict it to carbohydrates, fats, and proteins which can be used directly as a source of energy when oxidized in respiration or can be used as building materials in the process of assimilation. Minerals and carbon dioxide usually are regarded by physiologists as raw materials, reagents, or accessory substances necessary for the synthesis of foods, rather than as foods.

General Functions of Minerals

Mineral nutrients have many functions in plants. Among their more important roles are constituents of plant tissues, catalysts in various reactions, osmotic regulators, constituents of buffer systems, and regulators of membrane permeability. Examples of minerals as constituents are calcium in cell walls, magnesium in the chlorophyll molecule, sulfur in certain proteins, and phosphorus in phospholipids and nucleoproteins. Although nitrogen is not a mineral element it often is included with them and its importance as a constitutent of protein should be noted. Several elements, including iron, copper, and zinc, are required in very small quantities but are essential because they are prosthetic groups or coenzymes of certain enzyme systems. Others such as manganese and

224

magnesium function as activators or inhibitors of enzyme systems. Some elements such as boron, copper, and zinc, which are required in small quantities in enzyme systems, are very toxic if present in larger quantities. Toxicity of these and other ions such as silver and mercury probably is related chiefly to their injurious effects on enzyme systems.

Although much of the osmotic pressure of cell sap is attributable to soluble carbohydrates, a measurable fraction results from the presence of mineral salts, and salt often is the major source of the high osmotic pressure of halophytes. Phosphates form one of the important plant buffer systems, and elements such as calcium, magnesium, and potassium form the cations of the organic acid buffer systems. The kinds of ions present often affect the hydration of protoplasm and the permeability of cell membranes, di- and trivalent cations usually decreasing and monovalent cations increasing permeability. Certain ions tend to counterbalance the effect of others, and this is known as an antagonistic or balancing effect. For example, a low concentration of calcium is required to balance sodium and prevent the injury which occurs in a solution of sodium chloride alone.

The importance of an adequate supply of minerals for good growth has been appreciated in agriculture and horticulture for many years but has been largely neglected in forestry until recently. Even now most of the research is on seedling growth in nurseries, but increasing costs of land and higher prices for timber are likely to change this situation. As tree improvement programs supply better planting stock it will be necessary to provide a better environment if the growth potential of the stock is to be realized. For these reasons it may become as important to fertilize forest tree plantations as it now is to fertilize agricultural crops. More research on the specific mineral requirements of trees is badly needed as a basis for silvicultural applications.

The Essential Elements

More than half of the elements in the periodic table have been found in plants, and it seems probable that every element occurring in the root environment is absorbed. At least 27 elements were identified in certain samples of white pine wood (Wilcox, 1940), and others doubtless occur in very small quantities. Not all the elements found in trees are essential, however. For example, Parker (1956a) found platinum, tin, and silver in leaves of ponderosa pine, and considerable quantities of silicon and sodium occur in plants, but none of these elements is regarded as essential.

The elements required in fairly large quantities are nitrogen, phosphorus, potassium, calcium, magnesium, and sulfur, and these sometimes are called the major or macronutrients. Elements required in smaller quantities include iron, manganese, zinc, copper, boron, and molybdenum, and it now seems that chlorine should be added to the list (Broyer et al., 1954). It is possible that this list will be expanded further with time. Those elements required in very small quantities often are called the minor elements or micronutrients. The relative amounts of the various essential elements likely to be found in samples of leaf tissue are shown in Table 9.1.

Relatively little intensive research has been done on the specific mineral requirements of forest trees, but experience with fruit trees suggests that they have the same requirements as herbaceous plants. It seems likely, however, that their quantitative requirements may be lower for at least some elements. This will be discussed later.

An element is regarded as essential only if lack of it causes marked reduction in growth, abnormal growth, or death and if no other element can be substituted for it. Generally this relationship should be demonstrated for plants of several unrelated species. The fact that an element improves growth does not prove that it is essential, because some elements improve growth although plants will grow without them. For

Table 9.1. Relative amounts of various elements found in dried leaf tissue of a healthy plant. (*From Bollard, 1955.*)

Element	Content, parts per million
Nitrogen	20,000
Potassium	15,000
Calcium	15,000
Magnesium	3,000
Phosphorus	2,500
Sulfur	2,000
Iron	100
Boron	40
Manganese	40
Zinc	40
Copper	25
Molybdenum	1

example, sodium seems to improve the growth of sugar beets and several other species, but it is not considered essential for them.

Functions of Various Elements

Most of the research on the roles of various elements has been done with herbaceous plants because their short life cycle permits shorter experimental periods, but some experiments have been performed on fruit trees and forest tree seedlings. The following discussion is based on the reasonable assumption that various elements perform the same functions in both herbaceous and woody plants. For more details the reader is referred to the recent review by Gauch (1957) and various papers cited in it and to textbooks of plant physiology. A few specific functions of each of the essential elements follow.

Nitrogen. The essential role of nitrogen as a constituent of amino acids, which are the building blocks of proteins, is well known. It occurs in a variety of other compounds such as the purines and alkaloids and in many vitamins (Chapter 5). Nitrogen-containing compounds make up 5 to 30 per cent of the dry weight of plants. Nitrogen deficiency is accompanied by failure to synthesize normal amounts of chlorophyll, resulting in chlorosis of the older leaves and of younger foliage in cases of extreme deficiency.

Phosphorus. This element is a constituent of nucleoproteins and phospholipids, and the high-energy bonds associated with phosphate groups seem to constitute the chief medium for energy transfer in plants. Phosphorus occurs in both organic and inorganic forms and is translocated readily, probably in both forms.

Potassium. Although large amounts of potassium are required, it is not known to occur in organic forms. It apparently is involved in enzyme activity, and a deficiency is said to hinder translocation of carbohydrates and nitrogen metabolism, but this may be an indirect rather than a direct effect. It is interesting to note that plant cells distinguish between potassium and sodium, and the latter cannot be substituted for the former. Potassium is highly mobile in plants.

Sulfur. Sulfur is a constituent of cystine, cysteine and other amino acids, of biotin and thiamin and occurs in the sulfhydryl group. Deficiency of sulfur causes chlorosis and failure to synthesize proteins, resulting in accumulation of amino acids. Sulfur is less mobile than nitrogen, phosphorus, or potassium.

Calcium. Calcium occurs in considerable quantities as calcium oxalate crystals; it occurs in cell walls and apparently influences their elasticity; and it is involved in some manner in nitrogen metabolism. Calcium is relatively immobile, and a deficiency results in serious injury to meristematic regions.

Magnesium. This element is a constituent of the chlorophyll molecule and is also involved in the action of several enzyme systems. A deficiency usually produces chlorosis. Magnesium is translocated readily in most plants.

Iron. One of the most common causes of chlorophyll deficiency at high soil pH values is inability to utilize iron properly. Iron probably plays some role in the synthesis of chloroplast proteins, and much of the iron in leaves occurs in the chloroplasts (Brown, 1956). It also occurs in a number of respiratory enzymes such as peroxidases and in cytochrome oxidase. Iron is relatively immobile, and deficiencies usually develop in new tissues because it is not translocated out of older leaves.

Manganese. This element also is essential for the synthesis of chlorophyll. Its principal function probably is the activation of enzyme systems, and it probably also affects the availability of iron. A deficiency often causes a malformation of leaves known as "frenching" and the development of chlorotic or dead areas. It is relatively immobile.

Zinc. A deficiency of zinc produces leaf malformations in several species of trees resembling virus diseases, possibly because it is involved in the synthesis of tryptophan, which is a precursor of indoleacetic acid. It also is a constituent of carbonic anhydrase. Smith and Bayliss (1942) described well-defined symptoms of zinc deficiencies in Monterey pine in Australia, including development of a flat top, and Bollard (1955) discusses boron, manganese, and zinc deficiencies of fruit trees.

Copper. Copper also is a constituent of certain enzymes, including ascorbic acid oxidase and tyrosinase. Very small quantities are needed, and too much is toxic. Benzian and Warren (1957) demonstrated the need of copper in spruce seedlings, and Smith (1943) demonstrated it in Monterey pine.

Boron. This is another element required in very small quantities, the specific requirements varying from 1 to 10 or 15 parts per million, depending on the species, and the concentration for best growth closely approaches the toxic concentration in some species. A deficiency causes serious injury to stem tips, and it seems to be necessary for sugar translocation (Gauch and Dugger, 1954). Plants deficient in boron contain more sugars and pentosans and have lower rates of water absorption and transpiration than normal plants. Smith (1943) produced strongly defined symptoms of boron deficiency in Monterey pine.

Molybdenum. This element is required in the lowest concentration of any essential element, only 1 part per million sufficing for most plants. It is involved in nitrogen fixation and a nitrate-reducing enzyme system and probably has other functions (Evans, 1956).

Chlorine. It has recently been reported that chlorine is essential (Broyer et al., 1954), and it may be involved in photosynthesis.

Other Elements. Aluminum, sodium, and silicon occur in large quantities in some plants, and although they sometimes increase growth, they are not usually regarded as essential. An excess of aluminum is highly toxic. It is claimed by Trelease and Trelease (1939) that selenium is essential to plants of certain species which normally accumulate high concentrations. There are numerous and complicated interactions among various elements, one element modifying the absorption and utilization of another, but lack of space prevents discussion of these interactions.

Symptoms of Mineral Deficiencies

Mineral deficiencies cause changes in biochemical and physiological processes which often produce morphological changes or visible symptoms. Growth sometimes is depressed by deficiencies before other symptoms appear (Ingestad, 1957). Some of the more important morphological and physiological reactions to mineral deficiencies will be discussed briefly.

Visible Symptoms of Deficiencies. The most important general effect of mineral deficiencies is reduced growth, but the most conspicuous effect usually is yellowing of the leaves caused by reduced chlorophyll synthesis. Leaves seem to be particularly sensitive indicators of deficiency, tending to be reduced in size, abnormal in shape or structure, or pale in color, and they sometimes even develop dead areas on the tips, the margins, or between the principal veins. In some instances leaves tend to occur in tufts or rosettes, and pine needles occasionally fail to separate properly, producing a disorder known as fused needles. Pessin (1937) reported that most fascicles of phosphorus-deficient longleaf pine seedlings contained only two instead of the usual three needles. A common symptom of certain types of mineral deficiency is frenching, in which stem elongation is inhibited and leaf blade growth is reduced, resulting in rosettes of slender leaves which often show a network of chlorotic areas. The visible symptoms of deficiencies of various elements are so characteristic that experienced observers can identify them by appearance. Some examples are shown in Figure 9.1.

Deficiencies sometimes cause trees to produce excessive amounts of gum, resulting in so-called "gummosis." In Australia resin exudation around buds is characteristic of a zinc-deficiency disease of Monterey pine (Kessel and Stoate, 1938). Gummy exudates also occur on the bark of fruit trees suffering from exanthema or dieback (Anderssen, 1932).

Severe deficiencies often cause death of leaves, shoots, and other tissues, resulting in symptoms described as dieback. Copper deficiency has been observed to cause dieback of shoots in citrus, olive, pear, and plum trees and some berry fruits (Anderssen, 1932). Dieback of terminal shoots of copper-deficient apple trees produces a stunted, bushy appearance (Dunne, 1938). Boron deficiency is said to cause hypertrophy and finally death of the cambium in citrus, and death of phloem in apple (Hildebrand, 1939) and olive (Ciferri et al., 1955). Lesions in bark (Hildebrand, 1939) and fruits have been attributed to mineral deficiencies. Deficiency of a single element sometimes produces several different symptoms. For example, boron deficiency in apple trees causes brittle deformed leaves, phloem necrosis, lesions in bark (Shannon, 1954), and injury to the fruit.

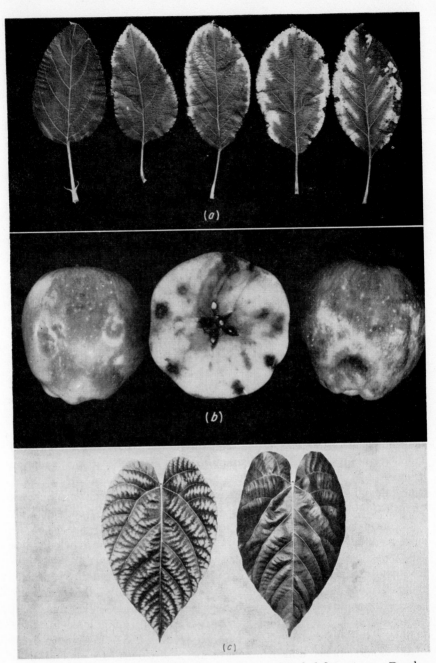

Figure 9.1 Examples of symptoms caused by mineral deficiencies. *a.* Development of symptoms on apple leaves associated with magnesium deficiency. *b.* Breakdown of tissue in apple fruits apparently caused by boron deficiency. *c.* Manganese-deficient (left) and normal (right) leaves of tung. (*Photographs a and b courtesy of Crops Research Division, U.S. Department of Agriculture; photograph c courtesy of R. D. Dickey, Florida Agricultural Experiment Station.*)

Mineral deficiencies also produce internal changes visible only under the microscope, as well as external symptoms. Davis (1949) found that calcium-deficient seedlings of loblolly pine not only had smaller buds and stem tips but smaller leaves with fewer and smaller cells and less xylem and phloem, less primary and more secondary tissue in stems, and abnormally blunt root tips with fewer mitotic figures than in normal seedlings. Cell division was reduced more than cell enlargement or differentiation by calcium deficiency, resulting in the lignification of xylem very close to the meristematic region.

Noticeable changes in cell structure often are caused by mineral deficiencies. Reed and Dufrenoy (1935) found that the palisade cells of zinc-deficient citrus leaves were wider than in normal leaves, rhomboidal instead of columnar in shape, and often transversely divided. Chloroplasts were reduced in number and abnormally high in fat, while starch grains were slender and elongated. Microchemical tests indicated the presence of phytosterol or lecithin in the vacuoles of cells of zinc-deficient leaves, but not in leaves of normal plants. Reed (1938) later observed that zinc deficiency retarded differentiation in leaves, resulting in a very compact mesophyll with reduced intercellular spaces.

The location of the symptoms of deficiencies of various elements seems to be related as much to the relative mobility of the various elements as to their specific functions. For example, symptoms of deficiencies of nitrogen, phosphorus, potassium, and magnesium appear in the older leaves while the young leaves are yet healthy, because these elements are readily translocated from old to young tissues. In contrast, symptoms of deficiencies of boron and calcium appear in the growing stem tips and those of iron, manganese, and sulfur deficiency in the younger leaves, because these elements are not readily translocated from old to new tissues (Müller, 1949). Bukovac and Wittwer (1957) rated the mobility of various elements. Rubidium, sodium, and potassium were highly mobile. The following ions showed decreasing mobility in the order in which they are listed: phosphorus, chlorine, sulfur, zinc, copper, manganese, iron, and molybdenum. Calcium, strontium, and barium were immobile. These rates are based on translocation of radioactive isotopes out of bean leaves. No extensive data of this type are available for trees.

Chlorosis. The most commonly observed symptom of a wide variety of deficiencies is chlorosis, caused by interference with chlorophyll synthesis. It varies in the pattern, the extent to which young and old leaves are involved, and the severity, according to the species, the element, and the degree of deficiency. Chlorosis most often is associated with lack of nitrogen, but it also is caused by deficiencies of iron, manganese, magnesium, potassium, and other elements. Furthermore, numerous unfavorable environmental factors other than mineral deficiency cause chlorosis, including an excess or deficiency of water, unfavorable temperatures, toxic substances such as sulfur dioxide, and an excess of minerals. Chlorosis also is caused by genetic factors, which produce plants ranging from albinos totally devoid of chlorophyll to various degrees of deficiency found in virescent seedlings and various types of striping of leaves.

The wide variety of factors producing chlorosis suggests that it usually is caused by general disturbances of metabolism rather than by the specific effects of deficiency of a particular element. Iljin (1951) concluded that lime-induced chlorosis of several species of woody and herbaceous plants growing on calcareous soils is caused by abnormal nitrogen and organic acid metabolism. He found 5 to 15 times as much soluble nitrogen and considerably more organic acids in chlorotic than in nonchlorotic leaves and suggested that the abnormal concentration interferes with chlorophyll synthesis. This view is also held by Steinberg (1951), who found an increased concentration of amino acids and decreased protein content in tobacco plants suffering from a variety of mineral deficiencies. He demonstrated that an excess of isoleucine caused typical frenching of tobacco and that other free amino acids caused characteristic chlorosis, necrosis, and abnormalities in leaf form. Steinberg suggested that probably all mineral deficiencies cause disturbance of nitrogen metabolism, and the resulting unbalance in nitrogen compounds produces such visible symptoms as chlorosis and leaf injury.

The nitrogen metabolism of at least some trees differs from that of many herbaceous plants because nitrate reduction occurs in the roots of at least several species (Bollard, 1957a and b). Nevertheless, the similarity of deficiency symptoms in most woody and herbaceous plants suggests that the same mechanism operates to produce them in both types of plants.

One of the most troublesome types of chlorosis is that found in a wide variety of fruit, shade, and forest trees growing on calcareous soil. This has often been attributed to the unavailability of iron at a high pH, but Iljin (1952) and others have found the iron content sometimes higher and sometimes lower in chlorotic plants than in normal ones, and it seems that deficiency of iron may not be the direct cause. Iljin claimed, as mentioned earlier, that the entire metabolism was disturbed and not just the process of chlorophyll synthesis. Often little difference in calcium or iron content is found between soils supporting healthy and chlorotic plants (Thorne et al., 1951). The most severe lime-induced chlorosis occurs on fine-textured, poorly aerated, cold soils, where conditions are unfavorable for mineral absorption. Much of the chlorosis of azaleas and some other plants often attributed to the presence of lime really is caused by drought because salt absorption is reduced in very dry soil. It appears that the causes of chlorosis on calcareous soils are not yet fully explained. Dale et al. (1955) found that pine seedlings caused to form mycorrhizae by adding humus grew normally on a calcareous soil with pH 8.2. However, this may have been due to the humus rather than to the development of mycorrhizae.

Chlorosis can often be decreased or eliminated by spraying the foliage, injecting salts into the stems or leaves, or adding them to the soil. Korstian et al. (1921) corrected chlorosis in forest nurseries by spraying the seedlings with ferrous sulfate, and Becker-Dillingen (1937) found sprays containing potassium and magnesium effective in some instances. In certain situations where chlorosis of apple was not corrected by spraying the leaves or applying ferrous sulfate to the soil, it was corrected by injecting ferrous sulfate into the stems. Driving iron nails into the stems was effective also. Chlorosis in 50-year-old poplar trees was cured by injecting ferric phosphate through holes in the stems (Starr, 1940). Iron chelate is very effective in correcting chlorosis of citrus on acid sands in Florida and is now being used successfully in other regions for shade trees and shrubs. Brown (1956) recently summarized the literature on iron chlorosis.

Physiological Effects of Mineral Deficiencies

The visible morphological effects or symptoms of mineral deficiencies are the result of changes in various internal biochemical and physiological processes, but it usually is difficult to determine exactly how deficiency of a particular element produces the observed effects because of the complex interactions which exist. For example, a deficiency of nitrogen might reduce growth because of a reduced supply of nitrogen for synthesis of protoplasm, but synthesis of enzymes and chlorophyll also is reduced and the photosynthetic surface is decreased. This causes reduction in photosynthesis, which decreases the supply of carbohydrates available for growth, and this may further reduce the uptake of nitrogen and minerals. A single element often has several roles in plants, and it is difficult to learn which role or combination of roles is responsible for the visible symptoms. Manganese, for example, is an activator of certain enzyme systems, it is necessary for chlorophyll synthesis, and a deficiency causes several physiological diseases, including frenching of tung trees.

Physiological Processes

Some interesting research has been done on the relation between mineral deficiency and major physiological processes such as respiration, photosynthesis, nitrogen metabolism, fat synthesis, and water relations, mostly on apple (Batjer and Degman, 1940; Childers, 1937; Heinicke and Hoffman, 1933) and tung (Drosdoff et al., 1947; Loustalot et al., 1950). Relatively little work of this type has been done on forest trees, and further research is badly needed, especially with respect to effects of mineral deficiencies and fertilization on photosynthesis and on water relations. Some of these effects will be discussed further in the chapters dealing with various major physiological processes.

Mineral deficiency usually decreases both the synthesis of carbohydrates and their translocation to growing tissues. Photosynthesis often is affected (Chapter 3) differently from respiration. For example, a marked deficiency of potassium causes reduced photosynthesis and increased respiration, thereby decreasing carbohydrates available for growth (Meyer and Anderson, 1952). Translocation of carbohydrates sometimes also is inhibited. This effect is pronounced in boron-deficient trees with phloem necrosis. The decreased availability of carbohydrates results in decreased growth of tissues, but on the other hand, decreased growth and utilization of carbohydrates may result in their accumulation. Seed production sometimes is decreased because of low carbohydrate reserves. Heavy applications of nitrogen fertilizer resulted in greatly increased seed production by beech and sugar maple trees, and the percentage of sound seeds and the dry weight of the maple seed were increased (Chandler, 1938). Cone and seed production of young loblolly pine also were increased greatly by adding fertilizer (Wenger, 1953b). When trees are not mineral-deficient, however, additions of large amounts of nitrogenous fertilizers may decrease seed production by enhancing vegetative growth (Chapter 13).

Disease

Susceptibility to disease often is increased by declining tree vigor correlated with lack of available minerals. Mineral-deficient seedlings of longleaf pine become infected with the brown spot needle blight more readily than vigorous ones. According to Parker et al. (1947), development of Dutch elm disease is much less severe in young trees on soils of high fertility than on soils deficient in mineral nutrients. Sometimes healthy, vigorous trees are less susceptible than unthrifty ones to attacks of certain insects. For example, DenUyl (1944) has suggested that additions of fertilizers might help control locust borer injury because there is a close relationship between damage by the borer and low tree vigor.

Species and Individual Differences in Response to Mineral Deficiency

Trees of various species react differently to mineral deficiencies. On flat sand plains in New York State that had been abandoned for agriculture because of low potash and general infertility, trees of red pine showed general stagnation, with little difference in deficiency symptoms among individual trees. White pine, however, showed wide variations among individual trees, dead trees occurring beside trees making considerable height growth. Norway spruce and white spruce showed even more pronounced deficiency symptoms, with many dead trees and large cone crops even on small trees. In contrast, mugo pine showed virtually no deficiency symptoms, while Scotch pine and jack pine showed only slight chlorosis (Heiberg and White, 1951).

Hobbs (1944) found that tip chlorosis of seedlings was followed by necrosis in four species of pine seedlings grown in magnesium-deficient cultures but that the severity of the symptoms varied with species, being more severe in the more rapidly growing white and red pine than in the more slowly growing pitch and shortleaf pines. Pessin (1937) found still different symptoms of magnesium deficiency in longleaf pine, which developed necrosis without prior yellowing. Stone (1953a) observed that the most conspicuous symptom of magnesium deficiency in several coniferous species in New York was a bright yellow discoloration of the needles of the current year. The chlorosis appeared in the autumn and affected the upper part of the tree most. Whenever severe deficiency developed, death or premature loss of needles followed the yellowing. Chlorosis was much less conspicuous on white than on red pine. Norway spruce, however, reacted by a generalized yellowing rather than the apical yellowing on new needles shown by the pines.

Walker (1956) reported potassium-deficient black cherry leaves to show strikingly bright red pigmentation in leaf margins, while leaves of gray birch which were potassium-deficient had chlorotic margins. Symptoms of potassium deficiency were different for leaves of red maple, which were uniformly chlorotic, and white pine, which were short, chlorotic, and often brown at the tips. Worley et al. (1941) observed that the behavior of Siberian elm, ailanthus, and northern catalpa grown from seed in sand cultures was somewhat different when subjected to deficiencies of various elements. For example, in the absence of potassium catalpa leaves were dark green, ailanthus intermediate, and elm yellowish. It therefore is necessary to observe the appearance of trees of various species known to suffer from deficiencies of certain elements in order to learn their characteristic reactions or symptoms. Even then it is possible that differences in climatic conditions may modify the reactions.

Symptoms of Excess Minerals

Forest soils rarely contain an excess of mineral nutrients, but heavy fertilization of orchards and nurseries sometimes produces a concentration of salts high enough to cause injury. This can occur because the osmotic pressure is increased, because of unfavorable changes in pH, or because the proportions of various ions become unbalanced.

Increased osmotic pressure of the soil solution reduces water absorption, increasing leaf water deficits and resulting in injury to tissues from desiccation on days when wind and high temperatures cause rapid transpiration. More prolonged and severe dehydration also causes stomatal closure and interferes with photosynthesis. High concentrations of salt in the soil also may injure the roots by plasmolysis, especially in sandy soils (Bear, 1942). Injury to leaves sometimes occurs from application of high concentrations of liquid fertilizers, and citrus leaves have been reported to accumulate injurious concentrations of sodium from sprinkling with irrigation water high in salt.

The amount of injury caused by excessive fertilization depends on the species, the type of fertilizer used, and the time of application. Mulberry trees are said to tolerate only one-fifth as concentrated a soil solution without injury as does apple, and different species and varieties of citrus vary in their salt tolerance (Gardner et al., 1952). Baxter (1943) states that *Juniperus* and *Thuja* are unusually susceptible to injury from an excess of fertilizer.

Considerable discussion has occurred concerning the relative importance of the osmotic pressure of the soil solution and its composition and pH as factors in causing injury from an excess of salts in soil. Investigators at the Salinity Laboratory at Riverside, California, consider the osmotic effects in reducing water absorption as most important, but some ionic effects also exist. Root growth of peaches was reduced more on Lovell than on Shalil rootstocks and was reduced more by sulfates than by chlorides at the same osmotic pressure (Hayward et al., 1946). Brown et al. (1953) found calcium chloride to be more toxic to stone fruits than isosmotic solutions of sodium chloride. Hayward and Magistad (1946) have reviewed the salt problem with respect to crop plants. Unpublished observations suggest that conifers are more susceptible to injury from excess salt than deciduous species.

It seems probable that good root growth can occur over a considerable pH range if all the essential mineral elements are available, although Leyton (1952) found best growth of Sitka spruce roots between pH 4 and 5. Much of the injury in very acid soils apparently is caused by the increased solubility of aluminum, while injury at higher pH values most often results from decreased availability of elements such as iron and manganese. Howell (1932) found that ponderosa pine seedlings survived over a pH range from 2.7 to 11 but only grew well over a pH range from 3.0 to 6.0, and Guest and Chapman (1944) found no direct injury to roots of sweet orange seedlings over a range from pH 4.0 to 9.0 although indirect effects were observed at both extremes. Another indirect effect of abnormal pH or chemical composition may be to increase injury from pathogenic organisms. *Fomes annosus* often attacks roots of trees on heavily limed soil. Chapman (1941) found that shortleaf pine seedlings died at or soon after emergence in soils containing an excess of soluble calcium and thrived only in acid soils. Wahlenberg (1930) reported that addition of bone meal or dried blood caused increased damping-off of conifer seedlings. Young seedlings are particularly susceptible to such injury.

Another result of excessive fertilization late in the season is to prolong the growing season until there is insufficient time for the trees to harden off before frost. Twigs formed too late in the season are likely to be very susceptible to frost injury. Overfertilization also sometimes stimulates the production of large numbers of branches, flowers, and fruits on older trees. Pines may respond by producing clusters of cones (Boyce, 1948). Other responses to overfertilization include fasciation or flattening of stems (Kienholz, 1932) and internal bark necrosis (Shannon, 1954). An undesirable effect on seedlings is to stimulate excessive top growth, producing a low ratio of roots to shoots, which often results in poor survival after outplanting.

Methods of Studying Mineral Requirements

There are several ways of studying the mineral requirements of trees and of determining the adequacy of the mineral supply. The essentiality of an element can be determined only under the most carefully controlled conditions which exclude the possibility of contamination with the element under study from the salts, the water, the containers in which the plants are grown, or even from dust in the air. The minimum amounts of various elements necessary for successful growth can be determined more easily, however, in experiments using soil, sand, or water cultures or by fertilization experiments in the field. The adequacy of the supply of various elements has been studied by analysis of soils or plant tissues and by observation of the effects of supplying various elements to the soil or directly to the foliage. The first number of Volume 62 of *Soil Science* and a paper by Hewitt (1952) describe various techniques for greenhouse studies of mineral nutrition. Some methods will be discussed briefly in the following pages.

Water Cultures. Plants have been grown in water culture at least from the time of the experiments of Woodward in 1697. In this method the plants are supported with their roots immersed in a dilute solution containing the necessary mineral elements. The containers used vary from small jars to large tanks containing hundreds of gallons of nutrient solution. Meyer and Anderson (1952) have summarized the precautions necessary in work with sand and solution cultures. The principal problems are aeration and maintenance of a suitable pH and constant osmotic pressure. There often is difficulty in compensating for the changing rate of removal of various ions by growing plants. The difficulty formerly

encountered in maintaining a supply of available iron has been eliminated by the use of iron chelate which can be prepared or purchased
ready for use. Water cultures have been used for forest trees by Howell
(1932), Steinbauer (1932), Pessin (1937), Leyton (1952), and others.

Sand Cultures. The use of sand or gravel cultures represents an improvement over water cultures because it provides anchorage for the

Figure 9.2 Apparatus for study of mineral deficiencies in pine seedlings. The
substrate (cracked quartz) is enclosed in polyethylene bags supported in porcelain
pots provided with drainage holes near the bottom. A constant level of nutrient
solution is maintained in each container. Air for aeration is forced in through the
washing bottle beside each jar and down through the solution-level-indicator tube
attached to each jar. In another arrangement the jars are flooded periodically with
nutrient solution, which then drains back by gravity into a reservoir below. (*Courtesy
of Department of Forestry, Ohio Agricultural Experiment Station.*)

roots and better aeration than water cultures. The plants can be grown
in pots, trays, or tanks provided with drainage and filled with a chemically inert, porous medium such as coarse sand, gravel, vermiculite, or
even glass wool or rock wool. A solution of the mineral elements is
supplied by dripping it on the surface or by periodically flooding the
medium. Usually the solution is pumped into the plant containers from
a reservoir below at regular intervals and allowed to drain back into
the reservoir by gravity.

This is perhaps the simplest method of growing plants with complete control of the mineral supply. The medium must be coarse enough to provide good drainage or the roots will suffer from inadequate aeration, and it is advisable occasionally to flush the medium with an excess of water to prevent salt accumulation on the surface from evaporation. Various modifications of the sand-culture technique have been used with trees by Mitchell (1934), Addoms (1937), Gast (1937), Shirley and Meuli (1939), Kopitke (1941), Smith (1943), Hobbs (1944), Wilson (1953), and others.

Soil Cultures. A somewhat less precise but useful modification of the sand-culture technique is to grow plants in containers of soil to which various combinations of elements or various amounts of fertilizer are added. This is particularly useful in determining the nature and the extent of deficiencies in natural soils for the growth of particular species. The work of Mitchell (1934) is an excellent example of effective use of this method.

Tree Injection. According to Roach (1939), various substances were injected into trees at least as early as the twelfth century in order to give unusual flavors to fruit and colors to flowers, and Leonardo da Vinci described the injection of arsenic into trees to make the fruit poisonous. In the seventeenth century substances such as mercury were injected in an attempt to kill insects, and in the nineteenth century Sachs injected solutions of iron salts to remedy chlorosis. More recently injection of leaves has been used as a means of diagnosing deficiencies and injection through the trunk as a means of curing them. Miller (1938, pp. 883–885) summarized much of the early literature on this topic.

The cause of a chlorosis sometimes can be determined by injecting various elements through leaf tips, petioles, or branches and noting which element causes disappearance of the symptoms (Roach, 1939; Roberts, 1946; Delap, 1950). Solutions of iron, zinc, and other elements have been injected into tree trunks to cure deficiency diseases, and solid salts have been placed in holes bored in trunks to provide a supply of the deficient element. Even driving zinc-coated glazier's points or iron nails into tree trunks has been reported to cure chlorosis and other evidences of deficiency of these elements. Trees usually respond rapidly to such injections because the materials are distributed rapidly. The techniques are discussed in detail by Roach (1939) and May (1941).

Some of the ancient uses of injection have been revived in modern times, such as curing diseases, preventing attacks by insects (Craighead et al., 1937, 1938), killing trees, and facilitating removal of bark (McIntosh, 1949). In recent years there has been considerable interest in "chemotherapy" or the control of diseases by introducing chemicals into plants. Dimond et al. (1949) used injection methods in experimental control of the Dutch elm disease, and readers are referred to papers by Horsfall and Zentmeyer (1941) and Stoddard and Dimond (1949) for discussions of this interesting field. The present interest in systemic insecticides and fungicides is likely to result in more research along these lines.

Soil Analysis. Trees absorb their minerals from the soil; hence it seems reasonable to suppose that an analysis of the mineral content of the soil would be a good indicator of the adequacy of the mineral supply for tree growth. Soil analyses have proved to be of limited value, however, for several reasons. The mineral content of a soil extract is not a reliable indicator of the availability to trees of the elements present. Furthermore, the root systems of trees spread so far and so deep that analysis of the areas which supply minerals to a particular tree often is difficult in heterogeneous soils. Different species also have quite different requirements; hence a concentration adequate for one species may be inadequate for another. While soil analyses give general indications of the fertility of a site, they are most useful when combined with other techniques such as fertilizer trials and analyses of plant tissues.

Foliar Diagnosis. Another method of evaluating the fertility of soil and the adequacy of the mineral supply for tree growth is to analyze the plants growing on them to learn if they contain sufficient amounts of the essential elements. This method faces two difficulties. One is the problem of deciding what constitutes an adequate amount of an element; the other is the fact that the presence of a certain amount of an element in plant tissue does not guarantee its availability for physiological processes. For example, plants showing symptoms of iron-induced chlorosis may contain as much iron as normal plants (Iljin, 1951; Thorne et al., 1951). Nevertheless, with proper safeguards and within certain limits, analyses of plant tissues are good indicators of the nutrient status of plants. The leaves of trees are particularly useful for this purpose because they are relatively sensitive indicators of deficiencies in nutrient supply.

Foliar analysis has been used extensively to determine the adequacy of mineral supply and to diagnose deficiencies. The mineral concentration of leaves is quite variable, depending on the species, the soil, the age and location of leaves, and climatic conditions. It therefore represents the interaction and integration of all the internal and external factors which influence the uptake of minerals by a particular tree. Lagatu and Maume (1924) made an early attempt to study mineral nutrition by leaf analysis, and Thomas (1937) developed the technique and stressed the necessity of evaluating both the quantity and the ratio of one element to another. Various adaptations of this method have been used successfully on forest trees (Mitchell, 1936; Mitchell and Chandler, 1939;

Heiberg and White, 1951; Finn, 1953; Aaltonen, 1955; Leyton and Armson, 1955; Walker, 1955, 1956; Leyton, 1956) and on fruit trees (Lilleland et al., 1940, 1942; Goodall and Gregory, 1947; Boynton et al., 1941, 1945; Drosdoff, 1944; Beattie and Judkins, 1952). Prevot and Ollagnier (1954) used foliar diagnosis successfully on the oil palm in Africa.

Because of the variations which normally occur in mineral content, foliar diagnosis depends more on relative concentrations than absolute amounts. A basis for comparison can be obtained under some sampling conditions by comparing the mineral content of leaves of trees which obviously are making excellent growth with leaves from trees making poor growth. Tables 9.2 and 9.3 show the nitrogen, phosphorus, and potassium content of leaves of some normal and deficient trees. A better basis for comparison can be obtained by growing seedlings or trees with known supplies of minerals and determining the mineral composition of their leaves. This provides information concerning the relation between growth, mineral content of the leaves, and mineral content of the soil, which is useful in evaluating the probable significance of the composition

Table 9.2. Potassium concentration of leaves as percentages of dry weight and of the plow layer of soil as parts per million. (*From Walker, 1956.*)

Species	Deficient specimens			Normal specimens		
	July	August	Soil	July	August	Soil
Pinus strobus	0.44	0.27	10.1	0.67	0.46	26.4
Prunus serotina	0.65	0.55	9.8	1.07	1.26	26.4
Betula populifolia	0.77	0.71	10.1	0.90	1.16	9.8
Acer rubrum	0.59	0.45	10.0	0.66	0.68	36.5

of leaves on sites of unknown fertility. This method is limited by the fact that the relationship varies from site to site because factors other than available nutrients often limit growth.

Such a use of foliar diagnosis was described by Mitchell and Chandler (1939) and is illustrated by Figure 9.3, obtained by determining mineral concentrations of leaves on plots to which varying but known amounts of nitrogen fertilizers were added. If 2.22 per cent is the average nitrogen concentration of leaves of red oaks growing on a site of unknown fertility to which 167 pounds of nitrogen per acre was added, the leaf analysis would show the nitrogen-supplying power of the site to be x plus 167 pounds per acre on the relative nitrogen scale. Since the scale is relative, the value x represents the unknown amount of nitrogen originally present in the soil which was the poorest studied in this experiment.

Table 9.3. Variations in amounts of N, P, and K in leaves at deficiency and optimum levels. Values given as percentages of oven-dry weights. (*From Leyton,* 1957.)

Species		Deficiency			Optimum			Authority
		N	P	K	N	P	K	
Pinus sylvestris	(S)	1.2 –1.3	0.08		3.0			Gast (1937)
	(F)							Tamm (1954)
Pinus strobus	(S)	0.70–1.33	0.10–0.28	0.82–1.02	3.26	0.67	1.72	Mitchell (1939)
	(F)							Heiberg and White (1951)
Pinus resinosa	(F)			0.34				Heiberg and White (1951)
Pinus corsicana	(F)			0.34		0.15		Leyton (1954)
Picea abies	(F)	0.80–1.0	0.06					Tamm (1954)
	(F)			0.13–0.21				Heiberg and White (1951)
Picea glauca	(F)			0.13–0.21				Heiberg and White (1951)
Picea stichensis	(F)				1.5–1.6	0.14		Leyton (1954)
Larix leptolepis	(F)	1.8 –2.2	0.08–0.10		2.8	0.40		Leyton (1957)
Betula spp.	(F)	2.0		0.29–0.34				Tamm (1954)
Populus tremuloides	(F)				2.6–2.8			Mitchell and Chandler (1939)
Acer saccharum	(F)	1.75			2.8–2.9			Mitchell and Chandler (1939)
Fraxinus americana	(F)	2.01			2.8–2.9			Mitchell and Chandler (1939)
Tilia americana	(F)	2.32			3.1–3.2			Mitchell and Chandler (1939)

(S) Seedling. (F) Established trees in field.

An internal concentration of 2.22 per cent for red oak leaves means that the nitrogen-supplying capacity of this site is equivalent in terms of foliar concentration to 167 pounds of nitrogen added to an acre of the poorest soil used in the experiment. Thus the method is useful for appraising mineral availability of sites in terms of actual species requirements since on each site growth increases with supply and concentration to about the same optimum level. In classifying relative nitrogen-supplying capacity of forest sites with foliar diagnostic technique in the northeastern United States, Mitchell and Chandler found 20 per cent of the sites to be nitrogen-deficient, 65 per cent to be fair to good, and only 15 per cent good to excellent. Walker (1955) used a similar application of leaf analysis for identifying soils deficient in potassium for normal

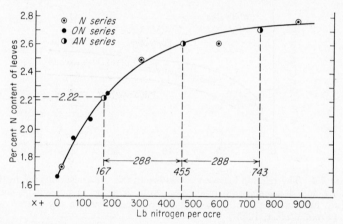

Figure 9.3 Diagram illustrating a method of correlating the nitrogen content of leaves and soil by observing the effects on leaf nitrogen of adding known quantities of nitrogen to the soil. (*From Mitchell and Chandler, 1939.*)

growth of conifers, but he used two sampling dates, early July and mid-August. White pine needle tissue collected in July from trees with deficiency symptoms had less than 0.59 per cent potassium, but in August the concentration had dropped this low in the healthy trees on a percentage basis (Figure 9.4). Foliage symptoms also were found useful in recognizing potassium deficiency on abandoned farm lands which should not be planted with species having a high potassium requirement.

Foliar analysis assumes a positive but not necessarily linear correlation between mineral concentration and growth, as above some particular concentration there may be further uptake of an element without any increase in growth (luxury consumption). Süchting (1939) pointed out that at a moderate level of deficiency, increase in mineral supply sometimes causes increased growth without any apparent increase in concentration. In cases of extreme deficiencies, especially of micronutrients, an increased supply may cause such a large increase in growth that a decrease in concentration occurs. In general, if an element is limiting, both growth and leaf concentration are increased by supplying more of that element, according to the law of diminishing returns. Over the lower part of the range, the relationship between growth and concentration is essentially linear; that is, growth is approximately proportional to concentration, but this is not true at higher concentrations of elements. Mitchell and Chandler (1939) analyzed foliage of hardwoods growing on sites of varying fertility which were fertilized with nitrogen. For each species a curve of diminishing returns was established between growth and nitrogen concentration of leaves, but the range of concen-

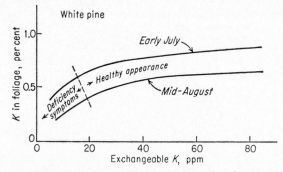

Figure 9.4 The relation between potassium in the soil and potassium in the leaves of healthy and deficient white pine trees. Note decrease in percentage composition from July to August, probably caused chiefly by increase in dry-matter content of leaves. (*From Walker, 1955.*)

trations over which this relationship was linear varied on different sites (Figure 9.8).

Leyton and Armson (1955) observed that increased concentrations of nitrogen or potassium in needles of Scotch pine were accompanied by increased growth, independently of the concentrations of other elements within the range encountered in this study. Leyton (1956) concluded that where multiple deficiencies occur, the contribution of each of several elements can be tested by regression analysis of the foliar-analysis data. Using this method he found height growth of Japanese larch to be limited significantly only by nitrogen and potassium among the several elements studied.

Boynton and Compton (1945) found the concentration of minerals in leaves of fruit trees to be influenced by a number of factors, including condition of the root system, conducting tissues, leaf injuries, age of leaves, climate, season, and species and variety of trees. They concluded that foliar diagnosis can be used together with observations of visible leaf and fruit symptoms, as well as past history of the trees, to provide information which neither observations nor analyses can provide alone. In spite of its defects it appears that when foliar diagnosis is used properly in comparison with data from healthy trees or fertilizer plots, it is one of the best methods of studying the mineral nutrition of trees. Some of the uses and limitations of foliar diagnosis are discussed by Goodall and Gregory (1947) and by Leyton (1958a).

Certain precautions are necessary in order to obtain reliable results. For example, leaves of the same stage of development should be used in comparison of different sites, and standards must be developed for trees of each species, as will be seen from the data presented in the next few pages. Leaves often are contaminated with dust and spray materials, especially in orchards, and this material must be removed before reliable analyses for certain elements can be made. Prolonged washing of leaves can leach out a portion of certain constituents (Kramer, 1957a), although Hammar (1956) did not find this a serious problem in pecan leaves. Exposure to rain also can leach out minerals from leaves, as shown by work cited in the next section.

It has been observed that browsing and grazing animals sometimes differentiate between plants which are deficient and those which have been fertilized. Mitchell and Hosley (1936) observed that deer preferred to browse on dogwood on plots fertilized with nitrogen, apparently because the leaves on these plots were higher in reducing sugars than those on unfertilized plots. According to Heiberg and White (1951), hares preferred seedlings fertilized with potassium chloride to unfertilized trees.

Analysis of Xylem Sap. Several workers have investigated the composition of the xylem sap of various trees. Dixon and Atkins (1916) measured the osmotic pressure and composition of the sap of trees of several species, and Oserkowsky (1932) measured the iron content of xylem sap from chlorotic and healthy pear trees. Bennett and Oserkowsky (1933) measured the copper and iron content of xylem sap of several tree species, and Bollard (1953, 1958) studied the xylem sap of apples on different rootstocks. He found large seasonal variations in concentrations of nitrogen, phosphorus, potassium, and magnesium. He concluded that sap displaced from the xylem vessels by air pressure provided good material for analysis because it need not be subjected to heat or chemical reagents. This appears to be a useful approach to some mineral nutrition problems.

Factors Affecting Mineral Composition

The mineral composition of individual trees and of trees of various species varies widely according to the soil on which they grow, the part sampled, and even the climatic conditions. As mentioned previously, the mineral content of leaves is of special interest and will therefore be considered in some detail.

Species Differences. There are rather consistent differences between species in ash content and in the composition of the ash. For example, Coile (1937a) found the ash content of dogwood, white oak, and sweetgum leaves to be about twice as high (7.0 to 7.2 per cent) as that of loblolly and shortleaf pine (3.0 to 3.5 per cent) growing on the same soils. Lyford (1941) found the ash content of red maple leaves to average 6.21 per cent compared with 2.62 per cent for white pine leaves grown on the same soil, and Mitchell and Finn (1935) found the phosphorus content of sugar maple leaves to be twice as high as that of red, chestnut, or white oak. They concluded that maple should be encouraged in certain stands because it will supply much more phosphorus to the soil in its litter than oak.

Differences in ability to absorb calcium are of particular interest because of the possible importance of calcium in favoring decomposition of litter. Coile (1937a) found that dogwood, yellow-poplar, redbud, white oak, and hickory leaves contained over 2 per cent of calcium while scarlet oak, post oak, and loblolly pine contained less than 1 per cent. Lutz and Chandler (1946) also differentiate between species high in calcium and those which are low, and they place most of the conifers in the latter group. In Europe beech is regarded as effective for the purpose of introducing calcium into the litter, but Lutz and Chandler list American beech as low in calcium, and this is supported by the data of Bard (1945), who also found that the calcium content of leaves varied more with species than with the calcium content of the soil on which the trees were growing. Differences between conifers and hardwoods are shown in Tables 9.7 and 9.8.

An interesting example of species differences in accumulation of micronutrients was reported by Beeson et al. (1955), who found that blackgum accumulated 0.70 to 58.9 parts per million of cobalt in its leaves on soil where other species accumulated only 0.01 to 0.25 parts per million. Gallberry growing on the same soil accumulates large amounts of zinc, and pepperbush accumulates large amounts of both cobalt and zinc. According to Wilson (1953), loblolly pine requires less zinc than shortleaf pine, but the differences observed might have been caused by differences in the amounts stored in the different sized seeds of the two species.

Age of Leaves. The mineral composition of leaves varies fairly consistently with their age and stage of development. Sampson and Samisch (1935) divided leaf development of oaks into three phases: (1) a period of rapid growth characterized by rapid accumulation of minerals and organic substances, (2) a period of maturation characterized by slow growth and reduced rate of increase in both organic and inorganic constituents, and (3) finally a period of senescence during which organic and inorganic constituents are translocated from the leaves back into the tree. There probably also is considerable loss by leaching during the senescent stage if rains occur.

This general situation has been found to exist in a wide range of species by several investigators. Mitchell (1936) warns of the importance of determining both the absolute content per leaf and the percentage content of each element under study because leaf dry weight continues to increase during the growing season and this may cause percentage concentrations of elements to decrease, while absolute amounts per leaf are

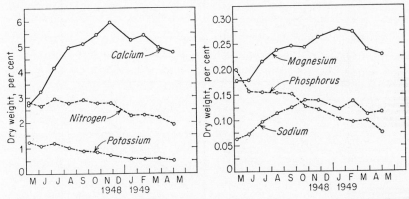

Figure 9.5 Seasonal variations in mineral concentration in leaves of Valencia orange trees. (*From Jones and Parker,* 1951.)

increasing, as shown in Figures 9.5 and 9.6. Mitchell (1936) observed that the concentration of nitrogen, phosphorus, and potassium decreased rapidly during the period of most rapid leaf growth, although the absolute amounts per leaf increased steadily until just before the leaves began to turn in the autumn. After the leaves began to yellow, the amount of nitrogen, phosphorus, and potassium decreased, indicating some migration out of the leaves. The concentration of calcium increased during the entire season and did not decrease after yellowing, as shown in Figure 9.6. Alway et al. (1934) found that several deciduous species of trees in Minnesota behaved in the same manner. McHargue and Roy (1932) reported that the percentage of nitrogen, phosphorus, and potassium in 23 species of trees was lower at the end of the growing season than at the beginning; the percentage of calcium, silica, and total ash increased; and there was no change in copper, manganese, or zinc. The concentration of most elements in Scotch pine needles decreases as they grow older, but calcium concentration continues to increase (Leyton and Armson, 1955). As shown in Figure 9.5, the nitrogen, phosphorus, and potassium concentration of orange leaves decreases during the summer while the concentration of calcium, magnesium, and sodium increases. The concentration of nitrogen, phosphorus, potassium, zinc, and copper decreased, but that of several other elements increased in peaches and the concentrations were altered by fruit production (McClung and Lott, 1956).

As long as leaves are growing they continue to accumulate minerals, but at least in hardwoods, as soon as leaves become senescent, some of the

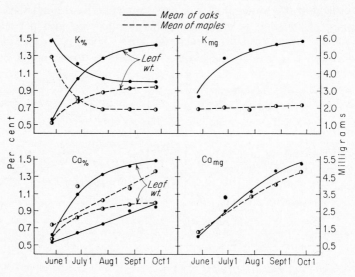

Figure 9.6 Seasonal trends in calcium and potassium content of leaves of oaks and maples expressed as percentages of dry weight and as milligrams per leaf. The curves for leaf dry weight indicate relative changes rather than absolute weights. (*From Mitchell, 1936.*)

nitrogen, phosphorus, and potassium appear to be translocated back into the trees. Ramann (1912) was one of the earlier workers to observe this, and Combes (1927a and b) made an extensive study of the subject. He also observed that some elements are leached out by rain. Sampson and Samisch (1935) concluded that translocation of nitrogen and phosphorus out of oak leaves begins as early as July, and potassium moves out later, but calcium and silicon do not move out. About 45 per cent of the nitrogen and potassium was translocated out of beech leaves in the autumn, but none of the calcium, iron, manganese, or silicon (Olsen, 1948). Much of the data on alleged translocation out of leaves before the end of the growing season is of doubtful value because, as mentioned earlier, the continued increase in dry weight causes the concentrations of some elements to decrease while absolute amounts are increasing. Unequivocal evidence of translocation can be obtained only by measuring changes in absolute amounts of elements per leaf.

There may be differences in composition of different parts of the same leaf which would be important in connection with determinations by methods using small samples of leaf tissue. Sayre (1957) found that some elements occur in greatest concentration near the tip, others near the base, and still others are distributed fairly uniformly throughout pine needles.

Samples for analysis preferably should be taken at a period when the mineral content is relatively constant. Reuther and Boynton (1940) found the potassium composition of apple leaves most constant during July and August, but most investigators prefer to sample near the end of the growing season (Leyton, 1957; Mitchell, 1936; Tamm, 1951). Conifers usually can be sampled in either late summer or winter (White, 1954; Tamm, 1955), but only needles of the current year should be used (Leyton and Armson, 1955). In general, leaves at the same stages of development should be chosen, rather than random samples, because this reduces variations due to differences in age (Gossard, 1943).

Some workers recommend collecting all samples at the same time of day (Mitchell and Chandler, 1939; Chapman, 1941) to eliminate possible diurnal variations. If appreciable diurnal variations in dry weight occur, as is known to be the case in some herbaceous plants, these could affect the apparent mineral content, even when expressed as percentage of dry weight.

Leaching. Another source of error is leaching of elements out of leaves by rain (Mitchell, 1936). Samples of litter collected after lying on the ground exposed to rain undoubtedly have undergone considerable changes in composition by leaching. Appreciable amounts of both inorganic and organic solutes also are leached out of healthy living leaves by rain and dew. Long et al. (1956) cited considerable data on this topic, and Tukey et al. (1958) have further data showing loss of carbohydrates by leaching. The data of Tamm (1951) shown in Table 9.4 indicate con-

Table 9.4. Leaching of minerals out of leaves by rain as indicated by difference in mineral content of rain water caught in open fields and under tree crowns, in milligrams per liter. (*Tamm,* 1951.)

Site	Ca	K	Na	P
Open field	0.4	0.2	0.4	0.02
	0.5	0.3	0.7	0.04
Under pine (*Pinus silvestris*)	4.0	6.3	2.0	0.12
Under oak (*Quercus robur*)	9.1	15.0	1.6	
Under birch (*Betula verrucosa*)	7.2	17.4	1.9	0.19

Physiology of Trees

siderable loss of several elements by leaching from attached leaves of
both coniferous and deciduous species. Tukey and Amling (1958) found
that the concentrations of several elements were significantly lower in
leaves of apple trees exposed to rain and dew than in leaves of trees
protected by a plastic roof. It seems probable that the importance of
leaching of solutes out of leaves may have been underestimated, although
its occurrence has been noted many times.

Location of Leaves on Tree. The effect of the position of leaves on a
tree on their mineral content seems rather variable. Wallihan (1944)
found no significant differences in composition of sugar maple leaves
from branches at different heights, although tip leaves had slightly lower
concentrations of nitrogen and potassium than leaves farther back on the

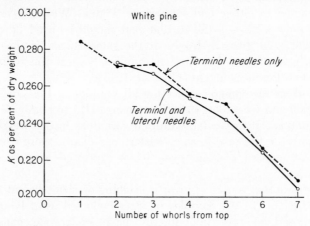

Figure 9.7 Effect of position of needles on potassium content of white pine
needles collected in September. (*White*, 1954.)

branches. Perhaps this is related to differences in age as well as in position. Leyton and Armson (1955) usually found the highest salt concentration in the terminal shoots at the top of the tree, and White (1954) found
a decrease in potassium content from top to bottom in white pine, as
shown in Figure 9.7. There were no significant differences between
needles from the north and south sides of trees, and White concluded
that the current year's needles from the middle of the crown constituted
a representative sample for potassium content. The lowermost whorls
were very unrepresentative because they carry on little photosynthesis
and the small increase in dry weight results in high concentrations of
minerals. In general, heavily shaded leaves probably should be avoided.

No standard procedure for sampling has been accepted. Some investigators have concentrated on a particular position (Leyton, 1954), while
others have sampled at various positions to obtain a composite represent-

ing the entire crown (Wallihan, 1944; White, 1954). The sampling method probably should be adapted to the objectives of the investigation.

Mineral Content of Soil. The mineral content of leaves naturally is affected by the mineral content of the soil in which the trees are growing. This is shown in Figures 9.3 and 9.4 and has been demonstrated in numerous fertilizer experiments. In fact, this assumption forms the basis for the foliar-analysis method of evaluating the supply of soil nutrients. Nevertheless, as pointed out in the section on species differences, there are species differences which are maintained on soils of widely different mineral content. This is particularly true of calcium (Lutz and Chandler, 1946; Bard, 1945). Dogwood, yellow-poplar, and basswood are high and most conifers are low in calcium regardless of the soil in which they are grown, and maple leaves have a much higher phosphorus content than oak leaves on a wide range of sites of varying fertility (Mitchell and Finn, 1935).

Other aspects of this problem are discussed in connection with soil factors affecting mineral absorption.

Handling of Samples. The manner in which leaf samples are handled can have considerable effect on the reliability of the results, as shown in Table 9.5. If leaves are not killed immediately after picking, continued

Table 9.5. Effect of treatment of leaf samples on nitrogen content and dry weight of foliage of *Pinus resinosa*. (*After White*, 1954.)

Constituent	Pretreatment	Composition, %	Weight per fascicle, mg
Nitrogen	Oven-dried, 70°C	1.25	1.38
	Air-dried, 6 weeks	1.38	1.41
	Air-dried on branch, 6 weeks	1.42	1.39
Phosphorus	Oven-dried, 70°C	0.147	0.164
	Air-dried, 6 weeks	0.161	0.161
	Air-dried on branch, 6 weeks	0.167	0.167
Dry weight	Oven-dried, 70°C		112.0
	Air-dried, 6 weeks		102.0
	Air-dried on branch, 6 weeks		98.0

respiration will cause measurable decrease in dry weight and the mineral content as percentage of dry weight will appear to increase. Methods of handling leaf samples after collection are discussed by Broyer (1939) and White (1954). Discussion of methods of analyzing leaf samples for minerals lies beyond the scope of this book, and readers are referred to recent papers on foliar analysis for methods.

Differences in Mineral Requirements of Forest Stands

In general, the annual mineral requirement of trees is less than that of agricultural crops (Rennie, 1955), and forest trees require less than orchard trees because an appreciable fraction of the minerals absorbed by the latter is removed in the fruit (Batjer and Rogers, 1952). However, logging may remove appreciable amounts of minerals from the site, especially if the bark is included.

It often is said that conifers have lower mineral requirements than hardwoods, but this depends on how data are interpreted. Data of Rennie (1955) indicate that mineral uptake of hardwood stands generally is higher than that of conifer stands (Table 9.6). Manshard (1933) reported

Table 9.6. Total nutrient uptake (excluding leaves and roots of thinnings and litter), in kilograms per acre. (*After Rennie, 1955.*)

Species	After 50 years' growth			After 100 years' growth		
	Ca	K	P	Ca	K	P
Pines	133	72	17	203	91	21
Other conifers	264	139	30	438	234	41
Hardwoods	463	126	29	879	225	50

that hardwood seedlings absorbed more minerals than conifers but they also weighed more, and when Leyton (1957) recalculated the data in terms of dry-weight increments he found little difference between the conifers and hardwoods. Ovington (1956a) also found that on certain sites mineral absorption of some conifers exceeds that of some hardwoods and although the ratio of minerals absorbed to dry-weight increase usually is higher in hardwoods than in conifers, exceptions are common (Leyton, 1957).

The mineral content of hardwood litter and leaves usually is higher than that of conifer litter, and Ovington (1956b) found that on the same soil hardwood leaves contained higher percentages of nitrogen, potassium, magnesium, and phosphorus but conifer leaves contained higher percentages of carbon, sodium, and manganese, and there were no consistent differences with respect to calcium, iron, or silicon. As mentioned previously, the mineral content of foliage is not always a good index of actual requirements, because absorption is not always related to needs, especially if there is an abundant supply.

There is good indirect evidence that species differ in their mineral requirements because some species occur only on fertile soils while others occur on sites of much lower fertility. Mitchell and Chandler (1939) divided hardwoods into the following three categories on the basis of their nitrogen requirements:

Group I. Species tolerant of low nitrogen
   Red oak
   White and chestnut oak
   Trembling aspen
   Red maple

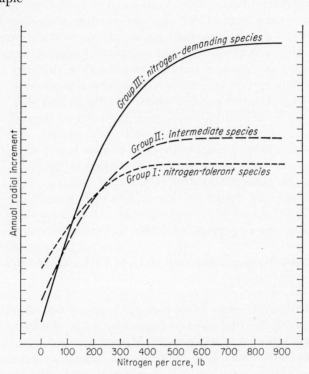

Figure 9.8 Relative growth response to increasing nitrogen supply of species with low (group I), intermediate (group II), and high (group III) nitrogen requirements. (*From Mitchell and Chandler, 1939.*)

Group II. Intermediate species
   Pignut hickory
   Sugar maple
   Beech
   Blackgum
Group III. Species requiring high nitrogen
   White ash
   Yellow-poplar
   Basswood

The relative growth responses of the three groups of trees to varying amounts of nitrogen applied to the soil are shown in Figure 9.8.

The greatest demand for minerals in a forest stand comes fairly early, probably about the time the canopy is fully closed, because most of the minerals occur in the leaves and twigs and maximum crown development of a good stand occurs at this time. Leyton (1958a) cites data of Morosow indicating that the maximum mineral requirements of Scotch pine occur at the age of 20 to 25 years on good sites and 30 to 35 years on poor sites. Maximum requirements of Norway spruce occur somewhat later, and those of beech do not come until the stands on good sites are 40 to 45 years old. Alten and Doehring (1952) stated that mineral requirements of stands reach a maximum at the time of greatest productivity of branch-wood. For pine, spruce, and beech on good sites this occurs at 20, 30, and 40 years of age, respectively, but somewhat later on poor sites.

We have only limited information on the range of internal concentrations of mineral elements within which good growth of forest trees occurs. Furthermore, it is not yet certain to what extent these ranges are affected by site and climatic factors. According to Mitchell (1939), the best range in concentration for white pine seedlings is for nitrogen 2.5 to 3.26 per cent, for phosphorus 0.56 to 0.67 per cent, for potassium 1.50 to 1.72 per cent, and for calcium 0.28 to 0.33 per cent, expressed as percentage of leaf dry weight. A lower concentration was accompanied by deficiency symptoms, a higher concentration by toxic effects. Some data on mineral concentrations are given in Tables 9.2 and 9.3.

The Mineral Cycle in Trees

The mineral cycle refers to the fact that much of the mineral absorbed by trees eventually is returned to the soil by decay of fallen litter. Some minerals are removed from forests by logging, and considerable amounts are removed from orchards in the fruits. An estimate of the mineral content of the various parts of trees is useful in evaluating the quantities removed in various plant parts.

The mineral content of wood is relatively low, compared with other parts of a tree, varying from 0.2 to 1.0 per cent (Kurth, 1949). One-third to one-half of the total ash usually is calcium, and potassium is the next most abundant element. Wood ash formerly was a common source of alkali for soap making, and 50 years ago many families kept a barrel of wood ashes which were leached to get "lye" with which to make soap from surplus fat. Considerable phosphorus and small amounts of many other elements, both essential and nonessential, occur in wood. Bark usually contains 3 to 10 times as high a concentration of minerals as wood, and calcium usually constitutes more than half of the total (Kurth, 1949).

Small branches and twigs contain more ash than older wood, and sapwood usually contains more ash than heartwood, but the reverse sometimes occurs. In general, the mineral concentration of roots is higher than that of stems (Ando, 1952; Gäumann, 1935). Buds and other growing regions tend to accumulate high concentrations of minerals, and Burstrom and Krogh (1947) state that the concentration of potassium in buds rose in the spring to 200 times that in the sap. The cambial region probably also is quite high in minerals, but no data seem to be available. In general, the mineral content of regions containing many living cells is likely to be higher than that of regions containing few living cells because living cells tend to accumulate mineral salts. The ash content of different parts of trees is shown in Table 9.7.

Table 9.7. Distribution of minerals in various parts of trees in fully stocked stands of European trees on average sites. (*From Baker, 1950, table 16.*)

Species	Mean annual increment, bd ft	Total use, lb per acre	Percentage of total amount found in:				
			Wood	Bark	Faggots	Thin-nings	Litter
		Phosphorus					
Spruce	680	10	1	3	7	17	72
Fir	760	14	3	3	5	17	72
Pine	370	6	5	3	6	17	69
Beech	420	14	13	2	6	6	73
Oak	370	11	8	2	5	15	70
		Calcium					
Spruce	680	68	3	1	2	8	86
Fir	760	78	1	1	2	4	92
Pine	370	26	10	2	4	16	68
Beech	420	101	3	1	2	4	90
Oak	370	78	3	1	3	9	84
Percentage of total dry matter in each part			50	5	7	32	6

Large quantities of minerals are accumulated in fruits and seeds, and Batjer and Rogers (1952) estimate that 75 pounds may be removed in the fruit from an acre of apple trees. A mature apple tree absorbs about 8 pounds of minerals annually, and about 3 pounds is removed in the fruit, the remainder eventually being returned to the soil.

Leaves usually contain the highest mineral content of any organ of trees, perhaps because salt tends to be concentrated there by the evaporation of water in the process of transpiration. Decay of fallen leaves therefore is the chief means by which minerals are returned to the soil, and soil fertility in forests is influenced by the rate of decomposition of fallen litter.

Considerable information has been published on the amount of leaf and twig litter which falls annually and on its mineral content. Some of this is summarized by Scott (1955). Pine forests in Minnesota produce an average of 2,122 pounds of litter per acre (Alway and Zon, 1930), while pine and hardwood forests in the South Carolina Piedmont produce about 4,400 pounds of litter, including 3,500 pounds of leaves on an oven-dry basis (Metz, 1952). In New York hardwoods produced 2,425 to 3,020 pounds of oven-dry leaves per acre and conifers produced 2,463 pounds (Chandler, 1941, 1944). Baker (1950) estimated the average litter fall in United States forests at 3,000 pounds per acre, and Ovington (1956b) gives the same value for well-stocked English forests, but the extreme values for European beech are said by Baker to range from 500 to 6,000 pounds on the poorest and best sites. Some data on the amount of minerals returned in the litter are given in Table 9.8. Some data on nitrogen content of litter are given in Chapter 5.

Table 9.8. Amounts of minerals returned to the soil annually by leaf fall, in pounds per acre.

	Annual litter fall	Minerals returned to soil by leaf fall					
		N	P	K	Ca	Mg	Total
New York:							
Hardwood *	2,716	16.6	3.3	13.5	65.6	9.2	108.2
Conifer †	2,463	23.6	1.8	6.5	26.5	4.5	62.9
South Carolina: ‡							
Hardwood	3,697	23.04			88.44	20.85	
Pine-hardwood	3,825	26.58			51.52	11.22	
Pine	2,938	13.22			17.32	5.58	

* Chandler (1941).
† Average of seven species of conifers. Chandler (1944).
‡ Metz (1952).

The generally higher mineral concentration of hardwood litter results in its returning more minerals to the soil than most coniferous litter, as shown in Table 9.8. The rate of decomposition is as important as the amount and composition of litter, however. Ovington (1954) found more organic matter accumulating under conifers than under hardwoods because coniferous litter decays slowly. Decomposition of pine litter is improved by the addition of hardwood litter high in calcium, such as dogwood leaves (Coile, 1937a), and under some conditions the presence of understory hardwoods may be an important factor in the maintenance of the fertility of forest soils.

Fertilization

The use of fertilizers is a well-established practice in orchards and on ornamental trees and shrubs, but their use in forestry has thus far been restricted largely to nurseries except on an experimental basis. Baker (1950) stated that under the conditions then existing fertilization was not profitable, but increased land costs and timber values, together with use of planting stock selected for rapid growth, seem to be changing this situation and there is considerable interest in the practicality of applying fertilizers to large acreages. This might be done by airplane (White, 1956).

Nursery soils often become deficient in mineral nutrients because considerable quantities are removed in the seedlings and lost by leaching. According to Switzer and Nelson (1956), a crop of loblolly pine seedlings removes as much of the mineral nutrients as a field crop. Where soil fertility is low and other environmental factors such as water and light are not seriously limiting, growth of seedlings usually is materially improved by fertilization. The kind and amount of fertilizer needed should be determined by soil and plant analyses, however, because no benefit will result from applying elements already present in sufficient quantities (Rosendahl and Korstian, 1945). Too high concentrations of fertilizer may even be toxic, especially early in the season while seedlings are small. Heavy shading and lack of water often reduce the effectiveness of fertilization because growth is then limited by carbohydrate supply or water rather than by mineral supply. Mitchell (1934), for instance, found that high light intensity was necessary to get increased yield with high nitrogen and that increasing nitrogen above a certain concentration caused dry weight to decrease.

Fertilization affects both the size and quality of seedlings. Heavy fertilization may produce seedlings of low quality which are unduly susceptible to injury from drought, cold, and parasites (Shirley and Meuli, 1939; Wilde and Voigt, 1948). White (1950) also concluded that unreasonably high levels of nursery soil fertility, too much nitrogen, and abnormal ratios of minerals tend to result in nursery stock vulnerable to drought, fungus diseases, and insects. On the other hand, Wilde et al. (1940) found that heavy applications of fertilizer at rates up to 1,100 pounds per acre to nursery beds markedly improved the height growth of jack, red, and Scotch pine after outplanting. Survival also was increased. Longleaf pine seedlings fertilized with a complete fertilizer survived drought better than unfertilized seedlings, but they did not respond to nitrogen alone (Allen and Maki, 1955). Obviously a good fertilization program will vary with the soil, climatic conditions, and species being grown. Readers are referred to the book by Wilde (1958) for a more detailed discussion of the fertilization of nurseries.

The essential factors in seedling survival after outplanting have not been analyzed satisfactorily, but they obviously include ability to form new roots promptly after transplanting and probably include a large root/shoot ratio. Too much nitrogen is likely to result in seedlings with a low root/shoot ratio and low carbohydrate reserves, while too little nitrogen may result in small seedlings which also are low in carbohydrates. More research is needed to learn what type of fertilization program will produce seedlings most likely to survive when outplanted.

Severe mineral deficiencies often develop in plantations on eroded or sandy soils, and these frequently can be corrected by fertilization. Stoate (1950) summarized many years of work on mineral-nutrition problems of pine in Australia, and Leyton (1954, 1956, 1957, 1958b) described some recent fertilization experiments in England. Stone (1955) summarized some European work in this field, and White and Leaf (1957) published a bibliography and abstracts on forest fertilization studies from all over the world. As might be expected, the results are variable.

Recent interest in stimulating seed production of superior trees has led to renewed interest in the effects of fertilization on the quantity and quality of seed produced. In general, fertilization has increased seed production. Allen (1953) found that fertilization increased the number of cones per tree of young longleaf pine from 1.3 to 13.5. This was double the number produced on trees which were released but not fertilized. Wenger (1953b) found that fertilizing loblolly pine increased cone production of trees 25 years old but not of trees 40 years old. Of course, results obtained from fertilization depend on the initial nutritional status of the trees.

Application of fertilizers by spraying them on the leaves is becoming increasingly common for shrubs and ornamental trees. This method of applying mineral nutrients is particularly effective where soil conditions tend to make them unavailable. Stoate (1950) stated that it is a common practice to spray zinc on plantations of Monterey pine in South Australia, and foliar applications of urea and various mineral nutrients are being used on nurseries and shade and fruit trees with success.

According to Tukey et al. (1952), nutrients are absorbed through the bark of trees as well as through the leaves. Harley et al. (1956) found no absorption through uninjured bark but measurable amounts of P^{32} and zinc were absorbed through naturally occurring cracks, splits, and ruptured lenticels. Greatest absorption occurred through pruning wounds, and application of zinc to pruning wounds cured zinc deficiency of grape.

It must be remembered that maximum results from applications of fertilizer will be obtained only if other factors are not seriously limiting. In dry summers water deficits can limit growth so severely that little or no increase in growth will result from application of fertilizers. Defoliation by insects and disease or shading can reduce photosynthesis until growth is limited by carbohydrates rather than by supply of mineral nutrients. Maximum use of minerals is possible only if water and light are not limiting (Mitchell, 1936). Weather and other environmental conditions must be taken into account in interpreting the results of fertilization experiments.

Use of Plant Cover to Improve Soil Fertility

In agriculture considerable use is made of cover crops and some attention has been paid by foresters to the use of certain tree species to build up the soil. It was mentioned earlier that dogwood litter is desirable because of its high calcium content (Coile, 1937a) and maple because of the high phosphorus content of its leaves. Some years ago Chapman (1935) reported that black locust stimulates the growth of other tree species growing beside it, apparently because nitrogen fixed by bacteria growing on its roots becomes available to neighboring trees. Chapman and Lane (1951) reported that black locust is a superior nurse crop for hardwoods planted on abandoned fields, but not for pines which suffer from shading. It was mentioned in Chapter 5 that alder often is interplanted in conifer plantations in Europe and Japan because nitrogen is fixed in the bacterial nodules on alder roots and this improves growth of the conifers. Broom has been used in Great Britain to increase growth of spruce on nitrogen-deficient soils, and lupine is used in Germany to improve forest soil fertility. It seems that more attention should be given to determining the best combinations of species to maintain soil fertility by natural methods.

SALT ABSORPTION

Much of the research on salt absorption deals with accumulation of salt in cells and tissues, but in studying growing plants we are more interested in the fraction which moves through the roots to the shoots than in the fraction which remains in the roots. The role of passive movement by diffusion and mass movement in the transpiration stream may be nearly as important as that of active transport and accumulation. Synthesis of organic nitrogen and possibly of organic phosphorus compounds in the roots may also be an important step preliminary to their translocation to the shoots. Several important questions must be answered concerning the movement of ions through the roots, including (1) what constitutes the salt-absorbing zone of woody roots, (2) by what path do ions move across the root tissues into the xylem, (3) what kinds of forces cause the inward movement, and (4) does the rate of water absorption have any important effects on salt absorption?

Terminology and Concepts

Before discussing the various details of absorption a few of the terms should be defined, because they are not always used with exactly the same meaning by all writers. "Absorption" and "uptake" are general terms applied to the entrance of a substance into a cell, tissue, or organ by any mechanism, while "accumulation" refers to entrance of a substance against a concentration or activity gradient. Accumulation generally requires the expenditure of metabolic energy in the cells or tissues in which it occurs, but nonmetabolic accumulation by adsorption also occurs.

Movement of ions or molecules along gradients of decreasing concentration, activity, or free energy, caused by their own kinetic energy, is termed "diffusion." Exit and entrance of gases in leaves is an example of diffusion. If movement is caused by gravity, hydrostatic pressure, or some other outside force, it is called "mass flow," and the ascent of sap under tension in the xylem of trees is an example. Movement by diffusion and mass flow is called "passive movement" in contrast to "active transport" of substances against a concentration or free-energy gradient brought about by the expenditure of metabolic energy. Active transport brings about "accumulation," which will be discussed in more detail in the next section of this chapter.

Accumulation can occur only within relatively impermeable membranes because otherwise the substances involved would leak out by diffusion as rapidly as they were transported in. A membrane, according to Ussing (1954), is a boundary that is less permeable or presents a higher resistance to the movement of materials than the phases separated by it. Plant membranes vary from monomolecular layers at interfaces to systems consisting of layers of cells such as the epidermis and endodermis, or many layers in corky tissues of bark. At the cellular level there are definite boundaries or membranes at the outer and inner surfaces of the cytoplasm (plasmalemma and tonoplast or vacuolar membrane) and surrounding the nucleus, plastids, and mitochondria. Robertson (1956) estimated that the impermeable barrier to ion diffusion might be about 10^{-6} centimeter thick, but Overstreet (1957) recently suggested that the entire layer of cytoplasm can be regarded as both membrane and carrier. The extent to which substances can pass through a membrane is termed its "permeability," and membranes which permit some substances to pass through more readily than others are termed "differentially permeable."

Collander (1957) has recently reviewed the subject of permeability in relation to plant cells.

The mechanism by which active transport across membranes occurs is not completely understood, but some form of carrier theory is most popular. According to this theory, ions form loose combinations with specific binding compounds or carrier molecules, somewhat similar to that formed between an enzyme and its substrate. This complex then moves across the membrane, which is impermeable to ions or carrier alone, but is permeable to a combination of the two, and breaks up on the inner side, releasing the ions. The exact nature of the hypothetical binding compounds is unknown, although proteins, amino acids, mitochondria, and high-energy phosphorylated compounds have been proposed. The relationship often observed between respiration, protein synthesis, and salt accumulation may be related in part to the synthesis of carriers and in part to energy required for transport. The reader is referred to papers by Epstein (1956), Kramer (1956a and b), and Robertson (1956) for more detailed discussions of these problems.

A relatively new concept in the field of salt absorption is that of apparent free space or outer space (Hope and Stevens, 1952; Briggs and Robertson, 1957; Epstein, 1955, 1956). Outer or free space is that part of a tissue or cell into and out of which ions can move freely by diffusion, as contrasted with the portion in which they are more or less irreversibly accumulated by active transport. Free space obviously includes the water-saturated cell walls which are as permeable to solutes as wet filter paper, but it apparently also includes part of the cytoplasm because the volume of the walls is too small to account for the fraction of ions which is free to move by diffusion. Various workers have estimated the free space in roots at from 10 to 35 per cent of the volume, and Epstein (1955) found that it amounted to 23 per cent for several ions in barley roots. The amount of free space probably varies with the nature of the solute used to measure it (Briggs and Robertson, 1957).

If a good part of the volume of the cytoplasm is accessible to ions by diffusion, the differentially permeable membrane behind which accumulation occurs is not the plasmalemma at the outer surface of the cytoplasm but the vacuolar membrane at the inner surface. Accordingly, part of the ions in a cell are more or less irreversibly accumulated in the vacuole, part are fixed on carrier molecules or binding sites in the cytoplasm, and part are free to move by diffusion. Levitt (1957b) argues that it is unnecessary to include cytoplasm in free space to explain the values published by Epstein and others, but Briggs and Robertson (1957) believe that at least part of it is included. Although outer or free space has been studied only in roots, it must occur in all organs of plants, and this has important implications with respect to the movement and distribution of minerals (Kramer, 1957a).

Salt Accumulation

Salt uptake by individual cells involves accumulation by which the concentration of certain ions is built up by active transport until it is much higher than in the environment. The process is highly selective, the concentration of some ions being increased much more than the concentration of other ions. The selectivity probably is related to the amount and kinds of carriers present to bring about active transport and the permeability of the cell membranes. Salt accumulation in roots usually is thought of as occurring in two stages, a nonmetabolic exchange-adsorption process followed by metabolic accumulation (Overstreet and Jacobson, 1946; Epstein and Leggett, 1954; Gauch, 1957). These two more or less concurrent steps can be characterized as follows:

Exchange adsorption	*Metabolic absorption*
Involves diffusion and adsorption	Involves carriers or ion-binding compounds
Rate decreases rapidly with time and approaches equilibrium within an hour	Rate slower, but absorption continues for long periods of time (hours or days)
Ions readily exchangeable stoichiometrically	Ions not readily exchangeable
Not highly selective with respect to various ions	Highly selective with respect to ions accumulated
Not dependent on metabolic energy. Occurs at low temperature or with poor aeration	Requires metabolic energy, hence greatly reduced by factors which reduce respiration
Ions adsorbed chiefly on binding sites in cytoplasm	Ions accumulated chiefly in vacuoles

The nonmetabolic adsorption step in salt absorption involves exchange of ions in the roots for ions in the root environment. Most of the ions leaving the roots probably are H^+ and HCO_3^- ions resulting from the carbon dioxide produced in respiration or else ions produced by dissociation of organic acids which exchange for cations and anions either in the soil solution or adsorbed on soil particles. There has been a tendency for soil physicists to treat the outer surfaces of roots as the place where such exchanges occur, but if the soil solution can diffuse into the roots, most of the exchange probably occurs at the cell surfaces inside the roots instead of at the outer surfaces. A typical curve for accumulation by excised roots is shown in Figure 9.9.

Accumulation is not restricted to roots, but probably occurs in all living, actively metabolizing cells. At one time it appeared that meristematic tissue accumulated ions most energetically, but it now appears that vacuolating cells are just as active (Steward and Millar, 1954). Enlarging buds, cambial cells, developing ovules, and other actively metabolizing tissues accumulate salt just as actively as roots. Burstrom and Krogh (1947) found that buds accumulate potassium to a concentration 200 times as great as in the xylem sap. In some instances accumulation of organic substances such as carbohydrates and nitrogenous compounds also occurs, although conversion of sugar into starch and soluble nitrogen compounds into insoluble forms usually maintains a concentration gradient in fruits, seeds, and other storage organs.

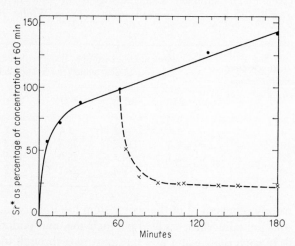

Figure 9.9 Curve showing uptake of radioactive strontium by excised barley roots. The rapid uptake during the first 30 minutes is largely nonmetabolic and easily reversible; that during the remainder of the period is by active transport and relatively irreversible. The curve with dashed line represents the fraction of radioactive strontium lost by exchange when the roots were transferred to nonradioactive strontium. (*From Epstein and Leggett, 1954.*)

Roots as Absorbing Surfaces

Most of the research on salt absorption has been done on young, excised roots or root systems of seedlings, and this probably has created a rather one-sided and incomplete view of the absorption process. In such roots most of the surface is unsuberized and ions must move through the epidermis, across a series of cortical parenchyma cells, and pass through the endodermis before entering the xylem (Figure 11.1). Considerable emphasis has been placed on the impermeability of the radial walls of endodermal cells because this forces water and solutes to pass through their protoplasts before entering the xylem. It was formerly believed that most of the salt was absorbed through the enlarging cells near the tip, but Wiebe and Kramer (1954) found that more salt is translocated away from the point of supply when supplied behind the root tip than when supplied to the apex (Table 9.9). In young roots most of the salt probably enters in the same region where most of the water enters, that is, in the region where the xylem is sufficiently differentiated to function in conduction but suberization has not progressed far enough seriously to reduce permeability.

Table 9.9. Translocation of radioactive isotopes from various regions of roots of barley seedlings. Each value represents the amount translocated away from the region to which it was supplied as a percentage of the total amount absorbed and is the average of two to four replications. (*From Wiebe and Kramer,* 1954.)

Approximate distance from root tip to point at which isotope was supplied, mm	Percentage of isotopes translocated away from region at which it was supplied				
	P^{32}	Rb^{86}	I^{131}	S^{35}	Ca^{45}
0– 4	1.3	4.2	1.0	1.7	1.3
7–10	8.5	14.3	28.3	5.2	3.1
27–30	34.4	14.7	28.9	11.8	11.2
57–60	24.9	9.4	22.7	9.2	3.6

In older woody plants most of the root system has undergone secondary thickening and the epidermis, cortical parenchyma, and endodermis have disappeared. In such roots water and salt must pass through the suberized outer layer, across the phloem, and through the cambium to reach the xylem. The role of suberized roots in absorption has been neglected because of the common opinion that they are impermeable to water. There is adequate evidence that measurable quantities of both water and salt enter through suberized roots and they comprise such a large proportion of the total root surface that they must play an important part in absorption (Kramer, 1949, pp. 116 and 242). Few data are available on the relative amounts of suberized and unsuberized root surfaces on trees, but during much of the year the latter probably constitute less than 5 per cent of the total surface. More work is needed on the amounts of unsuberized root surface found on trees at various seasons of the year and on the amounts of water and minerals absorbed through such roots.

Mycorrhizal Roots

There has been much discussion concerning the importance of mycorrhizae to the trees on which they grow. At first it was believed that they were involved in nitrogen absorption, but later it was decided that they are involved in mineral absorption in general and phosphorus in particular. Numerous attempts to grow coniferous trees in grassland and other localities where they had not been grown previously and to grow them on infertile soil have been failures, but in many instances treatments which resulted in development of mycorrhizae, such as adding organic matter containing fungi to the soil, are accompanied by successful growth. Well-known examples are the work of Rayner in England (Rayner and Neilson-Jones, 1944), of Hatch (1937), Mitchell and others in the United States, and Björkman (1942, 1956) in Sweden. Hatch (1937), Mitchell et al. (1937), and Finn (1942) all found that conifer seedlings grown in infertile soil inoculated with soil or organic matter containing mycorrhizal fungi made more growth and absorbed more mineral nutrients than those not inoculated. Similar results have been reported from other parts of the world. In Iowa and elsewhere conifers are said to grow successfully on alkaline, calcareous soils only if mycorrhizae are present, and chlorosis cannot be prevented by supplying iron or other micro- or macronutrients in the absence of mycorrhizae (Dale et al., 1955). Many other investigators have found that the presence of mycorrhizae is accompanied by increased uptake of minerals and improved growth (Table 9.10).

Table 9.10. Effects of fertilization and presence of mycorrhizae on dry weight and mineral content of 2-year-old white pine seedlings grown in a very infertile mixture of sand, sawdust, and clay. (*From Mitchell et al., 1937, table 3.*)

Fertilizer treatment	Mycorrhizae	Av. dry wt., mg	Mineral content as percentage dry wt.		
			N	P	K
None	Few	181	1.20	0.07	0.45
None	Abundant	337	1.60	0.21	0.63
Heavily fertilized	None	550	2.50	0.24	1.10

Recently it has been shown that inoculation of strawberry plants and apple seedlings and cuttings with a species of *Endogone* caused the development of endotrophic mycorrhizae. This was accompanied by increased growth and uptake of potassium, iron, and copper but reduced manganese content as compared with apple seedlings free of mycorrhizae (Mosse, 1957). Perhaps the role of mycorrhizae in horticultural plants deserves more study than it has thus far received.

Hatch (1937) proposed that the chief effect of mycorrhizae is to increase the absorbing surface of the root systems. This is certainly true,

but it is very difficult to estimate the amount of the increase in surface
and it is not known how the efficiency of the fungal hyphae as absorbing
organs compares with that of roots. Melin and Nilsson (1950) demonstrated that fungal hyphae could absorb radioactive phosphorus and

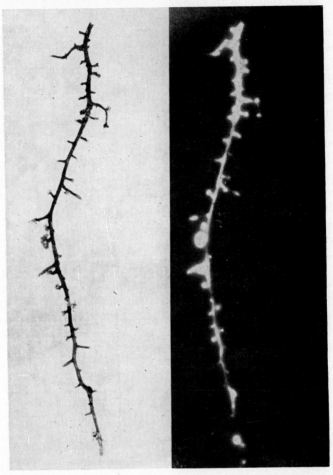

Figure 9.10   Left, a pine root showing mycorrhizal branches. Right, autoradio-
graph of the same root after exposure for 3 hours to a solution containing radioactive
phosphorus.

transfer it to pine seedlings, and later they showed that fungi could
transfer other substances from the medium to seedlings (Melin and
Nilsson, 1955). It also has been shown that mycorrhizal roots of several
species absorb more phosphorus, potassium, sodium, and other elements
per unit of surface or weight than nonmycorrhizal roots (Kramer and
Wilbur, 1949; Harley, 1956). It has been suggested that the high rate of

metabolism of mycorrhizal roots is a factor in their high salt-absorbing capacity (Routien and Dawson, 1943), but mycorrhizal roots of loblolly pine appear to have a lower rate of respiration per unit of dry weight than nonmycorrhizal roots, although they absorb considerably more phosphorus (Hodgson, 1954). There is some evidence that the high salt-accumulating capacity of the fungus results in its absorbing most of the minerals and especially phosphorus and only gradually releasing them to the root tissue (Harley, 1956). On the other hand, Melin et al. (1958) found that radioactive sodium was absorbed from the substrate through mycorrhizal roots and translocated into the tops of pine seedlings within 48 hours.

Mycorrhizal formation seems to be favored by deficiencies of one or more mineral nutrients, and few or no mycorrhizal roots develop in very fertile soils. Björkman (1942) showed that mycorrhizal development depends on a surplus of carbohydrates in the roots and is decreased by shading seedlings. Wenger (1955a) also found that loblolly pine seedlings produced more mycorrhizae in the sun than in the shade. A severe deficiency of nitrogen or phosphorus reduces mycorrhizal formation as well as growth, but a moderate deficiency stimulates their formation because it hinders use of carbohydrates in growth more than it hinders photosynthesis, resulting in a surplus in the roots. Severe deficiencies reduce both photosynthesis and growth while an abundance of mineral nutrients causes rapid use of carbohydrates in growth, and in both situations no surplus occurs in the roots to stimulate mycorrhizal development. Work in Melin's laboratory indicates that the fungi which form mycorrhizae require simple carbohydrates and various accessory substances in contrast to most fungi found in forest litter. This probably explains why their growth is stimulated in roots containing an abundance of sugar.

MacDougal and Dufrenoy (1944, 1946) considered the synthetic activities of mycorrhizal fungi to be important and suggested that they supply vitamins, nitrogen compounds, and carbohydrates to the plants on which they grow. McComb and Griffith (1946) also attributed their stimulating effect in part to the transfer of growth substances as well as minerals from the fungus to the seedlings. This seems questionable in view of the fact that the fungi require simple carbohydrates and vitamins for their own growth. There is no doubt, however, about their importance in increasing the absorption of minerals from infertile soils.

In view of the importance of mycorrhizae in bringing about increased absorption of minerals and especially of phosphorus from soils of low fertility, they should receive more attention in nursery practice. It may be advantageous to inoculate nursery beds with the proper fungi in order to ensure the presence of mycorrhizal roots on seedlings when transplanted. It is possible that the fungi ought to be selected for survival on the site where the seedlings are to be planted, especially if this possesses any unusual features such as a high pH or excess of calcium.

Readers are referred to Harley (1956), Hatch (1937), Melin (1953), Kelley (1950), and Wilde (1954) for more extensive discussions of various aspects of the mycorrhizal problem. Some Russian literature was reviewed by Buchholz (1951).

Mineral-absorption Mechanisms

Ion accumulation often is regarded as the dominant process in mineral absorption (Hoagland, 1948), but there is increasing evidence that passive movement by diffusion and mass flow also is involved.

Passive Movement. Many years ago Scott and Priestley (1928) proposed that the soil solution diffuses into roots as far as the endodermis along the water-saturated cell walls and the protoplasts of the cortical cells accumulate ions from the surrounding solution. This view was revived by Hylmö (1953) and Epstein (1955, 1956) with the addition that if part of the cytoplasm is included as free space, diffusion can occur in it as well as in the walls. Thus ions can move across roots without entering the vacuoles of the intervening cells. The importance of the endodermis probably has been overestimated, because it is pierced by root initials and sloughs off during secondary growth and is absent in older roots. In most roots of woody plants, if water and solutes can pass through the outer suberized layer, there are continuous passageways along the cell walls in which ions can move by diffusion to the xylem. If ions can enter roots by diffusion, they also can be carried inward by the transpiration stream.

There has been much debate concerning the extent to which increased intake of water affects intake of salt, and many writers state that there is no direct connection between the two processes. It has been shown by a number of investigators that increasing the rate of transpiration does increase the absorption of salt and its movement to the shoots (Freeland, 1937; Wright, 1939; Hylmö, 1953; Brouwer, 1954; Smith, 1957), but this has been explained as an indirect effect caused by more rapid removal of salt from the root xylem increasing the rate of active transport to the xylem, rather than because of increased mass flow across the root tissues into the xylem. Brouwer attributed his results to increased permeability of the roots to water and solutes at higher rates of transpiration. If water and salt enter roots in the same general region, as indicated by the data of Wiebe and Kramer (1954) and Canning and Kramer (1958), and if free space exists throughout the root, then it seems almost certain that increasing the inward movement of water across the root tissues to the xylem by increasing transpiration must also cause increased movement of solutes into the root xylem as well as increased rate of translocation away from the roots to the shoots.

Active Transport. Although it is probable that a varying but important fraction of salt is carried passively to the xylem in the transpiration stream, active transport must also occur, because at times the concentration of salt in the root xylem exceeds that in the solution surrounding the roots. There is no fully satisfactory explanation of how this active transport comes about, but it resembles accumulation in individual cells in its sensitivity to factors which affect metabolism, such as oxygen and carbohydrate supply and respiration inhibitors. Crafts and Broyer (1938), Lundegardh (1954), and others have suggested that ions move from cell to cell across the roots along gradients of decreasing accumulatory capacity, caused by decreasing aeration toward the center and especially within the endodermis. According to this hypothesis the well-aerated epidermal cells accumulate ions which move by diffusion and cytoplasmic streaming through the living cells into the stele, where they leak out of the poorly aerated cells and diffuse into the xylem vessels. The traditional view of the endodermis as having impermeable radial walls is essential to this scheme because it forms a barrier within which salt is trapped and accumulates to a concentration higher than in the external solution. If free space includes part of the cytoplasm, the endodermis is a less effective barrier than formerly supposed, and the data of Wiebe and Kramer (1954) suggest that salt passes through it fairly readily.

Hylmö (1953) attempted to eliminate the difficulty of explaining "secretion" into the xylem by assuming that the protoplasts of xylem initials continue to accumulate ions even after their upper transverse walls are ruptured. These ions are released into the xylem sap as the xylem vessels form, providing a continuous supply of solutes as long as xylem differentiation continues. This plausible hypothesis is consistent with what is known about the relation between root growth and the development of root pressure, but as yet there are no experimental data to support it. More research is needed on the nature of the process by which ions are accumulated in the root xylem.

Interrelated Absorption Processes. According to the views presented in the preceding sections, accumulation in the root cells is not necessarily an integral part of the process of salt absorption by intact plants. In plants low in salt, growing in dilute solutions, accumulation in the root cells may actually compete with the shoots by removing salt from the entering soil solution which otherwise would have moved on to the shoots. As suggested by Broyer (1950) and Hylmö (1953), salt entering the roots may (1) be accumulated in the root cells, (2) be moved by active transport into the xylem, or (3) move passively by diffusion and mass flow into the xylem without entering the vacuoles of the root cells. This is supported by the work of Kylin and Hylmö (1957), while Brouwer (1956) thinks that only a small fraction of salt enters passively. Arisz (1956) thinks that salt moves inward through the symplast formed by strands of cytoplasm (plasmodesms) which connect the protoplasts of the root cells.

It is not surprising that contradictory results have been obtained in experiments on the relation between transpiration and salt absorption because so many factors are involved in salt absorption. Of the salt entering roots, a variable fraction is accumulated by the root cells and the remainder moves on to the shoot. If the roots are initially low in salt, the fraction accumulated in the roots is large and relatively less moves to the shoot than if the roots are high in salt. When plants high in phosphorus are placed in a solution containing radioactive phosphorus, the fraction moved to the shoot depends on the rate of transpiration, but if the roots are low in phosphorus, so much is accumulated in the root cells that little is left to move to the shoot in short-term experiments and the effects of transpiration are less noticeable or are even undetectable. Another factor is the fraction of salt transferred to the xylem by active transport. This is apt to be large in rapidly growing seedlings with many young roots, but in older plants or in plants with inactive root systems passive movement is likely to be dominant, and then a relation between absorption and transpiration is more likely to be detectable.

Factors Affecting Salt Absorption

The kinds and quantities of mineral elements absorbed by plants depend on the kind of plant, the composition and concentration of the soil solution, the extent and efficiency of their root systems, and general physiological activity of both roots and shoots.

Chemical Composition of Soil Solution. The mineral elements in the soil which are directly available for absorption occur in ionized form either in the soil solution or adsorbed on the negatively charged clay micelles. Roots apparently can absorb ions either from the soil solution or from the soil particles with which they come in contact. Anions occur in the soil solution because they are not bound by negatively charged soil particles. The soil solution is a dilute but complex solution whose concentration and composition vary with the water content and pH. According to Reitemeier (1946), a kind of negative adsorption occurs, resulting in a considerably higher concentration of some ions at low moisture content than expected from calculations based on the concentrations at higher moisture contents. Several workers have published data indicating that absorption is greater from dilute systems where the roots are in contact with solid particles bearing adsorbed ions than where the ions must be absorbed from a solution (Jenny and Overstreet, 1939; Gonzalez, 1958).

The concentration of most ions in the soil solution is very low, and continuous replacement must occur to supply the quantities removed by growing plants (Stout and Overstreet, 1950). Most of this occurs by solution of more or less insoluble salts of the soil minerals, but nitrogen is supplied entirely by the activity of soil organisms. The reactions between the liquid and solid phases are very complex and beyond the scope of this discussion. There likewise are complex interactions between various ions by which the presence of one ion affects the availability of another. For example, phosphorus precipitates iron as ferric phosphate on root surfaces, and at higher pH values calcium combines also. This inhibits absorption of more iron (Biddulph, 1951).

The effects of soil pH on the absorption of mineral nutrients also are complex, involving effects on the solubility of various elements as well as effects on the activity of soil organisms which carry on nitrification and other biological processes. At extreme pH values root growth also is affected (Leyton, 1952). In alkaline soils the solubility of iron, copper, manganese, and zinc is greatly decreased, resulting in deficiencies of these elements, whereas in acid soils the increased solubility of manganese and aluminum may result in toxic concentrations. If the proper concentrations of the essential mineral elements are maintained, plants can be grown over a wide pH range, and it is doubtful if plants have very rigid pH requirements if the secondary effects of pH on availability of mineral elements are eliminated. The effects of the pH on absorption of phosphorus by mycorrhizal and nonmycorrhizal roots of beech were studied by Harley and McCready (1950).

Soil water content affects the availability of mineral elements in various ways. Drying of soil reduces the availability of minerals in general and potassium in particular (Volk, 1934), and in dry soil both root growth and the efficiency of roots as absorbing surfaces are reduced. Mineral deficiencies often become apparent during droughts because of reduced availability of solutes and reduced efficiency of absorption. Too much soil water is even worse because the resulting deficient aeration may become so injurious that it not only interferes with absorption but even kills the roots. Very dry and very wet soils are unfavorable for the biological activity necessary for the release of nitrogen and other elements from organic matter and for nitrogen fixation.

Root Activity. In soils with a moisture content below field capacity water movement is very slow; hence continued extension of roots into previously unoccupied soil is an important factor in making water and minerals available. Soil conditions favorable to the growth of roots and to their functioning as absorbing systems thus become an essential factor in successful growth of trees and other plants. Root extension of healthy trees is limited chiefly by lack of oxygen and occurrence of mechanically impervious soil horizons; hence the physical properties of soils often are as important as their chemical properties with respect to tree growth. In fact, Coile (1948) reported that most of the differences in site quality for loblolly and shortleaf pine in the North Carolina Piedmont can be explained in terms of the depth of the A horizon and the imbibitional water value of the B horizon.

It already has been mentioned that accumulation of salt by cells is related to their metabolic activity and is affected by low temperature, oxygen supply, and other factors which reduce the metabolic activity of roots. Most of the research on these phenomena has been done with herbaceous roots, but the data available indicate that tree roots behave

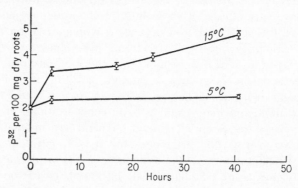

Figure 9.11 Effect of temperature on movement of radioactive phosphorus from the fungal sheath into the core of mycorrhizal roots of beech. (*From Harley, 1956.*)

in the same manner. As shown in Table 9.11, respiration inhibitors reduce uptake of P^{32} by both mycorrhizal and nonmycorrhizal roots. The effects of low temperature on phosphorus transfer are shown in Figure 9.11, and the effects of oxygen supply in Figure 9.12. Brierley (1955) measured oxygen and carbon dioxide in the humus and litter layer under beech and found that the oxygen never fell low enough nor did the carbon dioxide rise high enough to interfere with salt absorption. Inadequate aeration doubtless often limits mineral absorption in wet and compact soils.

Even in rapidly transpiring plants where accumulation may be less important than passive movement of ions, factors which reduce metabolism reduce absorption of minerals, just as they reduce passive absorption of water. Low temperatures and deficient aeration reduce water absorption by reducing the permeability of the protoplasm in membranes across which most of the water moves, and movement of ions must be reduced as much as or more than water movement. Thus the fact that salt absorption is reduced by factors which reduce root metabolism is not inconsistent with the view that some passive absorption of salt occurs.

The relation between synthetic activities of roots and mineral absorption seems to deserve more attention. In many trees inorganic nitrogen is converted into organic nitrogen compounds in the roots, before moving to the shoots (Bollard, 1958). There is evidence that in at least some plants a part of the phosphorus is converted into an organic compound. It may be that the synthetic activity of roots is an important step in absorption of some elements.

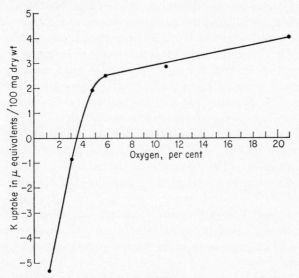

Figure 9.12 Effect of oxygen concentration on uptake of potassium by excised mycorrhizal roots of beech. (*From Harley,* 1956.)

Table 9.11. Effect of respiration inhibitors on accumulation of radioactive phosphorus by mycorrhizal and nonmycorrhizal loblolly pine roots. (*From Kramer,* 1951a.)

Treatments at pH 4.7–4.8	Root tips		Mycorrhiza segments	
	Counts per min	Activity as % of control	Counts per min	Activity as % of control
Control	81,713		77,306	
0.025 *M* malonic acid	77,330	94.6	67,405	87.2
0.001 *M* sodium azide	308	0.4	965	1.2
0.005 *M* sodium fluoride	986	1.2	1,620	2.1

Shoot Activity. Root growth and metabolism depend on a continuous supply of carbohydrates produced by photosynthesis in the tops. Roots probably also require growth substances synthesized in the tops, but this has not yet been demonstrated for tree roots. It has been shown frequently that factors which reduce photosynthesis reduce root growth more than shoot growth, and this tends to reduce mineral absorption. The effect of decreased light intensity on root growth and the root/shoot ratio is shown in Figure 16.2.

Various insecticides, fungicides, and herbicides applied to soils also affect the absorption of minerals. Voigt (1954) reported that such commonly used materials as aluminum sulfate and benzene hexachloride decreased both root growth and phosphorus absorption. In contrast, formaldehyde and allyl alcohol increased phosphorus uptake and seedling growth. It seems that more attention ought to be given to the physiological effects of various chemicals used to control insects, fungi, and weeds, because some of them undoubtedly reduce growth of seedlings significantly. On the other hand, if the soil treatments eliminate serious pests such as nematodes, growth will be increased.

Seasonal Periodicity in Absorption. Büsgen and Münch (1931) cited work indicating that trees of different species, at least in their seedling stages, absorb most of their minerals at different times during the growing season. This was not confirmed by Süchting (1939), and the data of Mitchell (1936) do not show any very marked differences in mineral uptake from June 1 to September 1 among the seven species studied. All species showed a fairly high rate of uptake of nitrogen, phosphorus, potassium, and calcium early in the season compared with the uptake in late summer.

If there is a pronounced seasonal periodicity in mineral absorption, this should be taken into account in applying fertilizer. Magness et al. (1948) reported no difference in effectiveness of spring and fall applications of nitrogen to mature apple trees, and this is generally true for older trees. Seedlings, however, need an adequate supply of minerals at the beginning of the growing season.

GENERAL REFERENCES

Childers, N. F. (ed.), 1954, Mineral nutrition of fruit crops, Hort. Pub. Rutgers Univ., New Brunswick, N.J.

Epstein, E., 1956, Mineral nutrition of plants: mechanisms of uptake and transport, Ann. Rev. Plant Physiology, 7:1–24.

Goodall, D. W., and F. G. Gregory, 1947, Chemical composition of plants as an index of their nutritional status, Imp. Bur. Hort. Plantation Crops Tech. Commun. 17.

Hewitt, E. J., 1952, Sand and water culture methods used in the study of plant nutrition, Imp. Bur. Hort. Plantation Crops, East Malling, Tech. Commun. 22.

Kelley, A. P., 1950, Mycotrophy in plants, Chronica Botanica Co., Waltham, Mass.

Lutz, H. J., and R. F. Chandler, 1946, Forest soils, John Wiley & Sons, Inc., New York.

Reuther, W., T. W. Embleton, and W. W. Jones, 1958, Mineral nutrition of tree crops, Ann. Rev. Plant Physiology, 9:175–206.

Ruhland, W. (ed.), 1958, Encyclopedia of plant physiology, vol. 4, Mineral nutrition of plants, G. Michael (subed.), Springer-Verlag, Berlin.

White, D. P., and A. L. Leaf, 1957, Forest fertilization, New York State Coll. Forestry Tech. Pub. 81, Syracuse, N.Y.

Wilde, S. A., 1958, Forest soils, The Ronald Press Company, New York.

CHAPTER 10   *Water Relations and Transpiration*

Over large parts of the earth's surface the occurrence of trees and the amount of growth they make are controlled to a greater extent by the water supply than by any other factor. Most grasslands areas and many deserts could support forests if enough water were available. Other large areas support only sparse stands of trees because of limited supplies of water.

The water relations of trees are just as important to their successful growth as the biochemical processes involved in the synthesis of food and its transformation into new tissue. The essential factor in plant-water relations is maintenance of a sufficiently high water content or turgidity to permit normal functioning of physiological processes and growth.

There are two interrelated aspects of plant-water relations. One deals with the water relations of the plant as a whole, the other with water relations of cells and tissues within the plant. Plant-water relations involve the absorption of water, the ascent of sap, and loss of water by transpiration. On warm, sunny days transpiration tends to exceed absorption, producing water deficits in trees and competition among the various parts for water. The resulting redistribution of water within the tree is controlled by the osmotic properties of its cells and tissues.

The importance of water in the life of trees can be shown by listing its more important functions, which can be grouped under four headings.

1. A constituent of protoplasm. Water forms 80 to 90 per cent of the fresh weight of actively growing tissue. Water content is invariably high in regions of high physiological activity, such as root and stem tips, and low in regions of low activity.

2. As a reagent. Water is just as essential a reactant in photosynthesis as carbon dioxide. It also is a reactant in hydrolytic reactions such as the digestion of starch to sugar.

3. As a solvent. Water is the solvent in which gases, salts, and other

276

solvents move in and out of cells and from organ to organ in trees. Water in the cell walls and xylem forms a practically continuous solvent system throughout trees.

4. Maintenance of turgidity. Sufficient water to maintain a certain minimum degree of turgidity is essential for cell enlargement and growth. Cell turgidity also is important in the maintenance of the form of leaves and other slightly lignified structures, in stomatal opening, and in movement of flower petals, leaf petioles, and other structures whose position is governed by the turgidity of cells.

Cell-Water Relations

Most of the space given to water relations deals with trees and stands of trees. However, some knowledge of the water relations of cells and tissues and the terminology used in dealing with them is necessary to an understanding of plant-water relations; hence a brief discussion follows.

Full consideration of cell-water relations involves discussion of cell structure, permeability of cell membranes, osmotic pressure, turgor and wall pressure, and diffusion-pressure deficit or suction force. For more detailed discussions of these topics readers are referred to Meyer and Anderson (1952) and Kramer (1955, 1956d).

Living plant cells consist of protoplasts surrounded by more or less rigid walls which severely limit changes in volume. The protoplast consists of a thin layer of cytoplasm in which a nucleus and sometimes plastids are embedded, enclosing a central vacuole filled with cell sap, consisting of water and organic and inorganic solutes. Often the protoplasts of adjacent cells are connected by strands of cytoplasm, called "plasmodesms," resulting in a continuous system sometimes termed the "symplast."

Typical cellulose and lignified cell walls are highly permeable to water and solutes. The cytoplasmic membranes of the protoplast are relatively permeable to water also, though less permeable than the walls, as indicated by the increase in permeability when cells are killed (Ordin and Kramer, 1956). The cytoplasmic membranes are relatively impermeable to sugars and most ions; hence solutes accumulated in the vacuoles tend to remain there, producing osmotic pressures ranging from 5 to 50 or more atmospheres.

Water movement in plants occurs along gradients of decreasing free energy or molecular activity. It is very difficult to measure the activity or free energy of water, but it is fairly easy to measure the difference between the free energy of pure water and that of water in a solution. This difference is termed the diffusion-pressure deficit by Meyer (1945) and the suction force or suction tension by many European workers. It is a measure of the pressure with which water tends to diffuse into a cell or tissue which is placed in pure water. The diffusion pressure of an unconfined solution is equal to its osmotic pressure, but the diffusion pressure of water is reduced and the diffusion-pressure deficit increased by the presence of solutes as in vacuoles, by surface forces as in water bound in cell walls and cytoplasm, by decrease in temperature, and by decrease in pressure. The diffusion pressure is increased and the diffusion-pressure deficit decreased by increased temperature or pressure.

Water moves through plants along a gradient of decreasing diffusion pressure or increasing diffusion-pressure deficit. The gradient in diffusion-pressure deficit from soil to plant to air is shown in Table 10.1.

Table 10.1. Gradient of diffusion-pressure deficit from soil to plant to air.

	Diffusion-pressure deficit, atm
Soil near field capacity	0.1
Roots at zero turgor	5– 6.0
Leaves at zero turgor	10–50.0
Air at 90% relative humidity	140.5

The osmotic relations of plant cells can be expressed by the following equation:

Diffusion-pressure deficit (DPD) = osmotic pressure (OP) − wall
               pressure (WP)   (wall pressure = turgor pressure)

Cells absorb water from the soil or from their neighbors if their diffusion-pressure deficit (hereafter to be termed DPD) exceeds that of their surroundings and lose water when it is lower than their surroundings. The DPD of cells and tissues varies from zero to a value equal to their osmotic pressure at incipient plasmolysis, and if the protoplasts are under tension because of negative wall pressure, the DPD can even exceed the osmotic pressure.

The osmotic relations of cells in various states of turgidity are shown in Table 10.2.

Table 10.2. Osmotic relations of cells in various states of turgidity.

	At incipient plasmolysis	Half turgid	Fully turgid
OP	10	9.5	9.0
WP	0	5.0	9.0
DPD	10	4.5	0.0

The decrease in osmotic pressure results from dilution of cell sap by water absorption with consequent increase in cell volume. As water diffuses into the cell, its volume tends to increase, producing outwardly directed turgor pressure. Cell walls resist extension, exerting an inwardly directed wall pressure against the cell sap, increasing its free energy and decreasing its DPD. When the wall pressure becomes equal to the osmotic pressure of the cell sap, the DPD becomes zero and entrance of water ceases because there is no longer a free-energy gradient from the environment into the cell. The relationships among cell volume,

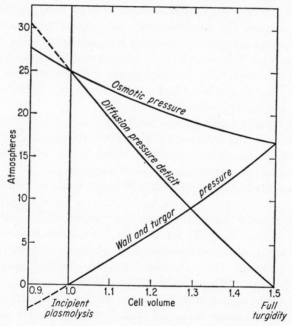

Figure 10.1 Interrelationships among cell volume, turgor pressure, osmotic pressure, and diffusion-pressure deficit. (*Modified from Höfler,* 1920.)

wall pressure, osmotic pressure, and DPD are shown graphically in Figure 10.1.

It has been suggested that there might also be nonosmotic uptake or "secretion" of water against a free-energy gradient, brought about by the expenditure of metabolic energy. This suggestion is based chiefly on occurrence of discrepancies between osmotic values determined cryoscopically and plasmolytically and on observations that auxin increases and respiration inhibitors decrease water uptake by plant tissues. It now seems more probable that auxin and respiration inhibitors operate through their effects on cell wall metabolism and wall pressure, rather than directly on a metabolic water-uptake mechanism. At present it appears improbable that any measurable nonosmotic uptake of water occurs in plant cells (Kramer, 1956d).

Importance of Transpiration

An amazing amount of water is lost by transpiration. A hardwood forest in the humid southern Appalachians transpires 17 to 22 inches of water per year (Hoover, 1944), and individual trees may lose 50 to 100 gallons on a sunny day. More than 95 per cent of the water used by a tree simply passes through it, replacing that lost by transpiration.

In view of the large quantities of water lost by transpiration it seems desirable to discuss the importance of the process to trees. There has been considerable disagreement among botanists concerning the role of transpiration, some regarding it as beneficial while others consider it to be harmful. Clements (1934) emphasizes the alleged benefits, while Curtis (1926) and Curtis and Clark (1950) emphasize its harmful effects. Some of the arguments follow.

Beneficial Effects. Transpiration has been claimed to be beneficial because (1) it cools the leaves; (2) it prevents development of excessive turgidity; (3) it causes movement of water to the leaves; and (4) it increases absorption and translocation of minerals.

There is no doubt that evaporation of water tends to cool leaves, and leaves in which transpiration has been reduced by wilting are warmer than unwilted leaves under the same conditions (Miller and Saunders, 1923). Nevertheless, they do not become hot enough to be injured because they are cooled by reradiation or thermal emission of heat to the surrounding air. The extensive literature on leaf temperature is discussed by Curtis (1936) and by Miller (1938).

It sometimes is argued that if it were not for transpiration, plants in moist soil would become so turgid that they would burst. Occasionally fruits and fleshy roots do burst from excessive turgor pressure, but in general attainment of full turgidity by plant cells stops the uptake of water.

The relation of transpiration to the ascent of sap will be discussed later, but any use of water in leaves produces forces causing movement of water to them; hence transpiration is not essential to move water to leaves. The relation of transpiration to salt absorption and translocation remains the subject of considerable disagreement, as stated in Curtis and Clark (1950) and Meyer and Anderson (1952). There is increasing evidence that increased water absorption is accompanied by increased salt absorption (Chapter 9). Gustafson (1934) found little difference in salt concentration of plants grown in low and high humidity, and there is no evidence that plants grown in a humid environment unfavorable to rapid transpiration suffer from lack of minerals. Nevertheless, it seems doubtful if sufficient minerals would move to the shoots if transpiration were stopped completely. Winneberger (1958) found that growth of sunflower plants was reduced materially in an extremely humid atmosphere. Although there was no visible evidence of mineral deficiency in the shoots of these plants, he suggested that transpiration may be essential for translocation.

Harmful Effects. The harmful effects of transpiration are more definite. Rapidly transpiring plants often lose so much water that the cells of their leaves and young twigs lose turgor and wilt during the middle of the day. This results in temporary cessation of growth, which is not too serious if the tissues recover their turgidity in the evening. If water loss so far exceeds absorption that recovery cannot occur, death from dehydration will eventually result. Even moderate loss of turgidity causes premature closure of stomates which interferes with photosynthesis, and dehydration often disturbs the starch-sugar balance, the rate of respiration, and various other biochemical processes. On the whole, excessive transpiration must be regarded as an evil which retards the growth of many plants and kills many others. The effects of transpiration are particularly serious to foresters in connection with planting projects because thousands of seedlings are killed each year by transpiration before they are able to produce a new root system large enough to absorb water as rapidly as it is lost.

Transpiration sometimes is termed an unavoidable evil. It is an evil for the reasons just outlined. It is unavoidable because of the structure of leaves. As shown in Figure 10.2, the interior of leaves consists of numerous cells with moist cell walls exposed to the air of the intercellular spaces, and the air of the intercellular spaces is connected with the outside air through the stomates. Whenever the stomates are open, water tends to evaporate from the cell walls and diffuse out. If leaves were so constructed that no water could escape from them, little or no carbon dioxide could enter.

Polster (1950) measured the rates of transpiration and photosynthesis of several tree species and found that the daily cycles of the two processes agreed in having a rapid early-morning rise and evening decrease. They differed because the maximum rate of photosynthesis usually occurred before noon, and the maximum rate of transpiration usually occurred after noon (Figure 10.3). On hot sunny days photosynthesis was reduced more than transpiration in birch, but not in beech.

It appears that during the evolution of land plants, a structure favorable for entrance of the carbon dioxide essential in photosynthesis has been more important to their success than a structure unfavorable to the loss of water. Thus the present structure of most plants has developed in a manner which makes transpiration unavoidable, even though it often is detrimental. The only exceptions are a few desert species which are covered with heavy layers of cutin and have few stomates. These species usually grow very slowly.

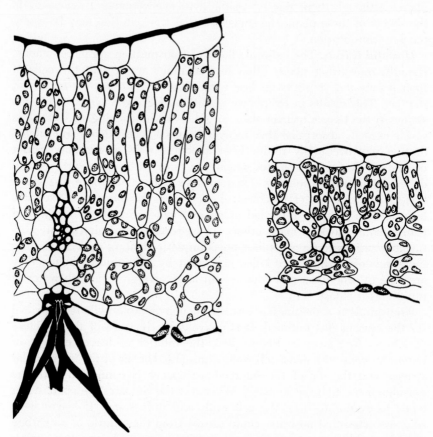

Figure 10.2 Cross sections through leaves of post oak (left) and beech (right). Post oak leaves are representative of the xeromorphic type, with thick cutin, double layer of palisade cells, bundle sheath extension, and a high ratio of internal to external surface. Beech leaves are of the mesomorphic type. They are thinner, with thin cutin and a single layer of palisade cells and less internal surface exposed to intercellular spaces. (*Courtesy of J. Philpott.*)

The Process of Transpiration

Transpiration is the loss of water from plants in the form of vapor. Basically it is an evaporation process, modified somewhat by plant structure and stomatal control. In leaves it usually occurs in two stages, evaporation from the moist cell walls into the intercellular spaces and diffusion of water vapor from the intercellular spaces into the outside

air. There are three principal pathways for the escape of water vapor from plants, the stomates, the epidermis, and the lenticels of twigs.
Lenticular Transpiration. The bare branches of deciduous trees lose

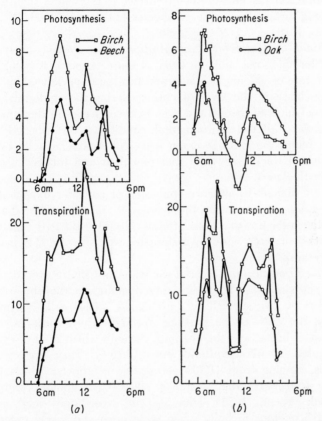

Figure 10.3 Transpiration and photosynthesis of trees on different kinds of days. *a.* Sunny and warm in the morning, hazy in the afternoon. *b.* Clear and hot. Transpiration is expressed as milligrams water per gram fresh weight per minute, photosynthesis as milligrams carbon dioxide per gram fresh weight per hour. Both processes show early-morning rise and evening decrease, but on a mild day (*a*) maximum photosynthesis was in the morning and maximum transpiration was in the afternoon. On a hot day (*b*) photosynthesis of birch was reduced more than that of oak, falling below the compensation point. Transpiration of both species was reduced to about the same extent. On day *a* birch used 337 grams of water per gram of dry matter produced while beech used only 257 grams of water. On day *b* birch used 506 grams of water per gram dry matter and oak used 372 grams. (*From Polster,* 1950.)

measurable amounts of water through their lenticels and other breaks in the corky layers which enclose them. Kozlowski (1943) found a winter rate of transpiration for yellow-poplar of about 2 grams per 100 square centimeters of twig surface per week, compared with August transpiration of 80 grams per 100 square centimeters of leaf surface per week. Cherry laurel, a broadleaf evergreen, had a winter transpiration rate of 10 to 15 grams per 100 square centimeters per week, but conifers lose little more water per unit of needle surface in the winter than is lost per unit of twig surface by deciduous species (Kozlowski, 1943; Weaver and Mogensen, 1919).

Epidermal or Cuticular Transpiration. The amount of water lost through the epidermis and the layer of cutin covering it is highly variable. The rate or amount of epidermal transpiration depends principally on the thickness of the layer of cutin covering the epidermis, and this varies widely among species and even between leaves of the same species grown under various environmental conditions. Swanson (1943), for example, found the cutin layer on leaves of American holly to be 7 to 10 microns in thickness, while that of coleus and tobacco was only 1 micron in thickness.

It is very difficult to measure epidermal or cuticular transpiration, but it is generally agreed that on the average it amounts to less than 10 per cent of the total transpiration. Stålfelt (1932) estimated that cuticular transpiration of birch with open stomates was only about 3 per cent of stomatal transpiration.

Stomatal Transpiration. Most of the water lost by transpiration escapes through the stomates. These are tiny openings in the epidermis, each surrounded by two specialized cells called "guard cells." Stomates are important not only as the passages through which most vapor passes out of leaves, but also as the openings through which most of the carbon dioxide used in photosynthesis enters leaves. They are exceedingly numerous, ranging from 11,500 per square centimeter in black poplar and yew (Salisbury, 1927) to over 100,000 per square centimeter in scarlet oak (Yocum, 1935). They also are exceedingly small, averaging 12.5 by 6.5 microns in holly when wide open and rarely exceeding 20 microns in length and 8 microns in width in any species. Thus their total area when open is often only about 1 per cent of the epidermal surface. Although they occur in both the upper and the lower epidermis of some species, they usually occur only in the lower epidermis of leaves of trees.

The relative importance of epidermal and stomatal transpiration varies widely among different species. Species with thick layers of cutin such as privet, magnolia, and many conifers lose water very slowly when the stomates are closed, but species with a thin layer of cutin continue to lose water through the epidermis even after the stomates are entirely closed. Such species usually lose water more rapidly and are injured more severely by droughts than species having little epidermal transpiration. Stålfelt (1956a) summarized the literature on cuticular transpiration.

Stomatal Behavior. Detailed discussions of stomatal behavior can be found in plant physiology texts; hence only a few important facts will be presented here. Perhaps most notable is the rapid rate of diffusion through stomatal pores. Although they usually occupy only about 1 per cent of the leaf surface, diffusion of water vapor through stomates often amounts to 50 per cent of the rate of evaporation from a free-water surface. Stålfelt (1932) found that under favorable conditions transpiration from birch leaves amounted to as much as 65 per cent of the evaporation from a water surface. Thus diffusion of water vapor through stomates sometimes occurs more than 50 times as rapidly as from a free-water surface of the same area.

This situation was studied over a half century ago by Brown and Escombe (1900), who found (1) that the smaller a pore, the more rapid the rate of diffusion through it per unit of area, and (2) that the rate of diffusion through small pores is more nearly proportional to their perimeter than to their area. These relationships have been verified by several other workers (Sayre, 1926; Sierp and Seybold, 1929; Huber, 1930; Bange, 1953). Thus the size and shape of stomates are such as to result in maximum efficiency as passages for gases. Also, stomates usually are spaced far enough apart so that their diffusion shells do not interfere seriously with each other. Furthermore, because of the elliptical shape of stomatal openings, partial closure has relatively little effect on their perimeter and the rate of diffusion through a stomate is not seriously reduced when it changes from fully open to half closed (Figure 10.4).

Stomates of most trees open when the guard cells become turgid and close when they lose their turgidity. This occurs because the inner walls are much thicker than the outer walls, resulting in the entire guard cell bending outward as its turgidity increases. In some conifers increased turgor causes changes in shape of the guard cells, which results in stomatal opening. The mechanism of the diurnal changes in turgidity is not completely understood, but it seems to be related to changes in the osmotic pressure of the cell sap caused by changes in the relative amounts of starch and sugar.

The opening and closing of stomates are controlled by light, the water content of leaves, and temperature. In general, stomates open in the light and close in darkness. The explanation usually offered is that accumulation of carbon dioxide in low light intensity or in darkness lowers the pH of the guard cells, causing conversion of sugar to starch, decrease in DPD, and loss of water to the surrounding cells, resulting in loss of turgidity and stomatal closure. When illuminated, photosynthesis probably removes excess carbon dioxide, raising the pH and causing conversion of starch to sugar. This raises the DPD of the guard cells, causing uptake of water, increase in turgidity, and opening of the stomates.

The mechanism of guard cell movement probably is considerably more complex than a mere change in osmotic pressure, but there is as yet no general agreement on the details. Virgin (1957) found that stomates of

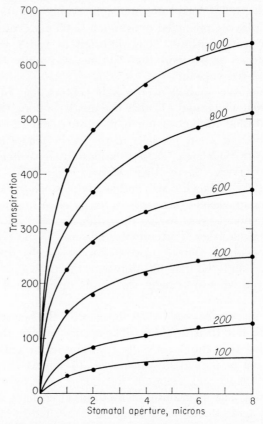

Figure 10.4 Relation between stomatal aperture and rate of transpiration with various potential rates of transpiration. The numbers on the curves indicate the relative rates of evaporation from blotting paper atmometers expressed in milligrams of water per hour per 25 square centimeters of surface. Transpiration is expressed in milligrams of water per 25 square centimeters of leaf surface. (*From Stålfelt, 1932.*)

plants completely lacking chlorophyll did not open in the light, suggesting that guard cell movement is related to photosynthesis. Readers are referred to papers by Scarth and Shaw (1951), Heath and Russell (1954), and Stålfelt (1955, 1956a) for more detailed discussions of the mechanism of stomatal movement.

If loss of water exceeds absorption, decrease in turgidity of leaf cells results and closure of stomates occurs. As the soil dries out, the stomates close earlier in the day. Stomates usually remain closed at temperatures near freezing, and Wilson (1948b) found that stomatal apertures increased with increased temperature up to 25 or 30°C in several woody and herbaceous species (Figure 10.5). There also is some evidence that the responsiveness of stomates is decreased by deficiencies of nitrogen and other mineral nutrients.

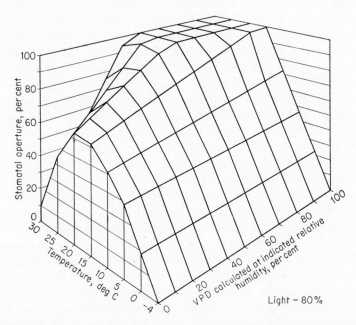

Figure 10.5 Effects of temperature and vapor-pressure deficit of the air on stomatal aperture of privet and camellia. (*From Wilson,* 1948b.)

Environmental Factors Affecting Transpiration

As mentioned earlier, transpiration is basically an evaporation process. The rate of evaporation of water is controlled by the steepness of the vapor-pressure gradient from the evaporating surface to the surrounding air. This depends on the temperature of the evaporating surface and the temperature and relative humidity of the surrounding air. In leaves the chief evaporating surfaces are the wet walls of the mesophyll cells and the principal pathway for escape of water vapor is the stomates. Visible light affects the rate of transpiration both by warming the leaves and by affecting the extent of stomatal opening. Wind also affects transpiration by sweeping away the water vapor from the vicinity of leaves. The chief environmental factors affecting transpiration will be discussed separately. An extensive review of factors affecting the rate of water loss from trees was made by Raber (1937).

Vapor Pressure. It is necessary to have a clear understanding of evaporation before it is possible to understand how various environmental factors affect the rate of transpiration. The molecules in a beaker of water or any other liquid are in continual motion, and some of the more energetic molecules escape from the surface into the atmosphere and exist as water vapor. If the beaker is placed under a bell jar, molecules accumulate in the air over the beaker until the rate at which they return to the water (condense) equals the rate at which they escape (evaporate) and no more net loss occurs. At this point the pressure of the water vapor in the air will have a definite value at any given temperature, which is known as the "vapor pressure." The vapor pressure increases greatly with increase in temperature. Therefore increase in temperature of leaves will tend to increase their rate of transpiration because it increases the vapor pressure of the water in the leaves. Plants transpire when the vapor pressure in their leaves exceeds that in the surrounding air, and anything which increases the steepness of this gradient increases the rate of transpiration.

Humidity of the Air. The actual amount of water present in the atmosphere is known as the "absolute humidity" and often is expressed as milligrams of water per liter of air. More often the moisture content of the air is expressed in terms of relative humidity, which is the percentage of saturation at the existing temperature. Thus a relative humidity of 50 per cent means that the air is 50 per cent saturated at that temperature. Occasionally the humidity is expressed as the saturation deficit, which is the difference between the relative humidity and saturation, or 100 per cent. For example, if the relative humidity is 60 per cent, the saturation deficit is 40 per cent, and at 80 per cent relative humidity, it is 20 per cent. Unfortunately, relative humidity is an unsatisfactory term for evaluating the moisture conditions of the air with respect to evaporation or transpiration because the rate of evaporation from a water surface would be more than three times as rapid at 30°C and 50 per cent relative humidity as at 10°C and 50 per cent relative humidity. It is obvious, therefore, that maintaining various systems at the same relative humidity does not guarantee similar rates of evaporation, unless the temperatures are also kept the same.

For studying evaporation and transpiration the humidity of the air can best be expressed in terms of its water vapor pressure. The vapor pressure of saturated air at 10°C is 9.21 millimeters of mercury, and at 30° it is 31.82 millimeters. At a relative humidity of 60 per cent, the air is 60 per cent saturated and its vapor pressure therefore is 60 per cent of the saturation vapor pressure. The vapor-pressure gradient between air at 10°C and 60 per cent relative humidity and saturated air at the same temperature is $9.21 - 5.53 = 3.68$ millimeters, and at 30°C it is $31.82 - 19.09 = 12.73$ millimeters. It usually is assumed in considering the effect of humidity on transpiration that we are dealing with diffusion from a saturated atmosphere in the intercellular spaces to an atmosphere of varying vapor pressure outside of the leaf. As shown by Thut (1939), the relative humidity in the intercellular spaces often drops considerably below saturation, but this will be neglected in our discussion because it is too difficult to measure precisely.

The misleading results produced by use of relative humidity alone to evaluate the moisture content of the air can be shown by what occurs if plant tissue is maintained at 60 per cent relative humidity at various temperatures. Assuming that the plant tissue is at its saturation vapor pressure for each temperature, the situation shown in Table 10.3 results.

Table 10.3. Vapor-pressure gradient from leaf to air at a fixed humidity and various temperatures.

Temperature, °C	Vapor pressure of tissue	Vapor pressure of air at 60% relative humidity	Vapor-pressure gradient
10	9.21	5.53	3.68
20	17.54	10.52	7.02
30	31.82	19.09	12.73

Here are three lots of material maintained at the same relative humidity, but with three different vapor-pressure gradients from the plant tissues to the air, and therefore with three different rates of water loss. If material is to be stored at different temperatures under conditions ensuring the same rate of water loss, then the relative humidity must be adjusted to various values which ensure the same water-vapor-pressure difference between plant tissue and air at all temperatures. This principle applies not only to plant tissue but to any other kind of material which loses water to its environment.

Temperature. It is well known that within the noninjurious range, the rate of transpiration increases with increasing temperature, but the reason for this increase is not always understood. If the temperature of an air mass is increased, its relative humidity decreases, and it sometimes is claimed that this decrease in relative humidity is responsible for the increased loss of water. This is not true. If the absolute humidity of the air (the water content per unit of volume) remains unchanged as the temperature increases, the water vapor pressure in the air increases in proportion to the increase in absolute temperature, but the vapor pressure of the saturated evaporating surfaces inside of the leaves increases so much faster that there is a marked increase in the water-vapor-pressure gradient from leaf to air. The situation is shown in Table 10.4.

Table 10.4. Effects of change in temperature on vapor-pressure gradient from leaves to air.

	10	20	30
Leaf and air temperature, °C	10	20	30
Relative humidity of air assuming no change in absolute humidity, %	80	44	25
Vapor pressure at evaporating surface of leaf, mm Hg	9.21	17.54	31.82
Vapor pressure of air at indicated temperatures	7.37	7.74	7.88
Vapor-pressure gradient from leaf to air	1.84	9.80	23.94

Actually, leaf temperatures fluctuate considerably and may be either warmer or cooler than the surrounding air. In bright sunlight leaves often are somewhat warmer than the surrounding air, but a breeze may cool them, or a passing cloud might cause them to cool down below the air temperature. The effects on transpiration of deviations of leaf temperature above or below air temperature can be explained in terms of their effects on the vapor-pressure gradient from leaf to air.

Light. Solar radiation includes both visible light and those wavelengths shorter and longer than visible light which reach the earth's surface from the sun. Visible light is an important factor affecting transpiration because of its effects on stomatal opening, as well as because some of it is absorbed by leaves, tending to raise their temperature. The stomates of most plants are closed in darkness, and many stomates close in light of low intensity, as on cloudy days. Stomates of some plants close in full sun also (Nutman, 1937; Polster, 1950). Leaves fully exposed to the sun tend to become somewhat warmer than the air. Leaves exposed to the sky on a clear night tend to become cooler than the air, and this is a major factor in the deposition of dew on leaves.

Wind. The effect of wind is twofold. It tends to decrease leaf temperature, which reduces transpiration, but it also removes water vapor from the vicinity of leaves. This helps to maintain a steep vapor-pressure gradient from the leaf to the air and therefore tends to increase the rate of transpiration. Most of the latter effect occurs at a very low velocity. Winds of high velocity sometimes cause reduction in transpiration, apparently because they cause closure of stomates. Most of the work on effect of wind has been done with herbaceous plants, but Satoo

(1955b) has reported similar results from experiments with three Japanese conifer species.

Supply of Water. Sustained high rates of transpiration require an adequate supply of water to the leaves. Otherwise the leaf water content decreases, incipient or visible wilting occurs, stomates close, and the rate of transpiration decreases. Thus a midday drop in transpiration

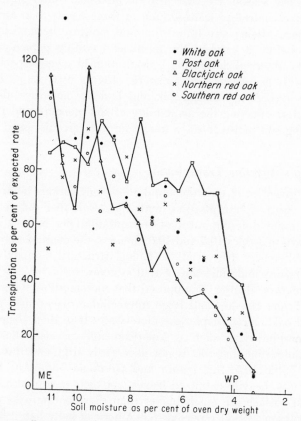

Figure 10.6 Effect of decreasing soil moisture content on transpiration rates of oak seedlings. (*From Bourdeau, 1954.*)

sometimes occurs even in well-watered plants on hot, dry days because water absorption cannot keep pace with water loss. As the soil moisture content decreases, absorption tends to lag further and further behind transpiration, resulting in permanent water deficits which greatly reduce the rate of water loss.

In the classic experiments of Hartig (1876) and Höhnel (1884) it was observed that the transpiration rate was higher for plants in moist soil than for plants in dry soil. Pearson (1924) showed that decreasing soil moisture content was accompanied by decreasing water loss from several species of conifers, and many other investigators all over the world have observed the same thing. Ringoet (1952) observed that the transpiration rate of oil palm was reduced by low soil moisture to such an extent that the trees actually transpire more in the rainy season than in the dry season, in spite of the fact that atmospheric conditions are more favorable in the dry season. He therefore decided that water supply was a more effective control on transpiration of these plants than atmospheric factors. Lemée (1956) also found that soil moisture became limiting to cacao long before it reached the permanent wilting percentage. Bourdeau (1954) observed decreasing transpiration in several species of oak seedlings with decreasing soil moisture (Figure 10.6), and Kozlowski (1949) observed it in overcup oak and loblolly pine (see also Figure 16.12). Factors affecting the availability of soil moisture and the effects of decreasing soil moisture on water absorption are discussed in Chapter 11.

Plant Factors Affecting Transpiration

Under a given set of environmental conditions various internal factors modify the rate of transpiration, with the result that different species may have quite different rates of transpiration per unit of leaf area. This is shown in Tables 10.5 and 10.6. Some of the characters responsible for these differences are variations in leaf structure, stomatal behavior, osmotic pressure, and efficiency of root systems.

Leaf Structure. It often is supposed that mesomorphic types of leaves with thin layers of cutin and large intercellular spaces such as yellow-poplar, red oak, or red maple lose more water than thick, heavily cutinized xeromorphic types such as American holly or magnolia. Maximov (1929) pointed out that this is not necessarily true, and this is further shown in Table 10.5. *Ilex glabra* and *Gordonia lasianthus* both have thick, leathery, heavily cutinized leaves, yet their transpiration rates per unit of leaf surface are much higher than those of the oaks or yellow-poplar. Swanson (1943) reported that American holly had a higher rate of transpiration than coleus, tobacco, or lilac on a sunny day. On a cloudy day, however, the transpiration rate of holly was lower than that of lilac.

Such differences can be explained at least in part by differences in leaf structure. Xeromorphic and mesomorphic leaf structures are shown in Figure 10.2. Turrell (1936, 1944) has shown that in general the xeromorphic types of leaves have considerably more cell wall surface exposed to the internal atmosphere than mesomorphic leaves. This provides more evaporating surface and seems to be largely responsible for the higher rate of water loss of this type of leaves when plants have

Table 10.5. Midsummer transpiration rates of various species of trees expressed as grams of water lost per square decimeter of leaf surface per day. All seedlings were growing in soil near field capacity.

Species	Location	Season	Duration, days	No. of plants	Av. transpiration, g per sq dm per day
Liriodendron tulipifera *	Columbus, Ohio	August	1	7	10.11
Liriodendron tulipifera †	Durham, N.C.	August	3	4	11.78
Quercus alba †	Durham, N.C.	August	3	4	14.21
Quercus rubra †	Durham, N.C.	August	3	4	12.02
Quercus rubra ‡	Fayette, Mo.	July	14	6	8.1
Acer saccharum ‡	Fayette, Mo.	July	14	6	12.2
Acer negundo ‡	Fayette, Mo.	July	14	6	6.4
Platanus occidentalis ‡	Fayette, Mo.	July	14	6	8.8
Pinus taeda †	Durham, N.C.	August	3	4	4.65
Clethra alnifolia †	Durham, N.C.	August	3	4	9.73
Ilex glabra †	Durham, N.C.	August	3	4	16.10
Myrica cerifera †	Durham, N.C.	August	3	4	10.80
Gordonia lasianthus †	Durham, N.C.	July	23	4	17.77
Liriodendron tulipifera §	Durham, N.C.	Aug. 26– Sept. 2	12	6	9.76
Quercus rubra §	Durham, N.C.	Aug. 26– Sept. 2	12	6	12.45
Pinus taeda §	Durham, N.C.	Aug. 26– Sept. 2	12	6	5.08

* Meyer. † Caughey. ‡ Biswell. § Kramer. Unpublished.

adequate water. In some leaves of this type there is relatively more water-conducting tissue and smaller but more numerous stomates, and these may also contribute to increased transpiration per unit of leaf surface. Although the transpiration rate of such plants is high in full sun if there is abundant soil moisture, it usually becomes much lower than that of mesomorphic leaves in dry soil or when the stomates are closed, because of their lower rate of epidermal transpiration. The effect of differences in amount of cutin is seen chiefly when the stomates are closed. Leaves with little cutin continue to lose water by epidermal transpiration, while leaves with thick layers of cutin lose little water after the stomates close and survive much longer in dry air.

The number and size of stomates probably are less important than their responsiveness. Differences in response of stomates to changes in light intensity and leaf water content may produce differences in loss of water from different plants. It is claimed that deficiencies of certain nutrients, particularly nitrogen, decrease the rate of response of stomates. Pleasants (1930) suggested that stomates of plants given an abundance of nitrogen closed more promptly than stomates of plants deficient in nitrogen when a water deficit occurred. This might explain why plants well supplied with nitrogen sometimes are more drought-resistant than plants deficient in nitrogen, even though they transpire more when water is readily available. On the other hand, Biebl (1952) reported that plants given an abundance of nitrogen transpired more because their stomates remained open all day while those of plants low in nitrogen closed by noon.

In some leaves, such as pine needles, the stomates are sunken in grooves or pits. This reduces transpiration because the pits become more or less saturated with water vapor, increasing the length of the diffusion path from the intercellular spaces to the outside air. Loblolly pine, for example, has only about half the transpiration rate per unit of leaf surface of deciduous species such as red oak.

Epidermal Hairs. It has been claimed that heavy coverings of epidermal hairs, such as are found on the undersurfaces of the leaves of some species of *Populus*, reduce transpiration by reducing the rate of air movement over the leaf surface. Large, living hairs might actually increase transpiration by increasing the evaporating surface. Sayre (1920) found that removal of the dead hairs from mullein (*Verbascum thapsus*) leaves had little effect on the transpiration rate, and in general hairs probably have little effect on the rate of water loss.

Orientation of Leaves. Orientation of leaves may have some effect on transpiration because leaves which are at right angles to the sun's rays are warmer than those which are parallel to the incident radiation. Most leaves grow in such a manner as to become oriented approximately perpendicular to the brightest light which strikes them, but a few exceptions occur. One notable exception is the tendency of the leaves of turkey oak seedlings to become oriented in the vertical plane. The needles of longleaf pine seedlings tend to grow upright, and it is claimed that their orientation aids seedlings of these two species to survive in the dry, hot sand hills. Pine needles which occur in bundles tend to shade each other, and this may reduce the water loss per unit of surface, but it also reduces the rate of photosynthesis (Uhl, 1937; Kramer and Clark, 1947).

Curling or rolling of wilted leaves reduces the exposed surface and is particularly effective in reducing transpiration from leaves with stomates only on the undersurface. Of course, wilting is evidence that an undesirable water deficit has already developed, but it probably materially prolongs the life of trees during droughts.

Leaf Area. Other things being equal, plants with large leaf areas transpire more than plants with small leaf areas. As shown in Table 10.6, the transpiration rate per unit of leaf area is much lower for loblolly pine than for several deciduous species but the total leaf area of a pine often is considerably greater than that of a deciduous tree of the same size. Thus a loblolly pine might transpire as much water per day as a hardwood tree having the same size of crown.

There is a definite tendency for some species to shed their leaves earlier than others, especially if subjected to a water deficit. Yellow-poplar tends to shed its leaves earlier than the oaks, and it seems probable that oaks therefore remove more water from the soil in the early autumn than yellow-poplar. If well-defined differences exist, it might be possible to increase stream flow in the late summer and early autumn by converting watersheds to those species which have the minimum rate of transpiration at that season. Some experiments also have been conducted on the feasibility of defoliating trees in late summer to increase water yield. If this could be done at a reasonable cost, it would be desirable, as it undoubtedly would result in increased stream flow. Growth would be reduced somewhat, but this would not be important where water is more valuable than timber, as often is true.

Root/shoot Ratio. The ratio of roots to shoots or of absorbing surface to transpiring surface is even more important than leaf surface alone, because if absorption lags behind transpiration, a water deficit develops and transpiration is reduced.

Table 10.6. Transpiration rates per unit of leaf surface and per seedling of loblolly pine and hardwood seedlings for period of August 22 to September 2. Average of six seedlings of each species. (*Unpublished data.*)

	Loblolly pine	Yellow-poplar	Northern red oak
Transpiration as g per day per sq dm	5.08	9.76	12.45
Transpiration as g per day per tree	106.7	59.1	77.0
Av. leaf area per tree, sq dm	21.0	6.06	6.18
Av. height of trees, cm	34	34	20

Parker (1949) found that the rate of transpiration per unit of leaf area of northern red oak and loblolly pine seedlings grown in moist soil increased as the ratio of root surface to leaf surface increased. Fowells and Kirk (1945) reported that removal of part of the roots reduced the transpiration of ponderosa pine seedlings. Loss of roots during lifting of seedlings undoubtedly is sometimes an important cause of losses in new plantations.

Plants with extensive, much-branched root systems, such as sorghum, do not suffer from water deficits as soon as plants with less-branched root systems such as corn (Miller, 1916). It has also been observed that although severe pruning of fruit trees reduces the transpiration per tree, the rate per unit of leaf surface is increased because of the larger ratio of roots to shoots (Miller, 1938, p. 454).

A large root/shoot ratio is particularly important to the survival of transplanted tree seedlings because the most common cause of death is desiccation, caused by excessive water loss in transpiration before an effective absorbing surface is developed. Seedlings with a low ratio of roots to shoots are particularly likely to be killed by desiccation, and it has been found useful to either clip off part of the needles or coat the foliage of pine seedlings with a material which reduces water loss. Clipping the needles of longleaf pine planting stock back to 5 inches in length has proved effective in reducing mortality after transplanting because it reduces the transpiring surface (Allen, 1955). Reducing the transpiring surface also reduces the photosynthetic surface, and this generally is undesirable.

Osmotic Pressure of Leaf Sap. At one time it was generally believed that the higher osmotic pressure of the cell sap found in the leaves of some trees must appreciably reduce the rate of water loss. This view was abandoned when it was realized that an increase in osmotic pressure of the cell sap lowers its vapor pressure very little. For example, at 20°C a 2 M solution of a nonelectrolyte with theoretical osmotic pressure of about 44.8 atmospheres has a vapor pressure only about 0.6 millimeter lower than that of pure water. It now appears, however, that the effect of the osmotic pressure of cell sap on evaporation from cells may be much greater than would be expected from its small effects on the vapor pressure of water. Boon-Long (1941) found that increasing the osmotic pressure of a solution lowered its rate of evaporation through a membrane much more than it lowered the rate of evaporation from an open solution surface. He also found that increasing the osmotic pressure of leaf cells decreased transpiration more than could be accounted for by the lowering of vapor pressure of the cell sap. Apparently, increase in osmotic pressure of the cell sap decreases the rate of water loss by decreasing the permeability of the cell membranes. There probably also is a concentration of solution at the surfaces of the cells which lowers the vapor pressure of the evaporating surface.

Effects of Fungi. It has been observed by a number of investigators that leaves infected with various fungi show considerably higher transpiration rates than healthy leaves (Miller, 1938). In some instances this increase has been attributed to rupture of the epidermis by developing fruiting bodies; in other instances, as with powdery mildews, the aerial mycelium may increase the evaporating surface. Stomatal closure may be prevented also, and permeability of cell membranes may be affected. Yarwood (1947) suggested that increased permeability of the host cells is the chief cause of increased water loss from mildew-infected leaves.

Effects of Sprays and Dusts. Deposits of nontoxic foreign matter on leaves may modify transpiration by affecting both leaf temperature and the permeability of the cuticle or epidermal cells. The results of the older experiments on the effect of sprays are summarized by Miller (1938). Apparently bordeaux mixture and presumably any other spray which leaves a light-colored residue reduce the leaf temperature and thereby tend to reduce transpiration, but bordeaux mixture increases cuticular transpiration; hence the effects of spray applications often are somewhat contradictory. Horsfall and Harrison (1939) thought that bordeaux mixture tended to reduce transpiration by clogging the stomates and to increase it by increasing cuticular transpiration by saponifying the cutin and increasing its permeability. Thus under some circumstances application of bordeaux might increase transpiration and under other conditions might decrease it, depending mostly on the relative importance of cuticular and stomatal transpiration. Southwick and Childers (1941) reported that in general bordeaux mixture slightly reduced the transpiration of young apple trees. Kobel (1952) reported that spraying bean leaves with a dilute solution of copper sulfate reduced transpiration in the light but increased it in darkness. According to Kelley (1926), oil sprays materially reduce transpiration of fruit trees if the lower surfaces of the leaves are coated. Beasley (1942) reported that only those dusts containing particles smaller than 5 microns in diameter increased transpiration, and those only at night. She concluded that their effect was brought about chiefly by particles becoming lodged in the stomates, preventing closure of the guard cells.

Several studies have been made of the effects on transpiration of applying various waterproofing substances such as latex, oil, or wax by dipping or spraying the foliage, with the hope that survival following transplanting would be increased. Some reduction in transpiration has been observed (Shirley and Meuli, 1938; Marshall and Maki, 1946; Miller et al., 1950), and some increases in survival and improvements in growth have been observed. Allen (1955) reported that dipping longleaf and loblolly pine seedlings in Dowax (a commercial compound consisting of paraffin wax and bentonite with ammonium linoleate as an emulsifier) gave increased survival under some circumstances. He suggested that further study of wax coatings should be made before recommending their use.

Measurement of Transpiration

The first quantitative measurements of transpiration known to the writers were those made by Stephen Hales, prior to 1727. He measured the rate of water loss from potted grapevines, apples, lemons, and various herbaceous species, using methods similar to those used today. A number of measurements of transpiration of trees were made during the latter half of the nineteenth century, of which the best known are those of von Höhnel, published in 1881 and 1884. This early work was summarized by Raber (1937).

A variety of methods have been used, and new ones are being developed. Miller (1938) has a rather detailed description of some of the older methods. A few of these methods will be described, and their advantages and disadvantages will be discussed.

Gravimetric Methods. Hales, von Höhnel, and many more recent investigators grew plants in pots of soil and measured the water lost by weighing the container at regular intervals. The essential factor is to enclose the soil mass containing the plant in a container from which water cannot evaporate and to replenish the water content frequently so that soil moisture does not become a limiting factor. The size of the plants grown is limited by the size of the container, and the size of the container is limited by the equipment available for handling and weighing it. Nutman (1941) used a balance with a capacity of 2.5 tons and a sensitivity of better than 1 ounce. Veihmeyer (1927) measured transpiration of trees growing in tanks of soil weighing about 1,000 pounds by means of an automatic recording scale. If properly managed this method gives very accurate measurements of the water loss by individual trees, but in many of the early experiments the containers appear to have been too small for best results.

The extent to which the results obtained from individual potted plants can be applied to plants growing in their normal environment is debatable. In the first place, the potted plants usually are in soil kept near field capacity, rather than subjected to cycles of decreasing soil moisture characteristic of field conditions. Secondly, they usually are exposed to abnormal atmospheric conditions. One way to approximate natural conditions is to set the containers in pits with their tops level with the soil surface in the habitats where the plants under study usually grow, as was done by Biswell (1935) and Holch (1931) in their studies of transpiration of tree seedlings in sun and shade in Missouri and Nebraska. In some other studies the containers have been immersed in water baths or covered with insulating material to prevent overheating.

Because of the limitations on size and the time and expense required to carry on experiments with potted plants, many workers have measured the transpiration of cut branches. The usual method is to cut off a twig or a single leaf if it is large and hang it on the arm of a sensitive balance set up in the immediate vicinity, so that the twig or leaf will remain in the same environment as before its removal. Usually loss of weight is measured for only a few minutes after cutting since the rate of transpiration tends to change with the passage of time. This sometimes is called the quick-weighing method. It has been used extensively by workers such as Huber (1927), Stocker (1929), Pisek and Cartellieri (1939), Polster (1950), Pisek and Tranquillini (1951), Ringoet (1952), Parker (1957), and Ivanov et al. (1951). Considerable difference of opinion has been expressed concerning the relation of the transpiration rate after cutting to the rate before detaching a branch (Halevy, 1956b; Andersson et al., 1954), but detached leaves have been used successfully to measure differences in rate on different sides of a tree and at different heights and for comparisons among species (Table 10.7). The merits of this method are discussed further in a later section.

Table 10.7. Relative transpiration rates of various tree species with spruce as 100. Eidmann's data are from potted plants; the other data are from rapid weighing of cut branches. (*From Huber,* 1953, *table* 1.)

	Eidmann	*Huber*	*Pisek and Cartellieri*	*Polster*
Birch	618		541	740
Oak	282	468 (377–559)	512	460
Beech	268	379 (218–541)	137	372
Douglas-fir	130			94
Spruce	100	100 (64 –136)	100	100
Pine	181	134 (118–150)	133	139
Larch	310	409 (341–476)	212	212

Volumetric Methods. Another long-used method of measuring water loss is to measure the volume of water absorbed by a cut branch. The base of a twig is immersed in a small reservoir of water, to which is connected a sidearm graduated so that the volume of water absorbed from the reservoir by the transpiring branch can be measured. These devices, usually called "potometers," permit very accurate measurement of the rate of water absorption. Unfortunately, however, the rate of transpiration of a detached branch may be quite different from what it was while attached to the tree because the attached branch was in competition with all the other branches of the tree for water, and water intake was also affected by the rate of absorption through the roots. Furthermore, the water intake of cut twigs often is reduced by plugging of the vessels by air or other materials. It seems, therefore, that although potometers are useful for laboratory demonstrations, they are very unreliable indicators of the rate of transpiration of entire plants.

Somewhat more reliable results are obtained with potometers arranged to contain the entire root system of small plants or seedlings. The chief error in the use of this type of apparatus arises from the fact that absorption lags considerably behind water loss in rapidly transpiring plants (Figure 11.9); hence the volume of water absorbed in a short period of time is not always identical with the amount lost.

Measurement of Transpired Water Vapor. More or less successful attempts have been made to measure the change in water-vapor content of the air caused by transpiration. A branch or even a single leaf is enclosed in a transparent container through which an air stream is passed, and the difference in water-vapor content of the air is determined before and after it has passed over the plant material. In the earlier experiments the water vapor in a given volume of air was measured by collecting it in an absorbent such as phosphorus pentoxide or calcium chloride. This method was used by Minckler (1936, 1939) to measure transpiration of branches of forest trees. Heinicke and Childers (1936) also used it to measure the transpiration of apple leaves.

Other methods of measuring the water-vapor content of the air are now available. Scarth et al. (1948), Huber and Miller (1954), and Decker and Wetzel (1957) used infrared gas analyzers built to measure photosynthesis for measurements of transpiration. Huber and Miller (1954) also developed what they called a Thermoflux, in which the water-vapor content of the air was measured by the heat produced in reacting with sulfuric acid. Glover (1941) used the difference in temperature between a wet and a dry thermocouple to measure the water-vapor content of the air, and Andersson et al. (1954) measured it by the amount of corona produced by a high-tension-spark discharge. The infrared absorption method seems promising, although the apparatus used is quite expensive. Another promising method is to measure the changes in humidity of air passing over plant material by a humidity-sensing device (Went, 1957, p. 301).

The use of attached branches was supposed to eliminate the errors caused by removal of branches from the tree, but other errors result from the effects on temperature and humidity of enclosing the branch in a container and passing an air stream over it. This can be minimized by enclosing the branch for only a short time to prevent overheating and by moving the air stream at a moderate velocity to prevent wind effects.

Cobalt Chloride Paper. Another method used to measure the water vapor escaping from leaves is to place the leaves in contact with some substance capable of absorbing water. Most commonly pieces of filter paper impregnated with cobalt chloride are held against the leaf surface by some kind of clamps and protected from the air on the outer surface by a transparent cover such as a piece of cellophane. Cobalt chloride turns from blue to pink as it absorbs water vapor, and the time required for the color change to occur is taken as a measure of the rate of transpiration. This method measures the rate of water-vapor loss under artificial conditions, and although it sometimes serves as an indicator of the relative rates of water loss and of stomatal opening of plants growing under similar conditions, it gives no indication of the actual rates of transpiration of plants growing under different environmental conditions (Milthorpe, 1955).

Comparison of Methods. Ringoet (1952) made an extensive comparison of the transpiration of detached shoots and potted seedlings. He found that the rates obtained by measuring water loss from leaves and leaflets for 2-minute intervals were too large as compared with results obtained with intact plants. This difference was greatest with sun plants such as the oil palm and least with shade plants. Weighing entire plants showed effects of soil moisture and atmospheric humidity better than weighing detached parts. Ringoet concluded that in general weighing detached plant parts measured the physical factors affecting evaporation, while weighing entire plants resulted in data which represented the sum of the biological and physical factors affecting transpiration. In spite of its defects Ringoet used the method of weighing leaves successfully to determine the daily course of transpiration of several species.

Halevy (1956a) found that on mild autumn days the rates of transpiration of orange leaves obtained by weighing individual leaves and potted plants were similar. On hot summer days transpiration rates of potted plants were 25 to 35 per cent lower than those of detached leaves, and on extremely hot, dry days they were as much as 50 per cent lower. The general shape of the daily curves obtained by the two methods was surprisingly similar in all kinds of weather, however. The error in this type of measurement is increased by the large variation in rate of transpiration encountered among individual leaves from the same plant and from different plants of the same species (Hölzl, 1955).

Transpiration Rates

Almost innumerable measurements have been made of rates of transpiration of various species and ages of trees under almost every conceivable condition. Many of the results of these studies have been summarized by Raber (1937), and only a few examples will be given here. In general, the range of transpiration rates of trees is similar to that of herbaceous plants. Variability is very great among individuals, and the differences

Physiology of Trees

in rate between old and young leaves of any individual may be greater than the differences between individuals of different species.

Some representative data on midsummer transpiration rates of tree seedlings are given in Table 10.5. Loblolly pine has a lower rate of transpiration per unit of leaf area than the broadleaf species, and species of *Ilex* and *Gordonia* with coriaceous leaves have rates as high as species with mesomorphic leaves such as yellow-poplar or red oak. Transpiration data for loblolly pine and two deciduous hardwoods are presented in Table 10.6, where it can be seen that although the hardwoods transpire about twice as much per unit of leaf surface as pine, the transpiration per tree is higher for pine because the leaf area of a pine seedling is often much greater than that of a deciduous seedling of similar size. Groom (1910) also found the transpiration rate of conifers to be lower per unit

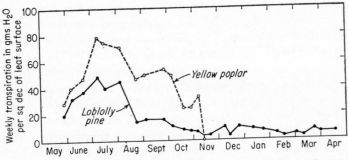

Figure 10.7 Seasonal course of transpiration of potted seedlings of an evergreen and a deciduous species at Durham, North Carolina.

of leaf area but as high per tree as in deciduous species because of the large leaf area of conifers. Weaver and Mogensen (1919) reported that deciduous seedlings transpired about 2.8 times as much per unit of leaf surface as coniferous seedlings, and Von Höhnel (1884), Kusano (1901), and others have reported the same general situation.

The seasonal cycle of transpiration for two species is shown in Figure 10.7. In this experiment measurement of the water loss from the deciduous species was stopped at the time of leaf fall, but Kozlowski (1943) continued measurements from late October to early January. Some of his results are shown in Table 10.8, where it can be seen that the winter transpiration rate of the pines is not significantly higher than the transpiration rate from the bare branches of the deciduous species. Weaver and Mogensen (1919) also reported the same situation in Nebraska, with respect to winter transpiration of conifers and deciduous species.

The relative amounts of water lost in winter and summer of course vary widely with seasonal conditions. Some water loss occurs even at temperatures well below freezing (Raber, 1937, p. 36), but it is lower in a very cold climate than in a warmer climate. For example, Ivanov (1924) and Weaver and Mogensen (1919) found winter transpiration rates of several species of conifers to be less than 1 per cent of the summer rates, but from the data shown in Figure 10.7 it can be seen that the winter transpiration rate of loblolly pine was about 13.5 per cent of the sum-

Table 10.8. Winter transpiration rates per unit of surface for coniferous and broadleaf seedlings. Data for December 22 to January 5. (*From Kozlowski,* 1943.)

	G per sq dm per day
Prunus laurocerasus *	1.65
Pinus taeda *	0.40
Acer saccharum †	0.26
Liriodendron tulipifera †	0.76
Quercus alba †	0.84

* Per unit of leaf surface.
† Per unit of twig and stem surface.

mer transpiration rate. This is doubtless the result of the higher temperatures and larger number of warm sunny winter days in North Carolina than at Leningrad, where Ivanov worked, or in Nebraska, where Weaver and Mogensen performed their experiments.

Even in the tropics seasonal cycles occur because of variations in rainfall and soil moisture. Ringoet (1952), for example, found seasonal differences in the transpiration of oil palms in the Belgian Congo.

Evapotranspiration

In general, foresters are more interested in the loss of water from entire stands of trees than from individual trees. Huber (1953) discussed the water usage of forests and commented on the surprisingly good agreement concerning relative rates of transpiration of various species rated according to water loss from potted specimens (Eidmann, 1943) and by weighing detached shoots (Pisek and Cartellieri, 1932–1939; Polster, 1950). From the rate of transpiration per gram of foliage and the total foliage per hectare, Polster calculated the average daily transpiration of stands of various species as shown in Table 10.9. In Russia, Ivanov et al. (1951) decided that the rate of transpiration can be determined from the weight of leaves per unit of area and the amount of radiation absorbed during the growing season. By this method they calculated the water loss from 10- to 80-year-old pine stands to be 260 millimeters, while the water loss from birch in the same region was 323 millimeters per year.

Huber (1953) discussed several methods of studying water losses from

Physiology of Trees

forest stands, including measurements of the water vapor of the air above the stand, calculation from the energy absorbed, from the difference between precipitation and runoff, and by means of lysimeters. Koch (1957) measured the water-vapor concentration of the air over vegetation at heights of 10 and 25 meters. From these data and measurements of wind velocity he was able to calculate the rate of water loss.

Table 10.9. Daily transpiration of stands of various species. (*From Polster,* 1950.)

Species	Av. daily transpiration	
	Liters per hectare	Millimeters
Betula verrucosa	47,000	4.7
Fagus silvatica	38,000	3.8
Pseudotsuga douglasii	53,000	5.3
Picea excelsa	43,000	4.3
Pinus silvestris	23,500	2.35

The use of lysimeters, as at San Dimas, California, and Coshocton, Ohio, and by Bartels (1933, 1937), in Germany, has given rather precise information on the water usage of various kinds of plant cover. Some rather reliable data on the use of water were obtained at Coweeta, North Carolina, by measuring precipitation, interception, and runoff of small watersheds, then removing all the woody vegetation from one of them (Hoover, 1944). This study indicated that a hardwood forest in the southern Appalachian Mountains loses 17 to 22 inches of water annually by transpiration. Burger (1943, 1945) has made similar studies on watersheds in Switzerland.

Several investigators have calculated water losses from evaporation and transpiration by systematically sampling the water content of the soil in the root zone. Some of the earlier studies were made on fruit trees. Magness et al. (1935) found that the trees in a Maryland apple orchard removed all the readily available water from the upper 24 to 30 inches of soil in less than three weeks. Wiggans (1937) estimated that 18- to 20-year-old apple orchards in eastern Nebraska lost 37.8 inches of water by evapotranspiration, or 15.2 inches more than the rainfall in that year.

The ease with which soil moisture changes can be followed with electrical-resistance blocks has encouraged extensive research on rates of depletion of soil moisture. Among the soil moisture studies dealing with forest trees are those of Bethlamy (1953), Fraser (1957a and b), Hoover et al. (1953), and Zahner (1955b, 1958). Zahner found good agreement between the actual rate of evapotranspiration from forest stands on moist soil (0.25 inch per day) and the rate calculated by Thornthwaite's formula (0.22 inch per day).

The present trend is toward estimation of evapotranspiration from areas by means of equations based on the amount of solar energy available to evaporate water. This approach has been developed by Albrecht, Geiger, and others on the Continent, by Schofield and Penman in England, and by Thornthwaite (1948) in the United States. This theory assumes that if the soil is moist and is completely covered by vegetation, then the water loss will be practically independent of the kind of vegetation. According to this view, the total water loss per acre during the growing season might be the same from a field of grain or grassland as from an adjacent forest. This view is supported by both theory and observation. The rate of water loss depends primarily on the amount of energy absorbed, and this is similar for forest and grassland. Thornthwaite and Hare (1955) reported that over 80 per cent of the available energy was used in evapotranspiration by a moist grassland. Little if any more energy would be available for evaporation of water from a forest. Individual trees and rows of trees along roads or streams might have higher rates of transpiration for limited periods than stands of trees. Huber (1953) concluded that there probably is little difference in the water loss from different forest species growing on similar sites. Rider's (1957) observations on rates of evapotranspiration from various crops caused him to advise caution in assuming that water loss is potentially similar from all types of plant cover. More research is needed on this problem.

In view of this concept of potential evapotranspiration as being controlled almost entirely by the water supply and atmospheric factors, Stone (1952) argued that it is useless to measure the transpiration of individual trees because such measurements cannot be applied quantitatively to stands. This might be partly true if we were interested solely in the behavior of stands, but we are often interested in the behavior of various components of mixed stands and in the effects of changing the composition of stands.

Estimates of evapotranspiration based on energy absorption depend on the assumption that the soil is always moist, that it is completely occupied by roots, and that the surface is completely covered by vegetation. In many forest areas soil moisture becomes low enough to limit evaporation and transpiration several times during the growing season. Furthermore, the root systems of different species occupy the soil to different depths, and deciduous trees present a different kind of coverage than evergreens during a part of the year. Thus some limitations exist in applying a purely physical formula to determination of water loss from forest areas, and actual evapotranspiration is apt to be somewhat lower than the calculated values, especially when soil moisture is limiting.

Considerable useful information can be obtained from pot experiments on seasonal differences among species and differences in reaction to decreasing soil moisture content and other environmental factors. More reliable information could be obtained from large lysimeters or small watersheds, but such experiments are expensive and require many years for completion. Perhaps pot experiments are most useful for preliminary studies to indicate what types of studies on the water relations of forest stands might be carried out profitably on a large scale.

Transpiration Ratio

There has been considerable interest in the amount of water required to produce a unit of dry matter. Miller (1938) summarized a large amount of data on the water requirement or transpiration ratio of crop plants. According to these data, the amount of water required to produce a pound of alfalfa varied from 657 to 1,068 pounds over a period of 7 years. The requirements for various crops varied from 216 pounds for Kursk millet to 1,131 pounds for *Franseria*, a native weed.

Few comparable data are available for trees, but Polster (1950) estimated that the amount of water required to produce a gram of dry matter varied from 170 grams in beech and Douglas-fir to 300 in Scotch pine, 317 in birch, and 344 in English oak. The transpiration ratio varies with the rate of photosynthesis, soil fertility, and other factors affecting growth, as well as with the factors affecting transpiration. Koch (1957) found that the ratio of photosynthesis to transpiration was more favorable in cloudy weather than in bright sunny weather because transpiration was reduced more than photosynthesis. This also is shown in Figure 10.3. Of course, very cloudy weather causes an undesirable reduction in photosynthesis, especially in closed stands. Koch suggested that the ratio of photosynthesis to transpiration is of considerable ecological importance and that it can be improved in some plants by fertilization.

GENERAL REFERENCES

Crafts, A. S., H. B. Currier, and C. R. Stocking, 1949, Water in the physiology of plants, Chronica Botanica Co., Waltham, Mass.
Kramer, P. J., 1952, Plant and soil water relations on the watershed, Jour. Forestry, 50:92–95.
Maximov, N. A., 1929, The plant in relation to water, trans., George Allen & Unwin, Ltd., London.
Meyer, B. S., and D. B. Anderson, 1952, Plant physiology, chaps. 9–11, D. Van Nostrand Company, Inc., Princeton, N.J.
Raber, O., 1937, Water utilization by trees, with special reference to the economic forest species of the North Temperate Zone, U.S. Dept. Agr. Misc. Pub. 257.
Ruhland, W. (ed.), 1956, Encyclopedia of plant physiology, vol. 3, Water relations of plants, O. Stocker (subed.), Springer-Verlag, Berlin.

CHAPTER 11 *Absorption of Water*

and Ascent of Sap

This chapter consists of two sections, one on the absorption of water and related phenomena such as root pressure and another on the ascent of sap. These two processes are important parts of the total picture of water relations. Water absorption is considered first chiefly because root pressure sometimes is regarded as a factor in the ascent of sap.

THE ABSORPTION OF WATER

Most of the water absorbed by trees enters through their roots. A small amount sometimes is absorbed through the leaves, and this may in certain special circumstances be of considerable importance for survival, but appreciable absorption through the leaves probably occurs only when the diffusion-pressure deficit in the plant is so high that little or no growth could occur. Absorption through roots is not an independent process but is closely related to transpiration (Figure 11.9). It is affected by the diffusion pressure in the tree, the efficiency of the root system as an absorbing organ, and various factors which affect the availability of soil moisture.

It will be easier to understand the process of water absorption if the reader has a sufficiently clear picture of the structure of a root to visualize the tissues through which water must pass in moving from the soil to the xylem. In Figure 11.1 are shown the tissues through which water must pass in a young root. The walls of the epidermal and cortical cells of young roots are comparatively thin and composed largely of cellulose, but the endodermal cell walls tend to become thickened and strips of suberized tissue, the casparian strips, develop on the radial walls. It usually is assumed that water and solutes move from cell to cell across the vacuoles of the epidermal and cortical cells, but experiments by Strugger (1949) and others suggest that considerable movement of water may occur in the cell walls. Apparently such movement would be stopped by the casparian strips of the endodermis, although there is increasing evidence that the endodermis is not as impermeable as it was once supposed to be.

As roots mature, the epidermis and root hairs often are destroyed by the activity of a cork cambium in the outer part of the cortex, but this suberization does not render the roots impermeable to water. The arrangement of tissue in older woody roots is shown in Figure 11.2. Water enter-

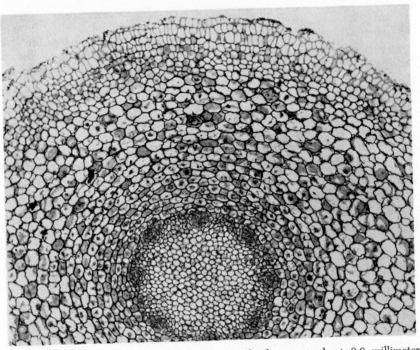

Figure 11.1 Cross section of a young *Liriodendron* root about 0.6 millimeter behind the apex. (*About* 80×. *From R. A. Popham, Developmental plant anatomy,* 1952. *By permission of the author.*)

ing such roots must pass through the layers of suberized tissue, the phloem, and the cambium on its way to the xylem. A much larger percentage of the area consists of walls in older roots than in younger roots; hence the possibility of movement through the walls is even greater in these roots.

Water-absorption Mechanisms

There appear to be two different mechanisms responsible for water absorption by trees and other plants. One mechanism, termed "active absorption" by Renner (1912, 1915), occurs only in very slowly transpiring plants which are well supplied with water. Active absorption is responsible for root pressure, guttation, and at least part of the exudation or "bleeding" from cut stems. The other mechanism, called "passive absorption," occurs in freely transpiring plants and seems to be responsible for most of the water intake of trees. In active absorption the forces responsible for water uptake are developed in the roots, while in passive absorption they are developed as a result of water loss by the shoots and

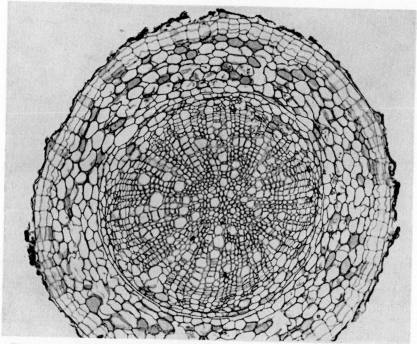

Figure 11.2 Cross section of an older *Liriodendron* root after part of the outer parenchyma tissue had sloughed off and a layer of cork had begun to develop. (*About* 60×. *From R. A. Popham, Developmental plant anatomy, 1952. By permission of the author.*)

transmitted through the xylem to the roots, which serve merely as passive absorbing surfaces.

It should be understood that all absorption of water occurs along diffusion-pressure-deficit gradients from the soil to the xylem in the roots. The difference between active and passive absorption is largely the result of the manner in which these gradients are produced. This will now be discussed in more detail.

Passive Absorption by Transpiring Trees. Sachs, Pfeffer, and Strasburger agreed that loss of water by transpiration produces the force causing the intake of water, and even Hales believed that the forces causing water absorption by transpiring plants were different from those causing root pressure. The exact mechanism by which this occurs was not understood until it was discovered that water confined in small tubes has a high tensile strength. This enabled Askenasy (1895), Dixon and Joly (1895), and others to explain that water absorption is coupled to water loss through the cohesive columns of water in the xylem elements.

The water in the xylem elements and saturated cell walls forms a continuous system, the hydrostatic system of some writers, which extends throughout the plant. Thus, as explained in more detail in the section on ascent of sap, the loss of water from the evaporating surfaces of the leaf cells produces a diffusion-pressure deficit which causes water to move into them from the xylem of the leaf veins. This reduces the pressure on the water in the xylem, and this reduction in pressure is transmitted throughout the hydrostatic system down to even the smallest branch roots. Reduction in pressure of water in the xylem produces a diffusion-pressure deficit along which water moves from the soil across the roots into the root xylem. If very rapid transpiration occurs, the pressure in the xylem often drops below zero and becomes a tension and water is pulled in through the roots by mass flow.

It usually is assumed that water moves across the tissues lying between the epidermis and xylem of roots by diffusion from vacuole to vacuole, but this probably is true only at low rates of transpiration. At higher rates of transpiration tension develops in the xylem sap and water probably passes into roots largely by mass flow. It has been demonstrated by many investigators that even a small pressure difference causes rapid movement of water through detopped root systems (Renner, 1929; Kramer, 1932; Mees and Weatherley, 1957).

There seems to be increasing reason to believe that considerable water moves across the roots in the cell walls, without passing through the vacuoles of the intervening cells. Fully hydrated cellulose walls are highly permeable to water and solutes, and movement through them has been demonstrated in various organs of plants (Strugger, 1949; Hulsbruch, 1956). If there is a continuous system of water-filled walls in roots, inward movement of water will occur by diffusion whenever a diffusion-pressure deficit exists in the xylem; but if tension develops in the water in the xylem, this will be transmitted directly through the water in the cell walls across the root, causing mass flow of water into the xylem. The only obstacles to such mass flow across roots are the casparian strips on the radial walls of the endodermal cells, but the endodermis probably is often considerably disrupted by branch roots and usually disappears during secondary thickening.

In young roots it appears that most of the water must move through the cytoplasm at some point, probably at the endodermis. This is indicated by the fact that killing the roots results in a large increase in the amount of water passing through them under a constant pressure (Kramer, 1933; Renner, 1929). Brouwer (1954) also found that treatment of roots with potassium cyanide and carbon dioxide, or deprival of oxygen, reduced water uptake, confirming and extending earlier work of Kramer (1940). Unfortunately, most of this research was done on root systems of young herbaceous plants. In trees such a small proportion of the total root surface possesses its original primary structure that much of the water intake probably occurs through older roots from which the cortex and endodermis have disappeared. It is possible that water enters such roots chiefly by mass flow. Absorption through suberized roots is discussed later in this chapter.

The absorption process outlined here was termed passive absorption by Renner (1915) because the roots act simply as passive absorbing surfaces through which water is absorbed. This does not alter the fact that healthy, growing root surfaces are essential for the continued absorption of water and minerals, because in soils below field capacity water movement toward roots is very slow and only by continuous extension of roots into new soil regions can sufficient water become available.

Active Absorption. The active absorption of water occurs as a result of forces developed in the roots themselves. Its occurrence is demonstrated principally by the fact that under certain conditions sap exudes from stumps if the tops are removed, or from wounds made in the stems. If this occurs it is assumed that root pressure occurs, caused by the active absorption of water. Active absorption and the resulting root pressure are common in herbaceous species growing in warm moist soil under conditions unfavorable for transpiration. Root pressure occurs commonly in only a few woody species, such as birch and grape, and in them only in the spring before the leaves have unfolded. Clark (1874) tested over 60 species of woody plants in Massachusetts and found exudation only from a few species of *Acer, Betula, Juglans, Ostrya,* and *Vitis.* Exudation of sap from stems of gymnosperms is rare, but White et al. (1958) reported exudation of sap from detached roots of several coniferous species. It will be shown in a later section that some examples of exudation from wounds, such as the flow of sap from maple and palms, are not caused by root pressure.

Active-absorption Mechanisms. Two explanations have been offered for the occurrence of active absorption and the resulting root pressure. One explanation assumes that water is secreted into the xylem by some non-osmotic mechanism, while the other assumes that roots behave as osmometers and water absorption occurs as the result of osmotic movement of water from a lower diffusion-pressure deficit in the soil solution to a higher diffusion-pressure deficit in the xylem. Ursprung (1929) regarded the endodermis as a secretory mechanism which forced water into the stele, and more recently Arnold (1952) also claimed that the endodermis controls the entrance of water and minerals. One basis for claiming that a nonosmotic, secretory type of water movement occurs is that the osmotic pressure of the exudate from the stumps of detopped plants sometimes is lower than the osmotic pressure of the solution required to stop exudation (van Overbeek, 1942). Root pressure also is reduced or stopped by respiration inhibitors (van Overbeek, 1942; Rosene, 1944, 1947) and lack of oxygen (Kramer, 1940; Rosene, 1950), suggesting that it is related to respiration in some way.

No satisfactory explanation of how water can be secreted into the xylem under pressure has been offered, and the most recent research indicates that no measurable nonosmotic water uptake by cells occurs (Kramer, 1956d). Nonosmotic explanations of root pressure have therefore been largely abandoned. Several investigators have suggested that electroosmosis might cause the inward movement of water responsible for root pressure (Keller, 1930; Lund, 1931; Heyl, 1933), but Lundegardh (1944) and Blinks and Airth (1951) regard the electrical potentials which exist between the surface and the interior of roots as much too small to cause appreciable movement of water. It seems more probable that active uptake of water can be explained as an osmotic process, resulting from the accumulation of sufficient solutes in the xylem to cause inward diffusion of water.

Osmotic Explanations of Root Pressure. Two problems arise in connection with an osmotic explanation of root pressure. One is what constitutes the differentially permeable membrane, and the other is the origin of the solutes in the xylem responsible for the DPD gradient from the soil to the xylem. Atkins (1916) regarded the cortical cells as forming a complex, multicellular, differentially permeable membrane, while Scott and Priestley (1928), Crafts and Broyer (1938), Arnold (1952), and others have emphasized the role of the endodermis as a specialized layer of cells which might act as a differentially permeable membrane. The radial walls of the endodermal cells usually are rendered more or less impermeable by bands of suberized tissue called casparian strips, forcing the water and salts which pass through them to move through the cytoplasm. If the differentially permeable membrane controlling the accumulation of ions is the plasmalemma, then the endodermis would certainly be a fairly effective membrane, but if the principal differentially permeable membrane is the vacuolar membrane, then the endodermis is relatively permeable to ions. More research will be necessary before a decision can be made concerning the location of the differentially permeable membrane responsible for root pressure. The problem is made more difficult by the claim that a considerable fraction of the root volume (the apparent free space or outer space of some authors) is accessible to ions by diffusion (Hope and Stevens, 1952; Butler, 1953; Epstein, 1956; Briggs and Robertson, 1957).

A question also exists concerning the source of the solutes found in xylem sap. In trees a considerable fraction of these solutes is composed of sugars, usually mostly sucrose, while in herbaceous plants most of the solutes are inorganic ions. Birch sap contains about 1.5 per cent of sucrose, maple sap 3.0 per cent or more, and a sample of grape sap analyzed by Priestley and Wormall (1925) contained 0.33 per cent of reducing sugars. Priestley (1922) proposed that the solutes in the xylem elements are released by the breakdown of the protoplasts of the cells which coalesce to form the elements. Lundegardh (1940, 1950), Crafts and Broyer (1938), and others have suggested that the ions are secreted into the xylem, or at least into the stele, from the cortical cells, but it is very difficult to see how cells which are accumulating ions can secrete them into the dead xylem elements. Hylmö (1953) offered an explanation resembling that of Priestley, suggesting that the protoplasts of the xylem cells continue to accumulate ions even after their upper ends are ruptured and these ions are released into the xylem vessels as the protoplasts disintegrate. This theory has not been proved actually to operate, and at the present time there is no satisfactory explanation of how ions can be accumulated in the xylem.

There is considerable evidence in favor of an osmotic explanation of root pressure, however. For example, the rate of absorption of water by detopped root systems seems to be proportional to the concentration of solutes in the xylem sap (Arisz et al., 1951; van Andel, 1953). Eaton (1943) also showed that the rate of exudation from detopped cotton plants was proportional to the difference in osmotic pressure between the solution in which the roots were immersed and the concentration of the xylem sap. Root pressure does not continue in roots kept in pure water, indicating that a supply of salt is essential, and it occurs only in healthy, growing roots in a well-aerated medium, suggesting that there is a relation between root growth and water intake.

The weight of evidence therefore suggests that root pressure is the result of osmotic movement of water which occurs when the concentration of solutes in the xylem becomes high enough to produce a DPD gradient across the roots from the soil solution to the stele. The effects of respiration inhibitors and aeration probably are exerted indirectly through their effects on the absorption of minerals. The absorption of minerals is discussed in Chapter 9.

Physiology of Trees

Relative Importance of Active and Passive Absorption

Ever since a distinction was made between active and passive absorption, debate has occurred concerning their relative importance (White, 1938). This has been particularly true with respect to herbaceous plants

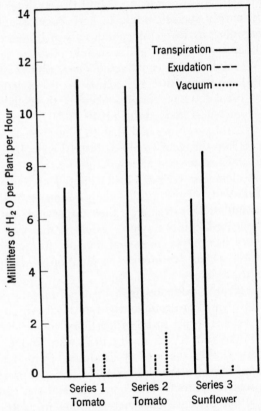

Figure 11.3 Comparison of rates of transpiration, exudation from detopped root systems, and water movement through tomato root systems under a pressure gradient of 0.8 atmosphere produced by attaching a vacuum pump to the stumps. The rates of transpiration and exudation are assumed to be measures of the rates of passive and active water absorption. (*From Kramer, 1949.*)

where root pressure is common and of relatively high magnitude. In trees root pressure is not often demonstrable, except in a few species early in the spring, and it is regarded as a negligible factor in supplying their normal water requirements.

It occasionally has been argued that absence of root pressure or exudation is not evidence that the active-absorption mechanism does not work.

Rufelt (1956), in fact, offers the suggestion that active absorption is occurring even in conifers or in rapidly transpiring plants where only subatmospheric pressure can be demonstrated in the xylem, because salt accumulation must be occurring in the xylem of such plants. It seems more probable that in rapidly transpiring plants the condition of the root cells makes the active-absorption mechanism inoperative. For example, the osmotic pressure of the xylem sap is almost always less than 2 atmospheres, and if the diffusion-pressure deficit in the living cells of the root exceeds the osmotic pressure of the xylem sap, then water could not move into the xylem by osmosis, although it might enter by mass flow along a gradient created by reduced pressure or tension in the xylem. Furthermore, actively transpiring plants can absorb water against much higher external DPDs than detopped root systems, indicating that the active absorption mechanism is ineffective in dry soils and concentrated soil solutions (Army and Kozlowski, 1951).

There is little doubt that active absorption is of negligible importance in the water economy of trees in terms of the quantity of water absorbed. Even under the most favorable conditions it probably supplies less than 5 per cent of the water lost by transpiration of herbaceous species (Figure 11.3), and it probably is of even less importance in trees.

It has been argued that in some tree species active absorption is important because the root pressure produced causes those xylem elements which become filled with air during the summer to be refilled with water during the winter or early spring. It is probable that this actually occurs in some species, but its importance is debatable.

Root and Stem Pressures

Probably from prehistoric times men have observed the exudation of sap from broken or wounded plants. In the Far East sap has been obtained from palms to make sugar and wine since before the beginning of recorded history, and the first European settlers found the Indians of Canada and New England tapping maple trees and boiling down the sap to make sugar. According to Evelyn (1670), birches have long been tapped in England and on the Continent and the sap was used for various purposes, especially to make beer.

The earliest writers indiscriminately grouped together all examples of "bleeding" or "weeping" without regard to their origin. Wieler (1893) listed nearly 200 species belonging to a wide variety of genera which exhibited exudation; but this included guttation, secretion from glandular hairs, and sap flow from wounds in stems. In trees a distinction should be made between sap flow caused by root pressure and that caused by some local stem pressure such as the flow of sap from tapped maple trees.

Although these phenomena have been of great interest to both casual

observers and to plant physiologists, they probably are of little importance to the trees in which they occur. The extensive literature which has
accumulated is the result of the uncertainty concerning their origin rather
than of their importance.

Guttation. In herbaceous plants the most conspicuous evidence of root
pressure is the exudation of droplets of water from the margins and tips
of leaves. This occurs only in plants growing in moist, warm soil, when
the air is humid and transpiration is very low. It seems to occur at times
when the active-absorption process greatly exceeds water loss, resulting
in development of root pressure great enough to force water up the
xylem and out through special pores in the leaves called "hydathodes."
In tropical rain forests guttation is a common phenomenon, but it is
uncommon in woody plants in the Temperate Zone, probably because the
necessary combination of soil and atmospheric conditions occurs less
frequently.

A few instances of guttation from the twigs of trees have been reported.
Raber (1937) observed sap flow from the leaf scars of deciduous trees,
especially the hackberry, in Louisiana, and Friesner (1940) observed exudation of sap from uninjured stems of stump sprouts of red maple in
February, in Indiana. These examples of sap flow are interesting but
probably of little importance to the life of trees.

Magnitude of Root Pressure. Hales (1727), who made the first recorded
measurements of root pressure, observed a pressure of more than 1 atmosphere in a grapevine. Clark (1874) in Massachusetts and Merwin and
Lyon (1909) in New York observed pressures of 2.6 atmospheres in birch.
The highest pressure observed by Merwin and Lyon would have supported a column of water higher than the tree in which it was observed.
Some higher pressures have been reported in stems, but they probably
are not caused by root pressure. Stem pressures will be discussed in
another section of this chapter.

Root pressures of trees vary widely in magnitude, both seasonally and
daily. In general, as trees leaf out, positive pressures disappear and negative or subatmospheric pressures appear, because the rate of water loss
exceeds the rate of active absorption (Figure 11.4). Wide daily fluctuations in root pressure of birch often occur because of variations in temperature and rate of transpiration from the bare branches, according to
Merwin and Lyon. According to Johnson, paper birch trees 20 to 44
centimeters in diameter yielded from less than 20 to over 100 liters of sap.
The volume of sap was not proportional to the size of the tree. Clark
reported that a paper birch 37.5 centimeters in diameter produced 28 liters
of sap in 1 day and 675 liters during the season. The sugar content of
birch sap is much lower than that of maple sap, and it consists largely
of reducing sugar while maple sap contains sucrose.

Maple Sap Flow. Not all sap flow from wounds occurs as a result of root pressure. The flow of maple sap, for example, seems to occur quite independently of root pressure because pressure gauges attached to roots of maple trees often show negative pressures at times when sap is flowing from the trunk (Figure 11.4). Furthermore, most of the sap flow into a

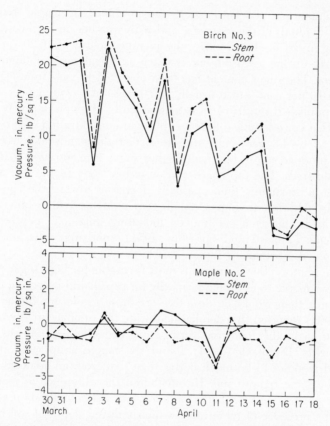

Figure 11.4 Simultaneous measurements of root and stem pressure in river birch and red maple. Root pressures in birch exceed stem pressures, and the two are closely correlated. Root pressures in maple are often below atmospheric pressure even when positive pressures occur in the stems.

hole occurs from above. Even more important is the fact that branches and sections of trunks removed from maple trees show sap flow when supplied with water and subjected to temperatures which rise and fall (Stevens and Eggert, 1945; Marvin and Greene, 1951). Clark (1874, 1875) published some of the most extensive observations ever made on maple sap flow. He reported that in Massachusetts sap flow might occur any time from October to late April if freezing nights were followed by days with temperatures above freezing. Sap flow ceases if temperatures are continuously above or below freezing, and it ceases in the spring when night temperatures no longer fall below freezing. In contrast, flow of sap from birch tends to increase as the temperature rises until increased transpiration caused by the opening of leaves brings an end to root pressure.

The volume and concentration of sap produced by maple trees vary among individuals of the same size and with weather and soil conditions. According to Bryan et al. (1937), the average yield is 10 to 20 gallons of sap per tree during a season, but as much as 40 gallons is obtained from a few trees. The sugar content has been observed to vary from 0.5 to 7.0 or even 10.0 per cent, but it usually is 2.0 to 3.0 per cent. Taylor (1956) recently published results of an extensive study of maple sap flow which indicate that considerable differences in sugar concentration exist between stands (2.2 to 4.8 per cent) and trees. Certain stands and trees consistently produce sap of relatively higher sugar concentration than other stands and trees. The sap concentration is low early in the season, rises quickly to a maximum, then gradually decreases toward the end of the season. In addition to sugars, maple sap contains minute amounts of organic acids, nitrogen compounds including ammonia, peptides, and amino acids (Pollard and Sproston, 1954), inorganic salts, and other undetermined substances (Taylor, 1956).

A large photosynthetic surface is most favorable for high sugar production; hence maple trees grown primarily for sap should be grown in more open stands than would be desirable for those grown for timber. Jones et al. (1903) reported that defoliation during the summer greatly reduced the sugar yield the following spring, and drought also reduces subsequent yields. Dambach (1944) found the maple sirup yield from an ungrazed woodlot to be much better than that from an adjacent grazed lot on the same type of soil. He attributed the difference to more non-capillary pore space with better aeration and better infiltration of water and to the presence of more litter, which reduced depth of soil freezing in the ungrazed woodlot, resulting in more vigorous growth and better conditions for water absorption in the spring.

The sugar of course comes from carbohydrates accumulated principally as starch during the preceding summer. The starch is converted into sucrose when the weather becomes cool, resulting in a relatively high concentration of sugar in the xylem sap. This sugar solution drains out of holes bored in the stems if conditions are favorable for the existence of pressure in the xylem. Such a sap flow has no relation to the rise of sap in transpiring plants. Apparently this loss of sugar is not injurious because trees have been tapped for many years without any visible damage. Jones et al. (1903) estimated that tapping maples would remove less than

10 per cent of the total sugar in the tree, a loss too small to be significant unless the tree was defoliated or other conditions were very unfavorable for photosynthesis the following summer.

The cause of maple sap flow is not yet known, in spite of numerous studies of the subject. It is generally agreed that a rise of temperature following a period of low, but not necessarily freezing, temperature is essential, and sap flow has been induced in cut stems in the laboratory by proper manipulation of temperature (Marvin and Greene, 1951). According to Marvin and Erickson (1956) and Marvin (1958), sap flow on a given day is closely related to the temperature of the preceding day. They also found that large flows tend to occur on successive days, indicating that a heavy flow one day does not deplete the sap supply enough to affect the flow on the succeeding day if the temperature conditions are favorable. Warming of the tree trunk undoubtedly produces an increase in gas and liquid pressure, and cooling produces a contraction, but these pressure variations do not adequately explain sap flow. Marvin (1958) suggests that maple sap flow results from the interaction of two or more factors. Evidently more research is needed on this interesting problem.

Other Examples of Stem Pressure. Two other plants which yield sap in commercial quantities are palms and agaves. In the tropics of India and Asia, palm sap probably was used as a source of sugar long before sugar cane was cultivated. The sap also was fermented to make palm wine. In most instances the sap is obtained by cutting off a part or all of the inflorescence, although Hill (1952) states that sap is obtained from the stem of the date palm by tapping. According to Molisch (1902), who studied the process in Java, sap flow in palms is caused by wounding. If the inflorescence is cut out at the proper stage, a flow of sap can be maintained for weeks or even months by repeatedly cutting and pounding the stem.

In Mexico large amounts of sap are obtained from several species of *Agave* and fermented to produce pulque or the distilled drink mescal. When the inflorescence of these plants begins to form it is cut out and a cavity holding a liter or more is scooped in the top of the stem. The tissue lining this cavity is bruised periodically to maintain the flow which continues for many days. Some botanists have attributed the sap flow to root pressure, but it seems more likely that it is the result of wounding the spongy parenchyma of the stem at a time when a large amount of sugar has been accumulated in connection with flowering. In Arizona *Agave americana* is said to flower in soil so dry that little or no water could be absorbed from it, and the water used in producing the large inflorescence comes from the fleshy leaves which decrease in both water content and dry weight during flowering. The entire plant dies after flowering.

A number of reports of high sap pressures in stems of trees occur in the literature, but Molisch (1902) regarded most of these as being caused by the effects of wounding rather than by root pressure. MacDougal (1926) reported that exudation pressures developed in holes bored in stems of tree cacti, Monterey pine, English walnut, and oak but that none of these were caused by root pressure. He attributed the pressures to exudation of various substances from the cells lining the wounds. He also observed exudation in *Juglans*, which he attributed to root pressure.

Occasionally flow of sap occurs from cracks and other wounds in trees, causing what is called "slime flux." According to Carter (1945), in elms this is associated with a water-soaked condition of the heartwood, called wetwood, caused by bacterial activity. Gas and liquid pressures of 5 to 30 pounds were often observed, and the gas from affected trees contained considerable methane.

Factors Affecting Water Absorption

For discussion it is convenient to classify the factors affecting water absorption into plant and environmental factors. The chief plant factors are the rate of transpiration, the diffusion-pressure deficit (DPD) existing in the plant, and the extent and efficiency of the root system. The principal environmental factors are the availability of soil moisture (in terms of its DPD), soil temperature, soil aeration, and occasionally the concentration and composition of the soil solution.

Terminology of Soil Moisture. Water absorption occurs whenever there is a gradient of decreasing free energy or increasing DPD from the water in the soil to the water in the roots (Chapter 10). The DPD of a root system is controlled largely by the rate of transpiration and the resulting tension in the xylem and to a lesser extent by the osmotic pressure of the xylem sap, while the DPD of the soil solution (often termed the "total soil moisture stress") depends largely on the surface forces which bind water to the soil particles ("soil moisture tension") and to a minor extent in forest soils on the osmotic pressure of the soil solution. In general, it may be assumed that the rate of water absorption depends on the steepness of the free energy or DPD gradient from soil to roots.

The water readily available for growth is that in the range between field capacity and permanent-wilting percentage. The relationship of these values to soil moisture content is shown in Figure 11.5. Field capacity can be regarded as the moisture content, expressed as percentage of oven-dry weight, of a soil which has been thoroughly wetted and then allowed to drain until the rate of drainage has become very slow. Permanent-wilting percentage is the moisture content of soil in which plants first become permanently wilted. These and other terms are discussed in soil texts such as that by Baver (1956) and a book by Kramer (1949).

Availability of Soil Water. If the water content of soil is much greater than field capacity, air is displaced from the noncapillary pore space, and root growth and water absorption are hindered by deficient aeration. If the water content is too low, the remaining water is held so firmly by the surface forces of the soil particles that it is unavailable to roots. A soil with a relatively wide spread between permanent-wilting percentage and

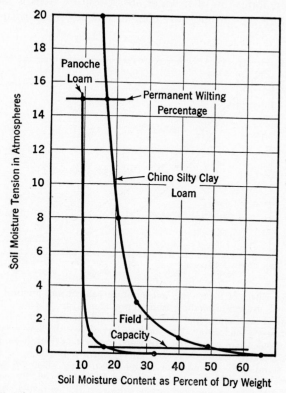

Figure 11.5 The relationship between soil moisture tension and soil moisture content in a sandy soil and in a clay soil. In soils low in salt the soil moisture tension is approximately equal to the soil DPD or total soil moisture stress. (*From Kramer,* 1949.)

field capacity is most favorable for tree growth because it contains more water available for growth.

As the moisture content of the soil decreases, the DPD increases from zero at saturation to about 0.1 atmosphere at field capacity and then to about 15 atmospheres at permanent wilting. In the range near permanent wilting a very small decrease in water content results in a very large increase in DPD so that the availability of soil water decreases very rapidly.

There has been some argument concerning the relative availability of water over the range from field capacity to permanent wilting. Theoretically, as the DPD of the soil increases, water absorption should decrease, but Veihmeyer (1956) and Veihmeyer and Hendrickson (1927, 1950) have argued that water absorption is not reduced until soil moisture is reduced almost to the permanent-wilting percentage. There are numerous data, however, indicating that water absorption by trees is reduced considerably before the soil moisture content reaches the permanent-wilting

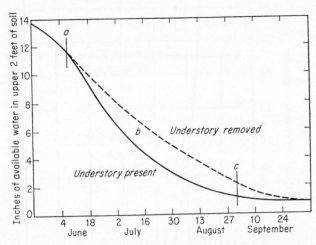

Figure 11.6 Effect of decreasing soil moisture content and removal of understory trees on rate of evapotranspiration from forest stands in Arkansas. The solid line shows removal of soil moisture under a 50-year-old stand of loblolly and shortleaf pine with hardwood understory. The broken line shows the lower rate of removal in a similar stand from which the hardwood understory had been removed. Soil moisture was abundant during May, but after point *a* it began to be limiting, especially in the stand with an understory, which lost water about 25 per cent faster than the stand from which the understory had been removed. By point *c* the soil water content was approaching permanent wilting in the untreated stand. Note that the rate of water loss from the untreated stand began to decrease before soil moisture approached the permanent-wilting percentage. (*From Zahner, 1958.*)

percentage (Bourdeau, 1954; Kozlowski, 1949; Schopmeyer, 1939; Zahner, 1955b, 1958). Furr and Taylor (1939) reported that lemon trees growing on a shallow soil underlain by dense subsoil showed reduction in fruit growth before the moisture content of all the soil in the surface was reduced to the permanent-wilting percentage. Kenworthy (1949) reported that diameter and shoot growth and leaf area of apple trees were reduced before the soil moisture content was reduced to permanent wilting. The effect of decreasing soil moisture on the rate of evapotranspiration from a forest stand is shown in Figure 11.6.

Most of the controversy on this subject results from failure to measure the internal water balance of the plants. Under conditions favoring high transpiration, water deficits large enough to reduce growth can occur in moist soil, but when transpiration is low, the soil might be dried nearly to permanent wilting before serious water deficits develop. Growth is controlled by the internal water balance of the plant, and this is controlled both by availability of soil moisture and by rate of water loss. Sometimes one factor is dominant, sometimes the other; hence contradictory results have been obtained from experiments on effects of decreasing soil moisture content. Hagan (1955) has an excellent discussion of this problem, and Stanhill (1957) has reviewed the results of 80 experiments dealing with effects of decreasing soil moisture.

There is little doubt that water becomes progressively less available as the soil DPD increases, but the practical importance of this varies with the soil type. In sandy soils practically all the water is held with a tension of less than 1 atmosphere, but in clay soils 50 per cent or more of the so-called readily available water often is held with a tension of more than 1 atmosphere. In such soils water actually does become significantly less available before the moisture content falls to the permanent-wilting percentage. The relations between moisture content and moisture tension in two different soils are shown in Figure 11.5. This problem is discussed in more detail by Richards and Wadleigh (1952).

Concentration and Composition of the Soil Solution. The DPD of soil water is controlled largely by two groups of forces, the surface-attractive forces of the soil (soil moisture tension) and the osmotic forces of the soil solution. If the osmotic pressure of the soil solution exceeds 2 or 3 atmospheres, plant growth is likely to be seriously retarded, even at field capacity, but this seldom is a problem in forest soils, where the soil moisture tension usually is the important factor determining the availability of water. In arid regions salt concentration may become high enough to be a limiting factor for absorption.

This is particularly important if the irrigation water is high in salt. The major effect of high salt concentration on water absorption is caused by reduction of the diffusion-pressure gradient from soil to roots. This not only reduces the uptake of water, but also produces a continual saturation deficit in the plant tissue which reduces growth. The reduction in growth and the more rapid suberization of roots exposed to soil solutions having an osmotic pressure of more than 1 or 2 atmospheres further reduce absorption.

Some debate has occurred concerning the relative importance of concentration or osmotic pressure versus the ionic composition of the solution. For example, it is often claimed that chlorides are more toxic than sulfates, and there is some evidence to support this. Brown et al. (1953)

found calcium chloride more toxic to several kinds of stone fruits than isosmotic solutions of sodium chloride. Data on toxicity of individual ions are summarized by Hayward and Magistad (1946). In general, it appears that the osmotic effects are more important than the ionic effects.

Diffusion-pressure Gradient from Soil to Roots. All other factors being equal, the rate of water absorption depends on the steepness of the diffusion-pressure gradient from soil to roots. The DPD of soils varies from about 0.1 atmosphere at field capacity to 15 atmospheres at permanent wilting, but rapidly increases to a very large value as the soil moisture content drops below the permanent-wilting percentage. In soils near field capacity the steepness of the gradient from soil to tree depends largely on the DPD in the tree. This varies from zero to a value of 30, 50, or even more atmospheres, depending on the internal water conditions. According to some investigators, the internal DPD may exceed 100 atmospheres in a very rapidly transpiring plant.

It must be admitted that over long periods of time the uptake of water is not always proportional to the steepness of the gradient from substrate to roots. If root systems are placed in a moderately concentrated solution, the osmotic pressure of the roots will increase, so approximately the same osmotic gradient from substrate to roots is maintained in a more concentrated solution as in a less concentrated solution, yet water absorption will be much less from the more concentrated solution (Eaton, 1942). Evidently plants subjected to a high external DPD undergo changes which reduce their transpiration rate and therefore decrease their rate of water absorption below what might be expected theoretically.

The fact that the osmotic pressure and DPD of plants increase when they are subjected to a severe moisture stress suggests that the usual concept of the permanent-wilting percentage requires reevaluation. The permanent-wilting percentage often is regarded as practically a constant, occurring at a soil moisture stress or DPD of approximately 15 atmospheres with all kinds of plants. According to Slatyer (1957a), the soil moisture stress or DPD at permanent wilting can vary over a considerable range, depending on the kind and condition of plant used. Permanent wilting occurs when the soil moisture stress increases until it is equal to the osmotic pressure of the leaves. Thus it is controlled by plant characteristics rather than by soil characteristics. General agreement that the soil moisture stress or DPD at permanent wilting is about 15 atmospheres results from the fact that sunflowers or other mesophytes are used to determine it. If plants are very gradually wilted, they may develop high osmotic pressures and the soil moisture stress at permanent wilting may be much higher than 15 atmospheres. For example, the DPD in privet plants near death from desiccation was about 70 atmospheres (Slatyer, 1957b).

Soil Temperature. Low soil temperatures often seriously reduce water absorption. Figure 11.7 shows the effects of low soil temperatures on the rate of transpiration of several woody species. It was assumed in these studies that the rate of water loss was a fairly accurate measure of the rate of water absorption, although it is probable that water absorption lagged somewhat behind water loss.

It can be seen that water absorption was reduced much more in the southern slash and loblolly pines than in the northern white and red pines. Kozlowski (1943) also found that absorption was reduced much more

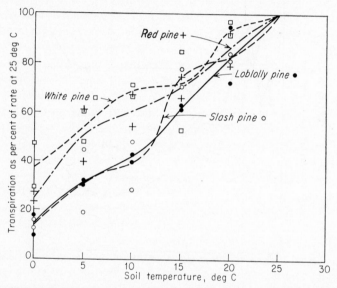

Figure 11.7 Effect of soil temperature on water absorption of four species of pine as measured by rate of transpiration. Absorption was reduced more by cold soil in the southern species of pine, slash and loblolly, than in the northern species, white and red pine. (*From Kramer,* 1942.)

between 15 and 5°C in loblolly pine than in white pine. It has been observed that when the soil is cooled rapidly absorption is reduced more than when it is cooled slowly. This observation suggests that there may be basic differences in permeability between the protoplasm of different species and also that the protoplasm may undergo changes in permeability if subjected to low temperatures for several days. Such a hypothesis would be consistent with reports that cells of cold-hardened plants are more permeable to water than the cells of unhardened plants (Levitt and Scarth, 1936).

Low soil temperatures materially reduce water absorption of citrus trees (Bialoglowski, 1936; Haas, 1936), and Cameron (1941) reported that in California orange trees often wilt severely during periods of cold weather. Cold soil also may be of some ecological significance. Whitfield (1932) and Clements and Martin (1934) believed that the low soil temperatures existing at high altitudes may limit plant growth, and Michaelis (1934) suggested that the position of timber lines may be partly determined by slow water absorption in cold soils.

Low soil temperatures reduce water absorption directly by decreasing the permeability of roots to water and by increasing the viscosity of water.

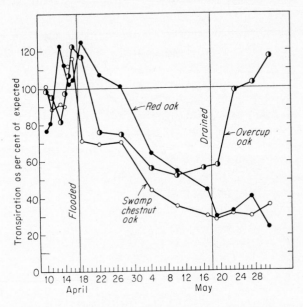

Figure 11.8 Effects of flooding the soil on water absorption as indicated by changes in rate of transpiration. These seedlings lost most of their leaves while flooded, but overcup oak was leafing out for the second time when the soil was drained. (*From Parker, 1950.*)

The combined effect of these changes is to greatly increase the resistance to water movement through roots. Water absorption is decreased indirectly by retardation of root elongation and decreased rate of water movement from soil to roots. The principal cause of decreased water uptake in cold soil is the increased resistance to water movement across the roots.

Soil Aeration. In saturated soils and soils containing a small amount of noncapillary pore space, root systems often suffer from deficiency of oxygen and excess of carbon dioxide. This reduces water and salt absorption directly and also indirectly by reducing root growth and the extent of the absorbing system. Effects of flooding the soil on water absorption and transpiration of three species of oak are shown in Figure 11.8.

In general, it seems that under field conditions low oxygen becomes a limiting factor more often than excess carbon dioxide, but it has been shown that a high concentration of carbon dioxide can cause wilting of herbaceous plants more rapidly than a deficiency of oxygen. This occurs because carbon dioxide produces an immediate decrease in permeability to water (Kramer and Jackson, 1954). The causes of injury to plants in flooded soil seem to be rather complex and are not attributable entirely to reduced water absorption (Jackson, 1956).

There are wide differences among species with respect to susceptibility to injury from inadequate soil aeration. Swamp species such as cypress and tupelo-gum survive and even thrive in soil saturated or flooded for long periods of time. In contrast Parker (1950) found that flooding severely injured dogwood within a week, and Kramer (1951b) found that yellow-poplar and ligustrum were killed in 3 weeks. Effects of flooding are discussed briefly with respect to respiration in Chapter 7 and with respect to growth in Chapter 16.

Extent and Efficiency of Roots. In terms of water relations the success of any plant depends on its ability to absorb water sufficiently rapidly to prevent development of prolonged or serious internal water deficits during periods of rapid transpiration. The effectiveness of the absorbing systems of trees depends on both the extent and the efficiency of their root systems. The growth and extent of roots is discussed by Kramer (1949, chaps. 5 and 6), and their role in absorption also is considered in some detail by Kramer (1956a).

Most trees have roots which not only extend well beyond the spread of the branches but also penetrate deeply into the soil. In forests the entire soil mass usually is completely occupied by roots to a depth which varies from several inches to several feet, depending on soil characteristics such as drainage and aeration. On a deep sandy loam soil at Davis, California, Proebsting (1943) found that maximum concentration of roots of various fruit trees occurred at depths of 2 to 5 feet and many roots penetrated 15 feet or more. According to Wiggans (1936), roots of 18-year-old apple trees on a deep loess soil in Nebraska were absorbing water from a depth of over 30 feet and fully occupied the soil between the rows, which were 33 feet apart. In contrast pears on a heavy, poorly drained adobe soil in Oregon developed nearly 90 per cent of their roots in the upper 3 feet, and Coile (1937b) found that 90 per cent of the small roots were in the top 5 inches of soil in forests of the North Carolina Piedmont. The heavy concentration of roots near the surface in North Carolina forests probably is partly related to poorer aeration at greater depths and partly to wetting of the surface layer by summer showers after the soil has been dried to permanent wilting to a considerable depth. In spite of the smaller number of roots usually found deep in the soil under forest stands, the soil often is dried to permanent wilting to depths of 5 or 6 feet (Hoover et al., 1953; Zahner, 1955b).

Water moves rather slowly in soils drier than field capacity, and a soil mass fully occupied by roots therefore tends to become depleted of water. Only by continual extension of roots and their branching and rebranching, so that every part of the soil mass is occupied, does the water in soils at or below field capacity become available. If root systems were to cease extension, trees would suffer from a serious lack of water, even though the soil at a short distance from the roots contained available water.

It has often been assumed that absorption of water and minerals occurs only through the growing unsuberized tips of tree roots, but this can scarcely be true because such roots form too small a percentage of the

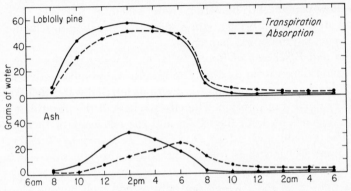

Figure 11.9 The relation between absorption and transpiration of two species of trees. Rates were measured simultaneously at 2-hour intervals. The seedlings were grown in autoirrigated pots. (*From Kramer, 1937a.*)

root surface of most trees to provide an adequate absorbing surface. For example, Roberts (1948) found that unsuberized tips and mycorrhizal branches formed only about 3.5 per cent of the total root surface under a 20-year-old loblolly pine stand in April, and about the same percentage of unsuberized surface was found on yellow-poplar root systems in April. It also is well known that citrus (Chapman and Parker, 1942; Reed and MacDougal, 1937) and pine trees (Reed, 1939) have very few growing root tips during the winter, yet they obviously absorb considerable quantities of water. Furthermore, it has been demonstrated by direct measurement that water can be absorbed through suberized roots of various trees (Hayward et al., 1942; Kramer, 1946).

In view of these facts it seems probable that considerable quantities of water, and probably of minerals, are absorbed through the suberized surfaces of the older roots of trees. In fact, in the winter most absorption must occur through such roots. No data are available on the role of mycorrhizal roots in water absorption, but they presumably increase the absorbing capacity by increasing the root surface.

Rate of Transpiration. In the end, rate of water loss controls rate of water absorption because it produces the internal water deficit which is transmitted through the xylem to the roots and also produces the forces responsible for water absorption. The relation between the two processes is shown when they are measured simultaneously and the rates are plotted over time, as illustrated in Figure 11.9. The causes of the lag of absorption behind transpiration will be discussed in Chapter 12.

THE ASCENT OF SAP

Because of their height the ascent of sap in trees is a more serious problem than in smaller plants. On a hot summer day a medium-sized tree may transpire a barrel or more of water. How such a large quantity of water reaches the leaves 100 to 300 feet or more above the soil surface has concerned botanists, foresters, and laymen for centuries.

Historical Review

The earliest writers on this subject, such as Merret and Ray in England, thought there was a circulation of sap much as in animals, involving both ascent and descent in the stems. Nehemiah Grew, who published from 1671 to 1682, believed that sap rose through the wood in the spring and through the bark in the summer. He believed that roots absorbed water by capillarity and the sap was then forced up the stem by a pulsatory action of the parenchyma cells. Hales (1727) made the first careful observations on this problem and observed that although sap pressure and exudation occurred in grape and a few trees in the spring, it always disappeared when the trees leafed out. After measuring transpiration of cut shoots and absorption by cut stems and observing no exudation of sap from the upper ends of cut shoots standing in water, Hales wrote: "These last three experiments all show that the capillary sap vessels imbibe moisture plentifully; but they have little power to protrude it farther without the assistance of the perspiring leaves, which do promote its progress." Thus Hales developed an explanation of the ascent of sap which foreshadowed our modern explanation, although he did not understand how transpiration could "promote its progress."

During the nineteenth century Godlewski, Westermaier, Janse, and others proposed various vital theories in which the parenchyma cells of the xylem exerted some sort of pumping action. Bose (1923) claimed that rhythmic waves of pulsatory activity in the living cells of stems caused the ascent of sap. These vital theories had all been disproved before they were proposed, because Boucherie (1840) found that a tree cut at its base would draw a poisonous liquid to its top which killed the cells en route, and then would draw up a second liquid. Schultze published results of a similar experiment in 1844. Strasburger performed several experiments in which poisonous substances were drawn up more than 10 meters in stems. His most notable experiment was with an oak tree 22 meters in height. The tree was cut off, and the base of the trunk placed in picric acid for 3 days, after which the dye fuchsin was added. The fuchsin rose to the top of the tree through tissues in which all living cells had almost certainly been killed by the poisonous picric acid. Overton (1911), Mac-Dougal et al. (1929), and others also have demonstrated the rise of sap through stem segments which had been killed in various ways.

Supporters of the role of living cells in the ascent of sap have objected to the conclusion that living cells are not involved because the leaves on a stem which has been partly or completely killed eventually die. Killing the stem probably results in partial plugging of the conducting stem by gum, and air doubtless penetrates dead stems more easily than living ones. It also is possible that toxic substances escape from the dead cells, move up in the ascending sap, and poison the leaves.

Toward the end of the nineteenth century Sachs and Strasburger concluded that the loss of water produced the pull causing the ascent of sap, but did not understand how it could be brought about. The final step was added by Dixon and Joly (1895) and Askenasy (1895), who demonstrated the large cohesive forces of water confined in small tubes such as the xylem elements in plant stems.

Cohesion Theory of the Ascent of Sap

The cohesion theory of the ascent of sap depends on the high tensile strength of water and the high adhesive or imbibitional forces of cell walls for water. According to this theory, all the water in a plant is connected together in a continuous system, the hydrostatic system of MacDougal and some other authors, and because of the great attraction existing between water molecules, a stress developed in any part of this system will be transmitted throughout the plant. Because of the high imbibitional attraction of the cell walls for water, the water in the xylem elements is not easily pulled away from the surrounding walls; hence the water in the plant may be subjected to high tension.

When water evaporates from the walls of the leaf cells and other surfaces, a DPD is developed in the walls which causes the movement of water into the evaporating surfaces from the adjacent cells and finally from the xylem. This reduces the pressure on the water in the xylem and increases its DPD, producing a gradient along which water moves from the soil into the xylem. If water loss is rapid, the pressure on the xylem sap falls below atmospheric pressure and becomes a negative pressure or tension. If the tension in the xylem exceeds the osmotic pressure of the root cells, the latter also are subjected to tension and the tension on the water in the xylem extends to the surfaces of the roots, causing water to enter by mass flow.

Levitt (1956a) calculated that movement of liquid water by diffusion along a DPD gradient across the root cells and the mesophyll cells of the leaves is so much slower than evaporation that it could not supply water to the evaporating surfaces of transpiring plants as rapidly as it is lost. In his opinion, mass movement in a cohesive column is the only way in which water can be supplied to the walls of the mesophyll cells as rapidly as it evaporates from them. According to this view, evaporation of water produces imbibitional forces in the drying cell walls which, when they become large enough to overcome gravity and friction, cause mass movement of water from the soil, through the roots, up the stems, and out to the evaporating surfaces. This explanation resembles that originally proposed by Dixon, who regarded the water as hanging suspended from the evaporating surfaces, anchored in the cell walls by imbibitional forces. It stresses mass movement of water in cohering columns more than some current theories which emphasize osmotic forces of the cells.

Objections to the Cohesion Theory. Various objections to the cohesion theory have been advanced. The more important of these concern the cohesive forces of water, the instability of water columns under tension, and the plugging of xylem elements with air.

The theoretical intermolecular attractive forces in water are equivalent to approximately 15,000 atmospheres per square inch, and Fisher (1949) estimated that fracture of stretched water columns theoretically would occur at a negative pressure or tension of 1,300 atmospheres. Such high values are not obtained experimentally, but Dixon (1914) demonstrated tensions up to 200 atmospheres in plant sap, and Ursprung (1915) found a tension of 315 atmospheres in annulus cells of fern sporangia. Briggs (1949) measured tension of 223 atmospheres in water subjected to centrifugal force. Greenidge (1954) quotes various workers who found that water columns usually break at much lower tensions and suggests that the highest tensions found in trees probably average about 30 atmospheres.

It is difficult to measure the tension in the xylem directly, but Arcichovskij and Ossipov (1931) measured DPDs of up to 142.9 atmospheres in a desert shrub and assumed that tension of this magnitude must exist in the xylem. Slatyer (1957b) measured a DPD of 70 atmospheres in privet plants and 77 atmospheres in cotton plants near death from desiccation. On the other hand, Stocking (1945) found the maximum tension in squash leaf petioles to be less than 6 atmospheres and in wilted leaves 9 atmospheres. Dixon (1914) calculated that a force equal to twice the height of the water column would be required to move water through stems at normal rates of transpiration. Thus in a tree 300 feet in height, a tension of about 20 atmospheres would be required, a value which seems to be well within even the minimum cohesive forces observed in water.

A common objection to the cohesion theory is based on the fact that water columns under tension in glass tubes are broken so easily by mechanical shock that it seems doubtful that the xylem contents can be maintained under tensions of several atmospheres in swaying tree trunks. Perhaps the size of the xylem elements in trees and the hydrophilic nature of their walls make their contents less susceptible to breakage than water columns in glass tubes. Furthermore, according to Crafts et al. (1949), many of the vessels which lose their liquid content become filled with water vapor rather than air during experimental manipulation, giving an exaggerated notion of the proportion of air-filled vessels in undisturbed stems. Apparently many of the bubbles of gas formed by mechanical shock contract and disappear, but during the summer an appreciable fraction of the xylem of many trees becomes occupied by air (Figure 12.2). This is not serious, because most trees have much more conducting tissue than is necessary to supply their crowns with water. The experiments of Scholander et al. (1957) suggest that air bubbles tend to remain confined to the xylem vessels in which they first appear and do not extend into others.

Preston (1952) and Greenidge (1955, 1957) questioned the existence of cohering water columns under tension because horizontal cuts made more than halfway through tree trunks, one above the other, did not prevent the ascent of sap. They assumed that such cuts must interrupt all the water columns. Scholander et al. (1955) questioned the cohesion theory because water continued to move up grapevine stems after the large vessels had been plugged with air. After further experiments Scholander et al. (1957) concluded that water moves through the smaller xylem elements after the larger ones are plugged with air but resistance to movement is much increased. Postlethwait and Rogers (1958) demonstrated movement of radioactive phosphorus around as many as four cuts made only 6 inches apart in trunks of hickory, blue beech, and red pine. It seems that even though many of the xylem elements are cut, air does not spread beyond the elements actually opened and water and solutes move around cuts and other interruptions. This fact, coupled with the fact that the average tree trunk possesses a much greater conducting capacity than is necessary for survival, means that trees can survive extensive injury to the water-conducting tissues.

Root pressure and capillarity cannot account for the rise of sap, and no plausible theory involving secretory or pumping activity by living cells has been proposed. As mentioned previously, transpiration, ascent of sap, and water absorption seem to be linked together so closely that if anything disturbs one process, the others are also modified. The only logical way in which such a relationship can be explained is by assuming that at least most of the time, the rate of water loss controls the rate of water absorption and ascent in the xylem. The simplest way in which these processes could be linked together is through the cohesive forces of the continuous water phase or hydrostatic system of the plant. It seems probable that further study will provide explanations for the objections now being raised against it, and in the end, instead of being abandoned, the cohesion theory will be strengthened.

Before leaving this subject an error which is frequently made should be cleared up. It sometimes is said that transpiration is useful or necessary because it brings about the ascent of sap. This is not true. Any use of water in the top of a tree, such as in growth of new cells or even in photosynthesis, will produce forces causing the ascent of sap. Transpiration is not indispensable in this connection, but merely uses many times as much water as all other processes combined and therefore causes the ascent of more sap.

The Water-conducting System

Practically all the water movement from roots to leaves occurs in the specialized water-conducting tissue known as the "xylem." Before water can enter the xylem of roots, however, it must pass through several layers of cells (Figures 11.1 and 11.2), and after it passes out of the xylem of the smallest veins of the leaves it again passes through several cells before reaching the cells which are losing water by evaporation. The xylem of trees is important both as a water-conducting system and because it provides mechanical support for the crowns. Although almost everyone knows that water moves through the xylem, this simple statement is not sufficient to explain the complex water-conducting system of trees. The xylem system differs in structure in angiosperms and gymnosperms, it differs in various species, and it differs in various parts of a tree. In the stem of a tree the effective conducting system usually consists of a cylindrical layer in the outer part of the wood, but it divides and subdivides repeatedly in the roots and branches, until it consists of millions of individual elements in the smallest veins of the leaves and the youngest roots.

Xylem Elements. The xylem of angiosperms contains vessels, tracheids, fibers, wood parenchyma cells, and ray parenchyma cells, but in gymnosperms vessels are absent. In fully differentiated xylem only the parenchyma cells are living, and as the xylem of a tree ages these die, so that no living cells remain in the heartwood. Tracheids are single cells which may be as much as 5 millimeters in length and 30 microns in diameter. In conifers water must therefore pass through thousands of cell walls as it moves up the stem, and although its passage is facilitated by pits in the walls, resistance to movement is much higher than in stems containing vessels. The vessels which form the chief path for water movement in angiosperms are complex tubular structures formed by the disappearance of the end walls and protoplasts of large numbers of cells located end to end, resulting in tubes 20 to 700 or 800 microns in diameter and from a few centimeters to many meters in length.

Length of Vessels. Numerous studies have been made of vessel length in trees by observing the distance to which mercury, suspensions of starch, India ink and certain dyes, or air can be forced through stem segments. By starting with a long piece of stem and cutting off successive segments until air bubbles or the substance used as an indicator appears at the cut surface, the maximum length of vessels can be determined. The results of many such studies indicate that in diffuse-porous species the vessels are relatively short while in at least some ring-porous species they extend the entire length of the stem and principal branches.

MacDougal et al. (1929) found the vessels of willow and alder to be 7 to 10 centimeters in length, while those of walnut were 30 centimeters and California live oak had vessels 35 centimeters in length. Malhotra (1931) found vessels 5 to 84 centimeters in length in various fruit trees, while Priestley concluded that in ring-porous species continuous vessels are differentiated from top to bottom of trees in the spring. Greenidge (1952) measured vessel length in various species of trees in Nova Scotia by felling the trees and forcing air through a twig in the crown under a pressure of 1 atmosphere. His results are shown in Table 11.1, where it can be seen that the vessels of diffuse-porous species were mostly about a meter in length but those of ring-porous species extended most of the length of the tree. The vessel lengths of diffuse-porous species reported in this study are somewhat greater than those given by most investigators. Liming (1934) measured vessel length in branches of American elm by forcing mercury through them under a pressure of 120 millimeters. He found vessels varying in length from 0.5 centimeter to 5.5 meters, the average length of the five longest open vessels in the current year's wood of a branch being 55 per cent of the length of the branch. The vessels in the wood of the preceding year were only 5 to 10 per cent as long as those in a corresponding segment of wood of the current year. Vessels in ring-porous wood usually tend to become blocked by gas bubbles, tyloses, masses of gum, or other stoppages, so that their effective length decreases rapidly and they cease to function in conduction after a year or two.

Cross Section of Stem Involved in Ascent of Sap. The amount of the cross section of a tree involved in water conduction varies widely. In most species a large amount of the xylem becomes heartwood and is no longer involved in conduction and, in fact, has no physiological function whatsoever. Not even all the sapwood is involved actively in conduction, although there is considerable difference in opinion concerning the distribution of the regions actually involved. In at least some species of ring-porous trees, including chestnut, ash, and red oak, water movement is largely confined to the outermost annual ring (Rumbold, 1920; Huber, 1935), although a small amount may occur in the summerwood of the preceding year. In diffuse-porous trees a considerable number of annual

Table 11.1. Apparent length of vessels in trunks of various hardwood trees. (*From Greenidge, 1952.*)

Species	Apparent vessel length, in.		
	Minimum	Maximum	Average
Diffuse-porous species:			
Acer saccharum	32	37	34.7
Betula lutea	34	56	46.8
Fagus grandifolia	192	219	119.1
Populus tremuloides	40	52	47.9
Alnus rugosa	34	48	41.3
			Av. percentage of height of tree through which air passed
Ring-porous species:			
Quercus rubra	336	600	94.8
Fraxinus americana	304	720	97.1
Ulmus americana	204	336	94.6

rings usually are involved in conduction, although it is probable that not all of each ring functions equally, because there naturally is a tendency for water movement through the regions of lowest resistance and the resistance is not uniform throughout the rings. MacDougal et al. (1929) reported upward movement of dyes in concentric columns of summerwood, but this has been questioned by Baker and James (1933) and others. Besides interference by tyloses, a considerable percentage of the total volume of the conducting system is rendered unavailable by accumulation of gases. According to MacDougal (1926), 20 to 40 per cent of the volume of a tree trunk may be occupied by gas. Data obtained by Clark and Gibbs (1957) are shown in Figure 12.2. Perhaps the discontinuities in distribution of dye in stems of root-pruned trees observed by Greenidge (1955) were the result of blockage by gas bubbles, caused by the high moisture stress produced by an inadequate absorbing system.

Effects of Injuries. Fortunately trees seem to have a very large safety factor in their water-conducting system so that reduction of the effective area by 50 per cent or more usually has little or no effect on growth. Although there normally is little lateral or circumferential movement of water in tree trunks, it can occur, compensating for injuries to a part of the conducting system. Auchter (1923) removed the roots from one side of apple, peach, oak, and privet and found that although the water content of the trees as a whole decreased, there was no difference in water content between the side with roots and that without, indicating that the water absorbed on one side was distributed uniformly throughout the top. Furr and Taylor (1939) observed that a water deficit produced by removal of roots on one side of a lemon tree affected the turgor of the fruits on both sides. Jemison (1944) observed that trees in which over 50 per cent of the circumference near the base had been killed by fire made as much growth over the next 10 years as uninjured trees. He also observed that such trees quickly formed new xylem oriented to produce an effective pathway for water around such wounds; hence the trunk above the wound was supplied by lateral conduction for only a short time (Figure 8.6). Disease and insect injuries also often interfere with the ascent of sap. This is discussed in Chapter 16.

Ring-porous versus Diffuse-porous Species. Huber (1935) has an interesting discussion of the significance of ring and diffuse porousness. Ring-porous species of trees have longer vessels of greater diameter than diffuse-porous species and usually have well-developed heartwood, while diffuse-porous species have shorter vessels of smaller diameter and often have no definite heartwood. Huber believes that the most significant difference is in diameter of vessels, because the wider vessels of ring-porous species greatly increase the probability of fracture of the water columns when placed under tension; hence they usually have a short life with respect to conduction. He regards the heartwood formation characteristic of ring-porous species as resulting from the rapid loss of conductive capacity, and formation of new vessels in the spring before leaves appear as a necessary accompaniment of this type of structure.

According to Huber (1935), the ring-porous type of structure seems quite as successful biologically as the diffuse-porous structure. In the dry region of the southern Tyrol ring-porous species predominate. Huber believes that ring porousness could scarcely be successful in evergreens, however, and even the evergreen oaks of the Mediterranean region are diffuse-porous.

It seems obvious that ring-porous trees with their localized conducting systems are usually more susceptible to mechanical injury than diffuse-porous species with a generalized conducting system. What has been said about diffuse-porous species also can be applied to the conifers, where water moves in the tracheids of several annual rings.

Efficiency of Conduction in Xylem. There are two ways of expressing the efficiency of the conducting system. Specific conductivity refers to the volume of water moved per unit of time under a given pressure through a segment of given length and cross section (volume per hour per square centimeter per atmosphere per meter length). The other expression is in terms of relative conducting surface, which is the ratio of conducting surface to transpiring tissue. Vité (1958) claims that the tendency toward spiral orientation of the xylem elements which occurs in many trees improves water distribution to the branches.

Farmer (1918) reported that the specific conductivity of stems of evergreen trees is much lower than that of stems of deciduous species. Huber

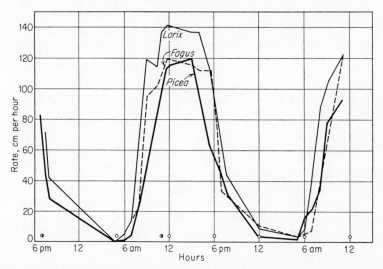

Figure 11.10 Diurnal variations in rate of ascent of sap in beech, larch, and spruce, measured by the thermoelectric method. (*From Schubert, 1939.*)

(1956) gives specific conductivities of 20 for conifers, 65 to 128 for deciduous broadleaf trees, 236 to 1,273 for vines, and even higher values for roots. According to Huber (1928), the specific conductivity of branches and twigs is lower than that of the trunk and the specific conductivity of the trunk decreases from bottom to top. This is compensated for by a considerable increase in relative conducting surface from the base to the top of the trunk. The resistance to water movement is not proportional to the length of the stem because of changes in specific conductivity. The relative conducting surface expressed as square millimeters of xylem per gram of leaf fresh weight increases from 0.02 in an aquatic plant to about 0.50 in trees and 3.4 in nonsucculent desert plants (Huber, 1956).

Huber (1928, 1956) concluded that movement of water through plants is not limited by resistance in the xylem but by the osmotic conductivity or resistance to movement through living cells in the roots and leaves. This conclusion accords with observations that killing the roots greatly increases the rate of water intake with a given pressure difference (Kramer, 1933).

Velocity of Sap Movement. The differences in conductivity between ring- and diffuse-porous species are brought out by measurements of the velocity of the ascent of sap. Some of the measurements have been made by injecting dyes (Greenidge, 1958) or radioactive tracers (Fraser and Mawson, 1953; Moreland, 1950; Kuntz and Riker, 1955). Measurements made by this method suffer from the possibility that the rate in opened xylem is not the same as in undisturbed xylem. Huber (1956) discussed the various methods in more detail. The most reliable measurements seem to be those made by the thermoelectric method devised by Huber and his students (Huber, 1932, 1935; Huber and Schmidt, 1937; Bloodworth et al., 1956). In this method heat is applied to the ascending sap

Table 11.2. Rates of water movement in xylem determined by various methods.

Investigator	Method	Material	Rate
Greenidge (1958)	Acid fuchsin	*Acer saccharum*	1.5–4.5 m per hr
	Acid fuchsin	*Fagus grandifolia*	3.6–4.2 m per hr
	Acid fuchsin	*Ulmus americana*	4.3–15.5 m per hr
Moreland (1950)	P^{32}	*Pinus taeda*	1.2 m per hr max.
Huber and Schmidt (1937)	Thermoelectric method	*Quercus pedunculata*	43.6 m per hr max.
	Thermoelectric method	*Fraxinus excelsior*	25.7 m per hr max.
	Thermoelectric method	*Ulmus effusa*	6.0 m per hr max.
	Thermoelectric method	*Juglans cinerea*	3.79 m per hr max.
	Thermoelectric method	*Liriodendron tulipifera*	2.62 m per hr max.
	Thermoelectric method	Conifers	Less than 0.5 m per hr
Kuntz and Riker (1955)	I^{131}	*Quercus ellipsoidalis*	27.5–60 m per hr max.
	Rb^{86}	*Quercus macrocarpa*	27.5–60 m per hr max.

stream by a small electrical heating element and the time required for the heated water to reach a thermocouple placed in the wood above the heater is measured. Marshall (1958) studied the theory and operation of the thermoelectric method. He concluded that although the sap speed exceeds the speed of the heat pulse, the method is useful for measuring relative rates of sap flow. The velocity at midday in diffuse-porous species

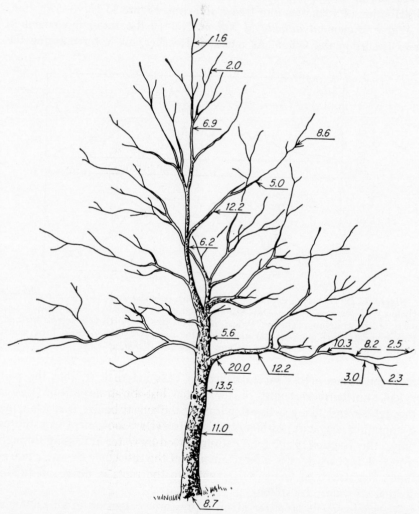

Figure 11.11 Rates of water movement in meters per hour in various parts of an oak tree at midday. The rate decreases toward the top because the relative conductivity (the ratio of xylem to leaf surface) increases. In birch the reverse occurs, the rate increasing toward the top. (*After Huber and Schmidt, 1937; from Huber, 1956.*)

ranged from 1 to 6 meters per hour, while in ring-porous species it was 25 to 60 meters per hour (Table 11.2). These results are what might be expected on the assumption that in ring-porous wood water moves rapidly in only one annual ring while in diffuse-porous species it moves more slowly in a number of annual rings. Movement also is very slow in the nonporous conifers, where a number of annual rings are involved. Diurnal variations in velocity of sap movement are shown in Figure 11.10, and the distribution of velocities in a tree is shown in Figure 11.11.

Water Movement outside of Xylem. Not all the water movement in trees occurs in the xylem. As mentioned earlier, all water entering the

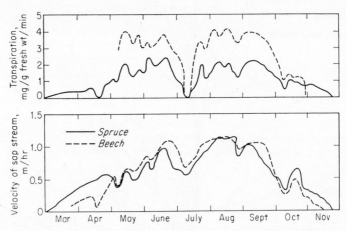

Figure 11.12 Seasonal course of transpiration (above) and rate of ascent of sap (below) of Norway spruce and European beech in Germany. Transpiration was measured by weighing detached twigs; ascent of sap by the thermoelectric method. Measurements were made about noon. Note the decreased rate in early July, which is said to be a normal occurrence. (*From Huber and Plankl, 1956.*)

roots must pass across several layers of cells before it reaches the root xylem. Furthermore, most of the water lost by transpiration passes through several living cells after leaving the xylem before it reaches the evaporating surfaces. Although this extraxylary movement constitutes only a tiny fraction of the total path traversed by water in passing through a tree, it appears to offer a large amount of the resistance to water movement. Resistance to water movement into the roots is discussed in the section on water absorption.

Mass movement of water along a pressure or tension gradient might occur through the cell walls as well as through the protoplasts. According to Butler (1953), 15 or 20 per cent of the water in wheat roots occurs in the cell walls. This suggests that the walls afford a pathway for the movement of considerable amounts of water and solutes. The relative amounts of water moving through the walls and across the protoplasts depend on the relative resistance in the two paths as well as on their relative areas. It has been shown that the protoplasm offers more resistance than the walls to water movement, because killing the protoplasm results in an increase in rate of water movement into roots, both by diffusion (Ordin and Kramer, 1956) and by mass flow (Kramer, 1933). It seems that there is less resistance to water movement through the walls than across the protoplasts. Therefore, in spite of the fact that the walls constitute a relatively small amount of the cross-section area, they may function as a pathway for the movement of significant amounts of water and solutes in both roots and leaves.

GENERAL REFERENCES

Dixon, H. H., 1924, The transpiration stream, University of London Press, Ltd., London.

Greenidge, K. N. H., 1957, Ascent of sap, Ann. Rev. Plant Physiology, 8:237–256.

Kramer, P. J., 1949, Plant and soil water relationships, McGraw-Hill Book Company, Inc., New York.

MacDougal, D. T., J. B. Overton, and G. M. Smith, 1929, The hydrostatic-pneumatic system of certain trees, Carnegie Inst. Washington Pub. 397.

Meyer, B. S., and D. B. Anderson, 1952, Plant physiology, chaps. 12–14, D. Van Nostrand Company, Inc., Princeton, N.J.

Ruhland, W. (ed.), 1956, Encyclopedia of plant physiology, vol. 3, Water relations of plants, O. Stocker (subed.), Springer-Verlag, Berlin.

CHAPTER 12 *Internal Water Relations*

The most important aspect of plant-water relations is the internal water balance, as indicated by the turgidity of cells and tissues. All the other processes considered in connection with water relations are important chiefly because they affect the internal water relations of trees and thereby modify the physiological processes and conditions which affect growth.

Various attempts have been made to coin terms which will express our concern with the internal water relations. Such terms as "water balance" and "water economy" emphasize the fact that internal water relations may be regarded somewhat like a budget in which water content (balance) is controlled by the relative rates of water absorption (income) and water loss (expenditures). Some physiologists have preferred to emphasize the condition of the water (Wasserzustand) in the plant, and Walter (1931) used the term *Hydratur* to describe the condition of water in plants as measured by its vapor pressure or osmotic pressure. Such terms as "suction force," "diffusion-pressure deficit," and "specific free energy" also represent efforts to evaluate the condition of the water in plants.

Another method of evaluating the internal water balance of a tree is in terms of its "saturation deficit" (Stocker, 1929) or its "relative turgidity" (Weatherley, 1950). These terms describe the actual water content of plants or plant parts relative to what it would be if the tissues were fully hydrated. If it is assumed that the healthiest tree is one in which the tissues are most nearly fully hydrated, this method gives a good indication of the state of the internal water balance. This approach will be discussed later.

Water Content of Various Parts of a Tree

Over 50 per cent of the total fresh weight of a tree consists of water, but the water concentration varies widely in different parts of a tree and also with species, age, site, season, and even the time of day. Although

342

the heartwood usually has the lowest water content, it often contains over 100 per cent on a dry-weight basis, and the sapwood of some species may contain up to 250 per cent (Gibbs, 1935). The water content of leaves varies with species, age, and season. Korstian (1933) reported leaf moisture contents ranging from 56 to 65 per cent of fresh weight in loblolly pine and from 52 per cent in 1-year-old leaves to 78 per cent in newly formed leaves of southern magnolia.

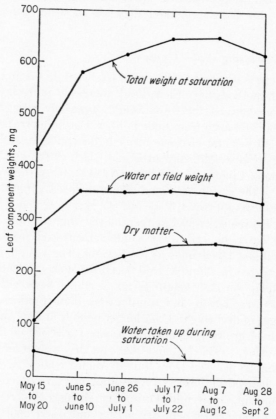

Figure 12.1 Seasonal changes in dry matter and water content of pear leaves in milligrams per leaf; also amount of water taken up during saturation and saturated weight. (*From Ackley, 1954a.*)

The highest water contents usually occur in growing regions such as the cambium, root and stem tips, and young fruits. Over 90 per cent of the fresh weight of young tips of loblolly pine roots consists of water. Such tissues consist largely of highly hydrated protoplasm and vacuoles enclosed in very thin, highly hydrated cell walls. As tissues mature, the increase in solid matter in the cell walls usually more than compensates for the increased amount of water in vacuoles, resulting in decrease in water content on a percentage basis. For example, Ackley (1954a) found the 6 A.M. water content of pear leaves to decrease from 73 per cent of their fresh weight in May to 59 per cent in August, although individual leaves actually contained a greater weight of water in August than in May (Figure 12.1). The water content of young poplar shoots in June was about twice that of 2-year-old shoots, but by September the water content of the maturing shoots was lower than that of the old ones (Butin, 1957). Seeds also show a marked decrease in water content as they mature.

Methods of Expressing Water Content

Water content is expressed either on a fresh-weight or on a dry-weight basis, but both methods have their disadvantages. The fresh-weight basis is unsatisfactory because the fresh weight, especially in leaves, changes from day to day and even from hour to hour. Furthermore, large changes in water content per unit of tissue result in deceptively small changes in percentage of fresh weight. As Curtis and Clark (1950, p. 259) show in discussing data of Livingston and Brown (1912), when the water content of the leaves of the shrub *Nicotiana glauca* decreased from 85 to 80 per cent on a fresh-weight basis, they lost 25 grams of water per original 100 grams of leaf tissue, or 29.4 per cent of the original water content. On a dry-weight basis the leaf water content decreased from 566 to 400 per cent, assuming no change in dry weight. The reader might check these figures to see for himself how deceptive such calculations can be.

Unfortunately, the dry weight is not a stable basis either, because photosynthesis, respiration, and translocation often produce measurable diurnal changes in dry weight. Over longer periods of time large increases in dry weight of growing tissues can occur as a result of thickening of cell walls. Ackley (1954a) found that the dry weight of pear leaves increased about 25 per cent from June to August while the water content remained unchanged (Figure 12.1), resulting in a large decrease in water content per unit of dry weight. Ordinarily, changes in percentage water content reflect changes in both dry matter and water content, although changes in the latter usually are much larger.

Miller (1917) expressed the moisture content of corn and sorghum leaves on the bases of dry weight, fresh weight, and leaf area. The trends on the fresh-weight and leaf area basis were similar to those on a dry-weight basis, but showed smaller differences. Unfortunately, leaf area also changes with water content, so it is not a uniform basis. Mason and Maskell (1928) and Denny (1932) attempted to reduce fluctuations in the base for calculating changes in water content and other constituents by using what they termed "residual dry weight." This was obtained by extracting the leaves in dilute HCl to remove the easily hydrolyzable materials, leaving the relatively inert cell walls and other resistant constituents. This decreases hour-to-hour variations caused by photosynthesis, respiration, and translocation, but does not eliminate long-term changes caused by increase in thickness of cell walls, as shown by Weatherley (1950). Obviously, there is no entirely satisfactory basis for calculating water content, and investigators, in interpreting their data, should remember the shortcomings of the method they use.

Water Content of Tree Trunks

By far the largest part of the water in a tree occurs in the trunk, but even in this relatively inactive structure the water content varies from bottom to top and from outside to inside. Luxford (1930) reported that the water content of the heartwood of redwood is highest at the base and lower toward the top, but the water content of the sapwood is just the reverse, being lowest at the base and highest toward the top. The combination of high water content of heartwood and high density of wood found in butt logs often results in their failure to float. Ito (1955) found that *Castanea crenata* trunks had the highest water content at the base, but in *Pinus densiflora* the water content was lowest at the base and increased upward. According to Ovington (1956a), the water content usually increases from base to top in trees, the increase being greatest in conifers.

In those trees whose heartwood is well differentiated the water content of the heartwood usually is considerably lower than that of the sapwood, but Gibbs (1939) reported that although the heartwoods of jack pine and white spruce always are very dry, those of balsam fir and hemlock often contain wet areas with a water content higher than that of the sapwood.

Hickory is exceptional because its heartwood consistently contains a higher concentration of water than its sapwood. Smith and Goebel (1952) sampled six species and found that the sapwood averaged 50 per cent water while the heartwood contained 70 per cent or more. There were no significant differences among the species and no definite seasonal trends, hence no advantage in cutting hickory at any particular season. Attempts to reduce the water content by "leaf seasoning" or leaving the top and its leaves attached for a time after felling were unsuccessful, although this method works well with some species. As a result of the peculiar distribution of water, hickory logs and lumber are difficult to season because of a tendency to split.

Seasonal Variations in Water Content of Wood. Large seasonal variations occur in the water content of the wood of most trees. These are not only interesting physiologically but also are important economically because they affect the rate of drying, flotation of logs, and the cost of transport. Logs of some species are so heavy at the season when they contain maximum water content that they float poorly and cannot be transported by water. The largest variations in water content occur in hardwoods, but some variations also occur in conifers, especially in the sapwood.

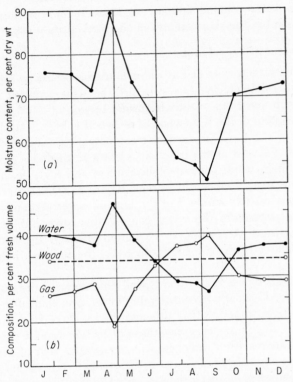

Figure 12.2 *a.* Seasonal changes in water content of yellow birch tree trunks calculated as percentage of dry weight from discs cut from the base, middle, and top of the trunks. *b.* Seasonal changes in gas and water content of yellow birch trunks calculated as percentages of total volume. (*From Clark and Gibbs, 1957.*)

An extensive study of the water content of the wood of various tree species was made by Gibbs in eastern Canada (Gibbs, 1935, 1939, 1950, 1958; Clark and Gibbs, 1957). The typical seasonal pattern, at least for diffuse-porous species, is that of birch, shown in Figure 12.2. In general, in eastern Canada, tree trunks attain their highest water content in the spring, just before the leaves open. The water content decreases during the summer to a minimum just before leaf fall as a result of heavy loss in transpiration, then increases again during the autumn after leaf fall greatly reduces transpiration. Most species show another decrease during the winter, presumably because cold soil hinders water absorption, and an increase after the soil thaws. This is typical of the birches, cottonwood, crack willow, and some aspens, but many aspens reach their maximum water content in the autumn instead of waiting until spring. White ash and American elm show no autumn increase, their water content remaining low all winter and increasing rapidly in the spring to a maximum at the time buds are opening. Silver maple and beech in contrast attain their maximum water content in late autumn, and silver maple shows some increase in the spring after a winter decrease, but beech is unique among all the species studied in showing no spring increase in water content. Twigs of several species of walnuts showed a large increase in

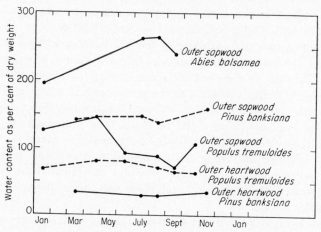

Figure 12.3 Seasonal variations in water content of heartwood and sapwood of several tree species. (*From Gibbs, 1935.*)

water content after leaf fall, but the two species of hickory studied did not, and *Pterocarya*, which taxonomically is closer to *Juglans* than to *Carya*, behaved like the former.

Gibbs's data (1935) indicate that jack pine, white spruce, and balsam fir undergo much smaller variations in water content than the deciduous species studied (Figure 12.3). Hemlock heartwood undergoes little change in water content, but the sapwood shows variations similar to those of birch and poplar. The sapwood of hemlock is so narrow, however, that these variations have little effect on the water content of the tree as a whole. According to Gibbs, R. Hartig and Münch reported definite seasonal changes in water content of European conifers. Ito (1955) reported from Japan that there are larger seasonal variations in water content of the wood of *Pinus densiflora* than in *Castanea crenata*, the minimum occurring in August in both species. Haasis (1933) reported a decrease in diameter of conifer trunks during dry weather, which presumably resulted from decrease in water content.

There are relatively few reliable data on water content of trees in other parts of the world, but Gibbs's results for birch are in general agreement with those of Hartig, as given by Büsgen and Münch (1931). Craib (1918) also presented considerable data. It seems probable that the general picture given here holds for all trees of the Temperate Zone, at least to the extent that the minimum water content occurs at the end of the summer and the maximum either in late autumn or more commonly during the early spring.

The summer decrease in water content is the natural result of an unfavorable water balance during periods of rapid transpiration. As a deficit develops in the leaves and the resulting tension is transmitted through the hydrostatic system, the less firmly held portion of the water in the trunk is removed. Apparently the wet patches which occur in the heartwood of balsam fir and hemlock are not available as reserve water, however, because they do not disappear during the summer. The upper parts of birch trunks contain a lower percentage of water in the winter and a higher percentage in the summer than the middle or base of the trunk. The same situation exists in aspen. The outermost rings at the bases of these trees had about the same water content as the tops, probably because the twigs are connected to the outer annual rings. Gibbs (1939) found no evidence of water movement into gray birch during January and February, and there was surprisingly little loss of water at this season.

Diurnal Variations in Water Content. Diurnal variations in water content of tree trunks were reported by Hartig and other early investigators. Gibbs (1935) found that the maximum water content occurs at or before sunrise, the content decreasing during the morning and middle of the day and rising in the late afternoon and evening. An example of such variations is shown in Table 12.1. The diurnal fluctuations in stem diameter

Table 12.1. Diurnal variations in water content of wood in birch trunks. (*From Gibbs*, 1935, *table* 13.)

	August 24			August 25		
Time	5 A.M.	1 P.M.	7 P.M.	5 A.M.	1 P.M.	7 P.M.
Weather	Clear	Clear, hot	Clear	Clear	Slightly overcast	Clear
Water content as per cent of dry weight	65	54	58	59	50	53

reported by MacDougal (1938) and others may also be considered as evidence of changes in water content as well as tension (Figure 15.2).

Variations in Water Content of Leaves

The leaves of most trees show a daily cycle in water content, even when growing in moist soil. Generally the minimum water content occurs in early afternoon or about the time of maximum transpiration, but the maximum water content often occurs near the middle of the night and decreases again toward morning, as shown in Figure 12.4. Maximum water content would be expected toward morning, and no explanation is available for this peculiar behavior, which has been observed in several species, unless translocation of water from leaves to other organs occurs,

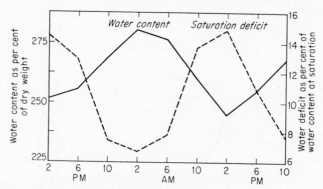

Figure 12.4 Diurnal variations in water content and water deficit (= relative turgidity) of pear leaves. (*From Ackley, 1954a.*)

perhaps as a result of redistribution of carbohydrates in the plant during the night.

Seasonal changes in water content of leaves also occur, the water content usually decreasing toward the end of the growing season. This trend is shown for pear leaves in Figure 12.5, but Ackley (1954a) points out that the apparent reduction in water content is not caused by reduced content per leaf but by increased dry-matter content, as shown by Figure 12.1. Gibbs (1939, table 8) summarized some data on water content of the twigs and leaves of several conifers, which also indicate a decrease in water content with increasing age of the twigs and leaves.

More or less characteristic species differences exist in water content. According to Meyer (1927), the leaves of woody plants usually have a lower water content than the leaves of herbaceous species, but the osmotic pressure of the cell sap is higher in woody plants.

Wilting. A frequent result of the midday decrease in water content is temporary wilting of leaves and succulent stems. Three degrees of wilting are recognized: incipient, temporary, and permanent.

Incipient Wilting. This condition refers to decrease in water content too small to produce visible loss of turgor. It occurs when water loss barely exceeds water intake and the water content of leaves and other

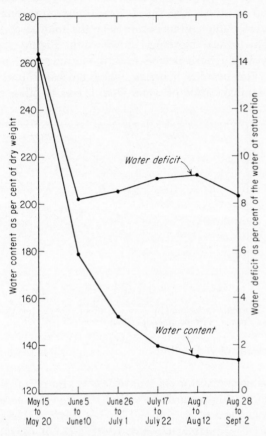

Figure 12.5 Seasonal change in water content expressed as percentage of dry weight and in water deficit of pear leaves. Most of the apparent decrease in water content results from seasonal increase in dry weight of leaves, as shown in Figure 12.1. (*From Ackley, 1954a.*)

structures decreases slightly. Incipient wilting also involves partial drying of the walls of the mesophyll cells by retreat of the water menisci into the submicroscopic pores, resulting in decreased vapor pressure and lowered evaporation of water. This may explain the tendency of transpiration to lag behind evaporation from a free-water surface although closure of stomates probably is a much more important factor.

Temporary Wilting. Incipient wilting probably occurs daily in weather favorable for transpiration, and when transpiration is rapid it often progresses into temporary wilting, in which visible drooping of leaves and succulent shoots occurs. Leaves wilt first, but the water deficit usually spreads throughout the plant, resulting in wilting of young twigs, shrinkage of fruits, reduction in water content of trunks, and development of tension in the hydrostatic system. Most of the structure of trees contains so much lignified tissue that visible wilting does not occur, regardless of the magnitude of the water deficit developed. Plants recover from temporary wilting overnight or whenever transpiration falls sufficiently below absorption for the water deficit to be eliminated.

Permanent Wilting. This is the condition in which plants cannot recover turgidity unless water is added to the soil. Temporary wilting gradually progresses into permanent wilting because as the soil dries out, absorption becomes slower and slower and the plants remain wilted longer and longer each day, until finally they fail to regain turgor overnight. Some shallow-rooted deciduous trees such as dogwood may remain wilted for many days during late summer droughts. Permanent wilting naturally interferes seriously with numerous physiological processes and usually stops growth completely. Eventually it causes death from desiccation. Some of its effects will be discussed later under drought injury.

Obviously, even in leaves, the degree of wilting cannot be regarded as a reliable indication of the amount of water lost or the severity of the water deficit because leaves of many trees contain so much lignified tissue that even when the parenchyma cells lose their turgor, little or no visible change in form occurs. Even in leaves containing little lignified tissue, differences exist in the amount of water which must be lost before wilting occurs. In some shade species wilting occurs when only 3 to 5 per cent of the total water is lost, while certain sun species lose 20 to 30 per cent of their water content before wilting visibly (Maximov, 1929).

Occurrence of leaf water deficits usually causes measurable decrease in area and thickness of leaves. Closure of stomates also occurs, and in those species with heavily cutinized leaves this hinders entrance of carbon dioxide and reduces photosynthesis.

Variations in Osmotic Quantities. Closely associated with the daily variations in water content of leaves are variations in osmotic pressure and diffusion-pressure deficit. Few data are available on diurnal variations in these quantities in trees, but they have been studied extensively in herbaceous plants. Osmotic pressure tends to increase during the day, both because decreasing water content increases the concentration of the cell sap and because photosynthesis adds to the concentration of solutes. The diffusion-pressure deficit (DPD) of the plant sap tends to vary over a much wider range than the osmotic pressure. In fully turgid plants the

DPD approaches zero, but as transpiration removes water, the concentration of the cell sap increases and cell volume and wall pressure decrease, causing rapid increase in DPD. If transpiration materially exceeds absorption, the resulting tension in the hydrostatic system may exceed the osmotic pressure of the cell sap, causing the DPD to become greater than the osmotic pressure. Chu (1936) claims that the DPD of tree leaves depends more on the tension in the water-conducting system than on the osmotic pressure of their cell sap.

Several investigators have followed seasonal changes in osmotic pressure because of its possible relation to cold and drought resistance. Korstian (1924) found the osmotic pressure of the leaf sap to be highest in those tree species growing in soil with the lowest moisture supply. He also reported that plants with high water contents usually had low osmotic pressures, and vice versa. Stanfield (1932) found a correlation between rate of evaporation from atmometers and osmotic pressure in pine needles in Colorado, but no correlation of osmotic pressure with soil moisture. He observed lowest osmotic pressures (13 atmospheres) in January and the highest in July (16.7 atmospheres). Walter (1951, p. 285) reported little difference between the osmotic pressure of needles of various conifer species growing on very dry and very moist sites and cites similar unpublished data of Pisek for spruce in Europe. Gail and Cone (1929) measured the osmotic pressure of ponderosa pine needles at monthly intervals in northern Idaho and found the highest values in December (25 to 30 atmospheres) and the lowest values in July (8 to 15 atmospheres). The osmotic pressure of first-year needles was lower than that of 3- or 5-year-old needles. Meyer (1928), working in Ohio, found the osmotic pressure of sap expressed from pitch pine needles to be higher in the winter than in the summer. Slatyer (1957b) has interesting data on the osmotic pressure, diffusion-pressure deficit, and relative-turgidity changes in *Ligustrum* during drying of the soil (Figure 15.1).

Walter (1951) presents an extensive collection of data on osmotic values of various plants and plant parts from all over the world.

Relative Turgidity. It is obvious that measurements of leaf water content alone do not indicate whether or not a favorable water balance exists in leaves and other tissues. Measurements of the diffusion-pressure deficit give a better indication, but reliable measurements are difficult. If it is assumed that a fully turgid plant is in the most satisfactory condition for growth and other physiological processes, then comparison of water content of the growing plant under field conditions with its water content when fully turgid should be a good indicator of internal water conditions. Two methods of doing this have been described, one by Stocker (1929), the other by Weatherley (1950).

Stocker's method, which has been used extensively in ecological studies, measures what he terms the "saturation deficit." This is the actual water content expressed as a percentage of the water content of the plant tissue when fully hydrated. To measure the saturation deficit, cut shoots or leaves are weighed carefully, placed in containers of water, and the stems or petioles are recut to eliminate plugging of vessels by air bubbles. They are then kept in a closed chamber at 100 per cent relative humidity until they attain equilibrium. This may require 2 or 3 days. The fully turgid tissue is again weighed, dried to constant weight, and the saturation deficit calculated as follows:

$$\frac{\text{Saturated weight} - \text{original weight}}{\text{Saturated weight} - \text{oven-dry weight}} \times 100 = \text{saturation deficit, \%}$$

Saturation deficits of leaves of several species of oak growing in soil near permanent wilting are shown in Table 12.2, and diurnal variations

Table 12.2. Saturation deficits of leaves of various species of oak growing in soil allowed to dry down to the permanent-wilting percentage. (*From Bourdeau,* 1954.)

Species	Saturation deficit, %
Chestnut oak	1.65
White oak	2.16
Northern red oak	4.84
Scarlet oak	5.23
Black oak	9.50
Southern red oak	15.66
Post oak	20.60
Blackjack oak	25.04

of the water deficit in pear leaves are shown in Figure 12.4. Seasonal changes in water deficits of pear leaves are shown in Figure 12.5.

Weatherley (1950) developed a method for measuring what he termed "relative turgidity," which can be expressed as follows:

$$\frac{\text{Original fresh weight} - \text{dry weight}}{\text{Fresh weight when fully turgid} - \text{dry weight}} \times 100 = \text{relative turgidity}$$

This usually can be determined by cutting discs of tissue about 1 centimeter in diameter out of leaves, weighing them, floating them on water in a closed container until they attain constant weight, reweighing, and oven-drying to obtain their dry weight. This method is relatively rapid, since the leaf discs usually attain full turgidity in a few hours, but care must be taken to make certain that the intercellular spaces of the leaf discs do not become injected with water. Some material such as pine needles cannot be floated on water, and the needles must be placed with their bases in water in a closed container to attain saturation (Rutter and Sands, 1958). The effects of decreasing soil moisture on relative turgidity of privet leaves is shown in Figures 15.1 and 16.12.

Causes of Variations in Water Content

The chief cause of diurnal and seasonal variations in water content is the lag of water absorption behind water loss. This is shown in Figure 11.9, from experiments in which the rates of absorption and of transpiration were measured simultaneously for loblolly pine and ash seedlings growing in pots of soil supplied with water by autoirrigators. The details of the apparatus are described elsewhere (Kramer, 1937a). Water deficits develop in plants because water loss exceeds water absorption. This often occurs even in plants in moist soil because of excessively rapid water loss on hot sunny days, but it usually is more severe when absorption is slowed down by lack of available water, low temperature, too concentrated a soil solution, or an inadequate root system.

In general, transpiration increases rapidly during the period after sunrise when the stomates open and rising temperatures increase the steepness of the vapor-pressure gradient from the intercellular spaces to the outside air. Absorption does not begin to increase, however, until the DPD or pull developed in the leaf cells by water loss is transmitted through the water in the xylem to the absorbing surfaces of the roots. Furthermore, the pull in the leaves must build up to a value high enough to overcome the friction in the water-conducting system and cause movement of water from soil to roots, a discussion of which will follow in the next section. This takes considerable time, during which an increasing water deficit develops in the top. Such deficits often become large enough to cause temporary wilting. Late in the afternoon as the temperature drops and stomates close, transpiration decreases rapidly but water absorption continues until the diffusion-pressure deficit of the plant is eliminated. This may require all night, and in dry soil the plant even then may not be saturated; hence some water absorption continues even in the early morning hours when negligible water loss is occurring.

The Absorption Lag

The existence of such a well-defined lag of absorption behind transpiration, even in plants growing in moist soil, indicates that there is considerable resistance to the absorption of water and its translocation to the leaves. This may be located in three places: (1) where water moves across the cells intervening between soil and root xylem, (2) in the xylem system of the tree, and (3) in the cells which occur between the final xylem elements of the leaf veins and the evaporating surfaces.

Some evidence is available which helps in evaluating the relative importance of the resistance in these three parts of the conducting system. Wilson and Livingston (1937) compared the duration of the absorption lag in willow cuttings with long and short stems and concluded that not over 16 per cent of the lag could be attributed to stem resistance in the willows with the longest stems. In general, it appears that relatively little of the resistance to water movement resides in the xylem, but there is good evidence that considerable resistance occurs in the roots. For example, removal of the roots decreased the lag period about 50 per cent in tomato and sunflower plants. In other experiments stems of sunflower plants were attached to a vacuum pump while the root systems were immersed in water. The rate of water movement was measured with a constant pressure difference, the roots were cut off, and the rate of movement again measured at the same pressure difference. The rate of water movement through the stems was 80 times as great as before the roots were removed (Kramer, 1938). In other experiments there was a very large increase in water movement with a constant pressure gradient when the roots were killed (Kramer, 1933; Renner, 1929).

Resistance to water movement undoubtedly occurs in the leaves (Mer, 1940; Wylie, 1938), but it appears to be much smaller than in roots. This is chiefly because most of the parenchyma cells of leaves are separated from the xylem elements by only a few cells, but in most roots water must pass across a considerable number of cells in order to reach the xylem elements. The resistance to water movement seems to be localized largely in the living protoplasm rather than in the walls, because killing the roots results in a large increase in permeability to water. Apparently this is not equally true of all tissues because Ordin and Bonner (1956) found that living cells of oat coleoptiles were no less permeable to water than dead cells, suggesting that most of the resistance to water movement occurs in the walls of this tissue. Ordin and Kramer (1956) found, however, that dead root cells of *Vicia faba* were six times as permeable to diffusion of water as living ones, which agrees in general terms with results obtained with entire root systems (Kramer, 1933; Brouwer, 1954).

Under some circumstances the absorption lag results from lack of an adequate absorbing surface (Figure 12.6). Wilting of recently transplanted trees and shrubs is an obvious example, and their tops are often pruned in order to bring their transpiring surfaces into a more satisfactory ratio with root systems reduced in extent by transplanting. Aldrich and Work (1934) found that when the ratio of root surface to leaf surface of pear was increased by removing part of the leaves, the midday water deficit in the fruits and remaining leaves was reduced; but when the ratio was decreased by removal of some roots, the internal water deficit was increased (Figure 12.6). Nutman (1934) concluded that absorption of water by coffee trees is limited by the extent of their root systems. This probably is true in the sense that if the roots offer the major resistance to the entrance of water, then the more extensive the absorbing surface the greater the quantity of water which can be absorbed per unit of time. Nevertheless, most trees can survive removal of a considerable fraction of their root system without permanent injury, although internal

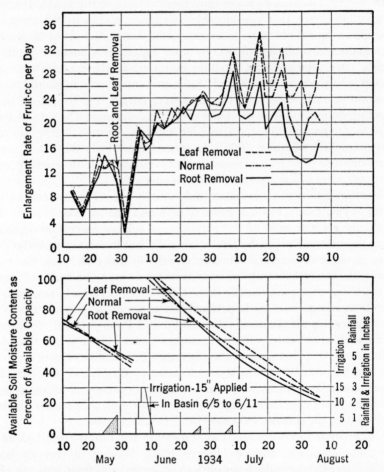

Figure 12.6 Effects on enlargement of pear fruits of changing the ratio of root surface to leaf surface. As the moisture content of the soil was reduced, the fruit on trees from which one-fifth of the roots had been removed showed greatest reduction in rate of enlargement. Fruit on trees from which one-fifth of the leaves had been removed showed least reduction in growth. (*From Kramer, 1949, after Aldrich and Work, 1934.*)

water deficits must be considerably increased by such decreases in absorbing surface.

Occasionally poor aeration or other injury reduces the absorbing surfaces so drastically that severe injury results to the top. There is some evidence that dieback of Monterey pine plantations in Australia, brown top of loblolly pine in North Carolina, pole blight of western white pine, birch dieback, and various "decline" diseases of trees in other regions may be caused in part by internal water deficits resulting from injury to root systems by poor aeration and other soil factors. This probably also is a factor in the littleleaf disease of shortleaf pine in the southeastern United States. Roots of trees of some species such as birch and shortleaf pine are more sensitive than those of other species to unfavorable environmental conditions, making them more susceptible to injury. This is discussed further in the section on the structural basis of drought resistance.

Internal Competition for Water

During the growing season the various parts of a tree usually are in competition with one another for water. If a tree in well-watered soil were surrounded by a saturated atmosphere, then it might be expected to become turgid throughout its structure and water movement would be negligible, but such a static condition seldom exists. Transpiration, changes in turgor and concentration of solutes, and growth produce changes in the relative diffusion-pressure deficits of various tissues, which cause more or less continual redistribution of water in trees.

In well-watered plants differences in diffusion-pressure deficit usually are small, but if a large water deficit develops, as when the soil begins to dry, competition occurs among the various tissues and those which can develop the highest diffusion-pressure deficits obtain water at the expense of those having lower diffusion-pressure deficits. For example, young leaves usually obtain water at the expense of older leaves and the latter die first during droughts. Shaded leaves also often die from desiccation during drought because they cannot develop as high diffusion-pressure deficits as unshaded leaves which are manufacturing more carbohydrates. Growing regions usually can obtain water at the expense of other tissues, probably largely because of their high imbibitional forces. Thus although the youngest leaves on a plant may wilt first, they usually are the last to die in plants suffering from drought. Wilson (1948c) found that stem tips continued to elongate even when the older parts were shrinking during the middle of the day. This indicated that the stem tips were obtaining water even though the older parts of the stem were losing it.

Leaves and Fruits. Best known, perhaps, is the competition between leaves and fruits. In general, the growth rate of fruits decreases when water deficits develop in trees (Figure 12.7), because leaves are able to develop larger diffusion-pressure deficits than fruits. Bartholomew (1926) observed shrinkage in lemons during the hours of rapid transpiration and increase in size at night, but when transpiration was very high for many days the fruits failed to recover overnight. Rokach (1953) found that water transfer from fruits to leaves of oranges did not occur in very young fruits but began when the fruits were about 35 millimeters in diameter. This agrees with the observation of Anderson and Kerr (1943) that leaves were unable to remove water from young cotton bolls, but older bolls showed the expected daily shrinkage caused by loss of water to transpiring leaves. Furr and Taylor (1939) concluded that decrease in growth rate of lemon fruits is a good indicator of development of a water stress in the trees. Hendrickson and Veihmeyer (1941) found that Bartlett pears increased in size from 6 P.M. to 8 A.M. but decreased slightly in size during the day. Growth of apples decreases when water deficits develop in the trees (Magness et al., 1935), and this probably is true of most fruits.

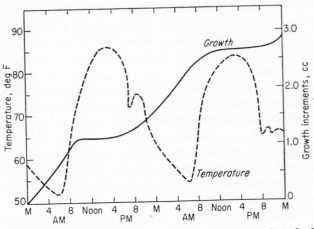

Figure 12.7 Diurnal variations in the rate of enlargement of apple fruit caused by midday water deficits. (*Redrawn from Harley and Masure, 1938.*)

Upper and Lower Branches. Death of the shaded lower branches of trees in closed stands appears to be related to their inability to compete with the exposed upper branches for water. The exact mechanism has never been completely worked out, but apparently the reduced light intensity decreases photosynthesis, resulting in lower concentration of solutes, lower osmotic forces, and decreased ability to compete for water with branches carrying on photosynthesis more actively. The relative importance of carbohydrate and water deficits in heavily shaded lower branches deserves further study.

In a certain sense all the branches of a tree compete with each other for water and the branches compete collectively with the roots. Water moves toward the top only when a diffusion-pressure gradient exists;

hence the leaves are supplied with water only when a higher diffusion-pressure deficit is developed in them than in the roots or in the soil surrounding the roots. As mentioned earlier, younger leaves and branches often seem able to obtain water at the expense of lower branches, but Baker (1950) mentions situations where water seems to become limiting to the tops of tall trees, resulting in decrease in growth and an unthrifty condition. It also was mentioned earlier that damage to root systems often results in dieback of the tops. The upper part of the crown probably suffers most severely because it is more exposed and is therefore subjected to higher water deficits.

Effects of Water Deficits

Almost every process of a tree is affected directly or indirectly by the occurrence of a water deficit in its tissues. Even the leaves of trees growing in moist soil are subjected to temporary water deficits on sunny days. Stocker (1935), for example, found appreciable water deficits occurring in leaves in the crowns of trees growing in the rain forests of Java. During droughts severe deficits often develop and persist for days or weeks, resulting in serious disturbance of many physiological processes and conditions. The over-all effect of internal water deficits is to reduce vegetative growth, but this is brought about both directly and indirectly. For example, growth is reduced both directly by loss of cell turgor and indirectly by closure of stomates, which often reduces the supply of carbon dioxide for photosynthesis.

Water deficits not only reduce the quantity of growth, but also change the quality, largely by increasing the amount of lignification and thickness of cell walls. Increased severity of internal water deficits may be an important factor in producing smaller, thicker walled cells in the wood laid down in the summer than in the earlywood. Water deficits also produce changes in chemical composition. Some of the effects of water deficits on plant processes have already been discussed in connection with the processes. Other effects are discussed in Chapters 15 and 16 in connection with effects of environmental factors on growth. The reader is also referred to Kramer (1949), Richards and Wadleigh (1952), and Volume 3 of the Encyclopedia of Plant Physiology for further discussion of effects of water deficits on physiological processes.

Drought Resistance

The most common cause of internal water deficits severe enough to limit growth is lack of available soil moisture, usually termed "drought." The causes of differences in susceptibility to drought are of considerable interest and importance.

As Parker (1956b) pointed out, there is no single satisfactory definition of drought nor is there general agreement concerning the causes of drought resistance. Ordinarily drought is thought of as a deficiency of available soil moisture which results in water deficits in plants severe enough to reduce plant growth. Although drought usually is associated with low soil moisture, its injurious effects often are greatly increased by atmospheric factors, such as low humidity, high temperature, and wind, which favor high rates of transpiration and increase the severity of internal water deficits. In general, however, deficient soil moisture is by far the most common cause of internal water deficits. Compton (1936), for example, found that at Riverside, California, wind and high temperature produced relatively small increases in saturation deficit in citrus trees growing in moist soil compared with those in trees in dry soil. Schimper (1898) introduced the term "physiological drought" to explain special instances where water deficits develop because cold soil or high osmotic pressure of the soil solution interferes with water absorption, but Walter (1951) excludes osmotic effects from this category.

It should be remembered that drought itself is an environmental condition which produces internal water deficits that interfere with physiological processes, causing reduction in growth or even death by dehydration. The effects of drought on physiological processes have been discussed in earlier chapters and will be taken up in Chapters 15 and 16; hence in this section we shall discuss principally the reasons for differences among species in resistance to drought.

The Nature of Drought Resistance. The causes of differences in drought resistance have been debated energetically for over half a century, and we still find considerable differences in opinion and terminology (Levitt, 1951; Parker, 1956b; Stocker, 1956). The earliest view seems to have been that drought-resistant plants have low rates of water loss, but Maximov (1929) and others attacked this concept because they found that many xerophytes transpire rapidly when well supplied with water. Emphasis then moved toward the idea that ability to endure dehydration is the primary factor in drought resistance (for example, Iljin, 1930, 1933, 1953; Maximov, 1929), and the possible control of water loss by structural and physiological factors was largely disregarded. At present there seems to be a trend toward a more reasonable viewpoint which admits that numerous factors are involved in drought resistance, including those which postpone dehydration, such as efficiency of the absorbing surface and the water-conducting system, leaf area, leaf structure, stomatal behavior, and osmotic pressure, and those which enable the plant to survive dehydration, such as cell size and shape and protoplasmic characteristics.

Perhaps in dealing with the tree as a whole we can differentiate between various kinds or degrees of drought resistance, as follows:

1. Plants which cannot endure drought at all, but are severely injured

or die as soon as soil moisture becomes deficient. Few or no woody plants occur in this category.

2. Plants such as the succulents which store large amounts of water and have very low water loss because of their small surface-to-volume ratio, thick cutin, and few stomates. The protoplasm of these plants usually is not very resistant to dehydration. There are relatively few trees in this category.

3. Plants which are truly drought-enduring in the sense that their protoplasm can be dehydrated without permanent injury, such as many ferns, mosses, and lichens. A few woody species, such as *Larrea* and various other desert shrubs and trees, belong to this group, although it is doubtful if any trees can be dehydrated to the extent of various nonwoody plants.

4. Plants with protoplasm having some capacity to endure dehydration, combined with morphological and anatomical characteristics which decrease the rate of water loss and postpone the development of critical internal water deficits. Most of the drought-resistant trees fall in this category (Oppenheimer, 1951).

Structural Basis of Drought Resistance. Among the general structural characteristics which postpone the development of internal water deficits and therefore delay the occurrence of drought injury are deep, widespreading root systems, an efficient conducting system, a small transpiring surface in proportion to root surface, reduction in leaf area when water deficit develops, thick layers of cutin, and few or deeply embedded stomates.

Root Systems. The importance of development of a deep root system for survival of tree seedlings has long been recognized by foresters, and much attention has been given to differences in initial root habit as a cause of differences in survival of various species (Haig, 1936; Holch, 1931; Toumey, 1929). Baldcypress and yellow birch, for example, can become established only in moist areas because their shallow roots do not enable them to survive summer drought, whereas most upland species have deep taproots which enable them to survive droughts, even during the first year or two. The failure of pine seedlings to survive under forest stands where hardwood seedlings survive can be attributed at least in part to their shallower root systems, which make them more susceptible to death during summer drought (Coile, 1940). Satoo (1956) observed that the extent of root systems is an important factor in survival of conifer seedlings in Japan, and Fowells and Kirk (1945) concluded that reduction in extent of the absorbing system by injury to roots during lifting and planting is an important cause of failure of ponderosa pine transplants.

These and many similar observations emphasize the importance of producing planting stock which has vigorous roots capable of resuming growth and a favorable ratio of roots to shoots. Experiments have shown that a low ratio of root surface to leaf surface is a limiting factor for water absorption (Bialoglowski, 1936; Parker, 1949), as shown in Figure 12.6. Rapid regeneration of roots following transplanting is often the most important factor in survival. Root growth probably is related to carbohydrate reserves and possibly to other as yet unidentified internal conditions.

Wilcox (1954, 1955) found a definite cycle in regeneration of roots on seedlings of *Abies procera*. He regarded this as independent of food reserves, but possibly related to the concentration of growth substances. Stone (1955) found that 15 to 40 per cent of ponderosa pine seedlings failed to produce roots when transplanted in the autumn under conditions favorable for root production. The season seems to be a factor also, because Stone and Schubert (1956) found that only 50 to 60 per cent of pine seedlings transplanted in October formed roots but all did when transplanted in April. Wakeley (1948) has emphasized the wide differences in survival of different lots of planting stock, and further study of what constitutes good-quality seedlings and how to produce them is greatly needed.

Some attempts have been made to obtain a higher ratio of roots to shoots by spraying the tops of seedlings with growth-regulating substances (Maki et al., 1946; Ostrom, 1945), but the results have not been encouraging. Attempts to stimulate root growth by soaking the roots in solutions of growth-regulating substances have not been successful either (Maki and Marshall, 1945).

The depth and extent of root systems of mature trees often are dominant factors in drought resistance. Many desert shrubs and trees grow only where their roots can penetrate to great depths and reach sources of water unavailable to shallow-rooted plants (Oppenheimer, 1951). It is well known that orchard, shade, and forest trees on shallow soil are more subject to drought injury than those on deep soils, and during the great drought of the 1930s the greatest mortality was among shallow-rooted species (Albertson and Weaver, 1945). Many examples of dieback and unthriftiness of trees such as "dead top" in Australia, "spot die-out" in the North Carolina Piedmont, and difficulties with red pine in New York (Stone et al., 1954) and white spruce in Quebec (Paine, 1953) seem to result from injury to root systems, resulting in failure to absorb enough water for survival during the summer. Ackley (1954b) found that leaves of pear growing on French rootstocks (*Pyrus communis*) have a lower water deficit than those on Japanese rootstocks (*P. serotina*) and suggested that this might explain the greater prevalence of the "hard end" condition of pears on Japanese rootstocks.

During severe soil droughts the roots often are subjected to conditions almost as severe as those affecting leaves. They must lose considerable water to soil drier than the permanent-wilting percentage, and this results in cessation of growth and suberization, which further reduce their efficiency as absorbing surfaces. Few or no growing roots are found in dry soil. Roots of herbaceous plants subjected to drought require several days to regain their previous efficiency for water absorption. This probably is true of tree roots also, but no supporting experimental data are available. Bourdeau (1954) reported that even after the tops of oak seedlings appeared to be dead from dehydration, some living white root tips were found on them, suggesting that the root cells survived higher diffusion-pressure deficits than the tops. Parker (1956b) found that root tips of ponderosa pine exposed to a relative humidity of less than 94 per cent (equivalent to a soil moisture tension of 80 atmospheres) were killed in 4 days. More study of the effects of dry soil on growth, structure, and functioning of tree roots is needed.

Stems and Conducting Systems. Stems probably play a relatively small part in drought resistance of trees, although in cacti they serve as a water reservoir. Tree trunks also serve to a limited extent as water reservoirs, as indicated by the fact that their water content usually decreases materially during the summer (Figures 12.2 and 12.3). Sometimes the dehydration is so severe and the tension so great that collapse of the wood occurs, forming cracks (Lutz, 1952). On the other hand, Gibbs (1939, p. 463) concluded that the large amount of water found in "wet patches" in the heartwood of aspen and balsam fir probably is not utilized by the tree. The physiological importance of the water in the trunk deserves further study.

Differences in water conductivity seem to be poorly correlated with differences in drought resistance. Ring-porous stems are most efficient, diffuse-porous stems are intermediate, and the nonporous conifers have the least efficient conducting systems (Huber, 1928, 1935), but this seems to have little or nothing to do with drought resistance. Ashby (1932) found the xylem of the drought-resistant shrub *Larrea* to have twice the resistance to water movement of that in the less drought resistant *Ligustrum*. There always is considerable resistance to water movement through plants, as shown by the fact that they wilt on bright sunny days, even in moist soil, and the differences between species seem to be much less important than many other factors.

Leaves. In the early part of the century much emphasis was placed on the importance of the xeromorphic structure of leaves of xerophytes as a means of reducing transpiration. When it was discovered that many plants having small thick heavily cutinized leaves transpire rapidly when growing in moist soil, the importance of leaf structure for water conservation was questioned. Perhaps this revision of an erroneous concept has gone too far, because there is evidence that certain leaf characteristics do help conserve water in plants growing in dry soil. Stomates which close promptly when leaf moisture begins to decrease, combined with a thick cuticle which decreases cuticular transpiration, certainly postpone the development of injurious water deficits. Oppenheimer (1932, 1951) found that almond and fig trees have high rates of transpiration but a low water deficit, because of their deep root systems, while olive trees have a much lower rate and very effective stomatal control. Almonds shed their leaves when they finally develop a serious water deficit. Oppenheimer (1953) found that the water loss from certain species of sclerophyllous shrubs of the Mediterranean maqui was greatly reduced by stomatal closure when the soil began to dry. The stomates of *Phillyrea media* remained open, however, and the continuing transpiration produced a severe water deficit and extremely high osmotic pressure in plants of this species. Several other investigators have found stomatal closure in woody plants to result in marked decrease in water loss (Ferri, 1953; Pisek and Winkler, 1953; Satoo and Hukahara, 1953; Stålfelt, 1932). This also is regarded as an important factor in drought resistance of crop plants (Slatyer, 1955).

Differences in rate of water loss from excised leaves of various species have been observed by many investigators. Parker (1951) found that detached leaves of Douglas-fir and ponderosa pine lost less water than those of arborvitae, white pine, Engelmann spruce, or grand fir. Parker (1954) also found that older leaves of ponderosa pine lost water more rapidly than younger leaves. He suggested that this might result from decreased activity of the guard cells and increased permeability of the cuticle in older leaves.

Another leaf characteristic which undoubtedly reduces water loss is reduction in leaf area by abscission. The leaves of many species tend to drop prematurely if late summer droughts cause internal water deficits. A few broadleaf trees and shrubs such as California buckeye regularly shed their leaves as soon as the soil begins to dry out. This also is characteristic of some desert shrubs, such as *Larrea tridentata*.

The possibility of absorption of water from fog and dew through the leaves must also be considered. There is little doubt that at least enough water for survival is absorbed in this manner by some plants (Stone et al., 1950, 1956; Gessner, 1956). This probably is of appreciable importance where fog is common, as in the fog belt along the Pacific coast of upper California and lower Oregon. Coast redwood, for example, is restricted to the fog belt.

Protoplasmic Basis of Drought Resistance. All the characteristics previously discussed merely postpone the evil day when water content falls to a critical level. In the final analysis, the drought resistance of plants depends on the degree of dehydration which their protoplasm can endure. Species differ widely in this respect, and individuals even differ from time to time.

Oppenheimer (1932) reported that the deep-rooted almond tree had a saturation deficit under field conditions of less than 10 per cent but the leaves could be dried to a saturation deficit of 70 per cent before serious injury occurred. Fig leaves had a saturation deficit of about 16 per cent, and the leaves were injured at a deficit of 25 per cent. Leaves of olive trees which are more shallow rooted than almond or fig had a saturation deficit in late summer of 27 to 51 per cent and were injured at a deficit of about 60 per cent. Runyon (1936) found that individual leaves of *Larrea tridentata* differed widely in their ability to endure dehydration. Those developed during moist weather were large, high in moisture content, and easily injured by drought, but leaves whose development was checked by drought often survived dehydration to a water content slightly less than 50 per cent of their dry weight. Bourdeau (1954) found no significant differences among the leaf water contents of various species of oak seedlings in soil at field capacity, but when the soil was allowed to dry to permanent wilting, the more drought resistant post and blackjack oaks had the highest saturation deficits (Table 12.2). It was concluded that their protoplasm can tolerate a higher water deficit than that of such species as white and northern red oak. Burstrom (1948b) found the dormant buds of *Carpinus betulus* and *Fagus sylvatica* quite resistant to dehydration, surviving a loss of up to 75 per cent of their normal water content.

Seasonal differences in ability to endure dehydration seem to occur. The differences in leaves of *Larrea* formed at various times have already been mentioned. Pisek and Larcher (1954) found a seasonal rhythm in drought resistance of several species of woody plants. Resistance increased during the autumn to a high in the winter, then decreased again in the spring. In the winter leaf moisture could be reduced to 60 to 80 per cent of the value which caused damage in the summer before injury resulted. Thus the yearly cycle of resistance to dehydration coincides with that for cold resistance, as shown in Figure 12.8.

At one time high osmotic pressure was regarded as an important factor in drought resistance, but later this was questioned because even a high osmotic pressure produces a negligible lowering of vapor pressure and therefore has little effect on evaporation of water. Perhaps the importance of high osmotic pressure in reducing transpiration was underestimated, because Boon-Long (1941) found that the osmotic pressure of the cell sap reduces transpiration much more than would be expected from the lowering of the vapor pressure. In general terms, high osmotic pressure doubtless is an advantage to plants in drying soil, but differences in drought resistance can seldom if ever be attributed entirely to differences in osmotic pressure. Oppenheimer (1932) found the osmotic pressure of the very drought resistant *Rosmarinus officinalis* to be only 15 atmospheres, and the highest osmotic pressures found in the species studied by him were only a little over 30 atmospheres, except in *Phillyrea media* with an osmotic pressure of over 50 atmospheres. The stomates of this species seldom close, and it becomes highly dehydrated (Oppenheimer, 1953). According to Oppenheimer (1951), the increase in osmotic pres-

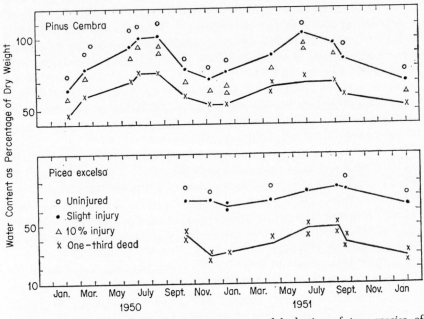

Figure 12.8 Seasonal changes in resistance to dehydration of two species of conifers. Note that resistance increases during the winter and decreases during the growing season. *Picea* can be dehydrated to a lower water content than pine without injury. (*From Pisek and Larcher, 1954.*)

sure accompanying dehydration is important in many plants because it enables them to absorb water from the drying soil.

Drought resistance was for a time believed to be related to bound-water content, but Schopmeyer (1939) could find no relation between bound-water content and drought resistance of shortleaf pine, and work by Meyer (1932) and others indicates that there probably is no causal relationship (Kramer, 1955). It is true that bound water and osmotic pressure tend to be higher in dry habitats and during droughts than in well-watered plants, but these increases are largely the result of dehydration rather than protective changes.

We agree with Parker (1956b) that there probably is no one cause of drought resistance in any woody species, although some factors are more important in certain species and other factors in other species. Efficient absorbing surfaces, thick cutin, and stomates which close promptly when a water deficit develops postpone the development of critical internal water deficits, but eventually the ability of the protoplasm to endure dehydration becomes the most important factor.

Iljin (1953) claims that tissues consisting of small elongated cells with a large ratio of surface to volume are most resistant to dehydration. Slowly dehydrated tissue also is claimed to be more resistant than that which is rapidly dehydrated or rehydrated. Although cell size and shape may be of importance, they cannot explain seasonal variations in dehydration endurance of the same leaves, such as were observed by Pisek and Larcher (1954). In such instances changes in the protoplasm itself must occur which render it more resistant to injury from dehydration.

Practical Applications. The existence of differences in drought resistance among species can be inferred from the fact that some species such as birch and willow are found in sites where soil moisture is seldom deficient and rarely occur in dry sites where species such as post oak and blackjack oak commonly occur. It generally is believed by foresters that shortleaf pine is more drought resistant than loblolly; hence it often is planted on dry sites. Likewise, longleaf pine is thought to be more drought resistant than slash or loblolly pines and therefore is preferred for dry sites, but this may be the result of a deep root system rather than any greater efficiency in the use of water. We have little reliable information concerning the relative efficiency of various species when subjected to drought during the growing season, and this deserves extensive investigation.

GENERAL REFERENCES

Gibbs, R. D., 1958, Patterns in the seasonal water content of trees, chap. 3 in K. V. Thimann (ed.), The physiology of forest trees, The Ronald Press Company, New York.

Iljin, W. S., 1957, Drought resistance in plants and physiological processes, Ann. Rev. Plant Physiology, 8:257–274.

Killian, C., and G. Lemée, 1956, Les xerophytes: leur economie d'eau, Encyclopedia of plant physiology, vol. 3:787–824.

Levitt, J., 1956, The hardiness of plants, Academic Press, Inc., New York.

Maximov, N. A., 1929, The plant in relation to water, Eng. transl., George Allen & Unwin, Ltd., London.

Parker, J., 1956, Drought resistance in woody plants, Bot. Rev., 22:241–289.

Richards, L. A., and C. H. Wadleigh, Soil water and plant growth, chap. 3 in B. T. Shaw (ed.), Soil physical conditions and plant growth, Academic Press, Inc., New York.

CHAPTER 13 *Reproduction*

One of the most important problems in forestry and horticulture is to produce trees of desirable kinds and quality for planting. Most trees reproduce in nature by seeds, but vegetative propagation also occurs by means of root suckers, layering, and stump sprouts. In horticulture plants are propagated extensively by budding, grafting, and cuttings, and these methods are beginning to be used in forestry for propagation of superior individuals. One of the chief hindrances to tree improvement programs is the difficulty of propagating trees of important forest species vegetatively.

It has been known for many centuries that fruit trees do not grow true to type from seed but must be propagated vegetatively. Most trees are highly heterozygous; and the embryo in a seed receives sets of chromosomes from both the pistillate and the pollen parents; hence it differs genetically from both parents, and the plant which develops from it is likely to differ from the parents in important characteristics. Even if an embryo is produced as a result of self-pollination, it will not be identical with the parent on which the seed is borne because of the high degree of heterozygosity and the random manner in which chromosomes separate during reductional division and recombine during the union of egg and sperm.

There are other reasons for propagating trees vegetatively in addition to ensuring that the offspring will resemble the parent. For example, by budding or grafting, a treetop with certain desirable characteristics can be combined with a root system of another type which grows more vigorously or is more resistant to disease, as when *Vinifera* varieties of grapes are grafted on American varieties of rootstocks which are resistant to phylloxera. Another example of vegetative propagation to produce a desired type of growth is the production of dwarf apple trees by grafting them on rootstocks known to cause dwarfing, such as Malling IX, and dwarf pears by grafting on quince rootstocks. Budding, grafting, and

368

cuttings all permit rapid multiplication of an individual with desired characteristics. Vegetative propagation sometimes is more reliable than seeds which may germinate poorly or slowly, and budded or grafted plants often begin flowering and fruiting much earlier than seedlings.

SEXUAL REPRODUCTION

Most forest trees are propagated from seed; hence the series of processes involved in seed production and the factors affecting seed quantity and quality will be discussed in some detail. Sexual reproduction includes initiation of flower buds, flowering, setting of fruits, and maturation of fruits and seeds. Increasing the certainty of flowering, and hence of fruit and seed production, is of great importance in both forestry and horticulture, and we need to learn much more about the internal processes and conditions which control these phenomena.

Flowering and Fruiting

The structures associated with sexual reproduction of trees are borne in clusters on specialized branches which usually are known as flowers in angiosperms and as cones or strobili in gymnosperms. Although botanists often restrict the term flower to angiosperms, it need not be so restricted. Foresters commonly speak of flowering in conifers, and the term will be used in its broader sense in this chapter. The flowers of many forest trees are inconspicuous and commonly overlooked, but functionally these inconspicuous structures are just as important as the larger flowers of ornamental plants.

Flower Bud Initiation. The first step in sexual reproduction is the initiation of flower buds. In most trees this occurs during the growing season preceding that in which flowering occurs. For example, apples usually produce flower buds for the following year in early summer, peaches produce them in late summer, and dogwood and many other forest trees produce them in late summer. The long period between flower bud initiation and fruit and seed production means that unless cultural practices intended to increase flower and seed production are applied early in the season they will not affect flowering until the second season after they are applied.

It was suggested by Sachs (1887) that flower formation is caused by a flower-forming substance or hormone produced in the leaves, and extensive research has been carried on to isolate this substance. Although it generally is believed that such flower-forming hormones or florigens exist, they have not yet been isolated. It has been well established that the chemical composition of trees has important effects on flower bud formation. Early in the present century Fischer (1905) and Klebs (1918)

suggested that the carbohydrate supply, and probably the nitrogen supply, affected flower differentiation. Perhaps the importance of carbohy-
drate-nitrogen relations was overemphasized by the researches of Kraus
and Kraybill (1918) on tomatoes and Hooker (1920) on apples. Davis
(1957) believes that change in the carbohydrate/nitrogen ratio is the
result rather than the cause of flowering. In general, it appears that a
relatively high concentration of carbohydrate is necessary for the initiation of flower buds. It seems probable that chemical composition operates
through its effects on the concentration of a flower-forming hormone,
but this has not yet been demonstrated.

Various environmental factors are known to affect the initiation of
flower buds, probably chiefly through their effects on such internal conditions as carbohydrate supply. Reduction in light intensity by shading
has been shown to reduce flower bud formation in apples and peaches
(Kraybill, 1923; Gourley and Howlett, 1941), and this seems to apply
to forest trees also, because opening up a stand usually results in increased seed production. Heavy applications of nitrogen sometimes reduce flower bud production because of increased use of carbohydrates
in growth, but light applications may increase flower bud production
of unthrifty trees. The beneficial effects of applying nitrogen may be
partly indirect because Heinicke (1934) found that a late application of
nitrogen caused leaves to carry on photosynthesis later in the autumn,
building up a higher carbohydrate reserve in the trees. The importance
of the carbohydrate supply also is indicated by the fact that anything
decreasing photosynthesis, such as heavy pruning, defoliation by insects
or fungi, or reduction in photosynthetic efficiency by sprays, tends to
reduce flower bud initiation. Reduction of carbohydrate translocation
out of the top by girdling also usually results in increased production
of flower buds and earlier production on young trees. It is said that on
a certain feast day the peasants in some parts of central Europe went
to the orchards and flogged the trunks of nonbearing trees. This may
have had the effect of temporarily blocking translocation by damaging
the phloem and might sometimes cause nonbearing trees to form flower
buds and produce fruit.

Flower bud formation and flowering of many herbaceous plants and
some woody shrubs are affected by the duration of light or photoperiod,
but there is not much evidence that photoperiod controls flowering of
either fruit or forest trees under natural conditions. Mirov (1956) recently investigated the flowering behavior of a number of species of
pine brought together at Placerville and Berkeley, California, from a
wide range of latitudes. He found that they seemed to be neutral with
respect to photoperiod because species from very different photoperiods
of more southern and northern latitudes flowered well with the inter-

mediate photoperiod of Placerville and Berkeley. Wareing (1956) cites several workers who found photoperiod to have little effect on flower initiation in azalea and apple. Citing Sceglova and Leisle, Wareing also points out that although long days are required for flower initiation in *Ulmus glabra*, some internal ontogenetic mechanism rather than photoperiod appears to control flowering in this species under natural conditions. The tendency to form flower buds seems to be correlated with cessation of vegetative growth. Flower buds usually differentiate about the time shoot growth stops and the greater the number of flower buds formed the less the amount of vegetative growth.

Biennial Flowering and Bearing. Development of floral primordia is correlated with the well-known phenomenon of alternate bearing of fruit trees. During off years when few flowers and fruits are produced a relatively higher percentage of fruit tree spurs form flower buds than in those years when heavy crops are borne. This results in alternate bearing in such trees as apple, orange, plum, prune, olive, and coffee. According to Davis (1957) alternate bearing probably occurs in all fruit trees to varying degrees. It also occurs in many species of forest trees. Biennial bearing appears to be internally controlled in individual trees and even in individual branches. On the same site some trees bear heavily in one year while neighboring trees produce heavy crops the following year. Some branches of a tree also bear heavily during a year when other branches produce no crop. The fruit crop exerts a regulatory effect on the bearing sequence because, as Davis (1957) points out, if a crop is removed early enough the bearing year can be changed.

Flowering. Actual opening of the flower buds often does not occur until many months after they have been differentiated. In the Temperate Zone buds usually remain inactive over winter and those of many species are physiologically dormant and will not open even if brought into a warm greenhouse early in the winter. Occasionally the dormant buds are killed by unusually cold weather, resulting in failure of the next year's crop, but in general they are quite resistant to cold and dehydration.

The time at which flowering, or the opening of flower buds, occurs varies widely among trees of different species. A few shrubs such as species of *Jasminum, Hamamelis,* and *Alnus* flower in midwinter, and many trees flower long before the danger of frost is past. Destruction of potential seed crops by freezing of opening flowers is not uncommon. In general, the time of flowering of trees of any species seems to be controlled chiefly by temperature.

The flower buds of many trees of the Temperate Zone resemble vegetative buds in requiring exposure to several hundred hours of low temperature to break their dormancy. As a result, flower buds of trees and shrubs planted toward the southern limits of their range sometimes fail to open properly after exceptionally mild winters. This has produced serious failures in the peach crop of the southeastern United States (Higdon, 1950; see also Figure 15.12). The need for low temperature to break dormancy of flower buds also has been observed in blueberries (Coville, 1920; Darrow, 1942) and many other species (Chandler et al., 1937). Crocker (1948) also has an extensive discussion of dormancy in buds of various kinds.

The opening of flowers consists principally of enlargement of cells already formed in the bud, and it occurs very rapidly under favorable conditions, many flowers attaining full size in 24 to 48 hours. Most flowers are open only a few days, and as the flowers of shade and forest trees typically are small and inconspicuous compared with those of fruit trees, their flowering often goes by unnoticed.

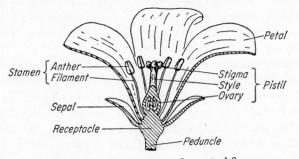

Figure 13.1   The structure of a typical flower.

Flowers of Angiosperms. As shown in Figure 13.1, a typical complete flower of an angiosperm consists of a flower stalk or peduncle, a calyx composed of sepals, a corolla composed of petals, a group of stamens, and one or more pistils. Some of these parts often are lacking. Willow flowers, for example, lack both calyx and corolla, and sweetgum flowers have no corolla. The only essential parts are the stamens, which produce pollen grains in which sperms are developed, and the pistils, in which the ovules containing eggs are developed. In perfect flowers such as those of apple, peach, and cherry, stamens and pistils occur in the same flower. In many trees the stamens and pistils occur in separate flowers. Those trees which bear staminate and pistillate flowers separately on the same tree, such as oaks, elms, and birches, are termed monoecious; those which bear them on separate individuals, such as holly, willow, and poplars, are termed dioecious species. Some trees such as maple and ash produce pistillate, staminate, and perfect flowers on the same individual. It is obvious that pistillate and staminate individuals of dioecious species must be grown near each other if fruit and seeds are to be produced.

Furthermore, if trees are grown chiefly for the ornamental value of their fruits, it is desirable to have mostly pistillate individuals because the staminate individuals produce no fruits.

Several types of flowers are shown in Figure 13.2.

Flowers of Gymnosperms. The reproductive structures of conifers are very different from those of angiosperms. In conifers the ovules are

Figure 13.2 Some examples of flowers produced by trees. *a*. Dogwood. *b*. Yellow-poplar. *c*. Staminate catkins of southern red oak. (*Courtesy of U.S. Forest Service.*)

borne on the upper surfaces of the scale leaves or bracts which form the pistillate or ovulate cones, while in angiosperms the ovules are enclosed in the pistils. Pollen grains of gymnosperms are produced in pollen sacs in staminate cones instead of in anthers on stamens, as in angiosperms. Typical ovulate and staminate cones are shown in Figure 13.3. Most conifers are monoecious and produce the two kinds of cones on the same tree.

Figure 13.3 Mature ovulate and staminate cones of Austrian pine. (*Courtesy of W. M. Harlow.*)

Age and Flowering. Most trees must attain an age of at least several years before they begin to flower, but there are wide differences among species. Peaches begin to flower in 2 or 3 years, and some varieties of apple, as Wealthy, may flower at the age of 3 or 4 years, but others such as Northern Spy may not flower until 15 or 20 years old.

Pine seedlings begin to produce cones at a rather early age. According to Righter (1939), the average minimum age at which ovulate cones were produced by a large number of species of pine at Placerville, California, was 5.2 years. Staminate cones were produced somewhat earlier, appearing at an average age of only 4.4 years. Wareing (1953) reported, however, that in England Scotch pine produced ovulate cones at the age of 7 years but no staminate cones until several years later. No significant amount of seed is produced until the trees are several years older.

Methods of inducing precocious flowering and seed production in trees would be very useful in breeding programs, but only limited success has been attained thus far. More information concerning the internal factors which control flower bud initiation must be obtained before we shall be able to cause precocious flowering on a large scale.

Seed Development.

The production of a seed begins with the development of an ovule. The details of the process differ somewhat in angiosperms and gymno-

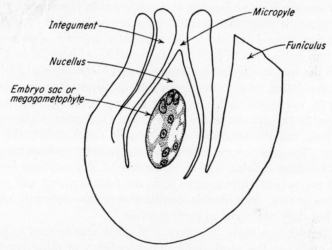

Figure 13.4 Ovule of elm containing an embryo sac. This embryo sac contains 8 nuclei, but up to 16 are reported. Two embryo sacs are found occasionally in a nucellus of elm, and it sometimes produces two embryos in a single embryo sac. (*Redrawn from Shattuck, 1905.*)

sperms; hence seed development will be discussed separately for the two groups.

Angiosperm Seed Development. An ovule develops into a structure consisting of an outer layer, the integuments, which finally become the seed coat, and a layer of tissue known as the nucellus, enclosing an inner structure called the embryo sac. A typical mature embryo sac contains eight nuclei. One of these functions as the egg. Two, called polar nuclei, unite to form the primary endosperm nucleus, while the other five do not function directly in reproduction. The arrangement of these structures is shown in Figure 13.4.

Pollen grains are produced in the anthers or pollen sacs of the stamens. When mature the anthers dehisce or split open and release the pollen grains, which usually contain two nuclei at this stage. Most tree pollen is distributed by wind, although insects are important in the pollination of many fruit trees. If the pollen grains are viable and if they fall or are deposited on a receptive stigma of a flower, they germinate and produce pollen tubes which grow down through the style into the ovary. One of the two nuclei in the pollen grain divides and produces two sperms.

The rate at which pollen tubes grow through the style varies greatly. Fertilization is said to occur in 12 to 14 hours after pollination in *Coffea arabica* (Mendes, 1941), and in *Juglans regia* it is said to occur in 2 to 5 days after pollination (Nast, 1935), but in some oaks the process requires 12 to 14 months (Bagda, 1948). There is said to be an interval of 5 to 7 months from pollination to fertilization in *Hamamelis*, probably at least partly because this shrub flowers in the late fall or winter and cold weather slows down physiological activity. In most angiosperms the period from pollination to fertilization probably is about 24 to 48 hours, although the rate is affected by temperature (Maheshwari, 1950).

After the pollen tube grows down into the ovary it enters the ovule through the micropyle, or by digesting its way in through the base, and discharges its two sperms in the embryo sac. One sperm unites with the egg nucleus, and the fertilized egg eventually develops into the embryonic plant. The other sperm unites with the primary endosperm nucleus, and the resulting cell has a triploid number of chromosomes because it received two sets of chromosomes from the female parent and one from the pollen parent. This double fertilization is characteristic of angiosperms but does not occur in gymnosperms.

After fertilization there is a period of great activity, not only in the ovule but also in the pistil itself, and sometimes in other surrounding structures. The endosperm grows rapidly by a series of cell divisions and usually digests and absorbs most or all of the tissue of the embryo sac. There is rapid translocation of food into the enlarging ovule. In some trees, such as coconut, much of this food is stored in the endosperm. In other trees, such as the legumes and oaks, the embryo absorbs the endosperm and enlarges until it occupies all the space within the seed coat and food is stored in the cotyledons. Occasionally, a part of the nucellus remains in the seed and is known as the perisperm. While the embryo is enlarging, the integument develops into the seed coat and the ovary wall develops into the fruit. In some instances the wall of the fruit becomes greatly thickened, and as in apple, it sometimes is modified by the presence of other stem or flower parts.

Occasionally, more than one embryo is found in seeds of angiosperms. Among the species in which multiple embryos have been found are

Alnus rugosa (Woodworth, 1930), *Ulmus americana* (Shattuck, 1905), and *U. glabra* (Ekdahl, 1941). Multiple embryos appear to be quite common in *Citrus*, as Frost (1926) found an average of up to 6.5 per seed in various citrus varieties. According to Maheshwari (1950), multiple embryos can develop in angiosperms by (1) cleavage of the proembryo, (2) development of more than one cell in the embryo sac into an embryo, (3) presence of more than one embryo sac in an ovule, or (4) apomictically by budding of cells of the nucellus or integument, which develop into embryos.

Apomictic embryos are developed asexually from the pistillate parent without any fusion of sperm and egg and therefore resemble genetically the pistillate plant on which they are produced. Occurrence of apomictic embryos therefore constitutes a kind of vegetative or asexual reproduction.

Gymnosperm Seed Development. Seed development in gymnosperms differs from that in angiosperms in several respects. One difference is the absence of true endosperm in gymnosperm seeds. The tissue in which the embryo is embedded, and which functions as does the endosperm of angiosperms, is the megagametophyte or embryo sac. It should not be called endosperm since it was produced solely from the tissue of the ovule and is haploid in chromosome number; true endosperm is triploid because it is formed by the fusion of two nuclei in the embryo sac plus a sperm nucleus. Polyembryony is fairly common. In *Pinus* and *Tsuga* the proembryo commonly splits to form two or more embryos (cleavage polyembryony), while in *Picea, Larix, Abies,* and *Pseudotsuga,* more than one egg is fertilized in each embryo sac. The interval between pollination and fertilization is unusually long in pines, pollination occurring one spring while the ovulate cones are very small and fertilization occurring the second spring. Development of mature seeds therefore requires two full growing seasons.

Fruit Development

Botanically a fruit is an ovary together with whatever parts adhere to it during development. Fruit development usually is stimulated by pollination and fertilization and occurs simultaneously with the development of the ovule into a seed. Many tree fruits are relatively complex structures because the receptacle, bracts, or other parts remain associated with the ovary during its development. In some instances, as in citrus, apple, and peach, the fruits become large and fleshy, but in other instances they dry out during maturation. Examples are the legumes, ash, maple, and various trees which produce nuts. The term "nut" often is applied to large seeds with hard coats such as Brazil nut, almond, and horsechestnut, but nuts really are fruits such as those of beech, oak, hickory, and walnut. In those fruits bracts arising from the base of the flower form a cup as in the acorn, a loose enclosure as in beechnut, or become fused to the seed as in hickory and walnut. Some examples of tree fruits are shown in Figure 13.5.

Early growth of fruits is by cell division, but after flowering growth is by cell enlargement (Figure 13.6). Cell division usually continues

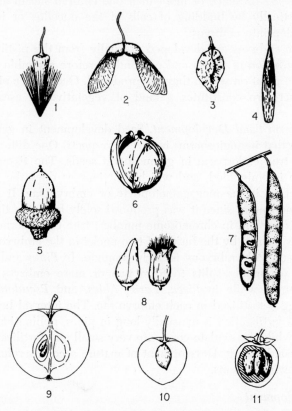

Figure 13.5 Examples of various types of tree fruits. 1, achene of sycamore; 2, double samara of maple; 3, simple samara of elm; 4, single samara of ash; 5, acorn (nut) of oak; 6, nut of hickory; 7, legume of black locust; 8, capsule of poplar; 9, pome of apple; 10, drupe of cherry; 11, berry of persimmon. (*From Harlow and Harrar*, 1958.)

longer in ovaries of species with large fruits (Nitsch, 1953). Intense physiological activity occurs in developing fruits and seeds, large quantities of soluble food being translocated into them and converted into new tissue and storage forms such as starch, fat, and proteins.

Many stone fruits such as cherry and peach develop in three stages: (1) rapid increase in size immediately following full bloom, (2) slow development in midseason, and (3) renewed rapid increase in size to fruit ripening (Tukey and Young, 1939). In early-ripening varieties the second period lasts only a few days, while in late-ripening varieties it may last over a month. The nucellus and integuments achieve maximum size during the first stage when the embryo remains very small. During the second stage the stony pericarp hardens and the embryo grows rapidly. As may be seen in Figure 13.6, most of the increase in size is the result of cell enlargement. The over-all development of the apple shows no retarded midseason development. Tukey and Young (1942) base this difference on the fact that the apple is an accessory fruit con-

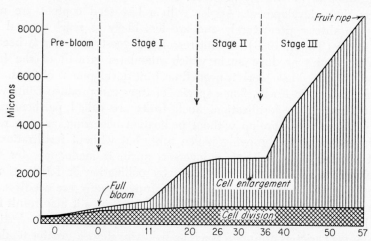

Figure 13.6 Diagram showing amounts of increase in thickness of ovary wall of sour cherry caused by increase in number of cells and amount caused by cell enlargement. Practically all increase after blooming is caused by enlargement of existing cells. (*From Tukey and Young, 1939.*)

sisting largely of stem tissue surrounding five relatively small carpels within the stem part. Growth of the carpels of apple fruits is rather similar to that of cherry and peach. The carpel blade achieves maximum length early, as do the nucellus and integuments, while the embryo does not develop for a long time after full bloom. In dry fruits only the first and second growth stages occur. During the first stage the fruit and ovules both grow, while in the second stage only the ovules grow (Nitsch, 1953).

Embryo Development and Fruit Growth

Embryo development has a definite relation to fruit development distinct from the effect of fruit and seed formation on the whole plant. Tukey (1936) observed that destruction of the embryo early in the second stage of development of peaches and cherries inhibited fruit development and caused shriveling and abscission. Destroying the embryo at the transition from the second to the third stage of pericarp development resulted in growth of the fruit for a limited time at a rate similar to that of untreated fruits, but fruits without embryos ripened sooner and did not achieve full size. When the embryo was destroyed in the third stage of pericarp development, there was increased growth and early ripening. Sometimes this resulted in greater size than that of untreated fruits. Apparently the relation between the embryo and pericarp is influenced by the stage of fruit development and the genetic composition of the variety involved. The number of seeds in fruits also affects their development. Apples with a low seed content are more likely to abscise prematurely and are less likely to reach normal size and shape (Tukey, 1936). Recent research suggests that this is because growing ovules produce auxin which stimulates growth of the fruits (Nitsch, 1953). More work is needed on fruit development of trees.

Parthenocarpic Fruits. Some species of trees can produce fruits without pollination or fertilization. Such fruits are called parthenocarpic fruits. These may develop without pollination occurring, or as a result of the stimulus of a growing pollen tube, but without fertilization. In most species the supply of endogenous auxin is inadequate for fruit development and must be reinforced by pollination or fertilization or both (Gustafson, 1942). Parthenocarpic fruits usually are seedless, but a seedless fruit is not necessarily parthenocarpic since it may result from a pollinated ovary in which ovules do not develop properly after fertilization. Some varieties of apples, such as Baldwin, show a greater tendency for production of parthenocarpic fruits than other varieties. Seedless fruits also form without fertilization in Japanese persimmon, fig, and navel orange. Gardner and Marth (1937) induced development of parthenocarpic fruits in American holly by spraying pistillate flowers with indoleacetic, indolepropionic, indolebutyric, or naphthaleneacetic acids. Osborne and Wain (1951) caused certain varieties of pear to form parthenocarpic fruits with auxin sprays. They also produced small parthenocarpic apples in the variety Bramley's Seedling. However, despite very extensive attempts at developing parthenocarpic pome fruits with sprays of growth regulators, the results generally have been disappointing. It is possible that further research may result in more success in this field.

Factors Affecting Seed Production

The great interest of foresters in seed production has resulted in numerous observations and considerable research on factors affecting quantity and quality of seed produced. Among the important factors are age, tree vigor, crown exposure, heredity, and climatic conditions.

Age and Size of Trees. Most trees produce seed in greatest quantities during middle age, after the period of most rapid height growth has occurred. As life span varies greatly among species, there are wide variations in the age at which trees begin to produce a significant amount of seed and the length of time over which seed production continues. Short-lived trees such as aspens, birches, and willows may begin to produce full crops of seed at the age of 10 to 20 years, but full production usually is not attained in long-lived trees such as oaks and hickories until they are 40 to 50 years of age. According to Wenger and Trousdell

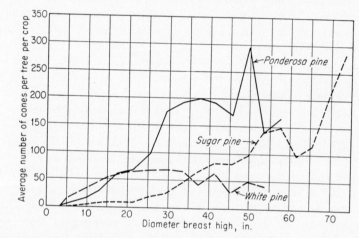

Figure 13.7 Average number of cones per tree per crop for various species and diameter classes in the Stanislaus National Forest, California. (*From Fowells and Schubert*, 1956.)

(1958), loblolly pine trees less than 10 years old occasionally produce a few cones, but dominant and codominant trees in even-aged stands usually do not begin to produce appreciable amounts of seed until they are 30 to 50 years of age.

In California, Fowells and Schubert (1956) observed a very gradual increase in cone production of sugar pine with increasing age. Ponderosa pine produced more cones in its early years and its production increased more rapidly with increasing age than did cone production of sugar pine. White fir was an even more prolific seed producer in its early years, but in older trees production declined more rapidly with increasing age than that of sugar or ponderosa pine (Figure 13.7). It often is stated that seed production declines in overmature trees (Baker, 1950), but this seems to vary among species. Wenger and Trousdell (1958) found that a 145-year-old loblolly pine stand produced as much seed as a 95-year-old stand.

Downs and McQuilkin (1944) observed that seed production of some species of oaks increased indefinitely with trunk diameter, but in other species it increased up to a certain diameter, then decreased with further increase in size. In loblolly pine stands which have reached the age of full bearing, seed production is closely related to trunk diameter (Wenger and Trousdell, 1958).

The ability of a tree to produce seed at a given age seems to be conditioned by its level of metabolic activity. For example, a middle-aged tree which is subjected to severe competition and is growing poorly usually is a poor seed producer. A tree that is growing at an abnormally rapid rate may also produce a small seed crop because large amounts of its reserve food are channeled into vegetative growth and are unavailable for seed production.

Occasionally, trees produce seeds several years before the average seeding age is reached for that species. Seed from such young trees often is of poor quality. Douglas-fir trees less than 20 years old produced viable seed, but the percentage of empty seed was high unless there was cross-pollination from older trees. Evidently the young trees produced little pollen (Allen, 1942). Similarly, Wakeley (1947) found that open-grown loblolly pine trees often produced as much as a bushel of cones per tree at the early age of 15 to 20 years, but the cones from these young trees contained few full seeds and he therefore emphasized the greater dependability of seeds from trees that were at least 25 years old. Apparently the low seed production of young pine trees results from inadequate pollination rather than from inability to develop good seed.

Although seeding capacity usually varies markedly with age, such differences may not occur during an unusually good seed year. Kolesnichenko (1949) and Gysel (1956) found, for instance, that oaks of all sizes often produce acorns during unusually good seed years.

Crown Exposure. Open-grown trees usually are the most prolific seeders. The physiological basis for their unusually high seeding capacity presumably is the large amount of available carbohydrates resulting from high photosynthetic activity in the open. In a forest most seeds are produced by dominant trees. Intermediate and suppressed trees are such poor seeders that they can be disregarded with respect to any significant role in seed production. Over a 16-year period, Fowells and Schubert (1956) observed that practically all the cones produced by ponderosa and sugar pines in California were on dominant trees while only 1 to 1.5 per cent of the pine cones were on codominant trees (Table 13.1). Trees of intermediate and suppressed crown classes produced only a negligible number of cones. Dominant trees of white fir produced about 88 per cent of the fir cones, while codominant trees accounted for only about 12 per cent. Although most cones were produced by dominant trees, all dominants were not equally prolific because there was considerable variation in crown vigor. Verne (1953) found that acorn production of oaks was greatest in the part of the crown that was exposed to direct light. Acorn production by black oak was 11 times greater in the exposed crown area than in the lower, shaded crown area. Outer exposed parts of border trees also produced more acorns than partly shaded crown areas. Verne further noted that south and west facing sides of crowns produced more acorns than those facing east or north. There are, of course, exceptions

Table 13.1. Cone production of conifers at the Stanislaus National Forest, California. Data are for 16 years. (*After Fowells and Schubert, 1956.*)

Crown class	Ponderosa pine, total cones produced		No. of cones per tree	Sugar pine, total cones produced		No. of cones per tree	White fir, total cones produced		No. of cones per tree
	No.	Per cent		No.	Per cent		No.	Per cent	
Dominant	82,692	99.03	996	41,836	98.46	291	138,334	87.56	221
Codominant	767	0.92	70	640	1.51	24	18,655	11.81	77
Intermediate and suppressed	38	0.05	6	13	0.03	4	995	0.63	27
Total	83,497	100.00		42,489	100.00		157,984	100.00	

to these generalizations, and it is not uncommon to find open-growth trees with large crowns that produce little or no seed. The inhibition of seed production in suppressed trees probably reflects competition for light, moisture, and minerals, and the reduction is often proportional to the severity of the deficiency. Wenger (1954) noted a large increase in cone crops of loblolly pine trees that were isolated by cutting. When he released trees from competition, he found they produced 10 times as many cones as did control trees. Bilan (1957) also found that releasing loblolly pine from competition increased the cone crop. Allen (1953), Cooper and Perry (1956), and Halls and Hawley (1954) observed that release from competition increased cone production of longleaf and slash pines.

Tree Vigor. Vigorous, fast-growing trees are much better seed producers than unthrifty ones. Since seed production requires large quantities of minerals, trees growing in soil of high fertility are usually prolific seed producers, especially if they are not competing with other trees. Wenger (1953b) observed that addition of a balanced fertilizer greatly increased cone production of 25-year-old loblolly pine. The next year, however, the effect of the fertilizer disappeared. Since the response to added minerals was observed only in the earliest possible year, Wenger concluded that the effect was directly nutritional rather than indirect through foliage development and increased carbohydrate supplies, as previously reported by Chandler (1938) for deciduous species. Gemmer (1932) also emphasized the relation of tree vigor to cone production. He found that a complete fertilizer plus irrigation greatly increased vigor of longleaf pine and produced 62 cones per treated tree compared with only 2 cones per untreated tree. Chandler (1938) and Detwiler (1943) also reported a large increase in seed production of broadleaf species after addition of fertilizer.

The importance for seed production of high carbohydrate reserves in the crown has been demonstrated by girdling and banding. For example, Pond (1936) observed that a knife-cut girdle stimulated 50 per cent of experimental black ash trees to produce seed compared with 10 per cent of the check trees. Similarly in Europe, Arnborg (1946) noted that girdling and banding caused pines to almost double cone production. Bilan (1957) found that girdling and banding were much less effective in increasing seed production of loblolly pine than opening up the stand. Wenger (1953b) found that release was more effective than fertilization. He later suggested that the larger seed crops produced after release of loblolly pine might be caused by increased soil moisture rather than increased light (Wenger, 1957). Both increased light and increased moisture might lead to increased photosynthesis and higher carbohydrate content.

As mentioned earlier, a relatively high concentration of carbohydrate promotes flower bud initiation, and it usually is assumed that a high carbohydrate content combined with moderate nitrogen content is most favorable for seed production. Excessive fertilization with nitrogen might divert so much carbohydrate to vegetative growth that flowering and seed production are reduced. Forest soils usually are low in nitrogen, however, and moderate increases probably will increase seed production of forest trees. The amount already available and the time at which additional nitrogen is applied will affect the results. More research is needed on the effects of fertilization on seed production.

Climate. Weather conditions exert control on seed production by influencing flower bud formation and existing flower crops. Conditions of high temperatures, adequate light, and soil moisture, which promote high rates of photosynthesis and carbohydrate accumulation, are conducive to production of large seed crops. Extended rainy periods during flowering may decrease seed production by suppressing pollen dispersal of wind-pollinated trees, thus resulting in less-than-normal amounts of fertilization. Heavy rains also interfere with pollination by preventing activity of pollinating insects. Rainy, cloudy weather may cause drop

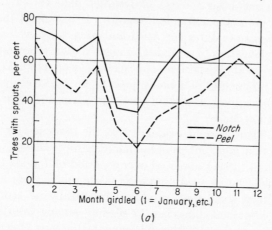

(a)

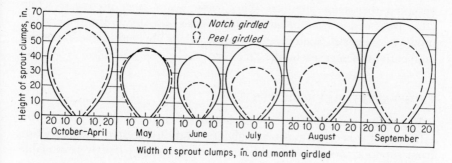

Width of sprout clumps, in. and month girdled

(b)

Figure 13.8 Effect of season of girdling on number and size of sprouts produced by blackjack oak trees. Observations were made six seasons after girdling. Above, number of trees producing sprouts after girdling in various months. Below, height and width of clumps of sprouts produced after girdling in various months. (*From Clark and Liming, 1953.*)

of young fruits because it reduces the amount of photosynthesis and lowers the carbohydrate supply. Wet soil interferes with absorption of nitrogen and mineral nutrients. Lack of moisture often inhibits seed maturation, and pine seed crops are reported to have been ruined by droughts. Weather conditions are particularly crucial in the spring, when frosts may kill flowers (Campbell, 1955; Gysel, 1956). Frost damage to flowers is of the greatest concern to orchardists because entire fruit crops often are destroyed in this way. Orchard managers often combat such spring frosts with smoke screens to reduce radiation and with various types of orchard heaters (Gardner et al., 1952). Occasionally late freezes seriously reduce the seed crop of forest trees, as occurred in the southeastern United States in the spring of 1955.

There is some basis for use of weather data for predicting size of future seed crops. For example, Maguire (1956) found that when average monthly temperatures for April and May were well above normal, ponderosa pine trees flowered abundantly the following spring and there was a good prospect of an excellent seed crop. Wenger (1957) found seed production of loblolly pine to be positively correlated with rainfall of the second preceding year and inversely correlated with the previous seed crop.

Heredity. There is some evidence that the tendency for heavy or light seed production is an inheritable characteristic (Downs, 1947). Downs and McQuilkin (1944) observed over a period of 7 years that some oaks were habitually heavy seed producers while others were habitually light seeders. In fact, some trees produced practically no acorns for several years. The continued difference in seeding among trees of similar size could not be correlated with environmental factors. Downs (1947) also observed that some shortleaf pines were heavy seed producers while other trees of the same or larger crown class and size in the same stand produced no cones. Such genetic considerations obviously have important implications in seed orchards.

VEGETATIVE REPRODUCTION

Vegetative reproduction is more important in horticulture than in forestry, but it is becoming increasingly important to foresters. Reproduction from superior specimens would be greatly facilitated if it were possible to propagate them vegetatively.

Sprouting

Sprouting is the most important type of vegetative propagation for hardwood forest stands. Sprouts of species that can develop from either seeds or sprouts are invariably of poorer form than trees from seed. Nevertheless, sprouting is important in certain instances, as in the reproduction of pond pine after fire and aspen, birch, and oak after cutting. Much of the New England hardwood forests and as much as 75 per cent of the oak forests of Pennsylvania originate from sprouts (Braun, 1950; McIntyre, 1936). Reproduction in the oak-hickory forests of the Ozarks also is largely of sprout origin (Liming and Johnston, 1944).

Sprouts originate from both adventitious and dormant buds. These are quite different in origin (Stone and Stone, 1943a). Adventitious buds originate *de novo*, usually from callus tissue around wounds. Most buds originate in the axils of the leaves on new shoots. Some of these develop new shoots the succeeding year, but many remain dormant indefinitely. As trees increase in diameter, these dormant buds grow just enough in length for the tips to remain outside of the wood but under the bark. Each year the increase in length equals the width of the new annual increment, resulting in a dwarfed, modified, embedded branch or bud trace. These dormant buds sometimes branch, giving rise to additional buds. This accounts for the numerous sprouts that arise from stumps of species such as sweetgum, which form few adventitious buds. When the physiological balance of a tree is upset by cutting, injury, fire, or disease, dormant and adventitious buds are stimulated to produce sprouts. In fact, the presence of sprouts near the bases of standing trees usually is symptomatic of some physiological disorder.

A distinction should be made between stump sprouts, stool shoots, and root suckers. Stump sprouts, which arise from root collars and the lower part of the tree trunk, develop from dormant buds which formed early and grew outward with the cambium. Stool shoots develop from adventitious buds which arise between the bark and wood of stumps. Ordinarily such shoots are short-lived and of no real importance in vegetative propagation. Root sprouts or root suckers arise from adventitious buds on roots, and their production is increased by mechanical injury. Reproduction by root suckers is rare among trees, except in black locust and several species of *Populus*. In pine, "root collar" sprouts arise from buds formed in axils of primary needles rather than from adventitious buds (Stone and Stone, 1954).

Although regeneration by sprouts is relatively unimportant in gymnosperms, a few coniferous species sprout prolifically, especially after fire. Among the conifers which have good sprouting ability are redwood, pitch pine, shortleaf pine, pond pine, and baldcypress. Cheyney (1942) states that only three American conifers, shortleaf pine, cypress, and redwood, produce sprouts that will grow to merchantable size. Although redwood is considered a good sprout producer, Person and Hollin (1942) found that sprouts provided less than 10 per cent of full stocking.

Epicormic Branches

When the environment of a tree is changed by exposure to light, its main stem or branches may produce branches from dormant buds. Such epicormic branches or water sprouts are a response to altered physiological balance which usually follows thinning or pruning. When trees are equally crowded on all sides, epicormic sprouts may be produced on the warmest side, but since forest trees are seldom equally crowded on all

Physiology of Trees

sides, most of the sprouts occur on the side which is most open (Wahlenberg, 1950). Most epicormic sprouts are located on the upper part of the clear bole, and few develop within the crown. Several epicormic branches in tufts may result from sudden growth of a cluster of lateral buds which formed at the base of the scales of a dormant bud during its prolonged suppression (Roth and Sleeth, 1939). Epicormic branches are more common on hardwoods than on conifers and are of concern to foresters because they produce quality-reducing knots. Second-growth timber is more susceptible to epicormic branching than old-growth trees. Jemison and Schumacher (1948) observed numbers of epicormic branches to vary significantly with species, site, merchantable height, and log position, but not with volume per acre or volume removed in logging.

Some species of pine bear dwarfed lateral branches or tufts of needle fascicles on the upper part of the bole long after the normal needles have fallen. Stone and Stone (1943a) observed that such sprouts arise from small buds at the intermediate nodes of multinodal stems, as well as from lateral buds at the winter nodes, which may remain dormant for a few years. If these buds grow, they become short branches of limited development, bearing isolated or few fascicles, but they can form normal long branches following injury to the tree. In pitch pine the branches of limited development give rise to lateral buds which often remain dormant for a considerable time in the bark of the parent tree. Stone and Stone suggested that stem sprouts in certain other multinodal pines, such as pond, shortleaf, Chihuahua, Table-Mountain, and digger pines, have a similar origin and development. According to Stone (1953b), dormant and adventitious buds have been confused in relation to sprouting in conifers. His observations demonstrated that adventitious stem buds are uncommon in many native coniferous genera, and he concluded that branching of conifers after pruning originates usually from dormant buds already present on the stems at the time of pruning.

Factors Affecting Sprouting

Among the important factors which influence sprouting are species, season of cutting, size of parent tree, and site. These will be discussed separately.

Species. It has already been stated that sprouting capacity is common among hardwoods and rare among conifers. There also is considerable variation among species in each of these two groups. For example, Little (1938) observed that white oak and post oak had more but shorter sprouts per stump than did black and scarlet oaks. Chestnut oak stumps gave rise to nearly as many stems as did white oak, yet the sprouts were more vigorous at the end of the first season than those in the black oak group. Before the fourteenth year, vigor, as measured by height, was greatest for scarlet oak, followed by black oak. These two species appeared to be the most intolerant, for persistence of sprouts ran in this order: post, white, chestnut, black, and scarlet.

All hardwoods do not sprout equally well throughout their ranges. For example, sugar maple, beech, and hophornbeam sprout vigorously in the northern but not in the southern part of their ranges. Many oaks, however, sprout vigorously through a greater part of their range (Braun, 1950).

Season of Cutting. Sprouting is least abundant from stumps cut in early summer when trees have just fully leafed out, and greatest from stumps of trees which were cut during the dormant season. As may be seen in Figure 13.8, Clark and Liming (1953) noted that in Missouri oak trees girdled in June had fewer trees sprouting, higher mortality of sprout clumps, fewer sprouts per tree, and smaller sprout clumps than trees treated during any other month. Stoeckeler (1947) found similar sprouting patterns for aspen and cherry in northeastern Wisconsin. Wenger (1953a) observed that sprouting of sweetgum in South Carolina followed a pronounced trend by date of cutting with two minima, the first when leaves that had emerged earliest reached full size and the second during the late-summer hardening period. Seasonal fluctuation in sprouting is of considerable silvicultural importance, as emphasized by Buell (1940), because weedings of undesirable species made in summer when sprout growth is less vigorous will give desirable crop trees the best chance of keeping ahead of competition from sprouts. However, if merchantable trees are cut and a crop is desired from sprouts, cutting during the dormant season will encourage a new stand of maximum density and vigor. When trees are cut in the latter part of the growing season, the abundant sprouts which follow usually fail to harden adequately and are killed by frost.

It generally has been held that sprouting vigor is closely related to availability of carbohydrate reserves. Seasonal fluctuations in carbohydrate reserves seem to parallel seasonal sprouting vigor, with a minimum occurring in early summer (Aldous, 1929). Furthermore, Clark and Liming (1953) found that practically all the sprouting of oaks took place during the first and second growing season after girdling. Sprouting was delayed to the second year for trees girdled late in the season. Many stumps will sprout for a number of years after cutting if the sprouts from the previous year are removed, but they usually sprout best during the first year after cutting. These observations suggest that sprouting vigor decreases as carbohydrate reserves are exhausted. However, Wenger (1953a) found that sprouting of sweetgum in South Carolina was not dependent on carbohydrate content. He suggested that a hormone system related to that controlling apical dominance governs sprouting vigor. At the present time the physiological control of sprouting is not satisfactorily explained, and this intriguing problem deserves further study.

Size of Parent Tree. The number of sprouts per stump increases with diameter up to the point where increasing thickness of the bark begins to hinder emergence of dormant buds. The possibility of bud traces being interrupted also increases with time. The increase in number of sprouts with increasing age and size occurs because the passage of time permits more branching of the original bud traces. It is possible that the dormant buds at the base of the tree also are less inhibited by active buds in the treetop as trees grow larger. In oaks, sprouting seems to increase with tree diameter up to about 5 inches and decreases with diameters above 6 inches (Little, 1938; Roth and Sleeth, 1939), but exceptions occur. For example, white oak stumps sprout prolifically up to 100 years of age and a diameter of 16 inches, and black and scarlet oak stumps sprout well up to 150 years of age and a diameter of 22 inches, but few sprouts are formed by older trees. Wenger (1953a) suggested that sprout size may be related to the effects of size of root system on the supply of water and mineral nutrients as well as the supply of food.

Site. Sprouting usually is more vigorous on good sites than on poor sites. Sprouts of quaking aspen and pin cherry on good sites were about 27 per cent taller than sprouts on poor sites, when the cut was made in the dormant season (Stoeckeler, 1947). The improved growth on better sites probably results from more available moisture and minerals, and perhaps more food stored in the stumps.

Cuttings

Many species of trees are multiplied by stem or root cuttings when they do not reproduce well by other means or when it is important that the new plants will be similar to the parent in all respects. According to Mahlstede and Haber (1957), more woody ornamentals are produced by cuttings than by seeds, grafting, budding, or layering. Attempts to root cuttings of many species of forest and orchard trees have been disappointing. Other species of forest trees root easily when cuttings are taken from young trees during a critical period of the year and treated with root-inducing chemicals.

Reproduction of forest trees by cuttings is important in developing clones or groups of plants which have originated by vegetative propagation from one seedling. As pointed out by Schreiner (1939a), considerable importance should be attached to the clone in practical forestry because it offers advantages of uniformity of growth and development and immediate availability of superior individuals for reforestation. The clone also is important in forest research because it eliminates differences in genetic constitution between trees. Forest geneticists have found the clone useful for improvement of forest trees, and pathologists have adapted it to work with tree diseases. Thomas and Riker (1950) believe that propagation of trees by cuttings holds promise for reproducing white pine trees selected for resistance to blister rust. Propagation by cuttings probably will receive more attention from foresters in the future than it has in the past. In Japan *Cryptomeria japonica* has been propagated by cuttings for centuries and many races have been developed. *Thujopsis dolabrata* also has been propagated by cuttings for many years.

Root Development on Cuttings. The types of adventitious roots which develop from cuttings vary with the species and the part of the tree from which the cuttings are taken. Root primordia may already be present when the cuttings are taken (morphological roots), or they may develop later (wound roots). Wound roots can develop from various tissues. Bannan (1942) found that they originated from dormant buds, from near dead or injured branches, and from the cambium. Satoo (1956) found that wound roots of conifer cuttings developed from the following tissues: (1) cambial and phloem regions of ray tissues, (2) leaf and branch traces, (3) bud meristems and bud traces, (4) irregularly arranged patches of parenchyma, and (5) callus tissue. However, in cuttings of species which were particularly difficult to root, practically all roots originated from callus tissue. According to Snyder (1954), callus tissue arises primarily from divisions of cambium and of phloem parenchyma, but it can form from any living cell which has not developed secondary walls (Buck, 1954).

Factors Affecting Rooting of Cuttings

Formation of roots on cuttings depends both on the internal condition of the plant from which they are taken and the environment in which they are placed. Little is known about the internal factors, but it seems clear that the physiological condition of the plant often is of paramount importance, because cuttings taken at one season may root readily while cuttings taken earlier or later in the season from the same plant fail to root regardless of how they are treated. Furthermore, cuttings taken from seedlings often root much better than cuttings from mature trees, as shown later in this chapter. The extensive literature on this subject was reviewed by Allen and McComb (1955) and Nienstaedt et al. (1958).

It often is stated that the carbohydrate and nitrogen reserves or the carbohydrate/nitrogen ratio is an important factor in the rooting of cuttings. A correlation between the starch content of cuttings and formation of callus and new roots was reported in evergreens by Durham (1934). Knight (1926) also emphasized the importance of carbohydrates for rooting and reported that rooting of cuttings of certain deciduous species was increased by soaking them in sucrose solution. According to Migita

(1955), poor rooting of heavily shaded cuttings is related to low carbo-hydrate content. Although the food supply obviously is an important factor, it seems likely that the control exercised over its utilization in root growth, probably through the action of hormones, is even more important.

Klein (1953) stated that it is generally agreed that metabolic factors are more important than hormonal factors in rooting of cuttings, but it is not clear which metabolites are most important. He found no correla-tion between sugar content and rooting of grape cuttings, although he cites work indicating that high carbohydrates promote rooting. Negisi and Satoo (1956) studied photosynthesis and respiration of *Cryptomeria* cuttings. Photosynthesis decreased rapidly after cuttings were made and often almost ceased. When roots were formed, photosynthesis increased to a relatively high level. The decrease was attributed to low water con-tent, which was eliminated after roots were formed. Respiration also fell to a low rate, then rose again after roots were formed.

Rooting Compounds. Cuttings of some species root easily, but their root-ing usually is improved by treatment with root-inducing growth sub-stances. Other species require such treatment for rooting (Thimann and Behnke, 1950). Indolebutyric acid, naphthaleneacetic acid, and indole-acetic acid and their potassium salts and esters are routinely used to treat cuttings for better rooting. Some species respond better to one or more of these compounds than to the others. In general, indolebutyric acid gives good results with cuttings of a number of species. Correct dosages are important, and optimum concentrations vary with the species. Root-ing is further improved in some species if mineral nutrients or fungicides are mixed with the growth substances.

After the base of a cutting has been treated with a root-inducing growth substance, carbohydrates are translocated to the treated area, the rate of respiration increases, and transformations of carbohydrates and organic nitrogen compounds occur. The growth substance accelerates normal metabolism and increases the number of root primordia (Snyder, 1954). Morphological development of the new roots is similar to that in untreated cuttings (Hiller, 1951). A natural supply of auxin from the tip of the cutting appears to stimulate rooting because debudding of cuttings usually decreases callus growth and root initiation. Removal of leaves from cuttings also decreases root formation. According to van Overbeek et al. (1946), the chief function of leaves in root initiation is to supply the cutting with sugars and nitrogenous substances. Garner (1944) discusses a number of methods that have been used for introduc-ing root-inducing substances into cuttings. The techniques are very simple. The two most popular methods will be mentioned briefly.

Solution Treatment. Prolonged immersion involves dipping about an inch of the basal ends of cuttings in glass containers of dilute hormone solutions for as long as 24 hours. Shorter-time immersions are used for species that are easy to root. Solution concentrations usually vary from 10 to 100 parts per million (Avery et al., 1947). During immersion, cuttings should not be exposed to strong sunlight, although some light is advisable (Pearse, 1939). Cuttings often are planted without rinsing after treatment, but it probably is safer to rinse them with water after prolonged immersion or immersion in very concentrated solutions. Solutions may be reused a few times, but succeeding treatments should be prolonged. The solutions deteriorate after a few days. Time of immersion and concentration are related, but a long-time immersion in a less concentrated solution generally will not equal a shorter time at higher concentration.

Short-time immersion consists in dipping basal ends of cuttings in glass beakers of concentrated hormone solutions for about 5 seconds. Hitchcock and Zimmerman (1939) used solutions varying in concentration from 1 to 20 milligrams of growth regulator per milliliter. Indolebutyric acid is dissolved in 50 per cent ethyl alcohol, or water is used instead of alcohol if sodium or potassium salts of indolebutyric acid are used. This method has been especially successful in rooting some species known to be difficult to root, including hemlock, apple, rhododendron, cinchona, and cacao (Avery et al., 1947).

Powder Treatment. The simplest and most popular method involves dipping the basal end of a cutting first in water and then in a hormone powder before planting. The hormone is distributed in a carrier, usually talc, but charcoal, bentonite, wheat flour, and soybean flour have also been used. Trade preparations of hormone powder in talc usually contain 1 to 8 milligrams of indolebutyric acid per gram of carrier. Powder mixtures may be reused.

After treatment, cuttings are inserted into benches containing a rooting medium, usually sand, loam, peat, vermiculite, or a mixture of these. For further details on techniques, time of year of taking cuttings, correct dosages of growth substances, and care of cuttings in the rooting benches, the reader is referred to Pearse (1939), Garner (1944), Avery et al. (1947), Thimann and Behnke (1950), and Mahlstede and Haber (1957).

Species. Cuttings of some species are much easier to root than others. There also is considerable variation among individual trees of the same species in their ability to root. Orchard trees such as apple, cherry, and peach and some deciduous forest trees including oak, beech, and maple are difficult to root. Cuttings of sugar maple have been rooted successfully, but there has been much difficulty in keeping the rooted cuttings alive over the first winter. If kept in the greenhouse over the first winter, the cuttings fail to resume growth outdoors the next spring (Doran, 1953). Many conifer cuttings root readily, but others are difficult to root.

Those of Norway spruce and eastern hemlock root more easily than those of white pine. Cuttings of the southeastern species of pine are very difficult to root (Mergen, 1955b). For ranking of species as to ease of rooting, the reader is referred to Avery et al. (1947), Thimann and Behnke (1950), and Doran (1957). Thimann and Delisle (1939) reported success in rooting several species that are normally considered difficult to root.

Age of Parent Tree. Cuttings usually root more readily if taken from younger than from older trees, if these were grown from seed. Thus, to ensure retention of certain characteristics of a particular tree, cuttings should be taken as soon as the desired features are evident. When cuttings were taken from 1-year-old seedlings of a number of orchard and forest trees, they rooted readily, but if 1-year-old wood from 2-year-old seedlings was used, rooting fell off appreciably (Gardner, 1929b). Among others, Thimann and Delisle (1939) and Mirov (1944) have shown that root formation on cuttings of forest trees decreases with increased age of the mother tree. Delisle (1954) grew rooted white pine cuttings to the age of 4 years. He then grew cuttings from these trees to the age of 4 years and made cuttings from them. The ability to form roots declined with each successive generation of cuttings. Patton and Riker (1958) also found that ability of white pine cuttings to root decreased with increasing age of the trees from which they were taken. Age of parent tree may or may not have an effect on "rootability" if cuttings are taken from trees which also originated from rooted cuttings. For example, Satoo et al. (1953) took cuttings from trees of *Cryptomeria japonica* of various ages belonging to the same clone, and their rooting was compared. Rooting of two of the four clones studied decreased with increasing age of the trees from which cuttings were taken, while the other two clones did not show a decrease. Even the form of the resulting plant may change with the age of the plant from which cuttings are obtained. Cuttings from young ivy plants (*Hedera*) always produce vines, but cuttings from adult, fruiting plants produce shrubs or small trees (Robbins, 1957).

Season. Stem cuttings of some species root well when taken over a period of from several weeks to several months, but for successful rooting, cuttings of other species must be taken within a critical period, which may last only from 1 to 2 weeks. Within limits, ability to form roots is related to the condition of the plant and the climate rather than time of year, so the best time for taking cuttings may vary somewhat from year to year (Garner, 1944). Considerable success has been obtained with cuttings of deciduous trees and conifers that were obtained in late autumn, winter, or early spring. Rooting of conifers usually is poor if stem cuttings are taken in late spring or early summer while shoots are still growing. On the other hand, best rooting of some species, such as azaleas, is obtained with softwood cuttings which are made before the wood has matured completely. According to Creech (1954), root cuttings should be made either in the autumn or during the winter months. Klein (1953) suggested that seasonal variations in rooting are related to variations in amount of a root-forming substance.

Part of Tree Sampled. Lateral shoots appear to root better than terminals (Knight, 1926; Grace, 1939). Ten weeks after planting Grace found that only 43 per cent of the cuttings taken from the upper regions of a Norway spruce rooted; 75 per cent of the lower cuttings rooted. In addition the lower cuttings produced twice the length of roots of the upper cuttings. When shoots are long enough to produce several cuttings, rooting of the basal cuttings usually is best. Podluzhnii (1940) noted that there was a progressive decrease in the rooting capacity of cuttings of olive as they were taken from the base of a shoot toward the tip. According to Tukey and Green (1934), moisture content, ash, and total nitrogen increased while starch decreased from the bases toward the tips of rose shoots. The basal cuttings of shoots may root better than cuttings from tips of shoots because of more available carbohydrates.

Grafting

Grafting and budding techniques are used extensively by horticulturists to propagate most fruit and ornamental trees because cuttings of such trees do not root easily and their seeds do not reproduce desirable characteristics. Foresters were slow to use such intensive methods, but they now have become an important tool in modern stand improvement programs. Grafting is used extensively in the development of seed orchards (Zobel et al., 1958) and for many other purposes. Mirov (1940) stressed the usefulness of grafting in propagating specimens for research and suggested that exotic species which do not thrive in a given environment can often be grown if grafted on local rootstocks. He found that inarching was the easiest way to graft pines in the semiarid conditions of California. Larsen and Magius (1944) and Pauley (1948) suggested that budding techniques might be used to introduce genetically superior forms of trees into forests and thereby improve stands of low quality.

Pathologists have found grafting to be very useful in studying tree diseases (Zak, 1955). Most of the known virus diseases of trees can be transmitted by grafting an infected part of the diseased tree, such as a twig, stem, bark patch, or a root piece, onto a susceptible healthy tree. Jackson and Zak (1949) adapted grafting techniques in studying little-leaf disease of shortleaf pine, and Graves (1950) found inarching or bridge grafting useful in saving diseased chestnut trees. Grafting also has been used to produce hardy and disease-resistant trees. For example, peach stems may be grafted on nematode-resistant rootstocks. To avoid frost injury in northern states "three-story" apple trees have been developed by grafting a cold-resistant stem on a seedling rootstock. A fruiting branch of a desired variety is then grafted on the cold-resistant stem (Wareing and Hilborn, 1942).

The anatomical changes which occur during formation of a graft union vary among different species. According to Nienstaedt et al. (1958), the following steps usually occur: (1) formation of a contact layer, (2) development of callus, (3) elimination of the contact layer and beginning of callus differentiation, (4) union of vascular elements, and (5) formation of a common cambium.

Successful grafting depends fundamentally on congeniality or compatibility of subjects and on good contact of cambial zones of stock and scion. Some cases of successful grafts between trees of different botanical families have been reported, but these are uncommon. However, permanent unions between genera in the same family occur often, as between *Crataegus* and *Pyrus*. Incompatability varies in degree from outright killing of the plant to various degrees of unthriftiness, failure to bear properly, and premature death. Incompatibility is indicated often by a smooth break at the point of union after one growing season. As pointed out by Eames and Cox (1945), this results from failure of the fibers of stock and scion to interlock. Some grafted trees will grow vigorously during the first year but show incompatibility in succeeding years. Zak (1955) concluded that success or failure of grafts in pine was largely a matter of water relationships in the scion stem, and later in the scion-stock combination. Rogers and Beakbane (1957) have a good discussion of stock and scion relations. For techniques and methods of grafting, the reader is referred to the book by Garner (1958) and the article by Nienstaedt et al. (1958) which cites most of the recent literature.

Natural Grafting. Natural fusion of roots of trees is common. There is much less opportunity for twigs and branches to graft naturally than there is for natural root grafts to occur, because the frequent movement and swaying of aboveground parts usually prevent their prolonged contact. Nevertheless, such grafts occur occasionally.

Root grafts are common in trees of Temperate and Tropical Zones (Rigg and Harrar, 1931; LaRue, 1934, 1952; Adams, 1940; Beddie, 1941). Roots appear to fuse best when they approach each other at an acute angle, but almost any angle of approach may result in a good graft. Even roots which approach each other from opposite directions may unite, and the elements of the new annual ring may twist so that they are oriented ultimately in the same direction (Büsgen and Münch, 1931, p. 39). Rigg and Harrar (1931) found that root fusions of conifers in peaty soils near Seattle, Washington, were promoted by the swaying of the trees, which caused bark abrasion and contact of their cambial regions. Although abrasion between roots stimulates graft unions, removal of the bark by friction does not appear to be necessary for grafts. LaRue (1934) found many fusions of white pine roots that were growing in stiff clay and reasoned that the trees could not have swayed enough to wear away the bark on the roots before the unions took place.

Root grafts are very important physiologically because trees can receive water, minerals, and presumably carbohydrates and hormones necessary for their growth from other trees through such grafts. This is discussed in Chapter 8, where examples of root grafts are pictured.

Layering

Layering refers to the formation of roots on attached branches, where they come into contact with a moist medium. Natural layering occurs where low-growing branches come into contact with the soil, and layering can be induced by wrapping branches in a water-retaining substance such as sphagnum. Layering can be used to good advantage to propagate plants that do not come true to type from seeds and are not readily reproduced by other vegetative methods.

Natural layering occurs fairly commonly among certain species of forest trees. For example, old spruces and hemlocks in open sites often develop vigorous lower branches that bend over, become covered by litter, and take root. Black spruce and northern-white cedar in northern peat swamps also reproduce by layering. According to Lutz (1939), layering frequently occurs in *Tsuga, Picea, Abies, Chamaecyparis, Thuja, Juniperus,* and *Taxus,* but only rarely in *Pinus.* Little (1944) described an interesting case of natural layering that was promoted by a heavy snowfall which bent branches to the ground. He observed that red maple, flowering dogwood, *Viburnum pubescens,* and *Clethra alnifolia* all layered readily.

Several modifications of artificial layering methods have been used by propagators. Probably the most useful of these are simple layering and trench layering; in the latter roots develop on shoots which arise from the buried part. In recent years interest has revived in air or Chinese layering, a very old method in which a tree branch is wounded in the spring or early summer, a growth-regulating compound is dusted into the wound, and moist sphagnum is wrapped around the wound. This is tightly wrapped in a thin sheet of waterproof paper or plastic which is tied at the top and bottom to retain moisture. After roots form, the rooted portion is severed from the mother plant. Both horticulturists (Wyman, 1951; Creech, 1954) and foresters (Mergen, 1955a; Zak, 1956) have found air layering useful in propagating trees.

GENERAL REFERENCES

Anonymous, 1948, Woody plant seed manual, U.S. Dept. Agr. Misc. Pub. 654.

Creech, J. L. (ed.), 1954, Vegetative propagation, Natl. Hort. Mag., vol. 33, no. 1.

Gardner, V. R., F. C. Bradford, and H. D. Hooker, Jr., 1952, Fundamentals of fruit production, McGraw-Hill Book Company, Inc., New York.

Garner, R. J., 1957, The grafter's handbook, Faber & Faber, Ltd., London.

Hawley, R. C., and D. M. Smith, 1954, The practice of silviculture, 6th ed., John Wiley & Sons, Inc., New York.

Nitsch, J. P., 1953, The physiology of fruit growth, Ann. Rev. Plant Physiology, 4:199–236.

Sheat, W. G., 1953, Propagation of trees, shrubs, and conifers, St. Martin's Press, New York.

Thimann, K. V., and J. Behnke, 1950, The use of auxins in the rooting of woody cuttings, Maria Moors Cabot Found. Pub. 1, Harvard Forest, Petersham, Mass.

Wenger, K. F., and K. B. Trousdell, 1958, Natural regeneration of loblolly pine in the South Atlantic coastal plain, U.S. Dept. Agr. Prod. Research Rept. 13.

CHAPTER 14 *Physiology of Seeds and Seed Germination*

The essential structure in a seed is the living embryo, and most of our concern in the storage of seeds is to provide conditions which will keep the embryo alive and ready to resume growth when the seed is planted. There also is a supply of food, either in the embryo itself or in the surrounding tissue, and the embryo and food supply are enclosed in a protective covering, the seed coat. Botanically, seeds are matured ovules, and their development was described in Chapter 13. Often part of the ovary remains attached to seeds, forming complex structures such as berries, drupes, nuts, or samaras, as shown in Figure 13.5. Botanically, such structures are fruits enclosing seeds, but they often are treated by foresters as special types of seeds.

Seed germination consists of the resumption of growth by the embryo and its development into a new, independent seedling. This involves most of the important processes included in the realm of plant physiology, such as water absorption, digestion of food, translocation, assimilation, and respiration.

Seed Structure

Tree seeds vary widely in size and complexity of structure, ranging from those which are barely visible, such as seeds of sourwood and rhododendron, to the large seeds of oaks and walnuts and, the largest of all, the coconut. They also vary considerably in structure, with respect both to the embryo and to the number and kind of parts associated with the embryo. Some examples of seed structure are shown in Figure 14.1.

Embryos. The embryo is a small, relatively simple plant, consisting of cotyledons or seed leaves attached to a rudimentary stem or hypocotyl which bears a stem tip or plumule at one end and a root tip or radicle at the other end. Plants are classified partly according to the number of cotyledons borne by the embryo. The seeds of most deciduous trees have two cotyledons and belong in the group known as dicotyledonous plants. The embryos of bamboo and palm seeds possess only one cotyledon, and they are classified with other monocotyledonous plants such as lilies and grasses. The embryos of conifer seeds bear from 2 to 15 cotyledons.

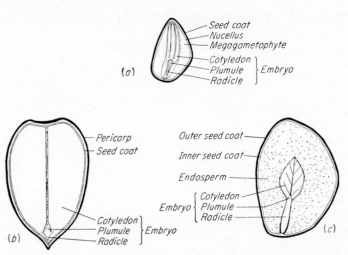

Figure 14.1 Structure of typical tree seeds. *a.* Pine seed. Food is stored in the megagametophyte, which is often termed "endosperm" but is different in origin and chromosome number from true endosperm. *b.* White oak acorn in which food is stored in cotyledons. The seed is enclosed in a fruit coat or pericarp. *c.* Persimmon seed containing its stored food in the endosperm. The cotyledons are thin and leaflike.

Cotyledons often are relatively large and thick and function as storage organs which supply food for seedling growth until the secondary leaves begin to carry on photosynthesis. Walnut, oak, beech, and leguminous species produce seeds with cotyledons of this type. Seeds of many other species such as dogwood and red maple possess thin cotyledons which expand, become green, and carry on photosynthesis as soon as they emerge from the ground. In such seeds food is stored outside of the embryo, usually in the endosperm, and is absorbed through the cotyledons, which are in close contact with the food-storage structure.

Seeds sometimes are classified according to the behavior of the cotyledons during germination. If the cotyledons emerge from the soil (beech, dogwood, most maples, and conifers), germination is called epigeous, but if they remain in the soil (oak, silver maple, walnut), it is called hypogeous (Figure 14.2).

Food Storage. As mentioned earlier, the food supply may be stored either in the cotyledons or in tissue surrounding the embryos, which usually is endosperm. True endosperm is triploid in chromosome number, having been formed following union of the diploid fusion nucleus and a sperm. It forms the principal food-storage tissue in many dicotyledonous species, including apple, ash, and dogwood. In ailanthus some food is

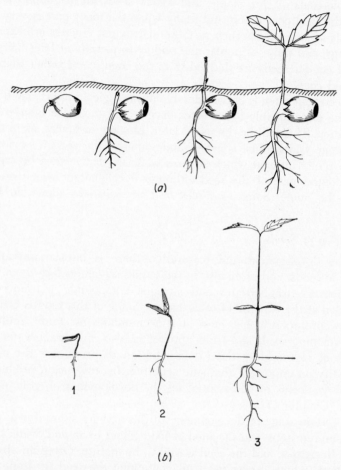

Figure 14.2 Stages in germination of seeds. *a.* Germination of white oak acorns in which cotyledons remain below ground (hypogeous). *b.* Germination of red maple in which cotyledons are pushed out of the ground (epigeous). (*Redrawn from various sources.*)

stored in the endosperm and some in the cotyledons. The so-called endosperm of conifer seed is megagametophyte tissue, haploid in chromosome number and quite different in origin from true endosperm although it serves the same function.

Seed Coats. The seed coat usually is a double layer of tissue which is derived from the integuments of the ovule. It protects the embryo from dehydration and mechanical injury, and even from attacks by insects and microorganisms. Seed coats vary from the hard, heavily cutinized, impermeable coats of black locust and holly to the relatively soft and permeable coats of elm, maple, and willow seeds. In magnolia the outer part of the seed coat is soft and fleshy while the inner part is very hard. The coats of some seeds such as those of trumpet creeper are expanded into wings, and those of poplar and willow form tufts of long hairs. The wings of conifer seeds are derived from the cone scales rather than from their seed coats.

The seed coat often is of considerable physiological importance because it may be impermeable to water or oxygen and therefore interfere with germination. This will be discussed later. In some instances, as in the so-called stone fruits, nuts, achenes, and samaras, the seed is enclosed in a pericarp or fruit coat which adheres so firmly that it must be regarded as an integral part of the seed although it originated from tissue outside of the ovule. Some examples of tree fruits are shown in Figure 13.5.

Maturation of Seeds

During development and maturation there is intense physiological activity in seeds, and often also in the tissues which enclose them. Large quantities of carbohydrates and nitrogen compounds are moved into them even at the expense of other tissues. Some of this food is converted into new protoplasm, but most of it accumulates as starch, protein, or fat. Developing seeds and fruits apparently also can obtain water at the expense of surrounding tissues. In addition to producing the embryo, seeds carry on important synthetic activities, because auxin produced by the embryo seems to be essential for the development of fruits of some species (Chapter 15).

At a certain stage of development all this activity slows down, growth of the embryo stops, translocation of food comes to an end, water content usually decreases, and the seed is said to be mature. Often an abscission layer forms which causes the fruit containing the seed to drop, or else the fruit dries, shrinks, and dehisces, and the seeds are shed. The sudden cessation of physiological activity which terminates maturation is as amazing as the burst of activity which follows fertilization and results in development of the seed and fruit. Further study of seed maturation would be interesting, possibly along the lines of the study of pea fruit maturation made by McKee et al. (1955). Some data on the chemical composition of seeds are presented in Table 14.1, and Crocker and Barton (1953) devote two chapters to this topic.

Seed Collection

The collection of seeds is not in itself a physiological problem, but the proper time to collect them is determined by their physiological and morphological condition. Physiologically, a seed is mature enough to

Table 14.1. Chemical composition of tree seeds as percentage of dry weight. (*From Woody-plant seed manual,* 1948.)

Species	Ash	Protein	Fat	Carbo-hydrates	Water content
Acorns, 1 month old, without pericarp:					
Northern red oak	2.62	7.16	22.50	34.47	49.0
White oak	2.56	7.42	6.81	47.93	65.4
Without seed coat:					
Digger pine	5.0	29.6	59.6	8.8	5.1
Pinyon pine	2.9	15.1	64.1	17.9	3.4
With seed coat:					
Eastern white pine	5.58	30.21	35.44	4.81	7.53
Longleaf pine	5.39	35.24	31.66	4.53	6.87

collect when it is no longer dependent on the tree for food or water. Considerable morphological and physiological changes may occur in seeds after this time, but in at least some species these normally occur long after the seeds are mature enough to collect. It is claimed that seeds of some species will germinate sooner if collected while somewhat unripe and planted immediately than if they are allowed to mature fully on the tree. On the other hand, seeds of other species are said to germinate better if collected late in the winter rather than in the autumn. This probably depends on how seeds collected early in the season are stored, however. For example, Silen (1958) reported that the seeds matured normally in Douglas-fir cones collected 3 or 4 weeks before the seeds were ripe if the cones were stored in moist peat, but not if they were exposed to the air.

Seed Storage

The storage of seeds requires careful consideration of the requirements for maintaining their embryos in a viable condition. This is particularly important if seeds are to be stored for more than one year. The best storage conditions vary widely, depending on the moisture content and other characteristics of the seed. The principal objectives in storage are to prevent excessive loss of water from seeds normally high in water and to prevent excessive respiration or other undesirable biochemical activity. In some instances storage conditions also should be designed to break dormancy of the embryos. In general, storage involves control of moisture and temperature, but control of the atmosphere may be beneficial in prolonging the life of some seeds.

Moisture Content. One of the most common causes of loss of viability of seeds which are high in water content at maturity is dehydration. Seeds of magnolia, silver maple, oak, hickory, and walnut are particularly susceptible to injury from dehydration. The effect of dehydration on germination of acorns is shown in Table 14.2. In contrast, the seeds of most coniferous and leguminous species and many others can be dried to the air-dry condition or even slightly lower without injury. These differences in tolerance of drying probably result from differences in ability of protoplasm to undergo dehydration without irreversible changes in structure. Sometimes the naturally occurring water content must be reduced by artificial drying to prevent injury to seeds by heating while in storage.

Dry seeds of many species can be stored at room temperature and exposed to the air for several months to a year, but a uniformly low humidity is most favorable for long periods of storage. According to

Table 14.2. Relation between moisture content of embryos and germination of acorns. (*From Korstian, 1927.*)

Species	Water content of embryos on dry-weight basis when planted	Percentage germinating
White oak	65.6	76
	59.8	65
	50.6	63
	32.1	12
	25.6	0
Northern red oak	55.8	59
	32.7	60
	20.7	24
	13.6	3
	8.7	0

Barton (1943), changes in moisture content caused by changes in atmospheric humidity are injurious to some seeds. For maximum longevity in storage, seeds probably should be sealed in airtight containers to prevent changes in water content.

Barton (1939) found that longevity of American elm seed was increased by drying it from 8 to 7 per cent of water before storage. Huss (1954) reported that conifer seed dried to less than 8 or 9 per cent kept better than seed higher in water content, especially at temperatures above freezing. He found that unfavorable storage conditions reduced seedling growth more than germination, and Stone (1957a) also found this to be true.

Temperature. Life of seeds usually is prolonged by storage at low temperatures. Allen (1957) recommended a constant low temperature, but found no advantage in storage of conifer seed at 0°F over storage at 32°F. Crocker and Barton (1953) found temperatures below freezing superior to temperatures above freezing for storage of elm seed over a period of many years, as shown in Table 14.3. Low temperatures prolong the life of most seeds many fold. The exact reason why storage at low temperature is effective in prolonging viability is unknown. Of course, it reduces the rate of metabolism, including the use of food in respiration, but seeds usually lose their viability long before they exhaust their food supplies. Perhaps low temperature acts by slowing down degenerative changes in the proteins of enzymes and nuclei (Crocker, 1948).

Gases. The storage life of some fruits is prolonged considerably by placing them in an atmosphere low in oxygen and high in carbon dioxide. It is probable that a similar treatment would be effective for storage of short-lived seeds. Kidd (1914) found that longevity of seeds of *Hevea brasiliensis* was greatly increased by storage in 40 to 45 per cent carbon dioxide, and storage in carbon dioxide is said to increase the longevity of sugar cane seed. The longevity of poplar seed was increased by storage in a vacuum. The use of special atmospheres combined with low temperature deserves more study in connection with preservation of special lots of seeds for long periods of time.

Longevity of Seeds

One of the most interesting characteristics of seeds is their wide variation in length of life, varying from a few days to several decades, or even several centuries. The literature is filled with fiction such as the stories concerning viable wheat from Egyptian tombs and equally surprising facts such as the behavior of the *Nelumbo* seeds from Manchuria. Ewart (1908) summarized much of the early data, and Crocker (1938, 1948) and Crocker and Barton (1953) present considerable data on longevity of seeds.

Ewart attempted to classify seeds in three groups. Short-lived or microbiotic seeds which survive less than 3 years include tree seeds high in water content, such as those of maple, elm, willow, and acorns and most nuts. Mesobiotic seeds have a medium life span varying from a few to

Table 14.3. Effects of storage conditions on retention of viability by seed of elm (*Ulmus americana*). (*Crocker and Barton*, 1953.)

| | Germination percentage after storage | | | | | | | | | | | | | | | | | |
| | In laboratory, years | | | | | | At 5°C, years | | | | | | At −4°C, years | | | | | |
Storage conditions	1	3	5	7	10	11	1	3	5	7	10	11	1	3	5	7	10	11
Open container	67	0					13	0					95	85	61	55	14	8
7 per cent moisture content	86	55	0				91	89	82	79	2	0	77	90	82	74	86	83
3 per cent moisture content	81	81	1				85	90	84	88	62	0	88	83	84	81	79	87
2 per cent moisture content	84	77	1				82	70	66	81	39	1	81	87	75	85	78	82

15 years, and macrobiotic seeds live more than 15 years. This sort of classification is fairly applicable under natural conditions but breaks down under laboratory conditions. Elm seeds retain their viability for only a few weeks in the open air but have been kept over 11 years in sealed containers at low temperatures (Table 14.3), and naturally short-lived poplar seeds were 90 per cent viable after 22 months when sealed in a vacuum.

Data on longevity of seeds of many woody species are given in the Woody-plant Seed Manual, and a few data are presented in Table 14.4.

Table 14.4. Longevity of seeds. (*Selected from Woody-plant seed manual, 1948.*)

Species	Storage conditions	Period of viability
Pinus banksiana	32–41°F	5+ years
	In cones on trees	15 years
Pinus contorta	32–41°F	7+ years
	In cones on trees	30+ years
Pinus echinata	32–41°F	7–9 years
Pinus ponderosa var.		
scopulorum	32–41°F	23+ years
Pinus palustris	32–41°F	2+ years
Quercus, various spp.	Sealed containers at 32–36°F	3–4 years
Robinia pseudoacacia	Sealed containers at 32–40°F	10+ years
Salix	Sealed containers	4–6 weeks
Tsuga canadensis	Sealed containers at 41°F	4+ years
Ulmus americana	Sealed containers near freezing	2 years
Acer saccharinum	Sealed containers at 32–50°F	1 year
Acer saccharum	Open or sealed containers at 36–40°F	1 year
Acer macrophyllum	Cannot be stored	
Albizia lophthantha	Dry, open, room temperature	50+ years
Betula lutea	Open, dry storage	18 months
	Sealed containers at 40°F	12 years
Carya spp.	Sealed containers at 41°F	3–5 years
Fagus grandifolia	Sealed containers at 41°F	1 year
Fraxinus excelsior	Open storage	2–3 years
	Dry seed in sealed containers	5–6 years
Fraxinus americana	Sealed in dry containers at 34–38°F	3+ years
Juglans cinerea	Sealed containers at near freezing	4–5 years

Seeds of legumes seem to be relatively long lived, probably because of their hard seed coats. Becquerel (1934) found that seeds of several species germinated after storage in the National Museum in Paris for 85 to 100 years. The oldest seeds to germinate were those of *Cassia multijuga*, which germinated after more than 150 years in storage. The oldest viable seeds found in their natural surroundings are those of *Nelumbo nucifera* from a bog in Manchuria. Their age has been estimated as from 150 to over 250 years, but radiocarbon dating indicates that they are about 1,000 years old (Libby, 1951).

The causes of loss of viability are not well understood. Dehydration of moist seeds such as those of elm, maple, and willow, and acorns usually causes death, but according to Crocker and Barton (1953), some seeds can be dehydrated at low temperatures and kept viable for years. Apparently changes in moisture content are injurious to many seeds, because storage in sealed containers usually prolongs their life. Seeds stored in open containers usually retain viability longer in a dry climate than in a moist climate.

Exhaustion of food has been suggested as a cause of loss of viability, but many seeds lose their viability without any visible decrease in food reserves. Stone (1957a) suggests that exhaustion of a specific metabolic substrate causes loss of viability. Perhaps this is a substance or substances necessary for the early stage of germination before digestion of reserve foods begins. Another possibility is loss of enzyme activity, but dead seeds sometimes contain active enzymes. Perhaps the cells lose their ability to form new enzymes.

It has been suggested that the proteins of seeds degenerate with age, or that mutations occur in the nuclei which hinder or prevent germination (Avery and Blakeslee, 1943). Gunthardt et al. (1953) reported that chromosomal aberrations and mutations increased with increasing age of seeds studied by them. These changes are similar to those produced by ionizing radiation. Further study of the biochemical and physiological changes in aging seeds might contribute worthwhile information on the general problem of aging.

Viability Tests

Consideration of the longevity of seeds naturally leads to consideration of methods of testing their viability. Knowledge concerning the viability or percentage of seeds capable of germinating is essential, not only in studies of storage conditions, but also in nursery work in order to determine the rate of seeding.

The ultimate test of seed quality is the ability to produce seedlings. Some workers differentiate between "germination," as evidenced by emergence of the radicle, and "plant percentage," based on the number of seedlings per 100 seeds which become established in the plant bed. Detailed discussion of methods is beyond the scope of this book, but it is obvious that the results obtained in germination tests depend on whether or not the conditions provided are favorable for the seeds being tested. The environmental factors affecting germination are discussed in a later section. The apparent viability of seeds may vary widely with different methods of germination. For example, Barton (1935) found that seeds of loblolly pine stored in sealed containers in a refrigerator for 7 years gave only 29 per cent germination if planted directly, but if they were stratified in peat moss at 5°C for a month before planting, 80 per cent germinated.

Harper et al. (1955) believe that the conventional laboratory tests of seed germination usually are poor indicators of their germination under the less favorable conditions often existing in the field. Stone (1957a) emphasizes the danger of evaluating seed quality from simple germination tests. For example, 80 per cent of sugar pine seed stored at 25°C for 3 months germinated but only 5 per cent produced a radicle 3 inches long, while 80 per cent of seed stored at −18°C for 30 months and 95 per cent of the fresh seed produced radicles of this length. Seedlings which produce long radicles are more likely to survive drought than those with weak roots.

Direct tests of germination often require long periods of time. This has resulted in attempts to develop more rapid tests of viability. Appearance of the seed, appearance of the embryo when the seed is cut, and the percentage of seeds which float in water or some other solvent are tests usable for seeds of some species. Some attempts have been made to judge viability by staining response with dyes, such as indigo carmine, which penetrates dead embryos but not living embryos, or by use of substances which are reduced by living embryos with a conspicuous change in color, such as tetrazolium chloride.

The most generally employed test of this type uses 2,3,5-triphenyl tetrazolium chloride, which is reduced from a colorless solution to an insoluble pink or red formazan in the presence of dehydrogenases. This method, which was developed in Germany by Lakon, is at least moderately successful for some kinds of seeds, but it requires cutting open the embryo to observe the color change, a difficult operation on some kinds of seeds. Lakon (1949, 1954) describes the technique, and Grano (1958), On (1952), and Parker (1953a) have found this method fairly satisfactory for seeds of a variety of tree species.

Germination tests often are delayed by hard seed coats or by substances in the endosperm or embryos. Flemion (1938, 1948) found that the time required for making viability tests of some seeds can be decreased by excising the embryos and germinating them on moist filter paper in petri dishes. The difficulty of removing embryos from many seeds restricts the usefulness of this method, however.

Germination

The essential event in seed germination is resumption of growth by the embryo and its development into an independent seedling. The physiological processes involved in seed germination can be summarized as follows: (1) absorption of water, largely by imbibition, (2) beginning of cell enlargement and cell division, (3) increase in enzymes and enzyme activity and digestion of stored food, (4) translocation of food to growing regions, (5) increase in respiration and assimilation, (6) increase in cell division and cell enlargement, (7) differentiation of cells into the various tissues and organs of a seedling. Germination can be regarded as complete when the seedlings have produced enough photosynthetic surface to supply their own food. According to Richardson (1956), the growth of northern red oak seedlings which have developed one whorl of leaves is independent of the food remaining in the acorns so long as conditions are favorable for photosynthesis. Toole et al. (1956a) recently reviewed the physiology of seed germination, and Huberman (1940) gives a good account of the morphological changes during germination and early growth of southern pines.

The exact order of the various steps is not entirely clear, but with few exceptions absorption of additional water is necessary to set in motion the chain of events resulting in germination. Imbibition of water softens hard seed coats, and the swelling of the embryo as it imbibes water bursts the seed coat, permitting emergence of the radicle. Stone (1957b) was able to separate water uptake required for afterripening of stratified seed from that required for germination in seed of Jeffrey pine. Enough water was absorbed in 48 hours for successful afterripening without further uptake, but additional water was necessary for germination. Increase in water content is followed by cell enlargement and cell division in the growing points, and this probably causes the release of hormone-like substances which stimulate enzyme formation and activity and the translocation of food to the growing regions. Increase in mitochondrial activity has been observed in some germinating seeds, and Stanley (1957) regards activation of mitochondrial enzyme systems as an important early step in germination. Much more needs to be learned about the physiological processes involved in germination.

Usually the primary root elongates first and grows down into the soil, anchoring the seedling. In epigeous germination the hypocotyl then elongates rapidly and arches upward, pulling the cotyledons up into the air, where they expand into photosynthetic organs. The seed coat usually is shed during this process, and the plumule soon produces a stem, bearing leaves. In hypogeous germination the hypocotyl does not elongate; hence the cotyledons remain inside the seed coat, underground, while the primary root grows downward and the epicotyl grows upward and develops photosynthetic leaves. The development of typical seedlings is shown in Figure 14.2. Where food is stored in the endosperm or megagametophyte, the cotyledons absorb food from the storage tissue and translocate it to the growing regions. Brown and Gifford (1958) found that excised embryos of sugar pine were able to absorb sucrose for growth much more effectively through their cotyledons than through their roots. Embryos of intact pine seeds presumably absorb food from the surrounding megagametophyte tissue chiefly through their cotyledons.

Factors Affecting Germination

In order to germinate, seeds require adequate water and oxygen and a suitable temperature. A few kinds of seeds also require exposure to light for prompt germination. Rapid germination is very desirable because the shorter the time required the less opportunity there is for injury by insects, fungi, or unfavorable weather conditions or for seeds to be eaten by birds or rodents. Most of the research on seed germination has been done on seeds of herbaceous plants, but the same principles apply to germination of seeds of woody plants.

Water. Most seeds must absorb additional water beyond that present at maturity in order to start off the biochemical and physiological processes involved in germination. For example, the water content of eastern white pine seeds with an original content of 7 per cent on a dry-weight basis increased to 45 per cent before germination started and reached 172 per cent in young seedlings (Woody-plant Seed Manual, p. 7).

The soil moisture tension or diffusion-pressure deficit of the medium can be a limiting factor for water absorption. Practically all seeds can absorb enough water for germination from soil at field capacity, and some vegetable seeds can germinate in soil dried nearly to permanent wilting (Doneen and MacGillivray, 1943). According to Kausch (1952), a diffusion-pressure deficit of less than 1 atmosphere has no noticeable effect on water uptake and seed germination, and Owen (1952) found that about 20 per cent of wheat seeds germinated at a diffusion-pressure deficit of 30 atmospheres. Failure of some seeds to germinate at high diffusion-pressure deficits where others germinated was not caused by failure to absorb water. Work cited by Baker (1950) indicates that tree seeds probably are sensitive to the osmotic pressure of the substrate, and this is supported by Satoo and Goo (1954). They found that germination of seeds of several conifer species was hindered by a soil moisture tension in excess of 8 atmospheres. Seeds of *Cryptomeria japonica* showed 10 per cent germination in 0.5 M sucrose, while germination of *Chamaecyparis obtusa* seed was little reduced at 0.4 M but fell to 25 per cent at 0.5 M, as shown in Figure 14.3. Excessive amounts of fertilizer may reduce seed germination more than seedling growth subsequent to germination. An excess of water reduces or prevents germination by reducing the oxygen supply.

Soaking seeds for a few hours often hastens germination, but pro-

longed soaking causes injury or even loss of viability of many kinds of
seeds. Even 6 hours of soaking is said to reduce germination of bean seed
(Barton, 1950). Toumey and Durland (1923) found that soaking tree
seeds 3 to 5 days did not decrease germination but soaking for 10 days

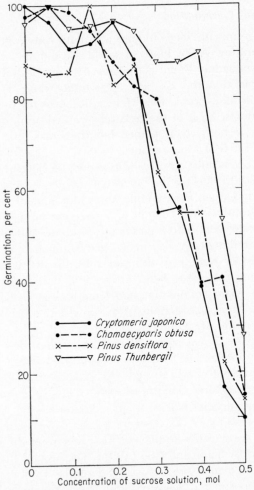

Figure 14.3 The effect of osmotic pressure of the substrate on germination of seed
of four species of trees. (*From Satoo and Goo, 1954.*)

reduced germination considerably and soaking for 30 days killed the seeds
of all upland species. Seeds of a few lowland species not only survived
soaking for 30 days but even germinated better than unsoaked seeds.

Soaking injury is not entirely the result of deprival of oxygen because
bubbling oxygen through the water in which the seeds are soaking does

not prevent and may even increase the injury (Barton, 1950). Bubbling carbon dioxide through the water decreased the injury somewhat and also decreased the absorption of water, suggesting that excessive water absorption might be involved in the injury. Leaching out of solutes and the activity of microorganisms also may contribute to injury from prolonged soaking.

Some seeds survive long periods of immersion in water. According to Demaree (1932), seeds of baldcypress remained viable after 30 months of submergence, and Shunk (1939) found that seeds of tupelo-gum

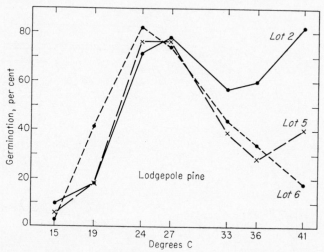

Figure 14.4 Germination of lodgepole pine seed of different origins at various temperatures. The lots were collected at increasing altitudes in British Columbia. Lot 2, collected at 350 to 450 meters, showed better germination at high temperatures than lot 5 from 1,300 meters or lot 6 from 1,350 meters. Seeds were germinated for 5 days on a 1 per cent agar gel in petri dishes. (*From Haasis and Thrupp*, 1931.)

survived 7 months of submersion. These seeds do not germinate under water, however. According to Larsen (1958), acorns of several species of oak can be submerged for at least 2 months without loss of viability and germination of overcup oak acorns was improved by prolonged soaking.

Oxygen. The oxygen requirements for germination appear to vary widely among seeds of different species. Seeds of a few species such as rice can germinate under water, although wheat and many other seeds will not germinate if kept submerged. Even the seeds of swamp species such as cypress and tupelo-gum which survive long periods of submergence will not germinate unless exposed to air. As a result, seedlings of these species become established in swamps only during dry summers when the soil is exposed for long periods of time (Demaree, 1932). A soil moisture content no higher than field capacity is unlikely to cause an oxygen deficiency.

Temperature. Germination of most tree seeds can occur over a rather wide range of temperatures, but most rapid germination of nondormant seeds usually occurs at fairly high temperatures. According to Haasis and Thrupp (1931), lodgepole pine seeds germinate best at about 25°C, poorly at 3 and 36°, but some seeds germinate better at 41 than at 36°. Haasis (1928) found this double maximum in a number of kinds of conifer seed. The effect of temperature on germination of pine seeds is shown in Figure 14.4. According to Critchfield (1957), lodgepole pine seed

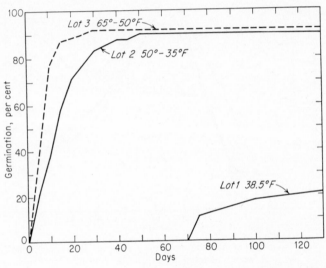

Figure 14.5 Germination of chestnut oak acorns at various temperatures. Lot 1 was kept constantly at 38.5°, but for lots 2 and 3 the day temperatures were higher than the night temperatures, as indicated on the graph. (*From Korstian, 1927.*)

germinates at about the same rate at 20 and 30°C but much slower at 10°. Coastal seed germinates more slowly than seed from the Rocky Mountain–Intermountain Region. Stearns and Olson (1958) found that eastern hemlock seed from Maine and Quebec germinated best at 12° and worst at 27°C while seed from Tennessee germinated well at 17 to 22°C and better than seed from any other source at 27°C.

In nature seeds usually are exposed to considerable temperature fluctuations from day to night, and they sometimes germinate better with the night temperature somewhat lower than the day temperature. A day temperature at 30° and night temperature at 20°C were found satisfactory for germination of most kinds of seeds, but some kinds of seeds germinate better with a day temperature of 25°C and a night temperature of 10° and a few do best at even lower temperatures (Woody-plant Seed Manual, p. 46). Figure 14.5 shows the germination of chestnut oak acorns at various temperatures, while Figure 14.6 shows differences between

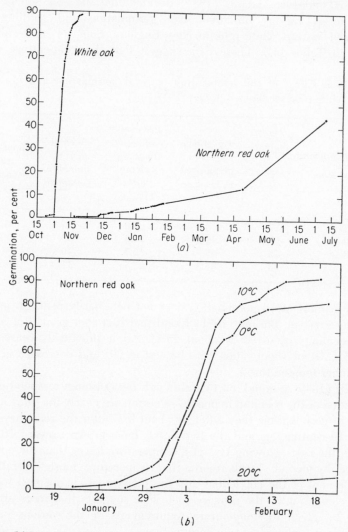

Figure 14.6 *a.* Behavior of white and northern red oak acorns planted in a greenhouse as soon as they were collected. *b.* Effect of storage at various temperatures on subsequent germination of northern red oak acorns. (*From Brown,* 1939.)

species of oaks. Acorns of the white oak group germinate much sooner than acorns of the red oak group, which usually exhibit embryo dormancy.

Ashby and Hellmers (1955) point out that temperature requirements for germination may have practical importance in choosing species for field planting because in some areas it is necessary to use species which will germinate with the field temperatures existing when there is adequate soil moisture. Adams (1934) decided that the cool soil under a dense forest canopy hindered seed germination and seedling root growth of eastern white pine in New England. Some of his results are shown in Table 14.5. These data suggest that the temperature which

Table 14.5. Effect of soil temperature on seed germination and growth of eastern white pine seedlings. (*Adams*, 1934.)

Soil temperature, °F		Percentage of seeds germinated in 117 days	Percentage of seedlings surviving after 117 days	Average days required to germinate	Root/shoot ratio of seedlings
Depth of 8 in.	Surface				
45	57	4.0	4.0	63	1.38
49	69	19.3	14.6	25	0.49
58	76	42.7	32.5	19	0.41
87	88	45.5	25.5	11	0.56

results in most rapid germination does not necessarily result in greatest seedling survival. Barney (1951) found that best root growth of loblolly pine seedlings occurred at about 25°C and it practically ceased at 5 and 35°C. Root/shoot ratios were highest at 20° and decreased at lower and higher temperatures.

Arndt (1945) pointed out that although the optimum temperatures for elongation of the root and hypocotyl of cotton are nearly the same in early stages of germination, they differ by about 9°C after the roots have elongated 10 centimeters and the hypocotyls have grown upward 16 centimeters, the roots growing best at a temperature lower than the optimum for the hypocotyl. Furthermore, the temperature most favorable for development of the cotyledons and secondary roots is not best for most rapid elongation of the primary root. This suggests that more attention might be given to temperature requirements of the various parts of seedlings at various stages in germination.

The mechanism by which fluctuating temperatures break dormancy is not fully understood. Possibly increase in temperature above the usual range causes a temporary increase in concentration of some substance to a critical level which permits germination. Cohen (1958) concluded that increasing the temperature to a critical level destroys an inhibitor. The physiological effects of alternating temperatures on seed germination and plant growth (thermoperiod) probably have some features in common.

Light. It has been known for many years that germination of some kinds of seed is hindered by exposure to light while germination of other kinds is promoted. Little is known about the effects of light on germination of tree seeds, but according to the Woody-plant Seed Manual, seeds of southern pines germinate more rapidly in diffuse light than in total darkness while jack pine seeds germinate in complete darkness.

Toole et al. (1956b) found that seed of Virginia pine failed to germinate in darkness but imbibed seed germinated well after exposure to red light for 32 minutes. Best germination was at 25°C, and germination was relatively poor at 20 and 30°C. The favorable effect of red light can be reversed by exposure to far-red radiation. The reversible photoreaction of seeds can be indicated as follows:

$$\text{Red-absorbing pigment and reactant} \underset{\text{peak about 7,350 A}}{\overset{\text{peak about 6,550 A}}{\rightleftharpoons}} \text{Far-red-absorbing pigment and changed reactant}$$

This photoreaction is involved in photoperiodism and a number of other processes (Toole et al., 1956a). The germination of light-sensitive seeds may be affected by the photoperiod, some seeds germinating well when exposed to daily periods of illumination but poorly if kept in continuous light or darkness.

There is a strong interaction between temperature and light requirement. For example, at 15°C unchilled seeds of *Betula pubescens* will germinate better with long days than with short days, but at 20° they germinate equally well with long and short photoperiods and will even germinate if given a single exposure to light (Black and Wareing, 1955). Chilled birch seed will germinate in complete darkness, and removal of the pericarp eliminates the light requirement of unchilled seed. Vaartaja (1956) obtained similar results with birch seed. According to Stearns and Olson (1958), temperature modifies the photoperiod requirements of eastern hemlock seed, the most favorable photoperiod being 8 or 12 hours at 17 to 22°C and 16 hours at 27°C.

Some kinds of seeds which require light for germination at a constant temperature will germinate in darkness with alternating temperatures, and some kinds of seeds not usually light-sensitive can be made sensitive by holding them in the imbibed condition at a certain temperature. In view of their sensitivity to light and temperature, it is not surprising that some very contradictory results have been reported concerning the effects of these factors on seed germination. It is essential to know the complete past history of seeds used in studies of dormancy and germination in order to obtain useful results.

Dormancy

Seeds of many tree species will germinate immediately if planted under favorable conditions, but the seeds of about two-thirds of our tree species exhibit some degree of dormancy. This means that they will not germinate promptly even when placed under the most favorable environmental conditions.

Dormancy probably has considerable survival value. For example, it often delays the germination of seeds produced in the autumn until the next spring when growing conditions are more favorable and there is no danger of frost injury. Different seeds in a crop often vary in their degree of dormancy, and this spreads out their germination over a longer period of time, increasing the probability that at least part of them will germinate under conditions favorable for survival. On the other hand, dormancy can be a nuisance to nursery operators who wish to have large quantities of seed germinate promptly in order to produce uniform crops of seedlings. The causes of dormancy and methods of breaking it are therefore of both physiological and practical importance.

Causes of Dormancy. Dormancy results from a number of causes, including impermeability of seed coats, conditions existing in embryos, and the presence of inhibitors in tissues outside of the seeds. Occasionally two causes of dormancy exist simultaneously, as in holly where hard seed coats and immature embryos occur, or in juniper where hard seed coats and dormant embryos are common.

Seed Coat Dormancy. A common cause of dormancy, especially among seeds of leguminous species, is impermeability of seed coats to water. This is common in seeds of black locust, honey locust, redbud, red cedar, and basswood. In other seeds, such as red ash (Cox, 1942), Jeffrey pine (Stone, 1957b), and eastern white pine (Kozlowski and Gentile, 1959), the seed coat is said to be relatively impermeable to oxygen. The classic example of this is cocklebur, where the lower seed in a fruit usually germinates the first season but the upper one remains dormant until the second season because its seed coat is impermeable to oxygen. Vegis (1956) believes that the low permeability of seed coats and other enclosing structures reduces the oxygen supply to the growing regions. As a result, anaerobic respiration occurs at high temperatures, causing the production of lipids and inhibiting substances which cause seeds to become dormant. Coats of seeds of some species are said to be mechanically resistant, preventing the embryo from bursting out (Haut, 1938).

Embryo Dormancy. Another common cause of failure to germinate promptly is some condition existing in the embryo. Sometimes the embryo is immature and requires a period of storage under favorable conditions to reach a certain stage of development before germination can occur, as in holly (Ives, 1923), European ash (Lakon, 1911), Swiss stone pine (Rohmeder and Loebel, 1940), and some viburnums (Giersbach, 1937). In other seeds the embryo is morphologically mature but physiologically incapable of germination. This probably is the most common type of dormancy. Examples are dogwood, red and black oaks, some pines, and seeds of many rosaceous species. This type of dormancy usually is attributed to the presence of inhibitors, either in the embryo itself or in surrounding structures. Cox (1942) attributed dormancy in northern red oak acorns to an inhibitor in the cotyledons which diffuses into the meristematic region. He also found inhibitors in the endosperm of black and white ash seeds. In birch the inhibitor appears to be in the pericarp (Redmond and Robinson, 1954; Black and Wareing, 1955).

Evenari (1949) listed about 100 species in which inhibitors of seed germination have been reported, and he also listed a wide variety of compounds which are believed to act as inhibitors in nature. Toole et al. (1956a) also discussed the role of inhibitors as causes of dormancy in seeds. Coumarin and related compounds are common and act by inhibiting root cell elongation. The mode of action of many inhibitors is unknown, but the variety of compounds listed indicates that they must act in many different ways. Some germination inhibitors are said to occur in the seed coat, or even in the fruit. That inhibitors sometimes occur outside of the embryo is shown by the fact that embryos removed from dormant seeds often germinate promptly on agar in culture bottles (Lammerts, 1942).

In a few species, including some viburnums and hophornbeam, the epicotyl is dormant but not the roots. Roots will start to grow at high temperatures, but a period of low temperatures is necessary to start stem elongation. In nature such seeds probably start to germinate one season and complete germination the next season after exposure to cold weather during the winter. Instances where one growing point is dormant but not another should afford an unusually good opportunity to study causes of dormancy.

Double Dormancy. More than 15 per cent of the seeds described in the Woody-plant Seed Manual are said to have both seed coat and embryo dormancy. Examples are ceanothus, cherry, and redbud. Stone's (1957b) results indicate that both seed coat and embryo dormancy occur in Jeffrey pine. It is probable that germination is controlled sometimes by one factor and sometimes by the other. The occurrence of double dormancy doubtless is responsible for much confusion and uncertainty concerning the causes of dormancy and the best method of breaking it in certain species.

Variations in Dormancy. Different species of a genus often vary widely in their germination behavior. White and post oak acorns are capable of germinating as soon as they drop, but northern red oak acorns require stratification at low temperature for a month or more before they will germinate (Figure 14.6). The percentage of dormant seeds and the degree of dormancy often vary widely in different lots of seed of the same species, resulting in quite different germination behavior under the same conditions. This often results in contradictory conclusions concerning the effectiveness of particular treatments in breaking dormancy. The reasons for such variations have not been explained. They may be partly genetic, but probably also are related to weather conditions during and after maturation. For example, red oak acorns collected early in the autumn often are much slower to germinate than those collected later, possibly because those collected late in the autumn have been exposed to more cold. The conditions under which the seeds are stored after collection also may affect their subsequent germination.

Methods of Breaking Dormancy

If the causes of dormancy are known, it usually is possible to apply treatments to break it and assure relatively prompt and uniform seed germination. This is particularly true if dormancy is caused by hard, impermeable seed coats. In nature, wetting and drying, freezing and thawing, or the activity of microorganisms softens hard seed coats and permit germination. Hard seed coats can be broken by scarification, which involves rubbing or blowing the seeds against coarse sandpaper or tumbling them with sharp gravel in a drum. Another effective treatment is to soak the seeds in concentrated sulfuric acid until their coats are soft and permeable. Soaking in hot water also usually increases the permeability of hard seed coats, and prolonged soaking in cold water will render some seed coats permeable. The effects of various treatments on germination of black locust seed are shown in Figure 14.7.

Embryo dormancy is not so easily eliminated, perhaps partly because the reasons for its occurrence are not fully understood. Experience has shown that most kinds of dormant seeds will germinate after 1 or 2 months of stratification in a moist medium at a temperature near freezing. According to Rudolf (1952), soaking seeds of pine, fir, and tamarack in water at 41°F for 7 days is as effective in breaking mild dormancy as stratification for a month. The breaking of embryo dormancy often is termed "afterripening." Alternating high and low temperatures are more effective in breaking dormancy of some seeds than continuous low temperature.

Various chemical treatments have been used to break dormancy, including immersion of seeds in dilute acids and exposure to vapors of various chemicals. Deuber (1932) found immersion in thiourea and exposure to vapor of ethylene chlorohydrin effective in hastening the germination of red and black oak acorns. McDermott (1941) also found that treatment with ethylene chlorohydrin increased the rate of germination of northern red oak acorns, but the effects varied with the crop. Apparently acorns exposed to some cold respond better to ethylene chlorohydrin than those not chilled.

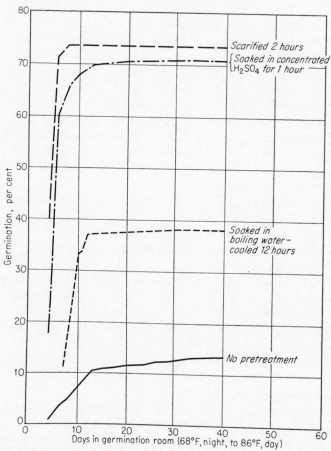

Figure 14.7 Effects of various treatments to soften seed coat on germination of black locust seed. (*From Woody-plant seed manual*, 1948.)

Chemical and Physiological Changes during Afterripening

It is obvious that a complex sequence of changes in composition and processes must occur in seeds during afterripening. A better understanding of these changes should aid in developing better methods of breaking dormancy. It was originally supposed that changes in chemical composition might be an important factor in afterripening. Jones (1920) reported that sucrose and polysaccharides decreased and reducing sugars increased in sugar maple seed during afterripening and the beginning of germination. He also observed increases in acidity, water-holding capacity, and catalase and peroxidase activity. According to Pack (1921), fat and protein decrease, and soluble nitrogen compounds, total carbohydrates, reducing sugars, and catalase activity increase, during stratification of juniper seed at 5°C for 100 days.

Korstian (1927) found that acorns of the red oak group which are dormant when mature are much higher in fat content than acorns of the nondormant white oak group (Table 14.1). He suggested that conversion of fat to protein might be an essential feature of afterripening. McDermott (1941) corroborated the fact that fats are converted to carbohydrates during afterripening of northern red oak acorns, but decided that this is not an essential feature of the process. He found a decrease in soluble nitrogen, starch, and lipids and an increase in reducing sugar and total sugar. He concluded that dormancy probably was caused by some substance present in amounts too small to be detected by the chemical methods available at that time.

Brown (1939) studied respiration, catalase activity, and germination of white and northern red oak acorns, stored at various temperatures for various periods of time. Catalase activity showed no correlation with afterripening, but the respiratory quotient and carbon dioxide uptake decreased during the winter in seeds stored at temperatures ranging from 2.5 to 17.5°C. Some results are shown in Figure 14.8. Brown suggested that a respiratory quotient of less than 0.3 indicated that dormancy of red oak acorns had been broken. The high oxygen consumption and low carbon dioxide production suggested that fats were being converted to carbohydrates, a fact verified later by McDermott (1941).

McDermott (1941) found decreases in starch, lipid, and insoluble nitrogen content and increases in reducing sugar and total sugar content of red oak acorns during the autumn and early winter. He also found a very low respiratory quotient in both red oak and willow oak acorns. Some data on respiration rates at various temperatures are shown in Figure 14.9. The drop in oxygen consumption at higher temperatures suggests a change in respiratory substrate from fats to carbohydrates, or a decrease in conversion of fats to carbohydrates, or possibly both. The chemical and physiological changes occurring in seeds during afterripening deserve further study. Haut (1938) found no significant changes in fats, sucrose, total sugar, reducing substances, or alcohol-soluble and -insoluble nitrogen during afterripening of apple, peach, and cherry seeds. Vegis (1956) claims there is a decrease in lipids and growth-inhibiting substances during afterripening.

If conversion of large amounts of stored food to soluble forms were the chief change during afterripening, it might be expected to proceed more rapidly at high temperatures, whereas it actually occurs more rapidly at temperatures near freezing. Perhaps a reduced rate of metabolism causes the accumulation of some substance to a critical concentration. Stone (1957b) suggests that breaking of embryo dormancy involves conversion

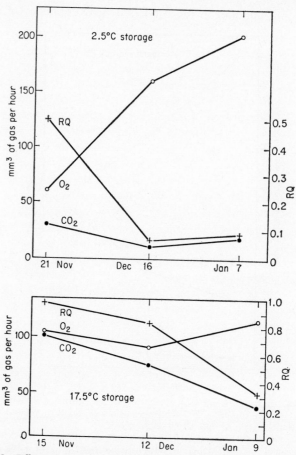

Figure 14.8 Effect of storage at low and intermediate temperatures on the respiration and respiratory quotients (RQ) of northern red oak acorns. Respiration was measured at the storage temperatures. (*From Brown*, 1939.)

of substrate into some intermediate which accumulates during stratification and permits growth to occur when temperature and oxygen supply are favorable. The fact that alternating low and high temperatures are favorable for breaking dormancy of some kinds of seeds suggests that the balance between processes is an important factor in afterripening. Various processes respond differently to changes in temperature, and this might result in either accumulation of a growth-promoting substance or elimination of a growth-inhibiting substance. Cohen (1958) suggests that temperatures act on a complex organized structure rather than on a sequence of reactions.

At present embryo dormancy usually is attributed to the presence of inhibitors. For example, dormancy of eastern red oak acorns has been attributed to an inhibitor in the cotyledons and dormancy of black and

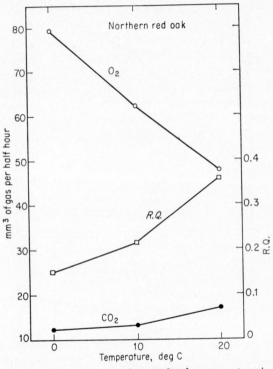

Figure 14.9 Respiration rates of northern red oak acorns at various temperatures. The high oxygen consumption at low temperatures probably is related to conversion of fats to carbohydrates. (*From McDermott, 1941.*)

white ash seed to inhibitors in the endosperm (Cox, 1942). So many different substances have been described as inhibitors that it is difficult to develop any general theory of inhibiting action. It is possible that not all these alleged inhibitors actually operate as inhibitors of seed germination in nature. It is certain that much more research must be done before we learn what constitute the basic factors in embryo dormancy.

Excised Embryos

One approach to the study of various problems of seed germination is by the use of excised embryos, because they can be subjected to various treatments without interference from surrounding tissues. Cox (1942) found that by removal of the endosperm he was able to bring about growth of the embryos of black and white ash, suggesting the presence of inhibitors in the endosperm. Excised embryos of birch do not show the sensitivity to light found in the intact seed (Black and Wareing, 1955; Redmond and Robinson, 1954), indicating that the light-sensitive reaction occurs outside of the embryo, probably in the pericarp.

Embryo culture is useful in growing seedlings from embryos of species which are difficult to germinate. Tukey (1938) grew thousands of excised embryos of cherry and plums, and Lammerts (1942) found embryo culture successful in producing seedlings of apricot and peach hybrids. Many seeds from these crosses possessed embryos which did not grow well after stratification but grew very well on agar in culture tubes. Seedlings from excised embryos can be potted in a few weeks, and seedlings 3 or 4 feet tall, ready to move to the field, can be produced in less than a year. This is much more rapid than stratifying seeds and germinating them in the usual fashion.

Effect of Seed Size and Source on Seedlings

It has been known for many years that seed size and seed source have some effects on subsequent growth of the seedlings. This involves both genetic and phenotypic factors. For example, large seeds might produce large seedlings simply because they supply more food for initial growth, but this might have little or no effect on their later growth. On the other hand, seed from fast-growing trees might be expected to carry genetic factors which would result in faster-growing offspring than seedlings from seed of slower-growing parents.

Seed Size. The size of seed is extremely variable, differing from year to year with weather conditions, from tree to tree, and even with location in the cone or fruit. For example, the largest seeds usually are produced in the largest fruits, and those near the middle of a fruit usually are larger than those at the ends. These differences probably are associated chiefly with differences in efficiency of food translocation to various fruits and parts of fruits.

Large seeds usually produce larger seedlings than do small seeds. Korstian (1927) found this to be true for acorns, and some of his data are presented in Table 14.6. He suggested that the better start obtained by seedlings from large acorns might give them a decided advantage in competition with smaller seedlings and other vegetation. Richardson (1956) made a study of the role of the acorn in seedling growth and concluded that red oak seedlings which have developed one whorl of leaves draw on reserve food in the acorns only if conditions are unfavorable for photosynthesis; hence the advantage of large acorns might last only until leaves are developed.

The effects of seed size probably are important only during the first season, although there is some uncertainty on this point. Mitchell (1934) and others have emphasized the importance of using seed of uniform size or else of applying a correction factor for seed size in mineral-nutrition studies involving rates of growth of first-year seedlings. Aldrich-Blake (1935) showed that seedling size was affected both by seed size and by nitrogen supply to the seedlings (Figure 14.10) and questioned Mitchell's method of correcting for seed size. It probably is more important to use seed of uniform size than seed which is similar genetically

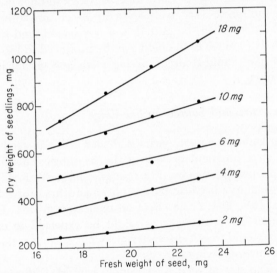

Figure 14.10 Effect of seed size and nitrogen supply on size of seedlings of Corsican pine. The number at the right of each line is the amount of nitrogen available per seedling, in milligrams. (*From Aldrich-Blake, 1935.*)

but dissimilar in size in short-term experiments. For longer experiments genetic differences are likely to become increasingly significant and genetic uniformity in seed becomes more important.

Seed Source. It has been well established that some tree species such as Douglas-fir, ponderosa, lodgepole, and loblolly pines and poplar, which have wide geographic distribution, have evolved distinct geographic races. These differ physiologically with respect to such characteristics as cold, drought, and disease resistance, photoperiod requirements, and length of growing season. As a result of natural selection over a long period of time, these strains have evolved physiological processes adapted to particular environments and they often do poorly when moved to dif-

Table 14.6. Effect of acorn weight on size of seedlings at end of one growing season. (*From Korstian, 1927.*)

Species and acorn size	Weight, g	Percentage surviving	Average height, in.	Average weight, g
Red oak:				
Small	2.5–3.5	60.7	5.19	4.88
Medium	5.0–6.0	64.6	6.78	8.74
Large	7.0–8.0	77.8	7.47	11.91
White oak:				
Small	0.5–1.5	16.0	3.42	2.18
Medium	2.0–3.5	57.0	4.45	5.74
Large	4.5–6.0	96.9	4.94	6.65

ferent environments. These differences are genetically controlled and transmitted through the seed. It therefore is desirable, so far as possible, to use seed from a local source or from a similar climate and latitude if local seed is unavailable. This problem is discussed further in Chapter 15.

Even individual trees of a species growing side by side differ genetically and physiologically, as indicated by differences in rate of growth, wood density, turpentine yield, and other characters. Realization that these characters often are transmitted to their offspring through the seed has given great impetus to more careful selection of seed trees as sources of seed for nursery planting. Even the offspring from such superior trees are more or less heterozygous and exhibit a wide range of variation in desirable characters. If we could learn more about the physiological processes controlling rate and quality of growth, it might become much easier to select desirable types both for parents and for planting stock.

GENERAL REFERENCES

Anonymous, 1948, Woody-plant seed manual, U.S. Dept. Agr. Misc. Pub. 654.

Baldwin, H. I., 1942, Forest tree seed, Chronica Botanica Co., Waltham, Mass.

Crocker, W., 1948, Growth of plants, Reinhold Publishing Corporation, New York.

—— and L. V. Barton, 1953, Physiology of seeds, Chronica Botanica Co., Waltham, Mass.

Stone, E. C., 1958, The seed dormancy mechanism in pine, chap. 33 in K. V. Thimann (ed.), The physiology of forest trees, The Ronald Press Company, New York.

Toole, E. H., S. B. Hendricks, H. A. Borthwick, and V. K. Toole, 1956, Physiology of seed germination, Ann. Rev. Plant Physiology, 7:299–324.

Toumey, J. W., and C. F. Korstian, 1942, Seeding and planting in the practice of forestry, John Wiley & Sons, Inc., New York.

CHAPTER 15 *Internal Factors Affecting Growth*

It was pointed out in Chapter 1 that plant growth is controlled by the interaction of hereditary and environmental factors operating through a complex of internal processes and conditions. In preceding chapters many of the important processes have been discussed individually and their reactions to environmental factors have been described. Two important aspects of plant growth remain to be discussed, the effects of external environmental factors on the plant as a whole and the interactions of processes within plants which produce the internal environment in which cells function. The effects of external environmental factors such as light, temperature, soil moisture, and cultural practices will be discussed in the next chapter. In this chapter we shall discuss the internal environment or internal conditions, such as growth substances, water balance, levels of food and minerals, and interactions among various organs, which affect the quantity and quality of growth.

Types of Correlating Systems

It should be emphasized that the various physiological processes of a tree do not operate independently of one another. Just as a plant is morphologically more than an assemblage of cells and organs, so it also is more than an assemblage of processes. Its success as an organism results from the efficient correlation of its various organs and processes so that it has the proper ratio of roots to shoots, of absorption to transpiration, of photosynthesis to respiration. This internal correlation of structures and processes takes many forms, but it probably is brought about principally by two general mechanisms. One mechanism operates through the action of hormones, the other through modification of the supplies of food, water, and minerals to the various organs. These two mechanisms probably often operate together in controlling growth (Gregory and Veale, 1957; Skoog and Miller, 1957). Examples of internal correlations are apical dominance, polarity, and relationships between reproductive

428

and vegetative growth, between shoot and diameter growth, and between root and shoot growth. Some of these correlations seem to be controlled chiefly by hormones, others chiefly through control over the distribution of metabolites and water. Skoog and Miller (1957) suggested that we are approaching a state of knowledge where sharp distinctions between stimuli and energy-supplying metabolites are disappearing. At present, however, it seems convenient to retain this distinction.

Another form of correlation is concerned with relative rates of processes. Relative rates often are much more significant than absolute rates. For example, the amount of food available for growth and accumulation depends more on the ratio of photosynthesis to respiration than on the absolute rate of photosynthesis alone. The internal water balance is controlled by the relative rates of absorption and transpiration, and a high rate of transpiration causes no injury if it is accompanied by an equally high rate of water absorption.

It is difficult to deal in a completely orderly and logical fashion with the internal factors which correlate growth activities of a tree, because they belong in overlapping categories. We shall discuss some examples of internal correlations, such as apical dominance and root/shoot ratios. We shall also discuss the effects of various internal conditions, such as the levels of hormones, food and water, and conditions such as aging and dormancy. The role of heredity also will be discussed in this chapter.

Growth Requirements

In simplest terms, successful growth requires adequate supplies of food, water, minerals, hormones, and oxygen and suitable temperatures. The food requirements are particularly high in meristematic regions where new tissues are being formed. Large amounts of nitrogenous compounds, such as amides and amino acids, are used in the formation of new protoplasm in the region of cell division. During cell enlargement and maturation carbohydrates are used in the formation of new cell walls and as a substrate for respiration. Most or perhaps all of the essential mineral elements are required in growing regions, plus hormones and vitamins. Some of the hormones and vitamins are formed in growing regions, while others must be supplied from other regions of the tree. In general, stem tips appear to be more self-sufficient in this respect than root tips. Sufficient water is required to maintain turgidity, and water deficit is one of the most common factors limiting growth (Loomis, 1934; Thut and Loomis, 1944).

Growth in one part of a tree is influenced materially by growth in other parts. Such internal correlations often involve competition for food, water, and minerals, as well as the effects of hormones. So marked does the internal competition for food and water sometimes become that

Murneek (1932) characterized fruit trees as loose metabolic aggregates of independent and competing units.

Foods and Minerals

The manufacture and translocation of food and the absorption and roles of various mineral elements were discussed in previous chapters; hence only their general role in growth will be discussed in this chapter. Some of the food used in growth comes from previously accumulated reserves, and some from current photosynthesis. Much of the height growth of deciduous trees appears to be made from reserve food accumulated the previous year, but trees with long growing seasons, such as the southern pines and yellow-poplar, presumably use the products of current photosynthesis for at least the latter part of their height growth (Kozlowski and Ward, 1957b). Phloem usually differentiates very close to the tips of roots and stems, providing a pathway for rapid translocation of organic substances to within a short distance of the meristematic regions. Carbohydrates for cambial activity come chiefly from current photosynthesis, and the close proximity of the phloem to the cambium ensures an adequate supply. Apparently much of the nitrogen is converted into organic compounds in the roots before being translocated to the growing regions, but most of the mineral elements probably move as ions (Chapter 9).

Correlations between vegetative and reproductive growth seem to be explainable largely in terms of competition for food, chiefly carbohydrates. Although flowers and very young fruits often drop off because they are unable to obtain enough carbohydrates, rapidly growing young fruits and seeds usually are able to obtain food at the expense of vegetative structures. Defoliation or shading can cause excessive abscission of flowers at the time of pollination, but a short time later the rapidly growing fruits can obtain food at the expense of vegetative growth. According to Loomis (1953), in most plants rapidly growing fruits usually obtain food at the expense of other plant structures. Vegetative buds are second in competitive ability, flowers next, and recently pollinated fruits last in order of competition for food. The competitive ability of these various regions probably is at least partly related to the relative amount of auxin produced by each.

Internal Water Deficits

Growth of plants probably is limited more often by internal water deficits than by any other single internal factor. The over-all effect of internal water deficits is to reduce vegetative growth, but this is brought about both directly and indirectly because water deficits affect almost every process occurring in a tree.

For more detailed discussion of various aspects of the water-relations problems discussed in this chapter, readers are referred to Crafts et al. (1949), Richards and Wadleigh (1952), and Volume 3 of the Encyclopedia of Plant Physiology. The causes of water deficits were discussed in Chapter 12.

Measurement of Water Deficits

One of the troublesome problems in connection with study of the water balance in plants is lack of a convenient and reliable method of

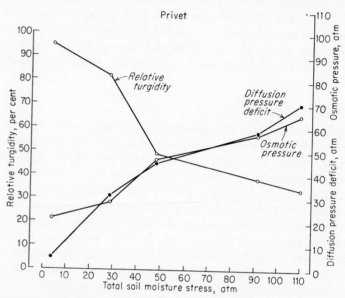

Figure 15.1 Changes in osmotic pressure, diffusion-pressure deficit, and relative turgidity of privet plants growing in drying soil. The plants were sampled early in the morning, and absorption of water vapor from the air is believed to explain the fact that the diffusion-pressure deficit of the leaves was lower than the soil moisture stress in severely dehydrated plants. (*From Slatyer*, 1957b.)

measuring water deficits or water stress in the various tissues. Probably this is the greatest current need in the field of water-relations studies. Early investigators measured the osmotic pressure of plant sap, and the work of Dixon and Atkins (1910, 1916), Korstian (1924), Meyer (1927), and Harris (1934) is well known. Walter (1951, 1955) measures the *Hydratur* or internal water balance in terms of osmotic pressure, but it is expressed more often in terms of suction force (Ursprung, 1933) or diffusion-pressure deficit (DPD). The DPD (Meyer and Anderson, 1952) is a desirable measurement because it indicates the pressure with which water would move into plant tissues if they were placed in pure water. It also is expressed in units comparable with those used to measure soil moisture tension or total soil moisture stress. Furthermore, as shown in Figure 15.1, DPD varies over a much wider range than osmotic pressure; hence it is a more sensitive indicator of water stress. The concept of diffusion-pressure deficit was discussed in Chapter 10.

Methods of measuring DPD were discussed recently by Slatyer (1958), who uses a vapor-equilibration method. Weatherley and Slatyer (1957) suggested that perhaps the DPD values equivalent to various relative turgidities might be determined for a species, and DPD values could then be calculated from relative-turgidity measurements, which are easier to make than DPD measurements. Slatyer (1957b) made an interesting series of measurements of relative turgidity, osmotic pressure, and DPD on plants growing in soil which was allowed to dry out, subjecting the plants to a severe water deficit. The results obtained with privet are shown in Figure 15.1.

Water Deficits and Growth

Everyone is aware that drought and the resulting internal water deficit reduce vegetative growth, but not enough consideration is given to the manner in which this reduction is brought about. Water deficit usually reduces enlargement more than cell division or cell differentiation. As a result, plants subjected to water deficits tend to differentiate earlier and to a greater extent than those which do not suffer from water deficits. Leaves are smaller, thicker, and more heavily cutinized, stems are shorter and more lignified, and annual rings of trees are narrower. Although plant growth as a whole is reduced by water deficit, meristematic regions such as stem tips sometimes continue to elongate while the older regions of the stems are shrinking (Wilson, 1948b; Burstrom, 1956).

Although there is no doubt that cell enlargement is closely related to water supply, the exact relationship between water absorption and cell enlargement is not as yet entirely clear. According to current views, as summarized by Burstrom (1956), the weight of evidence suggests that cell enlargement is caused chiefly by active growth of the wall, and this results in water absorption. It appears, however, that continued absorption of water is essential for continued cell enlargement because cells cease growth if even slightly plasmolyzed. Apparently enough turgor pressure must exist to keep the cytoplasm in contact with the wall in order for cell wall formation and cell enlargement to continue.

The smaller size of plants subjected to water deficit appears to be the result of decreased cell enlargement and earlier differentiation of cells. Roots of Valencia orange trees become differentiated almost up to the tip when growth is checked by dry soil or too concentrated soil solution (Hayward and Long, 1942), and this probably is true of the other tissues in trees. The rapid maturation of tissues stunted by water deficit reduces the opportunity of recovery, and if tree growth is checked by an early-season drought, both shoot and diameter growth usually are reduced for the entire season.

Loomis (1934) and Thut and Loomis (1944) concluded that an adequate supply of water to the growing region is the most important single factor for growth. The effect of even moderate, temporary water deficits is shown by the fact that young trees of loblolly and shortleaf pines

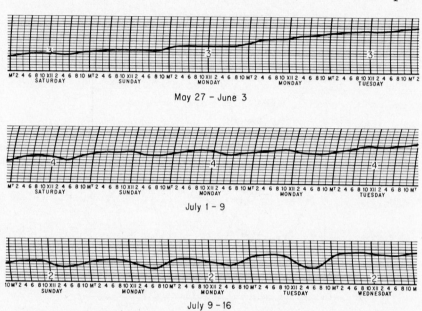

Figure 15.2 Daily variations in diameter in the trunk of a beech tree growing in Ohio. The upper graph was made early in the season while soil moisture was abundant and growth rapid; the lower graph shows slower growth and larger diurnal variations related to lower soil moisture and more rapid transpiration. Shrinkage occurred each afternoon, but was especially severe on Tuesday of the lower graph. A heavy rain replenished soil moisture, and little shrinkage occurred the next day. One unit on the ordinate equals 0.0005 inch. (*From Fritts and Fritts, 1955.*)

made nearly twice as much shoot growth during the night as during the day in late June and early July, apparently because transpiration caused midday water deficits (Reed, 1939). The effects of midday water deficits on diameter growth are shown in Figure 15.2. Many investigators have found growth and survival of tree seedlings reduced by water deficits (for example, Kozlowski, 1949; Ferrell, 1953; Bourdeau, 1954).

The importance of water supply to tree growth has been brought out in studies of competition, where reduction of competition for water by trenching has almost always resulted in improved growth and survival

(Korstian and Coile, 1938; Shirley, 1945; Toumey and Kienholz, 1931). This aspect of the problem will be discussed in more detail in Chapter 16. The cambium is affected by water deficit as much as the stem tips, and lack of available soil moisture results in reduced width of annual rings. This well-known phenomenon is discussed in Chapter 2. Fruit growth also is reduced by water deficits (Harley and Masure, 1938; Schroeder and Wieland, 1956). Some effects of water deficits are shown in Figure 15.3.

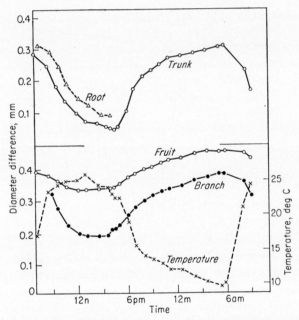

Figure 15.3 Shrinkage of various parts of an avocado tree, caused by internal water deficits. (*From Schroeder and Wieland, 1956.*)

As mentioned earlier, water deficit not only reduces the amount of growth but also changes its character. The thicker cuticle and palisade layers of sun leaves probably are caused by the more frequent and severe water deficits developed in full sun. Cell walls usually are thicker, and more supporting tissue usually develops around the vascular bundles. The vascular bundles usually are closer together in sun leaves also. The thicker walls of summerwood or latewood, as compared with earlywood, probably are related to the more severe water deficits developed in the summer.

Australian workers have made some particularly interesting studies of the effects of water deficits on growth and other processes in herbaceous plants. Gates (1955) found that even a short period of moderate wilting affects plant growth, decreasing leaf weight relative to stem weight, but growth rate increased above controls when the plants were rewatered. Williams and Shapter (1955) warned that effects of water deficits vary with the stage of growth at which plants are subjected to wilting. They found that in addition to reducing growth, water deficits reduced photosynthesis per unit of leaf area and reduced phosphorus uptake, while the nitrogen content of leaves was reduced and that of stems increased. Studies of this type on trees are needed.

It should be pointed out that moderate water deficit sometimes is beneficial, especially in the production of seedlings for transplanting. An abundance of water often results in large and succulent seedlings, with a high ratio of shoots to roots, which do not survive transplanting as well as smaller, more woody seedlings with a lower ratio of shoots to roots. It therefore is necessary to control the water supply to nursery beds carefully to produce good-quality seedlings. An abundance of water is necessary early in the season to promote growth, but it should be reduced later in the season to harden the seedlings (Stoeckeler and Aamodt, 1940; Toumey and Korstian, 1942), although severe water deficits may be injurious even at this stage. Other examples of the beneficial effects of reduced water supply will be discussed later in this chapter.

Water Deficits and Stomatal Closure

One of the well-known and important effects of internal water deficit is closure of stomates. Stålfelt (1955, 1956a) claims that of all the factors affecting the movement of guard cells, water deficit is most important. A number of investigators have found stomatal aperture to be a sensitive indicator of the internal water balance of plants. Jones (1931) found that the stomates of peach trees in moist soil remained open much longer each day than stomates of trees in dry soil. Yocum (1935) observed that stomates of seedlings of several species of oak remained closed all day after the soil became dry, and according to Magness et al. (1935), reduction in length of time stomates remain open is the first visible evidence of internal water deficit in apple trees. Stomates of apple trees began to close earlier than normal considerably before the soil moisture in the root zone had fallen to permanent wilting. Oppenheimer and Elze (1941) found that stomates of citrus trees also begin to close abnormally early when the soil begins to dry out and regarded this as a reliable indicator of the need for irrigation. Figure 15.4 shows the effects of decreasing soil moisture on stomatal opening of pears.

Closure of stomates as a result of internal water deficit may be beneficial to plants in dry habitats because it decreases water loss and postpones development of injurious or fatal water deficits. It can also be detrimental because it usually reduces the entrance of carbon dioxide and thus reduces photosynthesis. The extent to which stomatal closure retards entrance of carbon dioxide seems to vary with the species. It probably depends chiefly on the thickness and permeability of the cuticle to gas, because photosynthesis has been observed in some thin-leaved species even when their stomates are closed. Freeland (1948) found that

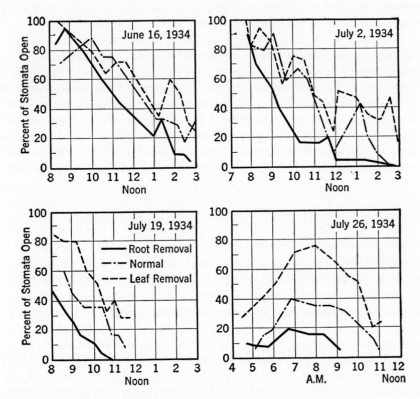

Figure 15.4 Effect of water deficit on daily closure of stomates of pear. As the soil dried out during the summer, internal water deficit developed earlier in the day and stomates closed earlier. Stomates closed earlier on trees with one-fifth of their roots removed than on trees with one-fifth of their leaves removed because the former developed an internal water deficit earlier in the day. (*From Kramer, 1949; after Aldrich and Work, 1934.*)

almost as much carbon dioxide entered through the epidermis of some species as through the stomates, but very little entered through the non-stomated surfaces of the heavily cutinized leaves of *Ficus elastica*. Dugger (1952) observed considerable diffusion of $C^{14}O_2$ through the cuticle of hydrangea leaves, but Nutman (1937) found that the midday closure of stomates which characteristically occurs in coffee was accompanied by a large reduction in photosynthesis. Schneider and Childers (1941) found that photosynthesis of apple decreased as the soil dried, but some photosynthesis occurred in leaves even after the stomates appeared to be closed. Heinicke and Childers (1937) found that photosynthesis was not much reduced in apple trees in the afternoon, although the stomates appeared to close. It is difficult to arrive at definite conclusions about the relationship between stomatal closure and photosynthesis because of the difficulty of deciding when stomates are actually closed.

According to Stälfelt (1928), both water loss and photosynthesis of Norway spruce are controlled largely by stomatal opening, although this species has some cuticular transpiration. Pisek and Tranquillini (1954) attributed the midday drop in photosynthesis of European beech and Norway spruce to closure of stomates produced by water deficit resulting from high transpiration, but other factors may be involved (Polster, 1950). In general, it seems probable that entrance of carbon dioxide into heavily cutinized leaves occurs principally through the stomates; hence in such leaves photosynthesis is controlled largely by stomatal opening but in leaves with thin cuticle it is not.

Water Deficits and Physiological Processes

In general, rates of physiological processes decrease when the water content of the plant tissue falls below normal. The rates of such processes as respiration and photosynthesis do not always decrease in proportion to the decrease in water content, however. In fact, photosynthesis may decrease while respiration is increasing, as Schneider and Childers found in apple trees. Usually, hydrolytic processes such as starch hydrolysis are favored and synthetic processes are decreased by water deficit, although some exceptions occur such as the accumulation of polysaccharides in certain succulents (Spoehr, 1919) and the formation of hemicelluloses in soybeans (Clements, 1937) subjected to drought. The effects of water deficit on various enzymatically controlled processes are discussed by Mothes (1956).

The effects of water deficits on photosynthesis were discussed in some detail in Chapter 3, and its effects on respiration in Chapter 7. Unfortunately, in most of these studies no actual measurements of water deficit were made. For example, photosynthesis was measured with decreasing soil moisture, and it was assumed that increasing water deficit was developing in the plants. However, if photosynthesis is measured in humid air at relatively low light intensities, transpiration might be relatively low and no serious water deficit would develop until the soil was dried nearly to permanent wilting. In future studies plant water deficits should be measured concurrently with plant processes as was done in *Theobroma cacao* by Lemée (1956).

Water Deficits and Chemical Composition

It is well known that plants grown with a reduced water supply often show differences in chemical composition when compared with those grown with an abundance of water. This problem was discussed in some detail by Mothes (1956) and by Stocker (1956), but most of the research reported was done on herbaceous plants and is not necessarily applicable to trees. One general effect of water deficits which seems to occur quite widely in the plant kingdom is the conversion of starch to sugar. Magness et al. (1933) found that deficient water supply caused an increase in the ratio of sugar to starch and a decrease in total carbohydrates in apple trees. According to Mothes (1956), Kursanov found that in tea leaves decreased water content resulted in decreased synthesis and increased hydrolysis of sucrose. Water deficiency causes accumulation of hemicelluloses and pentosans in some species, and it may cause changes in nitrogen metabolism, but this shows no consistent pattern. A low water supply decreased the total alkaloid and quinine sulfate content of cinchona seedlings, but increased the calcium, magnesium, and total salt content (Loustalot et al., 1947). It is generally agreed that fruits of plants subjected to water deficits are somewhat different from those grown on plants supplied with an abundance of water. Fruit from pear trees in dry soil are firmer, sweeter, and less acid than those from trees in moist soil (Ryall and Aldrich, 1944), but the differences are not commercially important if the fruits receive enough water to attain merchantable size.

Several studies have been made of the effect of different levels of water supply on size and rubber content of guayule. A generous water supply results in the largest bushes, but plants grown with a lower supply of water and therefore subjected to appreciable water deficits contained a higher percentage of rubber, resin, and lignin (Kelley et al., 1945). The relationships between fresh weight and rubber content and soil moisture stress are shown in Figure 15.5. Plants subjected to considerable moisture stress and internal water deficits also are higher in soluble carbohydrates and resume growth better when transplanted (Traub et al., 1946).

Water deficit undoubtedly affects such properties of the protoplasm as viscosity and permeability, but there is considerable difference of opinion concerning the nature of these effects (Levitt, 1951). There also is wide difference of opinion as to how water deficits bring about the various physiological and biochemical effects associated with them. Mothes (1956) and Stocker (1956) cite Russian work claiming that change in water content changes the activity of enzymes by freeing them from surfaces, or vice versa, but other factors certainly are involved.

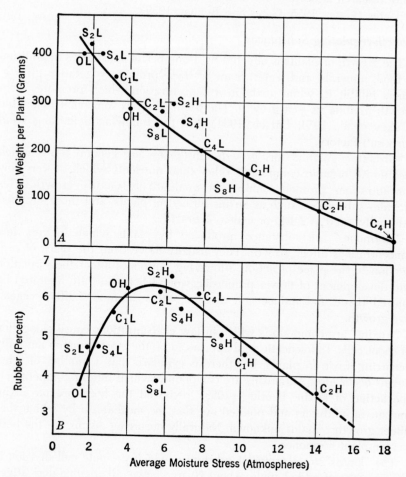

Figure 15.5 Relation between average soil moisture stress (soil DPD), the growth of guayule plants (*A*), and their rubber content (*B*). The symbols refer to various treatments used to increase soil moisture stress.

O = no salt added
C_1 = 0.1% NaCl added
C_2 = 0.2% NaCl added
C_4 = 0.4% NaCl added

S_2 = 0.2% Na_2SO_4 added
S_4 = 0.4% Na_2SO_4 added
S_8 = 0.8% Na_2SO_4 added

L = low tension. Water was added to bring soil moisture back to field capacity when a tension of 300 to 400 centimeters of water was indicated by tensiometers. H = high tension. Water was added when average moisture content fell to permanent-wilting percentage. Increasing soil moisture stress decreased growth regardless of the method used to produce it. (*From Kramer, 1949; after Wadleigh et al., 1946.*)

More research is needed in this field along the lines suggested in papers by Gates (Gates, 1955; Gates and Bonner, 1959).

Growth-regulating Substances

The growth of plants is affected by a number of substances in addition to food, minerals, and water. Some of these promote vegetative growth, others inhibit it, while auxin in a concentration which promotes stem growth inhibits its root growth. The terminology is somewhat debatable (Tukey et al., 1954; Larsen, 1954), but the following definitions seem fairly satisfactory.

"Growth regulators" or "growth substances" are general terms which include all organic compounds other than nutrients which at very low concentrations promote, inhibit, or qualitatively modify growth. This includes substances, such as auxins formed in plants, and those supplied externally, such as 2,4-D or maleic hydrazide.

"Hormones" are substances produced by plants which in very low concentrations affect growth. They usually move from the place of production to the place of action. Flowering hormones affect the formation and development of flower primordia; wound hormones are liberated by injured tissue and induce cell division; other hormones affect vegetative growth.

"Auxins" are compounds which in low concentrations cause elongation of shoot cells. Indoleacetic acid appears to be the most common naturally occurring auxin in plants, but there is evidence that a number of other auxins occur also. Antiauxins are compounds which inhibit competitively the action of auxin. Bentley (1958) reviewed the literature on auxins and auxin inhibitors and pointed out that the mechanism by which they affect growth remains unknown. Naturally occurring auxins are the best-known plant hormones.

The "kinins" are a group of substances which promote cell division in the presence of added auxin. About 20 are known, all adenine derivatives. The first one to be isolated was kinetin (Skoog and Miller, 1957).

"Gibberellins" are a group of substances with an ability to increase stem elongation by increasing cell elongation. It now appears that cell division also is stimulated. Stowe and Yamaki (1957) suggest that they should be defined as that "class of compounds which cause internodal elongation when applied to certain intact genetically dwarfed plants." Gibberellic acid often causes dramatic increase in stem elongation of tree seedlings, and its possible usefulness is being investigated by a number of workers (Marth et al., 1956; Nelson, 1957; Wittwer and Bukovac, 1958). Hacskaylo and Murphey (1958) found that gibberellic acid broke dormancy when injected into hybrid poplars. One of the authors observed that it also broke dormancy when sprayed on sweetgum seedlings.

The idea that plant growth is modified by specific substances is an old one. Sachs suggested that development of plant organs might be controlled by specific substances, and many other writers suggested that stimulating hormonelike substances might occur in plants. Went (1928) developed the agar block method of measuring auxin activity quantitatively, and this gave great impetus to the study of plant hormones.

Numerous examples of plant hormones are known. At least some young leaves require small amounts of a specific substance formed elsewhere in the plant if normal enlargement is to occur. For example, pea leaves require adenine, and this can be regarded as a hormone necessary for leaf expansion. Stem elongation requires auxin produced in the stem tips and young leaves, and there is evidence that shoot growth requires special substances formed in the roots (Went, 1938; Jackson, 1956). Substances of a hormonal nature seem to be involved in flower bud initiation, fruit development, wound healing, and a variety of other processes.

Substances such as thiamine, pyridoxine, and nicotinic acid, which function as coenzymes, are termed vitamins in animal nutrition. In plants the distinction between vitamins and hormones is very indefinite. All the vitamins apparently are synthesized in plants, but not all organs synthesize enough for normal growth. For example, the roots of at least some species of plants are dependent on their shoots for supplies of thiamine and other vitamins. In such instances these substances seem to function as hormones.

Growth inhibitors thus far have received less attention than growth-promoting substances, but they may prove to be equally important. It seems probable that growth is controlled by quantitative changes in proportions of growth-promoting and growth-inhibiting substances rather than by qualitative changes alone.

Auxins

The best-known plant hormones are the auxins. They seem to be produced in greatest amounts in stem tips, young leaves, flowers, and embryos of seeds, but presumably at least traces occur in all living cells. Their distinguishing characteristic is their ability to cause elongation of cells of shoots. Another characteristic of auxins is their tendency to be transported downward in stems. Auxin also stimulates cambial activity, causes initiation of root primordia in stems and formation of callus tissues, and brings about development of tumors and galls. At certain concentrations, auxin inhibits leaf abscission, the development of lateral buds (see section on apical dominance), and root growth. A concentration of auxin which stimulates stem elongation inhibits cell elongation in roots and the growth of lateral buds. A number of synthetic chemicals produce the same effects as natural auxin. Some effects of auxin on plant organs and processes will be described in the following section.

Shoot Growth. There seems to be a good correlation between rate of shoot growth and auxin supply from terminal buds (Zimmerman, 1936). Auxin can be extracted readily from growing buds (Czaja, 1934), and Mirov (1941) found the auxin content was higher in rapidly growing young ponderosa pine trees than in slowly growing trees. The yield of auxin from buds increases rapidly to a maximum, then falls to a negligible amount within a period of a few weeks in the spring. In at least some species, it appears that although the initial supply of auxin which stimu-

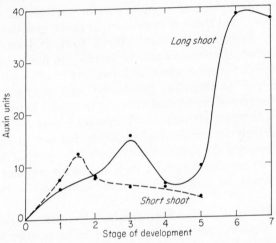

Figure 15.6 The yield of auxin from long- and short-shoot lateral buds at various stages in their development. Stages: 0, buds dormant; 1, buds swelling; 2, first green visible; 3, scales beginning to open; 4, scales folding back and petioles beginning to elongate; 5, petioles elongated and leaf blades expanding; 6, internodes visible in long shoots; 7, long shoots 25 millimeters in length. (*After Gunckel and Thimann, 1949.*)

lates shoot elongation comes from the bud and young leaves, after growth starts sufficient auxin is produced by the shoot itself. The lower parts of growing shoots may contain more auxin than the buds.

Gunckel and Thimann (1949) studied the relation of auxin to long and short shoot development in Ginkgo, where some of the shoots elongate much more than others. Production of the long shoots seems to be associated with high production of auxin, first at the apex and later in lower internodes (Figure 15.6). As Ginkgo grows older, the number of long shoots decreases, causing a change in form from excurrent to globose. According to Gunckel et al. (1949), the terminal long shoots produce so much auxin that lateral short shoots are prevented from elongating. It is possible, however, that auxin operates indirectly to inhibit lateral buds by curtailing their food supply. This will be discussed further in connection with apical dominance.

Diameter Growth. It generally is believed that auxin from opening buds moving down stems causes the initiation of cambial activity. Cambial activity usually begins at the base of buds and progresses downward, presumably as auxin moves downward. In conifers and ring-porous hardwoods cambial activity progresses downward so rapidly that diameter growth begins almost as soon at the bottom as at the top of the trunk. In diffuse-porous trees 8 or 10 weeks sometimes elapse between the beginning of cambial activity at the top and the bottom of a tree trunk, presumably because auxin moves downward more slowly. Diameter growth and its relations to shoot growth are discussed in more detail in Chapter 2.

Root Growth. Care must be taken to distinguish between the effects of auxin on root formation and on root elongation. Root elongation is stimulated by an exceedingly low concentration of auxin, but is inhibited by concentrations which stimulate root formation. Thus root systems treated with auxins sometimes produce numerous new laterals, but these fail to elongate because the concentration which caused their formation is high enough to inhibit their elongation. If the auxin concentration is lowered below the inhibiting level, these roots will elongate (Audus, 1953).

Application of auxin to roots of intact trees and shrubs when they are transplanted sometimes improves root growth. If this effect could be obtained consistently, it would be of considerable practical importance in increasing survival after transplanting, but the results obtained thus far are quite variable. Tilford (1938) reported that soaking roots of Elberta peaches, American elm, and red oak in a solution containing 40 parts per million of indolebutyric acid for 48 hours stimulated root growth. Gossard (1942) found similar treatments successful on peaches. According to Maki and Marshall (1945), soaking roots of red oak seedlings in indolebutyric acid increased the volume of new roots produced during the following growing season but it also increased mortality.

Use of indolebutyric acid was reported to increase root growth of *Viburnum dilatatum* (Chadwick, 1937) and root and shoot growth of crabapple, pfitzer juniper, and fragrant honeysuckle (Swartley, 1941). Smith and Romberg (1939) increased root production of 5- and 7-year-old pecan trees by inserting toothpicks impregnated with indolebutyric acid into their taproots. Results have been less successful with gymnosperms. Maki and Marshall (1945) obtained inconsistent results with loblolly pine, and Fowells (1943) found that indoleacetic acid was not effective on ponderosa pine seedlings.

Samantarai (1955) caused roots to form on attached twigs by applying synthetic auxin, and it is used rather commonly in propagating plants by air layering. Use of auxin to produce roots on cuttings is discussed in Chapter 13. Possibly auxin accumulation is connected with certain other instances of root formation. For example, Nesbitt (1942) described production of aerial roots from the callused area surrounding an old fire wound high up on the stem of a mature northern red oak tree. Perhaps accumulation of auxin in the vicinity of wounds causes adventitious root formation.

Apparently auxin produced by the fungus involved in the formation of mycorrhizal roots is responsible for their characteristic dichotomous branching. MacDougal and Dufrenoy (1944) concluded that auxin produced by the fungal hyphae is translocated into the root tissue. Slankis (1948) demonstrated that dichotomous branching can be produced in detached pine roots by supplying exudates of mycorrhizal fungi. Later he showed that treating cultures of isolated pine roots with low concentrations of indoleacetic and naphthaleneacetic acid caused production of dichotomous branches resembling those of mycorrhizal roots. Slankis (1958) recently summarized his work concerning the effects of auxin from mycorrhizal fungi on root growth.

Hypertrophies, Overgrowths, and Tumors. Auxin seems to play a part in the production of various hypertrophies, galls, and tumors which occur on plants. For example, outgrowths of cells, termed "intumescences" by Sorauer (1899), occur on the leaves of various trees. Intumescences may be hypertrophies which result simply from cell enlargement, hyperplasias caused by increased numbers of cells of normal size, or a combination of the two. LaRue (1936) caused intumescences to form by spreading the contents of crushed intumescence-bearing leaves or indoleacetic acid into healthy leaves. This suggested that auxin supply had some effect on their development.

Crown gall is an example of a hypertrophy or tumorous growth. It is caused by the bacterium *Agrobacterium tumefaciens* and is a common disease of both herbaceous and woody plants. It is characterized by overgrowths or galls which develop on roots and occasionally on stems, as a result of excessive division and enlargement of cells in the cortical parenchyma. According to Klein and Link (1955), growth substances play a multiple role in the development of crown gall tumors. Stimulation of cell division and enlargement by growth substances produced by invading fungi doubtless are responsible for many other hypertrophies in plants, such as those produced on trees by various species of rust fungi. The root nodules of legumes represent still another type of overgrowth hypertrophy, which is related to auxin supply. It is not clear, however, whether the excess auxin is produced by the bacteria or by host cells stimulated by the bacteria (Allen and Allen, 1958).

The galls produced on leaves by insects presumably also are caused by growth-stimulating substances. Usually the size, shape, and other characteristics of the galls vary widely, even on leaves of the same species, according to the kind of insect laying eggs (Wells, 1915). This suggests that each kind of insect larva produces a different kind of substance which either directly or indirectly determines the kind of gall produced.

Fruit Development. Naturally occurring auxins seem to play an important role in fruit development. Luckwill (1957) warns that we must distinguish between hormones initiating fruit growth after fertilization and those controlling its subsequent enlargement. The auxin content of ovaries is very low before pollination, but it usually increases rapidly after fertilization. In some species the pollen tube appears to supply enough auxin to start fruit enlargement but not enough to complete the process. After fruit enlargement starts, auxin produced in the ovules or embryos is needed to stimulate further development (Luckwill, 1948). Evidence for this view comes from observation of correlations between the size of mature fruits and the number of viable seeds in them, the relation between auxin production and rate of fruit growth, and the stimulation of fruit growth by applications of synthetic auxin (Luckwill, 1957). According to Luckwill, in apple the developing endosperm seems to be the first source of auxin after fertilization occurs, but later it is supplied by the embryos. Failure of seeds to develop in a carpel of pome fruits usually results in failure of the adjacent region of the fruit to enlarge properly.

There seem to be wide differences in the degree of dependence of fruit development on exogenous supplies of auxin. Strawberry fruits are dependent on their seeds for auxin during the entire course of their development, but navel orange and pineapple fruits evidently produce their own auxin because they contain no seeds. Luckwill (1957) cited work by Abbott, who demonstrated by removing seeds at various stages of development that growth of apple fruits is dependent on the seeds until they are about half grown. After the stage at which embryo growth is completed, fruit growth no longer depends on the presence of seeds.

Some indirect evidence of the importance of auxin for fruit development comes from experiments on fruit set and development by the use of synthetic growth substances. Gardner and Marth (1937), for example, caused parthenocarpic fruits to develop on American holly by applying dilute solutions of growth substances. The parthenocarpic fruits were indistinguishable from those produced by pollination, except for the absence of seeds. Sprays of synthetic auxins have been used to produce parthenocarpic fruits in figs (Crane and Blondeau, 1951), pears (De Tar et al., 1950), and apples (Osborne and Wain, 1951). Luckwill (1957) points out, however, that most attempts to produce parthenocarpic fruits by applying auxin to tree fruits have been unsuccessful. Evidently fruit set depends on other factors in addition to a supply of auxin.

Synthetic growth regulators have been used with limited success in horticulture to increase the size of some kinds of fruits and to shorten the time necessary for ripening. For example, application of synthetic auxin decreased the time required for ripening of apples, peaches, and figs (Crane and Blondeau, 1949; Harley et al., 1950; Marth et al., 1950) and increased the size of citrus fruits (Erickson and Brannaman, 1950) and seedless varieties of grapes (Weaver, 1953).

Abscission. Plant structures such as leaves, flower parts, and fruits are shed periodically, by a process called abscission. Dead twigs and branches are cast off in some genera of trees (*Ulmus, Quercus, Populus,* and *Agathis*). After the branches fall, protective layers of periderm seal off the exposed surfaces.

Healthy, young, physiologically active organs do not abscise, and it seems that senescence or a physiological disturbance invariably precedes abscission. A number of unfavorable environmental factors such as water deficit, low light intensity, unfavorable photoperiod or temperature, mineral deficiency, and injury by insects or fungi cause premature abscission of leaves. Some of these external factors bring about abscission by influencing the auxin supply, which is believed to be the primary, internal regulator (Addicott et al., 1955). For example, deficiencies of oxygen, nitrogen, and zinc and injury by insects and fungi seem to inactivate auxin or decrease the supply and thereby favor abscission. In healthy tissues continuous synthesis of auxin apparently counteracts a natural tendency of plant parts to abscise. The situation in leaves and fruits differs somewhat because leaves seem to synthesize auxin at a fairly uniform rate while fruits appear to produce auxin in surges, corresponding to developmental stages.

Abscission of Leaves. Abscission zones of simple leaves form along the petiole or at its base. Compound leaves have a number of abscission zones located at the base of the petiole and at the bases of leaflets. Such zones are characterized by lack of collenchyma, weakly developed or absent sclerenchyma tissue, thin and short vascular elements, and dense cytoplasm in parenchyma cells. Since most of the cells in the abscission zone are parenchymatous, the only strengthening material is in the vascular elements. Before the leaves actually fall, the middle lamella and outer walls of the cells in the abscission zone usually swell, become gelatinous, and finally break down (Eames and MacDaniels, 1947). According to Facey (1950), chemical changes in abscission zones include conversion of calcium pectates to pectic acid, which in turn is converted to water-soluble pectin. Cellulose becomes gelatinous but is unaltered chemically. The leaf usually is supported temporarily by vascular connections, but these are readily broken. After leaves are severed at the abscission zone, primary protective layers of parenchyma cells and normal periderm layers seal over the wound. There is considerable variation between species in the time and method of formation of these protective layers.

Several lines of evidence support the view that a continuous auxin supply from leaves is necessary to prevent leaf abscission. For example, it has often been observed that a leaf petiole abscises after the leaf blade, which is the source of auxin, has been removed (Shoji et al., 1951). Wetmore and Jacobs (1953) found that the inhibiting effect of leaf blades on abscission could be replaced by applications of synthetic auxin.

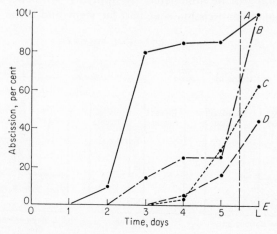

Figure 15.7 Relation between amount of leaf blade removed and rate of leaf abscission in Valencia orange. A, all leaf blade removed; B, 90 per cent of leaf blade removed; C, 75 per cent of leaf blade removed; D, 50 per cent of leaf blade removed; E, none of blade removed. (*From Livingston, 1950.*)

According to Livingston (1950), the amount of leaf petiole abscission in Valencia orange was proportional to the amount of leaf area removed (Figure 15.7).

Insect injury to leaf blades also stimulates abscission of leaves. An interesting case of leaf abscission in coffee trees, caused by the fungus *Omphalia flavida*, was described by Sequeira and Steeves (1954). Premature defoliation associated with leaf lesions caused by this fungus is regarded as the most destructive disease of coffee in the American tropics. Usually many lesions occur on a leaf, but even a single lesion at the base of the blade or on the petiole may cause abscission. Sequeira and Steeves found that abscission of leaves which were inoculated with the fungus could be delayed by applying synthetic auxin to leaf petioles. They concluded that the fungus produced an oxidative enzyme which stimulated abscission by inactivating auxin.

According to Addicott and Lynch (1955), abscission is not controlled by the amount of auxin in the abscission area but rather by the auxin gradient across the abscission zone. As may be seen in Figure 15.8, abscission does not occur when there is a steep gradient, that is, when there is a high auxin supply between the blade and the abscission zone and a low auxin supply between the abscission zone and the stem. Abscission occurs when the gradient is not steep, and it is accelerated when the amount of auxin is high between the abscission zone and the stem but low between the abscission zone and the leaf. It has been observed that the auxin gradient across the abscission zone is lowered prior to abscission. Abscission can be stimulated by applying synthetic auxin to the petiole between the abscission zone and the stem, and it can be inhibited

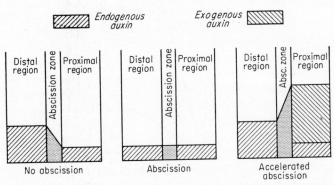

Figure 15.8 Effect of auxin gradient across the abscission zone on abscission of leaves. (*From Addicott and Lynch, 1955.*)

by applying auxin distal to the abscission zone. On the other hand, Gaur and Leopold (1955) stated that high concentrations of auxin inhibit abscission while low concentrations promote abscission. They concluded that abscission is controlled primarily by the quantity of auxin rather than the auxin gradient. Perhaps more research will reconcile these varying viewpoints.

Abscission of Fruits. Fruits abscise at the base of the pedicel or, less commonly, at the base of the fruit. As in leaves, abscission of fruits occurs primarily because of breakdown of calcium pectate of the middle lamella and primary walls in the abscission zone. Abscission is normally prevented in growing fruits by auxin supplied by the developing fruit to the abscission zone. Removal of a growing fruit causes rapid initiation of an abscission layer. This situation is somewhat analogous to the formation of an abscission zone in leaf petioles when leaf blades are removed.

Three normal waves of fruit drop are recognized. These include the abscission of unpollinated or unfertilized blossoms, the June drop of young fruits, and the preharvest drop. The abscission of immature fruit in the June drop is associated with embryo abortion.

Luckwill (1953) has shown that periods of low fruit drop in apple trees coincide with surges of hormone production in the fruit. He concluded that hormonal stimuli from developing seeds prevented abscission. Fruits with the smallest number of seeds are among the first to abscise, further indicating the necessity of seeds for preventing abscission.

Luckwill (1957) suggested that different auxins are involved in growth control and in abscission of fruit. Both Luckwill (1953) and Wright (1956) found auxins in apple and black currant which showed negative correlation with fruit drop but no correlation with growth of fruit. According to Luckwill (1957), the fruit drop auxin is not found in apple seeds until about 2 weeks after petal fall. However, 3 to 4 weeks after petal fall a small surge of auxin production occurs, and this is correlated with the end of fruit abscission. Later, as the embryo grows and primary endosperm disappears, auxin production decreases and the June drop of fruits occurs. When embryo growth stops and the secondary endosperm achieves maximum volume, auxin supply reaches a maximum and the June drop terminates. After this time the correlation between auxin content of the seed and abscission of fruit no longer seems to hold. Auxin production in the seed remains low until the preharvest drop begins. The preharvest drop may be linked to low auxin levels, but Luckwill (1957) suggests that other abscission-promoting substances such as ethylene may also be involved.

Preharvest fruit drop is a serious problem to horticulturists because the prematurely dropped fruit has low market value. Gardner et al. (1939) demonstrated that sprays of synthetic auxin checked abscission of fruits before picking time. Van Overbeek (1952) believes that such sprays inhibit abscission by preventing breakdown of calcium pectate in the middle lamella. Control of preharvest drop by spraying with hormones has become standard practice in apple and pear orchards, and it is estimated that loss of these fruits caused by preharvest drop has been decreased by 60 to 80 per cent (Batjer, 1954). Several growth-regulating chemicals are effective, but naphthaleneacetic acid or its sodium salt is the active ingredient in most sprays. The stimulus of these synthetic auxins appears to be transmitted chiefly through leaves. Therefore the success of spraying depends to a large extent on physiologically active leaves. Fruit drop is most easily controlled in vigorous trees with large carbohydrate reserves. It is difficult to control in winter-injured or diseased trees as well as in trees lacking vigor because of mineral deficiencies.

Tropisms. Another group of processes in which auxin seems to play a role are tropisms. In fact, auxin was discovered in connection with research on tropisms. Tropisms are movements caused by differences in the intensity of an environmental factor such as light or gravity which is applied in greater intensity to one side of a plant structure than to the other side. Phototropism or the tendency of stems to bend toward the light and geotropism or the tendency of stems to grow upward and roots to grow downward are the best known of these phenomena.

Phototropism not only causes stems to grow toward the light, but also causes leaf blades to become oriented in such a manner that they form a mosaic in which all blades receive maximum exposure to light. This orientation is particularly noticeable in vines growing on a wall, but it also occurs to some extent in the leaves of trees. One example of phototropism is the tendency of leaves of turkey oak seedlings to become oriented in a vertical plane. Phototropism is brought about by unequal growth on the shaded and unshaded sides of stems and petioles, the shaded side elongating more rapidly than the exposed side. Most of this difference in rate of elongation is attributed to differences in auxin concentration on the shaded and unshaded sides of stems, auxin being either inactivated or caused to move out of the unshaded side. There probably also is a limited amount of direct inhibition of bright light on cell elongation, although the importance of this is uncertain.

Geotropism also appears to be caused by unequal distribution of auxin, in this case unequal distribution between the upper and lower halves of horizontally oriented stems and roots. The greater concentration of auxin tends to occur in the lower halves of horizontally placed stems and roots, and this stimulates cell elongation on the undersides of stems, causing them to grow up. High concentrations of auxin inhibit elongation of root cells; hence the lower sides grow more slowly than the upper sides, causing them to bend downward.

Of course, there are wide differences in the sensitivity of roots and stems to light and gravity, resulting in varying degrees of response. Main stems and taproots appear very sensitive to gravity, but branch roots and stems show less response and tend to grow more or less horizontally. It is possible that the explanations of tropisms offered here are too simple, and views on the mechanisms causing tropisms may change when more information becomes available.

Examples of Internal Correlations

We shall now turn from discussion of correlating mechanisms to consideration of some examples of internal correlations which occur in plants. These include such phenomena as polarity, apical dominance, root/shoot ratios, cambial activity versus shoot growth, reproduction versus vegetative growth, and growth versus dormancy.

Polarity. As soon as a fertilized egg begins to divide and form an embryo, it begins to exhibit polarity. One end begins to develop differently from the other, and an embryo in a seed soon possesses apical and basal regions. Development of an embryo results in differentiation of the radicle, hypocotyl, epicotyl, and cotyledons, and finally results in the roots, shoots, and other organs of mature plants. In some plants polarity continues to exist even in detached stem segments which will produce roots only at the morphologically lower end.

Accompanying the morphological polarity, which usually is self-evident, there are various manifestations of physiological polarity. In Chapter 8 it was stated that there is a tendency toward polarity in translocation of food in the sense that carbohydrates and other metabolites tend to move toward actively growing regions such as stem tips and young fruits, even at the expense of more slowly growing regions. The means by which this polarized transport is brought about cannot be explained satisfactorily until we learn more about the mechanism of translocation. Auxin shows a well-defined tendency toward downward movement in stems, and its polar distribution probably is an important factor in controlling the polar distribution of food.

Another example of polarity is the distribution of electrical potentials in a spruce tree. The leader is negative to lower parts of the stem, and the tips of branches to their bases. Lund (1931) and Rosene and Lund (1953) regarded these patterns of electrical polarity as the controlling factors in determining polarity, but they might be the result of gradients in metabolic activity instead of the cause.

Apical Dominance. Somewhat related to polarity is the phenomenon of apical dominance. This refers to the fact that active terminal meristems or stem tips often inhibit development of lateral buds below them. This phenomenon is common in herbaceous plants, but is particularly important in certain trees and shrubs where differences in degree of apical dominance often determine the habit of growth.

Palms have a columnar habit of growth because no lateral branches develop and all growth occurs from one terminal meristem, resulting in a tuft of leaves at the top of an unbranched trunk. In most conifers and some nonconiferous trees a central stem or leader grows much more rapidly than the lateral branches below it. This produces a more or less conical tree form, often described as having excurrent branching. In many other kinds of trees, such as oaks and elms, numerous lateral buds grow at approximately the same rate, producing many branches and a rounded top. These trees are said to have decurrent branching. This growth habit is particularly marked in elm, which generally loses its terminal buds, resulting in branching and rebranching from lateral buds until the main stem loses its identity in the broadly spreading top. This type of branching sometimes is called deliquescent, because the main stem is lost in its branches. Some examples of tree form are shown in Figure 15.9.

If the terminal bud of a tree with well-defined apical dominance is removed or damaged, one of the lateral branches below usually outgrows its neighbors and forms a new leader. Occasionally, however, two or more laterals grow at so nearly the same rate that neither can exert control over the other and undesirable forked trunks and candelabrum-shaped tops result. According to some observers, late summer growth or lammas shoots are likely to produce forked stems and trees of poor form (Carvell, 1956; Leitbundgut, 1955).

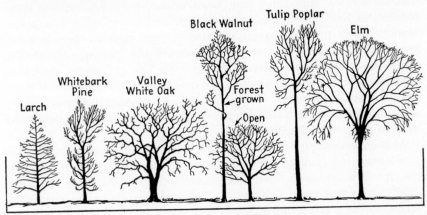

Figure 15.9 Various growth forms of trees, ranging from the strongly excurrent branching of larch to the decurrent branching of open-grown oak and walnut and the deliquescent branching of elm. (*From Baker, 1950.*)

Removal of terminal buds causes loss of apical dominance. This is undesirable if trees are being grown for timber, but removal of terminal buds is used effectively to produce a dense, shrubby type of growth. Many kinds of trees can be maintained as shrubs and even used as hedges by persistently pruning away the terminal growth. Removal of terminal buds removes their inhibiting effect and permits growth of numerous lateral buds which otherwise would remain dormant, producing a dense, bushy type of growth. An example is the dense cluster of shoots produced by pollarded trees, which are cut back to the trunk to produce long slender shoots for baskets and furniture.

Apical dominance usually is attributed to the inhibiting effects of auxin produced by the terminal bud on lateral buds below it (Skoog and Thimann, 1934; Thimann, 1937). This is based on observations that if auxin is supplied to stem tips from which the terminal bud has been removed, growth of lateral buds is inhibited just as if the terminal bud were present. Went (1936, 1939) proposed that the effect of auxin is exerted by diverting food and growth substances to regions of high auxin content, such as terminal buds. Thus lateral buds fail to grow because of lack of food and growth substances.

Gregory and Veale (1957) suggest that the degree of apical dominance depends on the supply of carbohydrate and nitrogen available for growth. There is competition for food among the various meristems, and if the supply of nitrogen is limited, only the most active meristem, usually the terminal bud, gets enough for growth. According to the view of Gregory and Veale, auxin plays an indirect role in apical dominance because a high concentration hinders or prevents formation of vascular connections to axillary buds. This blocks transport of food into them and prevents growth. The mechanism by which apical dominance is maintained probably will not be understood fully until more is known about the mechanism of translocation and the factors affecting it.

Leaf and Bud Correlations. Some correlative or competitive interrelationships between leaf and bud activity seem to exist in many kinds of plants. Buds grow in the axils of leaves, but after attaining a certain stage of development they cease growth and usually remain dormant until the following spring. However, if the leaves are removed from the plant during the growing season, these apparently dormant buds often produce shoots bearing a new crop of leaves. This behavior suggests that their inactivity is not caused by internal conditions but by the inhibiting influence of the leaves. The situation somewhat resembles apical dominance, and the inhibitory action of the leaves may be exerted through competition for water and nutrients, through hormones, or even by a combination of the two mechanisms.

Root/shoot Ratios. The ratio between the water- and mineral-absorbing surface and the transpiring and photosynthetic surface of a plant is an important factor in its growth. A small root system limits shoot growth by curtailing the supply of water and minerals to the top, while reduction in the photosynthetic surface limits growth of roots by curtailing their supply of carbohydrates. In general, this interaction tends to maintain a reasonably efficient ratio of roots to shoots, but the most desirable ratio often is disturbed by unfavorable environmental factors or cultural treatments.

Plants of various species have characteristic root/shoot ratios. Shading, pruning, defoliation, and flowering and fruiting all reduce root growth either by reducing photosynthesis or by diverting carbohydrates to fruit and seed production. Heavy applications of nitrogen usually stimulate shoot growth more than root growth; hence, although the amount of roots may be increased, the ratio of roots to shoots usually is decreased. Most of the data on root/shoot ratios have been obtained from herbaceous plants, but Heinicke (1936) observed that early-autumn defoliation of apple trees greatly reduced root growth during the autumn. An excess of soil water and very compact soil interfere with aeration and reduce root growth.

The interaction of roots and shoots is particularly evident when apples and other woody plants are grafted on various kinds of rootstocks. It is well known that many kinds of woody plants can be dwarfed by grafting or budding them on so-called dwarfing rootstocks or increased in vigor by grafting or budding them on other types. Sax (1958) has summarized some information on control of growth in this manner. The vigor of growth, fruitfulness, salt absorption, and other characteristics of the shoot frequently are modified by the root system. According to Swarbrick and Roberts (1927), the kind of top also affects the amount of root growth. Various aspects of stock and scion relationships have been discussed by Rogers and Beakbane (1957).

Height Growth and Diameter Growth. The correlation between height growth and diameter growth was mentioned in Chapter 2 and in the section dealing with auxin and diameter growth. It will suffice to point out here that apparently the beginning of height growth provides the stimulus, probably auxin, needed to start diameter growth, but diameter growth usually continues for some time after height growth ceases. The two processes do not appear to be competitive for food, at least not in trees with a relatively normal photosynthetic surface.

Reproductive and Vegetative Growth

It was mentioned earlier in the book that fruit and seed production often seriously lower food reserves. Growing fruits seem to be able to divert food from vegetative growth and cause it to be translocated to them. Heavy crops of fruit and seed would be expected to reduce growth, and there is some evidence that this sometimes occurs. Huber and von Jazewitsch (1956) state that the minimum width of annual rings in beech occurs in years when a heavy seed crop is produced. However, Huber et al. (1949) reported that heavy crops of acorns were not consistently correlated with narrow annual rings in oak. According to Loomis (1935), corn plants make little root growth after pollination, but if the young ears are removed, root growth continues until frost. Development of bolls also reduces root growth of cotton plants (Eaton, 1931). Root growth of woody plants probably also is reduced by heavy crops of fruit and seed.

In herbaceous annuals, flower and fruit production is accompanied by cessation of growth and death of the plants. Such behavior usually is attributed to exhaustion of food reserves, but there is a possibility that maturing fruits produce some factor inducing senescence. Nothing is known about any effects of hormones from maturing fruits on tree growth, or even if they are produced.

Dormancy

No matter how favorable the environment, woody plants do not grow continuously, but alternate between flushes or periods of active growth and periods of inactivity or dormancy. Many tropical trees and shrubs make several flushes of growth during a year (Klebs, 1915; Quetel, 1939), and this has been studied carefully in tea and cacao. Tea makes four or five flushes of growth (Bond, 1945; Wight and Barua, 1955). Growth of some

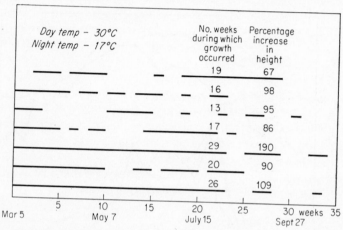

Figure 15.10 Diagram showing number of flushes or growing periods for 2-year-old loblolly pine seedlings growing in a constant environment in the Earhart Laboratory. The trees were grown in a greenhouse 8 hours at 30°C and 16 hours at 17°C and normal photoperiod.

trees is not continuous during the summer in the Temperate Zone but occurs in two or three periods, separated by periods of temporary dormancy. This fact often is obscured because growth data usually represent averages of a number of trees which grow at different times, and curves for averages hide the fact that individual trees may start and stop growth several times during a season, as shown in Figure 15.10. In the Temperate Zones cold winter weather provides a season when growth is impossible because of low temperatures, but growth of most woody plants normally ceases long before temperatures are low enough to stop it.

It appears that two kinds of dormancy exist in woody plants. One type is temporary summer dormancy, which occurs between flushes of growth, lasts a few days to a few weeks, and is broken spontaneously. The other type is permanent dormancy, which lasts for many weeks or months and usually is not broken in plants of the Temperate Zone until they have been exposed to low temperature for 1 or 2 months or given some special treatment. Samish (1954), in his review on dormancy in woody plants, terms cessation of visible growth caused by unfavorable environmental conditions "quiescence" and cessation of growth caused by internal factors "rest."

The two principal problems in connection with dormancy are to explain why growth ceases and what causes it to be resumed. We shall deal with causes of growth cessation first.

Causes of Dormancy. It often is assumed that in the Temperate Zones dormancy is caused by cold weather, but this seldom is true. As shown

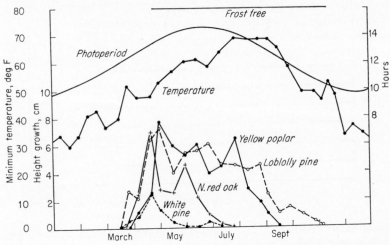

Figure 15.11 Height growth of seedlings of several tree species in the open. The natural photoperiod and the average minimum temperature also are shown. (*From Kramer, 1957b, based on data of Kramer, 1943.*)

in Figures 2.9, 2.10, and 15.11, growth commonly ceases long before the temperature is low enough to check growth. Furthermore, even in a warm greenhouse trees cease growth about as soon as out of doors. Drought or other unfavorable conditions sometimes stop growth temporarily in the middle of the season, but if the water supply is replenished, growth is resumed. Finally, however, no matter how favorable the environment, growth ceases and will not be resumed until the trees have been chilled or subjected to some special treatment. Thus the condition of temporary or summer dormancy progresses into permanent or winter dormancy.

This situation indicates that although either temporary or permanent dormancy can be caused by some environmental conditions, it usually is caused by some internal condition. The tendency toward intermittent growth shown in Figure 15.10 suggests that perhaps growth itself produces the conditions which bring about its cessation. This condition might be the exhaustion of something essential for growth or the accumulation of some kind of inhibitor. Klebs (1915) suggested that cessation of growth in tropical trees might be caused by temporary deficiency of minerals, but such a deficiency could not operate in pot experiments supplied with an abundance of nutrients. Hemberg (1949), Pollock (1953), and Vegis (1956) all believe that accumulation of inhibitors in buds causes dormancy to develop. Nitsch (1957a) found that development of dormancy in dogwood was correlated with a change in relative proportions of growth-promoting and growth-inhibiting substances rather than accumulation of a single inhibitor.

Even if it is established that cessation of growth is caused by changes in concentrations or proportions of growth-controlling substances, this does not explain why they accumulate. It already has been shown that low temperatures are not involved. Decreasing photoperiod might be a factor because, as shown in Chapter 16, the growing period of many woody plants can be prolonged by supplementary illumination. However, as indicated in Figure 15.11, growth commonly begins to slow down or even ceases before the photoperiod is short enough to be limiting; hence it probably is not usually the cause of dormancy in nature. Another possibility is that the hot weather of midsummer, especially the warm nights, may cause the beginning of dormancy. This idea is supported by Pollock (1953) and Vegis (1956), who claim that anaerobic respiration in buds at high temperatures causes development of inhibitors which stop growth. Furthermore, loblolly pine trees grown with various combinations of day and night temperatures made the most late-season growth when grown with cool nights (Kramer, 1957b). Much more research probably will be necessary before the causes of dormancy are understood fully.

Breaking Dormancy. The internal changes responsible for breaking dormancy will not be known until the causes of dormancy are known, but in temperate climates dormancy ordinarily is broken by exposure to low temperatures. After exposure to winter cold, buds usually are in a condition to resume growth as soon as the temperature rises in the spring. The amount of cold required to break dormancy varies greatly among different species and varieties. According to data collected by Samish (1954), the chilling requirement for peaches varies from 200 hours below 45°F for the Saucer peach to 1,150 hours for the Mayflower variety, but according to Hill and Campbell (1949), leaf buds of most peach and pear varieties require 600 to 900 hours and apples require 900 to 1,200 hours. In Georgia accumulation of about 1,000 hours below 45°F by February 15 will break dormancy of most peach varieties (Weinberger, 1950). Concord grapes are said to require as much as 3,500 hours, but

Vinifera grapes and plants native to mild climates have quite low requirements.

The southward extension of many northern tree species into warm climates is limited by lack of enough cold to break dormancy. According to Chandler et al. (1937), growth of many ornamental shrubs and fruit trees is delayed in California by lack of cold weather to break dormancy. The warm winter of 1940–1941 caused severe bud drop of apricots and

Figure 15.12 An Elberta peach tree suffering from prolonged dormancy following a mild winter. Buds on the older wood opened first, then the tip buds on the new shoots. Only a few flower buds opened and set fruit. (*Photograph courtesy of U.S. Department of Agriculture.*)

failure to produce fruit in 1941 (Brooks, 1942), while the mild winter of 1950–1951 in northern California caused blossom bud drop of almond, apricot, peach, plum, and cherry, and flowers of apple and pear died (Brown, 1952). In the southeastern United States peaches occasionally fail to flower properly, or if they flower, fruit set is poor because the trees fail to develop sufficient leaf area to manufacture food for fruit growth (Weinberger, 1950). A typical example of failure of peaches to break dormancy properly after a mild winter is shown in Figure 15.12. Lack of sufficient chilling also sometimes results in delayed resumption of growth by pecan trees (Van Horn, 1941).

Failure of buds to resume growth without chilling prevents the growth of most deciduous fruits in warm climates. According to Hill and Campbell (1949), this difficulty has been observed in Africa, Australia, India, and Palestine, as well as in the Americas. They suggest that selection and breeding for low cold requirements may at least partly solve this problem. According to Humphries (1944), warmer-than-average weather breaks dormancy in cacao, and he suggests that high temperatures may be as essential to resumption of growth by tropical trees as low temperatures are for trees of temperate climates.

In some instances a long photoperiod will at least partly substitute for cold in breaking dormancy (Gustafson, 1938; Kramer, 1936). A wide variety of other treatments have been found more or less successful in breaking dormancy. Doorenbos (1953) listed over 80 chemical compounds which have been found more or less successful in breaking dormancy. Ether formerly was used to break dormancy, and ethylene chlorohydrin vapor often is effective. Application by spraying of mineral oils and dinitro compounds also has been known to break dormancy. Immersion of branches in warm water and even rubbing stems just below the buds sometimes cause resumption of growth.

The wide variety of treatments effective in breaking dormancy makes the problem more puzzling because they do not point clearly toward any particular mechanism. Dormancy usually is localized in the buds, and it often is possible to break dormancy in individual buds or branches without disturbing their neighbors. Apparently much more research must be done on the causes and cures of dormancy. It sometimes would be useful to prolong dormancy in the spring until the chances of late frosts have passed. Peach crops often are destroyed by late frost, and other fruit crops suffer severe injury. Sell et al. (1944) estimated that tung production is reduced 25 per cent by frost injury. Attempts have been made to prolong dormancy by spraying with synthetic auxin, but concentrations which delay bud opening usually cause injury (Marth et al., 1947; Mitchell and Cullinan, 1942; Tukey and Hamner, 1949). Delayed growth of bulbs and potato tubers and blooming of raspberries were obtained with maleic hydrazide (Samish, 1954). Perhaps further research will supply a reliable method of retarding the resumption of growth.

Aging in Relation to Growth

Trees generally are regarded as the world's oldest living organisms, but there are wide variations in length of life of various species. For example, gray birch is senescent when 50 years of age, but some oaks continue to grow vigorously when 10 times that age. A number of redwoods are known to be in excess of 3,000 years old, and several bristlecone pines over 4,000 years of age were found recently in the White Mountains of

California. One specimen proved to be 4,600 years old (Schulman, 1958).

Almost everyone is familiar with the general symptoms of senescence in trees, such as a general decline in vigor characterized by a decrease in rate and amount of height and diameter growth, decrease in root growth, increase in number of dead branches, and a decreased rate of wound healing. With approach of senescence, trees also tend to lose their resistance to attack by pathogens and insects.

It should be remembered that even in the oldest trees there are relatively few living cells. Most of these probably are not more than a year or two old, and only a few may exceed a decade in age. The old bristlecone pines reported by Schulman (1958) have very short stems with small amounts of growing stem tissue and very small crowns. Continuity of life has been maintained in such organisms as a whole for several thousand years, but rapid death of cells occurs continuously in the various tissues during their development. Some tissues, such as cambia, apical meristems, and cork cambia, continue to function throughout the life of a tree, but most other tissues are relatively short lived. Even in meristems there is a continual replacement of cells as division and differentiation proceed. Flowers have only a brief life span. Leaves of most angiosperms live for 1 year, but in a number of species they remain alive and functional for several years. Gymnosperm leaves generally are longer-lived, but with minor exceptions they too are shed after only a few years. In stems the protoplasts of vessels and tracheids are lost very early, so that the bulk of the wood consists of dead cells. Pith cells and longitudinal and ray parenchyma cells seem to be the oldest living cells in tree stems. In birch, for example, the pith may remain alive for 40 years. In *Carnegiea gigantea*, pith cells have been reported to live for 100 years (MacDougal and Long, 1927). It generally is acknowledged that heartwood is composed essentially of dead cells. However, MacDougal and Smith (1927) reported a few living cells in the heartwood of redwood trees that apparently were about a century old. Cork cells die rapidly, and sieve tubes usually function for one season and then die, although in some species sieve tubes live for 2 years and in a few species for several years. Root hairs usually are very short lived. Because of continuous death of cells, an old tree consists of an accumulation of billions of dead cells with only a small percentage of living cells. In general, then, trees are much older than their living cells.

Aging in Relation to Ontogeny. During ontogeny the adult condition of many woody plants is preceded by a juvenile stage. Juvenile and adult stages may differ in one or more characteristics such as leaf shape, phyllotaxy, leaf abscission, ease of rooting of cuttings, thorniness, growth habit, and flowering (Robbins, 1957). For example, young plants of English ivy,

Hedera helix, have creeping or climbing shoots with three-lobed leaves, but in the adult stage English ivy is arborescent and has entire leaves. It does not flower while in the juvenile condition. According to Robbins (1957), juvenile and adult forms occur in beech, oaks, pecans, citrus, apple, and apricots. Schaffalitzky de Muckadell (1954) cites investigators who reported juvenility in *Chamaecyparis, Juniperus, Eucalyptus, Acacia, Hevea,* and several species of fruit trees. He believes that juvenile stages are quite common but that there is much variation in how well defined the stages are, probably because various degrees of topophysis exist within the juvenile stages. The peripheral portions of some older trees show adult characteristics, while inner portions show juvenility. Beech begins shedding leaves at tips of branches, and in winter the inner juvenile parts of trees retain leaves while leaves of the outer, adult twigs are shed. The juvenile, leaf-retaining part of young beech trees can often be circumscribed by a cone (Schaffalitzky de Muckadell, 1954). The juvenile or nonflowering stage of citrus shows unusually vigorous growth, an erect habit, and an abundance of thorns (Furr et al., 1947). While trunks of thorny seedlings continue to produce thorny branches for some time, shoots from the outermost branches lose their capacity for thorniness (Frost, 1943). Thus it appears that the older parts of trees retain their juvenile characteristics while the new growth is changing to the adult condition.

Of first importance to growth of trees are the metabolic changes which take place in growing leaves. It was pointed out in Chapter 3 that the rate of photosynthesis falls off in senescent leaves. In angiosperms leaves invariably have higher rates of photosynthesis immediately following the attainment of full size than do older leaves. Richardson (1957) suggested that during leaf expansion chlorophyll content, moisture content, and capacity of enzyme systems control photosynthesis. During senescence, however, moisture content and enzyme systems probably largely control photosynthesis rather than chlorophyll content. The decrease in chlorophyll content observed in senescent leaves probably is only a symptom of disturbances in basic metabolic processes.

During the first year of growth, ontogenetic changes occur in gymnosperm leaves which are related to a rapidly changing capacity for photosynthesis (Bormann, 1958). For example, very young loblolly pine seedlings have juvenile leaves borne singly, but later in the first year these seedlings develop secondary needles which are borne in fascicles. Thus photosynthesis is first centered in juvenile needles alone. Bormann (1958) has shown that while the seedling still has juvenile needles, maximum rates of photosynthesis are attained at relatively low light intensities. However, when the secondary needles form, the seedling shows increasing photosynthesis with increasing light up to full sunlight. Furthermore, juvenile leaves have considerably higher rates of photosynthesis per unit of surface than secondary needles. Bormann suggested that more light may reach the chlorenchyma of the relatively simple primary leaves whereas light is screened from the photosynthesizing cells of secondary needles by the thick cutin, thick-walled epidermal cells, and a hypodermis of thick-walled sclerenchyma cells as well as by mutual shading. Bormann reviewed the important ecological implications of such changes and stated that early establishment and later failure of loblolly pine seedlings to survive under hardwood overstories may be related to changes in photosynthetic capacity during ontogeny.

Several other changes occur in aging leaves. Respiration rates per unit of leaf surface decrease with increasing age of leaves in gymnosperms (Parker, 1954) and in angiosperms (Kelley, 1930). Parker also observed that the older the leaves of ponderosa pine, the sooner they died when removed from the tree. The early death of old leaves was caused by a rapid water loss. Osmotic pressure and pH have been reported to increase as ponderosa pine leaves age (Gail and Cone, 1929). There also are changes in protein metabolism with age of leaves. Protein content of young leaves increases, while in older leaves hydrolysis predominates to produce soluble nitrogen compounds which are translocated out of the leaves (McKee, 1958). Molisch (1938) believed that accumulation of minerals in aging leaves contributed to their change in physiological activity and helped to bring about senility.

Some controversy exists about the occurrence of aging in clones. Perhaps there is less aging in clones propagated by cuttings than in those propagated by budding and grafting. Lombardy poplar and *Cryptomeria* have been propagated from cuttings for centuries without apparent symptoms of old age, and many varieties of fruit trees have been propagated vegetatively through many generations. On the other hand, there is considerable evidence of aging in relatively young citrus clones. Hodgson and Cameron (1938) compared two clones of the Paper Rind variety of orange. One clone had been propagated vegetatively for many years; the other was a young clone produced by budding from a seedling originating from a nucellar embryo. The young clone showed greater vigor, a more upright growth habit, tendency toward thorniness, and lower seed content of fruits, while the older clone showed earlier and heavier bearing. Frost (1938) also reported that loss of vegetative vigor in citrus clones occurs regularly with increasing age. He observed that the tendency to thorniness decreased gradually in clones resulting from genetic seedlings and that varying amounts of thorniness were transmissible by budding in the same clone. According to Frost, both nucellar and gametic embryos cause conspicuous increases in vigor of vegetative growth; hence aging in citrus clones cannot be attributed to genetic changes.

The reasons for great differences in longevity of different trees are not fully understood. According to Robbins (1957), several physiological changes occur in aging trees and attempts have been made to link these to longevity. They include decrease in absorption and conduction of water, changes in photosynthetic capacity, resistance to decay, protein degeneration, and ash accumulation. Went (1942) stressed the importance of disturbed water relations in promoting senescence of trees. He stated that there is a rapid decrease in water availability to leaves as trees age and that this decrease occurs more rapidly in short-lived trees than in those which attain great age. It appears that as trees grow older and distance from roots to leaves increases, translocation slows down, water deficits in leaves grow more severe, and water supply to some branches falls so low that they die. Possibly an important factor responsible for decreased growth in old trees is the change in the ratio of food produced in photosynthesis to food used in respiration.

It was pointed out earlier that a larger percentage of carbohydrates produced in photosynthesis is used in respiration in older than in younger trees (Chapter 7). This occurs because the ratio of respiring tissue to photosynthetic tissue increases with age. Leaf area remains rather constant in trees over a wide age span, while the total amount of living tissue increases and food production decreases somewhat (Möller et al., 1954). Because of these changes less carbohydrate is available for production of new tissues.

The possibility exists that enzyme systems decrease in activity and hormone supplies become inadequate since the whole level of metabolism apparently slows down with increasing age. Gunckel et al. (1949) reported that the capacity of Ginkgo trees to produce long shoots, which depends on auxin supply, declined with age. This suggests decreased auxin supplies in the older trees. Much more research needs to be done on the physiology of aging in woody plants.

According to Wagener (1954), unusual longevity usually is associated with a favorable environment, absence of aggressive insect enemies, presence of vigorous root systems, and ability to adjust to temporary changes in water supply or loss of part of the crowns. Where longevity is associated with adverse environmental conditions, as in the trees studied by Schulman, the environment also is unfavorable to insects and pathogenic organisms and the trees often are relatively isolated and less subject to attack by various pests.

Genetics and Tree Improvement

Horticulturists have carried on improvement and breeding programs for many years, especially with small fruits. Selection for disease resistance has been made among shade and forest trees. Increased knowledge of European work and observation of the progress made in producing improved varieties of crop plants have stimulated interest in tree improvement programs in the United States.

The general objectives of tree improvement programs vary with the purposes for which the trees are grown. The criteria used in evaluation of trees differ widely, depending on whether the trees are grown for timber, pulp, naval stores, fruit, or as ornamental specimens. The chief methods used in improvement of trees are the selection of superior individuals and hybridization. When selection and hybridization are followed by thorough testing of progeny, desirable characteristics can be combined and retained and undesirable ones eliminated. Selection of superior types as a source of seed and material for vegetative reproduction seems most likely to yield immediate returns with many species, but hybridization has given good results, notably with such rapid-growing species as poplar.

Selection. Selection can be applied both to the geographic or ecological races of which many species are composed and to individual trees in a stand. Most species of trees which cover a wide geographic range consist of varying numbers of ecotypic or geographic races that have become adjusted through centuries of natural selection to the various environmental regimes occurring within the range of the species. Among the species having well-defined ecotypic races which have been studied are poplar (Pauley and Perry, 1954), lodgepole pine (Critchfield, 1957), and oak (Irgens-Moller, 1955). Often when seed from trees growing in one part of the range is planted in another part, the trees grow poorly, have poor form, are subject to disease, or even die prematurely (Schreiner, 1939b).

Selection of superior individuals obviously is the first step in any tree breeding program. This requires careful definition of the characteristics to be used as a basis for selecting parents and progeny. Most selection of forest trees is based on visible characteristics, such as growth rate, height, straightness of bole, crown size, and resistance to disease. Fruit trees usually are selected on the basis of yield and quality of fruit. Resistance to various diseases, cold, and drought are other desirable characteristics. It is relatively easy to carry out selection based on morphological characteristics, but in the long run physiological characteristics are more important. Unfortunately, they also are more difficult to evaluate.

Some progress has been made in selecting strains of trees resistant to the more important diseases (Riker, 1954). For example, Riker and his colleagues have found that resistance to the organism causing white pine blister rust is genetically controlled and transmitted to the offspring of resistant trees. When resistant trees were propagated by open-pollinated seed and exposed to the causal organism, most seedlings showed little resistance, but a number of individuals propagated vegetatively showed a high degree of resistance. Development of disease-resistant strains is likely to progress more rapidly after more is learned concerning the causes of injury and the physiological or biochemical nature of disease resistance. This problem is discussed further in Chapter 16.

Internal characteristics such as specific gravity, cellulose content, and fibril angle are beginning to be used as criteria in selecting trees for tree improvement programs, especially where the chief use is as pulpwood. According to Mitchell (1957), a unit of northern pine wood of high density will produce twice as much pulp as the same volume of wood of low density. Zobel and McElwee (1958a) found a range in specific gravity from 0.40 to 0.68 in mature wood of loblolly pine. The work of Zobel and Rhodes (1956) indicates that by selection and controlled breeding it may be possible to develop strains producing wood of both higher- and lower-than-average specific gravity.

Some important characteristics are expressed quite early in life, others not until the trees are many years of age. Barber et al. (1955) observed distinct differences in crown width of slash pine from different seed trees when the seedlings were only 3 years old. According to Wenger (1955b), the previous year's growth is a good indicator of subsequent growth of loblolly pine seedlings. On the other hand, the specific gravity of wood of northern pines is said to increase with age (Mitchell, 1958), although Zobel and McElwee (1958a) found little relationship between age or rate of growth and specific gravity of wood more than 10 years old in southern pines, specific gravity being controlled chiefly by hereditary factors. In southern pines there is a core of six to eight annual rings of juvenile wood, surrounded by so-called mature wood which has a significantly higher specific gravity. According to Zobel and Rhodes (1956), it is possible to predict whether or not a mature tree will produce wood of high specific gravity from measurements of the specific gravity of the juvenile wood. Zobel and McElwee (1958b) also found it possible to predict cellulose yield of mature wood from juvenile wood.

Mergen et al. (1955) concluded that gum yield and viscosity of gum of slash pine are genetically controlled. Bourdeau and Schopmeyer (1958) found that the ratio of gum pressure to gum viscosity is significantly related to gum yield. This ratio can be measured on young trees; hence it might be useful in selecting high-yielding trees in the seedling stage.

It would be very useful if some simple tests could be developed which would predict the future rate of growth of small seedlings. For example, if it were possible to measure a physiological process such as photosynthesis or the ratio of photosynthesis to respiration and use this to predict growth rate, selection of desirable individuals out of a large population of progeny would be greatly speeded up. Huber and Polster (1955) found a correlation between rate of growth of poplar hybrids and rate of photosynthesis, but there are insufficient data to justify generalization on this point. Nor do we know whether transpiration or drought resistance in seedlings is a reliable indication of what will be found in the adult tree. More work is needed on the relations between the physiological and morphological characteristics of seedlings and mature trees as an aid to tree improvement work.

Hybridization. Hybridization and selection of superior offspring have been used to increase production of wood, resin, cork, tannin, and maple sugar and resistance to disease, cold, and insects. It is primarily a means of increasing variation by producing new combinations of genes. A number of useful hybrids have been produced. The offspring of a cross between Jeffrey and Coulter pine is more desirable than either parent because it has the weevil resistance of Coulter pine, which is lacking in Jeffrey pine, and grows faster and branches less than Coulter pine (Duffield, 1954). The hybrid offspring of the poorly formed jack pine of the Lake States and the lodgepole pine of the Sierra Nevada region grows faster than either parent and is better formed than jack pine (Stockwell and Righter, 1947). Another excellent hybrid is that between selected parents of European and Japanese larch, because it shows the rapid growth and good stem form of the former and the resistance to canker characteristic of the latter. Duffield and Snyder (1958) summarized the behavior of a number of hybrids of American tree species.

Certain poplar hybrids are outstanding examples of what can be done by hybridization and selection. Schreiner (1950) stated that the best 50 per cent of the hybrids he studied could produce 40 cords of pulpwood per acre in 15 years, but the most rapid growing naturally occurring forms would require at least 35 years to produce this amount of wood.

The increased rate of growth of hybrid pines and poplars can be ascribed to hybrid vigor or "heterosis." This term refers to the fact that the F_1 offspring of crosses between varieties and species sometimes grow more vigorously than either parent type. Sprague (1953) discussed various theories of heterosis and concluded that no satisfactory genetic explanation is available. It sometimes has been claimed that the more rapid growth of the offspring occurs because the seeds contain a larger embryo and sometimes a larger supply of food. Buchholz (1945) compared embryos of hybrid pines with those of their parents and found that although hybrid embryos grew more rapidly at first, their final size was no greater than that of embryos of the parental type. He concluded, therefore, that hybrid vigor "is definitely a physiological vigor of growth." Sprague (1953, p. 120) suggests that hybrid vigor may result from more efficient utilization of nutrients, increased rate of cell division, greater ability to synthesize growth substances, and possibly from other causes not yet recognized.

Tree breeding procedures are somewhat simpler than those for crop plants because the same degree of uniformity is not required in tree crops as in field crops. As many as 80 per cent of the individuals will be eliminated during development of a forest stand; hence slow-growing trees are eliminated automatically. If a mixed population is planted, only the superior individuals will survive natural selection and thinning operations (Righter, 1946).

GENERAL REFERENCES

Audus, L. J., 1953, Plant growth substances, Interscience Publishers, Inc., New York.

Leopold, A. C., 1955, Auxins and plant growth, University of California Press, Berkeley, Calif.

Lindquist, B., 1948, Genetics in Swedish forestry practice, Chronica Botanica Co., Waltham, Mass.

Luckwill, L. C., 1957, Hormonal aspects of fruit development in higher plants, Soc. Exptl. Biol. Symp., no. 11.

Molisch, H., 1938, The longevity of plants, transl. by E. H. Fulling, The Translator, New York.

Robbins, W. J., 1957, Physiological aspects of aging in plants, Am. Jour. Botany, 44:289–294.

Samish, R. M., 1954, Dormancy in woody plants, Ann. Rev. Plant Physiology, 5:183–204.

Tukey, H. B. (ed.), 1954, Plant regulators in agriculture, John Wiley & Sons, Inc., New York.

Wain, R. L., and F. Wightman, 1956, The chemistry and mode of action of plant growth substances, Academic Press, Inc., New York.

CHAPTER 16 *Environmental Factors*
Affecting Growth

In the preceding chapter some of the internal factors affecting growth were discussed. In this chapter we shall discuss some of the important environmental factors and cultural practices and indicate through what internal processes and conditions they operate in affecting growth.

The general environmental requirements for successful growth of plants are sufficient light, water, oxygen, and mineral nutrients and suitable temperatures. In terms of physiological processes, the environmental requirements are conditions favorable for the manufacture of sufficient food for growth and maintenance of a satisfactory internal water balance. These apparently simple requirements actually involve a large number of environmental factors and physiological processes. The plant environment consists of numerous factors of varying importance which interact on one another as well as on plants. Some of these interrelationships are shown in Figure 16.1, and some environmental factors are listed in Table 16.1.

Limiting Factors

Many of the most important problems facing ecologists, foresters, and horticulturists require evaluation of the relative importance of various factors of the environment and identification of the physiological processes through which they affect growth. It sometimes is questioned if a single factor can be identified as controlling growth in a particular situation. It certainly is not as simple as Liebig (1843) supposed when he formulated the law of the minimum, later modified by Blackman (1905) and by Mitscherlich (1909). The principle of limiting factors, as proposed by Blackman, states that if a process is affected by a number of separate factors, its rate is limited by that factor which is present in least amount relative to its minimum requirement. Application of the principle of limiting factors to physiological processes is discussed by Meyer and Anderson (1952, pp. 335–338, 612–613). The importance of interaction of factors sometimes is recognized by speaking of the most significant factor, indicating that although several factors may be affecting growth, one is more important than the others at a given time.

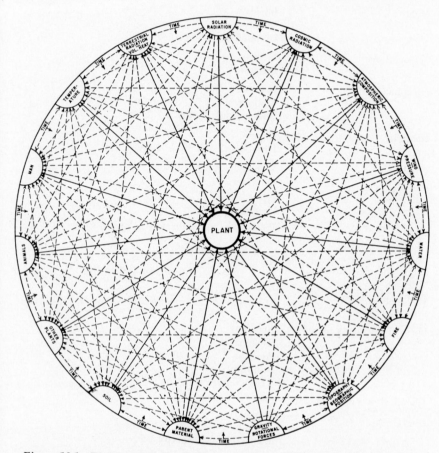

Figure 16.1 Diagrammatic representation of the interrelationships among environmental factors and plants. Relations among factors are shown by dashed lines; relations between factors and plants are shown by solid lines. (*From Billings, 1952.*)

Cain (1944) argued that as physiological processes are multiconditioned, study of the effects of variations in a single factor cannot indicate accurately the role of that factor in nature. Furthermore, similar growth patterns can be produced by different combinations of several factors; hence Cain believes that it is incorrect to regard a single factor as limiting. Mason and Stout (1954) also point out that the range of tolerance

Table 16.1. Important factors of the environment

Factors	Important aspects
Climatic factors	
Light	Intensity Quality Duration or photoperiod
Temperature	Degree Duration
Precipitation	Amount Frequency Seasonal distribution
Humidity	Degree Duration
Wind	Velocity Duration
Gases	Oxygen Carbon dioxide Pollutants (sulfur dioxide, halogens, smog, etc.)
Edaphic factors	
Origin and classification of soil	
Topography, slope, and exposure of soil	
Physical properties of soil	Structure Texture Aeration Moisture Temperature
Chemical properties of soil	pH Minerals Organic compounds Base exchange capacity, etc.
Biotic properties of soil	Organic matter Plants Animals
Biotic factors	
Man	Clearing Drainage Fire Cultivation and other cultural treatments (fertilization, pruning, thinning, weeding, girdling, irrigation, vegetative reproduction, etc.)

Table 16.1. Important factors of the environment (*Continued*)

Factors	Important aspects
Insects	Defoliation Stem and root feeding Disease transmission Pollination, etc.
Plants	Competition (light, water, minerals, space) Parasitism Symbiosis, etc.
Animals	Grazing animals, rodents, birds, etc.

of an environmental factor can vary at different stages of development. In spite of these difficulties, it seems that one or more factors often can be regarded as more important than others in the over-all success or failure of plants in a particular environment. Perhaps the view of Billings (1952) that limiting factors operate within an environmental complex describes the situation most accurately.

The study of diameter growth of beech by Fritts (1958) represents an interesting attempt to evaluate the relative importance of various environmental factors on tree growth. Radial growth was measured with a dendrograph (Fritts and Fritts, 1955), and temperature, rainfall, soil moisture, percentage of sunshine, evaporation, relative humidity, and average wind velocity were recorded for two growing seasons. A multiple-regression analysis of tree growth and the environmental factors was made for 112 days during each growing season. About 50 per cent of the variation in growth was caused by variations in maximum temperature and soil moisture, the former being more important in the spring, the latter more important in summer when soil moisture content tended to be lower. Relative humidity was third in importance, percentage of sun on the preceding day fourth, and precipitation fifth. Wind velocity was positively correlated with growth, but this probably was an indirect effect rather than a causal relationship. There also was an underlying seasonal trend in the growth potential which reached its maximum early in June and then declined until growth stopped in August.

In the following pages considerable attention will be given to the effects of variations in various factors on the physiological processes affecting growth. Sometimes it is difficult to distinguish between direct and indirect effects. For example, low temperature can cause direct killing of plant tissue but it also can interfere with water absorption, resulting in injury or death from dehydration. Both an excess and a lack of water can reduce growth directly, and also indirectly by interfering with mineral absorption, and an excess of minerals in the soil can reduce growth as much as a deficiency. Furthermore, as shown in the study by Fritts, the relative importance of various factors varies during the growing season. For example, temperature is relatively more important in the spring than during the summer and soil moisture becomes more important during the summer.

Light

The effects of light on plant growth depend on its intensity, its quality or wavelength, and its duration and periodicity. Variation in any of these characteristics can modify both the quantity and quality of growth. For example, seedlings grown in light of low intensity differ not only in height and dry weight from those grown in full sun but also in root/shoot ratio and leaf and stem structure. Duration or photoperiod affects both vegetative growth and flowering, and wavelength affects other processes in addition to photosynthesis.

Light Quality or Wavelength. Consideration often is given to the role of visible light alone in plant growth, but it should be remembered that visible radiation forms only part of the spectrum of radiant energy, which extends from radio waves to cosmic radiation. In nature, plants are exposed to a very wide range of invisible radiation. This includes infrared, which is longer in wavelength than visible light, and ultraviolet and cosmic radiations, which are of shorter wavelengths than visible light. Plants also often are exposed experimentally to irradiation by X rays and radioactive materials. All these invisible wavelengths are capable of affecting growth if the exposure is of sufficient duration and intensity.

Variations in the wavelength or quality of light in nature probably are too small to be of any physiological importance, but light quality is of great importance in connection with the growth of plants under artificial illumination. Excessive stem elongation tends to occur under incandescent lamps, but elongation is below normal under cool white or daylight-type fluorescent lights. A few incandescent lights added to banks of fluorescent tubes provide the far-red wavelengths missing from fluorescent lights, and this combination produces more satisfactory growth. Fluorescent lights are deficient in output of light of longer wavelengths which is supplied by incandescent lights.

Plants seem to be particularly susceptible to the relative amounts of red light (wavelength about 6,550 angstrom units) and far-red light (wavelength about 7,350 angstrom units) to which they are subjected. Red light promotes seed and spore germination, coloration of tomato cuticle, and elongation of dark-grown seedlings, while exposure to far-red reverses the effect of previous exposure to red light. Far-red light, in contrast, promotes the elongation of light-grown seedlings. Incandescent lights are superior to fluorescent lights as supplementary illumination to produce long photoperiods because of the far-red light emitted by them. This has been demonstrated for loblolly and ponderosa pine, red maple, catalpa, and hydrangea and for various herbaceous plants (Downs and Piringer, 1958; Downs et al., 1958). Some data are given in Table 16.2.

The greatest increase in dry weight usually occurs in the full spectrum of sunlight. Expansion of leaf blades is prevented by darkness, retarded

Table 16.2. Effects of quality of light used as supplemental illumination on growth of tree seedlings. (*From Downs et al., 1958.*)

Photoperiod, hr	Supplemental light	Loblolly pine			Ponderosa pine	
		Stem length, mm	Needle length, mm	No. of fascicles	Stem length, mm	Needle length, mm
8	None	37	36	1	22	0
16	Incandescent	149	84	25	55	76
16	Fluorescent	80	57	12	26	45

in green light, intermediate in blue, and greatest in white light. The photochemical reactions by which light produces these and other morphogenic effects are not yet fully understood. Wassink and Stolwijk (1956) have reviewed the literature dealing with effects of light quality on plant growth, but it is obvious that much more remains to be learned about this interesting problem.

Light Intensity. The effects of light intensity on plant growth have been observed since very early times. According to Baker (1949), Pliny, who died A.D. 79, observed that grass grew under sycamore trees but that no vegetation grew under pines. As shown in Chapter 3, light intensity affects tree growth through its direct effects on photosynthesis, stomatal opening, and chlorophyll synthesis. Its effects on cell enlargement and differentiation affect height growth, leaf size, and the structure of leaves and stems.

Light intensity varies daily and seasonally and is modified by latitude (Kimball, 1935). Insolation received per unit area is greater at high elevations than at low ones and greater on south-facing slopes than on north-facing slopes. Clouds, fog, dust, and smoke screen out light to varying degrees, and in industrial areas as much as 90 per cent of light may be intercepted by smoke (Daubenmire, 1959). In plant communities the effect of overtopping vegetation in screening light from subordinate vegetation is of paramount ecological significance. Shirley (1929a and b) reported that the range of light intensities under forest canopies often varies from 0.1 to 20 per cent of full daylight. Buell and Gordon (1945) found light penetration of less than 5 per cent through a conifer canopy in Minnesota, and Oosting and Kramer (1946) observed that the midday light intensity in the interior of a shortleaf pine forest in North Carolina averaged only 5.9 per cent of full sunlight.

There is an extensive literature on the effect of light intensity on tree growth and on variations in the response of different species to reduced light intensities. Only a few examples will be cited. Bates and Roeser (1928) reported that redwood had a very low light requirement and that Engelmann spruce and Douglas-fir required approximately twice as much light for appreciable growth. Shirley (1929a) showed that a number of species of plants could survive for several months at low light intensities but none were able to make appreciable increase in dry weight. Increase in dry matter produced was almost directly proportional to the light intensity received. Gast (1930) reported that leader growth of white pine appeared to be directly proportional to radiation up to full light intensity. Shirley (1932) stated that both establishment and growth of young pines in a virgin Norway pine stand are definitely correlated with light intensity. Shirley (1945) concluded that in the Lake States at least 20 per cent of full sun was necessary for satisfactory establishment and growth of seedlings of red pine, white pine, jack pine, and white spruce. White pine and jack pine attained maximum dry weight in 43 and 46 per cent of full sun, respectively; red pine and white spruce in 98 per cent.

High light intensities bring about important morphological changes in trees. Root development and root/shoot ratios are increased. Leaves that are grown in full sun are thicker than those grown in the shade. High light intensity favors development of long palisade cells, which often form two to three layers, whereas shading favors production of more spongy parenchyma tissue. Sun leaves also have more numerous stomates, thicker cell walls and cuticle, fewer and larger chloroplasts, and a higher ratio of internal to external leaf surface than leaves grown in the shade.

Effects of light intensity on height growth, dry weight, and root/shoot ratios of white pine seedlings are shown in Figure 16.2. The decreased height and increased dry weight in full sun are typical. Data for loblolly pine and overcup oak seedlings grown in sun and shade are given in Table 16.6.

The Concept of Tolerance. The concept of tolerance often is considered in connection with the effects of light intensity because tolerance frequently has been defined as the capacity of a species to endure shade. By this definition trees with marked capacity to endure shade are classed as tolerant while those lacking such capacity are considered intolerant (Baker, 1950). Thus trees often are assigned tolerance ratings in several classes representing various degrees of ability to endure shade (Table 16.3). The capacity to endure shade varies with age of trees and environmental conditions. According to Baker (1950), trees tend to show the

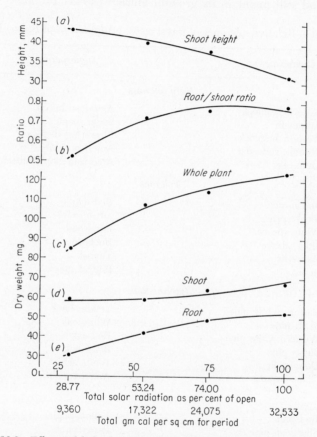

Figure 16.2 Effects of light intensity on height, dry weights of roots and shoots, and root/shoot ratios of white pine seedlings grown in a nursery for 100 days. (*From Mitchell*, 1936.)

greatest tolerance in their youth and those on good sites and in the southern parts of their range are more tolerant to shade than those on poor sites or in the northern part of their range.

As pointed out in Chapter 3, there are some differences of opinion among foresters concerning the proper definition of tolerance. Toumey and Korstian (1947) believed that tolerance should not be defined as the capacity of a tree to endure shade as long as this capacity is measured by survival of various species under different canopy densities. They pointed out that survival is dependent on a complex of factors, of which light intensity is but one factor, and proposed that tolerance be defined as the ability of a tree to develop and grow in the shade of, and in competition with, other species, or as the ability of a tree to withstand competition and still maintain its growth. Shirley (1943) proposed that use

Table 16.3. Relative tolerance of forest trees. (*Adapted from Baker,* 1950.)

Gymnosperms	Angiosperms
Very tolerant	
Eastern hemlock	American beech
Balsam fir	Sugar maple
Western hemlock	Flowering dogwood
Western redcedar	American holly
Alpine fir	American hophornbeam
Tolerant	
Red spruce	Red maple
Black spruce	Silver maple
White spruce	Basswood
Sitka spruce	Buckeye
White fir	Tanoak
Redwood	Bigleaf maple
Intermediate	
Eastern white pine	Yellow birch
Slash pine	White oak
Western white pine	Red oak
Sugar pine	Black oak
Douglas-fir	White ash
Giant sequoia	American elm
Intolerant	
Red pine	Yellow-poplar
Shortleaf pine	Paper birch
Loblolly pine	Sweetgum
Ponderosa pine	Black cherry
Lodgepole pine	Hickories
Noble fir	Black walnut
Very intolerant	
Longleaf pine	Quaking aspen
Jack pine	Gray birch
Tamarack	Willows
Digger pine	Cottonwood
Western larch	Black locust
Whitebark pine	

of tolerance as an unqualified term be discontinued and that "shade tolerance" be used to express capacity of species to survive under low light intensities. He argued that the new term is unrelated to ability to withstand deficiencies in moisture or minerals and to efficiency of photosynthesis at low light intensities. Shirley's concept implied an ability to survive at a low level of metabolic activity, but not necessarily an ability to outgrow associated plants in light of low intensity. He objected to "an omnibus concept of tolerance as ability to withstand all deficiencies which result from competition because the implied parallelism in tolerance of various deficiencies does not exist." Decker (1952) objected to emphasis on tolerance as a description and an explanation of tree behavior and also as the cause of that behavior. He preferred to define tolerance simply as "the degree of being tolerant" and visualized tolerance as representing "a whole pattern of behavior with the separate segments not necessarily with common causes and mechanisms." Decker advocated that tolerance be considered a descriptive and technical term only and believed it should not be concerned with an explanation of forest succession. These varying points of view have been emphatically expressed and probably will continue to be a subject for vigorous debate.

Photoperiod

In temperate regions large seasonal differences occur in the length of the daylight period. For example, Boston, Massachusetts, has about 9 hours of daylight on the shortest day of the year and about 15 hours on the longest day. At Key West, Florida, the shortest days are about 10.5 hours long while the longest days of the year last about 14 hours. Vancouver, British Columbia, has about 8 hours of light on its shortest day and 16 hours on its longest day. It has been recognized ever since the classic research of Garner and Allard (1920) that changes in length of exposure to light or photoperiod influence both vegetative and reproductive phases of plant growth. Among the processes known to be influenced by length of day are shoot growth, diameter growth, breaking of dormancy, leaf abscission, frost resistance, seed germination, and flowering. Responses to photoperiod have been demonstrated experimentally for many species under controlled conditions, but it must be remembered that under natural conditions photoperiod does not always control these processes. For example, species with very long growing seasons may be affected by the shortening days of autumn, but growth of species with short growing seasons usually is not controlled by photoperiod under natural conditions because their growth stops long before the days are short enough to influence growth (Wareing, 1956). Effects of photoperiod on reproduction are discussed in Chapter 13, and the effects on

seed germination are discussed in Chapter 14. Some of the more important effects of photoperiod on various types of vegetative growth will be
discussed in the following sections.

Shoot Growth. Both the length of time during which shoot growth
occurs and the amount of shoot elongation are influenced by photoperiod.
As may be seen in Figure 16.3, long days usually increase the rate and
duration of shoot growth while short days decrease growth rate and promote bud formation. Klebs (1914) reported that beech, oak, ash, and
hornbeam grew all winter when placed under continuous light, but he
failed to develop clearly the idea that length of light period was involved.

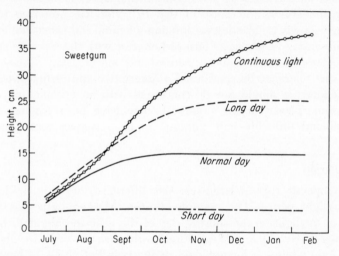

Figure 16.3 Effects of varying photoperiods on shoot growth of potted seedlings
of sweetgum grown in a greenhouse. (*From Kramer, 1936.*)

Garner and Allard (1923) worked with several species of woody plants
and concluded that length of day might be an important factor in determining the time of beginning and ending of dormancy. Moshkov (1932)
and Bogdanov (1935) observed that long days prolonged the growing
season of several woody species. Kramer (1936) observed that seedlings
of beech, black locust, yellow-poplar, redgum, post oak, white oak, and
loblolly pine made more growth and grew later in the autumn when daylight was supplemented by electric light to give a photoperiod of 14.5
hours. Several of these species also were grown with a short (8.5-hour)
day, and most of them made less growth and became dormant sooner
than with a normal day. Apparently some species will continue to grow
in a greenhouse throughout a winter if the length of day exceeds some
critical value characteristic for the species. For example, Kramer (1936)
found that with a 16-hour day or continuous light sweetgum grew nearly

all winter and yellow-poplar grew all winter (Figure 16.3). Some species do not respond to photoperiod in this way, but form buds after a certain definite growth period even when they are illuminated continuously (Wareing, 1956). Downs and Borthwick (1956) emphasized differences among species in response to long days. They found that catalpa, elm, birch, red maple, and dogwood could be kept growing continuously near Washington, D.C., by a day length of 16 hours, but paulownia, sweetgum, and horsechestnut could not. Growth of pine seedlings was intermittent on 16-hour days, but on 14-hour days they grew continuously for nearly a year. Downs and Borthwick (1956) found that most of their test trees stopped growing after about 28 days of exposure to short (8-hour) days. However, yellow-poplar responded more rapidly and stopped growing after about ten 8-hour days. At the other extreme American elm did not stop growing until after 140 days of exposure to short photoperiods.

Nitsch (1957b) published a table listing the shoot growth reaction to photoperiod for all the woody species for which information was available. Following Chouard (1946), he proposed grouping these species into four general classes, as follows:

	Class	Examples
I. Long days prevent onset of dormancy		
1. Short days cause dormancy		
a. Long days cause continuous growth	A	*Weigela*
		Acer rubrum
		Populus
b. Long days cause periodic growth	B	*Quercus*
		Rhododendron
2. Short days do not cause dormancy	C	*Juniperus*
		Thuja
II. Long days do not prevent dormancy	D	*Syringa*
		Buxus

There probably are all degrees of intergradation from Class A to Class D.

Diameter Growth. Exposure to short days brings about a cessation of cambial activity in some species of trees, while exposure to long days prolongs it (Wareing, 1956). Wareing (1951a) demonstrated that cambial activity in Scotch pine seedlings was maintained longer under 15-hour photoperiods than under 10-hour photoperiods and that it could be prolonged in the autumn by supplementary illumination to provide a 15-hour day. He concluded that natural changes in day length in the autumn affect the duration of cambial activity of this species. Wareing and Roberts (1956) found that in black locust cambial activity ceased under short days whereas it could be maintained for many weeks under long-day conditions. They believed that the effects could not be due primarily to effects on photosynthesis because cambial activity could be maintained with supplementary illumination of very low intensity. Wareing and Roberts suggested that a cambial stimulator, presumably auxin, developed in the mature leaves under long-day conditions. This view was reinforced by the observation that cambial activity was maintained when the stem was in complete darkness if the upper leaves were exposed to long days. Mollart (1954) also demonstrated photoperiodic effects on cambial growth in black locust by exposing seedlings to short days until shoot growth stopped. He then transferred half the seedlings to a long-day environment and found several weeks later that the cambium was active in this group but was inactive in the group maintained under short-day conditions. It should be remembered that these effects were observed in species whose diameter growth continues for some time after shoot growth stops. However, in many species, diameter growth stops early in the summer and shortening day length probably occurs too late to affect their diameter growth.

Breaking of Dormancy. Dormancy of the buds of many species can be broken by long exposure to light. Trees vary greatly in this response, depending on whether their buds are in a state of temporary or permanent dormancy, whether they have been previously exposed to low temperature, or whether lateral or terminal buds are involved. Temporary or summer dormancy usually is broken much more easily by photoperiod than winter or permanent dormancy. Dormancy of lateral buds usually is broken more easily than dormancy of terminal buds. Wareing (1951a) found that summer dormancy of Scotch pine was broken by continuous light but after buds became fully dormant in autumn their dormancy could be broken only with great difficulty and growth of new shoots was very restricted. Winter dormancy of many species can be broken readily by exposure to long days. When dormant seedlings of beech, yellow-poplar, sweetgum, and red oak were brought indoors early in January in North Carolina and subjected to long and short days, those receiving additional light resumed growth before those with a short day (Figure 16.4). Certain sweetgum trees kept in the greenhouse all winter under short days began to grow as soon as those kept under normal days, but only the lateral buds opened, growth was very slow, and the leaves were small and pale in color. These trees never caught up in height with those receiving normal or long photoperiods (Kramer, 1936). The time required for breaking winter dormancy by photoperiod varies greatly for different species. Dormancy of sweetgum was broken in 30 days of long photoperiod, but in other species breaking of dormancy occurred much more slowly (Kramer, 1936). Olmsted (1951) found that 54 per cent of unchilled sugar maple buds grew after 4 months of long-day treatment whereas only 35 per cent grew in those subjected to short-day treatment. Several months of long-day treatment were also necessary to break winter dormancy in *Populus robusta* (Veen, 1951). In some species winter-dormant buds do not respond to photoperiod, except after exposure to low temperatures. Wareing (1954) induced dormancy in seedlings by short days and then transferred them to long days. Buds of European larch, beech, and birch grew, but those of Norway maple and black locust remained dormant. However, after

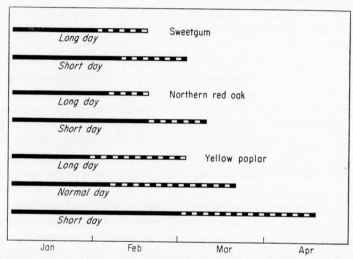

Figure 16.4 Effect of photoperiod on length of time required to break dormancy in tree seedlings brought indoors after exposure to low temperatures. Solid lines indicate completely dormant condition; barred lines, interval from opening of first bud until buds were open on all trees. (*From Kramer, 1936.*)

exposure to chilling, these two species readily broke dormancy under a number of day-length conditions. In some species such as catalpa which require chilling to break dormancy, the cold requirement develops gradually. Before the cold requirement builds up, long photoperiods alone may induce resumption of growth. In other species, such as dogwood (Olmsted, 1951) and red pine (Gustafson, 1938), continuous light may substitute for chilling in breaking dormancy. According to Olmsted (1951), the terminal bud in birch apparently requires chilling while dormancy of axillary buds can be broken by long photoperiods alone.

Leaf Abscission. In some species of deciduous trees leaf abscission is delayed when normal day length is supplemented by added light. When exposed to shorter-than-normal days these species lose their leaves early.

Garner and Allard (1923) observed that when daylight was supplemented with electric light until midnight, smooth sumac retained its leaves all winter while leaf fall of winged sumac was retarded only a few weeks. According to Kramer (1936), yellow-poplar grown with a long photoperiod will retain its leaves all winter in a greenhouse. In New York City, some trees near street lamps retained leaves at least a month longer than normal. A very weak light as much as 45 feet from the tip of a branch caused leaf retention (Matzke, 1936). Olmsted (1951) concluded that leaf abscission of sugar maple under natural conditions is caused by the shortening days of autumn. Age of leaves had a limited relation to abscission since the youngest leaves were retained a few days longer than older leaves. Temperature also has a marked effect on time of leaf fall and modifies the effects of the lengthened photoperiod (Wareing, 1956).

Frost Resistance. Woody plants which are induced to grow late in the season by long photoperiod often do not harden adequately and are more susceptible to winter killing than those grown under normal days. Kramer (1937c) described localized winter-frost injury to an abelia hedge in the vicinity of street lamps where the hedge failed to go into winter dormancy because of photoperiodic stimulation. Plants in the hedge that were midway between the lamps were uninjured. Winter-frost injury also has been described in shoots of trees near street lamps (Matzke, 1936). Bogdanov (1935) and Moshkov (1932) observed that certain southern species transferred to the long days of northern Russia continued to grow in the autumn until killed by frost. If the photoperiod was artificially shortened, they stopped growing before freezing weather occurred and survived the winter without injury. Species with long growing seasons whose growth is not readily stopped by shortening days of autumn may be subject to frost injury. Downs and Borthwick (1956) found under experimental conditions that American elm in the vicinity of Washington, D.C., stopped growing only after 140 days of exposure to short days. In the Washington area branch tips of elm often are killed by frost, probably because of its long growing season, which apparently is related to its lack of sensitivity to the shortening days of autumn.

Photoperiodic Ecotypes. There is considerable evidence that there are genetically controlled ecotypic variations within species which are related to photoperiod (Pauley and Perry, 1954; Vaartaja, 1954; Irgens-Moller, 1957; Critchfield, 1957). According to Sylven, as cited by Wareing (1956), when races of *Populus tremula* from northern Sweden were moved southward they made less growth than races that were native to this southern station. Similarly, southern races moved northward showed delayed dormancy and frost damage. When Pauley and Perry (1954) obtained clones of *Populus* from a wide range of latitudes and grew them at Weston, Massachusetts, they found that height growth of species from higher latitudes ceased much earlier than growth of species from lower latitudes. They concluded that the adaptation of *Populus* ecotypes to various habitats with frost-free seasons of varying length is brought about by a genetic mechanism which controls the length of their growing season. When Douglas-fir seedlings collected from a wide range of altitudes were grown at Corvallis, Oregon, opening of buds of those from high altitudes appeared to be controlled by photoperiod but no such effect was observed in seedlings from low altitudes (Irgens-Moller, 1957). Seedlings of lodgepole pine collected from various altitudes and latitudes were grown in Yosemite National Park by Critchfield (1957). Those from high latitudes or high elevations were the first to cease growth and form terminal buds. Such data emphasize that the natural photoperiodic regime has considerable influence on the amount and the time of cessation of growth.

Pauley and Perry (1954) emphasized that ecotypic variations have great practical significance and should not be overlooked when considering sources of seeds for planting in a particular habitat. Use of seed from northern long-day races should be avoided for planting in southern latitudes with short summer days because the trees developing from such seed will stop growing early and will be small. However, such seeds might be selected for sites with short growing seasons at high elevations in southern latitudes. Pauley and Perry also emphasized that ecotypes with long growing seasons in a particular latitude should be avoided as seed sources for habitats with short seasons at the same latitude, because the trees which develop from these seeds may be subject to frost damage. Such seeds should not be moved northward into a long-day environment because of possible frost damage.

Mechanism of Photoperiodism. Wareing (1949) noted that certain growth processes such as cambial activity and internode elongation were sensitive to both photoperiod and auxin supply and suggested that photoperiodic reactions may be caused by the effect of light on auxin availability and that the light intensities involved may be very low. Long days presumably favor high auxin levels, and short days favor lower availability of auxin. Wareing (1950) further observed that light appears to promote growth of buds under long-day conditions and to check growth through the action of an inhibitor which is translocated from the leaves under short days. He advanced a hypothesis that two mutually antagonistic systems were involved in Scotch pine during the dark period:

1. A system which promotes growth of shoots. This depends on a substance, presumably auxin, which is formed during the preceding light phase and is effective during the first hours of darkness.

2. An inhibitor system which becomes effective after 4 hours of darkness and results in the earlier cessation of growth in proportion to the length of the dark system.

There are several pieces of evidence which, when put together, support the view that such mutually antagonistic systems may be involved under alternating periods of light and dark. Avery et al. (1937) concluded that light was necessary for auxin production of green plants, and Leopold (1949) extracted more auxin from leaves under long-day than under short-day conditions. Growth-inhibiting substances occur in terminal buds, as demonstrated by Hemberg (1949). Downs and Borthwick

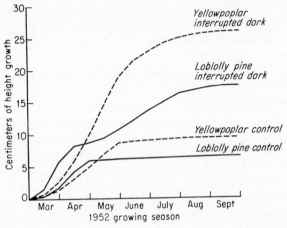

Figure 16.5 Effect of interrupted dark period on growth of loblolly pine and yellow-poplar seedlings. The seedlings were grown with a 9.5-hour photoperiod, and the dark period was interrupted in the middle by a 30-minute light period. The controls were subjected to the same photoperiod regime, but the dark period was not interrupted. (*From Zahner, 1955a.*)

(1956) proposed that an inhibiting condition originated in the leaves and its effects were transmitted to the buds of main and lateral axes. Wareing (1950) found that Scotch pine made better growth when subjected to interrupted dark periods than when grown with continuous dark periods. Zahner (1955a) found this to be true of yellow-poplar and loblolly pine seedlings. He subjected seedlings to 9.5 hours of light alternating with 14.5 hours of darkness. Another group was subjected to the same conditions except that the dark period was interrupted in the middle by a half-hour period of artificial light. As may be seen in Figure 16.5, the rate of height growth of those trees subjected to the interrupted dark-period treatment was greater than the rate of growth of trees subjected to an uninterrupted dark period. Thus a stable inhibitor could have accumulated during the long, uninterrupted dark period, causing growth to cease early. However, interruption of the dark period prevented the accumulation of a stable inhibitor and the checking of growth, as proposed earlier by Wareing.

Temperature

Fluctuations in soil and air temperature influence growth and distribution of trees by altering rates of various important physiological processes such as photosynthesis, respiration, cell division and elongation, enzymatic activity, chlorophyll synthesis, and transpiration. Growth usually increases with an increase in temperature until a critically high temperature for a species is reached, and then declines rapidly. As pointed out earlier, the decrease in growth may result from excessive respiration which reduces carbohydrates, from decreased rates of photosynthesis, from excessive transpiration which causes wilting, or from a combination of these.

There is considerable difference in the range of temperatures in which certain species make their best growth. According to DeVilliers (1943), mean summer temperatures of 62 to 68°F are said to be optimum for plums in South Africa, while apricots do best at 69 to 75°F. Peaches require mean temperatures above 75°F for best development. Different species also vary greatly in the temperature extremes which they can survive. Some subarctic conifers can survive temperatures of −80°F, while, at the other extreme, some desert shrubs survive air temperatures up to 140°F (Oosting, 1956). Species are arranged in altitudinal and latitudinal zones partly because of suitable temperature ranges within these zones. Because south-facing slopes receive more heat than north-facing slopes, some species are found at higher elevations on south slopes than on north slopes. Northern latitudinal limits of tree growth are controlled chiefly by temperature. Daubenmire (1943) stated that the upper altitudinal limits of trees on mountains are determined chiefly by low temperatures. However, Griggs (1946) places more emphasis on wind in the establishment of timber line on mountains.

Several attempts have been made to correlate vegetational distribution with some measure of temperature alone. For example, Merriam (1898) attempted to correlate life zones in the United States with temperature summations during the growing season, and Mayr (1909) outlined vegetation zones of the Northern Hemisphere on the basis of mean temperatures of four summer months (May, June, July, and August). Daubenmire (1938) criticized methods of correlating life zones with temperature summations as theoretically unsound since they assumed each degree of temperature to have the same significance. He pointed out that biochemical processes in plants tend to double or triple with each increase of 10°C until high temperatures cause injury. Winter temperatures certainly cannot be ignored because they also influence plant distribution (Daubenmire, 1938). In attempting to correlate vegetational distribution with temperature, some investigators have used averages, rather than sums, of daily maximal temperatures. Such studies have also been criticized by Daubenmire (1956) on the ground that high temperatures of midday are not necessarily nullified by night temperatures. Actually, there appears to be great difficulty in enclosing areas defined by isoclimatic lines and referring to them as life zones, despite many attempts to do this. The interacting phases of climate tend to make isoclimatic lines impractical as guides to the distribution of vegetation.

Thermoperiodism. It is well known that normal development of Temperate Zone woody plants occurs only when the high temperatures of summer alternate with periods of low winter temperatures. The relation between day and night temperatures, a phenomenon termed thermoperiodism by Went (1948, 1953), also has important effects on plant growth. Went (1953) believes that differences in optimum day and night temperatures are more useful than heat sums in expressing relationships between climate and plant growth. The importance of thermoperiodism in growth of trees was emphasized by Kramer (1957b), who grew loblolly pine seedlings with various combinations of day and night temperatures. He found that growth was related more closely to the difference between day and night temperature than it was to the actual temperatures within the range used. Best growth occurred with the greatest spread between day and night temperatures, and poorest growth when nights were as warm as days. Kramer suggested that loblolly pine may thrive better in the northern than in the southern part of its range because there is a greater difference between day and night temperatures in the northern part. Effects of various combinations of day and night temperatures on growth of loblolly pine are shown in Table 16.4.

Effects of Low Temperatures. Decreases in temperature slow down physiological activity, as emphasized earlier in discussions of individual processes. Sudden drops in temperature or very low temperatures often cause serious injuries. Winter injury commonly is caused by actual freezing, but sometimes it is caused by desiccation of tissues. A less important type of injury which is more frequent in plants of warmer regions is called chilling injury.

Freezing. There has been much discussion concerning the causes of injury from freezing (Belehradek, 1957; Levitt, 1956b). In early days it was claimed that expansion during freezing caused rupture of cells and tissues, but this view had to be abandoned when it was discovered that plant tissues actually shrink when they freeze. The splitting of tree trunks, for instance, usually results from uneven shrinkage rather than from expansion. Shrinkage occurs because formation of ice crystals usu-

Table 16.4. Effects of various combinations of day and night temperatures on height growth of loblolly pine seedlings. Average height increase over the entire growing season of 8 months is given in centimeters and as percentages of the original height. The values are averages for 8 trees, and a difference of 2.8 centimeters is significant at the 5 per cent level. (*From Kramer*, 1957b.)

Day temp., °C	Night temp., °C		
	11	17	23
	Average height growth, cm		
30		33.2	19.9
23	30.2	24.9	15.8
17	16.8	10.9	
	Height growth as percentage of initial height, cm		
30		106	62
23	97	69	51
17	50	35	

ally starts in the intercellular spaces, causing withdrawal of water from the cells. The decrease in volume sometimes is accompanied by collapse of the cells (Levitt, 1956b). Occasionally large masses of ice form locally, causing rupture of tissues. Removal of water during formation of extracellular ice concentrates the cell sap and dehydrates the protoplasm. Some of the early workers considered this dehydration to be the cause of death.

Formation of ice crystals within cells probably occurs only rarely, but it has been reported in laboratory experiments under conditions of very rapid freezing (Siminovitch and Scarth, 1938). Formation of ice crystals within cells invariably kills them, but ice crystals in intercellular spaces may or may not injure cells. According to Pfeiffer (1933) and Day and Peace (1937), rapid freezing usually is more harmful than slow freezing. In tissues which are not fully hardened the amount of injury is influenced by the rate of thawing: the faster the thawing the greater the injury (Dorsey and Strausbaugh, 1923; Hildreth, 1926; Pfeiffer, 1933).

Desiccation. Much winter and early spring injury in evergreens occurs as a result of an excess of transpiration over absorption. It is not uncommon for the air to warm up sufficiently for a short time during sunny days of winter or spring to bring about a high rate of transpiration. Since the soil is cold or frozen, water is not absorbed through the roots rapidly enough to replace transpirational loss and the tops dry out. Rhododendrons and other broadleafed evergreens are particularly sensitive to such injury. Munger (1916) described this type of injury on

Douglas-fir and called it "parch blight." Patton and Riker (1954) referred to desiccation injury of red pine as "needle droop." Voigt (1951) found desiccation injury in several conifers in Wisconsin and referred to it as "winter-drought injury." The injury was confined to parts of trees which were most exposed to warm southerly winds and subject to high transpiration. Curry and Church (1952) observed similar injury to conifers during the winter of 1947–1948 over extensive areas of the Adirondack Mountains in New York State. Entire mountainsides were covered with discolored trees. Red spruce, hemlock, white pine, and balsam fir showed severe browning and defoliation, but white-cedar, black spruce, white spruce, and red pine were only slightly injured. About 50 per cent of all stands examined were affected, and it was estimated that 10 per cent of all trees had at least one-fourth of their crowns killed by winter drying of their tops.

Chilling. Injury on exposure to low temperatures a few degrees above freezing often occurs in tropical and subtropical trees. Such injury is fairly common in fruits of Temperate Zone trees, but uncommon in their vegetative tissues, probably because they readily develop hardiness to chilling. Chilling injury may develop slowly or rapidly. It often is attributed to "metabolic disturbances," but the mechanism of chilling injury is not really understood and deserves further study (Eaks and Morris, 1956).

Winter Injury. Injury traceable to direct low-temperature effects or to desiccation during the cold months of the year may affect tissues above and below ground. Widely recognized forms of winter injury include killing back of shoots, frost cracks, frost heaving, winter sunscald, cambial injury, and root injury. These will be discussed separately.

Killing Back of Shoots. Sudden drops in temperature often kill back leaves, buds, twigs, and branches (Figure 16.6). If the temperature drops during the winter when tissues are dormant, relatively little frost damage occurs but late spring frosts can cause extensive injury. Most late-frost injury is to young succulent shoots of the current season. Late-frost injury is most severe when cold temperatures are preceded by warm days. When young, newly opened leaves are killed in spring, adventitious buds usually form and send out a new crop of leaves. However, a tree will not survive repeated freezing of its young shoots because eventually reserve carbohydrates are depleted. Kienholz (1933) described severe damage to red pine shoots in New Hampshire by frost after a month of warm weather in the spring, and Wagener (1949) observed dying of tops of Coulter pine from a sudden freeze in California.

Buds which begin to open in the spring are very tender and especially susceptible to frost injury, but unopened buds may also be killed when large and sudden temperature drops occur. Belyea and MacAloney

(1926) found frost killing of buds of Scotch pine, white pine, red pine, and ponderosa pine after a period of warm weather in April. When Belyea and MacAloney (1926) subjected opened and unopened buds to artificial freezing, they found that buds that were dry and unopened were undamaged by freezing but partially opened buds showed a shat-

Figure 16.6 An example of freezing damage to western white pine, photographed 5 years after the freeze. All the foliage and buds in the middle of the crown were killed. (*Courtesy of U.S. Forest Service.*)

tering of tissue and plasmolysis which probably was caused by extraction of water. Chaplin (1948) studied the influence of prevailing temperature conditions before freezing on susceptibility of buds to frost injury. He found that the killing temperatures of peach flower buds might rise as much as 11°F after a warm period and fall as much as 5 or 6°F after a cold spell. Horticulturists generally have found that susceptibility of fruit buds to frost injury is correlated with the degree of bud advancement in the spring, the more developed the buds the greater the chances of their being killed by spring frosts (Gardner et al., 1952, pp. 375–376).

Frost Cracks. When air temperatures suddenly drop below freezing, tree trunks sometimes split radially and longitudinally. Such injury results from rapid cooling and contraction of the bark and outer wood while the inner wood remains at a higher temperature and contracts less. Frost cracks are more common in forest trees than in orchard trees. Conifer stems usually are less susceptible than those of deciduous trees, and young trees less susceptible than old ones. According to Fisher (1907), species with large wood rays such as oak, beech, walnut, elm, ash, and chestnut are most subject to frost cracks. Fenska (1954) adds maple, sycamore, horsechestnut, weeping willow, and cherry to the list of susceptible trees. When injury to conifers does occur, it may be very severe. For example, Baxter (1943) described frost cracks in Norway spruce in Michigan which made 5 per cent of the trees worthless. According to Gardner et al. (1952), fruit trees are relatively resistant to frost cracks because they are low-headed and have small stems with short areas free of branches. An interesting case of stem splitting in apple trees in West Virginia following an autumn application of nitrate of soda was described by Sudds and Marsh (1943). Severe cracking of the bark occurred shortly after temperatures dropped below freezing in early January. The longitudinal cracks, which were confined to the south side, began about 5 to 10 centimeters above the ground and extended as much as a meter up the trunk. The bark was loosened radially for one-fourth to one-third of the stem circumference. Varietal differences in susceptibility were apparent since about 20 per cent of the Golden Delicious but only 10 per cent of Summer Rambo, Jonathan, and Rome Beauty trees were affected. Frost-crack injury also has been described on forest trees by Fisher (1907), Orr (1925), Heald (1933), and Boyce (1948); on orchard trees by Gardner et al. (1952); and on shade trees by Pirone (1941) and Fenska (1954).

Trunk splitting usually occurs during the night. Frost cracks, which usually are vertical but sometimes tend to be spiral, start near the base of the stem and work upward. With warming of air, frost cracks usually close but affected trees often sustain more injury from subsequent frosts. Frost cracks form an infection site for fungi. Healing of frost cracks is accompanied by growth of callus tissue, which forms a protruding, vertically oriented ridge or "frost rib." Occasionally, sudden warming of the outer bark and wood may produce a separation along part of an annual ring (Figure 16.7). Such internal injury is called "cup shake."

Frost Heaving. Roots of nursery stock and plantation trees may become frozen in a mass of ice and tend to be lifted out of the ground when additional ice layers form below (Haasis, 1923; Cooper, 1940). As the air warms temporarily and ice melts, the trees remain partially lifted out of the soil. During subsequent freezing they tend to be pushed out even more. Injury or death usually follows because roots are broken or the shoots and exposed roots dry out. Frost heaving is most common in heavy soils and may be decreased by snow cover, brush, ground cover, and various mulches. Schramm (1958) published a thorough discussion of the mechanism of frost heaving of tree seedlings.

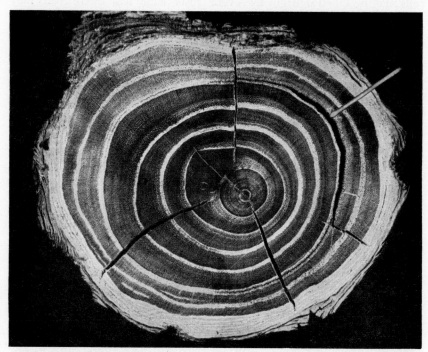

Figure 16.7   Frost crack in wood of Chinese elm, caused by a severe freeze. The crack, indicated at the end of the pointer, follows a growth ring. (*From Glock, 1951.*)

Winter Sunscald. Lesions which may be up to several feet long sometimes develop on south sides of tree stems when alternate freezing and thawing occur during the winter and early spring. According to Gardner et al. (1952), rapid freezing of stems after sundown is largely responsible for winter sunscald lesions. The injury often can be recognized by dead-bark patches which sometimes peel and expose the wood, or the injury may be characterized by sunken cankers which are sites for fungus and insect attack. Winter sunscald almost never occurs in old, thick-barked trees. Since the lesions damage the phloem, downward translocation of organic solutes is impeded. Mix (1916) made a study of winter sunscald and found large temperature differences of tissues of trees on the side exposed to the sun and the unexposed side. Eggert (1944) also reported differences of 50 to 55°F between bark temperatures on north and south sides of tree trunks, suggesting that the south sides of trees undergo violent temperature fluctuations. Winter sunscald injury can be lessened by shading trunks or by whitewashing them.

Cambial Injury. Dormant and active cambium layers of trees often are injured by frost. Studhalter and Glock (1942) observed that cambial cells may be killed outright by severe frosts, while less severe frosts may

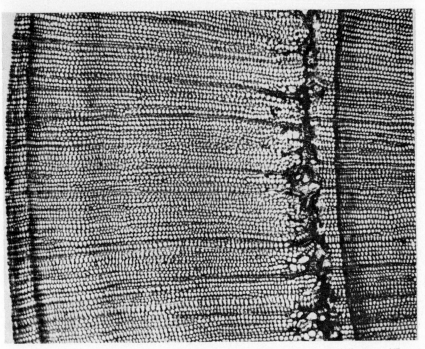

Figure 16.8 Frost ring in an Arizona cypress, caused by a late freeze. (*From Glock*, 1951.)

produce abnormal cells which form frost rings (Figure 16.8). Day and Peace (1934) cited Mayr (1893) as the first to recognize that these abnormal zones of tissue develop as a result of freezing. Frost rings have been reported to occur widely on many species of orchard and forest trees, including gymnosperms and angiosperms (Rhoads, 1923; Bailey, 1925; Day, 1928; Harris, 1934; Glock, 1951). Frost rings, which may appear within annual rings and sometimes are mistaken for them, often reduce the quality of lumber. According to Day and Peace (1934), both lightning injury and lack of water may cause formation of zones of abnormal tissue that are very similar to frost rings, although sometimes varying in detail. They stated that formation of zones of abnormal wood invariably appears to depend on collapse of cells in the developing cambial zone because of withdrawal of water.

Root Injury. Stem tissues are much hardier than root tissues, but roots are injured less in winter because the soil protects them from exposure to freezing air temperatures. However, whenever the soil freezes, roots are killed readily, and in northern areas where the soil usually freezes to a considerable depth, many of the surface roots are killed back each

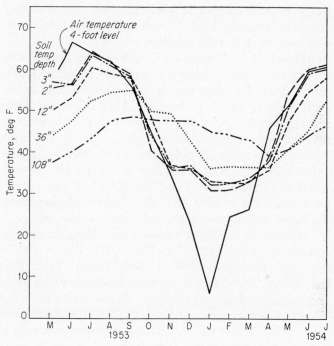

Figure 16.9 Soil and air temperatures in a hardwood stand near Chalk River, Canada. (*From Fraser,* 1957b.)

winter. According to Gardner et al. (1952), dormant roots of orchard trees are injured by soil temperatures in the range of 14 to 5°F, the critical temperature varying with the species. Snow cover prevents much winter injury to roots because it prevents deep freezing. For example, at Petawawa, Ontario, the soil usually freezes to a depth of only 2 or 3 inches under the snow although the average air temperature is below freezing for several months each winter (Fraser, 1957b). Some soil temperature data are shown in Figure 16.9. In British Columbia, Mann et al. (1953) found that during the exceptionally cold winters of 1935–1936 and 1949–1950 air temperatures dropped as low as −16 and −22°F but apple rootstocks were uninjured because of the presence of a snow blanket. Winter injury to roots appears to be greater in light than in heavy soils, probably because lower minimum temperatures occur in the lighter soils as a result of their greater conductivity. Injury also appears to be greater in drier soils. The extent of damage to orchard trees varies considerably with the rootstock used. Anderson (1935) reported considerable root killing of cherry trees in New York State during the winter of 1933–1934 on Mazzard rootstocks but relatively little damage on Mahaleb rootstocks. Gardner et al. (1952) suggest that root injury by freezing can be controlled by deep planting and mulching, use of hardy rootstocks, pruning back of tops of injured trees, and care in handling nursery stock in cold weather.

Frost Hardiness. Many Temperate Zone trees can survive winter temperatures as low as −50°C, or even lower, without injury. However, the same trees are killed by temperatures only a few degrees below 0°C if they are artificially frozen in midsummer. Under field conditions hardiness or resistance to injury by freezing develops in trees each year with the onset of the lowering temperatures of autumn. In late winter trees lose their capacity to resist injury by freezing. As may be seen in Figure 16.10, hardiness develops and disappears rather quickly. Several studies with orchard trees and forest trees in the United States and Europe emphasize a consistent pattern of a slow increase in hardiness in late summer, a rapid autumn increase, and finally a late winter decrease. Often the decrease in hardiness occurs long before dangers of severe frosts are over (Pfeiffer, 1933; Cartellieri, 1935; Ulmer, 1937; Meeder and Blake, 1943; Pisek and Schiessl, 1946; Parker, 1955; Tranquillini and Holzer, 1958). The ability to develop hardiness varies greatly with species and varieties of the same species. It also varies with the age of trees and with different tissues. Young, rapidly growing tissues usually are very susceptible to frost injury, and in fact hardiness usually develops only in tissues which have stopped growing.

Development of Frost Hardiness. Hardening of cells is accompanied by a number of biochemical and physical changes. Levitt and Scarth (1936) found that in cells which have become cold-hardened the viscosity of the protoplasm is decreased and permeability to water is increased as compared with cells which have not become cold-hardened. Parker (1958b) observed that the viscosity of the cytoplasm in phloem parenchyma cells of white pine decreased in the winter but content of the vacuoles of leaf endodermal cells changed from a sol to a gel in late autumn. With onset of hardening there may also be reduction in moisture content, at least in some species. However, attempts to develop cold hardiness by reducing the moisture content of plants have proved disappointing. There is some evidence that more bound water occurs in hardier cells, but Meyer (1932) could find no evidence that an increase in bound-water content played any part in increasing the cold resistance of pitch pine.

Increase in sugar concentration and in osmotic pressure of cells usually accompanies increase in cold resistance. This has been demonstrated

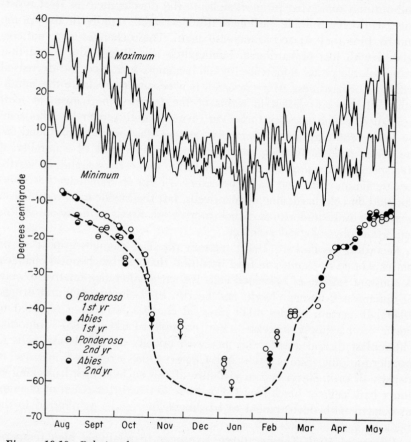

Figure 16.10 Relation between air temperature and development of hardiness in ponderosa pine and fir. Maximum and minimum temperatures are shown above. The lower curve shows the temperature necessary to produce visible injury. The arrows on some points indicate that no killing occurred at that temperature. (*From Parker, 1955.*)

many times in herbaceous plants, orchard trees (Levitt and Scarth, 1936), and forest trees (Korstian, 1924; Gail, 1926; Pisek et al., 1935). As pointed out in Chapter 4, this increase in sugars is correlated with starch digestion as a result of autumnal decrease in temperature. Levitt (1956b) believes that such conversion of starch to sugar is not precisely correlated with changes in hardiness and cannot in itself account for hardiness, although he later found that increasing cell sap concentration by infiltration with glycerin did increase cold hardiness (Levitt, 1957a).

Siminovitch and Briggs (1949) also emphasized that sugars are not primary factors concerned with the mechanism of hardening. They found that soluble sugars of bark cells of black locust increased in late summer and autumn somewhat proportionally to the development of frost resistance. However, soluble carbohydrates decreased rapidly in the spring, and by June they started to increase again. These changes were not correlated with loss of hardiness. Siminovitch and Briggs also found that water-soluble proteins increased when hardiness increased and decreased with loss of hardiness. More research is necessary to evaluate the significance of this correlation in terms of the primary mechanism of frost resistance, which appears to be very complicated and to be influenced by both protoplasmic and vacuolar factors. Parker (1958a) found increases in protein nitrogen and sugar in the inner bark of a number of tree species in the autumn. As a result of the pioneer researches of Scarth, Levitt, Siminovitch, and their coworkers, a fund of knowledge has accumulated on cold hardening of plant cells, but the biochemical mechanism is not yet fully understood. Much more work needs to be done on this important physiological problem.

According to Parker (1957), certain physical changes appear to be better related to changes in frost hardiness than are biochemical changes. A constant feature of hardened cells is their smaller size relative to cells of unhardened tissues (Levitt and Scarth, 1936; Siminovitch and Briggs, 1949). In certain species other physical changes have been reported to occur as hardiness increases. For example, Parker (1957) reported chloroplast disappearance and increased opacity of endodermal cells in ponderosa pine. Siminovitch and Chater (1958) reported increase in density of protoplasm and in visibility of the nucleus with hardening of inner bark cells of black locust. For more detailed discussion of changes associated with development of hardiness, the reader is referred to the book by Levitt (1956b).

Effects of High Temperatures. Exposure to relatively high temperatures often causes reduced growth and injury in trees. These effects may be the result of direct heat injury or of metabolic disturbances associated with very high respiration rates or even with desiccation of tops.

Direct Effects of High Temperatures. Direct heat injury is much more common in seedlings and young transplants than in older trees. Exposure to high air temperatures often causes stem lesions known as stem girdle, heat canker, sunscald, and various other names. Hartley (1918) described sunken stem lesions in young conifer seedlings in a Nebraska nursery and called the disease "whitespot." This type of injury, which is most prevalent on the south sides of stems, resembles damping-off injury except that the spots are lighter in color and restricted to aboveground tissues. Münch (1913, 1914) described similar injury to tree seedlings in Germany. Korstian and Fetherolf (1921) described harmful effects of stem girdle on growth and development of Engelmann spruce transplants. They were able to control the injury by inclining the trees slightly to the south at the time of transplanting. Toumey and Neethling (1923) observed that stem lesions formed when the beds were protected by half shade. In southern pecan nurseries high-temperature injury in the form of stem girdling and bud killing is called "sand burn" (Demaree, 1927).

Another type of lesion caused by drying out of the cambium and inner bark is known as sunscald or "bark scorch." Sunscald usually is found on south and southwest sides of stems of smooth-barked, older trees which have been transplanted or exposed by thinning (Figure 16.11). The large lesions may extend for several feet up the stem. Often long, dead strips of bark peel and expose the sapwood (Huberman, 1943). Sunscald degrades logs and provides an entrance for insects and fungi, which cause further deterioration. Huberman (1943) and Daubenmire (1959) believe sunscald is caused primarily by large temperature fluctuations rather than by high temperatures alone. As a precaution against sunscald, arborists often wrap stems of transplanted trees with paper tape or burlap or spray them with latex or wax. Sunscald of fruits commonly occurs also and is of serious concern to horticulturists (Harvey, 1925).

According to Levitt (1956b), protein denaturation of protoplasm at high temperatures probably is the cause of direct high-temperature injury to living tissues. This view was advanced by Sachs as early as 1864. However, from time to time other theories have been advanced to explain the mechanism of heat injury to protoplasm. These are summarized by Lorenz (1939).

The thermal death point of most active plant cells varies from 50 to 60°C (Meyer and Anderson, 1952). However, as stressed by Lorenz (1939), lethal temperatures vary with species, methods of application, age of tissue, and especially with the time of exposure to high temperatures. Lorenz found that cortical parenchyma cells of catalpa, American elm, red pine, eastern white pine, and white spruce seedlings were killed in 30 minutes when exposed to temperatures between 57 and 59°C, but only 1 minute of exposure was necessary to kill cortical parenchyma cells of the same species at 65 to 69°C. The five species did not vary greatly in relative heat resistance. Shirley (1936) concluded from tests with conifer seedlings varying in age from 1 to 4 years that resistance to heat increased with increasing age and with increasing size of plants. He also reported that tops were more resistant than roots. Differences in resistance to fire injury probably are related to differences in insulating effect of bark rather than to differences in heat tolerance of protoplasm.

Indirect Effects of High Temperatures. It was emphasized in Chapter 3 that apparent photosynthesis begins to decline rapidly after a critical high temperature is reached, because respiration usually continues to

Figure 16.11   Example of sunscald on aspen, showing repeated attempts at healing. (*Courtesy of U.S. Forest Service.*)

increase above that temperature while actual photosynthesis does not (Decker, 1944; Tranquillini, 1955). Therefore exposure of trees to high temperatures may cause decreased growth because of respiratory loss of large amounts of carbohydrates which otherwise would be available for growth. Poor development of nursery stock at high temperatures has been attributed, at least in part, to such a mechanism. Nightingale (1935) found that orchard trees were able to accumulate more carbohydrates at moderate temperatures than at higher ones. If unusually high temperatures are maintained for a long time, trees may die because of starvation. Tukey (1956) found that the rate of fruit growth was increased by maintaining branches at high night temperatures for several weeks after petal fall but flowering and growth the following year were reduced by exposure to abnormally high night temperatures.

High temperatures can also decrease growth of trees indirectly and promote injury by desiccation of leaves resulting from high transpiration rates. Hot, drying winds and prolonged periods of drought are conducive to this type of injury. Growth often is decreased because stomatal closure in wilted leaves results in decreased photosynthesis (Chapter 3). Injury may vary from death of parts of leaves to death of whole trees when they are desiccated to a critically low level.

Soil Moisture

Soil moisture often becomes a limiting factor because of its effects on the internal water balance, which in turn affects the processes controlling growth. The internal water balance and its relations to physiological processes were discussed in Chapter 15, and this section will deal chiefly with effects of variations in soil water content on growth. As mentioned earlier in this chapter, Fritts (1958) found a high degree of correlation between variations in soil moisture and diameter growth of beech trees, especially late in the summer when soil moisture often is low.

There is considerable uncertainty concerning the extent to which soil moisture must be depleted before it hinders growth. Theoretically, any increase in soil moisture stress above 1 or 2 atmospheres should reduce growth, but Veihmeyer (1956) and Veihmeyer and Hendrickson (1927, 1950) claimed that water was equally available for growth from field capacity almost to the permanent-wilting percentage. On the other hand, Richards and Wadleigh (1952) presented considerable evidence that soil moisture begins to limit growth considerably before it reaches the permanent-wilting percentage.

Many experiments dealing with the effect of soil moisture on growth have been performed on herbaceous plants, but few have been done with woody plants. The results of a study on young apple trees are shown in Table 16.5. Kenworthy (1948) grew apple trees in pots and timed his irrigations so that various percentages of the available water were removed before rewatering the pots. In the most severe treatment the trees were allowed to wilt before rewatering them. The data presented are the average of 6 trees for a 3-month growing period for 2 years. Apparently the true field capacity of the soil was higher than the moisture content at 60 centimeters tension, because the wettest soil was too wet for best growth; hence this experiment shows the effect of both wet and dry

Table 16.5. Growth and chlorophyll content of young apple trees as influenced by the percentage of available water in the soil when irrigated. (*From Kenworthy,* 1948.)

Character measured	Percentage of available water used before irrigation					L.S.D.* at 5%
	20	40	60	80	100	
Soil moisture tension before irrigation, cm H₂O	60	97	243	570	†	
Shoot growth, cm	193	208	194	142	92	59
Increase in trunk diameter, cm	0.36	0.36	0.34	0.18	0.10	0.8
Increase in dry weight, g	83	93	83	49	26	21
Total leaf area, sq dm	28	28	26	18	11	6.8
Chlorophyll, mg per tree	253	272	243	169	95	59

* Least Significant Difference.
† Trees wilted.

soil on tree growth. It is obvious that growth was reduced in soils in which the moisture content was not allowed to fall to permanent wilting, but not all characters were reduced to the same extent. Shoot growth was reduced 68 per cent, but diameter growth was reduced only 50 per cent.

In any discussion of the relation between soil moisture and growth, it must be remembered that growth is not controlled directly by soil moisture content or soil moisture stress but by the water balance of the plant. The internal water balance of the plant is controlled by the relative rates of absorption and transpiration; hence it is affected by both soil and atmospheric moisture conditions. Furthermore, it seems probable that the effects of decreasing soil moisture may depend largely on the characters measured, because the effects on height growth, diameter growth, fruit size, and yield of seed may be quite different. Stanhill (1957) examined 80 studies dealing with the effects of soil moisture content on growth and found that in 66 of them plant growth appeared to be affected before soil moisture was depleted to the permanent-wilting percentage. Most of the experiments where no significant effects were observed until the soil water fell to permanent wilting were performed on fruit trees, and the results were measured in terms of fruit yield.

The effects of decreasing soil moisture content and increasing soil moisture stress or DPD on height growth, dry weight, transpiration, and relative turgidity of privet are shown in Figure 16.12. The effect of soil moisture tension on diameter growth of avocado trees is shown in Figure 16.13. Both experiments indicate that growth is reduced before soil moisture tension reaches the value of 15 atmospheres usually assumed to be in the range where permanent wilting occurs.

There may be some doubt whether growth is limited by soil moisture above the permanent-wilting percentage, but there is no doubt that it is stopped when the soil moisture content falls below the permanent-wilting percentage. Soil moisture rarely is at the optimum moisture content during the entire growing season, and large losses occur annually because of

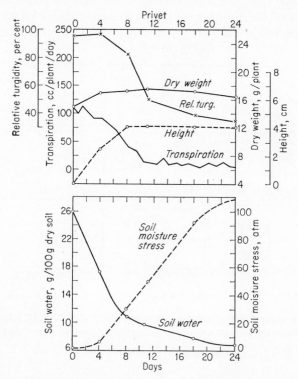

Figure 16.12 Effect of decreasing soil moisture content and increasing soil moisture stress on height growth, increase in dry weight, transpiration, and relative turgidity of privet plants. Growth began to be slowed down at a soil moisture stress of about 5 atmospheres. (*From Slatyer*, 1957b.)

deficient soil moisture. Even in the relatively humid southern United States, droughts 2 to 6 weeks in length are common (Moyle and Zahner, 1954), and in many other supposedly well watered regions soil moisture often falls low enough by midsummer to limit growth (Boggess, 1956; Fritts, 1956; Gaiser, 1952; Kozlowski, 1958). An intensive study of changes in soil moisture under a hardwood stand in Canada was made by Fraser (1957a).

In general, diameter growth is affected more than height growth by

deficient soil moisture. Diameter growth appears to be more dependent
on current photosynthesis than height growth. Furthermore, height
growth of many species is largely completed early in the season, before
soil moisture is reduced to a limiting level, while diameter growth usually
continues much later.

Some attempts have been made to correlate growth and rainfall. It
appears that height growth usually is correlated better with rainfall of
the preceding year than with rainfall of the current year. According to
Hustich (1948), height growth is related to the weather of the preceding
year in areas where soil moisture is abundant in the spring, but if spring

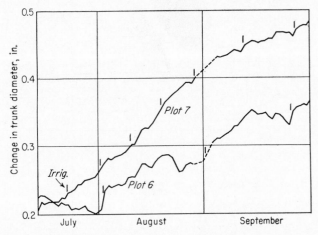

Figure 16.13   The relationship between soil moisture stress and diameter growth
of avocado trees. Trees in plot 7 were watered whenever the soil moisture tension
reached approximately 0.5 atmosphere. Trees in plot 6 were watered whenever the soil
moisture tension reached 10 atmospheres. The short vertical bars indicate irrigations.
Note cessation of growth and actual shrinkage of trunks before irrigation at high soil
moisture tension. (*From Richards et al.*, 1958.)

rainfall is low, growth can be correlated with rainfall. According to Tryon
et al. (1957), height growth of yellow-poplar in West Virginia is related
to May and June rainfall but the relationship is not as good as for rainfall
and diameter growth.

Diameter growth seems more sensitive to annual rainfall than height
growth. In fact, this sensitivity of diameter growth to moisture supply
provides the basis for predicting past weather conditions from relative
widths of annual rings produced in different years. There is a closer relationship between precipitation and ring width in regions where rainfall is
limited, as in northern Arizona (Glock, 1937), than where it is abundant.
In regions where rainfall is abundant, a few inches more or less may
have little effect on growth.

Figure 16.14 shows the effect of decreasing soil moisture on growth of 15-year-old shortleaf pine. These trees were growing on soil underlain by a hardpan layer, which hinders downward movement of water and

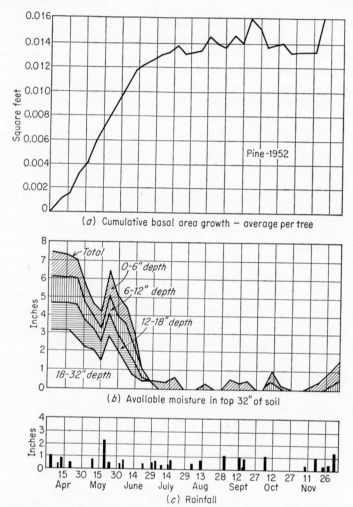

(*a*) Cumulative basal area growth – average per tree

(*b*) Available moisture in top 32" of soil

(*c*) Rainfall

Figure 16.14 Seasonal trends in growth of shortleaf pine trees in southern Illinois in relation to soil moisture and precipitation. Note rather uniform extraction of soil moisture at all depths and the reduction in growth which began when two-thirds of the available soil moisture was removed. A relatively impermeable layer limited water and root penetration below 30 to 36 inches. (*From Boggess, 1956.*)

root penetration. The 32-inch layer of soil above this hardpan must have been thoroughly occupied by roots because water was removed quite uniformly from all horizons sampled for soil moisture. It also is obvious that summer showers replenished the water in only the surface 6 inches of soil.

Soil Aeration

A deficiency of oxygen in the soil often causes cessation of root growth together with injury to or death of root systems. Root injury usually is followed by yellowing and death of leaves, reduced stem growth, and even death of trees. These symptoms may be brought about by flooding, poor drainage, or soil compaction. Trampling in public areas compacts soil and interferes with diffusion of gases and downward infiltration of water. Taylor (1949) has shown that diffusion of oxygen is greatly influenced by the degree of soil compaction. Lutz (1945) found in Connecticut parks that pore volume and air capacity of soil were decreased greatly by public use. Soil in one area which received intensive use was only about one-twentieth as permeable as soil in a nonused area. Soil compaction often occurs in woodlands where cattle are allowed to graze. Trampling of sandy soils usually is less harmful than trampling of heavier soils which pack more easily. Hardpans or impermeable layers hinder aeration, because they impede diffusion of gases and prevent water from draining out of the surface soil layers. Such impermeable layers are especially harmful if they are close to the soil surface. The greatest amounts of root injury occur in soils which do not allow free diffusion of gases between the soil and aboveground atmosphere. Aeration problems therefore occur primarily in heavy soils with small pores and poor drainage, and they almost never occur in coarse-textured soils. Boynton and Reuther (1938) found much higher oxygen percentages in light than in heavy soils.

Various species of trees differ greatly in their susceptibility to poor aeration. Parker (1950) found that growing dogwood was severely injured or killed within a week by flooding the soil but red, white, and overcup oak survived flooding longer. Hunt (1951) found seedlings of loblolly, shortleaf, and pond pine to be unexpectedly resistant to flooding. Most kinds of fruit trees are rather susceptible to flooding injury, but pear trees seem unusually resistant. Kienholz (1946) described a flooded pear orchard in Oregon where early spraying was routinely conducted from a barge. Complete submergence of the orchard for 3 months during the growing season did not kill the trees but did affect fruit development. Large variations among forest tree species in susceptibility to water impoundment were reported by Green (1947). Graham and Rebuck (1958) found that pond pine made nearly twice as much growth on a well-drained site as on a poorly drained site, although it is regarded as tolerant of poor aeration.

Roots require a continuous supply of oxygen. Respiration of roots and soil organisms tends to deplete soil oxygen and increase its carbon dioxide content. The oxygen content of the soil is replenished by diffusion from the atmosphere, while the excess carbon dioxide diffuses out of the soil, each gas moving in response to its own partial-pressure gradient. When soil is saturated with water the air which normally occupies the non-capillary pore space of the soil is displaced; hence water content and

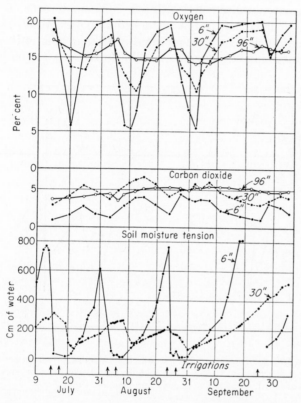

Figure 16.15 Variations in oxygen, carbon dioxide, and water content of soil at various depths. Changes in soil moisture content were measured by changes in soil moisture tension. An increase in soil moisture tension, indicating a decrease in soil water content, was accompanied by an increase in oxygen content. (*From Furr and Aldrich*, 1943.)

oxygen content of soils vary inversely. Furr and Aldrich (1943) illustrated the inverse relationship between soil moisture content and aeration in irrigated date gardens in California. As may be seen in Figure 16.15, the oxygen content of the soil air decreased from about 20 to 5 per cent as a result of irrigation and carbon dioxide content was increased. Oxygen content at a 30-inch depth also fluctuated inversely with soil moisture content but less so than at a 6-inch depth. At a depth of 96 inches oxygen content fluctuated only slightly. Carbon dioxide content at depths of 30 and 96 inches fluctuated very little and remained close to 5 per cent. Chemical properties of poorly aerated soils often differ radically from those of well-aerated ones. In flooded soils organic-matter decomposition is slowed down and there is a tendency for nitrogen to be bound to the accumulated organic matter. Anaerobic decomposition of organic matter produces partly oxidized and reduced compounds such as methane, methyl compounds, and complex aldehydes (Van't Woudt and Hagan, 1957). In addition, toxic concentrations of ferrous iron, nitrites, sulfides, and manganese may accumulate in submerged soils (Robinson, 1930).

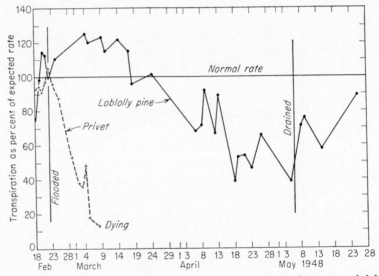

Figure 16.16 Effect of flooding the soil on transpiration of privet and loblolly pine. Privet was dying in 2 weeks, but loblolly pine began to recover when the soil was drained after 10 weeks of flooding. (*From Kramer*, 1951b.)

Reactions to Poor Aeration. Several physiological processes in trees are influenced by poor soil aeration even before changes in growth are observed. In general, flooding causes a decrease in the capacity of roots to absorb and conduct water, resulting in reduced transpiration. Permeability of root cells is decreased by high accumulations of carbon dioxide in the soil. Plants wilt sooner when soil air is displaced with carbon dioxide than when it is displaced with nitrogen. Saturating soil with carbon dioxide displaces oxygen and nitrogen, while saturating soil with nitrogen displaces both oxygen and carbon dioxide. This suggests that an excess of carbon dioxide decreases root permeability sooner than a deficiency of oxygen (Kramer and Jackson, 1954). Decrease in water absorption with prolonged flooding probably is caused by plugging of the conducting system by bacterial activity in the dying roots and by accumulation of gummy materials (Kramer, 1951b).

There is considerable variation in transpiration of different species after flooding. As may be seen in Fig. 16.16, transpiration of privet decreased rapidly after flooding the soil and the plants died after 12 days while transpiration of loblolly pine did not decrease greatly until after about a month of flooding. Parker (1950) found that transpiration of redcedar declined rapidly after flooding while that of cypress did not decrease until much later. The transpiration of flooded plants often returns to its original level after the soil is drained, but this may require several days or weeks.

Root injury and decreased formation of new roots associated with poor aeration decrease the rate of mineral uptake by decreasing the absorbing surface. Absorption of minerals depends at least in part on expenditure of energy released by respiration, so it is markedly reduced by a deficiency of oxygen. For example, phosphorus absorption of pine roots was reduced to only 5 per cent of the controls by displacing oxygen with nitrogen. Mineral absorption was also greatly reduced by saturating the solution in which roots were immersed with carbon dioxide (Kramer, 1951a). Loustalot (1945) found that ash content of pecan seedlings was lowered by flooding the soil. Anaerobic conditions in the soil also interfere with mineral nutrition because they impede activities of soil microorganisms concerned in nitrification.

Poor aeration often causes roots to carry on anaerobic respiration, with a consequent accumulation of by-products which may be toxic to the roots when present in large amounts.

Flooding of orchard trees often decreases fruit quality by causing early ripening and poor flavor. Sometimes cork formation occurs on fruits of flooded trees, suggesting mineral deficiency (Heinicke et al., 1939).

Oxygen Requirements. Oxygen requirements for roots of different species of trees vary greatly. For example, cypress roots require lower oxygen concentrations than dogwood roots. Roots also require much more oxygen during the growing season than when dormant. Heinicke (1932b) found that winter flooding did not cause injury to apple tree roots if the excess water was drained off before growth started. However, if any leaf surface was present, flooding was likely to cause severe damage especially when transpiration was high. Cannon (1925) reported that oxygen concentrations of 8 to 10 per cent were required for good root growth but roots of many species grew slightly with oxygen contents of only 2 per cent or less. While more than 10 per cent oxygen was required for good root and top growth of apple trees, roots grew slowly with 3 to 5 per cent oxygen and survived in atmospheres varying from 0.1 to 3.0 per cent oxygen (Boynton et al., 1938). Apparently at depths below 3 feet there is enough oxygen for good root growth in many northeastern orchard soils only during a short period of the year. Boynton and Reuther (1938) observed that for at least 6 months of the year the oxygen content at a depth of 3 feet in a light silty clay was less than 5 per cent.

A higher oxygen level is required for producing new roots than for keeping roots alive. Boynton (1940) noted a marked decrease in formation of new roots as the oxygen level was reduced below 15 per cent, at least when the carbon dioxide content increased by about the same amount. When oxygen content dropped below 10 per cent and carbon dioxide increased above 5 per cent so few new roots were produced that top growth subsequently was greatly reduced. According to Boynton and Compton (1943), best growth of roots of apple, prune, and peach in nutrient solutions in tanks occurred in solutions which were aerated with gas containing 20 per cent oxygen. A decrease in oxygen pressure to three-fourths of that found in air caused a substantial decrease in root and top growth.

Causes of Injury to Flooded Plants. Although deficient aeration caused by flooding the soil reduces water and salt absorption and injures or kills roots, this does not fully explain the symptoms which develop in the tops of flooded plants. Decreased absorption of water explains wilting of leaves, but it does not explain such reactions as curvature of leaf tips, epinasty, development of red pigments in leaves, stem hypertrophy at the water line, and production of adventitious roots. None of these reactions can be caused by dehydration, and production of adventitious roots and buttressed bases indicates that the water content is adequate for growth.

It has been suggested that epinasty and curvature of leaves might be caused by toxic substances released from the dying roots and carried upward in the transpiration stream (Kramer, 1951b). It also is possible that the leaves suffer from lack of some essential substance produced by healthy roots (Jackson, 1956). Perhaps the various results of flooding the soil have different causes.

One characteristic effect of flooding trees of several species is the production of buttressed bases. This possibly occurs because accumulation of food and auxin near the water line stimulates vegetative growth. It has been demonstrated that lack of oxygen interferes with translocation in the phloem (Curtis, 1929; Mason and Phillis, 1936) and flooding the lower part of stems probably produces a physiological girdle which stops downward translocation. Cypress knees apparently develop because excessive growth occurs in those portions of horizontal roots which happen to be better aerated than the remainder (Whitford, 1956).

Site Quality and Site Index

The interaction of the environmental factors of a particular habitat or site on the trees growing there often is expressed in terms of volume of wood produced, but height growth seems to be a more satisfactory measure because it is not greatly affected by density of the stand. Site quality therefore commonly is expressed in terms of site index or the average height of dominant trees in a stand at an age of 50 years.

Where fully stocked stands of sufficient age are available, site quality can be determined directly by measuring the age and height of the dominant trees. It often is necessary, however, to estimate the quality of sites on which no trees or trees of an undesired species are growing. Some use has been made of indicator plants to evaluate site quality (Heimburger, 1934; Oosting, 1956), but in recent years attention has been concentrated chiefly on measurement of soil properties. Climatic conditions such as rainfall, length of growing season, and photoperiod affect growth of species with very extensive ranges, but within moderately broad geographic areas site quality is controlled more by soil than by climatic factors.

Extensive studies by Coile and his students (Coile, 1948; Coile and Schumacher, 1953) indicate that site quality for southern pines is determined largely by soil properties which influence the quality and quantity of growing space for roots. For example, growth of loblolly and shortleaf pine in the Piedmont increases with increasing depth of the A horizon and decreases with decreasing friability of the subsoil, presumably because the poor aeration of less friable subsoils hinders root development. The suitability of the subsoil as a medium for root growth can be measured fairly conveniently and accurately in terms of its imbibitional water value (Coile, 1948). The imbibitional water value is the difference between the moisture equivalent and the xylene equivalent. It changes with the amount and kind of clay in the subsoil, friable, well-aerated soils having low imbibitional water values while plastic, poorly aerated soils have high values.

In well-drained, sandy soils of the Virginia and North Carolina Coastal Plain water often is limiting during the summer. Here site quality increases with decreasing friability of the subsoil, presumably because less friable subsoils store more water than sandy subsoils. Zahner (1958) states that site quality in southern Arkansas and northern Louisiana is closely correlated with soil factors which affect moisture and aeration.

Under some circumstances topography becomes important, although its effects are complex. Einspahr and McComb (1951) found that site-index values were 8 to 12 points higher on north and east slopes than on south and west slopes with similar soil. This difference probably occurs because south and west slopes are warmer and dry out faster than north and east slopes. They also found that where eastern white pine and oak grew together, the pine had the higher site index and the difference was greatest on the poorest soil. This emphasizes the fact that different species have different requirements for optimum growth; hence trees of one species often have a higher site index than those of another species growing on the same site.

The physical properties of the soil have been emphasized thus far in connection with site quality, but as indicated in Chapter 9, the chemical properties in terms of mineral nutrients often limit tree growth. This is particularly true on deep sands where nutrients leach out and on eroded sites where the topsoil has washed away. On very fertile soils no correlation between tree growth and nutrients would be expected because their minimum concentration is above that limiting growth. For example, Tarrant (1949) found that the nutrient content of forest soils in the Douglas-fir region of the Pacific Northwest seems to be so high that it is not a limiting factor for growth. On the other hand, Woodwell (1958) found evidence that deficiencies of nitrogen and phosphorus limit growth of pond pine in pocosins in the Carolina Coastal Plain.

Competition

Trees in dense stands continually compete above ground for light and below ground for water, minerals, and oxygen. They also compete with nonwoody plants in the same communities. Thus trees become involved in a dynamic struggle for existence in which many finally are eliminated through natural selection. Young forest stands with several thousand trees per acre may be reduced to less than a hundred trees when mature. As trees increase in size, their individual requirements for growth increase. The ability of surviving trees to overtop and suppress less vigorous ones expresses their greater physiological activity under environmental stress. Thus variations in rates of physiological processes, especially photosynthesis, are major factors in plant succession and development of climax communities with more or less stable species composition.

For many years light and soil moisture have been regarded as the most important factors in competition, and an extensive literature has accumulated which stresses the importance of one or the other of these factors. Until the researches of Fricke (1904), most emphasis was placed on the importance of competition for light. Fricke surrounded small areas with trenches and thereby freed the trees within these areas of root competition. Within the trenched areas a luxurious growth of woody and herbaceous plants developed, while vegetation failed to develop in untrenched plots. Soil moisture was higher in trenched than in untrenched plots, and Fricke concluded that soil moisture was the factor of paramount importance in competition. Trenched plots were subsequently used by other investigators, who also concluded that soil moisture was the most important factor in competition (Toumey and Kienholz, 1931; Korstian and Coile, 1938).

The importance of light intensity in competition was indicated by other investigations, of which only a few will be cited. For example, Shirley (1929a and b) concluded that the low light intensities in forests, which often varied from 0.1 to 20 per cent of full daylight, could support growth for some time but were too low to ensure survival because root development was poor and food reserves were inadequately developed under these intensities. From another study Shirley (1932) concluded that establishment and growth of young pines in a virgin Norway pine stand were correlated with light intensity. Olmsted (1941) reported that in an oak-maple forest in Wisconsin survival and growth of maple, even during the drought year of 1936, showed no real relation to root competition but were closely related to light intensity. Buell and Gordon (1945) studied the importance of water and light in a hardwood-conifer contact zone in Minnesota. They reported a substantial increase in soil moisture due to trenching. But in spite of the increased soil moisture they found no evidence of maple-basswood reproduction invading either the trenched plots in the spruce-fir forest or the spruce-fir end of their plot across the contact zone. They concluded that light was the factor limiting the invasion of the hardwood community into the spruce-fir zone.

The factors involved in competition have been under investigation for a number of years in the Piedmont plateau of the southeastern United States, where the difficulty of regenerating pine stands is a serious forestry problem. In this region the natural course of succession is from pine forests to climax hardwood forests. Cutting of pine releases understory hardwoods, which then outgrow pine seedlings. Pine stands are readily established on open fields, however, and in 10 to 15 years closed pine stands are established. The understory of such young stands is composed of hardwoods, and the overstory pines are thinned out by the time they reach overmaturity. Eventually climax hardwood communities are established. Korstian and Coile (1938) demonstrated with trenched plots that in several closed stands with light of approximately equal intensity a deficiency of soil moisture probably caused death of young pine seedlings on untrenched plots. In contrast, the hardwoods were able to survive, and Korstian and Coile concluded that soil moisture was the controlling factor in competition. However, within 6 to 10 years the pine trees on the trenched plots set up by Korstian and Coile began to die, and after 10 to 15 years nearly all died, suggesting that shading may have been a major factor in their ultimate death (Korstian and Bilan, 1957). The importance of light intensity in competition was shown earlier by Kramer and Decker (1944), who observed that photosynthetic rates of pine seedlings increased progressively with added light up to full sunlight (Chapter 3). Hardwoods, however, showed maximum photosynthesis at one-third or less of full sunlight. The principal reason for the lower photosynthetic efficiency of pine in the stands appears to be the self-shading of the needles (Kramer and Clark, 1947). In still another approach Oosting and Kramer (1946) investigated light and soil moisture conditions in transects extending from open fields into adjoining shortleaf pine stands. They concluded that the differential survival of pine reproduction at the margins and in the stands was related to differences in light intensity rather than to differences in available soil moisture. This was supported by further work in which seedlings were planted along the transects and their survival observed (Kramer et al., 1952). Kozlowski (1949) observed that growth of pines was affected by deficiencies of both light and soil moisture. Shading reduced the growth of loblolly pine seedlings much more than it reduced the growth of hardwood seedlings. More important, perhaps, it reduced the root/shoot ratio of pine seedlings more than that of oak seedlings (Table 16.6). Furthermore, the carbohydrate con-

Table 16.6. Effects of light intensity on growth and root/shoot ratio of loblolly pine and overcup oak grown for 2 years in sun and shade. (*From Kozlowski, 1949.*)

	Height, cm	Oven-dry roots	Weight, g		Root/shoot ratios
			Shoots	Entire plants	
Loblolly pine:					
Sun *	42	25.2	20.1	45	1.25
Shade	35	6.1	7.2	13	0.84
Overcup oak:					
Sun	59	44.1	21.1	65	2.01
Shade	66	38.7	20.1	59	1.92

* Light intensity on the shaded plants was about one-third of full sun.

tent was lowered more by shading in pine than in oak. Root and shoot growth of pines also was decreased by low soil moisture supplies. With decreasing available soil moisture, photosynthesis of pine began to decrease at a higher moisture content than did photosynthesis of hardwoods. On the basis of these several observations, Kozlowski (1949, 1955) concluded that ultimate failure of pine in competition is caused by significant effects of both shading and low soil moisture content. At a particular time both factors may contribute effects of similar magnitude or either one may contribute a greater effect. The survival and growth of pines appear to require a light intensity high enough for them to produce enough carbohydrates to develop roots which can absorb adequate amounts of water. In field experiments Korstian and Bilan (1957) reduced both crown competition and root competition of 7-year-old loblolly pines by killing all woody plants around the pines. They also reduced crown competition by tieing back all woody plants capable of shading the pines, leaving root competition undisturbed. They observed that either deficient soil moisture or inadequate light intensity can become a limiting factor in the growth of pine, a conclusion reached earlier by Kozlowski (1949). According to Ferrell (1953), the effects of soil moisture and light on seedling growth are additive.

Thus it appears that in competition a complex of environmental factors exists, with light and water as major components. Under natural conditions the effects of these factors are interacting and interdependent. There probably is a shifting in the importance of these factors, especially with variations in shading and soil moisture. When both light intensity and soil moisture operate as limiting factors, a sudden marked improvement in one of the factors alters the limiting effect of the interaction. The relative importance of each factor at any time depends on the physiological tolerances of the species involved and on fluctuations in physical factors of the environment.

Cultural Practices

Cultural practices generally are attempts to produce a more favorable environment for tree growth and reproduction, and they are effective only if they increase the over-all efficiency of the physiological processes which control growth and fruit and seed production. Irrigation helps maintain the turgid tissues necessary for growth. Fertilization provides the minerals required in building new tissues and in various biochemical processes. Thinning provides more light for photosynthesis and more water and minerals per individual tree. Pruning removes unproductive branches, improves tree form, and makes it easier to spray fruit trees and pick fruit.

The reasons for irrigation and fertilization were discussed earlier. Most of the emphasis in this chapter will be placed on such practices as thinning and pruning, as practiced by foresters. Horticultural practice varies so much for different species and in different regions that it cannot be treated adequately. Nevertheless, many of the same general principles apply to fruit and forest trees.

Thinning. It is well known that thinning usually results in increased diameter of the remaining tree trunks (Mann, 1952; Schantz-Hansen, 1939; Wahlenberg, 1952), but it also changes other characteristics. For example, Senda et al. (1952) and Satoo et al. (1955) studied the effect of spacing on the growth of *Pinus densiflora* up to the age of 16 years. Decreasing stand density was accompanied by decreased mortality, basal area, surface area of stem, percentage of total volume (stems plus branches) in stems, annual stemwood production per unit weight of needles, and the ratio of needles to branches. Decreasing stand density was accompanied by increase in average diameter at breast height, volume of stem, volume of stem increment per year, volume of branches per tree, ratio of branches to stem, size of crown, and amount of needles per tree. Height, total volume of wood (stems and branches), and amount of needles per hectare were affected relatively little by stand density. The results of these experiments are summarized in Table 16.7.

Table 16.7. Effect of stand density on total volume and volume of stem- and branchwood produced by a 13-year-old stand of *Pinus densiflora.* (*From Senda et al.,* 1952.)

| Spacing, m | Volume per hectare, cu m | | | | Total volume |
| | Stemwood | | Branchwood | | |
	Volume	Per cent of total wood	Volume	Per cent of total wood	
0.5	137.14	88	18.44	12	155.58
1.0	119.90	85	21.50	15	141.40
1.5	114.19	79	29.54	21	143.73
2.0	109.50	68	52.33	32	161.83

The thinning of stands influences growth and form of trees by reducing competition and altering the environment so that it is more favorable for the processes controlling growth of the remaining trees. According to Möller (1946), the total dry matter produced by a closed stand of trees varies little over a considerable time span whether the stand is thinned or not (Table 16.7 and Figure 7.3). However, thinning concentrates the production of dry matter in fewer trees, which are selected for their large size, quality, and growth potential.

The data of Burns and Irwin (1942) show the effect of spacing on the annual increment of bolewood of 28-year-old white and red pine trees growing in Vermont. As shown in Table 16.8, wider spacing resulted in greatly increased increments of bolewood per tree and per unit of leaf surface but a greatly decreased increment per acre.

Proper thinning should not attempt to cause sudden large increases in diameter growth of dominant trees but rather should prevent suppression of their growth. In fact, very large increases in diameter growth of residual trees immediately after thinning suggest that the stand should have been thinned earlier (Hawley and Smith, 1954). Thinning also tends to increase the number and size of branches, size of crown, size of root systems, and taper of the trees left in the stand. Height growth generally

Table 16.8. Effect of spacing on growth, wood production, and leaf efficiency of red and white pine trees. The data are for trees 28 years old. (*From Burns and Irvin, 1942.*)

Species	Spacing, ft	Trees per acre	Average height, ft	Average diameter, in.	Increment of bole-wood, cu ft per acre	Increment of bole-wood, cu in. per tree	Leaf area, sq m per acre	Increment, cu in. per sq m leaf surface
Red pine	2 × 2	10,890	20.6	1.95	170	27.17	84,803	3.48
	4 × 4	2,722	23.9	2.88	137	87.06	55,677	4.26
White pine	2 × 2	10,890	22.1	2.43	331	52.59	162,226	3.53
	4 × 4	2,722	22.7	2.83	148	93.69	62,134	4.10

is not affected greatly over a wide range of thinning, possibly because a small and more or less fixed amount of carbohydrate is used in height growth.

The rate of growth is increased or maintained after thinning primarily because the greater availability of light, water, and minerals to remaining trees favors increased rates of photosynthesis. A less immediate but very important effect is the increased rate of photosynthesis, which results from an increased photosynthetic surface as the crown increases in size. With more water available to trees left after thinning, photosynthesis is increased through increased hydration of leaf tissue and greater stomatal opening caused by increased leaf turgidity (Chapter 3). When Moyle and Zahner (1954) killed large hardwoods in forest stands in Arkansas, soil moisture supplies were higher for the remaining trees as a result of decreasing the amount of transpiring surface per acre. Moyle and Zahner recommended that methods of treating forest stands be considered which would both conserve the moisture supply and permit its use by the more desirable trees.

The response of trees to thinning varies greatly with age of a stand largely because the ratio of the amount of live crown to stem height decreases with age in unthinned stands. Trees in stands that remain unthinned until tree crowns become very small often do not respond to thinning, possibly because their release increases total respiration more than total photosynthesis. Large amounts of carbohydrates are consumed in respiration in cambial tissues. Therefore exposure of stems of trees with small crowns to the heating effect of direct sun may result in greatly increased respiration of stem tissues without a parallel increase in photosynthesis. The net effect may be to decrease carbohydrate reserves, at least until the crown increases in size. It therefore is important that thinnings be made early while crowns are sufficiently large to shift the carbohydrate balance in favor of photosynthesis over respiration (Hawley and Smith, 1954).

It is possible that trees in overcrowded stands possess insufficient food reserves to quickly develop an enlarged crown capable of increased photosynthesis. Furthermore, it is possible that the canopy of such stands contains a large proportion of shade leaves which are injured by sudden exposure to full sun.

In the North Carolina Piedmont, Miller (1951) found that thinning of old-field Virginia pine 12 years old or older was not practical because of poor growth response and the hazards of ice and wind damage. However, thinning of stands that were 5 or 6 years old resulted in accelerated growth.

Taper of tree stems is related to size of crown, and exposed trees with large crowns usually taper more than trees with small crowns. The relationship of thinning to stem taper was demonstrated by Bickerstaff (1946), who reported that diameter increase in red pine following thinning was greatest near the ground and decreased with increasing distance up the trunk. Satoo et al. (1955) and Burns and Irwin (1942) also found that stand density affected diameter growth and stem taper.

Pruning. The pruning of woody plants has been practiced for centuries and was even recorded in the Bible. Horticulturists, arborists, and foresters prune trees routinely, although often with somewhat different objectives. Pomologists usually prune primarily to improve fruit quality and reduce breakage of stems and branches, whereas arborists may prune largely from an aesthetic viewpoint. Thus arborists often remove branches to provide better landscape effects, to prevent crowding, to avoid street wires and improve public safety, and to eliminate diseased, mechanically injured, or insect-infested branches. On the other hand, foresters prune trees primarily to produce knot-free lumber. This is desirable for some conifers such as spruces, white pine, and Douglas-fir because they do not prune naturally and may retain lower branches for many years. According to Anderson (1951), artificially pruned Douglas-fir trees began to produce clear lumber rather than knotty common grades in one-tenth the time required for trees which were allowed to prune naturally. Foresters also prune less commonly to remove diseased branches, and they root-prune to prepare nursery stock for transplanting.

Natural Pruning. In densely grown stands natural pruning of lateral branches occurs in both angiosperms and gymnosperms, but it generally is slower in gymnosperms. Natural pruning involves several sequential phases, including weakening of branches, infection with wood-decomposing fungi, wood decay, severance of the branch from a tree, and wound healing. Natural pruning is set in motion in dense stands by low rates of photosynthesis in leaves of lateral branches which are heavily shaded. According to Mayer-Wegelin (1936), such branches are limited to the carbohydrates which are produced by their own foliage. They have relatively small amounts of leaf tissue and relatively large amounts of respiring surface and actually starve because of their low rates of photosynthesis and because there apparently is little or no translocation of carbohydrates into them. It seems probable that water deficit also contributes to their decline. Death of these branches is preceded by an extended period of retarded growth. After a branch is severed, a protective layer develops between the outer dead stub and the inner living part of the branch. In angiosperms the protective area consists of tyloses or wound gum, while in gymnosperms accumulations of resin occur. After severance of the branch the wound heals as stemwood grows over it.

Artificial Pruning. Most artificial pruning removes dead and live branches, but under certain conditions pruning of roots and buds has been found useful. Nurserymen may prune roots to retard stem growth and to increase flower and fruit production. There apparently are differences in growth responses of root-pruned trees because Smith (1940) found that seedlings of hardy catalpa, green ash, and black locust could be root-pruned without reducing growth the next year but growth of American elm and hackberry was reduced by root pruning.

It has been assumed that bud pruning, which is accomplished by rubbing off lateral buds or removing very young branches, does not materially reduce height or diameter growth. This is based on the assumptions that bud pruning decreases the wood volume produced in the crown, less carbohydrate will be used in growth in the crown, and therefore

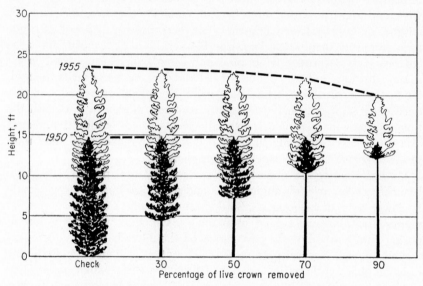

Figure 16.17   The effect of removal of various percentages of live crown on height growth of red pine. (*From Slabaugh*, 1957.)

more carbohydrate will be available for stem growth in a bud-pruned tree than in a normal one. However, the reduced photosynthesis in bud-pruned trees actually reduces stem growth in some species (Chapman and Taylor, 1951). Bud pruning has not been practiced extensively in the United States, but its limited usefulness has been shown with a few conifers such as red pine, longleaf pine, and slash pine (Rowland, 1950; Marts, 1950; Chapman and Taylor, 1951).

Effects of Pruning on Growth. Pruning of live branches decreases the amount of photosynthetic surface, but it also decreases the respiratory surface. Because many suppressed basal branches with only a few leaves may consume all the carbohydrates in respiration which they produce in photosynthesis, they do not contribute to stem growth (Labyak and Schumacher, 1954; Lehtpere, 1957). Pruning of such branches is obviously desirable because it will not lessen stem growth and will produce clearer lumber.

Removal of dead branches does not influence tree growth, but severe pruning of the live crown retards diameter and height growth by reduc-

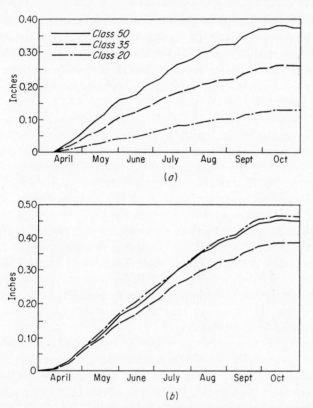

Figure 16.18 The effect on diameter growth of pruning loblolly pine trees to various percentages of their height. *a*. Diameter growth at 4.5 feet. *b*. Diameter growth at 80 per cent of tree height. Class 50 trees were pruned to 50 per cent of their height, class 35 trees to 35 per cent of their height, and class 20 trees to 20 per cent of their height. Reducing crown size reduced diameter growth much more at 4.5 feet than at 80 per cent of height. (*From Young and Kramer, 1952.*)

ing photosynthesis (Downs, 1944; Marts, 1951). Talbert (1931) observed that the heaviest type of pruning had the greatest dwarfing effect on apple trees. In many conifers as much as a third of the crown can be removed without much reduction in height or diameter growth (Dahms, 1954). Takahara (1954) found that moderate pruning of *Cryptomeria japonica* and *Chamaecyparis obtusa* had little effect on growth because it removed primarily shade leaves which have slow rates of photosynthesis and contribute little food for growth. As may be seen in Figure 16.17, removal of 30 to 70 per cent of the live crown of red pine had little effect on height growth (Slabaugh, 1957). Young and Kramer (1952) observed marked reduction in diameter growth of loblolly pine but no reduction of height growth after pruning. Lehtpere (1957) reported a similar response in pruned Douglas-fir. Lückhoff (1949) found that removal of 25 per cent of the crown did not affect height or diameter growth of conifers while removal of 50 per cent of the crown reduced diameter growth but not height growth. Labyak and Schumacher (1954) concluded that a branch in the lower half of the crown with less than three branchlets, or one in the lower fourth with less than five branchlets, contributes nothing to diameter growth in loblolly pine.

Height growth proceeds at the expense of carbohydrates produced in the vicinity of the leader, and a large part of the crown can be removed by pruning from below without seriously depleting the carbohydrates which will be used for height growth. However, diameter growth at any point on the trunk depends on carbohydrates produced by branches above rather than branches below that point. According to Young and Kramer (1952), pruning also decreases the taper of a stem because the reduction in diameter growth is greater near the ground than at upper levels of the stem (Figure 16.18). Exposing stems to sunlight by pruning often stimulates growth of epicormic branches. Cosens (1952) questioned the wisdom of pruning white fir because the epicormic branches which followed were a serious obstacle to production of clear lumber. Stem exposure after pruning may also cause thin-barked trees in open stands to suffer from sunscald.

Since root growth depends on adequate supplies of carbohydrates from the crown, the removal of photosynthetic tissue by pruning may reduce growth of roots. Light pruning reduces root growth less than heavy pruning (Savage and Cowart, 1942). The effects of pruning young cherry trees for several years are shown in Table 16.9.

Table 16.9. Effects of pruning on root and shoot growth of young cherry trees. Data show cumulative effects over a 5-year period. (*From Chandler,* 1923.)

	Percentage reduction caused by pruning
Total leaf surface	34
Fresh weight of tops	45
Fresh weight of tops plus prunings	31
Fresh weight of roots	50
Total dry weight of tops plus prunings	35
Total dry weight of roots	50

Effects of Pruning on Fruit Production. Pruning of orchard trees decreases the number of fruit spurs and fruit buds formed and usually decreases the total yield of fruit (Gardner et al., 1952). Nevertheless, pruning is widely practiced by horticulturists because it results in increased size and quality of fruit. If pruning is very severe, the size of fruit may be reduced because of too great a reduction in photosynthetic surface. Orchard trees often set more fruit than can be supplied adequately with carbohydrates, and removal of part of the crop reduces competition for available carbohydrates, thereby increasing the growth of the remaining fruit.

Healing of Pruning Wounds. Pruning and other stem injuries are followed by considerable physiological activity in the vicinity of the wound. Angiosperms respond promptly by producing a viscous substance resembling wound gum in their ray cells. This substance leaves the ray cells and blocks up the vessels. Such changes occur only during the growing season, so wounds made during the dormant season usually remain open until early in the following growing season, when they also become blocked. The rapid blocking of tissues against fungus entry in the growing season often is given as an argument for pruning during that time. The production of wound gum is associated with disappearance of starch from parenchyma cells (Swarbrick, 1926).

Actual wound healing begins with the appearance of soft parenchymatous tissue called callus, which is produced by the cambium or by division of parenchyma cells in the phloem and cortex (Eames and Mac-Daniels, 1947). In some species the cambium takes no part in the early development of callus, which is formed predominantly from rays. In such trees there may be no cambial activity until after the callus cushion is completely laid down (Sharples and Gunnery, 1933). Juliano (1941) has also called attention to the origin of callus from tissues other than the cambium. According to Buck (1954), callus can form from any living cell whose walls have not undergone secondary thickening. The callus, which begins to fill the wound, forms more rapidly from the sides than from the top or bottom. Closing of wounds also is more rapid from the top than from the bottom, presumably because the top receives larger amounts of carbohydrates and growth substances by downward translocation. In conifers the occluding tissue is characterized by abundance of resin canals which exude resin in the wound (Paterson, 1938). The cambium is active just below the cut surface and produces a ring of new tissue which gradually fills in the exposed wood and buries the ends of severed wood elements under living tissue. After a wound fills in, the cambium layers unite, until finally the healed wound is covered with callus, wound wood, and wound bark.

The rate of healing varies greatly with different species. Of 10 species investigated by McQuilkin (1950), white oak healed most rapidly and Virginia pine slowest. Red maple wounds closed slowly because of excessive dieback of callus. The rate of wound healing depends largely on the rate of diameter growth of the wounded stem or branch. Live-pruned branches heal more rapidly and cause less distortion of the grain than dead-pruned branches. Callus formation requires adequate amounts of food and growth regulators as well as suitable conditions of temperature, moisture, and aeration (Shippy, 1930). The rate of wound healing appears to be greatest when wounds are made shortly before or during the early part of the growing season. Marshall (1931) found that wounds made between February 15 and May 15 on six species of hardwoods in Connecticut healed faster than did wounds made at any other time of year. According to Takahara (1949), pruning wounds on some conifers heal more rapidly in the shade than in the sun.

Wound dressings retard infection, but in general they appear to have little effect on promoting healing. A few dressings, which check dieback by preventing drying, promote early differentiation of callus. Once callus starts to form, its rate of spread does not seem to be affected much by the presence of the dressing. There is some evidence that compounds containing sulfhydryl groups such as glutathione may speed up wound closing (Davis, 1949). McQuilkin (1950) favored lanolin as a wound dressing. Its beneficial effects were attributed largely to protection of the wound against drying and dieback. Without this protection the cambium and phloem died back as much as an inch or more under the bark. Growth of callus may be inhibited by chemicals present in some wound dressings or by slime flux.

Girdling. Ringing a stem so that a strip of bark and cambium and often some sapwood are removed affects both reproductive and vegetative aspects of growth. The removal of inner bark cuts the active phloem and blocks downward translocation of carbohydrates and growth substances from the crown. Therefore carbohydrate accumulation just above a girdle results in abnormally thick growth in that area. However, stem growth below the girdle is decreased and stops when carbohydrate reserves and hormones are exhausted. Root growth also is decreased, and girdled trees eventually die. Girdling of trees sometimes increases the amount of seed produced and increases fruit size because it confines carbohydrates to upper parts of the tree. Whenever girdling extends into the sapwood, it disrupts the upward movement of water, thus causing drying of leaves, which eventually decreases photosynthesis. Girdling causes leaves to dry out sooner in ring-porous than in diffuse-porous trees because in the former group upward movement of water usually is confined to a few outer rings of sapwood at most (Chapter 11). However, in diffuse-porous trees water normally moves in several rings of the outer sapwood. Death of girdled trees probably often is caused by desiccation resulting from injury of the root system by lack of carbohydrates.

Diseases

Many pathologists consider a plant to be diseased "when it is so impaired as a whole or in any of its parts that its usefulness to itself or to mankind is seriously reduced" (Riker and Riker, 1936). Both pathogenic and nonpathogenic diseases are recognized within the framework of this definition. The nonpathogenic diseases caused by too little or too much water, heat, light, minerals, etc., have already received considerable attention in this chapter and in other chapters. The present discussion therefore will be concerned with parasitic diseases caused by viruses, bacteria, fungi, parasitic seed plants, and nematodes.

The greatest loss of timber resources results from decrease in growth rather than from mortality. The total "growth impact," consisting of mortality plus growth loss, was recently reported to be 92 per cent of saw-timber growth in the United States. Some idea of the great importance of pathogens on growth and mortality of trees may be gained from the recent report that 45 per cent of the total reduction (mortality plus growth loss) was caused by disease, largely heart rots. Forest diseases accounted for more than half the loss in saw-timber growth from all causes (Hepting and Jemison, 1958).

Physiological processes of trees are altered unfavorably by disease, resulting in reduction of growth or death. Disease symptoms vary widely and may be expressed in color changes, necrosis, vein clearing, wilting, and leaf spots on leaves; atrophy, hypertrophy, and rotting of tissues; and dieback or abscission of various parts. Malformations such as cankers, galls, intumescences, witches'-brooms, rosettes, fasciation, and leaf crinkling or rolling commonly indicate a diseased condition. Some of these localized responses in turn affect important physiological processes adversely. For example, chlorosis and necrosis of leaves cause decreased photosynthesis, root diseases decrease absorption of water and minerals, and stem diseases hinder translocation. For comprehensive discussions of diseases attacking forest trees the reader is referred to books by Baxter (1943) and Boyce (1948). Disease resistance is discussed briefly in Chapter 15.

Leaf Diseases. Leaf diseases affect tree growth primarily by reducing photosynthetic tissue and by reducing the efficiency of the remaining tissue (Chapter 3). Photosynthesis is reduced chiefly by localized destruction of photosynthetic tissue by invading fungi. Virus diseases often reduce the amount of photosynthetic tissue or reduce the chlorophyll content of parts of leaves. Injury by fungi to leaves often causes abscission and thereby deprives the tree of the carbohydrates which such leaves would otherwise produce. For example, needle casts of conifers greatly decrease growth because of carbohydrate loss. Additional carbohydrate loss occurs when trees use stored food to put out a new crop of leaves following defoliation early in the season. Pathogens sometimes cause unsightly leaf galls.

Stem Diseases. Bacterial and fungus pathogens located in the outer sapwood interfere with water movement and cause wilting of leaves. In early stages of wilt diseases the wilted leaves recover turgor at night, but in later stages they do not. Eventually leaves may turn yellow and abscise or they may turn brown and dry up before abscission, as in Dutch elm disease. Interference with water conduction has been attributed to a variety of causes, including blocking of xylem by fungal hyphae, dislodged conidia, tyloses, gums, and hydrophilic compounds. Vessel occlusion has also been attributed to gas locks caused by carbon dioxide given off by the pathogen, effects of toxins, and disintegration of vessel walls into substances which increase viscosity of tracheal fluids. According to Dimond (1955), physical blocking of vessels by mycelium generally does not account for more than a small amount of the reduction in water transport in diseased stems. Dimond also questions whether the role of toxins in the wilting of infected plants has been clearly demonstrated. There is convincing evidence that, in some species at least, pathological wilts are caused largely by blocking of vessels with tyloses and gums. Such plugging of the vascular system has been observed in Dutch elm disease, oak wilt, verticillium wilt of elm and maple, and mimosa wilt. In trees affected with oak wilt, Struckmeyer et al. (1954) found extensive plugging of vessels with tyloses and gums prior to wilting of leaves. Tyloses formed primarily in earlywood vessels of the last annual ring of diseased trees and less abundantly in the smaller latewood vessels. In later stages gum formed in smaller vessels, rays, xylem parenchyma, tracheids, and among tyloses of large vessels. Gum formed less abundantly in root tissues. Wilting apparently resulted from physical blocking of the vessels rather than from toxic materials. Kuntz and Riker (1955) demonstrated that upward movement of water in northern pin oak trees which were inoculated with the oak wilt fungus was reduced by as much as 85 per cent 3 to 4 days before leaf wilt was evident. In trees with advanced wilt symptoms movement of water was negligible.

Various rust fungi cause abnormal stem growths, including swellings, cankers, galls, burls, and witches'-brooms. Growth of the host tree is decreased or distorted, and trees often are killed, especially when young trees are attacked. Cankers, which vary greatly in form and size, may cause death of patches of bark on branches and stems. These may be superficial and do little damage, while other cankers may kill trees by girdling them. Canker fungi kill living tissue by hyphal invasion or by toxic secretions. The mycelium often grows in the inner bark and cambium. Annual cankers may heal over and are not nearly as destructive as perennial cankers. Cankers also serve as points of entry for wood-decaying organisms such as the heart rots which drastically reduce accumulated growth.

Attacks by mistletoes, a group of parasitic seed plants, also decrease growth. Mistletoe haustoria enter the bark through lenticels and other openings. The host is further penetrated as the haustoria push cells aside and possibly secrete enzymes which soften the walls of host cells. Cortical strands develop from the haustoria, and sinkers then develop from the cortical strands. The sinkers grow down into the cambium and later are buried in the wood as new annual rings form. Mistletoes parasitize the host tree by absorbing water, mineral salts, and probably carbohydrates. They rarely kill trees, but often retard their growth. Individual branches may die beyond the point of attack or may be stimulated to produce swellings, cankers, and witches'-brooms. Necrotic areas also commonly occur (Kuijt, 1955). The vigor of the host often is reduced so that it becomes susceptible to other pathogens.

Root Diseases. Root diseases often destroy part of the root system and thereby interfere with absorption of water and minerals. For example, Nutman and Sheffield (1949) found clove trees in Zanzibar dying from "sudden death" disease caused by water shortage. The crown was desiccated as a direct consequence of death of absorbing roots. A branch from a wilting tree could be kept alive and fresh if placed in water. Injection of water into branches on dying trees also kept them alive and green until after the rest of the tree died.

Root diseases cause various distortions, as in the case of bacterial crown gall. Root rots cause wood and bark to decay and may eventually cause death. Diseases of roots sometimes spread to stems. For example, phloem necrosis of elm affects fibrous roots first and then progresses into larger roots. After the roots die, phloem necrosis may extend into the stem and branches before the whole tree dies (McLean, 1944).

Several species of ecto- and endoparasitic nematodes also cause important diseases of forest and orchard trees (Ark and Thomas, 1936; Lownsbery, 1956; Chitwood and Birchfield, 1956; Hansbrough and Hollis, 1957). Nematodes are especially serious pests of citrus trees. Baines and Clarke (1952) reported that the top 2 feet of California citrus soils frequently contains 2 to 7 million nematode larvae per cubic foot, indicating the seriousness of the nematode problem in some areas. The root-knot nematodes of the genus *Meloidogyne* cause knotlike swellings or galls to form on roots of a number of woody plants. By killing young feeder roots they impede water absorption and cause affected trees to wilt readily when the soil begins to dry. Eventually infested trees become chlorotic and their growth is reduced, probably because of decreased photosynthesis. The root lesion nematodes of the genus *Pratylenchus* enter root tissues of a number of woody plants and are followed by fungi and bacteria which cause black, decaying lesions and longitudinal root cracks. The smaller roots usually are killed, leaving a small tufted root system. Tops eventually show chlorosis, decreased growth, death of branches, and a reduction in fruit crops. Lownsbery (1956) observed potassium deficiency in leaves of walnut seedlings attacked by root lesion nematodes and suggested that the deficiency was due to use of potassium by the nematode, interference with potassium absorption, or both.

Spreading decline, caused by the burrowing nematode *Radolpholus similis,* is one of the most serious diseases of citrus in Florida. Diseased trees appear in clumps and show an abnormal deterioration of small feeder roots. Trees are usually small and of low vigor. They have sparse foliage and produce small fruit crops.

Insects

Insects affect growth of trees primarily by chewing plant tissues, sucking fluids from tissues, ovipositing, pollinating flowers, and causing gall formation. They also influence growth by acting as vectors of some of the most important fungus, bacterial, and virus diseases of trees. Graham (1952) emphasized that no stage in the life cycle of a tree is free from insect attack. Seeds may be attacked even before they are collected, and they may be attacked later in storage. Seedlings and saplings are attacked and often killed by a wide variety of insects.

In general, trees appear to acquire some resistance to insect attack once they get beyond the sapling stage. However, as they approach maturity and their physiological activity declines, trees again become subject to widespread insect depredations. There appears to be good correlation of physiological activity in trees with insect attack and mortality. Vigorous, fast-growing trees are less susceptible to attack by some types of insects or more likely to recover from attack than unthrifty trees. For example, DenUyl (1944) reported that there was more locust borer injury to trees of low vigor than to healthy, vigorous trees. Craighead (1925) also emphasized a relation between physiological activity and recovery from attack when he observed that the more rapid the rate of growth before insect attack, the lower the resulting mortality from spruce budworm defoliation. For our purposes the principal groups of insects which check tree growth or kill trees will be classed as defoliating, meristem, and sucking insects. These will be discussed separately.

Defoliating Insects. Defoliation by insects checks growth of trees primarily by reducing the amount of photosynthetic tissue and thereby decreasing the amount of carbohydrates available for growth. Reduction in growth of partially defoliated trees often is proportional to the amount of foliage removed (Church, 1949).

There is considerable variation between angiosperms and gymnosperms as well as between different species and individual trees in ability to survive defoliation. Angiosperms generally withstand defoliation better than gymnosperms, presumably because they have more reserve carbohydrates and readily put out new foliage (Graham, 1952). Gymnosperms often die after one complete defoliation. Beal (1942) found that young, open-grown shortleaf and loblolly pine trees did not survive if

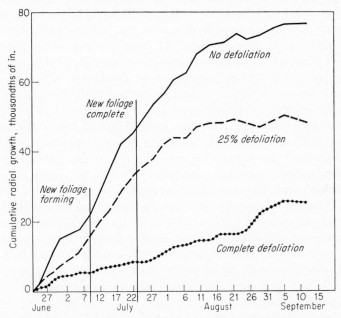

Figure 16.19 Effect of insect defoliation on diameter growth of aspen trees. Defoliation was first observed on June 6. (*From Dils and Day, 1950.*)

three-fourths or more of their needles were removed by the red-headed pine sawfly. Some pine trees which were growing in shade died after only 50 per cent defoliation. The effects of a single defoliation usually are overcome by deciduous trees. However, repeated defoliation results in progressively reduced growth, smaller crops of leaves, and eventually starvation and death. Understory trees which are undergoing severe competition usually succumb readily to defoliation because of their low carbohydrate reserves.

Growth response of the lower trunk to partial defoliation may occur in the same season, or there may be a lag in response for one or more years, depending on the severity of defoliation, the time of its occurrence, and amount of reserve carbohydrates in the tree. According to Belyea (1952), defoliation of current-year foliage in conifers must occur for more than one season before growth is severely decreased but reduced growth often occurs in deciduous trees shortly after they are defoliated (Figures 16.19 and 16.20). Dils and Day (1950) observed checking of growth from mid-June to late June in aspen trees that were defoliated only a week or two previously by tent caterpillars. Completely defoliated trees started to leaf out by the second week of July and eventually recovered from 60 to 75 per cent of their former leaf area, but their growth at the end of the season was only about a third of that of undefoliated trees. According to Rose (1958), when aspen is completely defoliated growth ceases and is not resumed that season. The double-growth rings reported by some workers in defoliated trees were not observed in defoliated aspen. In contrast, McLintock (1955) found a lag of 3 to 6 years between severe defoliation of balsam fir trees by spruce budworm and decreased diameter growth at the base. There also was a lag at the end of the epidemic, with depressed growth continuing after defoliation ended. In the early stages of attack the trees apparently had adequate carbohydrate reserves, and since the young caterpillars feed on new needles only, the old needles carried on photosynthesis and may even have produced more carbohydrate than before the attack because they were no longer shaded by new needles. With continued defoliation, carbohydrate supplies presumably eventually were exhausted and growth finally decreased. By the time the attack subsided, the trees were undoubtedly depleted of carbohydrate reserves and required more than one year to build up sufficient leaf surface to maintain normal rates of growth. According to Stark and Cook (1957), reduction in growth first appeared after defoliation in two successive years by the lodgepole needle miner, indicating a lag in carbohydrate depletion as previously reported by McLintock. Belyea (1952) emphasized the lag in tree response to partial defoliation of balsam fir by spruce budworm. As may be seen in Figure 16.20*a*, defoliation in 1946 and 1947 did not materially decrease growth during those years. The effect of defoliation was obviously cumulative because growth was suppressed for several years beginning in 1948, even though defoliation in 1948 and thereafter was lighter than in 1947. Figure 16.20*b* shows that more severe defoliation beginning in 1942 caused progressively decreased growth from 1946 to 1949, and trees began to die in 1947. Before trees died, several signs of physiological disturbances were apparent, including failure of buds to develop in early summer, suppressed bud and shoot development, wilting of leaves, failure to produce new xylem cells in early summer, and early growth cessation. These effects undoubtedly resulted from inadequate carbohydrate production by the repeatedly defoliated trees.

Removal of a given amount of foliage by insects often is more harmful to trees than the removal of an equal amount of foliage by artificial pruning. In pruning many of the lower shaded branches are removed. Such physiologically inefficient branches have low rates of photosynthesis and contribute little or no carbohydrates for growth of the main stem.

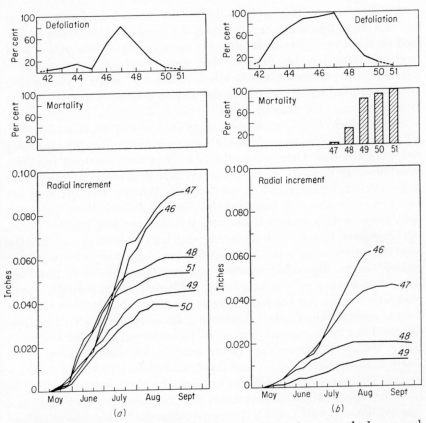

Figure 16.20 Relation between severity of defoliation by spruce budworm and growth and mortality of balsam fir in the Lake Nipigon region of Ontario. *a*. The Southern Border area. *b*. Black Sturgeon Lake area. Note that in area *b* heaviest mortality occurred several years after heaviest defoliation and there was a considerable lag in the effects of defoliation on growth. (*From Belyea, 1952.*)

On the other hand, defoliation by insects often removes photosynthetically active leaves which normally contribute large amounts of carbohydrates for stem growth. Insect defoliation is especially harmful because it leaves the stems and twigs on the tree and they continue to consume carbohydrates in respiration. Tree survival is further endangered because insects often defoliate the less vigorous trees which have low carbohydrate reserves. Defoliation of dominant trees may increase the amount of light available to understory trees and may decrease transpirational depletion of soil moisture. Duncan and Hodson (1958) found that defoliation of aspen by tent caterpillar resulted in increased diameter growth of understory balsam fir, presumably because of increase in available light and soil moisture.

Meristem Insects. This group includes insects which feed primarily on root and shoot tips and living tissues of the cambial region. Insects that feed on shoot tips such as the pine tip moth and the white pine weevil rarely kill trees, but they decrease their growth and cause stem deformities. When the terminal shoot is killed, apical dominance is temporarily lost. Removal of the leader upsets the hormonal balance, and one of the laterals becomes the leading shoot.

Insects which feed on roots, such as grubs and weevils, often interfere with absorption of water and minerals because they reduce the absorbing system of the tree. Decrease in the root/shoot ratio resulting from destruction of the root system by insects results in desiccation of tops, which in turn reduces photosynthesis and growth. When a large part of the root system is removed, trees usually die rapidly. Seedlings and small trees are especially susceptible to attack by root-feeding insects.

The phloem insects, such as borers and bark beetles, are among the most destructive tree pests. Bark beetles are classed as primary or secondary insects, depending to some extent on their ability to resist the flow of resin or sap (Graham, 1952). Vigorous, physiologically active trees with copious flows of sap and resin are better able than less vigorous trees to repel invading insects. Entrance galleries of bark beetles penetrate the cambium, phloem, and surface of the sapwood. The insects ingest living tissues which contain large amounts of carbohydrates. Thus meristematic cells are killed and the host tree is depleted of carbohydrates. The galleries often girdle or partially girdle trees, resulting in blocking of downward translocation of carbohydrates through the phloem. Normal physiological activity is seriously disrupted under the combined impact of death of meristematic tissues, carbohydrate depletion, and interference with carbohydrate translocation and water conduction. Caird (1935) observed that after attacks by bark beetles the outer rings of shortleaf pine trees lost their capacity to conduct water upward successively from the outermost ring inward. As a result the tops dried up and died. Failure to conduct water was related to drying of the wood and accumulation of air in the outer rings. It also was suggested that failure of the outer wood to conduct water was associated with penetration of the wood by fungi. However, drying of the wood could occur in the absence of fungi. Callaham (1955) observed pronounced drying of sapwood directly beneath adult galleries of the red turpentine beetle

(*Dendroctonus valens*). Drying of wood beneath beetle galleries probably reduces ability of infected trees to resist further attacks because it undoubtedly impedes resin flow. When beetle galleries encircle the stem and roots, rapid desiccation of tops follows.

Sucking Insects. Insects with sucking mouth parts, such as the aphids and scale insects, do not always kill trees but invariably decrease their growth by depriving them of carbohydrates and injuring and dehydrating tissues. These insects also are well known as vectors of plant diseases.

A good example of damage by a sucking insect was given by Balch (1952), who described attacks on balsam by the balsam woolly aphid, *Adelges piceae*. Heavy stem attacks kill trees in 1 or 2 years, but under light attacks trees may live for many years. The larva inserts its stylets between cells into twigs, penetrates the cortex or phelloderm, and feeds by dialysis through cell walls. The saliva which the larva injects may contain a growth hormone, or there is a concentration of hormone in the region of feeding, either because its production is stimulated in adjoining cells or because it is translocated from other tissues. Whatever the nature of the stimulus, the tree responds by producing large thick-walled cells, with large nuclei in the area adjoining the path of the stylets. Hyperplasia follows in surrounding tissues, and hypertrophied pockets of tissue often become surrounded by wound cork. The cambium also responds to the salivary stimulus and produces thick-walled, rounded tracheids which resemble those in compression wood. Trees die under heavy attack because of inhibited bud growth, starvation associated with lack of new foliage, death of bark tissues, and decreased conduction of water because of resistance to its movement in the abnormal tracheids of the outer sapwood.

Fire

Fire causes considerable damage by interference with physiological processes, in addition to direct destruction of trees. The most serious cause of injury is reduction in photosynthetic surface by defoliation. This is particularly serious in young stands, which are more likely to be completely defoliated than older, larger trees. A study by Harper (1944) showed that loss of one-third of the needles in March by fire reduced gum yield of longleaf and slash pine the following year by 11 per cent, loss of two-thirds of the needles reduced it 19 per cent, and complete defoliation reduced yield 32 per cent. Defoliation by fire in May or June caused much greater reduction in yield than defoliation early in the season.

Ground fires often kill an area of bark and cambium, producing girdles such as that shown in Figure 8.6. It has been assumed that such injury interferes with translocation and reduces growth, but a study by

Jemison (1944) indicates that fire injury to the base of tree trunks seldom reduces either translocation or diameter growth of hardwoods in subsequent years. New xylem and phloem are laid down in newly oriented paths during the next growing season, quickly providing new translocation pathways around wounds. The trees involved in this study suffered no crown injury. It should be remembered that even though growth was not reduced, timber quality was reduced by fire wounds. Furthermore, the possibility of infection by fungi is increased by such injury. The insulating properties of the bark often determine the severity of injury to the living phloem and cambium, and older trees with thicker bark are less subject to injury than younger trees with thinner bark. Species differences in fire resistance also depend largely on the characteristics of the bark.

Fire indirectly affects growth by decreasing the nitrogen supply. On the other hand, it may stimulate growth by quickly making available quantities of minerals in the ash which would not be available otherwise until after the litter decomposed.

Air Pollution

With increased industrialization and greater concentration of people there is growing concern about increasing damage to plants by air contaminants. The atmosphere is continuously polluted by discharges from industrial plants, stoves, incinerators, gas mains, and automobiles. Exposure of trees to contaminated air checks their growth and often injures or kills them. The extent of injury depends on the nature of the contaminants, their concentration, the duration of exposure, and the kind of plant (Middleton et al., 1956). Gaseous contaminants in the air cause more injury than solids or liquid aerosols (Thomas, 1951). Sulfur dioxide, produced by combustion of many fuels, is an important phytotoxicant. Fluorides and halogens also are toxic, but they are less prevalent and do not cause the extensive damage which is attributable to sulfur dioxide. Considerable local damage to crops and trees has been traced to gases present in smog, especially in the coastal area of southern California. Injury also is caused by illuminating gas which escapes from mains because of improper packing of joints, shaking by traffic, frost heaving, soil settling, construction work, and corrosion (Marsden, 1950–1951). Occasionally damage is caused by careless use of herbicides. Some of the more important gaseous pollutants will be discussed briefly. For comprehensive discussions and extensive bibliographies on gas damage to trees the reader is referred to the review article by Thomas (1951) and to the reports sponsored by the Interdepartmental Committee on Air Pollution (McCabe, 1952) and by the National Research Council of Canada (Katz et al., 1939).

Sulfur Dioxide. Reduced growth and injury to some kinds of trees are caused by sulfur dioxide when its concentration in the air exceeds about 0.3 to 0.5 part per million. Conifers are more susceptible than hardwoods, and seedlings more susceptible than older trees. Both acute and chronic (chlorotic) forms of injury are known. Acute injury occurs during the period of most rapid growth and is characterized by small discolored and collapsed areas in the leaves, or by discoloration of the whole leaf following rapid diffusion of sulfur dioxide into intercellular spaces. This is followed by shedding of leaves. When chronic injury occurs, symptoms such as chlorophyll breakdown, decreased photosynthesis, and decreased growth appear rather slowly. Chronic injury results from slow accumulation of sulfur in leaves and eventually causes leaves to drop. Sometimes it is difficult to distinguish between sulfur dioxide and hydrofluoric acid injuries. Usually, however, hydrofluoric acid causes more injury to leaf margins than sulfur dioxide. Trees are especially susceptible to sulfur dioxide injury during the early part of the growing season when the young leaves are emerging from the bud (Katz and McCallum, 1952). Growth of trees is reduced after exposure to sulfur dioxide, probably because of reduced photosynthesis. In Connecticut, Toumey (1921) found that growth of conifers was reduced 25 to 50 per cent by smoke, presumably because of the sulfur dioxide in it. In British Columbia, growth of conifers was depressed as far as 40 miles from the source of sulfur dioxide emission (Katz, 1949). Katz and McCallum (in McCabe, 1952) found western larch to be especially susceptible to injury, followed in order by Douglas-fir, Engelmann spruce, white pine, western yellow pine, cedar, lodgepole pine, silver fir, and white fir.

Illuminating Gas. Positive identification of injury by illuminating gas often is troublesome because symptoms may be indefinite in early stages or they may resemble those caused by other unfavorable environmental conditions such as high temperatures, deficiency or excess of water, mineral deficiency, and attacks by insects and fungi. Gas leaks cause injury to the roots, and this is followed by responses in leaves, twigs, and stems. Symptoms vary and depend on the amount of gas to which the roots are exposed. Slow leaks cause chlorosis and limited amounts of leaf abscission, followed by dieback of branches and crown discoloration. Exposure to rapid leaks causes almost immediate injury throughout the tree. Root symptoms include dieback, loss of bark, curvatures, and presence of tubercles. Leaves wilt, turn brown, and abscise. Buds dry out and die, and dormant buds may produce weak shoots. Dieback of branches commonly occurs, and as the cambium of the main stem and larger branches dies, the bark splits longitudinally and often peels. Injury to surrounding ground vegetation and odor of gas in the vicinity often foretell injury to trees (Marsden, 1950–1951).

Manufactured gas varies in composition, but it usually contains, among other constituents, several toxic substances, including ethylene and unsaturated hydrocarbons such as cyanogen compounds and hydrocyanic acid. The harmful effects of manufactured gas appear to be brought about through the direct action of the toxic unsaturated hydrocarbons as well as by displacement of air in the soil. Experiments at the Boyce Thompson Institute indicated that hydrocyanic acid and cyanogen compounds are important killing agents of manufactured gas. Hitchcock and his coworkers (1934) reported that removal of hydrocyanic acid by scrubbing rendered gas much less toxic to vegetation. Hydrogen cyanide usually is removed from manufactured gas during its manufacture. Natural gas consists largely of saturated hydrocarbons such as methane, ethane, and propane, which are not very toxic to plants, and it appears to injure plants chiefly by displacing oxygen from the soil.

Smog. An increasing cause of injury to plants is atmospheric pollution by the complex of substances called smog. Although many other substances occur in a smoggy atmosphere, most of the injury is attributed to substances produced by the reaction of unsaturated hydrocarbons with ozone in the atmosphere. These substances produce symptoms which are different from those produced by sulfur dioxide, illuminating gas, and other common air contaminants (Bobrov, 1955). Ozonated hexene has been used extensively as a synthetic smog in experimental work. It reduces photosynthesis and increases respiration in several kinds of plants. It also reduces growth of avocado seedlings (Taylor et al., 1958; Todd, 1958). Todd believes that smog has direct effects on growth processes in addition to its effects on photosynthesis and respiration.

GENERAL REFERENCES

Baker, F. S., 1950, Theory and practice of silviculture, McGraw-Hill Book Company, Inc., New York.
Billings, W. D., 1952, The environmental complex in relation to plant growth and distribution, Quart. Rev. Biology, 27:251–265.
Daubenmire, R. F., 1959, Plants and environment, John Wiley & Sons, Inc., New York.
Kozlowski, T. T., 1949, Light and water in relation to growth and competition of Piedmont forest tree species, Ecol. Mons., 19:207–231.
Levitt, J., 1956, The hardiness of plants, Academic Press, Inc., New York.
Lundegardh, H., 1931, Environment and plant development, Eng. transl., Edward Arnold & Co., London.
Oosting, H. J., 1956, The study of plant communities, W. H. Freeman Co., San Francisco.
Thomas, M. D., 1951, Gas damage to plants, Ann. Rev. Plant Physiology, 2:293–322.
Toumey, J. W., and C. F. Korstian, 1947, Foundations of silviculture upon an ecological basis, John Wiley & Sons, Inc., New York.

Wareing, P. F., 1956, Photoperiodism in woody plants, Ann. Rev. Plant Physiology, 7:191–214.

Wassink, E. C., and J. A. J. Stolwijk, 1956, Effects of light quality on plant growth, Ann. Rev. Plant Physiology, 7:373–400.

Went, F. W., 1957, The experimental control of plant growth, Chronica Botanica Co., Waltham, Mass.

Appendix

Common and Scientific Names of Species Mentioned in the Text [1]

COMMON NAMES

Abelia	*Abelia* spp.
Acacia	*Acacia* spp.
Agave or century plant	*Agave americana* L.
Ailanthus	*Ailanthus altissima* (Mill.) Swingle
Akamatu (*see* Pine)	
Albizia or "mimosa"	*Albizia* spp.
Alder, speckled	*Alnus rugosa* (Du Roi) Spreng.
Almond	*Prunus amygdalus* Batsch
Apple	*Malus pumila* Mill.
Apricot	*Prunus armeniaca* L.
Arborvitae (*see* Cedar)	
Ash, American mountain	*Sorbus americana* Marsh.
black	*Fraxinus nigra* Marsh.
European	*Fraxinus excelsior* L.
European mountain	*Sorbus aucuparia* L.
green or red	*Fraxinus pennsylvanica* Marsh.
prickly	*Zanthoxylum americanum* L.
white	*Fraxinus americana* L.
Aspen, European	*Populus tremula* L.
largetooth or bigtooth	*Populus grandidentata* Michx.
quaking or trembling	*Populus tremuloides* Michx.
Avocado	*Persea americana* Mill. (*P. gratissima* Gaertn.)
Baldcypress (*see* Cypress)	
Bamboo	*Phyllostachys edulis* A. & C. Riviere
Banana	*Musa sapientum* L.
Basswood, American, or American linden	*Tilia americana* L.
Oriental	*Tilia miqueliana* Maxim.

[1] Names of North American forest trees are based on E. L. Little, 1953, Check List of Native and Naturalized Trees of the United States, Agriculture Handbook No. 41, U.S. Forest Service, Washington, D.C. Names of other species are from various sources.

537

Batai   *Albizia falcata* L.
Bay, loblolly   *Gordonia lasianthus* (L.) Ellis
Bayberry (*see* Waxmyrtle)
Beech, American   *Fagus grandifolia* Ehrh.
  blue, or American hornbeam   *Carpinus caroliniana* Walt. (*Carpinus betulus virginiana* Marsh.)
  copper   *Fagus sylvatica* var. *atropunicea* West.
  European   *Fagus sylvatica* L.
Birch, gray or field   *Betula populifolia* Marsh.
  river   *Betula nigra* L.
  silver (European)   *Betula verrucosa* Ehrh.
  sweet   *Betula lenta* L.
  white or paper   *Betula papyrifera* Marsh.
  white (European)   *Betula alba* L. (*B. pubescens* Ehrh.)
  yellow   *Betula alleghaniensis* Britton (*B. lutea* Michx.)

Blackgum (*see* Gum)
Bluebeech (*see* Beech)
Blueberry, highbush   *Vaccinium corymbosum* L.
  lowbush   *Vaccinium angustifolium* Ait.
Boxelder (*see* Elder)
Boxwood   *Buxus sempervirens* L.
Brazil nut   *Bertholletia excelsa* Humb. & Bonpl.
Broadbean   *Vicia faba* L.
Broom   *Cytisus* spp.
Buckeye, California   *Aesculus californica* (Spach) Nutt.
  yellow   *Aesculus octandra* Marsh.
Buffaloberry, silver   *Shepherdia argentea* (Pursh) Nutt.
Butternut   *Juglans cinerea* L.
Buttonwood (*see* Sycamore)
Cacao   *Theobroma cacao* L.
Cactus (*see* Saguaro)
Camellia   *Camellia* spp.
Camphor-tree   *Cinnamomum camphora*, Nees Ederm.
Canelo   *Drimys winteri* Forst.
Carob   *Ceratonia siliqua* L.
Cassia   *Cassia multijuga* Rich.
Casuarina, horsetail   *Casuarina equisetifolia* L.
Catalpa, northern or hardy   *Catalpa speciosa* Warder
  southern   *Catalpa bignonioides* Walt.
Ceanothus, feltleaf   *Ceanothus arboreus* Greene
Cedar, eastern red   *Juniperus virginiana* L.
  northern white, or eastern arborvitae   *Thuja occidentalis* L.
  Oriental, or hiba arborvitae   *Thujopsis dolabrata* S. & Z.
  western red   *Thuja plicata* Don
Century plant (*see* Agave)
Cherry, black   *Prunus serotina* Ehrh.
  laurel   *Prunus laurocerasus* L.
  mahaleb   *Prunus mahaleb* L.
  pin   *Prunus pensylvanica* L. f.

Chestnut, American	*Castanea dentata* (Marsh.) Borkh.
Japanese, or kuri	*Castanea crenata* S. & A. (*C. sativa* var. *pubinervis* Mak.)
Chestnut oak (*see* Oak)	
Cinchona	*Cinchona* spp.
Citrus	*Citrus* spp.
Clove	*Syzygium aromaticum* (L.) Merr. & L. M. Perry
Cocklebur	*Xanthium* spp.
Coconut (*see* Palm)	
Coffee	*Coffea arabica* L.
Coffeetree, Kentucky	*Gymnocladus dioicus* (L.) K. Koch
Coleus	*Coleus blumei* Benth.
Cottonwood (*see* Poplar)	
Coyote bush (*see* Kidneywort)	
Cranberry, large or American	*Vaccinium macrocarpon* Ait.
small	*Vaccinium oxycoccus* L.
Creosote bush	*Larrea tridentata* (DC.) Coville [*Covillea tridentata* (DC.) Vail]
Cryptomeria or sugi	*Cryptomeria japonica* (L.F.) D. Don
Cuprea	*Remijia pedunculata* Triana
Currant, black	*Ribes nigrum* L.
Cypress, bald	*Taxodium distichum* (L.) Rich.
Hinoki	*Chamaecyparis obtusa* Endl.
Monterey	*Cupressus macrocarpa* Hartw.
Date palm (*see* Palm)	
Devils-walkingstick or Hercules-club	*Aralia spinosa* L.
Dogwood, flowering	*Cornus florida* L.
Douglas-fir (*see* Fir)	
Elder, American	*Sambucus canadensis* L.
Box	*Acer negundo* L.
European	*Sambucus nigra* L.
Elm, American or white	*Ulmus americana* L.
European white	*Ulmus laevis* Pall. (*U. pedunculata* Foug. *U. effusa* Willd.)
rock or cork	*Ulmus thomasii* Sarg.
Siberian	*Ulmus pumila* L.
slippery	*Ulmus rubra* Muhl.
wych	*Ulmus glabra* Huds.
Eucalyptus or eucalypt	*Eucalyptus* spp.
Feltleaf ceanothus (*see* Ceanothus)	
Fig, common	*Ficus carica* L.
Filbert	*Corylus avellana* L.
Fir, alpine or subalpine	*Abies lasiocarpa* (Hook.) Nutt.
balsam	*Abies balsamea* (L.) Mill.
Douglas	*Pseudotsuga menziesii* (Mirb.) Franco (*P. taxifolia*) (Poir.) Britton ex Sudw. *P. douglasii* (Lindl. Carr.)
European silver	*Abies alba* Miller [*A. pectinata* (DC.)]
grand or lowland white	*Abies grandis* (Dougl.) Lindl.

Fir (*continued*)
  noble

Abies procera Rehd. [*A. nobilis* (Dougl.) Lindl.]

  Pacific silver or silver
  white

Abies amabilis (Dougl.) Forbes
Abies concolor (Gord. and Glend.) Lindl.

Gallberry   *Ilex coriacea* (Pursh) Chapm.

Ginkgo   *Ginkgo biloba* L.

Grape   *Vitis* spp.

Grapefruit   *Citrus paradisi* Macf.

Guayule   *Parthenium argentatum* L.

Gum, black, or black tupelo   *Nyssa sylvatica* Marsh.

  red or sweet   *Liquidambar styraciflua* L.

  tupelo, or water tupelo   *Nyssa aquatica* L.

Hackberry   *Celtis occidentalis* L.

Hawthorn   *Crataegus* spp.

Hemlock, eastern   *Tsuga canadensis* (L.) Carr.

  western   *Tsuga heterophylla* (Raf.) Sarg.

Hercules-club (*see* Devils-walkingstick)

Hiba arborvitae (*see* Cedar)

Hickory, bitternut   *Carya cordiformis* (Wangenh.) K. Koch

  mockernut   *Carya tomentosa* Nutt.

  pignut   *Carya glabra* (Mill.) Sweet

  shagbark   *Carya ovata* (Mill.) K. Koch

Hinoki-cypress (*see* Cypress)

Holly, American   *Ilex opaca* Ait.

Honeylocust (*see* Locust)

Honeysuckle   *Lonicera* spp.

Hophornbeam, eastern   *Ostrya virginiana* (Mill.) K. Koch

Hornbeam (*see* Beech)

Horsechestnut   *Aesculus hippocastanum* L.

Horsetail casuarina (*see* Casuarina)

Inkberry   *Ilex glabra* (L.) Gray

Ivy, English   *Hedera helix* L.

Jasmine   *Jasminum* spp.

Juniper   *Juniperus* spp.

Kauri   *Agathis australis* Salisb.

Kentucky coffeetree (*see* Coffee)

Kidneywort or Coyote bush   *Baccharis pilularis* DC.

Konara (*see* Oak)

Kuri (*see* Chestnut)

Larch, American, or Tamarack   *Larix laricina* (Du Roi) K. Koch

  European   *Larix decidua* Mill. (*L. europaea* DC.)

  Japanese   *Larix leptolepis* Murr.

Laurel, cherry (*see* Cherry)

Lemon   *Citrus limon* (L.) Burm. f.

Ligustrum (*see* Privet)

Lilac   *Syringa vulgaris* L.

Linden (*see* Basswood)

Locust, black or yellow   *Robinia pseudoacacia* L.

  honey   *Gleditsia triacanthos* L.

Lodgepole pine (*see* Pine)

Lotus, East Indian	*Nelumbo nucifera* Gaertn.
Magnolia, southern	*Magnolia grandiflora* L.
Mahaleb cherry (*see* Cherry)	
Mahogany	*Swietenia macrophylla* King.
West Indies	*Swietenia mahogani* Jacq.
Mangrove	*Rhizophora mangle* L.
black	*Avicennia nitida* Jacq.
Maple, bigleaf	*Acer macrophyllum* Pursh.
black	*Acer nigrum* Michx. f.
Japanese	*Acer palmatum* Thunb. (*A. polymorphum* S. and Z.)
Norway	*Acer platanoides* L.
red (including trident)	*Acer rubrum* L.
silver	*Acer saccharinum* L.
striped	*Acer pensylvanicum* L.
sugar	*Acer saccharum* Marsh.
sycamore	*Acer pseudoplatanus* L.
Mazzard	*Prunus avium* (L.) L.
Mimosa or sensitive plant	*Mimosa pudica* L.
"Mimosa" (*see* Albizia)	
Mistletoe, American	*Phoradendron* spp.
dwarf	*Arceuthobium* spp.
Mountain-ash (*see* Ash)	
Mulberry, red	*Morus rubra* L.
white (European)	*Morus alba* L.
Mullein	*Verbascum thapsus* L.
Oak, black	*Quercus velutina* Lam.
blackjack	*Quercus marilandica* Muenchh.
bur	*Quercus macrocarpa* Michx.
California black	*Quercus kelloggii* Newb.
California live	*Quercus agrifolia* Nee
chestnut	*Quercus prinus* L.
cork	*Quercus suber* L.
English	*Quercus robur* L.
Gambel	*Quercus gambelii* Nutt.
Japanese, or konara	*Quercus acutissima* Carr.
Japanese live, or shirakashi	*Quercus myrsinaefolia* Blume
live	*Quercus virginiana* Mill.
northern pin	*Quercus ellipsoidalis* E. J. Hill
northern red or eastern red	*Quercus rubra* L. [*Q. borealis* var. *maxima* (Marsh.) Ashe]
overcup	*Quercus lyrata* Walt.
pedunculate (European)	*Quercus pedunculata* Ehrh.
pin	*Quercus palustris* Muenchh.
post	*Quercus stellata* Wangenh.
scarlet	*Quercus coccinea* Muenchh.
southern red	*Quercus falcata* Michx.
swamp white	*Quercus bicolor* Willd.
turkey	*Quercus laevis* Walt. (*Q. catesbaei* Walt.)
willow	*Quercus phellos* L.
Oleaster	*Elaeagnus angustifolia* L.

Olive	*Olea europaea* L.
Orange, sweet	*Citrus sinensis* Osbeck
Osage-orange	*Maclura pomifera* (Raf.) Schneld.
Palm, attalea	*Attalea excelsa* Mart.
carnauba	*Copernicia cerifera* Mart.
coconut	*Cocos nucifera* L.
date	*Phoenix dactylifera* L.
oil	*Elaeis guineensis* Jacq.
raffia	*Raphia pedunculata* Beauv. (*R. ruffia* Mart.)
wax	*Ceroxylon andicola* Humb.
Papaya	*Carica papaya* L.
Paulownia, Royal	*Paulownia tomentosa* (Thunb.) S. and Z.
Pawpaw	*Asimina triloba* (L.) Dunal
Peach	*Prunus persica* (L.) Batsch
Pear, common	*Pyrus communis* L.
Japanese	*Pyrus serotina* var. *culta* Rehd.
Pecan	*Carya illinoensis* (Wangenh.) K. Koch
Pedunculate oak (*see* Oak)	
Pepperbush, sweet	*Clethra alnifolia* L.
Persimmon, common	*Diospyros virginiana* L.
Japanese	*Diospyros Kaki* L. f. (*D. chinensis* Blume)
Phillyrea	*Phillyrea media* L.
Pine, Austrian	*Pinus nigra* Arnold (*P. laricio* Poir.)
black	*Pinus nigra* var. *austriaca* Aschers. & Graebn.
bristlecone	*Pinus aristata* Engelm.
Chihuahua	*Pinus leiophylla* var. *chihuahuana* (Engelm.) Shaw
Corsican	[*Pinus nigra* var. *calabrica* (Loud.) Schneider] (*P. laricio corsicana* Loud.) [*Pinus nigra* var. *poiretiapa* (Ont.) Aschers. & Graebn.]
Coulter	*Pinus coulteri* D. Don
Digger	*Pinus sabiniana* Dougl.
eastern white	*Pinus strobus* L.
jack	*Pinus banksiana* Lamb.
Japanese red, or akamatu	*Pinus densiflora* S. & Z.
Jeffrey	*Pinus jeffreyi* Grev. and Balf.
loblolly	*Pinus taeda* L.
lodgepole	*Pinus contorta* Dougl.
longleaf	*Pinus palustris* Mill.
Monterey	*Pinus radiata* D. Don
Mugo or Swiss mountain	*Pinus mugo* Turra
pinyon	*Pinus edulis* Engelm.
pitch	*Pinus rigida* Mill.
pond	*Pinus serotina* Michx.
ponderosa or western yellow (Rocky Mountain form)	*Pinus ponderosa* Laws. *Pinus ponderosa* var. *scopulorum* Engelm.
red or Norway	*Pinus resinosa* Ait.

Pine (*continued*)
  sand
  Scotch
  shortleaf
  slash
  sugar
  Swiss stone or Siberian
  table-mountain
  Virginia or scrub
  western white
  whitebark
Pineapple
Pinyon (*see* Pine)
Pittosporum

Plane, London
Plum, garden
Poplar, balsam
  black (European)
  California, or black cottonwood
  Eastern, or eastern cottonwood
  Lombardy
  "robusta"

  yellow, or tuliptree
Poppy, opium
Prickly-ash (*see* Ash)
Privet or ligustrum
Prune (*see* Plum)
Quince
Redbud, eastern
Redcedar (*see* Cedar)
Redwood
Rhododendron
Rose
Rosemary
Rubber
Saguaro or giant cactus

Sandalwood, white
Sapodilla
Sassafras
Sausage-tree
Sawa-gurumi (*see* Wingnut)
Sea-buckthorn
Sequoia, giant
Serviceberry, downy, or shadbush
Shii
Shirakashi (*see* Oak)
Sourwood
Spruce, black

Pinus clausa (Chapm.) Vasey
Pinus sylvestris L.
Pinus echinata Mill.
Pinus elliottii Engelm.
Pinus lambertiana Dougl.
Pinus cembra L.
Pinus pungens Lamb.
Pinus virginiana Mill.
Pinus monticola Dougl.
Pinus albicaulis Engelm.
Ananas comosus (L.) Merr.

Pittosporum tobira, Ait. (*Euonymus tobira*, Thunb.)
Platanus acerifolia Willd.
Prunus domestica L.
Populus balsamifera L.
Populus nigra L.
Populus trichocarpa Torr. and Gray
Populus deltoides Bartr.
Populus nigra var. *italica* Dur.
Populus robusta (*angulata x nigra plantierensis*)
Liriodendron tulipifera L.
Papaver somniferum L.

Ligustrum spp.

Cydonia oblonga Mill. (*C. vulgaris* Pers.)
Cercis canadensis L.

Sequoia sempervirens (D. Don) Endl.
Rhododendron spp.
Rosa spp.
Rosmarinus officinalis L.
Hevea brasiliensis Muell. Arg.
Cereus giganteus Engelm.
(*Carnegiea gigantea* Britt. & Rose)
Santalum album L.
Achras zapota L.
Sassafras albidum (Nutt.) Nees
Kigelia africana (Lam.) Benth.

Hippophaë rhamnoides L.
Sequoia gigantea (Lindl.) Decne.
Amelanchier arborea (Michx. f.) Fern.
Shiia Sieboldi Makino

Oxydendrum arboreum (L.) DC.
Picea mariana (Mill.) B.S.P.

Spruce (*continued*)
blue
Engelmann
Norway

red
Sitka
white
Spurge
Sugi (*see* Cryptomeria)
Sumac, staghorn
winged or shining
Sunflower
Sycamore, America, or
Sycamore maple (*see* Maple)
Tamarack (*see* Larch)
Tanoak

Tea
Tobacco
tree
Tomato
Tuliptree (*see* Poplar)
Tung
Tupelo (*see* Gum)
Viburnum
Walnut, black
English
Waxmyrtle or southern bayberry
Weigela
Willow, arctic
arroyo
black
crack
weeping
white
Willow oak (*see* Oak)
Wingnut or sawa-gurumi
Witch-hazel
Yama-guruma
Yellow-poplar (*see* Poplar)
Yellowwood
Yew
Zelkowa

Picea pungens Engelm.
Picea engelmannii Parry
Picea abies (L.) Karst. (*Picea excelsa* Link)
Picea rubens Sarg.
Picea sitchensis (Bong.) Carr.
Picea glauca (Moench) Vosa
Euphorbia spp.

Rhus typhina L.
Rhus copallina L.
Helianthus annuus L.
Platanus occidentalis L.

Lithocarpus densiflorus (Hook. & Arn.) Rehd.
Thea sinensis L. (*Camellia Thea* Link.)
Nicotiana tabacum L.
Nicotiana glauca Graham
Lycopersicon esculentum Mill.

Aleurites fordii Hemsl.

Viburnum spp.
Juglans nigra L.
Juglans regia L.
Myrica cerifera L.
Weigela spp.
Salix glauca L.
Salix lasiolepis Benth.
Salix nigra Marsh.
Salix fragilis L.
Salix babylonica L.
Salix alba L.

Pterocarya rhoifolia S. and Z.
Hamamelis virginiana L.
Trochodendron aralioides S.

Cladrastis lutea (Michx. f.) K. Koch
Taxus spp.
Zelkowa serrata Makino

GENUS NAMES

Abelia spp.
Abies alba
amabilis
balsamea

Abelia
European silver fir
Pacific silver or silver fir
Balsam fir

Abies (*continued*)	
concolor	White fir
grandis	Grand or lowland white fir
lasiocarpa	Alpine or subalpine fir
procera	Noble fir
Acacia spp.	Acacia
Acer macrophyllum	Bigleaf maple
negundo	Boxelder
nigrum	Black maple
palmatum	Japanese maple
pensylvanicum	Striped maple
platanoides	Norway maple
pseudoplatanus	Sycamore maple
rubrum	Red maple (including trident)
saccharinum	Silver maple
saccharum	Sugar maple
Achras zapota	Sapodilla
Aesculus californica	California buckeye
hippocastanum	Horsechestnut
octandra	Yellow buckeye
Agathis australis	Kauri
Agave americana	Agave or century plant
Ailanthus altissima	Ailanthus
Albizia spp.	Albizia or "mimosa"
falcata	Batai
Aleurites fordii	Tung
Alnus rugosa	Speckled alder
Amelanchier arborea	Downy serviceberry or shadbush
Ananas comosus	Pineapple
Aralia spinosa	Devils-walkingstick or Hercules-club
Arceuthobium	Dwarf mistletoe
Asimina triloba	Pawpaw
Attalea excelsa	Attalea palm
Avicennia nitida	Black mangrove
Baccharis pilularis	Kidneywort or coyote bush
Bertholletia excelsa	Brazil nut
Betula alba	White birch (European)
alleghaniensis or *lutea*	Yellow birch
lenta	Sweet birch
nigra	River birch
papyrifera	White or paper birch
populifolia	Gray or field birch
verrucosa	Silver birch (European)
Buxus sempervirens	Boxwood
Camellia spp.	Camellia
Carica papaya	Papaya
Carpinus caroliniana	Bluebeech or American hornbeam
Carya cordiformis	Bitternut hickory
glabra	Pignut hickory
illinoensis	Pecan
ovata	Shagbark hickory

Carya (*continued*)
  tomentosa   Mockernut hickory
Cassia multijuga   Cassia
Castanea crenata   Japanese chestnut or kurí
  dentata   American chestnut
Casuarina equisetifolia   Horsetail casuarina
Catalpa bignonioides   Southern catalpa
  speciosa   Northern or hardy catalpa
Ceanothus arboreus   Feltleaf ceanothus
Celtis occidentalis   Hackberry
Ceratonia siliqua   Carob
Cercis canadensis   Eastern redbud
Cereus giganteus   Saguaro or giant cactus
Ceroxylon andicola   Wax palm
Chamaecyparis obtusa   Hinoki cypress
Cinchona spp.   Cinchona
Cinnamomum camphora   Camphor-tree
Citrus spp.   Citrus
  limon   Lemon
  paradisi   Grapefruit
  sinensis   Sweet orange
Cladrastis lutea   Yellowwood
Clethra alnifolia   Sweet pepperbush
Cocos nucifera   Coconut palm
Coffea arabica   Coffee
Coleus blumei   Coleus
Copernicia cerifera   Carnauba palm
Cornus florida   Flowering dogwood
Corylus avellana   Filbert
Crataegus spp.   Hawthorn
Crypotomeria japonica   Cryptomeria or sugi
Cupressus macrocarpa   Monterey cypress
Cydonia oblonga   Quince
Cytisus spp.   Broom
Diospyros Kaki   Japanese persimmon
  virginiana   Common persimmon
Drimys winteri   Canelo
Elaeagnus angustifolia   Oleaster
Elaeis guineensis   Oil palm
Eucalyptus spp.   Eucalyptus or eucalypt
Euphorbia spp.   Spurge
Fagus grandifolia   American beech
  sylvatica   European beech
  sylvatica var. *atropunicea*   Copper beech
Ficus carica   Common fig
Fraxinus americana   White ash
  excelsior   European ash
  nigra   Black ash
  pennsylvanica   Green or red ash
Ginkgo biloba   Ginkgo
Gleditsia triacanthos   Honeylocust

Gordonia lasianthus	Loblolly bay
Gymnocladus dioicus	Kentucky coffeetree
Hamamelis virginiana	Witch-hazel
Hedera helix	English ivy
Helianthus annuus	Sunflower
Hevea brasiliensis	Rubber
Hippophaë rhamnoides	Sea-buckthorn
Ilex coriacea	Gallberry
glabra	Inkberry
opaca	American holly
Jasminum spp.	Jasmine
Juglans cinerea	Butternut
nigra	Black walnut
regia	English walnut
Juniperus spp.	Juniper
virginiana	Eastern red cedar
Kigelia africana	Sausage-tree
Larix decidua	European larch
laricina	American larch or tamarack
leptolepis	Japanese larch
Larrea tridentata	Creosote bush
Ligustrum spp.	Privet or ligustrum
Liquidambar styraciflua	Red- or sweetgum
Liriodendron tulipifera	Yellow-poplar or tuliptree
Lithocarpus densiflorus	Tanoak
Lonicera spp.	Honeysuckle
Lycopersicon esculentum	Tomato
Maclura pomifera	Osage-orange
Magnolia grandiflora	Southern magnolia
Malus pumila	Apple
Mimosa pudica	Mimosa or sensitive plant
Morus alba	White (European) mulberry
rubra	Red mulberry
Musa sapientum	Banana
Myrica cerifera	Waxmyrtle or southern bayberry
Nelumbo nucifera	East Indian lotus
Nicotiana glauca	Tree tobacco
tabacum	Tobacco
Nyssa aquatica	Tupelo-gum or water tupelo
sylvatica	Blackgum or black tupelo
Olea europaea	Olive
Ostrya virginiana	Eastern hophornbeam
Oxydendrum arboreum	Sourwood
Papaver somniferum	Opium poppy
Parthenium argentatum	Guayule
Paulownia tomentosa	Royal paulownia
Persea americana	Avocado
Phillyrea media	Phillyrea
Phoenix dactylifera	Date palm
Phoradendron spp.	American mistletoe
Phyllostachys edulis	Bamboo

Picea abies	Norway spruce
engelmannii	Engelmann spruce
glauca	White spruce
mariana	Black spruce
pungens	Blue spruce
rubens	Red spruce
sitchensis	Sitka spruce
Pinus albicaulis	Whitebark pine
aristata	Bristlecone pine
banksiana	Jack pine
cembra	Swiss stone or Siberian pine
clausa	Sand pine
contorta	Lodgepole pine
coulteri	Coulter pine
densiflora	Japanese red pine or akamatu
echinata	Shortleaf pine
edulis	Pinyon pine
elliottii	Slash pine
jeffreyi	Jeffrey pine
lambertiana	Sugar pine
leiophylla	Chihuahua pine
monticola	Western white pine
mugo	Mugo or Swiss mountain pine
nigra	Austrian pine
nigra var. *austriaca*	Black pine
nigra var. *calabrica*	Corsican pine
nigra var. *poiretiapa*	
palustris	Longleaf pine
ponderosa	Ponderosa or western yellow pine
ponderosa var. *scopulorum*	Ponderosa pine, Rocky Mountain form
pungens	Table-mountain pine
radiata	Monterey pine
resinosa	Red or Norway pine
rigida	Pitch pine
sabiniana	Digger pine
serotina	Pond pine
strobus	Eastern white pine
sylvestris	Scotch pine
taeda	Loblolly pine
virginiana	Virginia or scrub pine
Pittosporum tobira	Pittosporum
Platanus acerifolia	London plane
occidentalis	American sycamore or buttonwood
Populus balsamifera	Balsam poplar
deltoides	Eastern poplar or eastern cottonwood
grandidentata	Largetooth or bigtooth aspen
nigra	Black poplar (European)
nigra var. *italica*	Lombardy poplar
robusta	"Robusta" poplar
tremula	European aspen
tremuloides	Quaking or trembling aspen

Populus (*continued*)	
trichocarpa	California poplar or black cottonwood
Prunus amygdalus	Almond
armeniaca	Apricot
avium	Mazzard
domestica	Garden plum
laurocerasus	Laurel cherry
mahaleb	Mahaleb cherry
pensylvanica	Pin cherry
persica	Peach
serotina	Black cherry
Pseudotsuga menziesii	Douglas-fir
Pterocarya rhoifolia	Wingnut or sawa-gurumi
Pyrus communis	Common pear
serotina	Japanese pear
Quercus acutissima	Japanese oak or konara
agrifolia	California live oak
bicolor	Swamp white oak
coccinea	Scarlet oak
ellipsoidalis	Northern pin oak
falcata	Southern red oak
gambelii	Gambel oak
glauca	Japanese live oak
kelloggii	or drakashi
laevis	California black oak
lyrata	Turkey oak
macrocarpa	Overcup oak
marilandica	Bur oak
myrsinaefolia	Blackjack oak
palustris	Japanese live oak or shirakashi
pedunculata	Pin oak
phellos	Pedunculate oak (European)
prinus	Willow oak
robur	Chestnut oak
rubra	English oak
stellata	Northern red or eastern red oak
suber	Post oak
velutina	Cork oak
virginiana	Black oak
Raphia pedunculata	Live oak
Remijia pedunculata	Raffia
Rhizophora mangle	Cuprea
Rhododendron spp.	Mangrove
Rhus copallina	Rhododendron
typhina	Winged or shining sumac
Ribes nigrum	Staghorn sumac
Robinia pseudoacacia	Black currant
Rosa spp.	Black or yellow locust
Rosmarinus officinalis	Rose
Salix alba	Rosemary
babylonica	White willow
fragilis	Weeping willow
	Crack willow

Salix (*continued*)
glauca — Arctic willow
lasiolepis — Arroyo willow
nigra — Black willow
Sambucus canadensis — American elder
nigra — European elder
Santalum album — White sandalwood
Sassafras albidum — Sassafras
Sequoia gigantea — Giant sequoia
sempervirens — Redwood
Shepherdia argentea — Silver buffaloberry
Shiia Sieboldi — Shii
Sorbus americana — American mountain-ash
aucuparia — European mountain-ash
Swietenia macrophylla — Mahogany
mahogani — West Indies Mahogany
Syringa vulgaris — Lilac
Syzygium aromaticum — Clove
Taxodium distichum — Baldcypress
Taxus spp. — Yew
Thea sinensis — Tea
Theobroma cacao — Cacao
Thuja occidentalis — Northern white-cedar or eastern arborvitae
plicata — Western redcedar
Thujopsis dolabrata — Oriental cedar or hiba arborvitae
Tilia americana — American basswood or American linden
miqueliana — Oriental basswood
Trochodendron aralioides — Yama-guruma
Tsuga canadensis — Eastern hemlock
heterophylla — Western hemlock
Ulmus americana — American or white elm
effusa — European white elm
glabra — Wych elm
pumila — Siberian elm
rubra — Slippery elm
thomasii — Rock or cork elm
Vaccinium angustifolium — Lowbush blueberry
corymbosum — Highbush blueberry
macrocarpon — Large or American cranberry
oxycoccus — Small cranberry
Verbascum thapsus — Mullein
Viburnum spp. — Viburnum
Vicia faba — Broadbean
Vitis spp. — Grape
Weigela spp. — Weigela
Xanthium spp. — Cocklebur
Zanthoxylum americanum — Prickly-ash
Zelkowa serrata — Zelkowa

Bibliography

Aaltonen, V. T., 1955, Die Blättanalyse als Bonitierungsgrundlage des Waldbodens, Inst. Forestry Fennica Commun., 45(2):1-21.

Abell, C. A., and C. R. Hursh, 1931, Positive gas and water pressure in oaks, Science, 73:449.

Ackley, W. B., 1954a, Seasonal and diurnal changes in the water contents and water deficits of Bartlett pear leaves, Plant Physiology, 29:445-448.

——, 1954b, Water contents and water deficits of leaves of Bartlett pear trees on the two rootstocks, Pyrus communis and P. serotina, Am. Soc. Hort. Sci. Proc., 64:181-185.

Adams, A. J. S., 1940, Observations on root fusions in Monterey pine, Australian Forests, 5:78-80.

Adams, W. R., 1934, The influence of soil temperature on the germination and development of white pine seedlings, Vermont Agr. Expt. Sta. Bull. 379.

Addicott, F. T., and R. S. Lynch, 1955, Physiology of abscission, Ann. Rev. Plant Physiology, 6:211-238.

——, ——, and H. R. Carns, 1955, Auxin gradient theory of abscission regulation, Science, 121:644-645.

Addoms, R. M., 1931, Notes on the nutrient requirements and the histology of the cranberry (Vaccinium macrocarpon Ait.) with special reference to mycorrhiza, Plant Physiology, 6:653-668.

——, 1937, Nutritional studies on loblolly pine, Plant Physiology, 12:199-205.

Ahrns, W., 1924, Weitere Untersuchungen über die Abhängigkeit des Gegenseitigen Mengenverhältnisse der Kohlenhydrate in Laubblatt vom Wassergehalt, Bot. Archiv, 5:234-259.

Albertson, F. W., and J. E. Weaver, 1945, Injury and death or recovery of trees in prairie climate, Ecol. Mons., 15:393-433.

Aldous, A. E., 1929, The eradication of brush and weeds from pasture lands, Am. Soc. Agron. Jour., 21:660-666.

Aldrich, W. W., and R. A. Work, 1934, Evaporating power of the air and top-root ratio in relation to rate of pear fruit enlargement, Am. Soc. Hort. Sci. Proc., 32:115-123.

Aldrich-Blake, R. N., 1935, A note on the influence of seed weight on plant weight, Forestry, 9:54-57.

Allen, E. K., and O. N. Allen, 1958, Biological aspects of symbiotic nitrogen fixation, in W. Ruhland (ed.), Encyclopedia of plant physiology, vol. 8, pp. 48-118, Springer-Verlag, Berlin.

551

Allen, G. S., 1942, Douglas fir seed from young trees, Jour. Forestry, 37:935–938.

——, 1957, Storage behavior of conifer seeds in sealed containers held at 0°F., 32°F., and room temperature, Jour. Forestry, 55:278–281.

Allen, R. M., 1953, Release and fertilization stimulate longleaf pine cone crop, Jour. Forestry, 51:827.

——, 1955, Foliage treatments improve survival of longleaf pine plantings, Jour. Forestry, 53:724–727.

—— and A. L. McComb, 1955, Über Faktoren, die Bewurzelung der Stecklinge von der *Populus deltoides* Bartr. beeinflussen, Zentralbl. Forstwesen, 74:199–220.

—— and T. E. Maki, 1955, Response of longleaf pine seedlings to soils and fertilizers, Soil Sci., 79:359–362.

Allmendinger, D. F., A. L. Kenworthy, and E. L. Overholser, 1943, The carbon dioxide intake of apple leaves as affected by reducing the available soil water to different levels, Am. Soc. Hort. Sci. Proc., 42:133–140.

Allsopp, A., and P. Misra, 1940, The constitution of the cambium, the new wood, and mature sapwood of the common ash, the common elm, and the Scotch pine, Biochem. Jour., 34:1078–1084.

Alten, F., and W. Doehring, 1952, Die Düngung in der Forstwirtschaft, Zeitschr. Pflanzenernähr. Düng. Bodenk., 59:145–157.

Alway, F. J., J. Kittredge, and W. J. Methley, 1933, Components of the forest floor layers under different forest trees on the same soil type, Soil Sci., 36:387–398.

——, T. E. Maki, and W. J. Methley, 1934, Composition of the leaves of some forest trees, Am. Soil Survey Assoc. Bull. 15.

—— and R. Zon, 1930, Quantity and nutrient contents of pine leaf litter, Jour. Forestry, 28:715–727.

Andel, O. M. van, 1953, The influence of salts on the exudation of tomato plants, Acta Bot. Neerl., 2:445–521.

Anderson, D. B., and T. Kerr, 1943, A note on the growth behavior of cotton bolls, Plant Physiology, 18:261–269.

Anderson, E., 1951, Healing time for pruned Douglas fir, U.S. Forest Prods. Lab. Rept. R1907, Madison, Wis.

Anderson, L. C., 1935, A survey of the behavior of cherry trees in the Hudson River valley with particular reference to losses from winter killing and other causes, New York State Agr. Expt. Sta. (Geneva) Bull. 653.

Anderssen, F. G., 1929, Some seasonal changes in the tracheal sap of pear and apricot trees, Plant Physiology, 4:459–476.

——, 1932, Chlorosis of deciduous fruit trees due to a copper deficiency, Jour. Pomology, 10:130–146.

Andersson, N. E., C. H. Hertz, and H. Rufelt, 1954, A new fast recording hygrometer for plant transpiration measurements, Physiologia Plantarum, 7:753–767.

Ando, A., 1952, On the seasonal variation of the nutrient elements in Sugi and Hinoki seedlings, Tokyo Univ. Forests Bull., 42:151–161.

Arcichovskij, V., and A. Ossipov, 1931, Die Saugkraft der baumartigen Pflanzen der zentralasiastischen Wüsten nebst Transpirationsmessungen am Saxaul (*Arthrophytum haloxylon* Litw.), Planta, 14:552–565.

Arisz, W. H., 1956, Significance of the symplasm theory for transport in the root, Protoplasma, 56:5–62.

——, R. J. Helder, and R. van Nie, 1951, Analysis of the exudation process in tomato plants, Jour. Exptl. Botany, 2:257–297.

Ark, P. A., and H. E. Thomas, 1936, *Anguillulina pratensis* in relation to root injury of apple and other fruit trees, Phytopathology, 26:1128–1134.

Army, T. J., and T. T. Kozlowski, 1951, Availability of soil moisture for active absorption in drying soil, Plant Physiology, 26:353–362.

Arnborg, T., 1946, A few successful results from bark ringing and strangulation, Skogen (Stockholm), 33:84–85.

Arndt, C. H., 1945, Temperature-growth relations of the roots and hypocotyls of cotton seedlings, Plant Physiology, 20:200–220.

Arnold, A., 1952, Über den Functionsmechanismus der Endodermiszellen der Wurzeln, Protoplasma, 41:189–211.

Arrhenius, O., 1942, Fettmängdens variation hos våra träd, Svensk. Bot. Tidskr., 36:95–99.

Ashby, E., 1932, Transpiratory organs of *Larrea tridentata* and their ecological significance, Ecology, 13:182–188.

Ashby, W. C., and H. Hellmers, 1955, Temperature requirements for germination in relation to wild-land seeding, Jour. Range Management, 8:80–83.

Askenasy, E., 1895, Ueber das Saftsteigen, Botan. Zentralbl., 62:237–238.

Atkins, W. R. G., 1916, Some recent researches in plant physiology, Whitaker and Co., London.

Auchter, E. C., 1923, Is there normally a cross transfer of foods, water, and mineral nutrients in woody plants? Maryland Agr. Expt. Sta. Bull. 257.

Audus, L. J., 1935, The effect of handling on the respiration of cherry laurel leaves, New Phytologist, 34:403–406.

———, 1947, The effects of illumination on the respiration of shoots of the cherry laurel, Ann. Botany, 11:165–201.

———, 1953, Plant growth substances, Interscience Publishers, Inc., New York.

Avery, G. S., and A. F. Blakeslee, 1943, Mutation rate in Datura seed which had been buried 39 years, Genetics, 28:69–70.

———, P. R. Burkholder, and Harriet B. Creighton, 1937, Production and distribution of growth hormone in shoots of *Aesculus* and *Malus,* and its probable role in stimulating cambial activity, Am. Jour. Botany, 24:51–58.

———, E. B. Johnson, R. M. Addoms, and B. F. Thomson, 1947, Hormones and horticulture, McGraw-Hill Book Company, Inc., New York.

Bagda, H., 1948, Morphologische und biologische Untersuchungen über Valonia Eichen (*Quercus macrolepis* Ky.) im Haci-Kadin-Tal bei Ankara, Univ. Ankara fac. sci. commun., 1:89–125.

Bailey, I. W., 1925, The "spruce budworm" biocoenose. I. Frost rings as indicators of the chronology of specific biological events, Bot. Gaz., 80:93–100.

———, 1954, Contributions to plant anatomy, Chronica Botanica Co., Waltham, Mass.

Bailey, L. F., 1948, Leaf oils from Tennessee Valley conifers, Jour. Forestry, 46:882–889.

Baines, R. C., and O. F. Clarke, 1952, Some effects of the citrus-root nematode on the growth of orange and lemon trees, Phytopathology, 42:1.

Baker, F. S., 1949, A revised tolerance table, Jour. Forestry, 47:179–181.

———, 1950, Principles of silviculture, McGraw-Hill Book Company, Inc., New York.

Baker, H., and W. O. James, 1933, The behaviour of dyes in the transpiration stream of sycamore (*Acer pseudoplatanus*), New Phytologist, 32:245–260.

Balch, R. E., 1952, Studies of the balsam woolly aphid *Adelges piceae* (Ratz.) and its effects on balsam fir, *Abies balsamea* (L.) Mill., Canadian Dept. Agr. Pub. 867.

Baldwin, H. I., 1931, The period of height growth in some northeastern conifers, Ecology, 12:665–689.

———, 1934, Some physiological effects of girdling on northern hardwoods, Torrey Bot. Club Bull., 61:249–257.

———, 1938, Forest tree seed, Chronica Botanica Co., Waltham, Mass.

Bange, G. G. J., 1953, On the quantitative explanation of stomatal transpiration, Acta Bot. Neerl., 2:255–297.

Bangham, W. N., 1934, Internal pressure in latex systems, Science, 80:290.

Bannan, M. W., 1942, Notes on the origin of adventitious roots in the native Ontario conifers, Am. Jour. Botany, 29:593–598.

———, 1951, The annual cycle of size changes in the fusiform cambial cells of *Chamaecyparis* and *Thuja*, Canadian Jour. Botany, 29:421–437.

———, 1955, The vascular cambium and radial growth in *Thuja occidentalis*, Canadian Jour. Botany, 33:113–138.

———, 1956, Some aspects of the elongation of fusiform cambial cells in *Thuja occidentalis* L., Canadian Jour. Botany, 34:175–196.

Barber, J. C., K. W. Dorman, and R. A. Jordan, 1955, Slash pine crown width differences appear at early age in 1-parent progeny tests, U.S. Forest Service Southeastern Forest Expt. Sta. Research Note, no. 860.

Bard, G. E., 1945, Mineral nutrient content of the foliage of forest trees on three soil types of varying limestone content, Soil Sci. Soc. America Proc., 10:419–422.

Barnes, R. L., 1958, Studies on physiology of isolated pine roots and root callus cultures, Ph.D. dissertation, Duke University, Durham, N.C.

Barney, C. W., 1951, Effects of soil temperature and light intensity on root growth of loblolly pine seedlings, Plant Physiology, 26:146–163.

Bartels, J., 1933, Verdunstung, Bodenfeuchtigkeit und Sickerwasser unter natür-lichen Verhaltnissen, Zeitschr. gesamt Forstwesen, 65:204–219.

———, 1937, Witterung und Bodenfeuchtigkeit im Jahre 1936, Zeitschr. gesamt Forstwesen, 69:295–306.

Bartholomew, E. T., 1926, Internal decline of lemons. III. Water deficit in lemon fruits caused by excessive leaf evaporation, Am. Jour. Botany, 13:102–117.

Barton, L. V., 1935, Storage of some coniferous seeds, Boyce Thompson Inst. Contribs., 7:379–404.

———, 1939, Storage of elm seeds, Boyce Thompson Inst. Contribs., 10:221–233.

———, 1943, Effect of moisture fluctuations on the viability of seeds in storage, Boyce Thompson Inst. Contribs., 13:35–45.

———, 1950, Relation of different gases to the soaking injury of seeds, Boyce Thompson Inst. Contribs., 16:55–71.

Bates, C. J., and J. Roeser, 1928, Light intensities required for growth of coniferous seedlings, Am. Jour. Botany, 15:184–195.

Batjer, L. P., 1954, Plant regulators to prevent preharvest fruit drop, delay foliation and blossoming, and thin blossoms and young fruits, chap. 8 in H. B. Tukey (ed.), Plant regulators in agriculture, John Wiley & Sons, Inc., New York.

——— and E. S. Degman, 1940, Effect of various amounts of nitrogen, potassium, and phosphorus on growth and assimilation in young apple trees, Jour. Agr. Research, 60:101–116.

——— and B. L. Rogers, 1952, Fertilizer applications as related to nitrogen, phosphorus, potassium, calcium, and magnesium utilization by apple trees, Am. Soc. Hort. Sci. Proc., 60:1–6.

Baver, L. D., 1956, Soil physics, 3d ed., John Wiley & Sons, Inc., New York.

Baxter, D. V., 1943, Pathology in forest practice, John Wiley & Sons, Inc., New York.

Beal, J. A., 1942, Mortality of reproduction defoliated by the red-headed pine sawfly (*Neodiprion lecontei* Fitch), Jour. Forestry, 40:562–563.

Bear, F. E., 1942, Soils and fertilizers, John Wiley & Sons, Inc., New York.

Beasley, E. W., 1942, Effects of some chemically inert dusts upon the transpiration rate of yellow coleus plants, Plant Physiology, 17:101–108.

Beattie, J. M., and W. P. Judkins, 1952, Status of Ohio peach trees with respect to certain elements, Ohio Agr. Expt. Sta. Research Circ. 17.

Becker-Dillingen, J., 1937, The "yellow tip" disease of pine trees: a symptom of magnesium deficiency, Ernähr. Pflanze, 33:1–7.

Becquerel, P., 1934, La longévité des graines macrobiotiques, Acad. sci. (Paris) Comptes rendus, 199:1662–1664.

Beddie, A. D., 1941, Natural root grafts in New Zealand trees, Proc. Roy. Soc. (New Zealand) Trans., 71:199–203.

Beeson, K. C., V. A. Lazar, and S. G. Boyce, 1955, Some plant accumulators of the micronutrient elements, Ecology, 36:155–156.

Belehradek, J., 1957, Physiological aspects of heat and cold, Ann. Rev. Physiology, 19:59–82.

Belyea, H. C., and H. J. MacAloney, 1926, Winter injury to terminal buds of Scotch pine and other conifers, Jour. Forestry, 24:685–690.

Belyea, R. M., 1952, Death and deterioration of balsam fir weakened by spruce budworm defoliation in Ontario, Jour. Forestry, 50:729–738.

———, D. A. Fraser, and A. H. Rose, 1951, Seasonal growth of some trees in Ontario, Forestry Chronicle, 27:300–305.

Bennett, C. W., 1956, Biological relations of plant viruses, Ann. Rev. Plant. Physiology, 7:143–167.

Bennett, J. P., 1924, The distribution of carbohydrate foods in the apricot tree, Am. Soc. Hort. Sci. Proc., 21:372–384.

——— and J. Oserkowsky, 1933, Copper and iron in the tracheal sap of deciduous trees, Am. Jour. Botany, 20:632–637.

Bentley, J. A., 1958, The naturally-occurring auxins and inhibitors, Ann. Rev. Plant Physiology, 9:47–80.

Benzian, B., and R. G. Warren, 1957, Copper deficiency in Sitka spruce seedlings, Nature, 178:864–865.

Beskaravainyi, M. M., 1956, The formation of groups in pine plantings of the Kamyshinsk forest improvement support point, Agrobiologya, 1956(1):143–146; 1958, Biol. Abs., 32:38517.

Bethlamy, N., 1953, Estimating summer evapotranspiration losses in a Pennsylvania scrub oak forest, Soil Sci. Soc. America Proc., 17:295–297.

Biale, J. B., 1950, Postharvest physiology and biochemistry of fruits, Ann. Rev. Plant Physiology, 1:183–206.

Bialoglowski, J., 1936, Effect of extent and temperature of roots on transpiration of rooted lemon cuttings, Am. Soc. Hort. Sci. Proc., 34:96–102.

Bickerstaff, A., 1946, The effect of thinning upon the growth and yield of aspen stands, Project P-19, Canadian Dom. Forest Service Silvicult. Research Notes, no. 80, pp. 1–27.

Biddulph, O., 1941, Diurnal migration of injected radiophosphorus from bean leaves, Am. Jour. Botany, 28:348–352.

———, 1951, The translocation of minerals in plants, in E. Truog (ed.), Mineral nutrition of plants, University of Wisconsin Press, Madison, Wis.

———, S. Biddulph, R. Cory, and H. Koontz, 1958, Circulation patterns for phosphorus, sulfur and calcium in the bean plant, Plant Physiology, 33:293–300.

Biddulph, O., and R. Cory, 1957, An analysis of translocation in the phloem of the bean plant using THO, P^{32}, and C^{14}, Plant Physiology, 32:608–619.

——— and J. Markle, 1944, Translocation of radioactive phosphorus in the phloem of the cotton plant, Am. Jour. Botany, 31:551–555.

Biddulph, S., O. Biddulph, and R. Cory, 1958, Visual indications of upward movement of foliar applied P^{32} and C^{14} in the phloem of the bean stem, Am. Jour. Botany, 45:648–652.

Biebl, R., 1952, Die Wirkung verschiedener Stickstoffdünger auf die Transpiration einiger Kulturpflanzen, Zeitschr. Pflanzenernähr. Düng. Bodenk., 59:60–75.

Bilan, M. V., 1957, The stimulation of cone and seed production in pulpwood-size loblolly pine, D.F. dissertation, Duke University, School of Forestry, Durham, N.C.

Billings, W. D., 1938, The structure and development of old field shortleaf pine stands and certain associated physical properties of the soil, Ecol. Mons., 8:437–499.

———, 1952, The environmental complex in relation to plant growth and distribution, Quart. Rev. Biology, 27:251–265.

———, 1957, Physiological ecology, Ann. Rev. Plant Physiology, 8:375–392.

Birch-Hirschfeld, L., 1920, Untersuchungen über die Ausbreitungsgeschwindigkeit gelöster Stoffe in der Pflanze, Jahrb. wiss. Bot., 59:171–262.

Biswell, H. H., 1935, Effect of the environment upon the root habits of certain deciduous forest trees, Bot. Gaz., 96:676–708.

Björkman, E., 1942, Über die Bedingungen der Mykorrhizabildung bei Kiefer und Fichte, Symbolae Botanicae Upsaliensis, vol. 6, no. 2.

———, 1956, Über die Natur der Mykorrhizabildung unter besonderer Berücksichtigung der Waldbäume und die Anwendung in der forstlichen Praxis, Forstwiss. Zentralbl., 75:265–286.

Black, M., and P. F. Wareing, 1955, Growth studies in woody species. VII. Photoperiodic control of germination in *Betula pubescens* Ehrh., Physiologia Plantarum, 8:300–316.

Blackman, F. F., 1895, Experimental researches on vegetable assimilation and respiration. II. On the paths of gaseous exchange between aerial leaves and the atmosphere, Roy. Soc. (London) Phil. Trans., B186:503–562.

———, 1905, Optima and limiting factors, Ann. Botany, 19:281–295.

——— and P. Parija, 1928, Analytical studies in plant respiration. I. Respiration of a population of senescent ripening apples, Roy. Soc. (London) Proc., B103:491–523.

Blinks, L. R., and R. L. Airth, 1951, The role of electro-osmosis in living cells, Science, 113:474–475.

Bloch, R., 1941, Wound healing in higher plants, Bot. Rev., 7:110–146.

———, 1952, Wound healing in higher plants, Bot. Rev., 18:655–679.

Bloodworth, M. E., J. B. Page, and W. R. Cowley, 1956, Some applications of the thermo-electric method for measuring water flow rate in plants, Agron. Jour., 48:222–228.

Bobrov, R. A., 1955, Use of plants as biological indicators of smog in the air of Los Angeles County, Science, 121:510–511.

Bogdanov, P., 1935, Photoperiodism in species of woody plants (in Russian), Expt. Sta. Rec., 73:22.

Boggess, W. R., 1956, Weekly diameter growth of shortleaf pine and white oak as related to soil moisture, Soc. Am. Foresters Proc., 1956:83–89.

Böhning, R. H., 1949, Time course of photosynthesis in apple leaves exposed to continuous illumination, Plant Physiology, 24:222–240.

Bollard, E. G., 1953, The use of tracheal sap in the study of apple-tree nutrition, Jour. Exptl. Botany, 4:363–368.

———, 1955, Trace element deficiencies of fruit crops in New Zealand, New Zealand Dept. Sci. Ind. Research Bull. 115.

———, 1956, The nitrogenous constituents of xylem sap, Am. Soc. Plant Physiology Proc., 31:9.

———, 1957a, Nitrogenous compounds in tracheal sap of woody members of the family Rosaceae, Australian Jour. Biol. Sci., 10:288–291.

———, 1957b, Translocation of organic nitrogen in the xylem, Australian Jour. Biol. Sci., 10:292–301.

———, 1958, Nitrogenous compounds in tree xylem sap, chap. 5 in K. V. Thimann (ed.), The physiology of forest trees, The Ronald Press Company, New York.

Bonck, J., and W. T. Penfound, 1944, Seasonal growth of twigs of trees in the battue lands of the New Orleans area, Ecology, 25:473–475.

Bond, G., 1955, An isotopic study of the fixation of nitrogen associated with nodulated plants of Alnus, Myrica and Hippophaë, Jour. Exptl. Botany, 6:303–311.

———, 1956, Evidence for fixation of nitrogen by root nodules of alder (*Alnus*) under field conditions, New Phytologist, 55:147–153.

———, 1957, The development and significance of the root nodules of *Casuarina*, Ann. Botany, 83:373–380.

——— and L. C. Gardner, 1957, Nitrogen fixation in non-legume root nodule plants, Nature, 179:680–681.

Bond, T. E. T., 1942, Studies in the vegetative growth and anatomy of the tea plant (*Camellia thea* Link.) with special reference to the phloem. I. The flush shoot, Ann. Botany, 6:607–629.

———, 1945, Studies in the vegetative growth and anatomy of the tea plant (*Camellia thea* Link.) with special reference to the phloem. II. Further analysis of flushing behavior, Ann. Botany, 9:183–216.

Bonner, J., 1944, Accumulation of various substances in girdled stems of tomato plants, Am. Jour. Botany, 31:551–555.

———, 1950, Plant biochemistry, Academic Press, Inc., New York.

——— and A. W. Galston, 1947, The physiology and biochemistry of rubber formation in plants, Bot. Rev., 13:543–596.

——— and ———, 1952, Principles of plant physiology, W. H. Freeman, San Francisco.

Boon-Long, T. S., 1941, Transpiration as influenced by osmotic concentration and cell permeability, Am. Jour. Botany, 28:333–343.

Bormann, F. H., 1953, Factors determining the role of loblolly pine and sweetgum in early old-field succession in the Piedmont of North Carolina, Ecol. Mons., 23: 339–358.

———, 1956, Ecological implications of changes in the photosynthetic response of *Pinus taeda* seedlings during ontogeny, Ecology, 37:70–75.

———, 1957, Moisture transfer between plants through intertwined root systems, Plant Physiology, 32:48–55.

———, 1958, The relationships of ontogenetic development and environmental modification to photosynthesis in *Pinus taeda* seedlings, chap. 10 in K. V. Thimann (ed.), The physiology of forest trees, The Ronald Press Company, New York.

——— and B. F. Graham, 1958, The experimental detection and possible ecological significance of root grafting in white pine stands, Ecological Soc. America Bull., 39(3):83.

Bose, J. C., 1923, The physiology of the ascent of sap, Longmans, Green & Co., Ltd., London.

——, 1927, Plant autographs and their revelations, The Macmillan Company, New York.

Bourdeau, P. F., 1954, Oak seedling ecology determining segregation of species in Piedmont oak-hickory forests, Ecol. Mons., 24:297–320.

——, 1958, Interaction of gibberellic acid and photoperiod on the vegetative growth of *Pinus elliottii*, Nature, 182:118.

—— and M. L. Laverick, 1958, Tolerance and photosynthetic adaptability to light intensity in white pine, red pine, hemlock and Ailanthus seedlings, Forest Sci., 4:196–207.

—— and C. S. Schopmeyer, 1958, Oleoresin exudation pressure in slash pine: its measurement, heritability, and relation to oleoresin yield, chap. 14 in K. V. Thimann (ed.), The physiology of forest trees, The Ronald Press Company, New York.

Boyce, J. S., 1948, Forest pathology, 2d ed., McGraw-Hill Book Company, Inc., New York.

Boynton, D., 1940, Soil atmosphere and the production of new rootlets by apple tree root systems, Am. Soc. Hort. Sci. Proc., 42:53–58.

—— and O. C. Compton, 1943, Effect of oxygen pressures in aerated nutrient solutions on production of new roots and on growth of roots and top by fruit trees, Am. Soc. Hort. Sci. Proc., 42:53–58.

—— and ——, 1945, Leaf analysis in estimating the potassium, magnesium, and nitrogen needs of fruit trees, Soil Sci., 59:339–351.

——, J. I. DeVilliers, and W. Reuther, 1938, Are there different critical oxygen levels for the different phases of root activity? Science, 88:569–570.

—— and W. Reuther, 1938, Seasonal variation of oxygen and carbon dioxide in three different orchard soils during 1938 and its possible significance, Am. Soc. Hort. Sci. Proc., 36:1–6.

——, ——, and J. C. Cain, 1941, Leaf analysis and apparent response to potassium in some plum and apple orchards: preliminary report, Am. Soc. Hort. Sci. Proc., 38:17–20.

Boysen-Jensen, P., 1932, Die Stoffproduktion der Pflanzen, Gustav Fischer Verlagsbuchhandlung, Jena, Germany.

Bradley, J. W., 1922, A plantation of remarkable growth, Indian Forester, 48:637–640.

Braun, E. L., 1950, Deciduous forests of eastern North America, McGraw-Hill Book Company, Inc., Blakiston Division, New York.

Brierley, J. K., 1955, Seasonal fluctuations in the oxygen and carbon dioxide concentrations in beech litter with reference to the salt uptake of beech mycorrhizas, Jour. Ecology, 43:404–408.

Briggs, G. E., and R. N. Robertson, 1957, Apparent free space, Ann. Rev. Plant Physiology, 8:11–30.

Briggs, L. J., 1949, A new method of measuring the limiting negative pressure in liquids, Science, 109:440.

Brooks, R. M., 1942, Climate in relation to deciduous fruit production in California. II. Effect of the warm winter of 1940–41 on apricot, plum, and prune varieties in northern California, Am. Soc. Hort. Sci. Proc., 40:209–211.

Brouwer, R., 1954, The regulating influence of transpiration and suction tension on the water and salt uptake by the roots of intact *Vicia faba* plants, Acta Bot. Neerl., 3:264–312.

——, 1956, Investigations into the occurrence of active and passive components in the ion uptake by *Vicia faba*, Acta Bot. Neerl., 5:287–314.

Brown, A. B., and R. G. H. Cormack, 1937, Stimulation of cambial activity locally in the region of application and at a distance in relation to a wound by means of heteroauxin, Canadian Jour. Research, C15:433–441.

Brown, C. L., and E. M. Gifford, Jr., 1958, The relation of the cotyledons to root development of pine embryos grown in vitro, Plant Physiology, 33:57–64.

Brown, D. S., 1952, Climate in relation to deciduous fruit production in California. IV. Effect of the mild winter of 1950–51 on deciduous fruits in northern California, Am. Soc. Hort. Sci. Proc., 59:111–118.

Brown, H. P., 1912, Growth studies in forest trees. I. *Pinus rigida* Mill., Bot. Gaz., 54:386–403.

——, 1915, Growth studies in forest trees. II. *Pinus Strobus* L., Bot. Gaz., 59:197–241.

—— and A. J. Panshin, 1940, Commercial timbers of the United States, McGraw-Hill Book Company, Inc., New York.

——, ——, and C. C. Forsaith, 1949, Textbook of wood technology, vol. I, McGraw-Hill Book Company, Inc., New York.

Brown, H. T., and F. Escombe, 1900, Static diffusion of gases and liquids in relation to the assimilation of carbon and translocation of plants, Roy. Soc. (London) Phil. Trans., B193:223–291.

—— and ——, 1905, Researches on some physiological processes of green leaves with special reference to the interchange of energy between the leaf and its surroundings, Roy. Soc. (London) Proc., B76:29–112.

Brown, J. C., 1956, Iron chlorosis, Ann. Rev. Plant Physiology, 7:171–190.

Brown, J. W., 1939, Respiration of acorns as related to temperature and after-ripening, Plant Physiology, 14:621–645.

——, C. H. Wadleigh, and H. E. Hayward, 1953, Foliar analysis of stone fruit and almond trees on saline substrates, Am. Soc. Hort. Sci. Proc., 61:49–55.

Broyer, T. C., 1939, Methods of tissue preparation for analysis in physiological studies with plants, Bot. Rev., 5:531–545.

——, 1950, Further observations on the absorption and translocation of inorganic solutes using radioactive isotopes with plants, Plant Physiology, 25:367–376.

——, A. B. Carlton, C. M. Johnson, and P. R. Stout, 1954, Chlorine: a micronutrient element for higher plants, Plant Physiology, 29:526–532.

Bryan, A. H., W. F. Hubbard, and S. F. Sherwood, 1937, Production of maple syrup and sugar, U.S. Dept. Agr. Farmers' Bull. 1366, revised.

Buchholz, E., 1951, Mykotrophe Ernährung der Bäume (Sammelreferat über neuere Sowjetische Forschungen), Zeitschr. Weltsforstwirtsch., 14:51–53.

Buchholz, J. T., 1945, Embryological aspects of hybrid vigor in pines, Science, 102:135–142.

Buck, G. J., 1954, The histology of the bud graft union in roses, Iowa State Coll. Jour. Sci., 28:587–602.

Buell, J. H., 1940, Effect of season of cutting on sprouting of dogwood, Jour. Forestry, 38:649–650.

Buell, M. F., and W. E. Gordon, 1945, Hardwood-conifer forest contact zone in Itasca Park, Minn., Am. Midland Naturalist, 34:433–439.

Bukovac, M. J., and S. H. Wittwer, 1957, Absorption and mobility of foliar applied nutrients, Plant Physiology, 32:428–435.

Burger, H., 1926, Untersuchungen über das Höhenwachstum verschiedener Holzarten, Mitteil. schweiz. Anst. först. Versuchswesen, 14:1–158.

————, 1943, Einfluss des Waldes auf den Stand der Gewässer. III. Der Wasserhaushalt im Sperbel- und Rappengraben von 1927–28 bis 1941–42, Mitteil. schweiz. Anst. först. Versuchswesen, 23:167–222.

————, 1945, Einfluss des Waldes auf den Stand der Gewässer. IV. Der Wasserhaushalt im Valle di Melera, Mitteil. schweiz. Anst. först. Versuchswesen, 24:133–218.

Burke, E., and H. E. Morris, 1933, Nutrient elements used by leaves and growth of apple trees, Plant Physiology, 8:537–544.

Burns, G. P., 1923, Studies in tolerance of New England forest trees. IV. Minimum light requirement referred to a definite standard, Univ. Vermont Agr. Expt. Sta. Bull. 235.

———— and E. S. Irwin, 1942, Studies in tolerance of New England forest trees. XIV. Effect of spacing on the efficiency of white and red pine needles as measured by the amount of wood production on the main stem, Vermont Agr. Expt. Sta. Bull., 499:1–28.

Burns, G. R., 1934, Long and short wave length limits of photosynthesis, Plant Physiology, 9:645–652.

Burstrom, H., 1948a, The rate of the nutrient transport to swelling buds of trees, Physiologia Plantarum, 1:124–135.

————, 1948b, Studies on the water balance of dormant buds, Physiologia Plantarum, 1:359–378.

————, 1956, Die Bedeutung des Wasserzustandes für das Wachstum, in W. Ruhland (ed.), Encyclopedia of plant physiology, vol. 3, pp. 665–668, Springer-Verlag, Berlin.

———— and A. Krogh, 1946, The biochemistry of the development of buds in trees and the bleeding sap, Kgl. Danske Vidensk. Selsk. Meddel., 20(2):1–27.

———— and ————, 1947, Bleeding and bud development in *Carpinus*, Svensk Bot. Tidskr., 41:2–44.

Büsgen, M., and E. Münch, 1931, The structure and life of forest trees, 3d ed., transl. by T. Thomson, John Wiley & Sons, Inc., New York.

Butin, H., 1957, Die jahreszeitlichen Wassergehaltschwankungen und die Verteilung des Wassers in Stecklingen und im Stamm 2 jähriger Pappeln, Ber. deut. bot. Ges., 70:157–166.

Butler, G. W., 1953, Ion uptake by young wheat plants. II. The "apparent free space" of wheat roots, Physiologia Plantarum, 6:617–635.

Byram, G. M., and W. T. Doolittle, 1950, A year of growth for a shortleaf pine, Ecology, 31:27–35.

Cain, S. A., 1944, Foundations of plant geography, Harper & Brothers, New York.

Caird, R. W., 1935, Physiology of pines infested with bark beetles, Bot. Gaz., 96:709–733.

Callaham, R. Z., 1955, Sapwood moisture associated with galleries of *Dendroctonus valens*, Jour. Forestry, 53:916–917.

Cameron, S. H., 1941, The influence of soil temperature on the rate of transpiration of young orange trees, Am. Soc. Hort. Sci. Proc., 38:75–79.

———— and D. Appleman, 1933, The distribution of total nitrogen in the orange tree, Am. Soc. Hort. Sci. Proc., 30:341–348.

———— and G. Borst, 1938, Starch in the avocado tree, Am. Soc. Hort. Sci. Proc., 36:255–258.

———— and O. C. Compton, 1945, Nitrogen in bearing orange trees, Am. Soc. Hort. Sci. Proc., 46:60–68.

Campbell, T. E., 1955, Freeze damages shortleaf pine flowers, Jour. Forestry, 53:452.

Campbell, W. A., and O. L. Copeland, 1954, Little leaf disease of shortleaf and loblolly pines, U.S. Dept. Agr. Circ. 940.

Canning, R. E., and P. J. Kramer, 1958, Salt absorption and accumulation in various regions of roots, Am. Jour. Botany, 45:378–382.

Cannon, W. A., 1925, Physiological features of roots with especial reference to the relation of roots to aeration of the soil, Carnegie Inst. Wash. Pub. 368.

Cartellieri, E., 1935, Jahresgang von osmotischen Wert, Transpiration, und Assimilation einiger Ericaceen der alpinen Zwergstrauchheide und von *Pinus cembra*, Jahrb. wiss. Bot., 82:460–506.

Carter, J. C., 1945, Wetwood of elms, Illinois Nat. History Survey, 23(4):401–448.

Carvell, K. L., 1956, Summer shoots cause permanent damage to red pine, Jour. Forestry, 54:271.
20:671–689.

Caughey, M. G., 1945, Water relations of pocosins or bog shrubs. Plant Physiology, 20:671–689.

Chadwick, L. C., 1937, Root development of *Viburnum dilatatum* and *Cotoneaster divaricata* with the use of growth substances, Arborists' News, 2(10):3–4.

Chalk, L., 1937, A note on the meaning of the terms early wood and late wood, Leeds Phil. Soc. Proc., 3:324–325.

Chandler, R. F., 1938, The influence of nitrogenous fertilizer applications on the growth and seed production of certain deciduous forest trees, Jour. Forestry, 36:761–766.

———, 1941, The amount and mineral nutrient content of freshly fallen leaf litter in the hardwood forests of central New York, Am. Soc. Agron. Jour., 33:859–871.

———, 1944, The amount and mineral nutrient content of freshly fallen needle litter of some northeastern conifers, Soil Sci. Soc. America Proc., 8:409–411.

Chandler, W. H., 1923, Results of some experiments in pruning fruit trees, Cornell Univ. Agr. Expt. Sta. Bull. 415.

———, 1934, The dry-matter residue of trees and their products in proportion to leaf area, Am. Soc. Hort. Sci. Proc., 31:39–56.

———, M. H. Kimball, G. I. Phillip, W. P. Tufts, and G. P. Weldon, 1937, Chilling requirements for opening of buds on deciduous orchard trees and some other plants in California, California Agr. Expt. Sta. Bull. 611.

Chaplin, C. E., 1948, Some artificial freezing tests of peach fruit buds, Am. Soc. Hort. Sci. Proc., 52:121–129.

Chapman, A. G., 1935, The effects of black locust on associated species with special reference to forest trees, Ecol. Mons., 5:37–60.

———, 1941, Tolerance of shortleaf pine seedlings for some variations in soluble calcium and H-ion concentration, Plant Physiology, 16:313–326.

——— and R. D. Lane, 1951, Effects of some cover types on interplanted forest tree species, Central States Forest Expt. Sta. Tech. Paper 125.

Chapman, G. L., and R. F. Taylor, 1951, Nine years of bud pruning in a red pine plantation, Univ. Maine Forestry Dept. Tech. Note 10.

Chapman, H. D., and E. R. Parker, 1942, Weekly absorption of nitrate by young bearing orange trees growing out-of-doors in solution cultures, Plant Physiology, 17:366–376.

Chapman, H. W., L. S. Gleason, and W. E. Loomis, 1954, The carbon dioxide content of field air, Plant Physiology, 29:500–503.

Chase, W. W., 1934, The composition, quantity and physiological significance of gases in tree stems, Minnesota Agr. Expt. Sta. Tech. Bull. 99.

Chen, S. L., 1951, Simultaneous movement of P^{32} and C^{14} in opposite directions in phloem tissue, Am. Jour. Botany, 38:203–211.

Cheyney, E. G., 1942, American silvics and silviculture, University of Minnesota Press, Minneapolis, Minn.

Childers, N. F., 1937, The influence of certain nutrients on the photosynthetic activity of apple leaves, Am. Soc. Hort. Sci. Proc., 35:253–254.

——— and F. F. Cowart, 1935, The photosynthesis, transpiration and stomata of apple leaves as affected by certain nutrient deficiencies, Am. Soc. Hort. Sci. Proc., 33:160–163.

——— and D. G. White, 1942, Influence of submersion of the roots on transpiration, apparent photosynthesis, and respiration of young apple trees, Plant Physiology, 17:603–618.

Chitwood, B. G., and W. Birchfield, 1956, Nematodes: their kinds and characteristics, State Plant Board Florida Bull. 9, vol. 2.

Chouard, P., 1946, Sur le photopériodisme chez les plantes vivaces I, Soc. bot. France Bull., 93:375–377.

Chu, C. R., 1936, Der Einfluss des Wassergehaltes der Blätter der Waldbäume auf ihre Lebensfähigkeit, ihre Saugkräfte und ihren Turgor, Flora, 130:384–437.

Church, T. W., 1949, Effects of defoliation on growth of certain conifers, Northeastern Forest Expt. Sta. Paper 22.

Ciferri, R., D. Rui, G. Scaramuzzi, R. Candussio, and S. Bonforte, 1955, La "leptonecrosi" da boracarenza dell' olivo I (The phloem-necrosis of olive trees from boron deficiency), Ann. della Sper. Agr., 9:1309–1342.

Clark, F. B., and F. G. Liming, 1953, Sprouting of blackjack oak in the Missouri Ozarks, Central States Forest Expt. Sta. Tech. Paper 137.

Clark, J., 1954, The immediate effect of severing on the photosynthetic rate of Norway spruce, Plant Physiology, 29:489–491.

——— and R. D. Gibbs, 1957, Studies in tree physiology. IV. Further investigations of seasonable changes in moisture content of certain Canadian forest trees, Canadian Jour. Botany, 35:219–253.

Clark, W. S., 1874, The circulation of sap in plants, Massachusetts State Board Agr. Ann. Rept. 21, pp. 159–204.

———, 1875, Observations upon the phenomena of plant life, Massachusetts State Board Agr. Ann. Rept. 22, pp. 204–312.

Clements, F. E., and E. V. Martin, 1934, Effect of soil temperature on transpiration in *Helianthus annuus*, Plant Physiology, 9:619–630.

Clements, H. F., 1934, Translocation of solutes in plants, Northwest Sci., 8:9–21.

———, 1937, Studies in drought resistance of the soy bean, State College Washington Research Studies, no. 5, pp. 1–16.

———, 1938, Mechanisms of freezing resistance in needles of *Pinus ponderosa* and *Pseudotsuga mucronata*, State College Washington Research Studies, no. 6, pp. 3–45.

———, 1940, Movement of organic solutes in the sausage tree, *Kigelia africana*, Plant Physiology, 15:689–700.

——— and C. J. Engard, 1938, Upward movement of inorganic solutes as affected by a girdle, Plant Physiology, 13:103–122.

Clore, W. J., 1935, The effect of Bordeaux, copper, and calcium sprays upon carbon dioxide intake of Delicious apple leaves, Am. Soc. Hort. Sci. Proc., 33:177–179.

Cockerham, G., 1930, Some observations on cambial activity and seasonal starch content in sycamore (*Acer pseudoplatanus*), Leeds Phil. Soc. Proc., 2 parts, 2:64–80.

Cohen, D., 1958, The mechanism of germination stimulation by alternating temperatures, Council Israel, Bull. Research, 6D:111–117.

Coile, T. S., 1937a, Composition of leaf litter of forest trees, Soil Sci., 43:349–355.

———, 1937b, Distribution of forest tree roots in North Carolina Piedmont soils, Jour. Forestry, 35:247–257.

———, 1940, Soil changes associated with loblolly pine succession on abandoned agricultural land of the Piedmont plateau, Duke Univ. School Forestry Bull. 5.

———, 1948, Relation of soil characteristics to site index of loblolly and shortleaf pines in the lower Piedmont region of North Carolina, Duke Univ. School Forestry Bull. 13.

——— and F. X. Schumacher, 1953, Relation of soil properties to site index of loblolly and shortleaf pines in the Piedmont region of the Carolinas, Georgia, and Alabama, Jour. Forestry, 51:739–744.

Collander, R., 1957, Permeability of plant cells, Ann. Rev. Plant Physiology, 8:335–348.

Combes, R., 1927a, Absorption et migration de l'azote chez les plantes ligneuses, Ann. physiol. physicochim. biol., 3:333–376.

———, 1927b, Emigration des substances azotées des feuilles vers tiger et les racines des arbres au cours du jaunissement automnal, Rev. gén. bot., 38:430–448, 510–517, 632–645.

Compton, C., 1936, Water deficit in citrus, Am. Soc. Hort. Sci. Proc., 34:91–95.

Cook, D. B., 1941a, Five seasons' growth of conifers, Ecology, 22:285–296.

———, 1941b, The period of growth in some northeastern trees, Jour. Forestry, 39: 957–959.

Cooper, R. W., and J. H. Perry, 1956, Slash pine seedling habits, Southern Lumberman, 193:198–199.

Cooper, W. E., 1940, Frost heaving and damage to black locust seedlings, Ecology, 21:501–504.

Cormack, R. G. H., 1935, Investigations on the development of root hairs, New Phytologist, 34:30–54.

———, 1944, The effect of environmental factors on the development of root hairs in *Phleum pratense* and *Sporobolus cryptandrus*, Am. Jour. Botany, 32:490–496.

Cosens, R. B., 1952, Epicormic branching on pruned white fir, Jour. Forestry, 50: 939–940.

Coville, F. V., 1920, The influence of cold in stimulating the growth of plants, Jour. Agr. Research, 20:151–160.

Cowart, F. F., 1935, Apple leaf structure as related to position of the leaf upon the shoot and to type of growth, Am. Soc. Hort. Sci. Proc., 33:145–148.

Cox, L. G., 1942, A physiological study of embryo dormancy in the seed of native hardwoods and iris, Ph.D. dissertation, Cornell University, Ithaca, N.Y.

Crafts, A. S., 1938, Translocation in plants, Plant Physiology, 13:791–814.

———, 1951, Movement of assimilates, viruses, growth regulators, and chemical indicators in plants, Bot. Rev., 17:203–284.

———, 1956, I, The mechanism of translocation: methods of study with C^{14} labeled 2,4-D, Hilgardia, 26:287–334.

——— and T. C. Broyer, 1938, Migration of salts and water into xylem of the roots of higher plants, Am. Jour. Botany, 25:529–535.

———, H. B. Currier, and C. R. Stocking, 1949, Water in the physiology of plants, Chronica Botanica Co., Waltham, Mass.

Craib, W. G., 1918–1923, Regional spread of moisture in wood of trees, Roy. Bot. Gard. Edinburgh Notes, 11:1–18, 1918; 12:187–190, 1920; 14:1–8, 1923.

Craighead, F. C., 1925, Relation between the mortality of trees attacked by spruce budworm and previous growth, Jour. Agr. Research, 30:541–545.

―――― and R. A. St. George, 1938, Experimental work with the introduction of chemicals into the sap stream of trees for the control of insects, Jour. Forestry, 36:26–34.

――――, ――――, and B. H. Wilford, 1937, A method for preventing insect injury to material used for posts, poles and rustic construction, U.S. Dept. Agr. Circ. E409.

Crane, J. C., and R. Blondeau, 1949, The use of growth-regulating chemicals to induce parthenocarpic fruit in the Calimyrna fig, Plant Physiology, 24:44–54.

―――― and ――――, 1951, Hormone-induced parthenocarpy in the Calimyrna fig and a comparison of parthenocarpic and caprified syconia, Plant Physiology, 26:136–145.

Creech, J. L., 1954, Layering, Natl. Hort. Mag., 33:37–42.

Critchfield, W. B., 1957, Geographic variation in *Pinus contorta*, Maria Moors Cabot Found. Pub. 3, Harvard University, Cambridge, Mass.

Crocker, R. L., and J. Major, 1955, Soil development in relation to vegetation and surface age at Glacier Bay, Alaska, Jour. Ecology, 43:427–448.

Crocker, W., 1938, Life-span of seeds, Bot. Rev., 4:235–274.

――――, 1948, Growth of plants, Reinhold Publishing Corporation, New York.

―――― and L. V. Barton, 1953, Physiology of seeds, Chronica Botanica Co., Waltham, Mass.

Curry, J. R., and T. W. Church, 1952, Observations on winter drying of conifers in the Adirondacks, Jour. Forestry, 50:114–116.

Curtis, J., and R. Blondeau, 1946, Influence of time of day on latex flow from *Cryptostegia grandiflora*, Am. Jour. Botany, 33:264–270.

Curtis, O. F., 1926, What is the significance of transpiration? Science, 63:267–271.

――――, 1929, Studies on solute translocation in plants: Experiments indicating that translocation is dependent on the activity of living cells, Am. Jour. Botany, 16:154–168.

――――, 1935, The translocation of solutes in plants, McGraw-Hill Book Company, Inc., New York.

――――, 1936, Leaf temperatures and the cooling of leaves by radiation, Plant Physiology, 11:343–364.

―――― and D. G. Clark, 1950, An introduction to plant physiology, McGraw-Hill Book Company, Inc., New York.

Czaja, A. Th., 1934, Der Nachweis des Wuchsstoffes bei Holzpflanzen, Ber. deut. bot. Ges., 52:267–271.

Dahms, W. G., 1954, Growth of pruned ponderosa pine, Jour. Forestry, 52:444–445.

Dale, J., A. L. McComb, and W. E. Loomis, 1955, Chlorosis, mycorrhizae and the growth of pines on a high-lime soil, Forest Sci., 1:148–157.

Dambach, C. A., 1944, A ten year ecological study of adjoining grazed and ungrazed woodlands in northeastern Ohio, Ecol. Mons., 14:255–270.

Darrow, G. H., 1942, Rest period requirements for blueberries, Am. Soc. Hort. Sci. Proc., 41:189–194.

Daubenmire, R. F., 1938, Merriam's life zones of North America, Quart. Rev. Biology, 13:327–332.

――――, 1943, Vegetational zonation in the Rocky Mountains, Bot. Rev., 9:325–393.

――――, 1945, An improved type of precision dendrometer, Ecology, 26:97–98.

――――, 1956, Climate as a determinant of vegetation distribution in eastern Washington and northern Idaho, Ecol. Mons., 26:131–154.

——, 1959, Plants and environment, John Wiley & Sons, Inc., New York.

—— and M. E. Deters, 1947, Comparative studies of growth in deciduous and evergreen trees, Bot. Gaz., 109:1–12.

Davis, D. E., 1949, Some effects of calcium deficiency on the anatomy of *Pinus taeda*, Am. Jour. Botany, 36:276–282.

Davis, E. A., 1949, Effects of several plant growth regulators on wound healing of sugar maple, Bot. Gaz., 111:69–77.

Davis, L. D., 1931, Some carbohydrate and nitrogen constituents of alternate bearing sugar prunes associated with fruit bud formation, Hilgardia, 5:119–154.

——, 1957, Flowering and alternate bearing, Am. Soc. Hort. Sci. Proc., 70: 545–556.

Day, M. W., 1941, The root system of red pine saplings, Jour. Forestry, 39:468–472.

Day, W. R., 1928, Damage by late frost on Douglas fir, Sitka spruce, and other conifers, Forestry, 2:19–30.

—— and T. R. Peace, 1934, The experimental production and the diagnosis of frost injury on forest trees, Oxford Forestry Mem. 16.

—— and ——, 1937, The influence of certain accessory factors on frost injury in forest trees. II. Temperature conditions before freezing. III. Time factors, Forestry, 11:13–29.

Decker, J. P., 1944, Effect of temperature on photosynthesis and respiration in red and loblolly pines, Plant Physiology, 19:679–688.

——, 1947, The effect of air supply on apparent photosynthesis, Plant Physiology, 22:561–571.

——, 1952, Tolerance is a good technical term, Jour. Forestry, 50:41–42.

——, 1954, The effect of light intensity on photosynthetic rate in Scotch pine, Plant Physiology, 29:305–306.

——, 1955a, The uncommon denominator in photosynthesis as related to tolerance, Forest Sci., 1:88–89.

——, 1955b, A rapid, postillumination deceleration of respiration in green leaves, Plant Physiology, 30:82–84.

——, 1957, Further evidence of increased carbon dioxide production accompanying photosynthesis, Jour. Solar Energy Sci. Eng., 1:30–33.

—— and M. A. Tio, 1958, Photosynthesis of papaya as affected by leaf mosaic, Univ. Puerto Rico Jour. Agriculture, 42:145–150.

—— and B. F. Wetzel, 1957, A method for measuring transpiration of intact plants under controlled light, humidity, and temperature, Forest Sci., 3:350–354.

Delap, A. V., 1950, An interveinal injection needle, Ann. Rept. East Malling Research Sta., Kent, for 1949, no. 118.

Delisle, A. L., 1954, The relationship between the age of the tree and rooting of cuttings of white pine, Indiana Acad. Sci. Proc., 64:60–61.

De Long, W. A., J. H. Beaumont, and J. J. Willaman, 1930, Respiration of apple twigs in relation to winter hardiness, Plant Physiology, 5:509–534.

Demaree, D., 1932, Submerging experiments with *Taxodium*, Ecology, 13:258–262.

Demaree, J. B., 1927, Sand burn of pecan seedlings, Phytopathology, 17:647–661.

Denny, F. E., 1930, The twin leaf method of studying changes in leaves, Am. Jour. Botany, 17:818–841.

——, 1932, Changes in leaves during the night, Boyce Thompson Inst. Contribs., 4:65–83.

DenUyl, D., 1944, Effect of fertilizer on planted black locust, Jour. Forestry, 42:450–451.

De Tar, J. E., W. H. Griggs, and J. C. Crane, 1950, The effect of growth-regulating chemicals applied during the bloom period on the subsequent set of Bartlett pears, Am. Soc. Hort. Sci. Proc., 55:137–146.

Detwiler, S. R., 1943, Better acorns from a heavily fertilized white oak tree, Jour. Forestry, 41:915–916.

Deuber, C. G., 1932, Chemical treatments to shorten the rest period of red and black oak acorns, Jour. Forestry, 30:674–679.

Deuel, H. J., 1951, The lipids: their chemistry and biochemistry, Interscience Publishers, Inc., New York.

DeVilliers, G. B. D., 1943, Farming in South Africa, 18:378–381.

Dils, R. E., and M. W. Day, 1950, Effect of defoliation upon the growth of aspen, Michigan Agr. Expt. Sta. Quart. Bull., 33:111–113.

Dimond, A. E., 1955, Pathogenesis in the wilt diseases, Ann. Rev. Plant Physiology, 6:329–350.

———, G. H. Plumb, E. M. Stoddard, and J. G. Horsfall, 1949, An evaluation of chemotherapy and vector control by insecticides for combating Dutch elm disease, Connecticut Agr. Expt. Sta. Bull. 531.

Dixon, H. H., 1914, Transpiration and the ascent of sap in plants, Macmillan & Co., Ltd., London.

———, 1922, Transport of organic substances in plants, Nature, 110:547–551.

——— and W. R. G. Atkins, 1910, On osmotic pressures in plants, and on a thermo-electric method of determining freezing points, Roy. Dublin Soc. Proc., 12:275–311.

——— and ———, 1916, Osmotic pressures in plants. VI. On the composition of the sap in the conducting tracts of trees at different levels and at different seasons of the year, Roy. Dublin Soc. Proc., 15:51–62.

——— and J. Joly, 1895, On the ascent of sap, Roy. Soc. (London) Phil. Trans., B186:563–576.

Doneen, L. D., and J. H. MacGillivray, 1943, Germination (emergence) of vegetable seed as affected by different soil moisture conditions, Plant Physiology, 18:524–529.

Doorenbos, J., 1953, Review of the literature on dormancy in buds of woody plants, Landbouwhogeschool Wageningen Med., 53:1–24.

Doran, W. L., 1953, The vegetative propagation of some forest trees, Proc. 1st Northeastern Forest Tree Conf., Williamstown, Mass., pp. 41–47.

———, 1957, The propagation of some trees and shrubs by cuttings, Massachusetts Agr. Expt. Sta. Bull. 491.

Dorsey, M. J., and P. D. Strausbaugh, 1923, Winter injury to plum during dormancy, Bot. Gaz., 76:113–143.

Downs, A. A., 1944, Growth of pruned eastern white pine, Jour. Forestry, 42:598.

———, 1947, Choosing pine seed trees, Jour. Forestry, 45:593–594.

——— and W. E. McQuilkin, 1944, Seed production of southern Appalachian oaks, Jour. Forestry, 42:913–920.

Downs, R. J., and H. A. Borthwick, 1956, Effect of photoperiod on growth of trees, Bot. Gaz., 117:310–326.

———, ———, and A. A. Piringer, 1958, Comparison of incandescent and fluorescent lamps for lengthening photoperiods, Am. Soc. Hort. Sci. Proc., 71:568–578.

——— and A. A. Piringer, 1958, Effects of photoperiod and kind of supplemental light on vegetative growth of pines, Forest Sci., 4:185–195.

Doyle, J., 1938, On the supposed accumulation of fat in conifer leaves in winter, New Phytologist, 37:375–376.

—— and P. Clinch, 1927, Seasonal changes in conifer leaves, with special reference to enzymes and starch formation, Roy. Irish Acad. Proc., B37:373–414.

Drosdoff, M., 1944, Leaf composition in relation to the mineral nutrition of tung trees, Soil Sci., 57:281–291.

——, H. M. Sell, and S. G. Gilbert, 1947, Some effects of potassium deficiency on the nitrogen metabolism and oil synthesis in the tung tree (*Aleurites fordii*), Plant Physiology, 22:538–547.

Duffield, J. W., 1954, The importance of species hybridization and polyploidy in forest tree improvement, Jour. Forestry, 52:645–646.

—— and E. B. Snyder, 1958, Benefits from hybridizing American forest tree species, Jour. Forestry, 56:809–815.

Dugger, W. M., 1952, The permeability of non-stomate leaf epidermis to carbon dioxide, Plant Physiology, 27:489–499.

Duncan, D. P., and A. C. Hodson, 1958, Influence of the forest tent caterpillar upon the aspen forests of Minnesota, Forest Sci., 4:71–93.

Dunne, T. C., 1938, "Wither tip" or "summer dieback": a copper deficiency disease of apple trees, Western Australian Dept. Agr. Jour., (2)15:120–126.

Durham, G. B., 1934, Propagation of evergreens under different temperatures at different times of year, Am. Soc. Hort. Sci. Proc., 30:602–606.

Eaks, I. L., and L. L. Morris, 1956, Respiration of cucumber fruits associated with physiological injury at chilling temperatures, Plant Physiology, 31:308–314.

Eames, A. J., and L. G. Cox, 1945, A remarkable tree-fall and an unusual type of graft-union failure, Am. Jour. Botany, 32:331–335.

—— and L. H. MacDaniels, 1947, An introduction to plant anatomy, 2d ed., McGraw-Hill Book Company, Inc., New York.

Eaton, F. M., 1931, Root development as related to character of growth and fruitfulness of the cotton plant, Jour. Agr. Research, 43:875–883.

——, 1942, Toxicity and accumulation of chloride and sulfate salts in plants, Jour. Agr. Research, 64:357–399.

——, 1943, The osmotic and vitalistic interpretations of exudation, Am. Jour. Botany, 30:663–674.

Eckey, E. W., 1954, Vegetable fats and oils, Reinhold Publishing Corporation, New York.

Eggert, R., 1944, Cambium temperatures of peach and apple trees in winter, Am. Soc. Hort. Sci. Proc., 45:33–36.

Eggler, W. A., 1955, Radial growth in nine species of trees in southern Louisiana, Ecology, 36:130–136.

Ehlers, J. H., 1915, The temperature of leaves of *Pinus* in winter, Am. Jour. Botany, 2:32–70.

Eidmann, F. E., 1943, Untersuchungen über die Wurzelatmung und Transpiration unserer Hauptholzarten, Schriftenreihe Akad. deut. Forstwiss., 5:1–44.

Einspahr, D., and A. L. McComb, 1951, Site index of oaks in relation to soil and topography in southeastern Iowa, Jour. Forestry, 49:719–723.

Ekdahl, I., 1941, Die Entwicklung von Embryosack und Embryo bei *Ulmus glabra* Huds., Svensk. Bot. Tidskr., 35:143–156.

Epstein, E., 1955, Passive permeation and active transport of ions in plant roots, Plant Physiology, 30:529–535.

——, 1956, Mineral nutrition of plants: mechanisms of uptake and transport, Ann. Rev. Plant Physiology, 7:1–24.

—— and J. L. Leggett, 1954, The absorption of alkaline earth cations by barley roots: kinetics and mechanism, Am. Jour. Botany, 41:785–792.

Erickson, L. C., 1957, Citrus fruit grafting, Science, 125:994.

—— and B. L. Brannaman, 1950, Some effects on fruit growth and quality of a 2,4-D spray applied to Bearss lime trees, Am. Soc. Hort. Sci. Proc., 56:79–82.

Esau, K., 1943, Vascular differentiation in the pear root, Hilgardia, 15:299–324.

——, 1953, Plant anatomy, John Wiley & Sons, Inc., New York.

——, H. B. Currier, and V. I. Cheadle, 1957, Physiology of phloem, Ann. Rev. Plant Physiology, 8:349–374.

Evans, H. J., 1956, Role of molybdenum in plant nutrition, Soil Sci., 81:199–258.

Evelyn, J., 1670, Sylva, J. Martyn and J. Allestry, London.

Evenari, M., 1949, Germination inhibitors, Bot. Rev., 15:153–194.

Ewart, A. J., 1908, On the longevity of seeds, Roy. Soc. Victoria Proc., 21:1–210.

Ewart, M. H., D. Siminovitch, and D. R. Briggs, 1954, Studies on the chemistry of the living bark of black locust in relation to its frost hardiness. VIII. Possible enzymatic processes involved in starch-sucrose interconversions, Plant Physiology, 29:407–413.

Facey, V., 1950, Abscission of leaves in *Fraxinus americana*, New Phytologist, 49:103–116.

Farmer, J. B., 1918, On the quantitative differences in the water conductivity of the wood in trees and shrubs. II. The deciduous plants, Roy. Soc. (London) Proc., B90:232–250.

Farnsworth, C. E., 1955, Observations of stem elongation in certain trees in the western Adirondacks, Ecology, 36:285–292.

Faust, M. E., 1936, Germination of *Populus grandidentata* and *P. tremuloides*, with particular reference to oxygen consumption, Bot. Gaz., 96:808–821.

Fenska, R. R., 1954, The new tree experts' manual, A. T. De La Mare Company, Inc., New York.

Fensom, D. S., 1958, The bioelectric potentials of plants and their functional significance. II., Canadian Jour. Botany, 36:367–383.

Ferguson, T. P., and G. Bond, 1953, Observations on the formation and function of the root nodules of *Alnus glutinosa* (L.) Gaertn., Ann. Botany, 17:175–188.

Ferrell, W. K., 1953, Effect of environmental conditions on survival and growth of forest tree seedlings under field conditions in the Piedmont region of North Carolina, Ecol. Mons., 34:667–688.

—— and F. D. Johnson, 1956, Mobility of calcium-45 after injections into western white pine, Science, 124:364–365.

Ferri, M. G., 1953, Water balance of plants from the "Caatinga": further information on transpiration and stomatal behavior, Rev. Brasil. Biol., 13:237–244.

Fielding, J. M., and M. R. O. Millett, 1941, Some studies of the growth of Monterey pine (*Pinus radiata*). I. Diameter growth, Forest Bur. Bull. (Australia) 27, pp. 1–33.

Finn, R. F., 1942, Mycorrhizal inoculation of soil of low fertility, Black Rock Forest Papers, 1:115–117.

——, 1953, Mineral content of leaves due to white oak site quality, Central States Forest Expt. Sta. Tech. Paper 135.

Fischer, A., 1891, Beiträge zur Physiologie der Holzgewächse, Jahrb. wiss. Bot., 22:73–160.

Fischer, H., 1905, Über den Blutenbildung in ihrer Abhängigkeit vom Licht und über die blutenbildenden Substanzen, Flora, 94:475–490.

Fisher, J. C., 1948, The fracture of liquids, Jour. Appl. Physics, 19:1062–1067.

——, 1949, Fracture of liquids: nucleation theory applied to bubble formation, Sci. Monthly, 68:415–419.

Fisher, W. R., 1907, Schlich's manual of forestry. IV. Forest protection, Bradbury Agnew and Company, London.

Flemion, F., 1938, A rapid method for determining the viability of dormant seeds, Boyce Thompson Inst. Contribs., 9:339–351.

——, 1948, Reliability of the excised embryo method as a rapid test for determining the germinative capacity of dormant seeds, Boyce Thompson Inst. Contribs., 15:229–241.

Fowells, H. A., 1941, The period of seasonal growth of ponderosa pine and associated species, Jour. Forestry, 39:601–608.

——, 1943, The effect of certain growth substances on root-pruned ponderosa pine seedlings, Jour. Forestry, 41:685–686.

—— and B. M. Kirk, 1945, Availability of soil moisture to ponderosa pine, Jour. Forestry, 43:601–604.

—— and G. H. Schubert, 1956, Seed crops of forest trees in the pine region of California, U.S. Dept. Agr. Tech. Bull. 1150.

Franck, J., and W. E. Loomis, 1949, Photosynthesis in plants, Iowa State College Press, Ames, Iowa.

Fraser, D. A., 1952, Initiation of cambial activity in some forest trees in Ontario, Ecology, 33:259–273.

——, 1956, The translocation of minerals in trees, Canadian Dept. Northern Affairs Natl. Resources Forest Research Div. Tech. Note 47.

——, 1957a, Annual and seasonal march of soil moisture under a hardwood stand, Canadian Dept. Northern Affairs Natl. Resources Forest Research Div. Tech. Note 55.

——, 1957b, Annual and seasonal march of soil temperature on several sites under a hardwood stand, Canadian Dept. Northern Affairs Natl. Resources Forest Research Div. Tech. Note 56.

—— and C. A. Mawson, 1953, Movement of radioactive isotopes in yellow birch and white pine as detected with a portable scintillation counter, Canadian Jour. Botany, 31:324–333.

Frear, D. E. H., 1935, Photoelectric apparatus for measuring leaf areas, Plant Physiology, 10:569–574.

Freeland, R. O., 1937, Effect of transpiration upon the absorption of mineral salts, Am. Jour. Botany, 24:373–374.

——, 1944, Apparent photosynthesis in some conifers during the winter, Plant Physiology, 19:179–185.

——, 1948, Photosynthesis in relation to stomatal frequency and distribution, Plant Physiology, 23:595–600.

——, 1952, Effect of age of leaves upon the rate of photosynthesis in some conifers, Plant Physiology, 27:685–690.

Frey-Wyssling, A., 1952, Latex flow, chap. 5 in Deformation and flow in biological systems, North-Holland Publishing Co., Amsterdam.

Fricke, K., 1904, "Licht und Schattenholzarten," ein wissenschaftlich nicht begrundetes Dogma, Zentralbl. ges. Forstw., 30:315–325.

Friesner, R. C., 1940, An observation on the effectiveness of root pressure in the ascent of sap, Butler Univ. Bot. Studies, 4:226–227.

——, 1942a, Vertical growth in four species of pines in Indiana, Butler Univ. Bot. Studies, 5:145–159.

——, 1942b, Dendrometer studies on five species of broadleaf trees in Indiana, Butler Univ. Bot. Studies, 5:160–172.

——, 1943a, Some aspects of tree growth, Indiana Acad. Sci. Proc., 52:336–344.

Friesner, R. C., 1943b, Correlation of elongation in primary, secondary, and tertiary axes of *Pinus strobus* and *P. resinosa*, Butler Univ. Bot. Studies, 6:1–9.

—— and G. Walden, 1946, A five-year dendrometer record of two trees of *Pinus strobus*, Butler Univ. Bot. Studies, 8:1–23.

Fritts, H. C., 1956, Radial growth of beech and soil moisture in a central Ohio forest during the growing season of 1952, Ohio Jour. Sci., 56:17–28.

——, 1958, An analysis of radial growth of beech in a central Ohio forest during 1954–1955, Ecology, 39:705–720.

—— and E. C. Fritts, 1955, A new dendrograph for recording radial changes of a tree, Forest Sci., 1:271–276.

Fritz, E., and J. Averell, 1924, Discontinuous growth rings in California redwood, Jour. Forestry, 22:31–38.

Frost, H. B., 1926, Polyembryony, heterozygosis, and chimeras in citrus, Hilgardia, 1:365–402.

——, 1938, Nucellar embryony and juvenile characters in clonal varieties of *Citrus*, Jour. Heredity, 29:423–432.

——, 1943, The citrus industry, vol. I, chap. 9, Genetics and breeding, University of California Press, Berkeley, Calif.

Fuller, H. J., 1948, Carbon dioxide concentration of the atmosphere above Illinois forest and grassland, Am. Midland Naturalist, 39:247–249.

Furr, J. R., and W. W. Aldrich, 1943, Oxygen and carbon dioxide changes in the soil atmosphere of an irrigated date garden on calcareous very fine sand loam soil, Am. Soc. Hort. Sci. Proc., 42:46–52.

——, W. C. Cooper, and P. C. Reece, 1947, An investigation of flower formation in adult and juvenile citrus trees, Am. Jour. Botany, 34:1–8.

—— and C. A. Taylor, 1939, Growth of lemon fruits in relation to moisture content of the soil, U.S. Dept. Agr. Tech. Bull. 640.

Gail, F. W., 1926, Osmotic pressure of cell sap and its possible relation to winter-killing and leaf fall, Bot. Gaz., 81:434–445.

—— and W. H. Cone, 1929, Osmotic pressure and pH measurements on cell sap of *Pinus ponderosa*, Bot. Gaz., 88:437–441.

—— and E. M. Long, 1935, A study of site, root development, and transpiration in relation to the distribution of *Pinus contorta*, Ecology, 16:88–100.

Gaiser, R. N., 1952, Readily available water in forest soils, Soil Sci. Soc. America Proc., 16:334–338.

Ganong, W. F., 1905, Leaf area cutter, Bot. Gaz., 39:150–152.

Gardner, F. E., 1925, A study of the conductive tissues in shoots of the Bartlett pear and the relationship of food movement to dominance of the apical buds, Univ. California Agr. Expt. Sta. Tech. Paper 20.

——, 1929a, Composition and growth initiation of dormant Bartlett pear shoots as influenced by temperature, Plant Physiology, 4:405–434.

——, 1929b, The relationship between tree age and the rooting of cuttings, Am. Soc. Hort. Sci. Proc., 26:101–104.

—— and P. C. Marth, 1937, Parthenocarpic fruits induced by spraying with growth-promoting compounds, Bot. Gaz., 99:184–195.

——, ——, and L. P. Batjer, 1939, Spraying with plant growth substances to prevent apple fruit dropping, Science, 90:208–209.

Gardner, I. C., and G. Bond, 1957, Observations on the root nodules of *Shepherdia*, Canadian Jour. Botany, 35:305–314.

Gardner, V. R., F. C. Bradford, and H. D. Hooker, Jr., 1952, Fundamentals of fruit production, McGraw-Hill Book Company, Inc., New York.

Garner, R. J., 1944, Propagation by cuttings and layers: recent work and its application, with special reference to pome and stone fruits, Imp. Bur. Hort. Plantation Crops. Tech. Commun. 14.

——, 1958, The grafter's handbook, 2d ed., Faber & Faber, Ltd., London.

Garner, W. W., and H. A. Allard, 1920, Effect of the relative length of day and night and other factors of the environment on growth and reproduction in plants, Jour. Agr. Research, 18:553–606.

—— and ——, 1923, Further studies in photoperiodism: the response of the plant to relative length of day and night, Jour. Agr. Research, 23:871–920.

Garratt, G. A., 1922, Poisonous woods, Jour. Forestry, 20:479–487.

Gast, P. R., 1930, A thermoelectric radiometer for silvical research with preliminary results on the relation of insolation to the growth of white pine, Harvard Forest Bull. 14.

——, 1937, Studies on the development of conifers in raw humus. III. The growth of Scots pine (*Pinus silvestris* L.) seedlings in pot cultures of different soils under varied radiation intensities, Statens Skogsförsöksanstalt Medd., 29:587–682.

Gates, C. T., 1955, The response of the young tomato plant to a brief period of water shortage. I. The whole plant and its principal parts, Australian Jour. Biol. Sci., 8:196–214.

—— and J. Bonner, 1959, The response of the young tomato plant to a brief period of water shortage. IV. Effects of water stress on the ribonucleic acid metabolism of tomato leaves, Plant Physiology, 34:49–55.

Gates, F. C., 1931, Positive gas pressure in poplar, Science, n.s., 74:153.

Gauch, H. G., 1957, Mineral nutrition of plants, Ann. Rev. Plant Physiology, 8:31–64.

—— and W. M. Dugger, 1954, The physiological action of boron in higher plants: a review and interpretation, Maryland Agr. Expt. Sta. Bull. A80.

Gäumann, E., 1927, Der jahrzeitliche Verlauf des Kohlenhydratgehaltes im Tannen- und Fichtenstamm, Ber. deut. bot. Gesell., 45:591–597.

——, 1935, Der Stoffhaushalt der Büche (*Fagus sylvatica* L.) im Laufe eines Jahres, Ber. deut. bot. Gesell., 53:366–377.

Gaur, B. K., and A. C. Leopold, 1955, The promotion of abscission by auxin, Plant Physiology, 30:487–490.

Gemmer, E. W., 1932, Well-fed pines produce more cones, Forest Worker, 8:15.

Gessner, F., 1956, Die Wasseraufnahme durch Blätter und Samen, in W. Ruhland (ed.), Encyclopedia of plant physiology, vol. 3, pp. 215–246, Springer-Verlag, Berlin.

Geurten, I., 1950, Untersuchungen über den Gaswechsel von Baumrinden, Forstwiss. Zentralbl., 69:704–743.

Gibbs, R. D., 1935, Studies of wood. II. The water content of certain Canadian trees, and changes in the water-gas system during seasoning and flotation, Canadian Jour. Research, 12:727–760.

——, 1939, Studies in tree physiology. I. General introduction: water contents of certain Canadian trees, Canadian Jour. Research, C17:460–482.

——, 1940, Studies in tree physiology. II. Seasonal changes in the food reserves of field birch (*Betula populifolia* Marsh.), Canadian Jour. Research, C18:1–9.

——, 1945, Comparative chemistry as an aid to the solution of problems in systematic botany, Roy. Soc. Canada Trans., 39(sec. V):71–103.

——, 1950, Seasonal changes in water contents of trees, 7th Internat. Bot. Congr. Proc., pp. 230–231.

Gibbs, R. D., 1958, The Mäule reaction, lignins, and the relationships between woody plants, chap. 13 in K. V. Thimann (ed.), The physiology of forest trees, The Ronald Press Company, New York.

Giersbach, J., 1937, Germination and seedling production of species of viburnum, Boyce Thompson Inst. Contribs., 11:445–464.

Glock, W. S., 1937, What tree rings tell, Carnegie Inst. Washington Bull., n.s., 4(20):175–178.

———, 1951, Cambial frost injuries and multiple growth layers at Lubbock, Texas, Ecology, 32:28–36.

———, 1955, Tree growth. II. Growth rings and climate, Bot. Rev., 21:73–188.

Glover, J., 1941, A method for the continuous measurement of transpiration of single leaves under natural conditions, Ann. Botany, 5:25–34.

Godwin, H., 1935, The effect of handling on the respiration of cherry laurel leaves, New Phytologist, 34:402–406.

Gonzalez, J. D. L., 1958, Modes of entry of strontium into plant roots, Science, 128:90–91.

Goodall, D. W., and F. G. Gregory, 1947, Chemical composition of plants as an index of their nutritional status, Imp. Bur. Hort. Plantation Crops Tech. Commun. 17.

Gooding, H. B., 1947, Studies in comparative physiology of trees, M.S. thesis, McGill University, Montreal, Canada.

Goodwin, R. H., and D. R. Goddard, 1940, The oxygen consumption of isolated woody tissues, Am. Jour. Botany, 27:234–237.

Gortner, R. A., 1938, Outlines of biochemistry, 2d ed., John Wiley & Sons, Inc., New York.

Gossard, A. C., 1942, Root and shoot production by young pecan trees treated with indolebutyric acid at the time of transplanting, Am. Soc. Hort. Sci. Proc., 41: 161–166.

———, 1943, A study of methods of sampling pecan leaves for total nitrogen analysis, Am. Soc. Hort. Sci. Proc., 42:109–114.

Gourley, J. H., and F. S. Howlett, 1941, Modern fruit production, The Macmillan Company, New York.

Grace, N. H., 1939, Vegetative propagation of conifers. I. Rooting of cuttings taken from the upper and lower regions of a Norway spruce tree, Canadian Jour. Research, C17:178–180.

Graham, B. F., 1957, Labelling pollen of woody plants with radioactive isotopes, Ecology, 38:156–158.

——— and A. L. Rebuck, 1958, The effect of drainage on the establishment and growth of pond pine (*Pinus serotina*), Ecology, 39:33–36.

Graham, S. A., 1952, Forest entomology, McGraw-Hill Book Company, Inc., New York.

Granick, S., 1955, Plastid structure, development and inheritance, in W. Ruhland (ed.), Encyclopedia of plant physiology, vol. 1, pp. 507–564, Springer-Verlag, Berlin.

Grano, C. X., 1958, Tetrazolium chloride to test loblolly pine seed viability, Forest Sci., 4:50–53.

Graves, A. H., 1950, A method of controlling the chestnut blight on partially resistant species and hybrids of *Castanea*, 41st Ann. Meeting Northern Nut Growers Assoc. Rept.

Green, J. R., 1936, Effect of petroleum oils on the respiration of bean plants, apple twigs and leaves, and barley seedlings, Plant Physiology, 11:101–113.

Green, W. E., 1947, Effect of water impoundment on tree mortality and growth, Jour. Forestry, 45:118–120.

Greenidge, K. N. H., 1952, An approach to the study of vessel length in hardwood species, Am. Jour. Botany, 39:570–574.

——, 1954, Studies in the physiology of forest trees. I. Physical factors affecting the movement of moisture, Am. Jour. Botany, 41:807–811.

——, 1955, Studies in the physiology of forest trees. II. Experimental studies of fracture of stretched water columns in transpiring trees, Am. Jour. Botany, 42: 28–37.

——, 1957, Ascent of sap, Ann. Rev. Plant Physiology, 8:237–256.

——, 1958, Rates and patterns of moisture movement in trees, chap. 2 in K. V. Thimann (ed.), The physiology of forest trees, The Ronald Press Company, New York.

Gregory, F. G., and C. R. Hancock, 1955, The rate of transport of natural auxin in woody shoots, Ann. Botany, 19:451–465.

—— and J. A. Veale, 1957, A reassessment of the problem of apical dominance, Soc. Exptl. Biol. Symp., no. 9, pp. 2–20.

Griggs, R. F., 1946, The timberlines of northern America and their interpretation, Ecology, 27:275–289.

Groom, P., 1910, Remarks on the ecology of coniferae, Ann. Botany, 24:241–269.

Guest, P. L., and H. D. Chapman, 1944, Some effects of pH growth of citrus in sand and solution cultures, Soil Sci., 58:455–465.

Gunckel, J. E., and K. V. Thimann, 1949, Studies of development in long shoots and short shoots of *Ginkgo biloba* L. III. Auxin production in shoot growth, Am. Jour. Botany, 36:145–151.

——, ——, and R. H. Wetmore, 1949, Studies of development in long shoots and short shoots of *Ginkgo biloba* L. IV. Growth habit, shoot expression and the mechanism of its control, Am. Jour. Botany, 36:309–318.

Gunthardt, H., L. Smith, M. E. Haferkamp, and R. A. Nilan, 1953, Studies on aged seeds. II. Relation of age of seeds to cytogenetic effects, Agron. Jour., 45:438–441.

Gustafson, F. G., 1934, The effect of a decrease in the amount of transpiration on the growth of certain plants, Mich. Acad. Sci., Arts, Letters, Papers, 19:65–82.

——, 1938, Influence of the length of day on the dormancy of tree seedlings, Plant Physiology, 13: 655–658.

——, 1939, Auxin distribution in fruits and its significance in fruit development, Am. Jour. Botany, 26:189–194.

——, 1942, Parthenocarpy: natural and artificial, Bot. Rev., 8:599–654.

Guttenberg, H. von, and H. Buhr, 1935, Studien über die Assimilation und Atmung Mediterraner Macchiapflanzen während der Regen und Trockenzeit, Planta, 24:163–265.

Gysel, L. W., 1956, Measurement of acorn crops, Forest Sci., 2:305–313.

Haaglund, E., 1951, Chemistry of wood, Academic Press, Inc., New York.

Haas, A. R. C., 1936, Growth and water losses in citrus as affected by soil temperature, California Citrograph, 21:467–469.

Haasis, F. W., 1923, Frost heaving of western yellow pine seedlings, Ecology, 4:378–390.

——, 1928, Germinative energy of lots of coniferous tree seed as related to incubation temperature and to duration of incubation, Plant Physiology, 3:365–412.

——, 1931, Expulsion of gas and liquids from tree trunks, Science, 74:311–312.

Haasis, F. W., 1933, Shrinkage and expansion in woody cylinders of living trees, Am. Jour. Botany, 20:85–91.

―――― and A. C. Thrupp, 1931, Temperature relations of lodgepole pine seed germination, Ecology, 12:728–744.

Hacskaylo, E., 1957, Mycorrhizae of trees with special emphasis on physiology of ectotrophic types, Ohio Jour. Sci., 57:350–357.

Hacskaylo, J., and W. K. Murphey, 1958, Response of 9-year-old McKee hybrid poplar to gibberellic acid, Ohio Agr. Expt. Sta. Research Circ. 54.

Hagan, R. M., 1955, Factors affecting soil moisture plant growth relations, 14th Int. Hort. Cong. Rept., pp. 82–98.

Haig, I. T., 1936, Factors controlling initial establishment of western white pine and associated species, Yale Univ. School Forestry Bull. 41.

Hales, S., 1727, Vegetable staticks, W. and J. Innys and T. Woodward, London.

Halevy, A., 1956a, Orange leaf transpiration under orchard conditions. IV. A contribution to the methodology of transpiration measurements in citrus leaves, Research Council Israel Bull., 5D:155–164.

――――, 1956b, Orange leaf transpiration under orchard conditions. V. Influence of leaf age and changing exposure to light on transpiration, on normal and dry summer days, Research Council Israel Bull., 5D:165–175.

Hall, R. C., 1944, A vernier tree growth band, Jour. Forestry, 42:742–743.

Halls, L. K., and N. R. Hawley, 1954, Slash pine cone production is increased by seed-tree release, Southeastern Forest Expt. Sta. Research Note 66.

Hammar, H. E., 1956, Effect of spray residues and other contaminants on leaf analysis, Plant Physiology, 31:256–257.

Hansbrough, T., and J. P. Hollis, 1957, The effect of soil fumigation for the control of parasitic nematodes on the growth and yield of loblolly pine seedlings, Plant Disease Reporter, 41:1021–1025.

Harley, C. P., P. C. Marth, and H. H. Moon, 1950, The effect of 2,4,5-trichlorophenoxyacetic acid sprays on maturation of apples, Am. Soc. Hort. Sci. Proc., 55:190–194.

―――― and M. P. Masure, 1938, Relation of atmospheric conditions to fruit enlargement rate and periodicity of Winesap apples, Jour. Agr. Research, 57:109–124.

――――, L. O. Regeimbal, and H. H. Moon, 1956, Absorption of nutrient salts by bark and woody tissues of apple and subsequent translocation, Am. Soc. Hort. Sci. Proc., 67:47–57.

Harley, J. L., 1956, The mycorrhiza of forest trees, Endeavour, 15:43–48.

―――― and C. C. McCready, 1950, The uptake of phosphate by excised mycorrhizal roots of the beech, New Phytologist, 49:388–397.

―――― and ――――, 1953, A note on the effect of sodium azide upon the respiration of beech mycorrhizas, New Phytologist, 52:83–85.

――――, ――――, and J. K. Brierley, 1953, The uptake of phosphate by excised roots of the beech. IV. The effect of oxygen concentration upon host and fungus, New Phytologist, 52:124–132.

――――, ――――, and J. A. Geddes, 1954, The development of respiratory response to salt, New Phytologist, 53:427–444.

Harlow, W. M., and E. S. Harrar, 1958, Textbook of dendrology, 4th ed., McGraw-Hill Book Company, Inc., New York.

Harper, J. L., P. A. Landragin, and J. W. Ludwig, 1955, The influence of environment on seed and seedling mortality. I. The influence of time of planting on the germination of maize, New Phytologist, 54:107–118.

Harper, V. L., 1944, Effects of fire on gum yields of longleaf and slash pines, U.S. Dept. Agr. Circ. 710.

Harrington, G. T., 1923, Respiration of apple seeds, Jour. Agr. Research, 23:117–130.

Harris, G. H., 1926, The activity of apple and filbert roots especially during the winter months, Am. Soc. Hort. Sci. Proc., 23:414–422.

Harris, H. A., 1934, Frost ring formation in some winter-injured deciduous trees and shrubs, Am. Jour. Botany, 21:485–498.

Harris, R. W., and D. Boynton, 1952, Nitrogen fertilization and cultural practices in relation to growth and fruitfulness of an Elberta peach orchard in New York, Am. Soc. Hort. Sci. Proc., 59:36–52.

Harris, W. B., 1950, Bud burst delay of stone fruits, South Australian Dept. Agr. Jour., 53:356–358.

Hartig, R., 1876, Beiträge zur Physiologie der Holzpflanzen, Allg. Forst- und Jagdzeit., 52:41–48.

Hartig, T., 1861, Ueber die Bewegung des Saftes in den Holzpflanzen, Bot. Ztg., 19:17–23.

Hartley, C., 1918, Stem lesions caused by excessive heat, Jour. Agr. Research, 14:595–604.

Harvey, R. B., 1925, Conditions for heat canker and sunscald, Jour. Forestry, 23:392–394.

Hatch, A. B., 1937, The physical basis of mycotrophy in *Pinus*, Black Rock Forest Bull. 6.

Haut, I. C., 1938, Physiological studies on after-ripening and germination of fruit-tree seeds, Maryland Agr. Expt. Sta. Bull. 420.

Hawley, R. C., and D. M. Smith, 1954, The practice of silviculture, 6th ed., John Wiley & Sons, Inc., New York.

Hayward, H. E., W. M. Blair, and P. E. Skaling, 1942, Device for measuring entry of water into roots, Bot. Gaz., 104:152–160.

—— and E. M. Long, 1942, The anatomy of the seedling and roots of the Valencia orange, U.S. Dept. Agr. Tech. Bull. 786.

——, ——, and R. Uhvits, 1946, Effect of chloride and sulfate salts on the growth and development of the Elberta peach on Shalil and Lovell rootstocks, U.S. Dept. Agr. Tech. Bull. 922.

—— and O. C. Magistad, 1946, The salt problem in irrigation agriculture, U.S. Dept. Agr. Misc. Pub. 607.

Heald, F. D., 1933, Manual of plant diseases, McGraw-Hill Book Company, Inc., New York.

Heath, O. V. S., and J. Russell, 1954, Studies in stomatal behavior. VI. An investigation of the light responses of wheat stomata with the attempted elimination of control by the mesophyll. 2. Interactions with external carbon dioxide and general discussion, Jour. Expt. Botany, 5:1–15.

Heiberg, S. O., and D. P. White, 1951, Potassium deficiency of reforested pine and spruce stands in northern New York, Soil Sci. Soc. Am. Proc., 15:369–376.

Heimburger, C., 1934, Forest type studies in the Adirondack Region, Cornell Univ. Agr. Expt. Sta. Mem. 165.

Heinicke, A. J., 1932a, The assimilation of carbon dioxide by apple leaves as affected by ringing the stem, Am. Soc. Hort. Sci. Proc., 29:225–229.

——, 1932b, The effect of submerging the roots of apple trees at different seasons of the year, Am. Soc. Hort. Sci. Proc., 29:205–207.

——, 1934, Photosynthesis in apple leaves during late fall and its significance in annual bearing, Am. Soc. Hort. Sci. Proc., 32:77–80.

Heinicke, A. J., 1936, Root growth in young apple trees made shortly before and after defoliation, Am. Soc. Hort. Sci. Proc., 33:164–165.

——, 1937a, How lime sulphur spray affects the photosynthesis of an entire ten year old apple tree, Am. Soc. Hort. Sci. Proc., 35:256–259.

——, 1937b, Some cultural conditions influencing the manufacture of carbohydrates by apple leaves, New York Hort. Soc. Proc., 149–156.

——, 1939, The physiology of trees with special reference to their food supply, 15th Natl. Shade Tree Conf. Proc., pp. 26–35.

——, D. Boynton, and W. Reuther, 1939, Cork experimentally produced on Northern Spy apples, Am. Soc. Hort. Sci. Proc., 37:47–52.

—— and N. F. Childers, 1936, Influence of respiration on the daily rate of photosynthesis of entire apple trees, Am. Soc. Hort. Sci. Proc., 34:142–144.

—— and ——, 1937, The daily rate of photosynthesis during the growing season of 1935, of a young apple tree of bearing age, Cornell Univ. Agr. Expt. Sta. Mem. 201.

—— and M. B. Hoffman, 1933, The rate of photosynthesis of apple leaves under natural conditions, I, Cornell Univ. Agr. Expt. Sta. Bull. 577.

Helder, R. J., and J. M. Bonga, 1956, The influence of light on the loss of labelled phosphorus from bean leaves, Acta Bot. Neerl., 5:115–121.

Hemberg, T., 1949, Growth inhibiting substances in terminal buds of *Fraxinus,* Physiologia Plantarum, 2:37–44.

——, 1958, The occurrence of acid inhibitors in resting terminal buds of *Fraxinus,* Physiologia Plantarum, 11:610–614.

Hendrickson, A. H., and F. J. Veihmeyer, 1941, Some factors affecting the growth rate of pears, Am. Soc. Hort. Sci. Proc., 39:1–7.

Henry, T. A., 1949, The plant alkaloids, McGraw-Hill Book Company, Inc., Blakiston Division, New York.

Hepting, G. H., 1945, Reserve food storage in shortleaf pine in relation to little-leaf disease, Phytopathology, 35:106–119.

—— and G. M. Jemison, 1958, Forest protection, pp. 185–220 in Timber resources for America's future, U.S. Forest Service Resource Rept. 14.

Hewitt, E. J., 1952, Sand and water culture methods used in the study of plant nutrition, Bur. Hort. Plantation Crops Tech. Commun. 22.

Hewitt, W. B., and M. E. Gardiner, 1956, Some studies of the absorption of zinc sulfate in Thompson seedless grape canes, Plant Physiology, 31:393–399.

Heyl, J. G., 1933, Der Einfluss von Aussenfaktoren auf das Bluten der Pflanzen, Planta, 20:294–353.

Higdon, R. J., 1950, The effects of insufficient chilling on peach varieties in South Carolina in the winter of 1948–49, Am. Soc. Hort. Sci. Proc., 55:236–238.

Hildebrand, E. M., 1939, Internal bark necrosis of Delicious apple: a physiogenic "boron deficiency" disease, Phytopathology, 29:10.

Hilditch, T. P., 1949, Chemical constitution of natural fats, John Wiley & Sons, Inc., New York.

Hildreth, A. C., 1926, Determination of hardiness in apple varieties and the relation of some factors to cold resistance, Minn. Agr. Expt. Sta. Tech. Bull. 42.

Hiley, W., and N. Cunliffe, 1922, An investigation into the relation between height growth of trees and meteorological conditions, Oxford Forestry Mem. 1.

Hill, A. F., 1952, Economic botany, McGraw-Hill Book Company, Inc., New York.

Hill, A. G. G., and G. K. G. Campbell, 1949, Prolonged dormancy of deciduous fruit trees in warm climates, Emp. Jour. Exptl. Agr., 17:259–264.

Hill, R., 1937, Oxygen evolved by isolated chloroplasts, Nature, 139:881–882.

—— and C. P. Whittingham, 1955, Photosynthesis, Methuen & Co., Ltd., London.

Hiller, C. H., 1951, A study of the origin and development of callus and root primordia of *Taxus cuspidata* with reference to the effects of growth regulator, M.S. thesis, Cornell University, Ithaca, N.Y.

Hitchcock, A. E., W. Crocker, and P. W. Zimmerman, 1934, Toxic action in soil of illuminating gas containing hydrocyanic acid, Boyce Thompson Inst. Contribs., 6:1–30.

—— and P. W. Zimmerman, 1939, Comparative activity of root inducing substances and methods for treating cuttings, Boyce Thompson Inst. Contribs., 10:461–480.

Hoagland, D. R., 1948, Lectures on the inorganic nutrition of plants, Chronica Botanica Co., Waltham, Mass.

Hobbs, C. H., 1944, Studies on mineral deficiency in pine, Plant Physiology, 19:590–602.

Hodgson, R. H., 1954, A study of the physiology of mycorrhizal roots on *Pinus taeda* L., M.A. thesis, Duke University, Durham, N.C.

Hodgson, R. W., and S. H. Cameron, 1938, Effects of reproduction by nucellar embryony on clonal characteristics in *Citrus*, Jour. Heredity, 29:417–419.

Hoffman, M. B., 1935, The effect of lime sulphur spray on the respiration rate of apple leaves, Am. Soc. Hort. Sci. Proc., 33:173–176.

Höfler, K., 1920, Ein Schema für die osmotische Leistung der Pflanzenzelle, Ber. deut. bot. Gesell., 35:706–726.

Höhnel, F. von, 1884, Über das Wasserbedürfniss der Walder, Zentralbl. ges. Forstw., 10:384–409.

Holch, A. E., 1931, Development of roots and shoots of certain deciduous tree seedlings in different forest sites, Ecology, 12:259–298.

Holdheide, W., B. H. Huber, and O. Stocker, 1936, Eine Feldmethode zur Bestimmung der momentanen Assimilationsgrosse von Landpflanzen, Ber. deut. bot. Gesell., 54:168–188.

Hölzl, J., 1955, Über Streuung der Transpirations werte bei verschiedenen Blattern einer Pflanze und bei artgleichen Pflanzen eines Bestandes, Osterr. Akad. Wiss. Sitzber., Mathnaturw. Kl., pt. I, 164(9):659–721.

Hooker, H. D., 1920, Seasonal changes in the chemical composition of apple spurs, Missouri Agr. Expt. Sta. Research Bull. 40.

Hoover, M. D., 1944, Effect of removal of forest vegetation upon water yields, Am. Geophysical Union Trans., 25:969–977.

——, D. F. Olson, and G. E. Greene, 1953, Soil moisture under a young loblolly pine plantation, Soil Sci. Soc. America Proc., 17:147–150.

Hope, A. B., and P. G. Stevens, 1952, Electric potential differences in bean roots and their relation to salt uptake, Australian Jour. Sci. Research, B5:335–343.

Horsfall, J. G., and A. L. Harrison, 1939, Effect of bordeaux mixture and its various elements on transpiration, Jour. Agr. Research, 58:423–443.

—— and G. A. Zentmeyer, 1941, Chemotherapy for vascular diseases of trees, 17th Natl. Shade Tree Conf. Proc., 17:7–15.

Howell, J., 1932, Relation of western yellow pine seedlings to the reaction of the culture solution, Plant Physiology, 7:657–671.

Howes, F. N., 1949, Vegetable gums and resins, Chronica Botanica Co., Waltham, Mass.

Huber, B., 1927, Zur Methodik der Transpirationsbestimmung am Standort, Ber. deut. bot. Gesell., 45:611–618.

——, 1928, Weitere quantitative Untersuchungen über das Wasserleitungssystem der Pflanzen, Jahrb. wiss. Bot., 67:877–959.

Huber, B., 1930, Untersuchungen über die Gesetze der Porenverdunstung, Zeitschr. Bot., 23:839–891.

——, 1932, Beobachtungen und Messungen pflanzlicher Saftströme, Ber. deut. bot. Gesell., 50:89–109.

——, 1935, Der Wärmehaushalt der Pflanzen, F. P. Datterer & Cie, Freising-München.

——, 1937, Wasserumsatz und Stoffbewegungen, Fortschr. Bot., 7:197–207.

——, 1939, Das Siebröhrensystem unserer Bäume und seine jahreszeitlichen Veränderungen, Jahrb. wiss. Bot., 88:176–242.

——, 1948, Physiologie der Rindenschälung bei Fichte und Eiche, Forstwiss. Zentralbl., 67:129–164.

——, 1950, Registrierung des CO_2-Gefälles und Berechnung des CO_2-Stromes über Pflanzengesellschaften mittels Ultravot Absorptionsschrieber, Ber. deut. bot. Gesell., 63:53–64.

——, 1952, Über die vertikale Reichweite vegetationsbedingter Tagesschwankungen im CO_2-gehalt der Atmosphäre, Forstwiss. Zentralbl., 71:372–380.

——, 1953, Was wissen wir vom Wasserverbrauch des Waldes? Forstwiss. Zentralbl., 72:257–264.

——, 1956, Die Saftströme der Pflanzen, Springer-Verlag, Berlin.

——, 1958a, Neue Ergebnisse der pflanzlichen Gaswechselschreibung, Ber. deut. bot. Gesell., 70:455–461.

——, 1958b, Anatomical and physiological investigations on food translocation in trees, chap. 17 in K. V. Thimann (ed.), The physiology of forest trees, The Ronald Press Company, New York.

——— and R. Miller, 1954, Methoden zur Wasserdampf- und Transpirations-registrierung im laufernden Luftstrom, Ber. deut. bot. Gesell., 67:223–234.

——— and L. Plankl, 1956, Der jahrzeitliche Gang des Transpirationsstromes als Grundlage der Lebendtränkung von Waldbäumen, Forstwiss. Zentralbl., 75:350–357.

——— and H. Polster, 1955, Zur Frage der physiologischen Ursachen der unterschiedlichen Stofferzeugung von Pappelklonen, Biol. Zentralbl., 74:370–420.

——— and E. Schmidt, 1937, Eine Kompensationsmethode zur thermoelektrischen Messung Langsamer Saftstrome, Ber. deut. bot. Gesell., 50:514–529.

———, ———, and H. Jahnel, 1937, Untersuchungen uber den Assimilatstrom I, Tharandt. forstl. Jahrb., 88:1017–1050.

——— and W. von Jazewitsch, 1956, Tree-ring studies of the Forestry-Botany Institutes of Tharandt and Munich, Tree-Ring Bull., 21(1–4):28–30.

———, ———, W. Wellenhofer, and A. John, 1949, Jahrringchronologie der Spessarteichen, Forstwiss. Zentralbl., 68:706–715.

Huberman, M. A., 1940, Normal growth and development of southern pine seedlings in the nursery, Ecology, 21:323–334.

——, 1943, Sunscald of eastern white pine, *Pinus strobus* L., Ecology, 24:456–471.

Hulsbruch, M., 1956, Die Wasserleitung in Parenchymen, in W. Ruhland (ed.), Encyclopedia of plant physiology, vol. 3, pp. 533–540, Springer-Verlag, Berlin.

Humphries, E. C., 1944, A consideration of the factors controlling the opening of buds in the cacao tree (*Theobroma cacao*), Ann. Botany, 8:259–267.

——, 1947, Wilt of cacao fruits (*Theobroma cacao*). IV. Seasonal variation in the carbohydrate reserves of the bark and wood of the cacao tree, Ann. Botany, 11:219–244.

Hunt, F. M., 1951, Effect of flooded soil on growth of pine seedlings, Plant Physiology, 26:363–368.

Hunter, J. A., E. E. Chamberlain, and J. D. Atkinson, 1958, Note on the transmission of apple mosaic by natural root grafting, New Zealand Jour. Agr. Research, 1: 80–82.

Huss, E., 1954, Undersökningar över vattenhaltens betydelse för barrträdsfröets kvalitet vid forvaring (Studies of the importance of water content for the quality of conifer seed during storage), Statens Skogsforskn. Inst. Medd., 44(7):1–60.

Hustich, I., 1948, The Scotch pine in northernmost Finland and its dependence on the climate in the last decades, Acta Bot. Fennica, 42:4–75.

Hylmö, B., 1953, Transpiration and ion absorption, Physiologia Plantarum, 6:333–405.

Hyre, R. A., 1939, The effect of sulfur fungicides on the photosynthesis and transpiration of apple leaves, New York Agr. Expt. Sta. Mem. 222.

Iljin, W. S., 1930, Die Ursachen der Resistanz von Pflanzenzellen gegen Austrocknen, Protoplasma, 10:379–414.

———, 1933, Über Absterben der Pflanzengewebe durch Austrocknung und über ihre Bewahrung vor dem Trockentode, Protoplasma, 19:414–442.

———, 1951, Metabolism of plants affected with lime-induced chlorosis (calciose). I. Nitrogen metabolism, Plant and Soil, 3:239–256.

———, 1952, Metabolism of plants affected with lime-induced chlorosis (calciose). III. Mineral elements, Plant and Soil, 4:11–28.

———, 1953, Causes of death of plants as a consequence of loss of water: conservation of life in desiccated tissues, Torrey Bot. Club Bull., 80:166–177.

Illick, J. S., 1919, When trees grow, Am. Forestry, 25:1386–1390.

Ingestad, T., 1957, Studies on the nutrition of forest tree seedlings. I. Mineral nutrition of birch, Physiologia Plantarum, 10:418–439.

Irgens-Moller, H., 1955, Forest tree genetics research: Quercus L., Econ. Botany, 9:53–71.

———, 1957, Ecotypic response to temperature and photoperiod in Douglas fir (*Pseudotsuga menziesii*), Forest Sci., 3:79–83.

Ishibe, O., 1935, The seasonal changes in starch and fat reserves of some woody plants, Kyoto Imp. Univ. Bot. Inst. Pub. 42.

Ito, M., 1955, On the water amount and distribution in the stems of Akamatsu (*Pinus densiflora* S. et Z.) and Kuri (*Castanea crenata* S. et Z.) grown at Kurokawa district in Gifu Prefecture, Fac. Arts Sci., Sci. Rept., Gifu Univ., 3:299–307.

Ivanov, L. A., 1924, Über die Transpiration der Holzgewächse im Winter, Ber. deut. bot. Gesell., 42:44–49, 210–218.

——— and N. L. Kossovitsch, 1929, Über die Arbeit des Assimilationapparates verschiedener Baumarten. I. Die Kiefer (*Pinus silvestris*), Planta, 8:427–464.

——— and I. M. Orlova, 1931, Kvoprosu o zimnem fotosinteze nashikh khvoinykh, Zhur. Russk. Bot. Obshchestva, 16:139–157.

———, A. A. Silina, and Y. G. Tselniker, 1951, Determination of the transpiration capacity of forest cover, Bot. Zhur. SSSR, 36:5–20; 1952, Bot. Abs., 26: 7125.

Ives, S. A., 1923, Maturation and germination of seeds of Ilex opaca, Bot. Gaz., 76: 60–77.

Jackson, L. W. R., 1952, Radial growth of forest trees in the Georgia Piedmont, Ecology, 33:336–341.

——— and B. Zak, 1949, Grafting methods used in studies of the littleleaf disease of shortleaf pine, Jour. Forestry, 47:904–908.

Jackson, W. T., 1956, Flooding injury studied by approach-graft and split root system techniques, Am. Jour. Botany, 43:496–502.

Jacobs, M. R., 1954, The effect of wind sway on the form and development of *Pinus radiata* D. Don, Australian Jour. Botany, 2:35–51.

James, W. O., 1953, Plant respiration, Oxford University Press, New York.

Jemison, G. M., 1944, The effect of basal wounding by forest fires on the diameter growth of some southern Appalachian hardwoods, Duke Univ. School Forestry Bull. 9.

—— and F. X. Schumacher, 1948, Epicormic branching in old-growth Appalachian hardwoods, Jour. Forestry, 46:252–255.

Jenny, H., and R. Overstreet, 1939, Cation interchange between plant roots and soil colloids, Soil Sci., 47:257–272.

Johansson, N., 1933, The relation between the respiration of the tree stem and its growth, Svenska Skogsvardsforen. Tidskr., 31:53–134.

Johnson, L. P. V., 1944, Sugar production by white and yellow birches. Canadian Jour. Research C22:1–6.

Johnston, J. P., 1941, Height growth periods of oak and pine reproduction in the Missouri Ozarks, Jour. Forestry, 39:67–68.

Jones, C. G., A. W. Edson, and W. J. Morse, 1903, The maple sap flow, Vermont Agr. Exp. Sta. Bull. 103.

Jones, C. H., and J. L. Bradlee, 1933, The carbohydrate contents of the maple tree, Vermont Agr. Expt. Sta. Bull. 358.

Jones, I. D., 1931, Preliminary report on relation of soil moisture and leaf area to fruit development of the Georgia Belle peach, Am. Soc. Hort. Sci. Proc., 28: 6–14.

Jones, J. A., 1920, Physiological study of maple seeds, Bot. Gaz., 69:127–152.

Jones, W. W., and E. R. Parker, 1951, Seasonal trends in mineral composition of Valencia orange leaves, Am. Soc. Hort. Sci. Proc., 57:101–103.

Juliano, J. B., 1941, Callus development in graft union, Philippine Jour. Sci., 75:245–254.

Jumelle, M. H., 1892, Sur les lichens. 2. Influence de basses températures sur l'assimilation, Rev. gén. bot., 4:305–320.

Kalela, E., 1954, Mantysiemenpuiden japuustojen juurisuhteista (On root relations of pine seed-trees), Acta Forest Fennica, 61(28):1–17.

Katz, M., 1949, Sulfur dioxide in the atmosphere and its relation to plant life, Ind. Eng. Chemistry, 41:2450–2465.

—— and A. W. McCallum, 1952, The effect of sulfur dioxide on the conifers, chap. 8 in L. C. McCabe (ed.), Air pollution, McGraw-Hill Book Company, Inc., New York.

—— et al., 1939, Effect of sulfur dioxide on vegetation, National Research Council of Canada, Ottawa.

Kaufert, F., 1937, Factors influencing the formation of periderm in aspen, Am. Jour. Botany, 24:24–30.

Kauffman, C. H., 1926, Klebs' theory of the control of developmental processes in organisms, and its application to fungi, Internat. Cong. Plant Sci. Ithaca, Proc., vol. II, pp. 1603–1611.

Kaufman, C. M., 1945, Root growth of jack pine on several sites in the Cloquet Forest, Minnesota, Ecology, 26:10–23.

Kausch, W., 1952, Physiologische Wirkungen kleinster Saugkrafte, Planta, 41:59–63.

Keller, R., 1930, Der elektrische Faktor des Wassertransports in Lichte der Vitalfarbung, Ergeb. Physiol., 30:296–407.

Kelley, A. P., 1950, Mycotrophy in plants, Chronica Botanica Co., Waltham, Mass.

Kelley, O. J., A. S. Hunter, and C. H. Hobbs, 1945, The effect of moisture stress of nursery-grown guayule with respect to the amount and type of growth response on transplanting, Am. Soc. Agronomy Jour., 37:194–216.

Kelley, V. W., 1926, The effect of oil sprays upon the transpiration of some deciduous fruits, Am. Soc. Hort. Sci. Proc., 23:321–325.

———, 1930, Effect of certain hydrocarbon oils on respiration of foliage and dormant twigs of the apple, Illinois Agr. Expt. Sta. Bull. 348, pp. 369–406.

Kenworthy, A. L., 1948, Soil moisture and growth of apple trees, thesis, Washington State College, Pullman, Washington.

———, 1949, Soil moisture and growth of apple trees, Am. Soc. Hort. Sci. Proc., 54:29–39.

Kessel, S. N., and T. N. Stoate, 1938, Pine nutrition, Western Australia Forests Dept. Bull. 50.

Kidd, F. L., 1935, Respiration of fruits, Nature, 135:327–330.

Kidd, F. M., 1914, The controlling influence of carbon dioxide in the maturation, dormancy, and germination of seeds, II, Roy. Soc. (London) Proc., B87:609–625.

Kienholz, J. R., 1946, Performance of a pear orchard with flooded soil, Am. Soc. Hort. Sci. Proc., 47:7–10.

Kienholz, R., 1932, Fasciation in red pine, Bot. Gaz., 94:404–410.

———, 1933, Frost damage to red pine, Jour. Forestry, 31:392–399.

———, 1934, Leader, needle, cambial, and root growth of certain conifers and their relationships, Bot. Gaz., 96:73–92.

———, 1941, Seasonal course of height growth in some hardwoods in Connecticut, Ecology, 22:249–258.

Kimball, H. H., 1935, Intensity of solar radiation at the surface of the earth and its variations with latitude, altitude, season, and time of day, Monthly Weather Rev., 63:1–4.

Kinman, C. F., 1932, A preliminary report on root growth studies with some orchard trees, Am. Soc. Hort. Sci. Proc., 29:220–224.

Klebs, G., 1913, Über das Verhaltniss der Aussenwelt zur Entwicklung der Pflanzen, Sitzsber. Heidelberg. Akad. Wiss. Abt. B, 5:1–47.

———, 1914, Über das Treiben der einheimischen Bäume, speziell der Buche, Heidelb. Akad. Wiss. Abh., Math.-Naturw. Kl.3; 1915, reviewed in Plant World, 18:19.

———, 1915, Über Wachstum und Ruhe tropischer Baumarten, Jahrb. wiss. Bot., 56:734–792.

———, 1918, Über die Blutenbildung von *Sempervivum*, pp. 128–151, Festschrift Stahl, Jena, Germany.

Klein, R. M., and G. K. K. Link, 1955, The etiology of crown gall, Quart. Rev. Biology, 30:207–277.

Klein, S., 1953, Some aspects of metabolism in rooting of vine cuttings, Palestine Jour. Botany (Jerusalem), 6:114–119.

Knight, H., J. C. Chamberlain, and C. D. Samuels, 1929, On some limiting factors in the use of saturated petroleum oils as insecticides, Plant Physiology, 4:299–321.

Knight, R. C., 1926, The propagation of fruit tree stocks by stem cuttings, Jour. Pomology, 5:248–266.

Knudson, L., 1913, Observations on the inception, season, and duration of cambial development in the American larch, Torrey Bot. Club Bull., 40:271–293.

Kobel, H., 1952, Untersuchungen über den Einfluss des Kupfers auf die pflanzliche Transpiration, Phytopath. Zeitschr., 20:39–74.

Koch, W., 1957, Der Tagesgang der "Produktivität der Transpiration," Planta, 48:418–452.

Kolesnichenko, M. V., 1949, Poldonoshinie dooba (The fruition of oak), Lesnoye Khoziastivo (U.S.S.R.), 7:26–28.

Kopitke, J. C., 1941, The effect of potash salts upon the hardening of coniferous seedlings, Jour. Forestry, 39:555–558.

Korstian, C. F., 1921, Diameter growth in box elder and blue spruce, Bot. Gaz., 71:454–461.

———, 1924, Density of cell sap in relation to environmental conditions in the Wasatch Mountains of Utah, Jour. Agr. Research, 28:845–907.

———, 1927, Factors controlling germination and early survival in oaks, Yale Univ. School Forestry Bull. 19, pp. 7–115.

———, 1933, Physicochemical properties of leaves and sap as indices of the water relations of forest trees, Union intern. inst. recherches forestières, Congrès de Nancy, 1932, Comptes rendus, pp. 312–325.

——— and M. V. Bilan, 1957, Some further evidence of competition between loblolly pine and associated hardwoods, Jour. Forestry, 55:821–822.

——— and T. S. Coile, 1938, Plant competition in forest stands, Duke Univ. School Forestry Bull. 3.

——— and N. J. Fetherolf, 1921, Control of stem girdle of spruce transplants caused by excessive heat, Phytopathology, 11:485–490.

———, C. Hartley, L. F. Watts, and G. G. Hahn, 1921, A chlorosis of conifers corrected by spraying with ferrous sulphate, Jour. Agr. Research, 21:153–171.

Kostychev, S., 1926, Lehrbuch der Pflanzenphysiologie, Berlin.

———, 1931, Kostychev's chemical plant physiology, transl. by C. J. Lyon, McGraw-Hill Book Company, Inc., Blakiston Division, New York.

Kozlowski, T. T., 1943, Transpiration rates of some forest tree species during the dormant season, Plant Physiology, 18:252–260.

———, 1949, Light and water in relation to growth and competition of Piedmont forest tree species, Ecol. Mons., 19:207–231.

———, 1955, Tree growth, action and interaction of soil and other factors, Jour. Forestry, 53:508–512.

———, 1957, Effect of continuous high light intensity on photosynthesis of forest tree seedlings, Forest Sci., 3:220–224.

———, 1958, Water relations and growth of trees, Jour. Forestry, 56:498–502.

——— and A. C. Gentile, 1958, Respiration of white pine buds in relation to oxygen availability and moisture content, Forest Sci., 4:147–152.

——— and ———, 1959, Effect of seed coats on germination, respiration, and water uptake of eastern white pine seed, Univ. Wisconsin Forestry Research Note 48.

——— and W. Scholtes, 1948, Growth of roots and root hairs of pine and hardwood seedlings in the Piedmont, Jour. Forestry, 46:750–754.

——— and F. X. Schumacher, 1943, Estimation of stomated foliar surface of pines, Plant Physiology, 18:122–127.

——— and R. C. Ward, 1957a, Seasonal height growth of conifers, Forest Sci., 3:61–66.

——— and ———, 1957b, Seasonal height growth of deciduous trees, Forest Sci., 3:167–174.

Kramer, P. J., 1932, The absorption of water by root systems of plants, Am. Jour. Botany, 19:148–164.

———, 1933, The intake of water through dead root systems and its relation to the problem of absorption by transpiring plants, Am. Jour. Botany, 20:481–492.

――――, 1936, Effect of variation in length of day on growth and dormancy of trees, Plant Physiology, 11:127–137.

――――, 1937a, The relation between rate of transpiration and rate of absorption of water in plants, Am. Jour. Botany, 24:10–15.

――――, 1937b, An improved photoelectric apparatus for measuring leaf areas, Am. Jour. Botany, 24:375–376.

――――, 1937c, Photoperiodic stimulation of growth by artificial light as a cause of winterkilling, Plant Physiology, 12:881–883.

――――, 1938, Root resistance as a cause of the absorption lag, Am. Jour. Botany, 25:110–113.

――――, 1940, Causes of decreased absorption of water by plants in poorly aerated media, Am. Jour. Botany, 27:216–220.

――――, 1942, Species differences with respect to water absorption at low soil temperatures, Am. Jour. Botany, 29:828–832.

――――, 1943, Amount and duration of growth of various species of tree seedlings, Plant Physiology, 18:239–251.

――――, 1946, Absorption of water through suberized roots of trees, Plant Physiology, 21:37–41.

――――, 1949, Plant and soil water relationships, McGraw-Hill Book Company, Inc., New York.

――――, 1951a, Effects of respiration inhibitors on accumulation of radioactive phosphorus by roots of loblolly pine, Plant Physiology, 26:30–36.

――――, 1951b, Causes of injury to plants resulting from flooding of the soil, Plant Physiology, 26:722–736.

――――, 1955, Bound water, in W. Ruhland (ed.), Encyclopedia of plant physiology, vol. 1, pp. 223–242, Springer-Verlag, Berlin.

――――, 1956a, Roots as absorbing organs, in Encyclopedia of plant physiology, vol. 3, pp. 188–214.

――――, 1956b, The uptake of salts by plant cells, in Encyclopedia of plant physiology, vol. 2, pp. 290–315.

――――, 1956c, Permeability in relation to respiration, in Encyclopedia of plant physiology, vol. 2, pp. 358–368.

――――, 1956d, The uptake of water by plant cells, in Encyclopedia of plant physiology, 2:316–336.

――――, 1957a, Outer space in plants: some possible implications of the concept, Science, 125:633–635.

――――, 1957b, Some effects of various combinations of day and night temperatures and photoperiod on the height growth of loblolly pine seedlings, Forest Sci., 3:45–55.

――――, 1958a, Photosynthesis of trees as affected by their environment, chap. 8 in K. V. Thimann (ed.), The physiology of forest trees, The Ronald Press Company, New York.

――――, 1958b, Thermoperiodism in trees, chap. 30 in K. V. Thimann (ed.), The physiology of forest trees, The Ronald Press Company, New York.

―――― and W. S. Clark, 1947, A comparison of photosynthesis in individual pine needles and entire seedlings at various light intensities, Plant Physiology, 22:51–57.

―――― and J. P. Decker, 1944, Relation between light intensity and rate of photosynthesis of loblolly pine and certain hardwoods, Plant Physiology, 19:350–358.

―――― and R. H. Hodgson, 1954, Differences between mycorrhizal and nonmycorrhizal roots of loblolly pine, 8th Internat. Bot. Cong. Proc., sec. 13, pp. 133–134.

Kramer, P. J., and W. T. Jackson, 1954, Causes of injury to flooded tobacco plants, Plant Physiology, 29:241–245.

——, H. J. Oosting, and C. F. Korstian, 1952, Survival of pine and hardwood seedlings in forest and open, Ecology, 33:427–430.

——, W. S. Riley, and T. T. Bannister, 1952, Gas exchange of cypress (*Taxodium distichum*) knees, Ecology, 33:117–121.

—— and K. M. Wilbur, 1949, Absorption of radioactive phosphorus by mycorrhizal roots of pine, Science, 110:8–9.

Kraus, E. J., and H. R. Kraybill, 1918, Vegetation and reproduction with special reference to the tomato, Oregon Agr. Expt. Sta. Bull. 149.

Kraybill, H. R., 1923, Effect of shading and ringing upon the chemical composition of apple and peach trees, New Hampshire Agr. Expt. Sta. Tech. Bull. 23.

Kremers, R. E., 1957, The occurrence of lignin precursors, Tappi, 40:262–268.

Kreusler, U., 1885, Über eine Methode zur Beobachtung der Assimilation und Athmung der Pflanzen und über einige diese Vorgänge beinflussende Momente, Landw. Jahrb., 14:913–965.

Krotkov, G., 1941, The respiratory metabolism of McIntosh apples during ontogeny, as determined at 22°C, Plant Physiology, 16:799–812.

Kuijt, J., 1955, Dwarf mistletoes, Bot. Rev., 21:569–626.

Kuntz, J. E., and A. J. Riker, 1955, The use of radioactive isotopes to ascertain the role of root grafting in the translocation of water, nutrients, and disease-inducing organisms, Internat. Conf. Peaceful Uses of Atomic Energy (Geneva, Switzerland) Proc., 12:144–148.

Kursanov, A. L., 1933, Über den Einfluss der Kohlenhydrate auf den Tagesverlauf der Photosynthese, Planta, 20:535–548.

Kurth, E. F., 1949, The chemical composition of barks, Northeastern Wood Utilization Council Bull. 25, pp. 19–41.

—— and J. K. Hubbard, 1951, Extractives from ponderosa pine bark, Ind. Eng. Chemistry, 43:896–900.

Kurz, H., and D. Demaree, 1934, Cypress buttresses and knees in relation to water and air, Ecology, 15:36–41.

Kusano, S., 1901, Transpiration of evergreen trees in winter, Imp. Univ. Tokyo Coll. Sci. Jour., 15:313–366.

Kusumoto, T., 1957a, Physiological and ecological studies on the plant production in plant communities. 4. Ecological studies on the apparent photosynthesis curves of evergreen broad-leaved trees, Bot. Mag. Tokyo, 70:299–304.

——, 1957b, Physiological and ecological studies on the plant production in plant communities. 3. Ecological consideration of the temperature-photosynthesis curves of evergreen broad-leaved trees, Jap. Jour. Ecol., 7:126–130.

Kylin, A., and B. Hylmö, 1957, Uptake and transport of sulphate in wheat: active and passive components, Physiologia Plantarum, 10:467–484.

Labyak, L. F., and F. X. Schumacher, 1954, The contribution of its branches to the main stem growth of loblolly pine, Jour. Forestry, 52:333–337.

Ladefoged, K., 1948, Analysis of the root sap of the birch, Plant and Soil, 1:127–134.

——, 1952, The periodicity of wood formation, Dansk. Biol. Skr., 7(3):1–98.

Lagatu, H., and L. Maume, 1924, Etude, par l'analyse périodique des feuilles, de l'influence des engrais de chaux, de magnésie et de potasse sur la vigne, Acad. sci. (Paris) Comptes rendus, 179:932–934.

Lakon, G., 1911, Beiträge zur forstlichen Samenkunde. II. Zur Anatomie und Keimungsphysiologie der Eschensamen, Natur. Zeitschr. Forst u. Landw., 9:226–237.

————, 1949, The topographical tetrazolium method for determining the germinating capacity of seeds, Plant Physiology, 24:389–394.

————, 1954, Neuere Beiträge zur topographischen Tetrazolium-Methode, Ber. deut. bot. Gesell., 67:146–157.

Lammerts, W. E., 1942, Embryo culture an effective technique for shortening the breeding cycle of deciduous trees and increasing germination of hybrid seed, Am. Jour. Botany, 29:166–171.

Larsen, C. S., and E. Magius, 1944, Podning og Okulering af Skovtraeer (Grafting and budding of forest trees), Dansk. Skovforen. Tidsskr., 29:25–48.

Larsen, H. S., 1958, Private communication.

Larsen, P., 1954, Nomenclature of chemical plant regulators: a criticism, Plant Physiology, 29:400–401.

Larson, P. R., 1956, Discontinuous growth rings in suppressed slash pine, Tropical Woods, no. 104, pp. 80–99.

LaRue, C. D., 1934, Root grafting in trees, Am. Jour. Botany, 21:121–126.

————, 1936, Intumescences on poplar leaves. III. The role of plant growth hormones in their production, Am. Jour. Botany, 23:520–524.

————, 1952, Root grafting in tropical trees, Science, 115:296.

Leach, W., D. R. Moir, and H. F. Battro, 1944, An improved arrangement for the measurement of carbon dioxide output of respiring plant material by the electrical conductivity method, Canadian Jour. Research, C22:133–142.

Lehtpere, R., 1957, The influence of high pruning on the growth of Douglas fir, Forestry, 30:9–20.

Leitbundgut, H., 1955, Untersuchungen über Augusttrieb und Zwieselbildung bei der Fichte, Schweiz. Zeitschr. Forstw., 106:286–290.

Lemée, G., 1956, Recherches écophysiologiques sur le cacaoyer, Rev. gén. bot., 63:41–93.

Leonard, O. A., and A. S. Crafts, 1956, Uptake and distribution of radioactive 2,4-D by brush species, Hilgardia, 26:366–415.

Leopold, A. C., 1949, The control of tillering in grasses by auxin, Am. Jour. Botany, 36:437–440.

Levitt, J., 1951, Frost, drought, and heat resistance, Ann. Rev. Plant Physiology, 2:245–268.

————, 1956a, The physical nature of transpirational pull, Plant Physiology, 31:248–251.

————, 1956b, The hardiness of plants, Academic Press, Inc., New York.

————, 1957a, The role of cell sap concentration in frost hardiness, Plant Physiology, 32:237–239.

————, 1957b, The significance of "apparent free space" (A.F.S.) in ion absorption, Physiologia Plantarum, 10:882–888.

———— and G. W. Scarth, 1936, Frost-hardening studies with living cells, Canadian Jour. Research, C14:267–305.

Lewis, F. J., and G. M. Tuttle, 1920, Osmotic properties of some plant cells at low temperatures, Ann. Botany, 34:405–416.

———— and ————, 1923, On the phenomena attending seasonal changes in the organization in leaf cells of *Picea canadensis* (Mill.) BSP, New Phytologist, 22:225–232.

Leyton, L., 1952, The effect of pH and form of nitrogen on the growth of Sitka spruce seedlings, Forestry, 25:32–40.

————, 1954, The growth and mineral nutrition of spruce and pine in heathland plantations, Imp. Forestry Inst. Oxford Paper 31.

Leyton, L., 1956, The relationship between the growth and mineral composition of the foliage of Japanese larch (*Larix leptolepis* Murr.), Plant and Soil, 7:167–177.

———, 1957, The mineral nutrient requirements of forest trees, Ohio Jour. Sci., 57:337–345.

———, 1958a, The mineral requirement of forest plants, in W. Ruhland (ed.), Encyclopedia of plant physiology, vol. 4, pp. 1026–1039, Springer-Verlag, Berlin.

———, 1958b, Forest fertilizing in Britain, Jour. Forestry, 56:104–106.

——— and K. A. Armson, 1955, Mineral composition of the foliage in relation to the growth of Scots pine, Forest Sci., 1:210–218.

——— and L. Z. Rousseau, 1958, Root growth of tree seedlings in relation to aeration, chap. 23 in K. V. Thimann (ed.), Physiology of forest trees, The Ronald Press Company, New York.

Libby, W. F., 1951, Radiocarbon dates, II, Science, 114:291–296.

Liebig, J., 1843, Chemistry in its application to agriculture and physiology, 3d ed., Peterson, Philadelphia.

Lilleland, O., 1930, Does potassium increase the sugar content of prunes? Am. Soc. Hort. Sci. Proc., 27:15–18.

——— and J. G. Brown, 1940, The phosphate nutrition of fruit trees. II. Continued response to phosphate applied at the time of planting, Am. Soc. Hort. Sci. Proc., 37:53–57.

———, ———, and J. P. Conrad, 1942, The phosphate nutrition of fruit trees. III. Comparison of fruit tree and field crop responses on a phosphate deficient soil, Am. Soc. Hort. Sci. Proc., 40:1–7.

Liming, F. G., 1934, A preliminary study of the lengths of the open vessels in the branches of the American elm, Ohio Jour. Sci., 34:415–419.

———, 1957, Homemade dendrometers, Jour. Forestry, 55:575–577.

——— and J. P. Johnston, 1944, Reproduction in oak-hickory forest stands of the Missouri Ozarks, Jour. Forestry, 42:175–180.

Little, E. L., 1944, Layering after a heavy snow storm in Maryland, Ecology, 25:112–113.

Little, S., 1938, Relationships between vigor of resprouting and intensity of cutting in coppice stands, Jour. Forestry, 36:1216–1223.

Livingston, B. E., and W. H. Brown, 1912, Relation of the daily march of transpiration to variations in the water content of foliage leaves, Bot. Gaz., 53:309–330.

Livingston, G. A., 1950, In vitro tests of abscission agents, Plant Physiology, 25:711–721.

Long, W. G., D. V. Sweet, and H. B. Tukey, 1956, The loss of nutrients from plant foliage by leaching as indicated by radioisotopes, Science, 123:1039–1040.

Loomis, W. E., 1934, Daily growth of maize, Am. Jour. Botany, 21:1–6.

———, 1935, Translocation and growth balance in woody plants, Ann. Botany, 49:247–272.

———, 1953, Growth correlations, chap. 11 in W. E. Loomis (ed.), Growth and differentiation in plants, Iowa State College Press, Ames, Iowa.

Lorenz, R. W., 1939, High temperature tolerance of forest trees, Minn. Agr. Expt. Sta. Tech. Bull. 141.

Loustalot, A. J., 1943, Effect of ringing the stem on photosynthesis, transpiration and respiration of pecan leaves, Am. Soc. Hort. Sci. Proc., 42:127–132.

———, 1945, Influence of soil moisture conditions on apparent photosynthesis and transpiration of pecan leaves, Jour. Agr. Research, 71:519–532.

———, F. Burrows, S. G. Gilbert, and A. Nason, 1945, Effect of copper and zinc deficiencies on the photosynthetic activity of the foliage of young tung trees, Plant Physiology, 20:283–288.

———, S. G. Gilbert, and A. M. Drosdoff, 1950, The effect of nitrogen and potassium levels in tung seedlings on growth, apparent photosynthesis, and carbohydrate composition, Plant Physiology, 25:394–412.

——— and J. Hamilton, 1941, The effect of downy spot on photosynthesis and transpiration of pecan leaves in the fall, Am. Soc. Hort. Sci. Proc., 39:80–84.

———, H. F. Winters, and N. F. Childers, 1947, Influence of high, medium, and low soil moisture on growth and alkaloid content of *Cinchona ledgeriana*, Plant Physiology, 22:613–619.

Lownsbery, B. F., 1956, *Pratylenchus vulnus*, primary cause of the root-lesion disease of walnuts, Phytopathology, 46:376–379.

Lückhoff, H. A., 1949, The effect of live pruning on the growth of *Pinus patula*, *P. caribaea* and *P. taeda*, South African Forestry Assoc. Jour., 18:25–54.

Luckwill, L. C., 1948, The hormone content of the seed in relation to endosperm development and fruit drop in the apple, Jour. Hort. Sci., 24:32–44.

———, 1953, Studies of fruit development in relation to plant hormones. I. Hormone production by the developing apple seed in relation to fruit drop, Jour. Hort. Sci., 28:14–24.

———, 1957, Hormonal aspects of fruit development in higher plants, Soc. Exptl. Biol. Symp., no. 11, pp. 63–85.

Lund, E. J., 1931, Electric correlation between living cells in cortex and wood in the Douglas fir, Plant Physiology, 6:631–652.

Lundegardh, H., 1931, Environment and plant development, transl. by E. Ashby, Edward Arnold & Co., London.

———, 1940, Anionenatmung und Bluten, Planta, 31:184–191.

———, 1944, Bleeding and sap movement, Arkiv Botanik, A31(2):1–56.

———, 1950, The translocation of salts and water through wheat roots, Physiologia Plantarum, 3:103–151.

———, 1954, Anion respiration: the experimental basis of a theory of absorption, transport and exudation of electrolytes by living cells and tissues, Soc. Exptl. Biol. Symp., no. 8, pp. 262–296.

Lutz, H. J., 1939, Layering in eastern white pine, Bot. Gaz., 101:505–507.

———, 1945, Soil conditions of picnic grounds in public forest parks, Jour. Forestry, 43:121–127.

———, 1952, Occurrence of clefts in the wood of living white spruce in Alaska, Jour. Forestry, 50:99–102.

——— and R. F. Chandler, 1946, Forest soils, John Wiley & Sons, Inc., New York.

Luxford, R. F., 1930, Distribution and amount of moisture in virgin redwood trees, Jour. Forestry, 28:770–772.

Lyford, W. H., 1941, Mineral composition of freshly fallen white pine and red maple leaves, New Hampshire Agr. Expt. Sta. Tech. Bull. 77.

McCabe, L. C. (ed.), 1952, Air pollution, McGraw-Hill Book Company, Inc., New York.

M'Clenahan, F. M., 1909, The development of fat in the black walnut, Jour. Am. Chem. Soc., 31:1093–1098.

McClung, A. C., and W. L. Lott, 1956, Mineral nutrient composition of peach leaves as affected by leaf age and position and the presence of a fruit crop, Am. Soc. Hort. Sci. Proc., 67:113–120.

McComb, A. L., and J. E. Griffith, 1946, Growth stimulation and phosphorus absorption of mycorrhizal and nonmycorrhizal northern white pine and Douglas fir seedlings in relation to fertilizer treatment, Plant Physiology, 21:11–17.

MacDaniels, L. H., and O. F. Curtis, 1930, The effect of spiral ringing on solute translocation and the structure of the regenerated tissue of the apple, Cornell Univ. Agr. Expt. Sta. Research Mem. 133.

McDermott, J. J., 1941, A physiological study of after-ripening in acorns, Ph.D. dissertation, Duke University, Durham, N.C.

MacDougal, D. T., 1921, Growth in trees, Carnegie Inst. Wash. Pub. 307.

——, 1926, The hydrostatic system of trees, Carnegie Inst. Wash. Pub. 373.

——, 1938, Tree growth, Chronica Botanica Co., Waltham, Mass.

—— and J. Dufrenoy, 1944, Mycorrhizal symbiosis in *Asplectrum, Corallorhiza* and *Pinus*, Plant Physiology, 19:440–465.

—— and ——, 1946, Criteria of nutritive relations of fungi and seed plants in mycorrhizae, Plant Physiology, 21:1–10.

—— and F. L. Long, 1927, Characters of cells attaining great age, Am. Naturalist, 61:385–406.

——, J. B. Overton, and G. M. Smith, 1929, The hydrostatic-pneumatic system of certain trees: movements of liquids and gases, Carnegie Inst. Wash. Pub. 397.

—— and G. M. Smith, 1927, Long-lived cells of the redwood, Science, 66:456–457.

—— and E. B. Working, 1933, The pneumatic system of plants especially trees, Carnegie Inst. Wash. Pub. 441, pp. 1–87.

McDougall, W. B., 1921, Thick-walled root hairs of *Gleditsia* and related genera, Am. Jour. Botany, 8:171–175.

McGregor, W. H. D., 1958, Seasonal changes in the rates of photosynthesis and respiration of loblolly pine and white pine, Ph.D. dissertation, Duke University, Durham, N.C.

McHargue, J. S., and W. R. Roy, 1932, Mineral and nitrogen content of the leaves of some forest trees at different times in the growing season, Bot. Gaz., 94:381–393.

McIntosh, D. C., 1949, Some further information on the chemical treatment experiments conducted at Stevens, Ont., during 1947 and 1948, Pulp Paper Mag. Canada, 50:128–130.

McIntyre, A. C., 1936, Sprout groups and their relation to the oak forests of Pennsylvania, Jour. Forestry, 34:1054–1058.

McKee, H. S., 1958, Nitrogen metabolism in leaves, in W. Ruhland (ed.), Encyclopedia of plant physiology, vol. 8, pp. 516–553, Springer-Verlag, Berlin.

——, R. N. Robertson, and J. B. Lee, 1955, Physiology of pea fruits. I. The developing fruit, Australian Jour. Biol. Sci., 8:137–163.

McLean, D. M., 1944, Histopathologic changes in the phloem of American elm affected with the virus causing phloem necrosis, Phytopathology, 34:818–826.

McLean, F. T., 1920, Field studies of the carbon dioxide absorption of coconut leaves, Ann. Botany, 34:367–389.

McLintock, T. F., 1955, How damage to balsam fir develops after a spruce budworm epidemic, Northeastern Forest Expt. Sta. Paper 75.

McNair, J. B., 1935, The taxonomic and climatic distribution of alkaloids, Torrey Bot. Club Bull., 62:219–226.

——, 1945, Plant fats in relation to environment and evolution, Bot. Rev., 11:1–59.

McQuilkin, W. E., 1950, Effects of some growth regulators and dressings on the healing of tree wounds, Jour. Forestry, 48:423–428.

Magness, J. R., 1928, Relation of leaf area to size and quality in apples, Am. Soc. Hort. Sci. Proc., 25:285–288.

——, L. P. Batjer, and L. O. Regeimbal, 1948, Apple tree response to nitrogen applied at different seasons, Jour. Agr. Research, 76:1–25.

——, E. S. Degman, and J. R. Furr, 1935, Soil moisture and irrigation investigations in eastern apple orchards, U.S. Dept. Agr. Tech. Bull. 491.

————, and L. O. Regeimbal, 1938, The nitrogen requirement of the apple. Am. Soc. Hort. Sci. Proc., 36:51–55.

————, ————, and E. S. Degman, 1933, Accumulation of carbohydrates in apple foliage, bark, and wood as influenced by moisture supply, Am. Soc. Hort. Sci. Proc., 29:246–252.

Maguire, W. P., 1956, Are ponderosa pine cone crops predictable? Jour. Forestry, 54:778–779.

Maheshwari, P., 1950, An introduction to the embryology of angiosperms, McGraw-Hill Book Company, Inc., New York.

Mahlstede, J. P., and E. S. Haber, 1957, Plant propagation, John Wiley & Sons, Inc., New York.

Maizel, J. V., A. A. Benson, and N. E. Tolbert, 1956, Identification of phosphoryl choline as an important constituent of plant saps, Plant Physiology, 31:407–408.

Maki, T. E., and H. Marshall, 1945, Effects of soaking with indolebutyric acid on root development and survival of tree seedlings, Bot. Gaz., 107:268–276.

————, ————, and C. E. Ostrom, 1946, Effects of naphthaleneacetic-acid sprays on the development and drought resistance of pine seedlings, Bot. Gaz., 107:297–312.

Malhotra, R. C., 1931, Influence of tracheae and leaves on the water conductivity, Ann. Botany, 45:591–620.

Mann, A. J., F. W. L. Keane, and K. Lapins, 1953, Apple frameworks and rootstocks in British Columbia, Canadian Dept. Agr. Pub. 898.

Mann, W. F., 1952, Response of loblolly pine to thinning, Jour. Forestry, 50:443–445.

Manshard, E., 1933, Untersuchungen über den Nährstoffgehalt der Aschen forstlicher Kulturpflanzen aus den Halstenbecker Forstbaumschulen, Tharandt. forstl. Jahrb. wiss. Bot., 84:105–158.

Markley, K. S., S. B. Hendricks, and C. E. Sando, 1932, Further studies on the wax-like coating of apples, Jour. Biol. Chemistry, 98:103–107.

————, ————, and ————, 1935, Constituents of the wax-like coating of the pear, *Pyrus communis* L., Jour. Biol. Chemistry, 111:133–146.

————, E. K. Nelson, and M. S. Sherman, 1937, Some wax-like constituents from expressed oil from the peel of Florida grapefruit, *Citrus grandis*, Jour. Biol. Chemistry, 118:433–441.

Marsden, D. H., 1950–1951, Gas injury to trees, Trees, II:1, November–December; II:2, January–February.

Marshall, D. C., 1958, Measurement of sap flow in conifers by heat transport, Plant Physiology, 33:385–396.

Marshall, H., and T. E. Maki, 1946, Transpiration of pine seedlings as influenced by foliage coatings, Plant Physiology, 21:95–101.

Marshall, R. P., 1931, The relation of season of wounding and shellacking to callus formation in tree wounds, U.S. Dept. Agr. Tech. Bull. 246.

Marth, P. C., W. W. Audia, and J. W. Mitchell, 1956, Gibberellic acid: a plant regulator, U.S. Dept. Agr., ARS, Hort. Crops Research Branch, Beltsville, Md. 8 pp. Mimeo.

————, L. Havis, and L. P. Batjer, 1947, Further results with growth regulators in retarding flower opening of peaches, Am. Soc. Hort. Sci. Proc., 49:49–54.

————, ————, and V. E. Prince, 1950, Effects of growth-regulating substances on development and ripening of peaches, Am. Soc. Hort. Sci. Proc., 55:152–158.

Marts, R. O., 1950, Wood quality of bud-pruned longleaf pine, Southern Lumberman, 181(2273):197–199.

————, 1951, Influence of crown reduction on springwood and summerwood distribution in longleaf pine, Jour. Forestry, 49:183–191.

Marvin, J. W., 1958, The physiology of maple sap flow, chap. 6 in K. V. Thimann (ed.), The physiology of forest trees, The Ronald Press Company, New York.

Marvin, J. W., and R. O. Erickson, 1956, A statistical evaluation of some of the factors responsible for the flow of sap from the sugar maple, Plant Physiology, 31:57–61.

—— and M. T. Greene, 1951, Temperature-induced sap flow in excised stems of *Acer*, Plant Physiology, 26:565–580.

Maskell, E. J., 1928, Experimental researches on vegetable assimilation and respiration. XVIII. The relation between stomatal opening and assimilation: a critical study of assimilation rates and porometer rates in cherry laurel, Roy. Soc. (London) Proc., B102:488–533.

Mason, H. L., and P. R. Stout, 1954, The role of plant physiology in plant geography, Ann. Rev. Plant Physiology, 5:249–270.

Mason, T. G., and E. J. Maskell, 1928, A study of diurnal variation in the carbohydrates of leaf, bark, and wood and of the effects of ringing, Ann. Botany, 42:188–253.

—— and E. Phillis, 1936, Further studies on transport in the cotton plant. V. Oxygen supply and the activation of diffusion, Ann. Botany, 50:455–500.

—— and ——, 1940, Concerning the upward movement of soil solutes, Ann. Botany, 4:765–771.

Matthaei, G. L. C., 1902, The effect of temperature on carbon dioxide assimilation, Ann. Botany, 16:591–593.

——, 1905, Experimental researches on vegetable assimilation and respiration. III. On the effect of temperature on carbon dioxide assimilation, Roy. Soc. (London) Phil. Trans., 197:47–105.

Matzke, E. B., 1936, Effect of street lights in delaying leaf-fall in certain trees, Am. Jour. Botany, 23:446–452.

Maximov, N. A., 1929, The plant in relation to water, transl. by R. H. Yapp, George Allen & Unwin, Ltd., London.

May, C., 1941, Methods of tree injection, Trees, 4:7–16.

Mayer-Wegelin, H., 1936, Astung, Schaper, Hannover, U.S. Forest Service Div. of Silvics Transl. 264.

Mayr, H., 1893, Das Harz der deutschen Nadelwaldbäume. II. Verteilung des Harzes. A. Anatomische Verhältnisse, Zeitschr. Forst. und Jagdw., 25:389–443.

——, 1909, Waldbau auf naturgesetzlicher Grundlage, 2d ed., P. Parey, Berlin.

Meeder, E. M., and M. A. Blake, 1943, Seasonal trend of fruit bud hardiness in peaches, Am. Soc. Hort. Sci. Proc., 43:91–98.

Mees, G. C., and P. E. Weatherley, 1957, The mechanism of water absorption by roots. II. The role of hydrostatic pressure gradients across the cortex, Roy. Soc. (London) Proc., B147:381–391.

Meginnis, H. G., 1934, The effect of cultivating young black locust, Jour. Forestry, 32:569–571.

Melin, E., 1953, Physiology of mycorrhizal relations in plants, Ann. Rev. Plant Physiology, 4:325–346.

—— and H. Nilsson, 1950, Transfer of radioactive phosphorus to pine seedlings by means of mycorrhizal hyphae, Physiologia Plantarum, 3:88–92.

—— and ——, 1955, Ca^{45} used as an indicator of transport of cations to pine seedlings by means of mycorrhizal mycelium, Svensk Bot. Tidskr., 49:119–122.

——, ——, and E. Hacskaylo, 1958, Translocation of cations to seedlings of *Pinus virginiana* through mycorrhizal mycelium, Bot. Gaz., 119:243–246.

Mendes, A. J. T., 1941, Cytological observations in *Coffea*. VI. Embryo 'and endosperm development in *Coffea arabica* L., Am. Jour. Botany, 28:784–789.

Mer, C. L., 1940, The factors determining the resistance to the movement of water in the leaf, Ann. Botany, 4:397–401.

Mergen, F., 1955a, Air layering of slash pines, Jour. Forestry, 53:265–270.

———, 1955b, Vegetative propagation of slash pine, Southeastern Forest Expt. Sta. Paper 54.

———, P. E. Hoekstra, and R. M. Echols, 1955, Genetic control of oleoresin yield and viscosity in slash pine, Forest Sci., 1:19–30.

Merriam, C. H., 1898, Life zones and crop zones of the United States, U.S. Dept. Agr. Biol. Survey Bull. 10.

Merrill, S., Jr., and W. W. Kilby, 1952, Effect of cultivation, irrigation, fertilization, and other cultural treatments on growth of newly planted tung trees, Am. Soc. Hort. Sci. Proc., 59:69–81.

Merwin, H. E., and H. Lyon, 1909, Sap pressure in the birch stem, Bot. Gaz., 48:442–458.

Messeri, A., 1948, L'evoluzione della cerchia legnosa in *Pinus halepensis* Mill. Bari., Nuovo giorn. bot. ital., 55:111–132.

Metz, L. J., 1952, Weight and nitrogen and calcium content of the annual litter fall of forests in the South Carolina Piedmont, Soil Sci. Soc. Am. Proc., 16:38–41.

Meyer, A., 1918, Die angebliche Fettspeicherung immergrüner Laubblätter, Ber. deut. bot. Gesell., 36:5–10.

Meyer, B. S., 1927, Studies on the physical properties of leaves and leaf sap, Ohio Jour. Sci., 27:263–288.

———, 1928, Seasonal variations in the physical and chemical properties of the leaves of the pitch pine with special reference to cold resistance, Am. Jour. Botany, 15:449–472.

———, 1932, Further studies on cold resistance in evergreens, with special reference to the possible role of bound water, Bot. Gaz., 94:297–321.

———, 1945, A critical evaluation of the terminology of diffusion phenomena, Plant Physiology, 20:142–164.

——— and D. B. Anderson, 1952, Plant physiology, D. Van Nostrand Company, Inc., Princeton, N.J.

Michaelis, P., 1934, Ökologische Studien an der alpinen Baumgrenze. IV. Zur Kenntnis des winterlichen Wasserhaushaltes, Jahrb. wiss. Bot., 80:169–247.

Middleton, J. T., A. S. Crafts, R. F. Brewer, and O. C. Taylor, 1956, Plant damage by air pollution, California Agriculture, June 9–12.

Migita, K., 1955, Effect of light intensity on the rooting of cuttings of a very old tree of *Cryptomeria japonica*, D. Don., Japanese Forestry Soc. Jour., 37:53–54.

Mikola, P., 1950, On variations in tree growth and their significance to growth studies, Inst. Forestry Fennica Commun., 38(5):1–131.

Milbraith, J. A., and F. P. McWhorter, 1946, Yellow mottle leaf, a virus disease of camellia, Am. Camellia Yearbook, 51–53.

Miller, E. E., 1916, Comparative study of the root systems and leaf areas of corn and the sorghums, Jour. Agr. Research, 6:311–332.

———, 1917, Daily variation of water and dry matter in the leaves of corn and the sorghums, Jour. Agr. Research, 10:11–46.

———, 1938, Plant physiology, 2d ed., McGraw-Hill Book Company, Inc., New York.

——— and A. R. Saunders, 1923, Some observations on the temperature of the leaves of crop plants, Jour. Agr. Research, 26:15–43.

———, C. A. Shadbolt, and L. Holm, 1956, Use of an optical planimeter for measuring leaf area, Plant Physiology, 31:484–486.

Miller, E. J., V. R. Gardner, H. G. Petering, C. L. Comar, and A. L. Neal, 1950, Studies on the development, preparation, properties and application of wax emulsions for coating nursery stock and other plant materials, Michigan Agr. Expt. Sta. Tech. Bull. 218.

Miller, W. D., 1951, Thinning in old-field Virginia pine, Jour. Forestry, 49:884–887.

Milthorpe, F. L., 1955, The significance of the measurement made by the cobalt paper method, Jour. Exptl. Botany, 6:17–19.

Minckler, L. S., 1936, A new method of measuring transpiration, Jour. Forestry, 34:36–39.

———, 1939, Transpiration of trees and forests, Jour. Forestry, 37:336–339.

Mirov, N. T., 1940, Tested methods of grafting pines, Jour. Forestry, 38:768–777.

———, 1941, Distribution of growth hormone on shoots of two species of pine, Jour. Forestry, 39:457–464.

———, 1944, Experiments in rooting pines in California, Jour. Forestry, 42:199–204.

———, 1954, Chemical composition of gum turpentines of pines of the United States and Canada, Forest Prods. Research Soc. Jour., 4:1–7.

———, 1956, Photoperiod and flowering of pines, Forest Sci., 2:328–332.

———, 1958, Distribution of turpentine components among species of the genus *Pinus*, chap. 12 in K. V. Thimann (ed.), The physiology of forest trees, The Ronald Press Company, New York.

Mitchell, H. L., 1934, Pot culture tests of forest soil fertility, Black Rock Forest Bull. 5.

———, 1936, Trends in the nitrogen, phosphorus, potassium and calcium content of the leaves of some forest trees during the growing season, Black Rock Forest Papers, no. 1, pp. 30–44.

———, 1939, The growth and nutrition of white pine (*Pinus strobus* L.) seedlings in cultures with varying nitrogen, phosphorus, potassium, and calcium, Black Rock Forest Bull. 9.

———, 1957, Applying forest tree improvement practices in the Lake States: production of quality wood, Forest Prods. Lab. Rept. 2103.

———, 1958, Wood quality evaluation from increment cores, Tappi, 41:150–156.

——— and R. F. Chandler, 1939, The nitrogen nutrition and growth of certain deciduous trees of northeastern United States, Black Rock Forest Bull. 11.

——— and R. F. Finn, 1935, The relative feeding power of oaks and maples for soil phosphorus, Black Rock Forest Papers, no. 1, pp. 5–9.

———, ———, and R. O. Rosendahl, 1937, The relation between mycorrhizae and the growth and nutrient absorption of coniferous seedlings in nursery beds, Black Rock Forest Papers, no. 1, pp. 57–73.

——— and N. W. Hosley, 1936, Differential browsing by deer on plots variously fertilized, Black Rock Forest Papers, no. 1, pp. 23–27.

Mitchell, J. W., 1936, Measurement of the area of attached and detached leaves, Science, 83:334–336.

——— and F. P. Cullinan, 1942, Effects of growth regulating chemicals in the opening of vegetative and floral buds of peaches and pears, Plant Physiology, 17: 16–26.

Mitscherlich, E. A., 1909, Des Gesetz des Minimums und des Gesetz des abnehmenden Bodenertrags, Landw. Jahrb., 38:537–552.

Mittler, T. E., 1958, Sieve-tube sap via aphid stylets, chap. 19 in K. V. Thimann (ed.), The physiology of forest trees, The Ronald Press Company, New York.

Mix, A. J., 1916, Sunscald of fruit trees: a type of winter injury, Cornell Univ. Agr. Expt. Sta. Bull. 382.

Molisch, H., 1902, Über localen Blutungsdruck und seine Ursachen, Bot. Zeitschr., 60:45–63.

———, 1938, The longevity of plants, transl. by E. H. Fulling, The Translator, New York.

Mollart, D. L., 1954, The control of cambial activity in *Robinia pseudoacacia*, M.S. thesis, University of Manchester, England.

Möller, C. M., 1946, Untersuchungen über Laubmenge, Stoffverlust und Stoffproduktion des Waldes, Det forstlige Forsögsväsen i Danmark, 17:1–287.

———, 1947, The effect of thinning, age, and site on foliage, increment, and loss of dry matter, Jour. Forestry, 45:393–404.

———, M. D. Müller, and J. Nielsen, 1954, Graphic presentation of dry matter production of beech, Det forstlige Forsögsväsen i Danmark, 21:327–335.

Molliard, M., 1913, Recherches physiologiques sur les galles, Rev. gén. bot., 25:252–255, 285–307, 341–370.

Mönch, I., 1937, Untersuchungen über die Kohlensäurebilanz von Alpenpflanzen am natürlichen Standort, Jahrb. wiss. Bot., 85:506–553.

Monsi, M., and T. Saeki, 1953, Über den Lichtfaktor in den pflanzengesellschaften und seine Bedeutung für die Stoffproduktion, Japanese Jour. Botany, 14:22–52.

Moose, C. A., 1938, Chemical and spectroscopic analysis of phloem exudate and parenchyma sap from several species of plants, Plant Physiology, 13:365–380.

Moreland, D. E., 1950, A study of translocation of radioactive phosphorus in loblolly pine (*Pinus taeda* L.), Elisha Mitchell Sci. Soc. Jour., 66:175–181.

Morris, R. F., 1951, The effects of flowering on the foliage production and growth of balsam fir, Forestry Chronicle, 27:40–57.

Morrow, R. R., 1950, Periodicity and growth of sugar maple surface layer roots, Jour. Forestry, 48:875–881.

Moshkov, B. S., 1932, Photoperiodism of trees and its practical importance (transl. from the Russian by C. P. de Blumenthal), Bull. Appl. Bot. Gen. and Plant Breed, A2:108–132.

Mosse, B., 1957, Growth and chemical composition of mycorrhizal and nonmycorrhizal apples, Nature, 179:922–924.

Mothes, K., 1956, Der Einfluss des Wasserzustandes auf Fermentprozesse und Stoffumsatz, in W. Ruhland (ed.), Encyclopedia of plant physiology, vol. 3, pp. 656–664, Springer-Verlag, Berlin.

——— and L. Engelbrecht, 1952, Über Allantoinsäure und Allantoin. I. Ihre Rolle als Wanderform des Stickstoffs und ihre Beziehungen zum Eiweisstoffwechsel des Alhorns, Flora, 139:586–616.

Mott, D. G., L. D. Nairn, and J. A. Cook, 1957, Radial growth in forest trees and effects of insect defoliation, Forest Sci., 3:286–304.

Moyer, L. S., 1937, Recent advances in the physiology of latex, Bot. Rev., 3:522–544.

Moyle, R. C., and R. Zahner, 1954, Soil moisture as affected by stand conditions, Southern Forest Expt. Sta. Occasional Paper 137.

Mulay, A. S., 1931, Seasonal changes in total soluble protein, non-protein and insoluble nitrogen in current year's shoots of Bartlett pear, Plant Physiology, 6:513–539.

Muller, C. H., 1946, Root development and ecological relations of guayule, U.S. Dept. Agr. Tech. Bull. 923.

Müller, D., 1928, Die Kohlensäureassimilation bei arktischen Pflanzen und die Abhängigkeit der Assimilation von der Temperatur, Planta, 6:22–39.

———, 1949, The physiological basis for the deficiency symptoms of plants, Physiologia Plantarum, 2:11–23.

Münch, E., 1913, Hitzeschäden an Waldpflanzen, Naturw. Forst. u. Landwirtsch., 11:557–562.

Münch, E., 1914, Nochmals Hitzeschäden an Waldpflanzen, Naturw. Forst. u. Landwirtsch., 12:169–188.

——, 1930, Die Stoffbewegungen in der Pflanze, Gustav Fischer Verlagsbuchhandlung, Jena, Germany.

Munger, T. T., 1916, Parch blight on Douglas fir in the Pacific Northwest, Plant World, 19:46–67.

Murlin, J. R., 1933, The conversion of fat to carbohydrate in the germinating castor bean. I. The respiratory metabolism, Jour. Gen. Physiology, 17:283–301.

Murneek, A. E., 1929, Hemicellulose as a storage carbohydrate in woody plants, with special reference to the apple, Plant Physiology, 4:251–264.

——, 1930, Quantitative distribution and seasonal fluctuation of nitrogen in apple trees, Am. Soc. Hort. Sci. Proc., 27:228–231.

——, 1932, Growth and development as influenced by fruit and seed formation, Plant Physiology, 7:79–90.

——, 1939, Some physiological factors in growth and reproduction of trees, Am. Soc. Hort. Sci. Proc., 37:666–671.

——, 1942, Quantitative distribution of nitrogen and carbohydrates in apple trees, Missouri Agr. Expt. Sta. Research Bull. 348.

—— and J. C. Logan, 1932, Autumnal migration of nitrogen and carbohydrates in the apple tree with special reference to leaves, Missouri Agr. Expt. Sta. Research Bull. 171.

Myer, J. E., 1922, Ray volumes of the commercial woods of the United States and their significance, Jour. Forestry, 20:337–351.

Nast, C. G., 1935, Morphological development of the fruit of *Juglans nigra*, Hilgardia, 9:345–381.

Negisi, K., and T. Satoo, 1954, The effect of drying of soil on apparent photosynthesis, transpiration, carbohydrate reserves and growth of seedlings of Akamatu (*Pinus densiflora* Sieb. et Zucc.), Japanese Forest Soc. Jour., 36:66–71.

—— and ——, 1956, Photosynthesis, respiration and consumption of reserves of Sugi (*Cryptomeria japonica*) cuttings, Japanese Forest Soc. Jour., 38:63–70.

——, ——, and K. Yagi, 1957, A method for the rapid measuring of leaf areas, Japanese Forest Soc. Jour., 39:380–384.

Nelson, T. C., 1957, Early responses of some southern tree species to gibberellic acid, Jour. Forestry, 55:518–520.

Nemec, A., and K. Kvapil, 1927, Über den Einfluss verschiedener Waldbestände auf den Gehalt und die Bildung von Nitraten in Waldböden, Zeitschr. Forst. u. Jagdw., 59:321–352.

Nesbitt, W. A., 1942, Aerial roots from old tree wound, Plant Physiology, 17:689–690.

Nienstaedt, H., F. C. Cech, F. Mergen, C. Wang, and B. Zak, 1958, Vegetative propagation in forest genetics research and practice, Jour. Forestry, 56:826–839.

Nightingale, G. T., 1935, Effects of temperature on growth, anatomy, and metabolism of apple and peach roots, Bot. Gaz., 96:581–639.

Niklewski, B., 1906, Untersuchungen über die Umwandlung einiger stickstoffreien Reservestoffs während der Winterperiode der Bäume, Beih. Bot. Zentralbl., 19:68–117.

Nitsch, J. P., 1952, Plant hormones in the development of fruits, Quart. Rev. Biology, 27:33–57.

——, 1953, The physiology of fruit growth, Ann. Rev. Plant Physiology, 4:199–236.

——, 1957a, Growth response of woody plants to photoperiodic stimuli, Am. Soc. Hort. Sci. Proc., 70:512–525.

——, 1957b, Photoperiodism in woody plants, Am. Soc. Hort. Sci. Proc., 70:526–544.

Nixon, R. W., and R. T. Wedding, 1956, Age of date leaves in relation to efficiency of photosynthesis, Am. Soc. Hort. Sci. Proc., 67:265–269.

Nutman, F. J., 1934, The root system of *Coffea arabica*. III. The spatial distribution of the absorbing area of the root, Emp. Jour. Exptl. Agr., 2:293–302.

——, 1937, Studies of the physiology of *Coffea arabica*. II. Stomatal movements in relation to photosynthesis under natural conditions, Ann. Botany, 1:681–694.

——, 1941, Studies of the physiology of *Coffea arabica*. III. Transpiration rates of whole trees in relation to natural environmental conditions, Ann. Botany, 5:59–82.

—— and F. M. L. Sheffield, 1949, Studies of the clove tree. I. Sudden-death disease and its epidemiology, Ann. Appl. Biology, 36:419–439.

Olmsted, C. E., 1941, The roles of light and root competition in an oak-maple forest, Ecol. Soc. of America Bull., 22:41.

——, 1951, Experiments on photoperiodism, dormancy, and leaf age and abscission in sugar maple, Bot. Gaz., 112:365–393.

Olsen, C., 1948, The mineral, nitrogen and sugar content of beech leaves and beech leaf sap at various times, Laboratoire Carlsberg Comptes rendus des travaux, 26:197–230.

On, D., 1952, 2,3,5-triphenyl tetrazolium chloride as a viability indicator of certain coniferous seeds, Jour. Forestry, 50:868.

Oosting, H. J., 1956, The study of plant communities, W. H. Freeman Co., San Francisco.

—— and P. J. Kramer, 1946, Water and light in relation to pine reproduction, Ecology, 27:47–53.

Oppenheimer, H. R., 1932, Zur Kenntnis der hochsomerlichen Wasserbilanz mediterraner Gehölze, Ber. deut. Bot. Gesell., 50:185–243.

——, 1951, Summer drought and water balance of plants growing in the Near East, Jour. Ecology, 39:356–362.

——, 1953, An experimental study on ecological relationships and water expenses of Mediterranean forest vegetation, Palestine Jour. Botany, 8:103–124.

—— and D. L. Elze, 1941, Irrigation of citrus trees according to physiological indicators, Palestine Jour. Bot., R4:20–46.

Ordin, L., and J. Bonner, 1956, Permeability of *Avena* coleoptile sections to water measured by diffusion of deuterium hydroxide, Plant Physiology, 31:53–57.

—— and L. Jacobson, 1955, Inhibition of ion absorption and respiration in barley roots, Plant Physiology, 30:21–27.

—— and P. J. Kramer, 1956, Permeability of *Vicia faba* root segments to water as measured by diffusion of deuterium hydroxide, Plant Physiology, 31:468–471.

Orr, M. Y., 1925, The effect of frost on the wood of larch, Roy. Scot. Arbor. Soc. Trans., 39:38–41.

Osborne, D. J., and R. L. Wain, 1951, Studies on plant growth regulating substances. III. The production of parthenocarpic pomaceous fruits by chemical treatment, Jour. Hort. Sci., 26:317–327.

Oserkowsky, J., 1932, Hydrogen-ion concentration and iron content of tracheal sap from green and chlorotic pear trees, Plant Physiology, 7:253–259.

Ostrom, C. E., 1945, Effects of plant-growth regulators on shoot development and field survival of forest planting stock, Bot. Gaz., 107:139–183.

Overbeek, J. van, 1942, Water uptake by excised root systems of the tomato due to non-osmotic forces, Am. Jour. Botany, 29:677–683.

Overbeek, J. van, 1952, Agricultural application of growth regulators and their physiological basis, Ann. Rev. Plant Physiology, 3:87–108.

———, 1956, Absorption and translocation of plant regulators, Ann. Rev. Plant Physiology, 7:355–372.

———, S. A. Gordon, and L. E. Gregory, 1946, An analysis of the function of the leaf in the process of root formation in cuttings, Am. Jour. Botany, 33:100–107.

Overholser, E. L., and L. L. Claypool, 1935, The relations of leaf area per cherry to physical properties and chemical composition, Gartenbauwissenschaft, 9:95–99.

Overstreet, R., 1957, Comments on the absorption of inorganic ions by root cells, Plant Physiology, 32:491–492.

——— and L. Jacobson, 1946, The absorption by roots of rubidium and phosphate ions at extremely small concentrations as revealed by experiments with Rb^{86} and P^{32} prepared without carrier, Am. Jour. Botany, 33:107–112.

Overton, J. B., 1911, Studies on the relation of the living cells to transpiration and sapflow in *Cyperus*, Bot. Gaz., 51:28–63, 102–120.

Ovington, J. D., 1954, Studies of the development of woodland conditions under different trees. II. The forest floor, Jour. Ecology, 42:71–80.

———, 1956a, The form, weights and productivity of tree species grown in close stands, New Phytologist, 55:289–388.

———, 1956b, The composition of tree leaves, Forestry, 29:22–28.

Owen, P. C., 1952, The relation of germination of wheat to water potential, Jour. Expt. Botany, 3:188–203.

Pack, D. A., 1921, The after-ripening and germination of *Juniperus* seeds, Bot. Gaz., 71:32–60.

Paine, L. A., 1953, Deterioration in white spruce, Canada Dept. Agr. Bimonthly Prog. Rept. 9, no. 6.

Panshin, A. J., E. S. Harrar, W. J. Baker, and P. B. Proctor, 1950, Forest products, McGraw-Hill Book Company, Inc., New York.

Parham, W. L., 1941, *Albizia falcata:* a quick growing tree, Agr. Jour. (Fiji), 12: 67–68.

Parker, J., 1949, Effects of variations in the root-leaf ratio on transpiration rate, Plant Physiology, 24:739–743.

———, 1950, The effect of flooding on the transpiration and survival of some northeastern forest tree species, Plant Physiology, 25:453–460.

———, 1951, Moisture retention in leaves of conifers of the northern Rocky Mountains, Bot. Gaz., 113:210–216.

———, 1952, Desiccation in conifer leaves: anatomical changes and determination of the lethal level, Bot. Gaz., 114:189–198.

———, 1953a, New methods for the determination of forest tree seed germinability, Jour. Forestry, 51:34–35.

———, 1953b, Photosynthesis of *Picea excelsa* (P. abies) in winter, Ecology, 34:605–609.

———, 1954, Differences in survival of excised ponderosa pine leaves of various ages, Plant Physiology, 29:486–487.

———, 1955, Annual trends in cold hardiness of ponderosa pine and grand fir, Ecology, 36:377–380.

———, 1956a, Variations in copper, boron, and manganese in leaves of *Pinus ponderosa*, Forest Sci., 2:190–198.

———, 1956b, Drought resistance in woody plants, Bot. Rev., 22:241–289.

———, 1957, Seasonal changes in some chemical and physical properties of living cells of *Pinus ponderosa* and their relation to freezing resistance, Protoplasma, 48:147–163.

——, 1958a, Changes in sugars and nitrogenous compounds of tree barks from summer to winter, Naturwissenschaften, 45:139.

——, 1958b, Sol-gel transitions in the living cells of conifers and their relation to resistance to cold, Nature, 182:1815.

Parker, K. G., L. J. Tyler, D. S. Welch, and S. Pope, 1947, Nutrition of the trees and development of Dutch elm disease, Phytopathology, 37:215–224.

Paterson, A., 1938, The occlusion of pruning wounds in Norway spruce (*Picea excelsa*), Ann. Botany, 2:681–698.

Patton, R. F., and A. J. Riker, 1954, Needle droop and needle blight of red pine, Jour. Forestry, 52:412–418.

—— and ——, 1958, Rooting cuttings of white pine, Forest Sci., 4:116–126.

Pauley, S. S., 1948, Budding as a silvicultural technique, Jour. Forestry, 46:524–525.

—— and T. O. Perry, 1954, Ecotypic variations of the photoperiodic response in *Populus*, Arnold Arboretum Jour., 35:167–188.

Pearse, H. L., 1939, Plant hormones and their practical importance in horticulture, Imp. Bur. Hort. Plantation Crops Tech. Commun. 12, pp. 1–88.

Pearson, G. A., 1924, Studies in transpiration of coniferous tree seedlings, Ecology, 5:340–347.

Pearson, L. C., and D. B. Lawrence, 1958, Photosynthesis in aspen bark, Am. Jour. Botany, 45:383–387.

Penfound, W. T., 1934, Comparative structure of the wood in the "knees," swollen bases, and normal trunks of the tupelo-gum (*Nyssa aquatica* L.), Am. Jour. Botany, 21:623–631.

Person, H. L., and W. Hollin, 1942, Natural restocking of redwood cutover lands, Jour. Forestry, 40:683–688.

Pessin, L. J., 1934, Annual ring formation in *Pinus palustris* seedlings, Am. Jour. Botany, 21:599–604.

——, 1937, The effect of nutrient deficiency on the growth of longleaf pine seedlings, Southeast Forest Expt. Sta. Occasional Paper 65.

Pfeiffer, M., 1933, Frost untersuchungen an Fichtentrieben, Tharandt. forst. Jahrb., 84:664–695.

Phillis, E., and T. G. Mason, 1940, The effect of ringing on the upward movement of solutes from the roots, Ann. Botany, 4:635–644.

Pickett, W. F., 1933, A comparative study of the intercellular spaces of apple leaves, Am. Soc. Hort. Sci. Proc., 30:156–161.

——, 1937, The relationship between the internal structure and photosynthetic behavior of apple leaves, Kansas Agr. Expt. Sta. Tech. Bull. 42.

—— and A. L. Kenworthy, 1939, The relationship between structure, chlorophyll content and photosynthesis in apple leaves, Am. Soc. Hort. Sci. Proc., 37:371–373.

Pirone, P. P., 1941, Maintenance of shade and ornamental trees, Oxford University Press, New York.

Pisek, A., and E. Cartellieri, 1932–1939, Zur Kenntnis des Wasserhaushaltes der Pflanzen. I. Sonnenpflanzen. Jahrb. wiss. Bot., 75:195–251 (1932); II, Schafften-pflanzen, *ibid.*, 75:643–678 (1932); III, Alpine Zwergsträucher, *ibid.*, 79:131–190 (1933); IV, Bäume und Sträucher, *ibid.*, 88:22–68 (1939).

—— and W. Larcher, 1954, Zusammenhang zwischen Austrocknungsresistenz und Frosthärte bei Immergrünen, Protoplasma, 44:30–46.

Pisek, A., and R. Schiessl, 1946, Die Temperaturbeeinflussbarkeit der Frosthärte von Nadelhölzern und Zwergsträuchern an der alpinen Baumgrenze, Naturw. med. Ver. Innsbruck Ber., 47:33–52.

————, H. Sohm, and E. Cartellieri, 1935, Untersuchungen über osmotischen Wert und Wassergehalt von Pflanzen und Pflanzengesellschaften der alpinen Stufe, Beit. Bot. Centralbl., 52:634–675.

———— and W. Tranquillini, 1951, Transpiration und Wasserhaushalt der Fichte (*Picea excelsa*) bei zunehmender Luft und Bodentrockenheit, Physiologia Plantarum, 4:1–27.

———— and ————, 1954, Assimilation und Kohlenstoffhaushalt in der Krone von Fichten (*Picea excelsa* Link) und Rotbuchenbäumen (*Fagus silvatica* L.), Flora, 141:237–270.

———— and E. Winkler, 1953, Die Schliesbewegung der Stomata bei ökologisch verschiedenen Pflanzentypen in Abhängigkeit vom Wassersatigungszustand der Blätter und vom Licht, Planta, 42:253–278.

Plaisted, P. H., 1956, Changes in the free amino acids that accompany aging in leaves of *Acer platanoides*, Plant Physiology Proc., 31, VIII.

Plakidas, A. G., 1948, Possibility of utilizing virus infection as a means of producing new varieties of camellias, Am. Camellia Yearbook, pp. 107–109.

Pleasants, A. L., 1930, The effect of nitrate fertilizer on stomatal behavior, Elisha Mitchell Sci. Soc. Jour., 46:95–116.

Podluzhnii, D. F., 1940, Propagation of the olive tree by cuttings (in Russian), Soviet Subtropics, 11–12:41–43.

Pollard, J. K., and T. Sproston, 1954, Nitrogenous constituents of sap exuded from the sapwood of *Acer saccharum*, Plant Physiology, 29:360–364.

Pollock, B. M., 1953, The respiration of *Acer* buds in relation to the inception and termination of the winter rest, Physiologia Plantarum, 6:47–64.

———— and F. C. Steward, 1949, An investigation of respiration and fermentation in buds of *Acer* using a new form of microrespirometer, Am. Jour. Botany, 36:827.

Polster, H., 1950, Die physiologischen Grundlagen der Stofferzeugung im Walde, Bayerischer Landwirtschaftsverlag Gmbh., Munich.

Pond, J. D., 1936, Girdling for seed production, Jour. Forestry, 34:78–79.

Popham, R. A., 1952, Developmental plant anatomy, Long's College Book Co., Columbus, Ohio.

Postlethwait, S. N., and B. Rogers, 1958, Tracing the path of the transpiration stream in trees by the use of radioactive isotopes, Am. Jour. Botany, 45:753–757.

Preston, J. F., and F. J. Phillips, 1911, Seasonal variation in the food reserve of trees, Forest Quart., 9:232–243.

Preston, R. D., 1952, Movement of water in higher plants: deformation and flow in biological systems, pp. 257–321, North Holland Pub. Co., Amsterdam.

Prevot, P., and M. Ollagnier, 1954, Peanut and oil palm foliar diagnosis interrelations of N, P, K, Ca, Mg, Plant Physiology, 29:26–34.

Priestley, J. H., 1922, Further observations upon the mechanism of root pressure, New Phytologist, 21:41–48.

————, 1930, Studies in the physiology of cambial activity. III. The seasonal activity of the cambium, New Phytologist, 29:316–354.

————, 1935, Sap ascent in the tree, Sci. Prog., 62:42–56.

———— and L. I. Scott, 1936, A note upon summer wood production in the tree, Leeds Phil. Lit. Soc. Proc., 3:235–248.

————, ————, and M. E. Malins, 1933, A new method of studying cambial activity, Leeds Phil. Lit. Soc. Proc., 2:365–374.

———— and A. Wormall, 1925, On the solutes exuded by root pressure from vines, New Phytologist, 24:24–38.

Printz, H., 1933, Granens of furens fysiologi og geografiska uffredelse (Physiology and geographical distribution of spruce and pine), Nyt. Mag. Naturvidensk (Oslo), 73:167–219.

Proebsting, E. L., 1943, Root distribution of some deciduous trees in a California orchard, Am. Soc. Hort. Sci. Proc., 43:1–4.

Quetel, R., 1939, IV, Les rythmes de la croissance dans les régions tropicales, Rev. gén. bot., 51:33–52.

Raber, O., 1937, Water utilization by trees, with special reference to the economic forest species of the North Temperate Zone, U.S. Dept. Agr. Misc. Pub. 257.

Rabideau, G. S., and G. O. Burr, 1945, The use of the C^{13} isotope as a tracer for transport studies in plants, Am. Jour. Botany, 32:349–356.

Rabinowitch, E. I., 1945, Photosynthesis and related processes, vol. I, Interscience Publishers, Inc., New York.

————, 1951, Photosynthesis and related processes, vol. II, part 1, Interscience Publishers, Inc., New York.

————, 1956, Photosynthesis and related processes, vol. II, part 2, Interscience Publishers, Inc., New York.

Ramann, E., 1890, Die Waldstreu und ihre Bedeuting für Boden und Wald, Springer-Verlag, Berlin.

————, 1912, Die Wanderungen der Mineralstoffe beim herbstlichen Absieben der Blätter, Landw. Vers., 76:157–164.

Rayner, M. C., and W. Neilson-Jones, 1944, Problems in tree nutrition, Faber & Faber, Ltd., London.

Rebel, K., 1920, Streunutzung, insbesondere im bayerischen Staatswald, Munich.

Rediske, J. H., and O. Biddulph, 1953, The absorption and translocation of iron, Plant Physiology, 28:576–593.

———— and A. A. Selders, 1953, The absorption and translocation of strontium by plants, Plant Physiology, 28:594–605.

Redmond, D. R., and R. C. Robinson, 1954, Viability and germination in yellow birch, Forestry Chronicle, 30:79–87.

Reed, H. S., 1928, Intra-seasonal cycles of growth, Natl. Acad. Sci. (U.S.) Proc., 14:221–229.

————, 1938, Cytology of leaves affected with little-leaf, Am. Jour. Botany, 25:174–186.

———— and J. Dufrenoy, 1935, The effects of zinc and iron salt on the cell structure of mottled orange leaves, Hilgardia, 9:113–137.

———— and D. T. MacDougal, 1937, Periodicity in the growth of the young orange tree, Growth, 1:371–373.

Reed, J. F., 1939, Root and shoot growth of shortleaf and loblolly pines in relation to certain environmental conditions, Duke University School Forestry Bull. 4.

Rees, T., 1958, Cytochrome oxidase in mycorrhizal and uninfected roots of *Fagus sylvatica*, Am. Soc. Plant Physiology Proc., Suppl., 33, X–XI.

Reimer, C. W., 1949, Growth correlations in five species of deciduous trees, Butler Univ. Bot. Studies, 9:43–59.

Reineke, L. H., 1932, A precision dendrometer, Jour. Forestry, 30:692–697.

Reitemeier, R. F., 1946, Effect of moisture content on the dissolved and exchangeable ions of soils of arid regions, Soil Sci., 61:195–214.

Renner, O., 1912, Versuche zur Mechanik der Wasserversorgung, Ber. deut. bot. Gesell., 30:576–580, 642–648.

Renner, O., 1915, Die Wasserversorgung der Pflanzen, Handworterbuch Naturwiss., 10:538–557.

——, 1929, Versuche zur Bestimmung des Filtrationwiderstandes der Wurzeln, Jahrb. wiss. Bot., 70:805–838.

Rennie, P. J., 1955, The uptake of nutrients by mature forest growth, Plant and Soil, 7:49–95.

Reuter, G., and H. Wolffgang, 1954, Vergleichende Untersuchungen über den Charakter der Stickstoff-Verbindungen von Baumblutungssaften bei *Betulaceae* und anderen Holzarten, Flora, 142:146–155.

Reuther, W., and D. Boynton, 1940, Variations in potassium content of the foliage from certain New York orchards, Am. Soc. Hort. Sci. Proc., 37:32–38.

—— and F. W. Burrows, 1942, Effect of manganese sulfate on the photosynthetic activity of frenched tung foliage, Am. Soc. Hort. Sci. Proc., 40:73–76.

Rhoads, A. S., 1923, The formation and pathological anatomy of frost rings in conifers injured by late frosts, U.S. Dept. Agr. Bull. 1131.

Rhoads, W. A., and R. T. Wedding, 1953, Leaf drop in citrus, California Agriculture, 7:9.

Richards, L. A., and C. H. Wadleigh, 1952, Soil water and plant growth, chap. 3 in B. T. Shaw (ed.), Soil physical conditions and plant growth, Academic Press, Inc., New York.

Richards, S. J., L. V. Weeks, and J. C. Johnston, 1958, Effects of irrigation treatments and rates of nitrogen fertilization on young Hass avocado trees, Am. Soc. Hort. Sci. Proc., 71:292–297.

Richardson, S. D., 1953, A note on some differences in root-hair formation between seedlings of sycamore and American oak, New Phytologist, 52:80–82.

——, 1956, On the role of the acorn in root growth of American oak seedlings, Landbouwhogeschool, Wageningen Med., 56:1–18.

——, 1957, The effect of leaf age on the rate of photosynthesis in detached leaves of tree seedlings, Acta Bot. Neerl., 6:445–457.

Rider, N. E., 1957, Water losses from various land surfaces, Meteorological Soc. Quart. Rev., 83:181–193.

Rigg, G. B., and E. S. Harrar, 1931, The root systems of trees growing in sphagnum, Am. Jour. Botany, 18:391–397.

Righter, F. I., 1939, Early flower production among the pines, Jour. Forestry, 37: 935–938.

——, 1946, New perspectives in forest tree breeding, Science, 104:1–3.

Riker, A. J., 1954, Opportunities in disease and insect control through genetics, Jour. Forestry, 52:651–652.

—— and R. Riker, 1936, Introduction to research on plant diseases, Swift and Co., New York.

Ringoet, A., 1952, Recherches sur le transpiration et le bilan d'eau de quelques plantes tropicales, Inst. natl. étude agron. Congo Belge Pub., ser. sci. 56.

Rissmüller, L., 1874, Über die Stoffwanderung in der Pflanze, Landw. Vers., 17:17–31.

Roach, W. A., 1939, Plant injection as a physiological method, Ann. Botany, 3:155–226.

Robbins, W. J., 1957, Physiological aspects of aging in plants, Am. Jour. Botany, 44:289–294.

Roberts, F. L., 1948, A study of the absorbing surfaces of the roots of loblolly pine, M.A. thesis, Duke University, Durham, N.C.

Roberts, W. O., 1946, Simplifications of the Roach method of diagnostic plant injection, Jour. Pom. Hort. Sci., 22:184–188.

Robertson, R. N., 1956, The mechanism of absorption, in W. Ruhland (ed.), Encyclopedia plant physiology, vol. 2, pp. 449–467, Springer-Verlag, Berlin.

Robinson, W. O., 1930, Some chemical phases of submerged soil conditions, Soil Sci., 30:197–217.

Roeckl, B., 1949, Nachweis eines Konzentrationshubs zwischen Palisadenzellen und Siebröhren, Planta, 36:530–549.

Rogers, W. S., 1939, Apple root growth in relation to root-stock, soil, seasonal and climatic factors, Jour. Pom. Hort. Sci., 17:99–130.

―――― and A. B. Beakbane, 1957, Stock and scion relations, Ann. Rev. Plant Physiology, 8:217–236.

Rohmeder, E., and M. Loebel, 1940, Keimversuche mit Zirbelkiefer, Forstwiss. Zentralbl., 62:25–36.

Rokach, A., 1953, Water transfer from fruits to leaves in the Shamouti orange tree and related topics, Palestine Jour. Botany, 8:146–151.

Rose, A. H., 1958, The effect of defoliation on foliage production and radial growth of quaking aspen, Forest Sci., 4:335–342.

Rosendahl, R. O., and C. F. Korstian, 1945, Effect of fertilizers on loblolly pine in a North Carolina nursery, Plant Physiology, 20:19–23.

Rosene, H. F., 1944, Effects of cyanide on rate of exudation in excised onion roots, Am. Jour. Botany, 31:172–174.

―――――, 1947, Reversible azide inhibition of oxygen consumption and water transfer in root tissue, Jour. Cell. Comp. Physiology, 30:15–30.

―――――, 1950, The effect of anoxia on water exchange and oxygen consumption of onion root tissue, Jour. Cell. Comp. Physiology, 35:179–193.

―――― and E. J. Lund, 1953, Bioelectric fields and correlations in plants, in W. E. Loomis (ed.), Growth and differentiation in plants, Iowa State College Press, Ames, Iowa.

Roth, E. R., and B. Sleeth, 1939, Butt rot in unburned sprout oak stands, U.S. Dept. Agr. Tech. Bull. 684.

Routien, J. B., and R. F. Dawson, 1943, Some interrelationships of growth, salt absorption, respiration, and mycorrhizal development in *Pinus echinata* Mill., Am. Jour. Botany, 30:440–451.

Rowland, C. A., 1950, Early results of bud-pruning in slash pine, Jour. Forestry, 48:100–103.

Rudolf, P. O., 1952, Cold-soaking of jack pine seeds, Jour. Forestry, 50:626.

Rufelt, H., 1956, Influence of the root pressure on the transpiration of wheat plants, Physiologia Plantarum, 9:154–164.

Rumbold, C., 1920, The injection of chemicals into chestnut trees, Am. Jour. Botany, 7:45–57.

Runyon, E. H., 1936, Ratio of water content to dry weight in leaves of the creosote bush, Bot. Gaz., 97:518–533.

Rutter, A. J., and K. Sands, 1958, The relation of leaf water deficit to soil moisture tension in *Pinus sylvestris* L., New Phytologist, 57:50–65.

Ryall, A. L., and W. W. Aldrich, 1944, The effect of water deficits in the tree upon maturity, composition, and storage quality of Bosc pears, Jour. Agr. Research, 68:121–133.

Sablon, L. du, 1896, Sur le formation des reserves non azotées de la noix et de l'amande, Acad. Sci. (Paris) Comptes rendus, 123:1084–1086.

―――――, 1904, Recherches physiologiques sur les matières de reserves des arbres, Rev. gén. bot., 16:341–368, 386–401.

Sachs, J. von, 1884, Ein Beitrag zur Kenntnis der Ernährungsthatigkeit der Blätter, Bot. Inst. Wurzburg Arbeit, 3:1-33.

———, 1887, Lectures on the physiology of plants, Oxford University Press, New York.

Saeki, T., and N. Nomoto, 1958, On the seasonal change of photosynthetic activity of some deciduous and evergreen broadleaf trees, Bot. Mag. Tokyo, 71:235-241.

Salisbury, E. J., 1927, On the causes and ecological significance of stomatal frequency, with special reference to the woodland flora, Roy. Soc. (London) Phil. Trans., B216:1-65.

Samantarai, B., 1955, A note on the induction of roots on the twigs of *Magnolia grandiflora* L. with the aid of synthetic hormones, Indian Jour. Horticulture, 12:32-33.

Samish, R. M., 1954, Dormancy in woody plants, Ann. Rev. Plant Physiology, 5:183-205.

Sampson, A. W., and R. Samisch, 1935, Growth and seasonal changes in composition of oak leaves, Plant Physiology, 10:739-751.

Sando, C. E., 1923, Constituents of the waxlike coating on the surface of the apple, Jour. Biol. Chem., 56:457-468.

Satoo, S., 1956, Anatomical studies on the rooting of cuttings in conifer species, Tokyo Univ. Forests Bull., 51:111-157.

Satoo, T., 1955a, The influence of wind on dry matter increase in leaves of *Quercus acutissima*, Tokyo Univ. Forests Bull., 50:23-26.

———, 1955b, The influence of wind on transpiration of some conifers, Tokyo Univ. Forests Bull., 50:27-35.

———, 1956, Drought resistance of some conifers at the first summer after their emergence, Tokyo Univ. Forests Bull., 51:1-108.

——— and M. Goo, 1954, Seed germination as affected by suction force of soil and saccharose solution, Tokyo Univ. Forests Bull., 46:159-168.

——— and N. Hukahara, 1953, Water relations of cuttings shortly after planting, Tokyo Univ. Forests Bull., 45:89-101.

———, K. Nakamura, and M. Senda, 1955, Materials for the study of growth in stands. I. Young stands of Japanese red pine of various density, Tokyo Univ. Forests Bull., 48:65-90.

———, K. Negisi, and K. Nakamura, 1953, Relations between the rooting and the age of the tree from which cuttings are taken: an experiment using clonal materials, Jap. Forest. Soc. Jour., 35:69-70.

——— and T. Takegosi, 1952, Seasonal change of starch content in *Quercus myrsinaefolia* and *Q. acutissima*, Tokyo Univ. Forests Misc. Inf., no. 9, pp. 17-23.

Savage, E. F., and F. Cowart, 1942, The effect of pruning upon the root distribution of peach trees, Am. Soc. Hort. Sci. Proc., 41:67-70.

Sax, K., 1958, Experimental control of tree growth and reproduction, chap. 32 in K. V. Thimann (ed.), The physiology of forest trees, The Ronald Press Company, New York.

Sayre, J. D., 1920, The relation of hairy leaf coverings to the resistance of leaves to transpiration, Ohio Jour. Sci., 20:55-86.

———, 1926, Physiology of the stomata of *Rumex patienta*, Ohio Jour. Sci., 26:233-267.

———, 1957, Spectrographic techniques and analysis of pine needles, Ohio Jour. Sci., 57:345-349.

Scarth, G. W., A. Loewy, and M. Shaw, 1948, Use of the infrared total absorption method for estimating the time course of photosynthesis and transpiration, Canadian Jour. Research, C26:94–107.

—— and M. Shaw, 1951, Stomatal movement in Pelargonium. II. Effects of water deficit and of chloroform: photosynthesis in guard cells, Plant Physiology, 26: 581–596.

Schaffalitzky de Muckadell, M., 1954, Juvenile stages in woody plants, Physiologia Plantarum, 7:782–796.

Schantz-Hansen, T., 1939, Ten-year observations on the thinning of fifteen-year-old red pine, Jour. Forestry, 37:963–966.

Schertz, F. M., 1928, The preparation of chlorophyll, Plant Physiology, 3:487–497.

Schimper, A. F. W., 1898, Pflanzengeographie auf physiologischer Grundlage, Gustav Fischer Verlagsbuchhandlung, Jena, Germany.

Schneider, G. W., and N. F. Childers, 1941, Influence of soil moisture on photosynthesis, respiration and transpiration of apple leaves, Plant Physiology, 16:565–583.

Schoch-Bodmer, H., 1945, Interpositionswachstum, symplastiches und gleitendes Wachstum, Ber. schweiz. bot. Gesell., 55:313–319.

Scholander, P. F., 1947, Analyzer for accurate estimation of respiratory gases in one-half cubic centimeter samples, Jour. Biol. Chemistry, 167:235–250.

——, 1958, The rise of sap in lianas, chap. 1 in K. V. Thimann (ed.), The physiology of forest trees, The Ronald Press Company, New York.

——, L. van Dam, and S. I. Scholander, 1955, Gas exchange in the roots of mangroves, Am. Jour. Botany, 42:92–98.

——, W. E. Love, and J. W. Kanwisher, 1955, The rise of sap in tall grapevines, Plant Physiology, 30:93–104.

——, B. Ruud, and H. Leivestad, 1957, The rise of sap in a tropical liana, Plant Physiology, 32:1–6.

Scholtes, W. S., 1953, The concentration of forest tree roots in the surface zone of some Piedmont soils, Iowa Acad. Sci. Proc., 60:243–259.

Schopmeyer, C. S., 1939, Transpiration and physico-chemical properties of leaves as related to drought resistance in loblolly pine and shortleaf pine, Plant Physiology, 14:447–462.

——, 1955, Effects of turpentining on growth of slash pine: first-year results, Forest Sci., 1:83–87.

Schramm, J. R., 1958, The mechanism of frost heaving of tree seedlings, Am. Phil. Soc. Proc., 102:333–350.

Schreiner, E. J., 1939a, The possibility of the clone in forestry, Jour. Forestry, 37:61–62.

——, 1939b, Some ecological aspects of forest genetics, Jour. Forestry, 37:462–464.

——, 1940, Cultivation increases length of growing season and amount of growth of poplar hybrids, Northeastern Forest Expt. Sta. Occasional Paper 8.

——, 1950, Genetics in relation to forestry, Jour. Forestry, 48:33–38.

Schroeder, C. A., and P. A. Wieland, 1956, Diurnal fluctuation in size in various parts of the avocado tree and fruit, Am. Soc. Hort. Sci. Proc., 68:253–258.

Schroeder, H., 1919, Die jährliche Gesamtproduktion der grünen Pflanzendecke der Erde, Naturwissenschaft, 7:8–12, 23–29.

Schroeder, R. A., 1936, The effect of some summer oil sprays upon the carbon dioxide absorption of apple leaves, Am. Soc. Hort. Sci. Proc., 33:170–172.

Schubert, A., 1939, Untersuchungen über den Transpirationstrom der Nadelhölzer und den Wasserbedarf von Fichte und Lärche, Tharandt. forstl. Jahrb., 90:821–883.

Schulman, E., 1958, Bristlecone pine, oldest known living thing, Natl. Geographic, 113:355-372.

Scott, D. R. M., 1955, Amount and chemical composition of the organic matter contributed by overstory and understory vegetation to forest soil, Yale Univ. School Forestry Bull. 62.

Scott, L. I., and J. H. Priestley, 1928, The root as an absorbing organ. I. A reconsideration of the entry of water and salts into the absorbing region, New Phytologist, 27:125-141.

Scully, N. J., 1942, Root distribution and environment in a maple-oak forest, Bot. Gaz., 103:492-517.

Sell, H. M., A. H. Best, W. Reuther, and M. Drosdoff, 1948, Changes in chemical composition and biological activity of developing tung fruit with references to oil synthesis, Plant Physiology, 23:359-372.

———, H. A. Taylor, and G. F. Potter, 1944, Effect of chemical treatments in prolonging dormancy of tung buds, Bot. Gaz., 196:215-223.

Senda, S., K. Nakamura, S. Takahara, and T. Satoo, 1952, Some aspects of growth in stands, Tokyo Univ. Forests Bull. 43.

Sequeira, L., and T. A. Steeves, 1954, Auxin inactivation and its relation to leaf drop caused by the fungus *Omphalia flavida*, Plant Physiology, 29:11-16.

Shannon, L. M., 1954, Internal bark necrosis of the Delicious apple, Am. Soc. Hort. Sci. Proc., 64:165-174.

Sharples, A., and H. Gunnery, 1933, Callus formation in *Hibiscus Rosasinensis* L. and *Hevea brasiliensis* Muell. Arg., Ann. Botany, 47:827-839.

Shattuck, C. H., 1905, A morphological study of *Ulmus americana*, Bot. Gaz., 40:209-223.

Shaw, S. T., 1942, Respiration studies of developing Jonathan apples, Plant Physiology, 17:80-90.

Sherman, H., 1921, Respiration of dormant seeds, Bot. Gaz., 72:1-30.

Shippy, W. B., 1930, The influence of environment on the callusing of apple cuttings and grafts, Am. Jour. Botany, 17:290-327.

Shirley, H. L., 1929a, The influence of light intensity and light quality upon the growth of plants, Am. Jour. Botany, 16:354-390.

———, 1929b, Light requirements and silvicultural practice, Jour. Forestry, 27:535-538.

———, 1932, Light intensity in relation to plant growth in a virgin Norway pine forest, Jour. Agr. Research, 44:227-244.

———, 1935, Light as an ecological factor and its measurement, Bot. Rev., 1:355-382.

———, 1936, Lethal high temperatures for conifers and the cooling effects of transpiration, Jour. Agr. Research, 53:239-258.

———, 1943, Is tolerance the capacity to endure shade? Jour. Forestry, 41:339-345.

———, 1945, Reproduction of upland conifers in the Lake States as affected by root competition and light, Am. Midland Naturalist, 33:537-612.

——— and L. J. Meuli, 1938, Influence of foliage sprays on drought resistance of conifers, Plant Physiology, 13:399-406.

——— and ———, 1939, The influence of soil nutrients on drought resistance of two-year-old red pine, Am. Jour. Botany, 26:355-360.

Shoji, K., F. T. Addicott, and W. A. Swets, 1951, Auxin in relation to leaf blade abscission, Plant Physiology, 26:189-191.

Shunk, I. V., 1939, Oxygen requirements for germination of seeds of *Nyssa aquatica* —tupelo gum, Science, 90:565-566.

Sideris, C. P., and B. H. Krauss, 1955, Transpiration and translocation phenomena in pineapples, Am. Jour. Botany, 42:707–709.

Sierp, H., and A. Seybold, 1929, Untersuchungen über die Verdunstung aus multiperforaten Folien mit kleinsten Poren, Planta, 9:246–269.

Silen, R., 1958, Artificial ripening of Douglas-fir cones, Jour. Forestry, 56:410–413.

Siminovitch, D., and D. R. Briggs, 1949, The chemistry of the living bark of the black locust tree in relation to frost hardiness. I. Seasonal variations in protein content, Arch. Biochemistry, 23:8–17.

—— and A. P. J. Chater, 1958, Biochemical processes in the living bark of the black locust tree in relation to frost hardiness and the seasonal cycle, chap. 11 in K. V. Thimann (ed.), The physiology of forest trees, The Ronald Press Company, New York.

—— and G. W. Scarth, 1938, A study of the mechanism of frost injury to plants, Canadian Jour. Research, C16:467–481.

——, C. M. Wilson, and D. R. Briggs, 1953, Studies on the chemistry of the living bark of the black locust in relation to frost hardiness. V. Seasonal transformations and variations in the carbohydrates: starch-sucrose interconversions, Plant Physiology, 28:383–400.

Sinnott, E. W., 1918, Factors determining character and distribution of food reserve in woody plants, Bot. Gaz., 66:162–175.

——, 1939, Growth and differentiation in living plant meristems, Natl. Acad. Sci. (U.S.) Proc., 25:55–58.

—— and R. Bloch, 1939a, Changes in intercellular relationships during the growth and differentiation of living plant tissues, Am. Jour. Botany, 26:625–634.

—— and ——, 1939b, Cell polarity and the differentiation of root hairs, Natl. Acad. Sci. (U.S.) Proc., 25:248–252.

Skoog, F., and C. O. Miller, 1957, Chemical regulation of growth and organ formation in plant tissues cultured in vitro, Soc. Expt. Biol. Symp., no. 9, pp. 118–131.

—— and K. V. Thimann, 1934, Further experiments on the inhibition of the development of lateral buds by growth hormones, Natl. Acad. Sci. Proc., 20:480–485.

Slabaugh, P. E., 1957, Effects of live crown removal on the growth of red pine, Jour. Forestry, 55:904–906.

Slankis, V., 1948, Einfluss von *Boletus variegatus* auf die dichotomische Verzweigung isolierter Kiefernwurzeln, Physiologia Plantarum, 1:390–400.

——, 1958, The role of auxin and other exudates in mycorrhizal symbiosis of forest trees, chap. 21 in K. V. Thimann (ed.), The physiology of forest trees, The Ronald Press Company, New York.

Slatyer, R. O., 1955, Studies of the water relations of crop plants grown under natural rainfall in northern Australia, Australian Jour. Agr. Research, 6:365–377.

——, 1957a, The significance of the permanent wilting percentage in studies of plant and soil water relations, Bot. Rev., 23:585–636.

——, 1957b, The influence of progressive increases in total soil moisture stress on transpiration, growth and internal water relationships of plants, Australian Jour. Biol. Sci., 10:320–336.

——, 1958, The measurement of diffusion pressure deficit in plants by a method of vapour equilibration, Australian Jour. Biol. Sci., 11:349–365.

Smith, C. L., and L. D. Romberg, 1939, A method for the treatment of cuttings and roots of the pecan with root-inducing chemicals, Plant Physiology, 14:177–178.

Smith, L. F., 1940, Influence of root pruning after digging on the growth of certain hardwoods, Jour. Forestry, 38:600–601.

Smith, M. E., 1943, Micronutrients essential for the growth of *Pinus radiata*, Australian Forestry, 7:22–27.

——— and N. S. Bayliss, 1942, The necessity of zinc for *Pinus radiata*, Plant Physiology, 17:303–310.

Smith, R. C., 1957, Studies on the relation of ion absorption to water uptake in plants, Ph.D. dissertation, Duke University, Durham, N.C.

Smith, W. R., and N. B. Goebel, 1952, The moisture content of green hickory, Jour. Forestry, 50:616–618.

Smock, R. M., and A. M. Neubert, 1950, Apples and apple products, Interscience Publishers, Inc., New York.

Snow, R., 1935, Activation of cambial growth by pure hormones, New Phytologist, 34:347–360.

Snyder, W. E., 1954, The rooting of leafy stem cuttings, Natl. Hort. Mag., 33:1–18.

Söding, F., 1936, Über den Einfluss von Wuchstoff auf das Dickenwachstum der Bäume, Ber. deut. bot. Gesell., 54:291–304.

Sorauer, P., 1899, Über Intumescenzen, Ber. deut. bot. Gesell., 17:456–460.

Southwick, F. W., and N. F. Childers, 1941, Influence of Bordeaux mixture and its component parts on transpiration and apparent photosynthesis of apple leaves, Plant Physiology, 16:721–754.

Spencer, H. J., 1939a, On the nature of the blocking of the laticiferous system at the leaf base of *Hevea brasiliensis*, Ann. Botany, 3:231–235.

———, 1939b, Latex outflow and water uptake in the leaf of *Ficus elastica*, Ann. Botany, 3:237–241.

Spoehr, H. A., 1919, The carbohydrate economy of cacti, Carnegie Inst. Washington Publ. 287.

———, 1926, Photosynthesis, New York Chemical Catalogue Co., New York.

——— and H. W. Milner, 1939, Starch dissolution and amylolytic activity of leaves, Am. Phil. Soc. Proc., 81:37–78.

Sprague, G. F., 1953, Heterosis, in W. E. Loomis (ed.), Growth and differentiation in plants, Iowa State College Press, Ames, Iowa.

Stålfelt, M. G., 1921, Till Kännendomen on förhallendet mellans solbladens och skuggbladens Kohlydratsproduction, Statens Skogsförsöksanst. Meddel., 18:221–280.

———, 1928, Die Physiologisch-ökologischen Bedingungen der Stomatäten Diffusionkapazität, Svenska Skogs. Tidskr., 26:818–843.

———, 1932, Der stomatäre Regulator in der pflanzlichen Transpiration, Planta, 17:22–85.

———, 1935, Die Spaltöffnungsweite als Assimilationsfaktor, Planta, 23:715–759.

———, 1955, The stomata as a hydrophotic regulator of the water deficit of the plant, Physiologia Plantarum, 8:572–593.

———, 1956a, Die stomatäre Transpiration und die Physiologie der Spaltöffnungen, in W. Ruhland (ed.), Encyclopedia of plant physiology, vol. 3, pp. 351–426, Springer-Verlag, Berlin.

———, 1956b, Wasserzustand und Photosynthese, in Encyclopedia of plant physiology, vol. 3, p. 654.

Stanfield, J. F., 1932, Osmotic pressure of leaves of *Pinus scopulorum* and certain environmental factors, Bot. Gaz., 93:453–465.

Stanhill, G., 1957, The effect of differences in soil moisture status on plant growth: a review and evaluation, Soil Sci., 84:205–214.

Stanley, R. G., 1957, Krebs cycle activity of mitochondria from endosperm of sugar pine seed (*Pinus lambertiana* Dougl.), Plant Physiology, 32:409–412.

———, 1958, Gross respiratory and water uptake patterns in germinating sugar pine seed, Physiologia Plantarum, 11:503–515.

——— and E. E. Conn, 1957, Enzyme activity of mitochondria from germinating seedlings of sugar pine (*Pinus lambertiana* Dougl.), Plant Physiology, 32:412–418.

Stark, R. W., and J. A. Cook, 1957, The effects of defoliation by the lodgepole needle miner, Forest Sci., 3:376–396.

Starr, G. H., 1940, Treating deciduous trees for chlorosis, Phytopathology, 30:23.

Stearns, F., and J. Olson, 1958, Interactions of photoperiod and temperature affecting seed germination in *Tsuga canadensis,* Am. Jour. Botany, 45:53–58.

Steinbauer, G. P., 1932, Growth of tree seedlings in relation to light intensity and concentration of nutrient solution, Plant Physiology, 7:742–745.

Steinberg, R. A., 1951, Correlations between protein-carbohydrate metabolism and mineral deficiencies in plants, in E. Truog (ed.), Mineral nutrition of plants, pp. 359–386, University of Wisconsin Press, Madison, Wis.

Stevens, C. L., 1931, Root growth of white pine, Yale Univ. School Forestry Bull. 32.

——— and R. L. Eggert, 1945, Observations on the causes of the flow of sap in red maple, Plant Physiology, 20:636–648.

Steward, F. C., and F. K. Millar, 1954, Salt accumulation in plants: a reconsideration of the role of growth and metabolism, Soc. Exptl. Biol. Symp., no. 8, pp. 367–406.

Stewart, C. M., 1957, Status of cambial chemistry, Tappi, 40:244–256.

Stoate, T. N., 1950, Nutrition of the pine, Forestry Bur. Australia Bull., 30:1–61.

Stocker, O., 1929, Das Wasserdefizit von Gefasspflanzen in verschiedenen Klimazonen, Planta, 7:382–387.

———, 1935, III, Ein Beitrag zur Transpirationsgrösse im javanischer Regenwald, Jahrb. wiss. Bot., 81:464–496.

———, 1956, Die Dürreresistenz, in W. Ruhland (ed.), Encyclopedia of plant physiology, vol. 3, pp. 696–741, Springer-Verlag, Berlin.

Stocking, C. R., 1945, The calculation of tensions in *Cucurbita pepo,* Am. Jour. Botany, 32:126–134.

Stockwell, P., and F. I. Righter, 1947, Hybrid forest trees, U.S. Dept. Agr., Yearbook Agr., pp. 465–472.

Stoddard, E. M., and A. E. Dimond, 1949, The chemotherapy of plant diseases, Bot. Rev., 15:345–376.

Stoeckeler, J. H., 1947, When is plantation release most effective? Jour. Forestry, 45:265–271.

——— and E. Aamodt, 1940, Use of tensiometers in regulating watering in forest nurseries, Plant Physiology, 15:589–607.

Stone, E. C., 1955, Poor survival and the physiological condition of planting stock, Forest Sci., 1:90–94.

———, 1957a, Embryo dormancy and embryo vigor of sugar pine as affected by length of storage and storage temperatures, Forest Sci., 3:357–371.

———, 1957b, Embryo dormancy of *Pinus jeffreyi* Murr. seed as affected by temperature, water uptake, stratification, and seed coat, Plant Physiology, 32:93–99.

——— and G. H. Schubert, 1956, New roots on pine seedlings, California Agriculture, March, pp. 11, 15.

———, A. Y. Shachori, and R. G. Stanley, 1956, Water absorption by needles of ponderosa pine seedlings and its internal redistribution, Plant Physiology, 31:120–126.

———, F. W. Went, and C. L. Young, 1950, Water absorption from the atmosphere by plants growing in dry soil, Science, 111:546–548.

Stone, E. L., 1940, Frost rings in longleaf pine, Science, 92:478.

——, 1952, Evaporation in nature, Jour. Forestry, 50:746–747.

——, 1953a, Magnesium deficiency of some northeastern pines, Soil Sci. Soc. Am. Proc., 17:297–300.

——, 1953b, The origin of epicormic branches in fir, Jour. Forestry, 51:366.

——, 1955, Observations on forest fertilization in Europe, Natl. Plant Food Institute, Natl. Joint Com. on Fertilizer Application, Proc.

——, R. R. Morrow, and D. S. Welch, 1954, A malady of red pine on poorly drained soil, Jour. Forestry, 52:104–114.

—— and M. H. Stone, 1943a, Dormant buds in certain species of *Pinus*, Am. Jour. Botany, 30:346–351.

—— and ——, 1943b, "Dormant" versus "adventitious" buds, Science, 98:62.

—— and ——, 1954, Root collar sprouts in pine, Jour. Forestry, 52:487–491.

Stout, P. R., and D. R. Hoagland, 1939, Upward and lateral movement of salt in certain plants as indicated by radioactive isotopes of potassium, sodium, and phosphorus absorbed by roots, Am. Jour. Botany, 26:320–324.

—— and R. Overstreet, 1950, Soil chemistry in relation to inorganic nutrition of plants, Ann. Rev. Plant Physiology, 1:305–342.

Stowe, B. B., and T. Yamaki, 1957, The history and physiological action of the gibberellins, Ann. Rev. Plant Physiology, 8:181–216.

Struckmeyer, B. E., C. E. Beckman, J. E. Kuntz, and A. J. Riker, 1954, Plugging of vessels by tyloses and gums in wilting oaks, Phytopathology, 44:148–153.

Strugger, S., 1943, Der aufsteigende Saftstrom in der Pflanze, Naturwissenschaft, 31:181–194.

——, 1949, Praktikum der Zell- und Gewebephysiologie der Pflanzen, 2d ed., Springer-Verlag, Berlin.

Studhalter, R. A., and W. Glock, 1942, Apparatus for the production of artificial frost injury in the branches of living trees, Science, 96:165.

Süchting, H., 1939, Untersuchungen über die Ernährungsverhältnisse des Waldes. IV. Prüfung ausgewählter Waldboden auf Nährstofflieferung durch Vegetationsversuche mit Lärche, Kiefer und Fichte sowie auf Nährstofflöslichkeit durch chemische Untersuchungsmethoden, Bodenk. Pfl. Ernähr., 13:73–117.

Sudds, R. H., and R. S. Marsh, 1943, Winter injury to trunks of young bearing apple trees in West Virginia following a fall application of nitrate of soda, Am. Soc. Hort. Sci. Proc., 42:293–297.

Swanson, C. A., 1943, Transpiration in American holly in relation to leaf structure, Ohio Jour. Sci., 43:43–46.

Swarbrick, T., 1926, The healing of wounds in woody stems, Jour. Pom. Hort. Sci., 5:98–114.

—— and R. H. Roberts, 1927, The relation of scion variety to character of root growth in apple trees, Wisconsin Agr. Expt. Sta. Research Bull. 78.

Swartley, J., 1941, Effects of synthetic growth substances on transplants, Am. Soc. Hort. Sci. Proc., 39:357–360.

Switzer, G. L., and L. E. Nelson, 1956, The effect of fertilization on seedling weight and utilization of N, P, and K by loblolly pine (*Pinus taeda* L.) grown in the nursery, Soil Sci. Soc. Am. Proc., 20:404–407.

Takahara, S., 1949, The influence of the shading on healing of the wounds due to artificial pruning in some conifers, Tokyo Univ. Forests Bull. 37.

——, 1954, Influence of pruning on the growth of Sugi and Hinoki, Tokyo Univ. Forests Bull. 46.

Talbert, T. J., 1931, Results of some experiments in pruning young apple trees, Am. Soc. Hort. Sci. Proc., 28:610–612.

Tamm, C. O., 1951, Seasonal variation in composition of birch leaves, Physiologia Plantarum, 4:461–469.

——, 1954, A study of forest nutrition by means of foliar analysis. Extrait d'Analyse des plantes et problèmes des engrais minéraux; Congr. intern. botan., VIII, L'Institut des recherches pour les huiles et oléagineux (ed.), Paris.

——, 1955, Studies on forest nutrition. I. Seasonal variation in the nutrient content of conifer needles, Medd. Skogsförskn. Stockholm, 45:5.

Tarrant, R. F., 1949, Douglas-fir site quality and soil fertility, Jour. Forestry, 47: 716–720.

Taylor, F. H., 1956, Variation in sugar content of maple sap, Vermont Agr. Expt. Sta. Bull. 587, pp. 1–39.

Taylor, O. C., E. A. Cardiff, J. D. Merseveau, and J. T. Middleton, 1958, Effect of air-borne reaction products of ozone and 1-n-hexene vapor (synthetic smog) on growth of avocado seedlings, Am. Soc. Hort. Sci. Proc., 71:320–325.

Taylor, S. A., 1949, Oxygen diffusion in porous media as affected by compaction and moisture content, Soil Sci. Soc. Am. Proc., 14:55–61.

Thimann, K. V., 1937, On the nature of inhibitions caused by auxins, Am. Jour. Botany, 24:407–412.

—— and J. Behnke, 1950, The use of auxins in the rooting of woody cuttings, Maria Moors Cabot Found. Pub. 1, Harvard Forest, Petersham, Mass.

—— and A. L. Delisle, 1939, The vegetative propagation of difficult plants, Arnold Arboretum Jour., 20:116–136.

Thom, L. A., 1951, A study of the respiration of hardy pear buds in relation to rest period, Ph.D. dissertation, Univ. of California, Berkeley.

Thomas, J. E., and A. J. Riker, 1950, Progress on rooting cuttings from white pine trees, Jour. Forestry, 48:474–480.

Thomas, M., S. L. Ranson, and J. A. Richardson, 1956, Plant physiology, 4th ed., J. and A. Churchill, London.

Thomas, M. D., 1933, Precise automatic apparatus for continuous determination of carbon dioxide in air, Ind. Eng. Chemistry, 5:193–198.

——, 1951, Gas damage to plants, Ann. Rev. Plant Physiology, 2:293–322.

—— and G. R. Hill, 1949, Photosynthesis under field conditions, in J. Franck and W. E. Loomis (eds.), Photosynthesis in plants, pp. 19–52, Iowa State College Press, Ames, Iowa.

Thomas, W., 1927, Nitrogenous metabolism of *Pyrus malus*. III. The partition of nitrogen in the leaves, one- and two-year branch growth and non-bearing spurs throughout a year's cycle, Plant Physiology, 2:109–137.

——, 1937, Foliar diagnosis: principles and practice, Plant Physiology, 12:571–599.

Thor, C. J. B., and C. L. Smith, 1935, A physiological study of seasonal changes in the composition of the pecan fruit during development, Jour. Agr. Research, 50:97–121.

Thorne, D. W., F. B. Wann, and W. Robinson, 1951, Hypotheses concerning lime-induced chlorosis, Soil Sci. Am. Proc., 15:254–258.

Thornthwaite, C. W., 1948, An approach toward a rational classification of climate, Geograph. Rev., 38:55–94.

—— and F. K. Hare, 1955, Climatic classification in forestry, Unasylva, 9:51–59.

—— and J. R. Mather, 1955, The water balance, Climatology, vol. 8, no. 1, Drexel Institute Technical Laboratory on Climatology, Centerton, N.J.

Thut, H. F., 1939, The relative humidity gradient of stomatal transpiration, Am. Jour. Botany, 26:315–319.

Thut, H. F., and W. E. Loomis, 1944, Relation of light to growth of plants, Plant Physiology, 19:117–130.

Tilford, P. E., 1938, Effect of some synthetic growth substances on root development of transplanted trees, 14th Natl. Shade Tree Conf. Proc., pp. 51–59.

Tingley, M. A., 1936, Double growth rings in Red Astrachan, Am. Soc. Hort. Sci. Proc., 34: 61.

Todd, G. W., 1958, Effect of ozone and ozonated 1-hexene on respiration and photosynthesis of leaves, Plant Physiology, 33:416–420.

Tolbert, N. E., and H. Wiebe, 1955, Phosphorus and sulfur compounds in plant xylem sap, Plant Physiology, 30:499–504.

Tolsky, A. P., 1914, Mensuration, finance and management, Forestry Quart., 12:277–278.

Tompkins, L. E., 1934, The effects of certain fertilizers upon the carbon dioxide intake of mature Jonathan apple leaves, Am. Soc. Hort. Sci. Proc., 32:97–100.

Toole, E. H., S. B. Hendricks, H. A. Borthwick, and V. K. Toole, 1956a, Physiology of seed germination, Ann. Rev. Plant Physiology, 7:299–324.

———, A. G. Snow, Jr., V. K. Toole, and H. A. Borthwick, 1956b, Effects of light and temperature on germination of Virginia pine seeds, Am. Soc. Plant Physiology Proc., Suppl., 31, XXXVI.

Toumey, J. W., 1921, Damage to forests and other vegetation by smoke, ash, and fumes from manufacturing plants in Naugatuck Valley, Conn., Jour. Forestry, 19:267–373.

———, 1929, Initial root habit in American trees and its bearing on regeneration, Internat. Cong. Plant Sci. Proc., Ithaca, N.Y., 1926, 1:713–728.

——— and W. D. Durland, 1923, The effect of soaking certain tree seeds in water at greenhouse temperatures on viability and the time required for germination, Jour. Forestry, 21:369–375.

——— and R. Kienholz, 1931, Trenched plots under forest canopies, Yale Univ. School Forestry Bull. 30.

——— and C. F. Korstian, 1942, Seeding and planting in the practice of forestry, 3d ed., John Wiley & Sons, Inc., New York.

——— and ———, 1947, Foundations of silviculture upon an ecological basis, 2d ed., John Wiley & Sons, Inc., New York.

——— and E. J. Neethling, 1923, Some effects of cover over coniferous seedbeds in southern New England, Yale Univ. School Forestry Bull. 9.

Towers, G. H. N., and R. D. Gibbs, 1953, Lignin chemistry and the taxonomy of higher plants, Nature, 172:25.

Tranquillini, W., 1954, Die Lichtabhängigkeit der Assimilation von Sonnen und Schattenblättern einer Buche unter ökologischen Bedingungen, 8th Internat. Bot. Cong. Proc., Paris, sec. 13, pp. 100–102.

———, 1955, Die Bedeutung des Lichtes und der Temperatur für die Kohlensäureassimilation von *Pinus cembra* Jungwachs an einem hochalpinen Standort, Planta, 46:154–178.

———, 1957, Standortsklima, Wasserbilanz und CO_2—Gaswechsel junger Zirben (*Pinus cembra* L.) an der Alpinen Waldgrenze, Planta, 49: 612–661.

——— and K. Holzer, 1958, Über das Gefrieren und Auftauen von Conifernadeln, Ber. deut. bot. Gesell., 71:143–156.

Traub, H. P., M. C. Slattery, and W. L. McRary, 1946, The effect of moisture stress on nursery-grown guayule with reference to changes in reserve carbohydrates, Am. Jour. Botany, 33:699–705.

Trelease, S. F., and H. M. Trelease, 1939, Physiological differentiation in *Astragalus* with reference to selenium, Am. Jour. Botany, 26:530–535.

Tryon, E. H., J. O. Cantrell, and K. L. Carvell, 1957, Effect of precipitation and temperature on increment of yellow-poplar, Forest Sci., 3:32–44.

Tryon, H. H., and R. F. Finn, 1937, Notes on the terminal growth of coniferous plantations in the Hudson Highlands, Black Rock Forest Papers, no. 1, pp. 54–56.

Tswett, M., 1906, Adsorptionsanalyse und chromatographische Methode: Anwendung auf die Chemie des Chlorophylls, Ber. deut. bot. Gesell., 24:384–393.

Tukey, H. B., 1936, Development of cherry and peach fruits as affected by destruction of the embryo, Bot. Gaz., 98:1–24.

——, 1938, Growth patterns of plants developed from immature embryos in artificial culture, Bot. Gaz., 99:630–665.

—— and E. L. Green, 1934, Gradient composition of rose shoots from tip to base, Plant Physiology, 9:157–163.

—— and C. L. Hamner, 1949, Form and composition of cherry fruits (*Prunus avium* and *P. cerasus*) following fall applications of 2,4-dichlorophenoxyacetic acid and naphthaleneacetic acid, Am. Soc. Hort. Sci. Proc., 54:95–101.

——, R. L. Ticknor, O. N. Hinsvark, and S. H. Wittwer, 1952, Absorption of nutrients by stems and branches of woody plants, Science, 116:167–168.

——, F. W. Went, R. M. Muir, and J. van Overbeek, 1954, Nomenclature of chemical plant regulators, Plant Physiology, 29:307–308.

—— and J. O. Young, 1939, Histological study of the developing fruit of the sour cherry, Bot. Gaz., 100:722–749.

—— and ——, 1942, Gross morphology and histology of developing fruit of the apple, Bot. Gaz., 104:3–25.

Tukey, H. B., Jr., and H. J. Amling, 1958, Leaching of foliage by rain and dew as an explanation of differences in the nutrient composition of greenhouse- and field-grown plants, Michigan Agr. Exp. Sta. Quart. Bull. 40, pp. 876–881.

——, H. B. Tukey, and S. H. Wittwer, 1958, Loss of nutrients by foliar leaching as determined by radioisotopes, Am. Soc. Hort. Sci. Proc., 71:496–506.

Tukey, L. D., 1956, Some effects of night temperatures on the growth of McIntosh apples, Am. Soc. Hort. Sci. Proc., 68:32–43.

Turner, L. M., 1936, Root growth of seedlings of *Pinus echinata* and *Pinus taeda*, Jour. Agr. Research, 53:145–149.

Turrell, F. M., 1936, The area of the internal exposed surface of dicotyledon leaves, Am. Jour. Botany, 23:255–264.

——, 1944, Correlation between internal surface and transpiration rate in mesomorphic and xeromorphic leaves grown under artificial light, Bot. Gaz., 105:413–425.

Tuttle, G. M., 1919, Induced changes in reserve materials in evergreen herbaceous leaves, Ann. Botany, 3:201–210.

——, 1921, Reserve food materials in vegetative tissues, Bot. Gaz., 71:146–151.

Uhl, A., 1937, Untersuchungen über die Assimilationverhältnisse und die Ursachen ihrer Unterschiede in der Gattung *Pinus*, Jahrb. wiss. Bot., 85:368–421.

Ulmer, W., 1937, Über den Jahresgang der Frosthärte einiger immer grüner Arten der alpinen Stufe, sowie der Zirbe und Fichte: unter Berücksichtigung von osmotischen Wert, Zuckerspiegel, und Wassergehalt, Jahrb. wiss. Bot., 84:533–592.

Ulrich, R., 1958, Postharvest physiology of fruits, Ann. Rev. Plant Physiology, 9:385–416.

Umbreit, W. W., R. H. Burris, and J. F. Stauffer, 1957, Manometric techniques, Burgess Publishing Co., Minneapolis.

Ursprung, A., 1915, Über die Kohäsion des Wassers im Farnanulus, Ber. deut. bot. Gesell., 33:153–162.

———, 1929, The osmotic quantities of the plant cell, Int. Cong. Plant Sci. Proc., Ithaca, 2:1081–1094.

———, 1933, Ueber die Beziehungen zwischen der Wasserbilanz und einigen osmotischen Zustandsgrössen, Ber. schweiz. bot. Gesell., 42:225–237.

Ussing, H. H., 1954, Ion transport across biological membranes, in H. T. Clark (ed.), Ion transport across membranes, pp. 3–22, Academic Press, Inc., New York.

Vaartaja, O., 1954, Photoperiodic ecotypes of trees, Canadian Jour. Botany, 32:392–399.

———, 1956, Photoperiodic response in germination of seed of certain trees, Canadian Jour. Botany, 34:377–388.

Van Horn, C. W., 1941, Delayed foliation of pecan trees in Arizona, Am. Soc. Hort. Sci. Proc., 39:87–94.

Van't Woudt, B. D., and R. M. Hagan, 1957, Crop responses at excessively high soil moisture levels, in J. N. Luthin (ed.), Drainage of agricultural lands, Am. Soc. Agron. Mon. VII, Madison, Wis.

Veen, R. van der, 1951, Influence of day length on the dormancy of some species of the genus *Populus*, Physiologia Plantarum, 4:35–40.

Vegis, A., 1956, Formation of the resting condition in plants, Experientia, 12:94–99.

Veihmeyer, F. J., 1927, Some factors affecting the irrigation requirements of deciduous orchards, Hilgardia, 2:125–291.

———, 1956, Soil moisture, in W. Ruhland (ed.), Encyclopedia of plant physiology, vol. 3, pp. 64–123, Springer-Verlag, Berlin.

——— and A. H. Hendrickson, 1927, Soil moisture conditions in relation to plant growth, Plant Physiology, 2:71–82.

——— and ———, 1950, Soil moisture in relation to plant growth, Ann. Rev. Plant Physiology, 1:285–304.

Verne, L. J., 1953, Production and utilization of acorns in Clinton County, Michigan, M.S. thesis, Michigan State University, Ann Arbor, Mich.

Virgin, H. I., 1957, Stomatal transpiration of some variegated plants and of chlorophyll-deficient mutants of barley. Physiologia Plantarum 10:170–186.

Virtanen, A. I., 1957, Investigations on nitrogen fixation by the alder. II. Associated culture of spruce and inoculated alder without combined nitrogen, Physiologia Plantarum, 10:164–169.

Vité, J. P., 1958, Über die transpirations-physiologische Bedeutung des Drehwuchses bei Nadelhölzern, Forstwiss. Zentralbl., 77:193–203.

Voigt, G. K., 1951, Causes of injury to conifers during the winter of 1947–48 in Wisconsin, Wis. Acad. Sciences, Arts, Letters, Trans., 40:241–243.

———, 1953, The effects of fungicides, insecticides, herbicides and fertilizer salts on the respiration of root tips of tree seedlings, Soil Sci. Soc. Am. Proc., 17:150–152.

———, 1954, The effect of fungicides, herbicides, and insecticides on the uptake of phosphorus by *Pinus radiata* as determined by the use of P^{32}, Am. Soc. Agron. Jour., 46:511–513.

Volk, N. J., 1934, The fixation of potash in difficultly available form in soils, Soil Sci., 37:267–287.

Wadleigh, C. H., H. G. Gauch, and O. C. Magistad, 1946, Growth and rubber accumulation in guayule as conditioned by soil salinity and irrigation regime, U.S.D.A. Tech. Bull. 925.

Wagener, W. W., 1949, Top dying of conifers from sudden cold, Jour. Forestry, 47:49–53.

——, 1954, Longevity under adversity in conifers, Science, 119:883–884.

Wahlenberg, G., 1930, Experiments in the use of fertilizers in growing forest planting material at the Savenac nursery, U.S. Dept. Agr. Circ. 125.

Wahlenberg, W. G., 1950, Epicormic branching of young yellow-poplar, Jour. Forestry, 48:417–419.

——, 1952, Thinning yellow-poplar in second growth upland hardwood stands, Jour. Forestry, 50:671–676.

Wakeley, P. C., 1947, Loblolly pine seed production, Jour. Forestry, 45:676–677.

——, 1948, Physiological grades of southern pine nursery stock, Soc. Am. Foresters Proc., 311–322.

Waksman, S. A., 1932, Principles of soil microbiology, The Williams and Wilkins Company, Baltimore.

—— and R. L. Starkey, 1931, The soil and the microbe, John Wiley & Sons, Inc., New York.

Walker, L. C., 1955, Foliar analysis as a method of indicating potassium deficient soils for reforestation, Soil Sci. Soc. Am. Proc., 19:233–236.

——, 1956, Foliage symptoms as indicators of potassium deficient soils, Forest Sci., 2:113–120.

Wallihan, E. F., 1944, Chemical composition of leaves in different parts of sugar maple trees, Jour. Forestry, 42:684.

Walter, H., 1931, Die Hydratur der Pflanze und ihre physiologische ökologische Bedeutung, Gustav Fischer Verlagsbuchhandlung, Jena, Germany.

——, 1951, Grundlagen der Pflanzenverbreitung, vol. 1, Standortslehre, E. Ulmer Verlag, Stuttgart.

——, 1955, The water economy and the hydrature of plants, Ann. Rev. Plant Physiology, 6:239–252.

Wardlaw, C. R., and E. R. Leonard, 1938, Studies in tropical fruits. III. Preliminary observations on pneumatic pressures in fruits, Ann. Botany, 2:301–315.

Wareing, J. H., and M. T. Hilborn, 1942, Developing apple trees on hardy stocks, Maine Ext. Bull. 310.

Wareing, P. F., 1949, Photoperiodic control of leaf growth and cambial activity in *Pinus silvestris*, Nature, 163:770.

——, 1950, Growth studies in woody species. I. Photoperiodism in first-year seedlings of *Pinus silvestris*, Physiologia Plantarum, 3:258–276.

——, 1951a, Growth studies in woody species. III. Further photoperiodic effects in *Pinus silvestris*, Physiologia Plantarum, 4:41–56.

——, 1951b, Growth studies in woody species. IV. The initiation of cambial activity in ring-porous species, Physiologia Plantarum, 4:546–562.

——, 1953, Experimental induction of male cones in *Pinus sylvestris*, Nature, 171: 47–48.

——, 1954, Experiments on the light break effect in short-day plants, Physiologia Plantarum, 7:157–172.

——, 1956, Photoperiodism in woody plants, Ann. Rev. Plant Physiology, 7:191–214.

—— and D. L. Roberts, 1956, Photoperiodic control of cambial activity in *Robinia pseudoacacia* L., New Phytologist, 55:356–366.

Wassink, E. C., S. D. Richardson, and G. A. Pieters, 1956, Photosynthetic adaptation to light intensity in leaves of *Acer pseudoplatanus*, Acta Bot. Neerl., 5:247-256.

Wassink, E. C., and J. A. J. Stolwijk, 1956, Effects of light quality on plant growth, Ann. Rev. Plant Physiology, 7:373–400.

Watson, D. J., 1956, Leaf growth in relation to crop yield, in F. L. Milthorpe (ed.), The growth of leaves, pp. 178–191, 3d Easter School in Agr. Sci. Proc., Butterworth & Co. (Publishers), Ltd., London.

Waugh, J. G., 1939, Some investigations on the assimilation of apple leaves, Plant Physiology, 14:463–477.

Weakley, H. E., 1943, A tree-ring record of precipitation in western Nebraska, Jour. Forestry, 41:816–819.

Weatherley, P. E., 1950, Studies in the water relations of the cotton plant. I. The field measurement of water deficits in leaves, New Phytologist, 49:81–97.

——— and R. O. Slatyer, 1957, Relationship between relative turgidity and diffusion pressure deficit in leaves, Nature, 179:1085–1086.

Weaver, J. E., and A. Mogensen, 1919, Relative transpiration of coniferous and broadleaved trees in autumn and winter, Bot. Gaz., 68:393–424.

Weaver, R. J., 1953, Further studies on effects of 4-chlorophenoxyacetic acid on development of Thompson seedless and Black Corinth grapes, Am. Soc. Hort. Sci. Proc., 61:135–143.

Weber, F., 1909, Untersuchungen über die Wandlungen des Stärke- und Fettgehaltes der Pflanzen, insbesondere der Bäume, Sitz. math.-naturw. Kl. K. Akad. Wiss. Wien, 118(1):967–1031.

Wedding, R. T., L. C. Erickson, and B. L. Brannaman, 1954, Effect of 2,4-dichlorophenoxyacetic acid on photosynthesis and respiration, Plant Physiology, 29:64–69.

———, L. A. Riehl, and W. A. Rhoads, 1952, Effect of petroleum oil spray on photosynthesis and respiration in citrus leaves, Plant Physiology, 27:269–278.

Weier, T. E., and C. R. Stocking, 1952, The chloroplast: structure, inheritance, and enzymology, Bot. Rev., 18:14–75.

Weinberger, J. H., 1950, Chilling requirements of peach varieties, Am. Soc. Hort. Sci. Proc., 56:122–128.

Wells, B. W., 1915, A survey of the zoocecidia on species of *Hicoria* caused by parasites belonging to the *Eriophydiae* and *Itonididae*, Ohio Jour. Sci., 16:37–59.

Wenger, K. F., 1953a, The sprouting of sweetgum in relation to season of cutting and carbohydrate content, Plant Physiology, 28:35–49.

———, 1953b, The effect of fertilization and injury on the cone and seed production of loblolly pine seed trees, Jour. Forestry, 51:570–573.

———, 1954, The stimulation of loblolly pine seed trees by preharvest release, Jour. Forestry, 52:115–118.

———, 1955a, Light and mycorrhiza development, Ecology, 36:518–520.

———, 1955b, Height growth of loblolly pine seedlings in relation to seedling characteristics, Forest Sci., 1:158–163.

———, 1957, Annual variation in the seed crops of loblolly pine, Jour. Forestry, 55:567–569.

——— and K. B. Trousdell, 1958, Natural regeneration of loblolly pine in the South Atlantic coastal plain, U.S. Dept. Agr. Prod. Research Rept. 13.

Went, F. W., 1928, Wuchstoff und Wachstum, Rec. trav. bot. néerl., 25:1–116.

———, 1936, Allgemeine Betrachtungen über das Auxin Problem, Biol. Zentralbl., 56:449–463.

———, 1938, Specific factors other than auxin affecting growth and root formation, Plant Physiology, 13:55–80.

———, 1939, Some experiments on bud growth, Am. Jour. Botany, 26:109–117.

———, 1942, Some physiological factors in the aging of a tree, 18 Natl. Shade Tree Conf. Proc., pp. 330–334.

———, 1944, Plant growth under controlled conditions. III. Correlation between various physiological processes and growth in the tomato plant, Am. Jour. Botany, 31:597–618.

———, 1948, Thermoperiodicity, in F. Verdoorn (ed.), Vernalization and photoperiodism: a symposium, The Chronica Botanica Co., Waltham, Mass.

———, 1953, The effect of temperature on plant growth, Ann. Rev. Plant Physiology, 4:347–362.

———, 1957, The experimental control of plant growth, Chronica Botanica Co., Waltham, Mass.

Wetmore, R. H., and W. P. Jacobs, 1953, Studies on abscission: the inhibiting effect of auxin, Am. Jour. Botany, 40:272–276.

White, D. P., 1950, The effect of nursery soil fertility on the resistance of jack pine (*Pinus banksiana* Lamb.) seedlings to adverse environmental and biotic factors, Ph.D. thesis, University of Wisconsin, Madison, Wis.

———, 1954, Variation in the N, P, and K contents of pine needles with season, crown position and sample treatment, Soil Sci. Soc. Am. Proc., 18:326–330.

———, 1956, Aerial applications of potash fertilizer to coniferous plantations, Jour. Forestry, 54:762–768.

——— and A. L. Leaf, 1957, Forest fertilization, New York State College Forestry Tech. Pub. 81.

White, P. R., 1938, "Root-pressure": an unappreciated force in sap movement, Am. Jour. Botany, 25:223–227.

———, E. Schuker, J. R. Kern, and F. H. Fuller, 1958, "Root-pressure" in gymnosperms, Science, 128:308–309.

Whitfield, C. J., 1932, Ecological aspects of transpiration. II. Pikes Peak and Santa Barbara regions: edaphic and climatic aspects, Bot. Gaz., 94:183–196.

Whitford, L. A., 1956, A theory on the formation of cypress knees, Elisha Mitchell Sci. Soc. Jour., 72:80–83.

Widdowson, E. M., 1932, Chemical studies in the physiology of apples. XIII. The starch and hemicellulose content of developing apples, Ann. Botany, 46:597–631.

Wiebe, H. H., and P. J. Kramer, 1954, Translocation of radioactive isotopes from various regions of roots of barley seedlings, Plant Physiology, 29:342–348.

Wieler, A., 1893, Das Bluten der Pflanzen, Beitr. biol. Pflanz., 6:1–211.

Wiggans, C. C., 1936, The effect of orchard plants on subsoil moisture, Am. Soc. Hort. Sci. Proc., 33:103–107.

———, 1937, Some further observations on the depletion of subsoil moisture by apple trees, Am. Soc. Hort. Sci. Proc., 34:160–163.

Wight, W., and D. N. Barua, 1955, The nature of dormancy in the tea plant, Jour. Exptl. Botany, 6:1–5.

Wilcox, H., 1940, The spectrographic analysis of white pine, M.S. thesis, New York State College Forestry, Syracuse, N.Y.

———, 1954, Primary organization of active and dormant roots of noble fir, *Abies procera*, Am. Jour. Botany, 41:812–821.

———, 1955, Regeneration of injured root systems in noble fir, Bot. Gaz., 116:221–234.

———, 1958, Personal communication.

———, F. Czabator, and G. Girolami, 1954, Seasonal variations in bark-peeling of some Adirondack pulpwood species, Jour. Forestry, 52:338–342.

Wilde, S. A., 1954, Mycorrhizal fungi; their distribution and effect on tree growth, Soil Sci., 78:23–31.

———, 1958, Forest soils, The Ronald Press Company, New York.

Wilde, S. A., and G. K. Voigt, 1948, Specific gravity of the wood of jack pine seedlings raised under different levels of soil fertility, Jour. Forestry, 46:521–523.

——— and ———, 1955, Analysis of soils and plants for foresters and horticulturists, J. W. Edwards, Publisher, Ann Arbor, Mich.

———, R. Wittenkamp, E. L. Stone, and H. M. Galloway, 1940, Effect of high rate fertilizer treatments of nursery stock upon its survival and growth in the field, Jour. Forestry, 38:806–809.

Williams, R. F., and R. E. Shapter, 1955, A comparative study of growth and nutrition in barley and rye as affected by low-water treatment, Australian Jour. Biol. Sci., 8:435–466.

Willstätter, R., and A. Stoll, 1913, Untersuchungen über das Chlorophyll, Springer-Verlag, Berlin.

——— and ———, 1918, Untersuchungen über die Assimilation der Kohlensäure, Springer-Verlag, Berlin.

Wilson, C. C., 1948a, Fog and atmospheric carbon dioxide as related to apparent photosynthetic rate of some broadleaf evergreens, Ecology, 29:507–508.

———, 1948b, The effect of some environmental factors on the movement of guard cells, Plant Physiology, 23:5–37.

———, 1948c, Diurnal fluctuations in growth in length of tomato stems, Plant Physiology, 23:156–157.

———, 1953, The response of two species of pine to various levels of nutrient zinc, Science, 117:231–233.

Wilson, J. D., and B. E. Livingston, 1937, Lag in water absorption by plants in water culture with respect to changes in wind, Plant Physiology, 12:135–150.

Wilson, P. W., 1940, The biochemistry of symbiotic nitrogen fixation, University of Wisconsin Press, Madison, Wis.

Winkler, A. J., 1932, The lateral movement of elaborated foods in the grape vine, Am. Soc. Hort. Sci. Proc., 29:335–338.

——— and W. O. Williams, 1938, Carbohydrate metabolism of *Vitis vinifera:* hemicellulose, Plant Physiology, 13:381–390.

——— and ———, 1945, Starch and sugar of *Vitis vinifera,* Plant Physiology, 20:412–432.

Winneberger, J. H., 1958, Transpiration as a requirement for growth of land plants, Physiologia Plantarum, 11:56–61.

Wise, L. E., and E. C. Jahn, 1952, Wood chemistry, vol. I, Reinhold Publishing Corporation, New York.

Withrow, R. B., 1935, A photoelectric device for the rapid measurement of leaf area, Jour. Agr. Research, 50:637–643.

Wittwer, S. H., and M. J. Bukovac, 1958, The effects of gibberellin on economic crops, Econ. Botany, 12:213–255.

Woodhams, D. H., and T. T. Kozlowski, 1954, Effects of soil moisture stress on carbohydrate development and growth in plants, Am. Jour. Botany, 41:316–320.

Woodroof, J. G., and N. C. Woodroof, 1934, Pecan root growth and development, Jour. Agr. Research, 49:511–530.

Woodwell, G. M., 1958, Factors controlling growth of pond pine seedlings in organic soils of the Carolinas, Ecol. Mons., 28:219–236.

Woodworth, R. H., 1930, Cytological studies in the *Betulaceae.* III. Parthenogenesis and polyembryony in *Alnus rugosa,* Bot. Gaz., 89:402–409.

Worley, C. L., H. R. Lesselbaum, and T. M. Mathews, 1941, Deficiency symptoms for the major elements in seedlings of three broad-leaved trees, Tennessee Acad. Sci. Jour., 6:239–247.

Wright, K. E., 1939, Transpiration and the absorption of mineral salts, Plant Physiology, 14:171–174.

Wright, S. T. C., 1956, Studies of fruit development in relation to plant hormones. III. Auxins in relation to fruit morphogenesis and fruit drop in the black currant (*Ribes nigrum*), Jour. Hort. Sci., 31:196–211.

Wylie, R. B., 1938, Concerning the conductive capacity of the minor veins of foliage leaves, Am. Jour. Botany, 25:567–572.

Wyman, D., 1951, Air layering with polyethylene film, Arnoldia, 11:49–62.

Yarwood, C. E., 1947, Water loss from fungus cultures, Am. Jour. Botany, 34:514–520.

Yocum, L. E., 1935, The stomata and transpiration of oaks, Plant Physiology, 10:795–801.

Young, G. W., 1934, Fish oil sprays as affecting the carbon dioxide intake by Jonathan apple leaves, Am. Soc. Hort. Sci. Proc., 32:101–103.

Young, H. E., 1952, Differential time of change from early wood to late wood along the bole of young loblolly pine trees, Jour. Forestry, 50:614–615.

——— and P. J. Kramer, 1952, The effect of pruning on the height and diameter growth of loblolly pine, Jour. Forestry, 50:474–479.

Zahner, R., 1955a, Effect of interrupted dark period on height growth of two tree species, Forest Sci., 1:193–195.

———, 1955b, Soil water depletion by pine and hardwood stands during a dry season, Forest Sci., 1:258–264.

———, 1958, Hardwood understory depletes soil water in pine stands, Forest Sci., 4:178–184.

Zak, B., 1955, The grafting of shortleaf pine and other species, Southeastern Forest Expt. Sta. Paper 59.

———, 1956, Experimental air-layering of shortleaf and loblolly pines, Southeastern Forest Expt. Sta. Paper 69.

Zeller, O., 1951, Über Assimilation und Atmung der Pflanzen im Winter bei tiefen Temperaturen, Planta, 39:500–526.

Zimmerman, M. H., 1957a, Translocation of organic substances in trees. I. The nature of the sugars in the sieve tube exudate of trees, Plant Physiology, 32:288–291.

———, 1957b, Translocation of organic substances in trees. II. On the translocation mechanism in the phloem of white ash (*Fraxinus americana* L.), Plant Physiology, 32:399–404.

———, 1958, Translocation of organic substances in the phloem of trees, chap. 18 in K. V. Thimann (ed.), The physiology of forest trees, The Ronald Press Company, New York.

Zimmerman, P. W., and M. H. Connard, 1934, Reversal of direction of translocation of solutes in stems, Boyce Thompson Inst. Contribs., 6:297–301.

Zimmerman, W. A., 1936, Untersuchungen über die räumliche und zeitliche Verteilung des Wuchsstoffes bei Bäumen, Zeitschr. Bot., 30:209–252.

Zobel, B. J., 1951, Oleoresin composition as a determinant of pine hybridity, Bot. Gaz., 113:221–227.

———, J. Barber, C. L. Brown, and T. O. Perry, 1958, Seed orchards: their concept and management, Jour. Forestry, 56:815–825.

——— and R. L. McElwee, 1958a, Natural variation in wood specific gravity of loblolly pine, and an analysis of contributing factors, Tappi, 41:158–161.

——— and ———, 1958b, Variation of cellulose in loblolly pine, Tappi, 41:167–170.

——— and R. R. Rhodes, 1956, Specific gravity estimations of mature loblolly pine from juvenile wood and seedling limb sections, Forest Sci., 2:107–112.

Zscheile, F. P., 1941, Plastid pigments, Bot. Rev., 7:587–648.

Name Index

Subject Index